Software Process Improvement

Software Process Improvement

Editor:

Gerard Ian Prudhomme

ArclerPress

www.arclerpress.com

Software Process Improvement

Editor: Gerard Ian Prudhomme

708 3rd Avenue, 6th Floor
New York
NY 10017
United States of America
www.arclerpress.com

ISBN: 978-1-68094-467-9

Library of Congress Control Number: 2016951160

About the Editor

Gerard Ian Prudhomme

Gerard I. Prudhomme has a graduate degree (M.S.) for Computer Science from University College London (UCL). He has also worked as a software programmer and tech writer for different Fortune 500 companies, and studied at UCL, Harvard, and Oxford.

Contents

List of Contributors

Yujia Ge
College of Computer and Information Engineering, Zhejiang Gongshang University, Hangzhou, Zhejiang, China
College of Information Engineering, Zhejiang University of Technology, Hangzhou, Zhejiang, China

Bin Xu
College of Computer and Information Engineering, Zhejiang Gongshang University, Hangzhou, Zhejiang, China

Nadja Damij
Faculty for Information Studies, Ulica talcev 8, Novo mesto, Slovenia

Pavle Boškoski
Department of Systems and Control, Jožef Stefan Institute, Jamova cesta 39, Ljubljana, Slovenia

Marko Bohanec
Department of Knowledge Technologies, Jožef Stefan Institute, Jamova cesta 39, Ljubljana, Slovenia

Biljana Mileva Boshkoska
Faculty for Information Studies, Ulica talcev 8, Novo mesto, Slovenia
Department of Knowledge Technologies, Jožef Stefan Institute, Jamova cesta 39, Ljubljana, Slovenia

Qi Xuan
Department of Automation, Zhejiang University of Technology, Hangzhou, China
Department of Computer Science, University of California Davis, Davis, CA, United States of America

Premkumar Devanbu
Department of Computer Science, University of California Davis, Davis, CA, United States of America

Vladimir Filkov
Department of Computer Science, University of California Davis, Davis, CA, United States of America

Radek Silhavy
Faculty of Applied Informatics, Tomas Bata University in Zlin, Zlin, Czech Republic

Petr Silhavy
Faculty of Applied Informatics, Tomas Bata University in Zlin, Zlin, Czech Republic

Zdenka Prokopova
Faculty of Applied Informatics, Tomas Bata University in Zlin, Zlin, Czech Republic

Markus Knauff
Department of Psychology, Experimental Psychology and Cognitive Science, University of Giessen, Giessen, Germany

Jelica Nejasmic
Department of Psychology, Experimental Psychology and Cognitive Science, University of Giessen, Giessen, Germany

Jeanette A. Mumford
Center for Investigating Healthy Minds at the Waisman Center, University of Wisconsin—Madison, Madison, WI, USA

Jean-Baptiste Poline
Helen Wills Neuroscience Institute, Brain Imaging Center, University of California, Berkeley, CA, USA

Russell A. Poldrack
Department of Psychology, Stanford University, Palo Alto, CA, USA

Sally Andrews
Division of Psychology, Nottingham Trent University, Nottingham, United Kingdom

David A. Ellis
Department of Psychology, Lancaster University, Lancaster, United Kingdom
School of Psychology, University of Lincoln, Lincoln, United Kingdom

Heather Shaw
School of Psychology, University of Lincoln, Lincoln, United Kingdom

Lukasz Piwek
Faculty of Business and Law, University of the West of England, Bristol, United Kingdom

Ling-Hong Hung
Institute of Technology, University of Washington, Tacoma, WA 98402, United States of America

Daniel Kristiyanto
Institute of Technology, University of Washington, Tacoma, WA 98402, United States of America

Sung Bong Lee
Institute of Technology, University of Washington, Tacoma, WA 98402, United States of America

Ka Yee Yeung
Institute of Technology, University of Washington, Tacoma, WA 98402, United States of America

Tadeusz Chełkowski
Kozminski University, Warsaw, Poland

Peter Gloor
Massachusetts Institute of Technology, Center for Cognitive Intelligence, Cambridge, Massachusetts, United States of America

Dariusz Jemielniak
Kozminski University, New Research on Digital Societies (NeRDS) group, Warsaw, Poland

Pablo Garaizar
Deusto Institute of Technology, DeustoTech, Universidad de Deusto, Bilbao, Spain

Miguel A. Vadillo
Cognitive, Perceptual and Brain Sciences, University College London, London, United Kingdom
Primary Care and Public Health Sciences, King's College London, London, United Kingdom

Diego López-de-Ipiña
Deusto Institute of Technology, DeustoTech, Universidad de Deusto, Bilbao, Spain

Helena Matute
Faculty of Psychology and Education, Universidad de Deusto, Bilbao, Spain

Eric Pante
Littoral, Environnement et Socie´te´s Joint Research Unit 7266 Centre National de la Recherche Scientifique, Universite´ de La Rochelle, La Rochelle, France

Benoit Simon-Bouhet
Littoral, Environnement et Socie´te´s Joint Research Unit 7266 Centre National de la Recherche Scientifique, Universite´ de La Rochelle, La Rochelle, France

Samreen Laghari
Computer Science Department, Islamabad Model College for Girls, Street #25, F-6/2, Islamabad, Pakistan

Muaz A. Niazi
Computer Science Department, COMSATS Institute of IT, Park Road, Islamabad, Pakistan

Evangelos Kontopantelis
Centre for Primary Care, NIHR School for Primary Care Research, Institute of Population Health, University of Manchester, Manchester, United Kingdom
Centre for Biostatistics, Institute of Population Health, University of Manchester, Manchester, United Kingdom
Centre for Health Informatics, Institute of Population Health, University of Manchester, Manchester, United Kingdom

David A. Springate
Centre for Primary Care, NIHR School for Primary Care Research, Institute of Population Health, University of Manchester, Manchester, United Kingdom
Centre for Biostatistics, Institute of Population Health, University of Manchester, Manchester, United Kingdom

David Reeves
Centre for Primary Care, NIHR School for Primary Care Research, Institute of Population Health, University of Manchester, Manchester, United Kingdom
Centre for Biostatistics, Institute of Population Health, University of Manchester, Manchester, United Kingdom

Ani Eloyan
Department of Biostatistics, Bloomberg School of Public Health, Johns Hopkins University, Baltimore, Maryland, United States of America

Shanshan Li
Department of Biostatistics, Indiana University Fairbanks School of Public Health, Indianapolis, Indiana, United States of America

John Muschelli
Department of Biostatistics, Bloomberg School of Public Health, Johns Hopkins University, Baltimore, Maryland, United States of America

Jim J. Pekar
F. M. Kirby Research Center for Functional Brain Imaging, Kennedy Krieger Institute, Baltimore, Maryland, United States of America
Department of Radiology, The Johns Hopkins School of Medicine, Baltimore, Maryland, United States of America

Stewart H. Mostofsky
F. M. Kirby Research Center for Functional Brain Imaging, Kennedy Krieger Institute, Baltimore, Maryland, United States of America
Department of Neurology and Psychiatry, The Johns Hopkins School of Medicine, Baltimore, Maryland, United States of America

Brian S. Caffo
Department of Biostatistics, Bloomberg School of Public Health, Johns Hopkins University, Baltimore, Maryland, United States of America

Rodrigo A. Henríquez
Inserm U 1127, F-75013, Paris, France
Sorbonne Universités, UPMC Univ Paris 06, UMR S 1127, F- 75013, Paris, France
CNRS, UMR 7225, F-75013, Paris, France
Institut du Cerveau et de la Moelle épinière, ICM, F-75013, Paris, France

Ana B. Chica
Department of Experimental Psychology, and Brain, Mind, and Behaviour Research Center, University of Granada, Granada, Spain

Pablo Billeke
Research Center for Social Complexity, Faculty of Government, University of Desarrollo, Santiago, Chile

Paolo Bartolomeo
Inserm U 1127, F-75013, Paris, France
Sorbonne Universités, UPMC Univ Paris 06, UMR S 1127, F- 75013, Paris, France
CNRS, UMR 7225, F-75013, Paris, France
Institut du Cerveau et de la Moelle épinière, ICM, F-75013, Paris, France
Department of Psychology, Catholic University Milan, Milan, Italy

Michaël C. Waumans
École polytechnique de Bruxelles CoDE-IRIDIA, ULB, Brussels, Belgium

Thibaut Nicodème
École polytechnique de Bruxelles CoDE-IRIDIA, ULB, Brussels, Belgium

Hugues Bersini
École polytechnique de Bruxelles CoDE-IRIDIA, ULB, Brussels, Belgium

Steven James Watson
Department of Psychology, Lancaster University, Lancaster, Lancashire, United Kingdom

Daniel John Zizzo
BENC and Newcastle University Business School, Newcastle University, Newcastle Upon Tyne, Tyne and Wear, United Kingdom

Piers Fleming
School of Psychology, University of East Anglia, Norwich, Norfolk, United Kingdom

Alberto Betella
SPECS Lab, N-RAS, DTIC, Universitat Pompeu Fabra, Barcelona, Spain

Paul F. M. J. Verschure
Institució Catalana de Recerca i Estudis Avançats, Barcelona, Spain

Iñaki Bildosola
Foresight, Technology and Management (FTM) Group, Industrial Organization and Management Engineering Department, Faculty of Engineering in Bilbao (ETSI Bilbao), University of the Basque Country UPV/EHU, Basque Country, Spain

Rosa Río-Belver
Foresight, Technology and Management (FTM) Group, Industrial Organization and Management Engineering Department, University College of Engineering of VitoriaGasteiz, University of the Basque Country UPV/EHU, Basque Country, Spain

Ernesto Cilleruelo
Foresight, Technology and Management (FTM) Group, Industrial Organization and Management Engineering Department, Faculty of Engineering in Bilbao (ETSI Bilbao), University of the Basque Country UPV/EHU, Basque Country, Spain

Gaizka Garechana
Foresight, Technology and Management (FTM) Group, Industrial Organization and Management Engineering Department, Escuela Universitaria de Estudios Empresariales de Bilbao, University of the Basque Country UPV/EHU, Basque Country, Spain

Olga Symonova
IST Austria, Klosterneuburg, Austria

Christopher N. Topp
Donald Danforth Plant Science Center, St. Louis, Missouri, USA

Herbert Edelsbrunner
IST Austria, Klosterneuburg, Austria

Preface

Every business possesses somewhat varied requirements for their software development methods. Software Process Improvement (SPI) includes an explanation of the evaluation methodology, a model for carrying out an evaluation, an explanation of the equipment that could be utilized for the evaluation methodology, along with a discussion of the elements that lead to results.

Software Process Improvement (SPI) makes up a guideline to carrying out an evaluation for software program development campaigns. Within a business, no two software program tasks may be handled utilizing exactly the same methodology. Therefore, Software Process Improvement (SPI) looks to explain the favored order whereby routines ought to happen during a software development task, with specific focus on an organization's administration. The first chapter analyzes dynamic resource allocation. Chapter 2 analyzes business processes. Chapter 3 scrutinizes working collaboratively. Chapter 4 suggests an estimation method for software engineering. Chapter 5 puts emphasis on a document preparation system. Chapter 6 evaluates collinearity in fMRI-based GLMs. Chapter 7 peruses quantifying mobile usage. Chapter 8 probes work-flows that use Graphical User Interfaces (GUIs). Chapter 9 evaluates OSS phenomenon. Chapter 10 gives an outline of specialized experimental software packages. Chapter 11 figures out the performance of PsychoPy. Chapter 12 evaluates marmap, a package designed for downloading data in R. Chapter 13 views adaptive communication networks. Chapter 14 features heterogeneity in meta-analysis methods. Chapter 15 evaluates statistical analysis of fMRI data using R. Chapter 16 is designed to develop online assessment of psychophysical performance. Chapter 17 scrutinizes complex networks. Chapter 18 deals with unlawful file sharing. Chapter 19 explains a digital self-reporting tool. Chapter 20 analyzes cloud computing. Chapter 21 studies a software platform for analyzing plant root system growth.

Editor
Gerard Ian Prudhomme
Hawaii, US

CHAPTER 1

DYNAMIC STAFFING AND RESCHEDULING IN SOFTWARE PROJECT MANAGEMENT: A HYBRID APPROACH

Yujia Ge[1,2], Bin Xu[1]

[1] College of Computer and Information Engineering, Zhejiang Gongshang University, Hangzhou, Zhejiang, China

[2] College of Information Engineering, Zhejiang University of Technology, Hangzhou, Zhejiang, China

ABSTRACT

Resource allocation could be influenced by various dynamic elements, such as the skills of engineers and the growth of skills, which requires managers to find an effective and efficient tool to support their staffing decision-making processes. Rescheduling happens commonly and frequently during the project execution. Control options have to be made when new resources are added or tasks are changed. In this paper we propose a software project staffing model considering dynamic elements of staff productivity with a Genetic Algorithm (GA) and Hill Climbing (HC) based optimizer. Since a newly generated reschedule dramatically different from the initial schedule could cause an obvious shifting cost increase, our rescheduling strategies consider both efficiency and stability. The results of real world case studies and extensive simulation experiments show that our proposed method is effective and could achieve comparable performance to other heuristic algorithms in most cases.

INTRODUCTION

Software project process is not a rigorous engineering process because scheduling schemes can be influenced by various dynamic elements including the skills of engineers, the growth of those skills, and cooperation in teams etc. It is difficult for software project managers to meet budget and schedule constraints set by its stakeholders. To solve this problem, researchers have developed several approaches to efficiently assign employees to tasks [1][2][3][4][5]. However, most resource-constrained scheduling techniques focus on the availability of resources instead of the resource productivity [6]. Significant productivity differences do exist among software developers. Therefore, to make a more realistic and reasonable schedule, productivity factors, such as learning, schedule pressure, should also be considered in software project management. When factors change or status becomes bad to projects, project control actions are taken and schedule must be revised to follow the change. To prevent ineffectual project control which is also the main cause of over-budget and behind-schedule projects [7], an efficient rescheduling approach needs to be carefully designed to make the project back to the track. However, the rescheduling problem is not emphasized sufficiently in the literature of scheduling models. To the best of our knowledge, the previous researches fall short of adequately explaining human capabilities to conquer the

Citation: Ge Y, Xu B (2016) Dynamic Staffing and Rescheduling in Software Project Management: A Hybrid Approach. PLoS ONE 11(6): e0157104. doi:10.1371/journal.pone.0157104.

complex and dynamic nature of software project management.

Therefore, the main goal of our current work is to do the scheduling and rescheduling model in which optimal control strategies could be computed with reasonable complexity. In this paper, the following work related to our model and approach is reported.

- Proposing a software project scheduling/rescheduling framework which supports dynamic staffing and rescheduling;
- Applying a hybrid approach based on a Genetic Algorithm (GA) and Hill Climbing (HC) considering both efficiency and stability;
- Conducting case studies and empirical studies.

RELATED WORK IN SOFTWARE PROJECT SCHEDULING AND RESCHEDULING

Our work is to investigate assigning employees to tasks and minimize the total project cost by stochastic search methods in project scheduling and rescheduling.

Software Project Scheduling

Several researchers compare the results from heuristic and metaheuristic techniques when solving resource-constrained scheduling problems [8]. Heuristic approaches are typically preferred for solving large-scale problems. One of these techniques is GA, introduced in the 1970s by John Holland [9]. Ever since, GAs have been used by many researchers to study scheduling problems and its variations [10]. In software project optimization fields, stochastic search methods have also been widely used. A general introduction and survey of recent achievements in Search Based Software Engineering can be found in the work by Harman *et al.* [11] including search-based software project scheduling in which GAs are considered popular methods. Since no single GA approach can consistently perform best in all problems, different GAs should be designed and tuned for software project scheduling problems. Our previous task-based model can be considered an early effort to apply GAs in the software project management environment [1], much as timeline-based model [3] does. Similar to our previous work, Alba and Chicano [4] also apply GAs for automated task assignments, showing that GAs are flexible and accurate for software project scheduling, and function as an important tool for automatic project management. In their work, an in-depth analysis was performed with an instance generator, where 48 different project scenarios were solved in software project management. Few human resource factors were considered in their model. To achieve better performance in a realistic setting, a more sophisticated model is required. There are some more recent research works on software project scheduling problems. Ferrucci *et al.* [12] proposed a multi-objective decision support approach to help software engineers balance project risks and duration against overtime. They had extensive experiments to show their effectiveness of their approach. Ren *et al.* [13] presented an approach based on Cooperative Co-evolution to optimize both developers' team staffing and work package scheduling to achieve early overall completion time which has different objectives from our research. The above works are all dealing with scheduling problems under software project circumstances. However none of them consider rescheduling problems during schedule execution.

Rescheduling Methods

Rescheduling techniques are also proposed in the areas, such as job shop problems [14][15][16]. Nevertheless there is still very limited support under software projects circumstances. Sukhodolsky uses discrete optimization techniques for finding optimal control actions the manager should take to meet project's deadline [17]. However, the situations in real projects may not be as simple as it is stated in the paper.

Software Project Effort Estimation

The task model of our approach is also related to the precision of software project effort estimation. Among these estimation models, COCOMO [18] and its improvement COCOMO II [19] are the most commonly used effort estimation models. Other estimation methods, e.g., analogy-based estimation [20] [21] and Bayesian analysis [22], also exist. Individual project effort estimation method using genetic programming [23] to predict the software development effort shows the accuracy results when these projects have been developed in a disciplined manner within a development-controlled environment. Most of the existing software task effort estimation methods could be employed before initiating the scheduling and rescheduling approach in this paper.

Software Development with System Dynamics

Human resource factors play an important role in software development. For example, pressure from tight schedules can cause an employee to speed up work. System Dynamics is a method to model a system by using continuous feedback loops. Since the first application in 1991 of system dynamics by Abdel-Hamid [24] on project management, there has been additional extension work within the realm of project management, such as the system dynamics extension modules [25][26]. Besides the continuous modeling approach, other researches focus on discrete-event approaches [27][28]. Hybrid software process simulation models combining discrete event and system dynamics approaches are also introduced to support software project estimation and project management [29][30][31]. Penta *et al.* [32] formalize communication overhead and use a search-based project staffing and scheduling approach on two large real world maintenance projects.

As described in this paper, our model incorporates system dynamics to illustrate team productivity and use stochastic search methods to solve the optimization problem in scheduling and rescheduling, and has the potential to become a more realistic model for project managers to adopt.

Project Scheduling Tools

There are many commercial project management tools such as *Microsoft Project* and *Symantec* Corporation's *Time Line*. None of these, however, provides automatic scheduling functionality. An early effort on software to help automatic scheduling for project management is *Opensched* [33]. It reads a file describing the project as input and produces textural descriptions of the generated project plan, Gantt charts and network diagrams. The input includes tasks which must be accomplished, resources (e.g., people, equipment, and facilities) which may work on tasks and work that has already been completed. However, the model supported in *Opensched* is very simple. A tool named *IntelliSPM* [34] is provided to support software project management by Computational Intelligence considering significant human factors. Although it is not always practical to use automated project scheduling in project management, research is still needed for improving the overall capabilities of current tools which is also what we are trying in this paper.

DYNAMIC STAFFING AND RESCHEDULING APPROACH

Our proposed approach for team productivity modeling and schedule/reschedule optimization process is illustrated in Fig 1. In this framework, "Schedule Optimizer based on GA and HC" is the key component. It helps to generate the project schedule at the beginning of a project, or re-generate schedules when tasks/team members change or differences between execution of the project and the plan become big. The inputs of the optimizer include model parameters of detailed task and employee information, the duration of each task which is achieved by simulation, and the fitness function according to management objectives and control actions. "Task and Employee models" includes the static part of task models (i.e., task estimated effort, task penalty model and required task skill lists, etc.) and employee models (i.e., skill lists, payment model, etc.). Before a project execution, the "schedule optimizer" generates the initial optimal schedule according to the planned tasks and assigned employees. During the project execution, real project progress is compared to the initial plan. When control actions are taken by a manager, rescheduling happens and accordingly the model parameters are changed. Re-calculation will be done to generate a new schedule for the remaining project. The new generated schedule is evaluated by a "rescheduling" objective function considering stability and efficiency. The dashed lines illustrate the process involved in the project control activities.

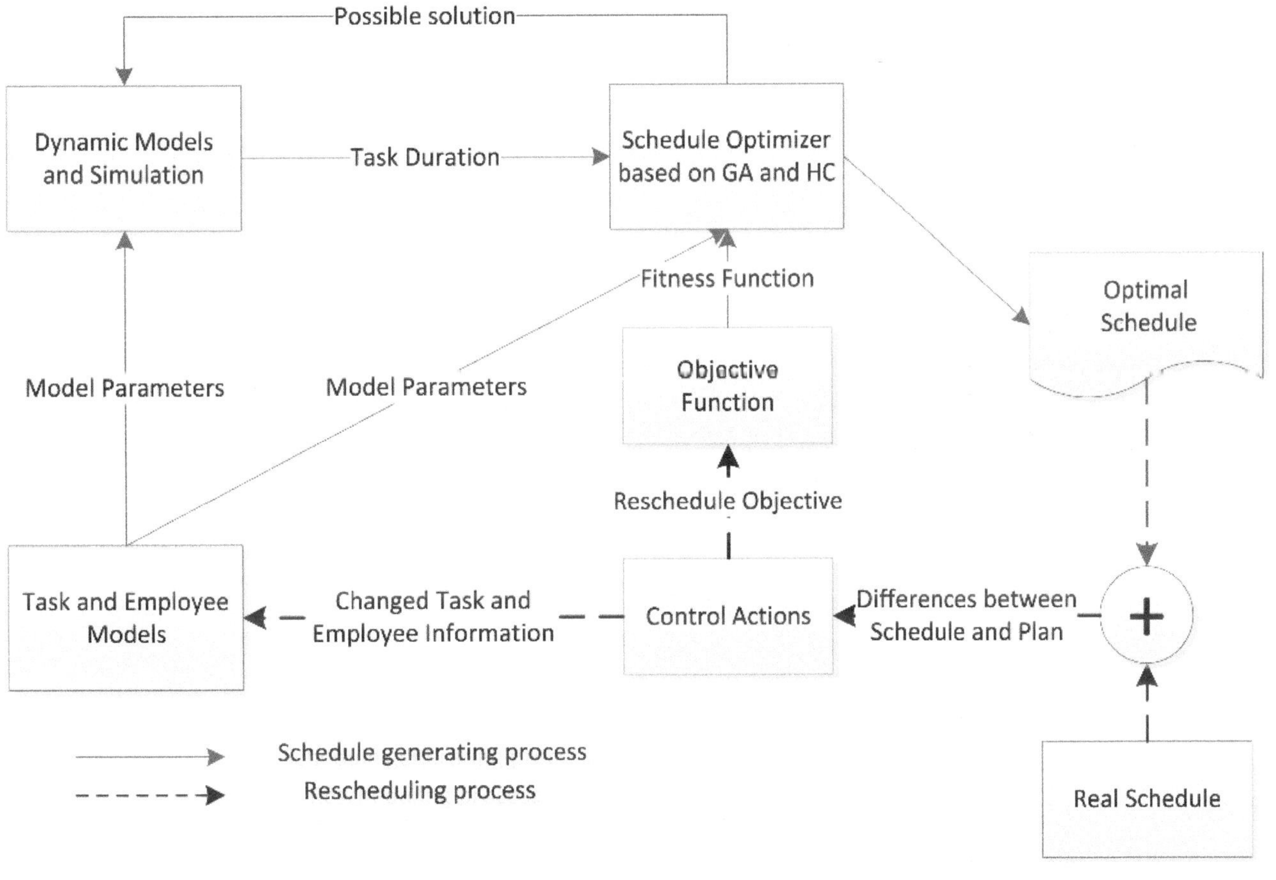

Figure 1. A Software Project Scheduling and Rescheduling Framework with Dynamic Factors.

Task and Employee Models

Task and employee models include the information about the tasks of a project and employees assigned to this task. A project is represented as a Task Precedence Graph (TPG), an acyclic directed graph consisting of a set of tasks $V = \{T_1, T_2,\ldots, T_n\}$ where T_k represents task k of the project, and precedence relations $P = \{(P_{ij}); i <> j, 1 \leq i \leq n, 1 \leq j \leq n\}$, where $P_{ij} = 1$ if T_i must be completed before T_j starts, and $P_{ij} = 0$ if not. Associated with each task T_k is the estimated effort, required skills, and deadline. Project team members $E = \{E_1, E_2,\ldots, E_n\}$ are the resources for the project where E_k represents employee k. Each E_k is associated with a list of skills he/she possesses with corresponding proficiency levels, salary rate, maximum workload (a limit to the amount of work load they can be assigned), and learning factor (a factor to reflect the improvement of their skill proficiency during working).

Dynamic Models and Simulation

Team productivity determines the overall project performance in a software development process. Fig 2 models this key component and its related factors. "Individual productivity" and "communication overhead" are major factors contributing to the "team productivity". "Individual productivity" is affected by "schedule pressure", "skill fitness" and "learning" factors. Although other factors, such as employee motivation, are also critical to individual productivity, we will not completely include all of them in this paper for the purpose of demonstrating key concepts. These factors are also controllable by project managers through a control parameter with value 0 or 1 to be turned on or off.

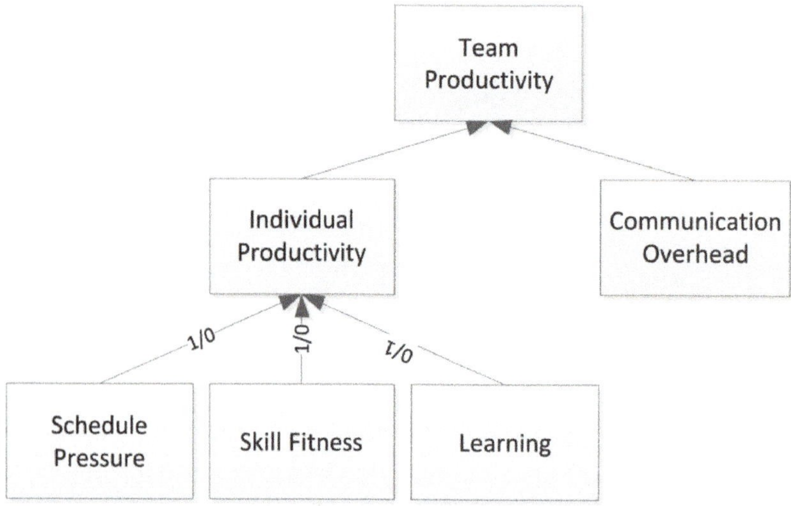

Figure 2. Team Productivity Model.

In the psychological model of group productivity by Ivan Steiner [24], the productivity of the software development group is stated as: Actual Productivity = Potential Productivity—Losses Due to Faulty Process, where losses due to faulty process refers basically to communication and motivation losses. Similarly, team productivity (P_{team}), i.e., the productivity of a team of people working on a given task in our work, is defined as the summation of individual productivity (InP_i) affected by communication overhead factor (*ComOverhead*(n)) in Eq (1).

$$P_{team} = (1 - ComOverhead(n)/100) * \sum_{i=1}^{n} InP_i \tag{1}$$

Abdel-Hamid and Madnick [24] demonstrated that communication overhead increases in proportion to n^2, where n is the size of the team, which can be expressed as Eq (2). When there is only one member in a team, it is obviously no need on team communication. As the size of the team increases, so does communication overhead. When the team size exceeds *MaxSize*, it is assumed to have 100% communication overhead in our work.

$$ComOverhead(n) = \begin{cases} 100 & n > MaxSize \\ 100 * (n-1)^2 * /(MaxSize - 1)^2 & 2 \le n \le MaxSize \\ 0 & n = 1 \end{cases} \tag{2}$$

Individual productivity is represented using Eq (3) which is affected by skill, learning, and schedule factor.

$$InP = nomP * f_{skill} * f_{learning} * f_{schedule} \tag{3}$$

where *InP* is the individual productivity; *nomP* corresponds to the nominal productivity which is generally the ideal individual productivity without considering factors such as schedule pressure and learning which is 1 by default; f_{skill}, $f_{learning}$, and $f_{schedule}$ correspond to the skill fitness factor, learning factor, and schedule pressure factor and defined in Eqs (4)–(6) respectively.

$$f_{skill} = \sum_{i=1}^{s} S_i / s \tag{4}$$

Eq (4) is to evaluate an employee's skill fitness to a task where S_i is the skill fitness level of the employee required for a given task and s is the number of skills required for a given task.

The learning curve has been studied for many years. Only a few papers, however, mention learning curve in Software Engineering, such as [24] where Eq (5) is adapted from. $f_{learning}$ represents the improvement of understanding the task along with the progress of the task itself and is a S-curve equation

$$f_{learning} = \begin{cases} 1.6 * (l_i - 1) * X^2 + 1 & 0\% <= X <= 50\% \\ 1.6 * (l_i - 1) * X + 1.4 - 0.4 * l_i & 50\% <= X <= 75\% \\ l_i - 3.2 * (l_i - 1) * (1 - X)^2 & 70\% <= X <= 100\% \end{cases} \quad (5)$$

where X is the percentage that a task has been completed and l_i is the learning property of an employee. To get $f_{schedule}$, *schedule pressure* is defined as a function of the current time (T_c) and the planned time (T_p) in Eq (6) derived from the research by Abdel-Hamid and Madnick [24].

$$\text{schedule pressure} = \begin{cases} 5 & T_c > T_p \\ \min\{Workflow_{required}/Workflow_{normal}, 5\} & T_c \leq T_p \end{cases} \quad (6)$$

Where

$$Workflow_{required} = effort_{remaining}/(T_p - T_c) \quad (7)$$

$$Workflow_{normal} = P_{team} \quad (8)$$

$f_{schedule}$ can then be obtained from *schedule pressure* using a lookup table from the Vensim documents [35] shown in Table 1. For example, if an employee's individual productivity is 100 LOC/day, then his productivity is 100 * $f_{schedule}$ which will range from 100-150 LOC/day, 100 being without schedule pressure.

Table 1. Lookup Table for $f_{schedule}$

schedule pressure (x)	$f_{schedule}$
$0 \leq x < 1.1$	1
$1.1 \leq x < 1.35$	1.2
$1.35 \leq x < 1.75$	1.4
$1.75 \leq x < 3.5$	1.45
$3.5 \leq x \leq 5$	1.5

doi:10.1371/journal.pone.0157104.t001

Objective Function for Scheduling/Rescheduling

Our objective function is set to be the minimum total cost for performing the whole project. Several assumptions have been made for our scheduling problem: (1) Tasks cannot be interrupted and resumed; (2) Different people can work on different tasks at the same time, but cannot do work over their maximum overwork level; (3) Every employee assigned to a task needs to do the work for the whole duration for each task. When rescheduling, other than the efficiency factor (i.e., the total cost of project execution), the stability factor also need to be considered since the cost of changing staffing profile could be high and managers are in favor of rescheduling strategies addressing continuity in practice.

$$\text{The objective function} = Efficiency * W_e + Stability * W_s \quad (9)$$

Our scheduling/rescheduling objective function considers both efficiency and stability is shown in Eq (9). W_e and W_s are the weights for the efficiency and stability factors controlled by project managers which are determined by their needs and their experiences. *Efficiency* and *Stability*are calculated by Eqs (10) and (11) respectively. In generating an initial project plan, the stability factor is set to 0. During the rescheduling process, if a newly generated schedule radically different from the initial one can produce a great cost in changing staffing profile, the stability factor could weight more.

$$Efficiency = 1/Cost_{norm} \quad (10)$$

where *Cost* is computed by the labor rates of each resource and the hours applied to the tasks of a schedule. $Cost_{norm}$ is achieved by dividing *cost* by the maximum cost in the population of a GA.

Stability in Eq (11) is applied to minimize the impact of disruptions induced by the new schedule or introduced by new team members.

$$Stability = 1/StabilityPenalty_{norm} \quad (11)$$

where $StabilityPenalty_{norm}$ is achieved by dividing *penalty for stability* by the *maximum penalty for stability* in the population of a GA. Two kinds of stability are recognized, i.e. ex post stability, ex ante stability [36]. Ex post stability is considered and Eq (12) [14] is adapted in our model. The value is achieved by adding starting time deviation and actuality penalty.

$$StabilityPenalty_{norm} = \sum_{j \in B}(|t_j' - t_j| + k/\sqrt{t_j - T})/n \quad (12)$$

where B is the set of tasks that need to be rescheduled. They are the tasks that remained unprocessed in the initial schedule and still need to be processed under new circumstances. N is the number of tasks in B. t_j is the predicted start time of task j in the new schedule. t'_j is the predicted start of job *j* in the initial schedule. *T* is the current time.

Project managers could control the rescheduling plan by changing the stability and efficiency weights. The results of the experiment given for different number of tasks to be rescheduled are shown in our previous work [37] in which we normalized the durations by dividing it by the maximum duration in each column. The outcome shows that the stability factor has more effect on the project when small number of tasks is to be rescheduled. It would encourage managers to adjust the stability factor when the rescheduled point is at the tail of the whole plan of the project.

Scheduler Optimizer based on Genetic Algorithm and Hill Climbing

With the GA's ability on global optimization and the HC's ability on local optimization, a hybrid algorithm combining GA with HC might be an ideal choice [3]. Based on the block theory, in the early stage of the GA computation, because there exist the many efficient, small blocks, under crossover operators, the probability that the small blocks can be united as big blocks are high. Therefore, the quality of the population is improved quickly. But in the later stage of GAs, when big blocks are becoming more and more similar, the efficiency of crossover operators is becoming much lower. At that time the quality of many individuals cannot be improved a lot which leads to low efficiency in the later stage of GAs. Therefore, we choose to use a GA at early stage followed by HC. The process of our optimizer is described in Fig 3. The first step is to set the parameters of the models, such as mutation probability, crossover probability, generation number, and population size of the GA. Then task and employee information is loaded into the GA. If it is a rescheduling process, the initial schedule plan also needs to be loaded. After these initialization steps, the GA runs until the generation number reaches the previously set one. Starting from the best individual generated from the last generation of the GA, HC runs to get an optimal schedule.

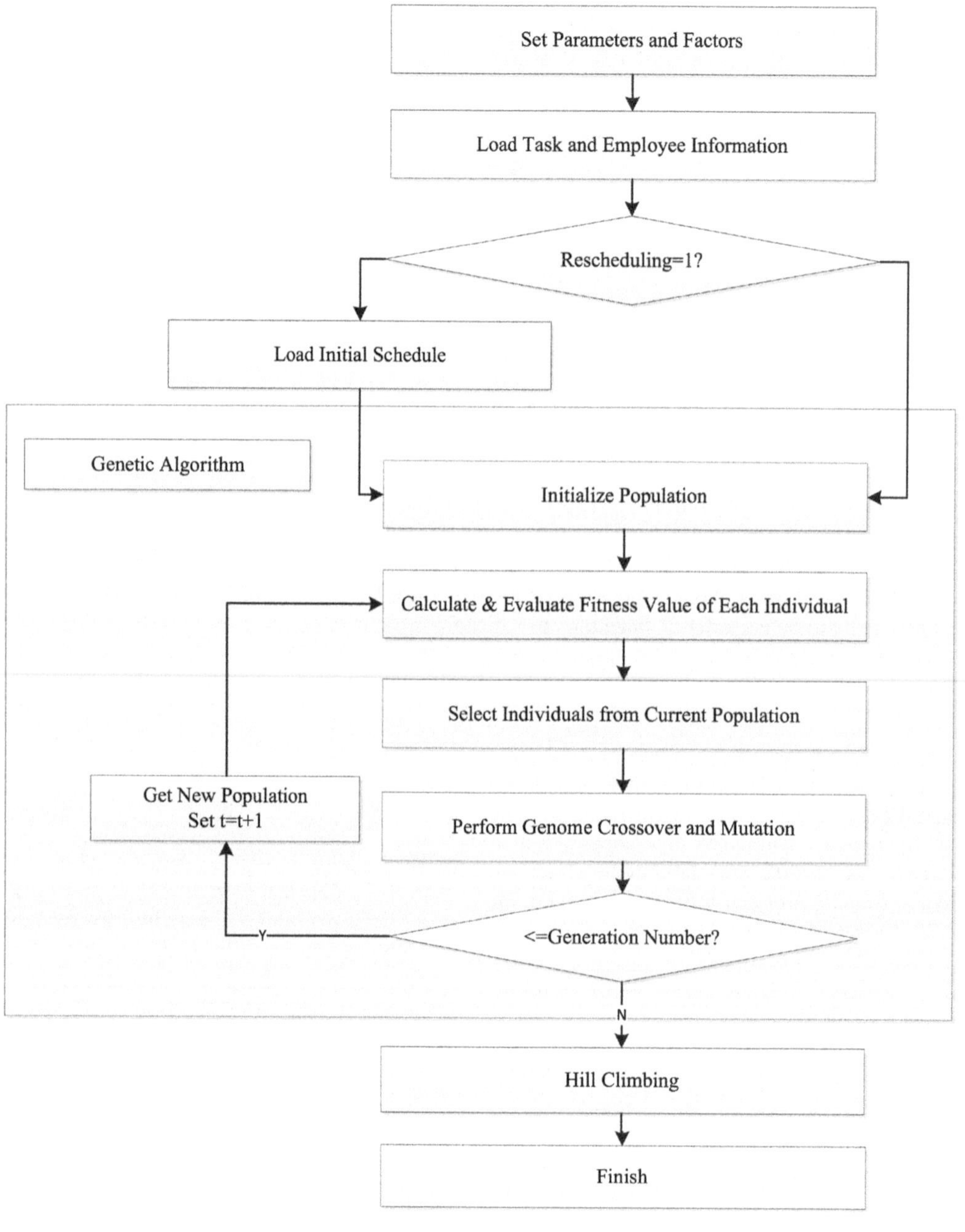

Figure 3. Process of Scheduler Optimizer.

Genome Representation

During the optimization, a candidate solution representation S is represented as {A, L}. Part A is a 1D task-employee assignment array that stores the information of task-employee assignments derived from 2D task-employee assignment array. For assigned tasks, an employee can work with a load of 0%, 25%, 50%, 75% or 100%. For example, 50% commitment means employee 1 can do 20 hours every week if he normally works 40 hours per week. A 2D task-employee assignment array can be squeezed into a 1D array according to the "possible" assignment matrix which is generated by the task-employee skill match. For example, in Fig 4, two employees are assigned to 6 tasks. Its task-employee possible-assignment matrix is derived according to their skill match, where 1 stands for possible assignment and 0 stands for no possible assignment. Since this possible assignment matrix is always stored in the model after the initial task-employee skill match calculation, the task-employee assignment 2D array could be squeezed into 1D array by taking out no-possible assignment elements (i.e., the "0" element). In this instance, there are 9 elements in task-employee assignment 1D array and the element order is the same as the order in task-employee possible assignment matrix in the row order.

Task-Employee Possible-Assignment Matrix

	Task1	*Task2*	*Task3*	*Task4*	*Task5*	*Task6*
Employee1	1	1	0	1	1	0
Employee2	0	1	1	1	1	1

1D Task-Employee Assignment Array (Genome S, Part A)

0.5	0.25	0.25	0.5	0.25	1	0.25	0.5	0.5

↕

2D Task-Employee Assignment Array

	Task1	*Task2*	*Task3*	*Task4*	*Task5*	*Task6*
Employee1	0.5	0.25	0	0.25	0.5	0
Employee2	0	0.25	1	0.25	0.5	0.5

Figure 4. Part A of Genome S Generated from Possible-Assignment Matrix and 2D Task-Employee Assignment Array.

Second part L is the priority list by which a certain topological-sort vector representing the execution order of the tasks in the schedule can be derived. Priority-based encoding, proposed by Gen and Cheng [38], can decide a certain order of tasks with information of tasks precedence information. Given a directed acyclic graph (DAG) $G = (V, E)$, a topological sort is an order of all the vertex and for each $(u, v) \in E$, u appears before v on the list. Each DAG may have more than one topological sort. When there are two tasks competing for one position, the task with the higher priority wins. For example, for a project including 3 tasks, namely T_1 to $T_3$where T_1 is the starting task and it is the direct precedence of T_2 and T_3, the task priority list [2 1 3] means T_3 whose priority value is 3 has higher priority than T_2 with value 1. A topological sort $\{T_1, T_3, T_2\}$ can be generated which satisfies task precedence relationship. Using task order as genome directly in our scheduling problem could generate invalid individuals which dissatisfies the DAG. But priority-based sort only manipulates the priority information which must combine with project DAG information to be interpreted as a project execution. Therefore, no invalid individual will be generated.

Genetic Operator.

To manipulate the two structures of candidate solution S, the following operators are chosen. The initialization operator randomly chooses any value from possible values (0, 0.25, 0.50, 0.75, 1) to be the allele (i.e., possible settings for an attribute of an individual) of the initial population of 1D task-employee array (A). The priority list (L) is initialized as the random order from 1 to the total number of tasks. When rescheduling is necessary, tasks and employees with changed profiles are updated first and then the previous schedule is set as the initial population of a new GA calculation. The crossover operator of S invokes the crossover operator for each of the genomes in the composite genome according to a random number P as illustrated in Fig 5. The standard one-point crossover function is applied in part A of the genome and Order Crossover is used in part L. Because the two structures of the genome representation are independent and the 1D array genome is derived from the possible-assignment matrix, the offsprings of the crossover operator are always valid.

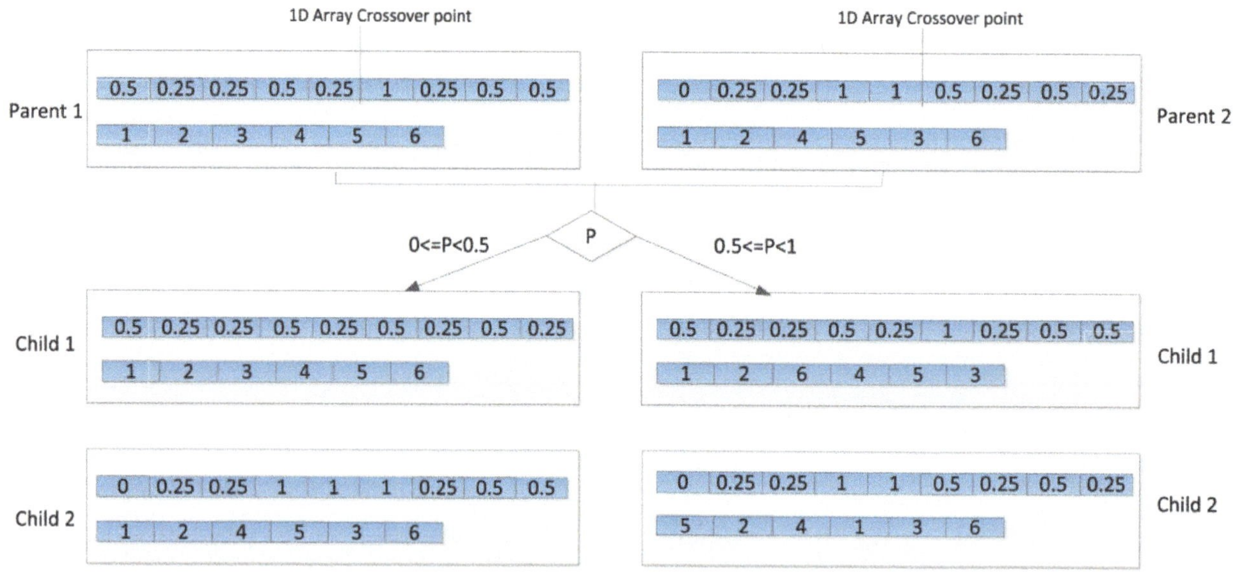

Figure 5. Crossover Operation of Genome S.

According to the mutation probability, we randomly select one of the two genomes to do the mutation shown in Fig 6. In the 1D array structure, we only change the certain elements while the certain elements are swapped in the task priority vector.

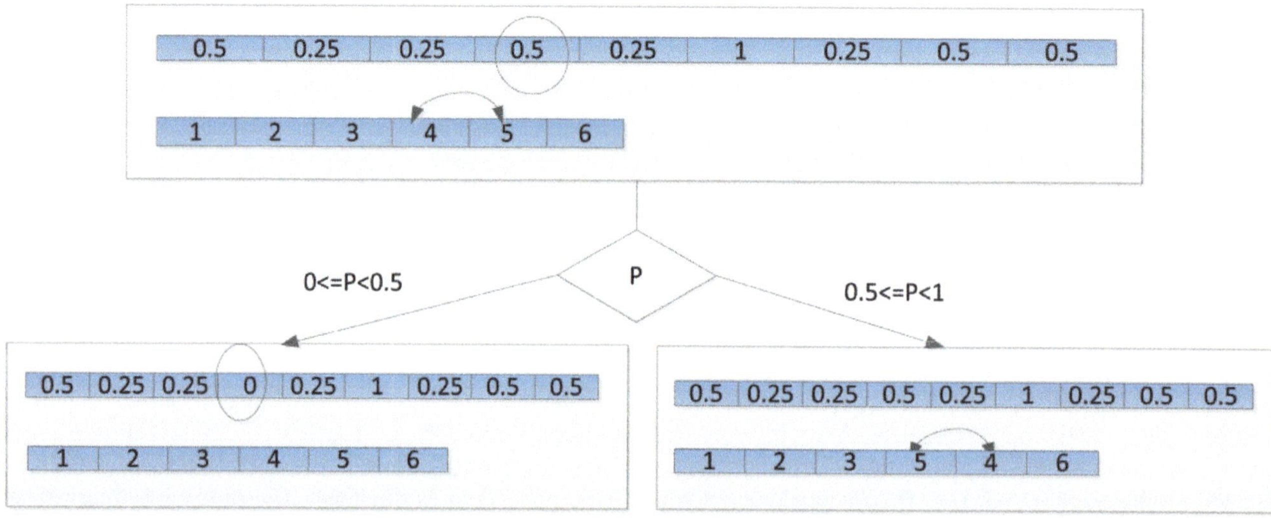

Figure 6. Mutation Operation of Genome S.

As stated in the subsection on genome representation, no invalid individual will be generated since operators only deal with possible task-employee assignment and priority task information.

Fitness Function Calculation

In our GA approach for software project scheduling, the fitness function calculation is the most complicated part. The detailed steps are illustrated in Fig 7: 1) Initialize the system by loading a task-employee assignment; 2) Set the number of the time unit; 3) Get the next task from a topological sorted list; 4) Check whether the task can start in this time unit or not by validating that all the; precedence tasks have been finished, all the employees are available, and all the employees do; not work over limit, if not, go to 2); 5) Do system dynamics simulation for each task; 6) At the end of execution of every task, calculate the cost, penalty and update the employee's; overall experience and certain skill proficiency; 7) If all the tasks are finished, return the fitness score; 8) Start another loop from 2).

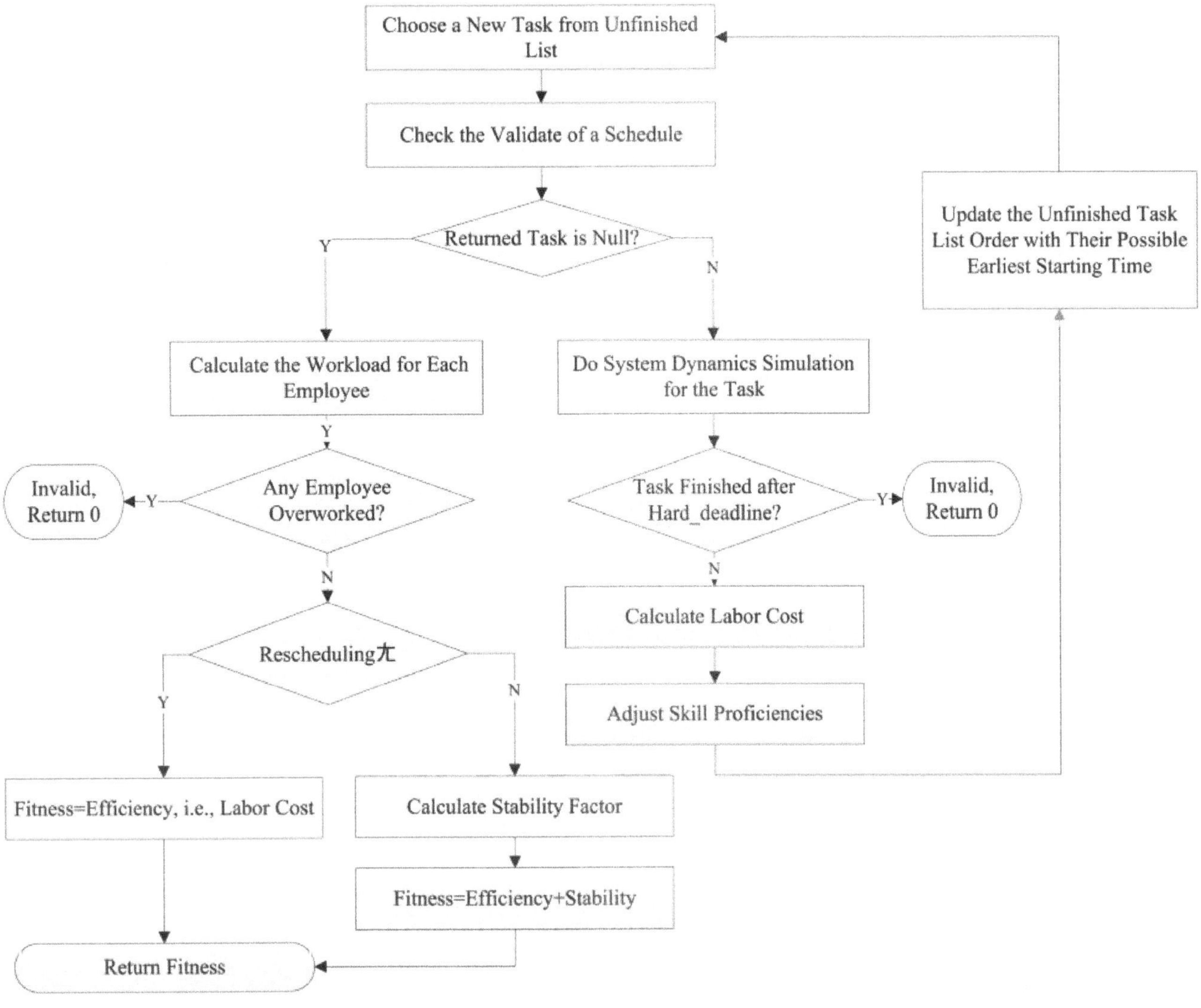

Figure 7. Fitness Function Calculation.

Hill Climbing.

Usually HC is much faster than GAs. However, the landscape in our problem has many local optima which makes HC difficult to achieve the global optimum. Therefore, in our algorithm, HC starts right after the end of our GA calculation. The HC algorithm that we use is that the best one is chosen as the start point. By using that best one, it is mutated at a randomly chosen single locus and the fitness is evaluated. If the mutation leads to a higher fitness, the new one replaces the old one. The procedure continues until the optimum is found.

EXPERIMENTS

A preliminary tool for our hybrid staffing and rescheduling model was implemented in C++ with GALib [39], an open-source toolkit of Genetic Algorithms in various platforms including Unix and Windows. The software *Sched-SPM* is available at http://sched-spm.sourceforge.net. The graphical user interface of *Sched-SPM* is shown in Fig 8. The input and output files of the software are required as XML format. The input file includes tasks' and employees' information according to predefined file format. The output XML file of the generated schedule is accordance with Microsoft Project 2010 and could be open and edited within it. The software runs on a Windows environment with 2.9GHz processor, 8G RAM. Several experiments were conducted under this setting to evaluate the performance of the model.

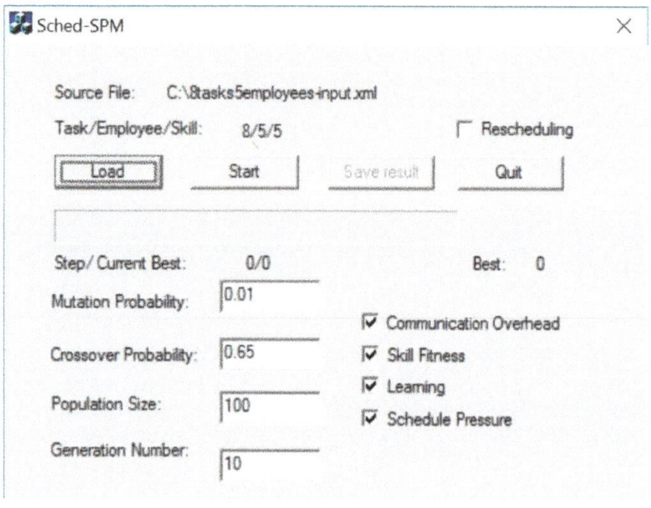

Figure 8. User Interface of *Sched-SPM.*

Parameter Settings

Genetic Algorithms are non-deterministic and factors such as the population size, generation number, mutation probability and crossover probability not only influence the time required to perform the GA algorithm, but also affect the quality of the result [3]. Several project simulation based tests were conducted to tune these parameters. Population size and generation number are set to 1000 and get the best results. It is reasonable to expect these two parameters set to 1000 to get good results for later larger and extensive experiments, although larger population size and generation number could result in better performance overall. The preliminary experiment results also show that the crossover probability set to 0.01-0.8 does not have a great impact on the performance of GAs. Hence, the crossover probability is set to 0.65 as our previous work [1][3]. The comparison of results by different mutation probabilities suggests that small mutation probabilities produce better results than the larger ones under some scenarios. Such a phenomenon is not unique [40]. This often occurs because higher mutation probabilities produce a greater percentage of not-so-good offspring. As the scheduling problem has many restrictions, it is easy to produce such kind of not-so-good offsprings by random mutation. In our experiments, mutation probabilities between 0.001 and 0.05 produced the best results. Accordingly, the default mutation probability is set to be 0.01 for the remainder of our work. To tune the value of k in Eq (12), experiments have been done in [37] where k is set to be 10, 100, 1000 and 10000 respectively. Stability Factor arrives from 0, 0.25, 0.5, 0.75 and 1. When stability factor weight more, the reschedule will favor on the schedule which is more similar to the initial plan and it will cause generated schedule with longer duration. We also expect that stability factor should increase steadily as the stability factor weights more. By this objective, $k$with 1000 seems more reasonable as the project includes about 12 tasks. When k is equal to 10 and 100, the line does not visibly going up which means k is too small to show the affect. As a result, we can consider k = 1000 outperform others.

Case Studies

One experiment is a small project from Boyuan Software Company (www.139erp.com) who commits to the development of mobile phone sales management software and provides corresponding services. This project is to develop a mobile phone sales management on JAVA. It is extracted from a real project and some parameters such as learning, max workload, are redefined for incorporating our case study. The project consisted of 19 tasks and 9 employees with the properties listed in Tables 2 and 3 respectively. The employees who are all available from Jan 1, 2013 to July 1, 2013, in turn, each possessed 6 skills (JAVA programming language, testing, analysis/requirements, design, SQL server, domain knowledge) to a greater or lesser extent. It is not immediately obvious, even to the most experienced software manager, what the optimal assignments would be in this case.

Table 2. Task Properties of a Project with 19 Tasks and 9 Employees

Task No.	Estimated Effort	Deadline	Precedence Tasks	Required Skills
1	0.3	Feb-01		3 6
2	0.6	Feb-01	1	3 5 6
3	0.8	March-01	1	3 5
4	0.3	March-01	1	3 6
5	0.5	March-01	3,4	3 4
6	0.4	March-0	1 2,5	3 4
7	0.4	Apr-01	2,3,5	6 4 5
8	0.4	Apr-01	6	3 4 5
9	0.7	Apr-01	4	6 4
10	0.5	Apr-01	7	4 5
11	0.5	Apr-01	8	1 3 5
12	0.4	Apr-01	9,10	1 6 4
13	0.5	May-01	7, 8, 9	1 2 6
14	0.8	May-01	11	1 4 6
15	0.5	May-01	13	1 4 5
16	0.5	June-01	12	1 2 5
17	0.2	June-01	14	1 2 6 4
18	0.2	July-01	14, 15	4
19	0.5	July-01	16,17,18	2 5 6

Table 3. Employee Properties of a Project with 19 Tasks and 9 Employees

EmpID	Hourly Salary	Max Workload	Learning	skill1	skill2	skill3	skill4	skill5	skill6
1	38	110%	1.5	3	4	0	5	5	4
2	33	120%	1.3	4	0	2	0	5	0
3	28	120%	1.3	0	4	2	0	3	4
4	35	150%	1.1	4	0	3	3	0	5
5	40	120%	1.1	5	5	0	0	5	4
6	30	110%	1.3	0	0	4	4	0	3
7	30	110%	1.1	0	0	3	4	5	0
8	35	110%	1.2	5	0	4	5	0	0
9	40	100%	1.5	0	3	5	0	0	5

Scheduling

The best result generated from the search algorithm is shown in Table 4. The cost of the schedule is 119358 RMB which involving all the dynamic factors. Table 5 shows the calculated costs with certain factors excluded. Without the learning factors or communication overhead, the overall cost increases as expected. Without schedule pressure, no solution is found in this highly constrained case. Although these results are intuitive in this simple scenario, in a more complicated situation data can help to analyze the influence of certain factors and to assist managers to make more sensible decisions.

Table 4. Generated Best Schedule from Our Algorithm

Task ID	Days	Start Date	End Date	*Resource*
1	13	Jan 1	Jan 13	Employee9
2	21	Jan 14	Feb 3	Employee3[50%]
3	24	Feb 4	Feb 27	Employee7, Employee3
4	19	Jan 14	Feb 7	Employee9[50%]
5	18	Feb 28	Mar 17	Employee3[25%], Employee7[75%]
6	6	Mar 18	Mar 25	Employee6
7	24	Mar 18	Apr 10	Employee1[50%]
8	11	Mar 26	Apr 5	Employee7[75%]
9	15	Mar 18	Apr 1	Employee4
10	12	Apr 11	Apr 22	Employee1
11	18	Apr 6	Apr 23	Employee2
12	18	Apr 23	May 10	Employee1
13	29	May 3	May 31	Employee5, Employee1[25%]
14	24	Apr 24	May 17	Employee4
15	12	Jun 1	Jun 12	Employee1
16	16	May 16	May 31	Employee5
17	9	May 18	May 26	Employee1[75%]
18	5	Jun 13	Jun 19	Employee7
19	12	Jun 20	Jul 1	Employee1

Table 5. Results without Considering Some Factors

Cost(RMB)	Best	Worst	Mean
With all the factors	119358	125759	121104
Without learning factor	131432	142992	141074
Without communication overhead factor	120202	128466	125936

Rescheduling

On Apr 3, T1, T2, T3, T4, T5, T6, T7, T10 have been completed and other tasks have not yet been initiated. The corresponding Gantt graph of the initial schedule and project execution is presented in Fig 9. The project is greatly behind the plan notified by real execution data.

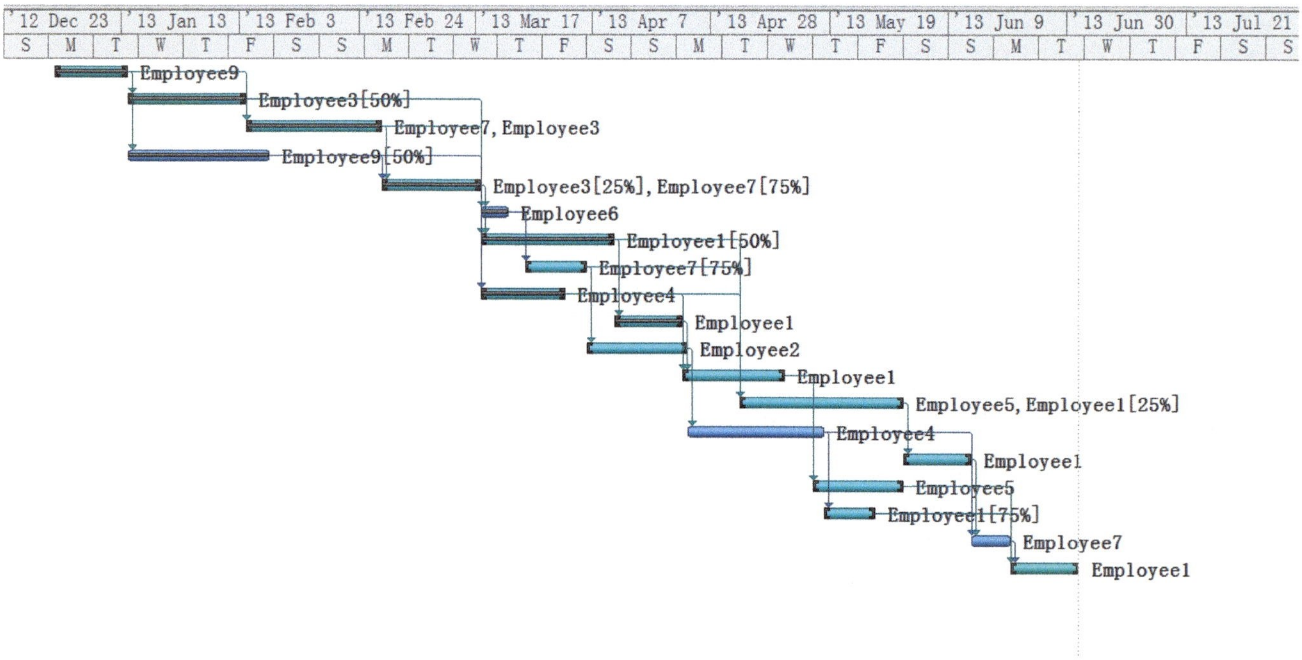

Figure 9. Initial Schedule and Project Execution.

To bring any remaining project tasks into alignment with the planned schedule, managers have various project control actions to take, such as, adding people to the project, extending the time to completion, cutting out non-essential or less essential requirements. If option 1 is taken, genetic algorithm can easily generate a new schedule with the updated employees' information and the updated tasks' information if any new estimation has been made. If option 2 is used, it is just right-shift rescheduling and no genetic algorithm calculation needs to be done. If option 3 is taken, our model still easily fits by updating original task information tables. The result going after option 1 is shown as follows. Suppose manager would like to add another engineer (as shown in Table 6) into this team to catch up the schedule.

Table 6. Newly Added Employee's Information

EmpID	Hourly Salary	Max Workload	Learning	skill1	skill2	skill3	skill4	skill5	skill6
10	32	150%	1.5	3	4	0	0	5	5

Our rescheduling approach is applied for the remaining tasks that have not been started and Table 7 shows the comparison from the best newly generated schedule versus the initial schedule. t_{start} lists the start time of a specific task and d means the duration of this task. Rescheduling approach produced acceptable results both with stability ($W_s = 0$, $W_e = 1$) and without stability ($W_s = 1$, $W_e = 1$).

Table 7. Generated Schedule versus Initial Schedule

Task ID	t_{start} in initial schedule	d	t_{start} in reschedule under Ws = 0, We = 1	d	t_{start} in reschedule under Ws = 1, We = 1	d
T8	Mar 26	11	Apr 3	10	Apr 3	12
T11	Apr 6	18	Apr 3	16	Apr 3	18
T12	Apr 23	18	Apr 3	10	Apr 3	11
T13	May 3	29	Apr 4	25	Apr 5	30
T14	Apr 28	24	Apr 29	18	May 5	19
T15	May 22	12	Apr 29	31	May 5	31
T16	May 16	16	May 19	11	May 24	12
T17	Jun 7	9	May 30	24	Jun 6	24
T18	Jun 13	5	May 30	9	Jun 6	10
T19	Jun 20	12	May 30	29	Jun 18	14
Duration (days)		130		121		136
Cost (RMB)		119358		128352		129327

The efficiency performance is affected by the stability measure. We can also see from the table that the schedule ($W_s = 0$, $W_e = 1$) has better efficiency performance over the schedule ($W_s = 1$, $W_e = 1$).

Discussion via Management Experts' Opinion

We decided to compare our model with experts' opinion to evaluate the performance. We invited two senior software project managers to assign the employees to tasks. Both of them are experienced software project manager. One has 20 years in managing software projects in IT department of an international bank. The other worked on software development for almost 20 years and over 15 years on planning and managing projects in a country-wide e-commerce company. The experts shared the same assumptions as our model does and the overall objective is to have lest cost. But since humans could not calculate the schedule under all the assumptions set in the problem, they have their own inclination when assigning employees to tasks. For example, one manager has more concerns on skill matching of the employees and communication overhead. One pays more attentions on the overall duration of the project. Based on their work shown in Figs 10 and 11, we obtained cost of 124580 and 128030 respectively. The average time the experts spent developing the assignments was 3 hours. The average run time for our program is 30 minutes. The average cost of the experiments was slightly below the experts' results. This is because the complexity of the problem makes humans difficult in achieving a schedule with minimal cost. When doing the rescheduling, experts change the schedules based on their previous plans. By adding Employee 10 to Task 13 and Task 16, the task duration is shorten to catch up the overall project duration. The results in Figs 12 and 13 are similar to our program's result but the overall costs are higher. The experts are reluctant to change other tasks other than the tasks affected by the newly added employees. During real project execution, experts may consider more factors such as the personality and experience factors which are currently difficult to model.

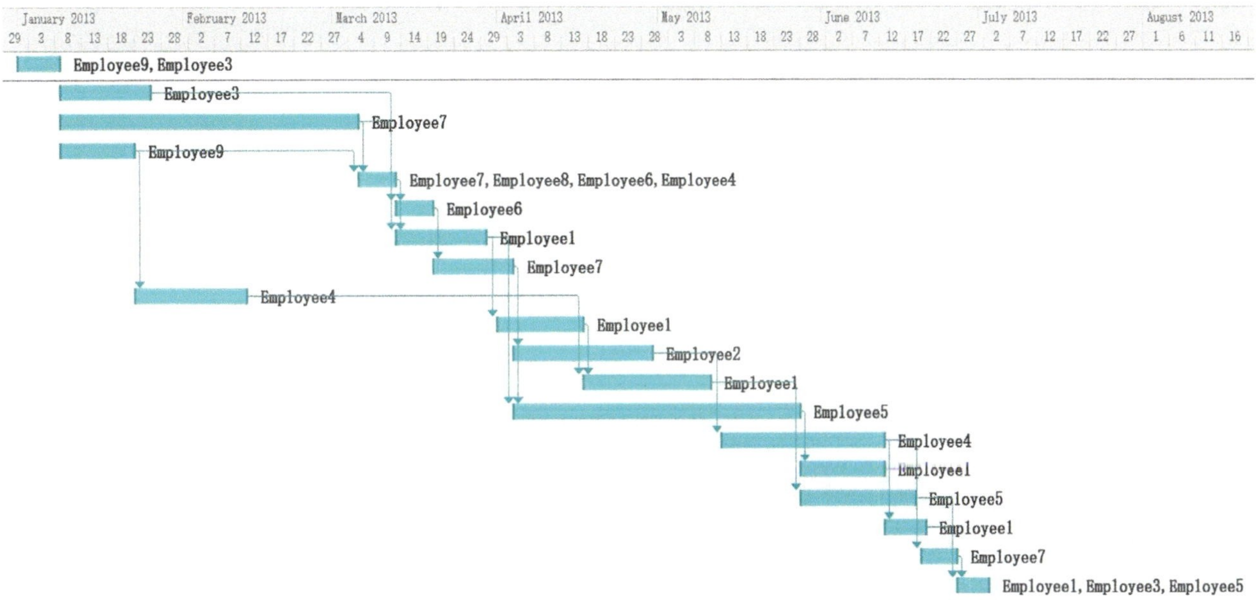

Figure 10. Scheduling Result from Expert 1.

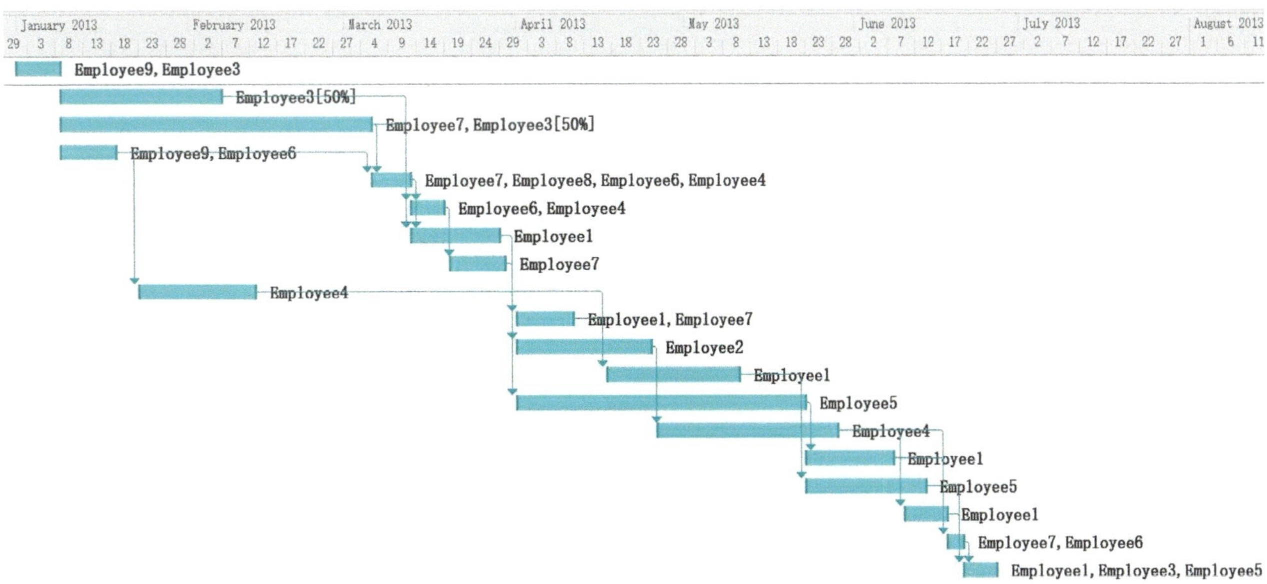

Figure 11. Scheduling Result from Expert 2.

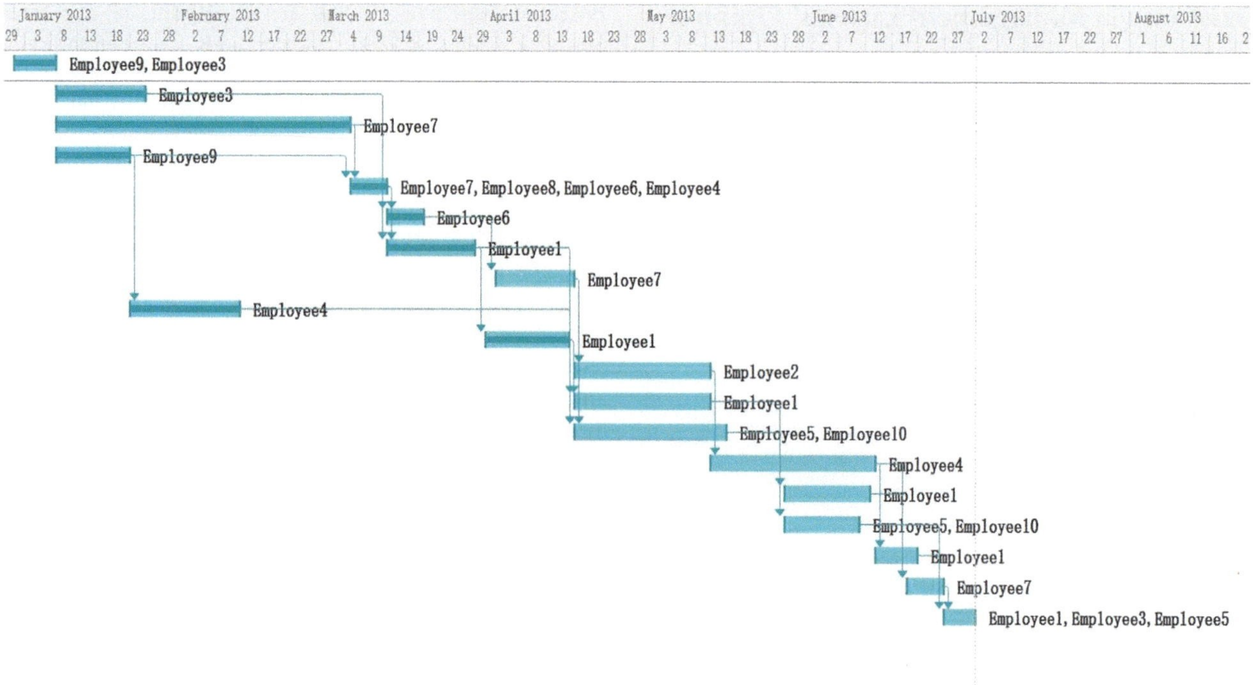

Figure 12. Rescheduling Result from Expert 1.

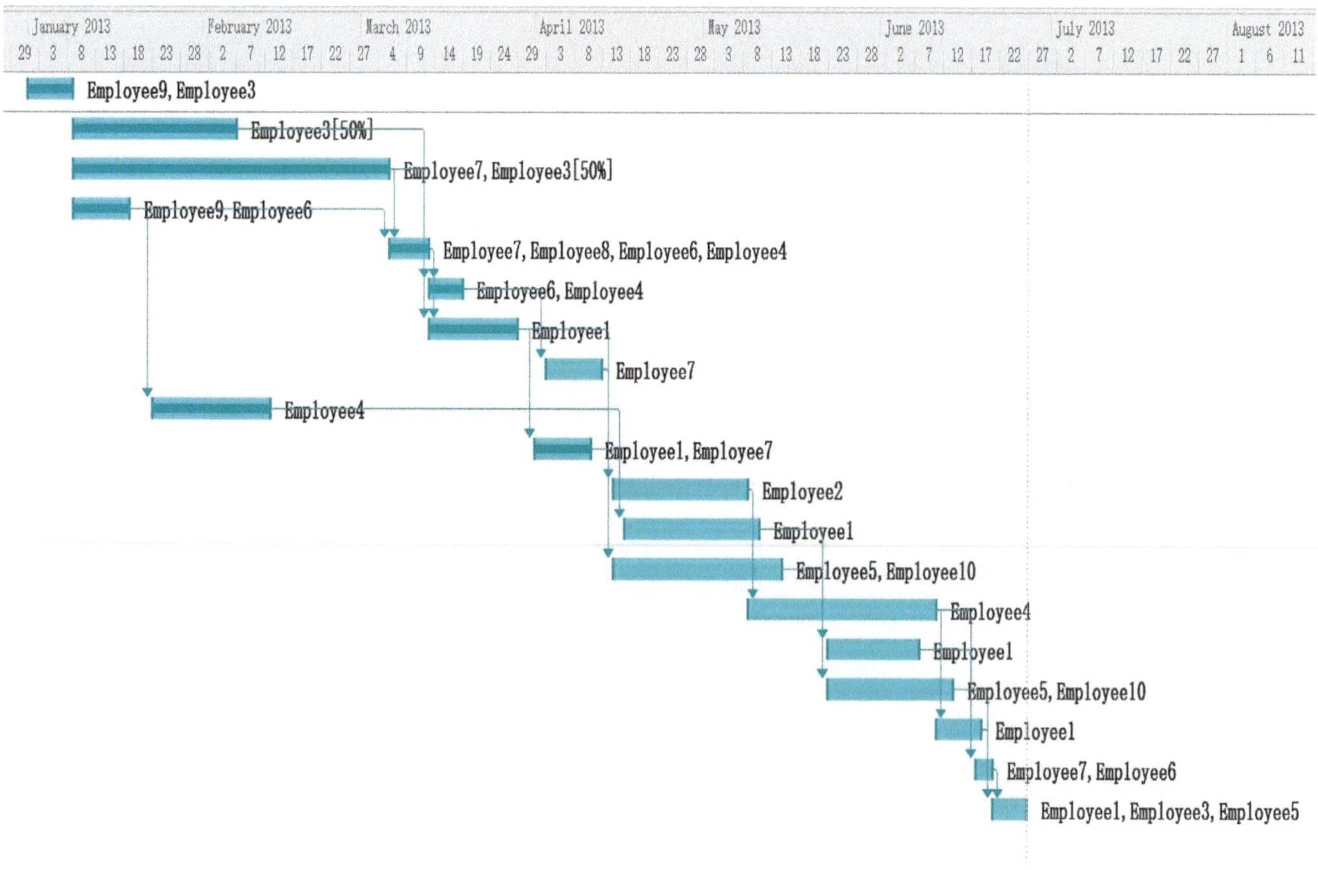

Figure 13. Rescheduling Result from Expert 2.

The experts also work on planning for a college web site project which represents a common category of software projects. The project is to develop a system for students and teachers to communicate in JSP technology. There are 28 tasks, 8 kinds of skills, and 10 employees available for this project. Work Breakdown Structure (WBS) of this project is illustrated in Fig 14. Skill lists include Planning, Personnel Training, Documentation, System Design, Requirements Analysis, Maintenance and Testing. Experts took about 3.5 and 3 hours to get the results. Our program run 25 minutes to get a scheduling result. Similar to previous cases, the average cost of our approach is slightly less than experts', i.e., 79000 and 77500 by experts respectively and 75800 by our program.

	Task Mode	Task Name	Predecessor
1		**Project Planning**	
2		Template Determination	
3		Planning Documentation	2
4		**Requirements Analysis**	
5		Requirements Acquisition	3
6		Requirements Analysis	5
7		Requirements Confirmation	6
8		Requirments Documentation	7
9		**Website Design**	
10		Architecture Design	8
11		Detailed Design	10
12		Database Design	10
13		User Interface Design	10
14		Design Documentation	10,11,12,13
15		**Hardware Procurement**	
16		Hardware and Software Planning and procurement	14
17		**Environmental Configuration**	
18		Environmental Configuration	16
19		**"Education" Subsystem Development**	
20		Coding 1	18
21		Unit Test 1	20
22		Coding and Unit Test Documentation 1	21
23		**"Communication" Subsystem Development**	
24		Coding 2	18
25		Unit Test 2	24
26		Coding and Unit Test Documentation 2	25
27		**"Authentification" Subsystem Development**	
28		Coding 3	18
29		Unit Test 3	28
30		Coding and Unit Test Documentation 3	29
31		**System Test**	
32		Integration Test	22,26,30
33		System Test	32
34		Test Documentation	33
35		**Acceptance Process**	
36		User Manuel Documentation	34
37		Personnel Training	34
38		Product Transition	37,36

Figure 14. WBS of a Web Site Development Project.

In conclusion, the schedules created by the experts were already acceptable but the results from the GA-HC program outperformed the experts' assignments in achieving the objectives and in execution time. Experts agree that the generated schedules can give good management suggestions and work as an auxiliary schedule for managers. Since our model considers more factors such as learning, communication overhead, skill fitness, managers can also take the generated results to inspect their management options.

EMPIRICAL STUDY AND DISCUSSION

To evaluate the effectiveness and performance of our approach, several problems with different sizes and constraints were designed and conducted. Analysis and discussion of the simulation results are reported.

Effectiveness of Our Approach

To confirm the effectiveness of our approach, smaller experiments were designed. It is a project with 4 tasks with task properties and employee properties in Tables 8 and 9.

Table 8. Task Properties of a Project with 4 Tasks and 3 Employees

Task No.	Estimated Effort	Deadline	Penalty Per Day	Precedence Tasks	Required Skills
Design	0.1	Jan-15	20000		Analysis C++ Word
Programming1	0.1	Jan-15	10000	1	Analysis C++
Programming2	0.2	Jan-15	10000	1	Analysis C++
Documentation	0.2	Jan-15	10000	2,3	Word

Table 9. Employee Properties of a Project with 4 Tasks and 3 Employees

EmpID	Hourly Salary	Max Workload	Learning	Analysis	C++	Word
1	15	100%	1.25	5	3	2
2	15	100%	1.15	4	4	4
3	18	100%	1.45	2	5	2

We also get good results in this simple example. The result from the GA-HC is shown in Table 10. After the soft deadline is changed to Jan. 10, the result in Table 11 shows that employees are assigned to the work more to get things done more quickly. By comparing these two results, the difference is that Employee 1 is also assigned to Task 3 and the execution time for Task 3 decreases from 6 days to 3 days. It can decrease the penalty cost by finishing tasks earlier. Since even Employee 1 is added to the team for Task 1, the time to finish tasks can only be decreased a little bit but not enough to decrease it from 3 days to 2 days. Therefore, Employee 2 and Employee 3 are considered as the best solution for Task 1 in this situation. Choosing Employee 3 for Task 1 and Task 4 instead of Employee 1 because Employee 3 has higher learning factor than Employee 1. From the above analysis, we can see the correctness of our model in some aspects.

Table 10. Generated Schedule for a Simple Project of 4 Tasks

Task ID	Days	Start Date	End Date	*Resource*
Design	3	Jan 1	Jan 3	Employee2, Employee3
Programming 1	5	Jan 4	Jan 8	Employee2
Programming 2	5	Jan 4	Jan 8	Employee1, Employee3
Documentation	6	Jan 9	Jan 14	Employee2, Employee3

Table 11. Generated Schedule for a Simple Project of 4 Tasks with More Tight Deadline

Task ID	Days	Start Date	End Date	*Resource*
Design	3	Jan 1	Jan 3	Employee2, Employee3
Programming 1	5	Jan 4	Jan 8	Employee2
Programming 2	5	Jan 4	Jan 8	Employee1, Employee3
Documentation	3	Jan 9	Jan 12	Employee1, Employee2, Employee3

Performance of Optimization Approach

To validate our approach, 10 simplified project management problems are designed with the objective to "Find a valid schedule that has lowest money cost, irrespective of other factors, such as learning, overwork". In such situations, any optimum solution should follow the rules that any available employees with lowest salary rate would be firstly assigned to a task. The GA parameter is the same as the previous section. All the results from the experiments obey our previous projections. We also design some moderately constrained problems, highly constrained problems, very small problems and large problems generated by simulation data. To find the GA-HC performance in those different examples, comparison experiments are conducted. The mean and standard deviation ( ) of the result data are reported in Table 12which shows that the GA-HC performance in the relative big problem (21 tasks, 10 employees) is good since all the results are close, while results are in a wider range in relatively simple problems.

Table 12. GA-HC Performance in a Relative Large Problem (21 Tasks, 10 Employees) and Small Problem (4 Tasks, 3 Employees)

Cost (RMB)	Mean	σ
Project A (21 tasks, 10 employees)	130311	4200
Project B (4 tasks, 3 employees)	5218	690
Project C (4 tasks, 3 employees with more tight constraints)	39085	1235

A number of researches have defined certain kinds of problems that GAs work better than other heuristic methods and the criteria to compare different problems and algorithms. Mostly the comparison focuses on GAs and HC algorithms [41]. To compare the performance between different heuristic methods, we chose Steady GA, Hill Climbing and Steady GA with HC on our model based on the criteria of the quality of the best, mean, worst solution from different algorithm. From the results shown in Tables 13–15 in large, medium and small cases, the steady GA and the GA-HC outperform the HC in most cases. Usually a HC algorithm is much faster than a GA. However, the landscape in our problem has many local optima which makes a HC algorithm difficult to achieve the global optimum. So in big cases, GAs outperforms HC algorithms on finding good quality solutions when the problems are becoming complicated, as is the case for many software projects. The experiment case consists of 30 tasks for which 20 employees were available. The employees, in turn, each possessed 5 skills to a greater or lesser extent. Each of the 5 skills was needed by at least one task and many tasks required multiple skills. The best cost computed by HC is 136760 with 1000 initial individuals in the population while the cost by the steady GA is 127448 which outperformed the best fitness achieved by HC, where lower number means lower cost and is better. In a smaller case of 15 tasks, 10 employees in which the GA outperforms the HC dramatically, and in a case of 8 tasks, 5 employees which do not show much difference in the two methods but the distribution of solutions from the HC is bigger than the GA in our experiment. Combining the GA's ability on global optimization and the HC's ability on local optimization, the performance of the GA and the GA-HC in a relative larger project scheduling problem shows similar result while GA converges very slowly in later stage and the running time of the GA-HC outperforms the GA apparently. When the project size increases, the calculation time of the GA could take several hours which becomes a burden to managers. Overall, the GA-HC is generally a good choice in the software project scheduling circumstance.

Table 13. Comparison between GA, HC, GA-HC in a Project of 30 Tasks and 20 Employees

Cost(RMB)	Best	Mean	Worst	Average Time
Steady GA (1000 generations)	127448	133019	142670	35m
Hill Climbing	136760	174203	256745	10m
Steady GA (500 generations) with HC	127448	133346	137023	19m

Table 14. Comparison between GA, HC, GA-HC in a Project of 15 Tasks and 10 Employees

Cost(RMB)	Best	Mean	Worst	Average Time
Steady GA (1000 generations)	38956	39822	43112	20m
Hill Climbing	44200	46297	54002	1m
Steady GA (500 generations) with HC	34248	39889	42344	12m

Table 15. Comparison between GA, HC, GA-HC in a Project of 8 Tasks and 5 Employees

Cost(RMB)	Best	Mean	Worst	Average Time
Steady GA (600 generations)	5460	5580	5736	60s
Hill Climbing	5504	6299	8686	3s
Steady GA (300 generations) with HC	5480	5590	5700	28s

Study on Dynamic Factors

Table 16 shows the calculated costs with certain factors excluded. Without the learning factors or communication overhead, the overall cost increases as expected. Without schedule pressure, no solution is found in this highly constrained case. Although these results are intuitive in this simple scenario, in a more complicated situation data can help to analyze the influence of certain factors and to assist managers to make more sensible decisions.

Table 16. Comparison of Schedule Costs with/without Factors

Cost(RMB)	Small Case	Medium Case	Large Case
With all the factors	4690	13110	234335
With only learning factor	6003	15117	285356
With only communication overhead factor	4200	12601	201314
With only schedule pressure factor	5230	13567	244500
Without all the factors	n/a	18670	342034

CONCLUSIONS AND FUTURE WORK

The main purpose of the model developed in this work is to assist managers in determining the best resource allocation. The unpredictable factors influencing a software development project are too many and complicate planning problems. This paper proposes a team productivity-based model to support generating project schedule. Our model is especially for modeling dynamic factors related to staff. A new genome of the GA is designed for the proposed model. It overcomes the complexities by generating only valid solutions in search space and decreases the computation burden. Additionally, HC is designed to make further efforts to alleviate the computation burden of the GA but achieve same quality of results. We also propose a software project rescheduling approach considering efficiency and stability. This approach is based on formulating software project scheduling and rescheduling situation as an optimization problem via a genetic algorithm. The proposed method will help a manager to do scheduling with the option he made to put the project back on track. Experiments and simulation results demonstrate that it has the ability to produce valid schedule and reschedule alternatives. Case studies with comparison to schedules generated by project management experts prove that it could provide reasonable decision-making support for managers.

Still, there are areas that can be improved. When formulating software project scheduling and rescheduling situation as an optimization problem via a genetic algorithm, studies should be directed to balance the parameters of the objective function in different situations. Evaluations of possible impact of all the available control options such as adding more people or leaving a project lag behind could be integrated. In rescheduling, sensitivity study of the parameters of stability and efficiency should be directed to balance the effect of stability and efficiency in different situations. In addition, evaluations of possible impact of all the available control options should be integrated in the model to support control decision making in software process. Currently the simulation is not taking into account the interactions between parallel tasks. For example, if an employee is assigned to two tasks at the same time, the factors relating to both tasks (such as $f_{learning}$) are calculated separately in each task. The issue is our future work and needs to be further studied. For more accurate estimation in project planning, tuning our simulation models is extremely important. The process of judging the validity of a model should be conducted, such as extreme condition test to test whether the model behaves reasonably under extreme conditions or extreme policies. Sensitive analysis could also be applicable for parameter tuning. Finally, case studies are necessary and essential to evaluate the performance of our work. After the models have been completely established, case studies will help customize these models to a specific organization when needed. Integration with current commercial software tools can help transfer current advanced techniques such as what our research group developed into industrial use.

ACKNOWLEDGMENTS

This work was partly supported by Scientific Research Fund of Zhejiang Provincial Education Department (No. Y201223642) and Zhejiang Provincial Natural Science Foundation (No. LY12F01018). We also thank Dr. Carl K. Chang and Dr. Hsin-yi Jiang for their valuable comments of revising and editing the paper.

AUTHOR CONTRIBUTIONS

Conceived and designed the experiments: YG. Performed the experiments: YG. Analyzed the data: YG BX. Contributed reagents/materials/analysis tools: YG. Wrote the paper: YG BX.

REFERENCES

1. Chang CK, Christensen MJ, Zhang T. Genetic Algorithms for Project Management. Annal of Software Engeering. 2001;11(1):107–139. doi: 10.1023/A:1012543203763.
2. Chao C. Software Project Management Net: a New Methodology on Software Management. PhD dissertation, University of Illinois at Chicago, Department of Electrical Engineering and Computer Science, 1994.
3. Chang CK, Jiang Hy, Di Y, Zhu D, Ge Y. Time-line Based Model for Software Project Scheduling with Genetic Algorithms. Information and Software Technology. 2008;50(11):1142–1154. doi: 10.1016/j.infsof.2008.03.002.
4. Alba E, Francisco Chicano J. Software Project Management with GAs. Information Sciences. 2007;177(11):2380–2401. doi: 10.1016/j.ins.2006.12.020.
5. Gueorguiev S, Harman M, Antoniol G. Software Project Planning for Robustness and Completion Time in the Presence of Uncertainty Using Multi Objective Search Based Software Engineering. In: Proceedings of the 11th Annual Conference on Genetic and Evolutionary Computation. GECCO'09. New York, NY, USA: ACM; 2009. p. 1673–1680.
6. Plekhanova V. On Project Management Scheduling Where Human Resource is a Critical Variable. In: Proceedings of the 6th European Workshop on Software Process Technology. EWSPT'98. London, UK: Springer-Verlag; 1998. p. 116–121.
7. Lederer AL, Prasad J. Causes of Inaccurate Software Development Cost Estimates. Journal of Systems & Software. 1995;31(2):125–134. doi: 10.1016/0164-1212(94)00092-2.
8. Hartmann S, Kolisch R. Experimental evaluation of state-of-the-art heuristics for the resource-constrained project scheduling problem. European Journal of Operational Research. 2000;127(2):394–407. doi: 10.1016/S0377-2217(99)00485-3.
9. Holland JH. Adaptation in Natural and Artificial Systems. Ann Arbor, MI, USA: University of Michigan Press; 1975. Available from: http://books.google.com/books?id=YE5RAAAAMAAJ.
10. Contreras-Bolton C, Parada V. Automatic Combination of Operators in a Genetic Algorithm to Solve the Traveling Salesman Problem. PLoS ONE. 2015;10(9). doi: 10.1371/journal.pone.0137724
11. Harman M, Mansouri SA, Zhang Y. Search-based Software Engineering: Trends, Techniques and Applications. ACM Comput Survey. 2012;45(1):11:1–11:61. doi: 10.1145/2379776.2379787.
12. Ferrucci F, Harman M, Ren J, Sarro F. Not Going to Take This Anymore: Multi-objective Overtime Planning for Software Engineering Projects. In: Proceedings of the 2013 International Conference on Software Engineering. ICSE'13. Piscataway, NJ, USA: IEEE Press; 2013. p. 462–471.
13. Ren J, Harman M, Penta MD. Cooperative Co-evolutionary Optimization of Software Project Staff Assignments and Job Scheduling. In: Proceedings of the Third International Conference on Search Based Software Engineering. SSBSE'11. Berlin, Heidelberg: Springer-Verlag; 2011. p. 127–141.
14. Pfeiffer A, Kadar B, L M. Stability-oriented Evaluation of Hybrid Rescheduling Methods in a Job-shop With Machine Breakdowns. In: Proceedings of the 39th CIRP ISMS; 2006. p. 173–178.
15. Cowling P, Johansson M. Using real time information for effective dynamic scheduling. European Journal of Operational Research. 2002;139(2):230–244. doi: 10.1016/S0377-2217(01)00355-1.
16. Katragjini Prifti K, Vallada Regalado E, Ruiz García R. Stability-oriented Evaluation of Rescheduling Strategies, by Using Simulation. International Journal

of Production Research. 2013;51(3):780–797. doi: 10.1080/00207543.2012.666856

17. Sukhodolsky J. Optimizing Software Process Control. SIGSOFT Softw Eng Notes. 2001;26(2):59–63. doi: 10.1145/505776.505791.
18. Boehm BW. Software Engineering Economics. 1st ed. Upper Saddle River, NJ, USA: Prentice Hall PTR; 1981.
19. Boehm BW, Abts C, Brown AW, Chulani S, Clark BK, Horowitz E, et al. Software Cost Estimation with COCOMO II. 1st ed. Upper Saddle River, NJ, USA: Prentice Hall PTR; 2000.
20. Azzeh M, Neagu D, Cowling PI. Analogy-based Software Effort Estimation Using Fuzzy Numbers. Journal of Systems and Software. 2011;84(2):270–284. doi: 10.1016/j.jss.2010.09.028.
21. Chiu NH, Huang SJ. The Adjusted Analogy-based Software Effort Estimation Based on Similarity Distances. Journal of Systems and Software. 2007;80(4):628–640. doi: 10.1016/j.jss.2006.06.006.
22. Pendharkar PC, Subramanian GH, Rodger JA. A Probabilistic Model for Predicting Software Development Effort. IEEE Transaction of Software Engineering. 2005;31(7):615–624. doi: 10.1109/TSE.2005.75.
23. Chavoya A, Lopez-Martin C, Andalon-Garcia I, Meda-Campaña M. Genetic Programming as Alternative for Predicting Development Effort of Individual Software Projects. PLoS ONE. 2012;7(11). doi: 10.1371/journal.pone.0050531
24. Abdel-Hamid T, Madnick SE. Software Project Dynamics: An Integrated Approach. Upper Saddle River, NJ, USA: Prentice-Hall, Inc.; 1991.
25. Barros M, Werner C, Travassos G. System Dynamics Extension Modules for Software Process Modeling. In: Proceedings of 2003 Software Process Simulation and Modeling Workshop. ProSim'03; 2003.
26. Pfahl D, Lebsanft K. Integration of System Dynamics Modeling with Descriptive Process Modeling and Goal-oriented Measurement. Journal of Systems and Software. 1999;46(2/3):135–150. doi: 10.1016/S0164-1212(99)00007-2.
27. Hansen GA. Simulating Software Development Processes. Computer. 1996;29(1):73–77. doi: 10.1109/2.481468.
28. Kouskouras KG, Georgiou AC. A Discrete Event Simulation Model in the Case of Managing a Software Project. European Journal of Operational Research. 2007;181(1):374–389. doi: 10.1016/j.ejor.2006.05.031.
29. Lakey PB. A Hybrid Software Process Simulation Model for Project Management. In: Proc. 2003 Software Process Simulation and Modeling Workshop. ProSim'03; 2003.
30. Martin RH, Raffo D. A model of the software development process using both continuous and discrete models. Software Process: Improvement and Practice. 2000;5(2–3):147–157. doi: 10.1002/1099-1670(200006/09)5:2/3%3C147::AID-SPIP122%3E3.0.CO;2-T.
31. Donzelli P. A Decision Support System for Software Project Management. IEEE Software. 2006;23(4):67–75. doi: 10.1109/MS.2006.90.
32. Penta Md, Harman M, Antoniol G, Qureshi F. The Effect of Communication Overhead on Software Maintenance Project Staffing: a Search-Based Approach. In: 2007 IEEE International Conference on Software Maintenance. IEEE Press; 2007. p. 315–324.
33. Shoham I, McIvor A. OpenSched; 2001-2006. http://opensched.sourceforge.net/.
34. Stylianou C, Gerasimou S, Andreou AS. A Novel Prototype Tool for Intelligent Software Project Scheduling and Staffing Enhanced with Personality Factors. In: 2012 IEEE 24th International Conference on Tools with Artificial Intelligence. vol. 1; 2012. p. 277–284.
35. Ventana Systems Inc. Vensim Software Tool; 2015. Available: http://vensim.com/.
36. Herroelen W, Leus R. Project scheduling under uncertainty: Survey and research potentials. European Journal of Operational Research. 2005;165(2):289–306. doi: 10.1016/j.ejor.2004.04.002.
37. Ge Y. Software Project Rescheduling with Genetic Algorithms. In: Artificial Intelligence and Computational Intelligence, 2009. AICI'09. International Conference on. vol. 1; 2009. p. 439–443.
38. Gen M, Cheng R. Genetic Algorithms and Engineering Optimization. New York, NY, USA: John Wiley & Sons; 2000.
39. Wall M. GALib; 1996-2007. Available: http://lancet.mit.edu/ga/.
40. Di Y. Timeline Based Model For Job Scheduling with Genetic Algorithms. Master's thesis, University of Illinois at Chicago, Department of Electrical Engineering and Computer Science, 2001.
41. Mitchell M, Holland JH, Forrest S. When will a Genetic Algorithm Outperform Hill Climbing. In: Cowan JD, Tesauro G, Alspector J, editors. Advances in Neural Information Processing Systems 6. San Francisco, CA: Morgan-Kaufmann; 1994. p. 51–58.

CHAPTER 2

RANKING OF BUSINESS PROCESS SIMULATION SOFTWARE TOOLS WITH DEX/QQ HIERARCHICAL DECISION MODEL

Nadja Damij[1], Pavle Boškoski[2], Marko Bohanec[3], Biljana Mileva Boshkoska[1,3]

[1] Faculty for Information Studies, Ulica talcev 8, Novo mesto, Slovenia

[2] Department of Systems and Control, Jožef Stefan Institute, Jamova cesta 39, Ljubljana, Slovenia

[3] Department of Knowledge Technologies, Jožef Stefan Institute, Jamova cesta 39, Ljubljana, Slovenia

ABSTRACT

The omnipresent need for optimization requires constant improvements of companies' business processes (BPs). Minimizing the risk of inappropriate BP being implemented is usually performed by simulating the newly developed BP under various initial conditions and "what-if" scenarios. An effectual business process simulations software (BPSS) is a prerequisite for accurate analysis of an BP. Characterization of an BPSS tool is a challenging task due to the complex selection criteria that includes quality of visual aspects, simulation capabilities, statistical facilities, quality reporting etc. Under such circumstances, making an optimal decision is challenging. Therefore, various decision support models are employed aiding the BPSS tool selection. The currently established decision support models are either proprietary or comprise only a limited subset of criteria, which affects their accuracy. Addressing this issue, this paper proposes a new hierarchical decision support model for ranking of BPSS based on their technical characteristics by employing DEX and qualitative to quantitative (QQ) methodology. Consequently, the decision expert feeds the required information in a systematic and user friendly manner. There are three significant contributions of the proposed approach. Firstly, the proposed hierarchical model is easily extendible for adding new criteria in the hierarchical structure. Secondly, a fully operational decision support system (DSS) tool that implements the proposed hierarchical model is presented. Finally, the effectiveness of the proposed hierarchical model is assessed by comparing the resulting rankings of BPSS with respect to currently available results.

INTRODUCTION

A business process (BP) is defined as a collection of related and structured activities with the aim to create outputs that are produced to serve customers' needs [1]. This is the fundamental differentiator between terms such as BP on one hand and support process, organizational department/unit, etc. on the other. In particular, BPs are considered to be value-added processes that are only executed when added value to the input or the activity from the customer's perspective can be achieved. BPs represent an essential part of every organization, regardless of size or industry. The clarity of their definition and regular optimization is essential for company's

Citation: Damij N, Boškoski P, Bohanec M, Mileva Boshkoska B (2016) Ranking of Business Process Simulation Software Tools with DEX/QQ Hierarchical Decision Model. PLoS ONE 11(2): e0148391. doi:10.1371/journal.pone.0148391

overall success and profitability. The process view looks at the functioning of the company from the customer's perspective [1, 2]. However, dealing with improper specification of a BP can have significant negative consequences. Introducing new or updating an existing BP without proper analysis may lead to significant deterioration of the company's performance. Optimization of BPs requires usage of modelling techniques and simulation tools [3]. The purpose of business process modelling is to develop a model that reflects the organization and functionality of an existing or new business process and is as such a predecessor to business process simulation that is usually executed by using of business process simulation tools or softwares [1]. BP analysis is usually performed by simulating the BP behavior under various conditions and potential "what-if" scenarios and/or sensitivity analysis prior to its implementation [4, 5]. Because of the algorithmic structure of a BP, it is generally possible to simulate it with special simulation tools referred to as business process simulations softwares (BPSSs) [6].

BPSS is increasingly being used to address a variety of issues from the strategic management of software development, to supporting process improvements, to software project management training with the scope of analyzing narrow focused portions of the life cycle to longer term product evolutionary models with broad organizational impacts [7]. Two main categories of BPSS are the general purpose discrete event simulation tools and business process modelling tools [8]. BPSS therefore can consist of either modelling tools (a graphical modelling environment, built-in simulation objects with defined properties and behavior, sampling routines, property sheets and visual controls), tools to execute the simulation (a simulation executive to run a model, animated graphic, virtual reality representation and user interaction with the simulation as it runs), tools to support experimentation, optimization, results interpretation and presentation, or links to other software (links to spreadsheets, databases, ERP systems) [9]. Selecting the most appropriate BPSS is a daunting task due to the vast number of available simulation tools. Since a multitude of, possibly conflicting, criteria influence this decision, the selection problem can be considered as a multi-criteria decision making problem. This paper addresses the problem of BPSS selection by proposing a hierarchical decision model implemented as a decision support system (DSS).

DSS are readily used for the process of software selection, predominantly for ranking purposes [10–17]. The effectiveness of a DSS is determined by the underlying model. In the context of BPSS, there is a set of characteristics that govern the selection of the optimal tool, for instance functionality, reliability, usability, efficiency, maintainability, portability and personalization [6, 8,11]. Each of these characteristics comprises several attributes which results into an attribute set with large cardinality. Despite having defined a comprehensive criteria set, the commonly used decision models comprise only a limited set of criteria [14–16, 18]. As a result, the employed DSSs provide rankings which can be considered as incomplete or partial.

Addressing this issue, a new hierarchical multi-criteria decision model is proposed that comprises 17 criteria grouped in logically interconnected segments covering every aspect of a BPSS packages. The newly designed model is employed for ranking of BPSS packages using a combination of DEX and qualitative to quantitative (QQ) methodologies [19].

The contributions of the proposed approach are the following:

- The hierarchical structure divides the large criteria set into smaller subsets thus providing more readable and easier to understand decision problem, allowing humans to achieve consistent decision making.
- The proposed hierarchical model can be easily extended by adding additional criteria groups and placing them accordingly in the model's structure.
- The hierarchical decision model is implemented in an operational and freely accessible DSS tool.
- In addition to commercially available BPSS tools, this analysis includes open-source BPSS tools that were previously mainly omitted.
- The effectiveness of the proposed model is assessed by comparing the evaluation results with those provided by proprietary tools, such as Gartner's [20].

Evaluation of software involves attributes that either indicate the presence of features or describe the quality level of their implementation. In both cases, it is easier to evaluate such attributes using a qualitative than quantitative scale. Consequently, the possible DSS solution should be sought in the class of qualitative decision making methods. In qualitative decision making, one may distinguish two groups of methods. The first group includes methods based on interactive questioning procedures for obtaining the decision makers preferences. Typical representatives are MACBETH [21] and ZAPROS [22]. The second group of methods apply the preference disaggregation principle. Typical methods that belong to this group are UTA [23], DRSA [24], Doctus [25] and DEX [19, 26]. From the possible candidates, this analysis is based on DEX methodology extended with the QQ method [27]. It employs the principle of decomposing the problem into smaller and easily understandable decision components. These are used for obtaining simple decisions that are propagated into the DEX tree structure from the bottom to the top of the tree leading to the final decision [28], which is completely in line with the designed hierarchical model structure. DEX has been previously used for building of hundreds of complex models in different areas, including health care, project management, quality and risk assessment, environmental management and many more [29]. In this work, DEX is extended with QQ in order to provide numeric evaluation results, which are used for BPSSs ranking.

The proposed DEX/QQ based DSS model is employed for evaluating 33 currently available BPSS tools. Both open-source and proprietary solutions are considered. The DSS ranking results are compared to currently available software rankings reports [20].

The paper is organized as follows. The description of the attributes characterizing a BPSS tool are presented in Section 2. The details about model building using DEX/QQ methodology is presented in Section 3. Finally, Section 4 presents the ranking results of the proposed DSS, by evaluating 33 different BPSS tools.

ATTRIBUTE SELECTION

BPSS tools are complex software packages. Therefore, many aspects have to be considered in order to perform a proper evaluation. This analysis focuses on the technical properties of these software tools. Consequently, the evaluation considers several aspects of the tool such as functionality, reliability, usability, efficiency, maintainability, portability and personalization [6,8, 11]. The attribute set used in this analysis is a union of the attributes characterizing each of these aspects.

From a decision maker's point of view, the attributes can be divided into two logical groups:

- technical/functional requirements and
- usability and personalization capabilities.

The qualitative evaluation of the attributes from the first group can be obtained from the technical specifications of the corresponding BPSS tool. This evaluation can be performed in a rather impartial manner, since the values of those attributes can be determined empirically. The values of the second group of attributes depend on the user's preferences.

Due to the large cardinality of the attribute set, it is preferable to group the attributes into smaller categories linked in a hierarchical structure based on their dependencies. Generally, the candidate BPSSs are ranked according to five different categories:

- statistical facilities
- experimental capabilities
- testing capabilities
- efficiency and
- visual aspects.

The first four categories belong to the group of technical/functional attributes. Characterizing these categories is directly related to the actual capabilities of the simulation tool. On the other hand, the visual aspects represent the personal appeal of the simulation tool and has generally little effect on the actual performance of the tool itself.

Statistical Facilities

Statistical facilities of a BPSS tool cover both simulation capabilities as well as the analysis of the simulation results. Each of these two segments have significantly different requirements and therefore they should be analyzed separately.

Stochastic simulation capabilities.

Typical analysis would focus on the most computationally demanding aspects, the most important ones being: random number generation, model parameter estimation and parallel processing capabilities.

In many cases, the execution of a BP is triggered by random events. In order to simulate such events, one has to be able to generate random numbers from a corresponding probability distribution. Notwithstanding the simplicity of the task, in many cases BPSS tools include only a limited set of probability distributions. Therefore it is of utmost practical importance to have rich library of probability distributions or some form of Markov Chain Monte Carlo sampling algorithms.

Similarly like the input, there are cases when the completion of a certain activity of the meta process can have a stochastic nature too. As a result the BP output can be regarded a random variable. For proper analysis of these results a powerful parameter estimation framework is needed.

Finally, an important aspect is the parallel processing capability i.e., executing a parallel discrete-event simulation with restricted common resource. Such environment would allow simulation of concurrent algorithm helping in determining synchronization issues.

It is hardly expected that all these requirements are met in a single BPSS. In many cases, the simulation tools provide a certain API interfaces that allow the users to introduce their own extensions which can certainly improve the capabilities of the simulation tool. This is particularly true for the open-source solutions.

Statistical reporting.

The statistical analysis of the results are crucial for proper understanding of the simulated BP. In its simplest form, the results are represented just with mean values, which can be misleading. In order to gain proper insight of the BP outcome, the statistical reporting should also include the calculation of confidence intervals for every simulated output variable, estimation of most likely probability distributions or at least typical moments and/or cumulant values.

Experiment Facilities

When simulating a BP, one usually opts for testing various "what-if" scenarios [5]. Therefore it is important to be able to perform various simulations with minimal effort from the user side. Three main attributes characterize the tool's experiment facilities: the ability to define the "warm-up" period, capability of executing batch runs and automatic determination of the run length.

Warm-up Period.

When performing random number generation, the underlying methods require the so-called "warm-up" time, i.e., the number of samples until the sampling algorithm reaches a steady state. All the samples, prior to that moment, should be discarded since they fail to represent the underlying distribution. The BPSS tool should be capable for incorporating this simulation parameter.

Batch Runs.

Capability of the software tool to run multiple parallel simulations with varying parameters can significantly speed up the simulation process. Such parallel simulations are also known as batch simulation runs [1].

Automatic determination of the run length.

For terminating simulations the run can be stopped as soon as the terminating event occurs. However, for simulations that enter a steady state, determining the run length is not a straightforward task, since the simulation can run indefinitely. Therefore, the simulation tool should implement some of the many available approaches for detecting a steady state. In such a way, the simulation run length will be kept in a reasonable interval while in the same time providing sufficiently long data sets enabling proper analysis of the BP.

Testing Capabilities

Powerful testing environment is of utmost practical importance. Typically, testing and debugging tools include features such as break points, watch points, execution flow control etc. However for the case of BP modelling, this set of features should also include tools for checking the correctness of chain of activity as well as powerful logging and tracing mechanisms.

Logic Checks.

A BP represents a chain of activities which usually includes branching and in some cases loops. Logical checks of such an architecture is helpful for determining dead branches, circularity, consecutiveness etc. These checks belong to the group of graph architecture checks and are useful during the modelling phase. Such architectural errors can be also detected during the simulation phase also, however their early detection can significantly shorten the design time.

Logging and Debugging Capabilities.

When performing demanding simulations it is expected to run into difficulties either with the model performance or parameter choice. Resolving these issues can be significantly improved by logging certain simulation values during the simulation itself. This can be achieved by employing well established logging services. In many cases, the logging data proves as a valuable source for bottleneck detection.

Efficiency

The efficiency of the BPSS tool addresses the way the models are build rather than the implementation of the simulation algorithms. In that manner, there are several aspects that are important: the allowed level of details that can be used when building either the process or its activities, the completeness of a library typical activities, capability of simulating various queuing scenarios and robustness of simulation.

Level of Detail.

Many BPs exhibit high level of complexity either in the process architecture itself or in the phenomena described by the encompassed activities. In either case, the BPSS tool should allow sufficiently detailed implementation which will lead to more accurate representation of the real-world BP.

Such a high level of modelling detail is usually achieved by offering high number of prepared activities that can be incorporated into a complex chain. In some other cases this can be achieved by allowing custom scripts to be written describing the underlying activity.

Modelling Quality.

Quality of modelling is directly related to the allowed detail level. It is expected that the BPSS tool includes a certain library of template processes and activities that can be used directly by setting certain set of parameters. When such a library is poorly implemented or non-existing the modelling process will become both time consuming and with degraded quality.

Queuing Policies.

Having predetermined set of queuing policies can significantly improve the quality of the model. In such a case, each activity can be associated with certain strategy of request behavior that corresponds with the real-world scenarios. In its simplest form, requests will wait for activity execution indefinitely.

Robustness.

It is expected that the most of the BPs are stateful i.e., there is record of the previous processing that influences any future actions. For such cases it is quite important how the BPSS handles fault recoveries. In the case of complex simulations, the BPSS tool should be able to store the BP state at certain milestones in a non-volatile memory. Afterwards, the fault recovery process would resume from the last checkpoint thus avoiding the need for restarting the simulation from the very beginning.

Visual Aspects

The graphical capabilities can help visualizing bottlenecks thus providing better understanding of the behavior of a BP. This category adds to the user-friendly aspect of the BPSS tool.

Apart from the simulation visualization, animation capabilities can significantly help in the process of debugging. If designed properly, it will allow visualization of execution paths, current input and output values as well as current property values of the actors in the BP.

DEX AND QQ METHODOLOGY

The evaluation of BPSS tools is performed by qualitative multi-criteria decision making method called DEX. DEX classifies qualitative multi-attribute alternatives into several qualitative classes [19, 26]. In context of DEX, each BPSS tools represents an alternative that is described by the attributes described in Section 2.

DEX methodology decomposes the complex decision problem at hand into smaller and easily understandable decision components, which are assembled into a hierarchical model. There are two types of attributes in DEX: *basic* and *aggregated* ones. The former are the directly measurable attributes, also called input attributes that are used for describing the alternatives at hand. The latter are obtained by aggregating the basic and/or other aggregated attributes.

The hierarchical attribute structure resembles a tree. The attributes are structured so that there is only one path from each attribute to the root of the tree. The path contains the dependencies among attributes such that the higher-level attributes depend on their immediate descendants in the tree. This structure is shown in Fig 1.

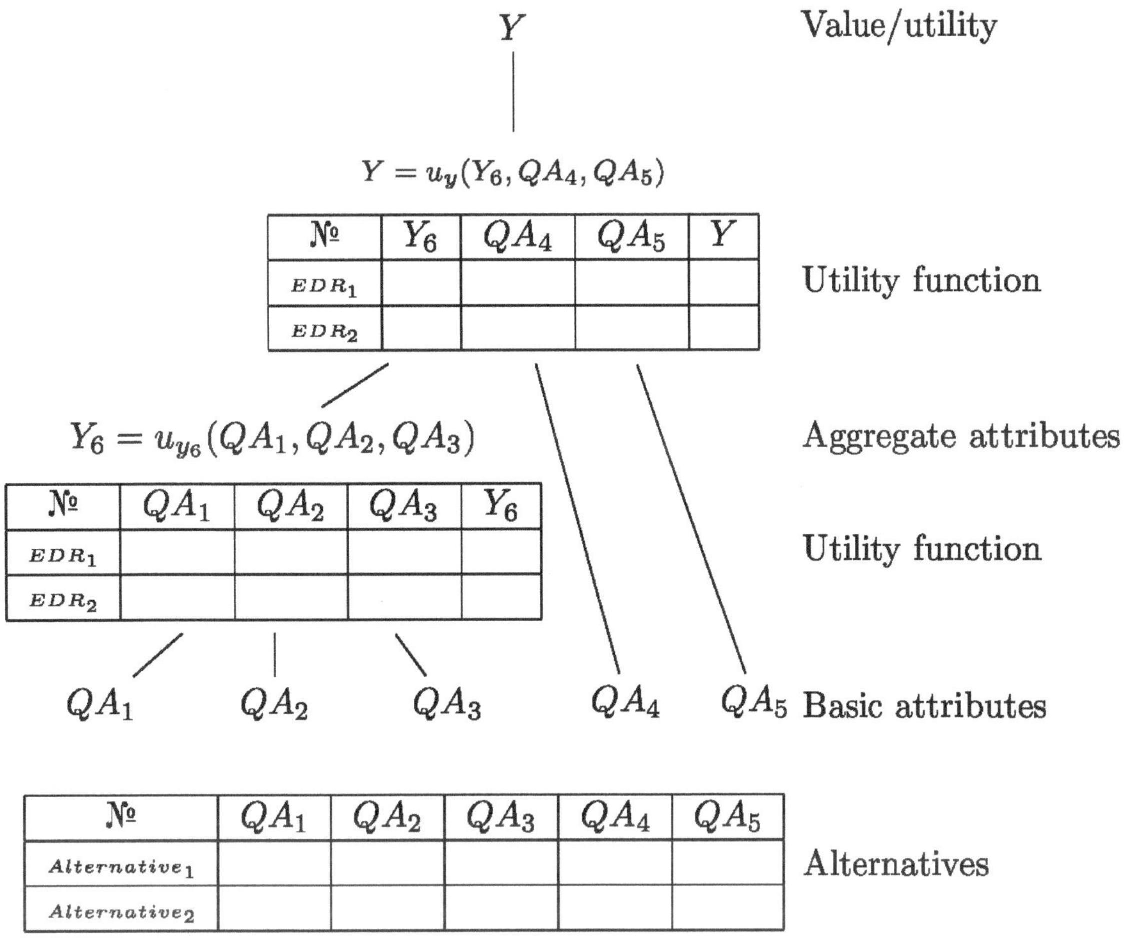

Figure 1. Hierarchical DEX model tree.

In DEX each of the n attributes is a discrete one i.e., the ith qualitative attribute QA_i, $i \in [1, n]$, can obtain values from a finite value set with N_i elements:

$$QA_i \in \{e_1^{(i)}, e_2^{(i)}, \ldots, e_{N_i}^{(i)}\}. \tag{1}$$

The dependency among the attributes is defined by a utility function. For every aggregated attribute y, the arguments of the corresponding utility function comprise its immediate descendants from the hierarchical tree. Consequently, the utility function reads as:

$$Y = u_y(QA_1, QA_2, \ldots, QA_n). \tag{2}$$

Due to the discrete nature of the attributes, the utility Function (2) is usually represented as a qualitative decision table, as shown in Fig 1 and Table 1. Each row in Table 1 represents an elementary decision rule. Such a rule consists of a subset of attributes and their evaluation into an aggregated attribute. In the decision table, each elementary decision rule can be interpreted as an *if-then* rule.

Table 1. Utility Function (2) in a form of a decision table. L is the number of elementary decision rules in the table.

№	QA_1	QA_2	…	QA_n	Y
1	qa_{11}	qa_{12}	…	qa_{1n}	y_1
2	qa_{21}	qa_{22}	…	qa_{2n}	y_2
⋮	⋮	⋮		⋮	⋮
L	qa_{L1}	qa_{L2}	…	qa_{Ln}	y_L

doi:10.1371/journal.pone.0148391.t001

Elementary decision rules that are almost equally preferred, have the same output y_i and are said to belong to the same qualitative class. Consequently, for DEX these elementary decision rules are indistinguishable. This can be resolved by employing the method QQ method [27]. The three step algorithm describing the DEX/QQ modelling approach is schematically shown in Fig 2.

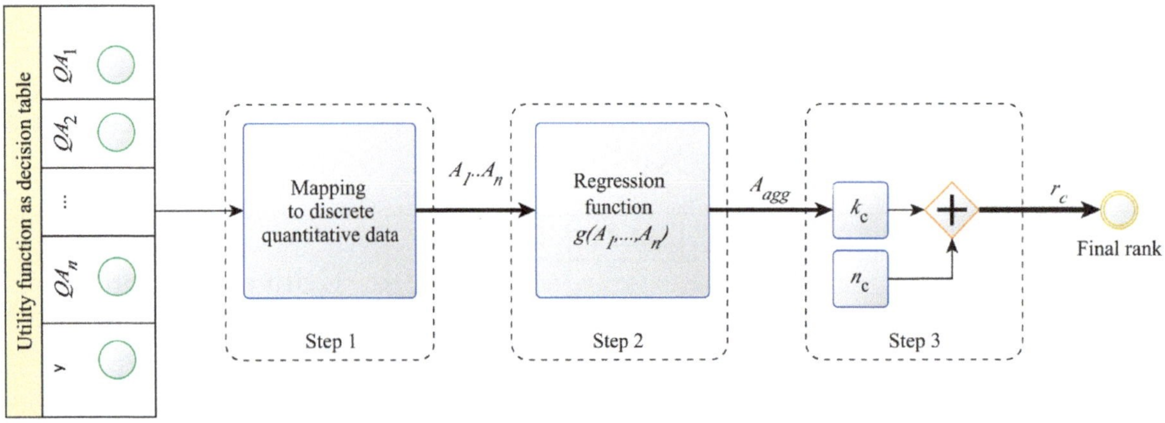

Figure 2. Workflow describing the transformation process from qualitative attributes and quantitative features to final quantitative evaluation.

First, the arguments and the output of the qualitative utility Function (2) are mapped into discrete quantitative ones as:

$$C = U_c(A_1, \ldots, A_n), \tag{3}$$

where $A_1, \ldots, A_n \in \mathbb{Z}$ (step 1 in Fig 2). The mapping function must preserve the preference order, i.e. the higher the preference of QA_i the greater the value of A_i. The goal is to preserve the preference order of attributes, and not the intensity of the preference. Consequently, the ordered qualitative attributes are mapped into ordered discrete values that are equally distanced. The resulting quantitative utility Function (3) is shown in Table 2.

Table 2. Utility Function (3) in a form of a decision table. L is the number of elementary decision rules and P is the number of distinct classes.

№	A_1	A_2	…	A_n	C
1	a_{11}	a_{12}	…	a_{1n}	c_1
2	a_{21}	a_{22}	…	a_{2n}	c_2
⋮	⋮	⋮		⋮	⋮
L	a_{L1}	a_{L2}	…	a_{Ln}	c_P

doi:10.1371/journal.pone.0148391.t002

In the second step, a utility function $g : \mathbb{R}^n \rightarrow \mathbb{R}$ is obtained such that

$$A_{agg} = g(A_1, \ldots, A_n). \tag{4}$$

The parameter's values are estimated by employing linear regression. The function defines the relation between the aggregated (dependent) attribute A_{agg} and input attributes A_1, A_2, …, A_n. Despite $A_i \in \mathbb{Z}$, the function $g(A_1, \ldots, A_n)$ is defined in $\mathbb{R}^n$.

The third step ensures consistency between the qualitative and quantitative models. It means that if an elementary decision rule belongs to a quantitative class c_i, $i \in \{1, \ldots, P\}$, then the output utility value must be in the interval $c_i \pm 0.5$. Additionally it improves the understandability of the quantitative model as it directly shows to which class a certain elementary decision rule belongs to. Therefore, for the utility Function (4), a set of functions f_{ci} is defined that ensures compliance with the original class c_i as:

$$f_{c_i}(A_1, \ldots, A_n) = k_{c_i} g(A_1, \ldots, A_n) + n_{c_i}, \tag{5}$$

where k_{ci} and n_{ci} are calculated as:

$$k_{c_i} = \frac{1}{max_{c_i} - min_{c_i}} \tag{6}$$

$$n_{c_i} = c_i + 0.5 - k_{c_i} min_{c_i}, \tag{7}$$

and max_{ci} and min_{ci} are the maximum and minimum value of the function $g(A_1, \ldots, A_n)$ for a class c_i.

The last two steps are presented with Algorithm 1 [28].

Algorithm 1 Algorithm steps 2 and 3

$U_C \leftarrow \{sort\ rows(U_c, \forall c)\}$ ▷ sort rows in utility table U_C Eq (3) according to class (output)C in ascending order to prepare for step 3 in QQ

$Agg = g(A_1, \ldots, A_n)$ ▷ find the utility function g that best describes the set of alternativesA_i

for $\forall el_i \in c_i$ where $el_i = (A_{1i}, A_{2i}, \cdots A_{ni})$ **do** ▷ for each elementary decision rule el_i that belongs to class c_i

$G_{ci} \leftarrow \{g(\forall A_{ji} \in el_i \pm 0.5)\}$ ▷ find all values of g for all combinations of $A_{ji} \pm 0.5$

$min_{ci} = \min(G_{ci})$ ▷ find the minimum of the function g in class c_i

$max_{ci} = \max(G_{ci})$ ▷ find the maximum of the function g in class c_i

$$k_{c_i} = \frac{1}{max_{c_i} - min_{c_i}}$$ ▷ calculate the coefficient k_{ci}

$$n_{ci} = c_i + 0.5 - k_{ci}\ max_{ci}$$ ▷ calculate the coefficient n_{ci}

end for

RESULTS AND DISCUSSION

DEX Hierarchical Model for Selection of BPSS Tool

For the problem of choosing the optimal BPSS tool, the hierarchical tree of the proposed DEX model is shown in Fig 3. The structure of the DEX model has been obtained by formulating the characteristics from section 2 in the form of hierarchically structured qualitative attributes. In the presented DEX model, the basic attributes are given with plain letters, while the aggregated attributes are shown with capital letters. For example, in the proposed DEX model, the **SIMULATION CAPABILITIES** of the evaluated BPSS tool are obtained by aggregating the values of the attributes **VISUAL ASPECTS**, **SIMULATION FACILITIES** and **STATISTICAL FACILITIES**. Similarly, the values of the aggregated attribute **SIMULATION FACILITIES** are obtained with aggregation of the values of the attributes **EXPERIMENT FACILITIES**,**TESTABILITY** and **EFFICIENCY**, and so on. The discrete value set Eq (1) is given alongside the corresponding attribute.

Attribute	Values
SIMULATION CAPABILITIES	poor, satisfactory, good, excellent
— **VISUAL ASPECTS**	poor, good, excellent
—— Animation quality	none, poor, good, excellent
—— Graphics quality	poor, good, excellent
— **SIMULATION FACILITIES**	poor, good, excellent
—— **EXPERIMENT FACILITIES**	poor, good, excellent
——— Automatic batch run	impossible, possible
——— Automatic determination of run length	impossible, possible
——— Warm-up period	impossible, possible
—— **TESTABILITY**	poor, good, excellent
——— Break points	impossible, possible
——— Logic checks	impossible, possible
——— Error reporting and tracing	poor, good, excellent
—— **EFFICIENCY**	poor, good, excellent
——— Level of detail	poor, good, excellent
——— Robustness	poor, good, excellent
——— Quality of modelling	poor, good, excellent
——— Queuing policies	impossible, possible
— **STATISTICAL FACILITIES**	poor, good, excellent
—— **DISTRIBUTIONS**	poor, good, excellent
——— Theoretical distributions	poor, good, excellent
——— User def ned distributions	impossible, possible
——— Distribution f tting	impossible, possible
—— **DATA ANALYSIS**	poor, good, excellent
——— Quality of data analysis facility	poor, good, excellent
——— Output data analysis	poor, good, excellent

Figure 3. DEX model attributes.

As the tree contains nine aggregated attributes, there are nine corresponding utility functions of the form Eq (2). One such utility function, for the attribute **VISUAL ASPECTS (VA)**, is presented in Table 3. From the hierarchical tree (Fig 3), it is clearly visible that the values of the the attribute **VISUAL ASPECTS** are obtained with aggregation of the values of the basic attributes *Animation quality (AQ)* and *Graphics quality (GQ)*. Therefore, the corresponding utility function has the following form:

$$y_{\mathrm{VA}} = u_y(QA_{AQ}, QA_{GQ}). \quad \textbf{(8)}$$

The decision table for the utility Function (8) is given with Table 3. In the context of *if-then* rules, the 8th row of the Table 3 can be read as:

IFanimation quality is **excellent** *AND Graphics quality* is **good**

THEN **VISUAL ASPECTS** are **good**.

Table 3. Utility function for the attribute VISUAL ASPECTS

№	Animation quality	Graphics quality	VISUAL ASPECTS
1	none	poor	poor
2	poor	poor	poor
3	good	poor	poor
4	excellent	poor	good
5	none	good	poor
6	poor	good	good
7	good	good	excellent
8	excellent	good	excellent
9	none	excellent	poor
10	poor	excellent	good
11	good	excellent	excellent
12	excellent	excellent	excellent

doi:10.1371/journal.pone.0148391.t003

The utility function presented in Table 3 defines a partial ranking. For example, for the 11th and the 12th elementary decision rule, the utility function obtains value **excellent**. However it is clear that the 12th elementary decision rule (EDR) is better than the 11th elementary decision rule since the attribute *Animation quality* acquires higher value for the 12th elementary decision rule.

This issue can be resolved by applying the QQ method. As a result, the original utility function presented in Table 3 is transformed into the one shown in Table 4. The mapped discrete quantitative values in Table 4 are employed for fitting the aggregating Function (4). The final rank (the last column in Table 4) is calculated by employing Eq (5). Each linear function in Eq (5) represents a model for the corresponding class in the originally defined qualitative decision table. These functions are used to rank the options in the classes.

Table 4. From qualitative to quantitative evaluations using QQ method

№	Animation quality	Graphics quality	VISUAL ASPECTS	Evaluation
1	1	1	1	0.72
2	2	1	1	0.91
3	3	1	1	1.09
4	4	1	2	1.28
5	1	2	1	0.97
6	2	2	2	1.82
7	3	2	3	2.75
8	4	2	3	2.96
9	1	3	1	1.22
10	2	3	2	2.18
11	3	3	3	3.04
12	4	3	3	3.25

doi:10.1371/journal.pone.0148391.t004

For the elementary decision rules given in Table 4, the Eq (4) has the form:

$$g = 0.833A_1 + 0.500A_2 - 0.778. \quad (9)$$

For the same table the functions f_{ci} Eq (5) reads as follows:

$$f_{c_i} = \begin{cases} 0.4013g + 0.5151, & \text{if } i = 1; \\ 0.5825g + 0.8859, & \text{if } i = 2; \\ 0.4580g + 1.8034, & \text{if } i = 3. \end{cases} \quad (10)$$

Ranking Results

For validation purposes, a set of 120 BPSS tools was identified. The list contained both proprietary as well as open-source tools. From the initial 120 tools, 33 were available either as a demo installation or as a completely operating tool. The latter group predominantly consists of open-source tools. Each of these tools was installed and evaluated. In cases for which the demo installations offered only limited capabilities, the technical data sheets were used in order to determine the appropriate evaluation grade for a particular attribute. The validation set was limited to 33 alternatives, since for the remaining 87 tools, it was impossible to determine the appropriate values for a substantial number of attributes.

It has to be noted that the selected set of 33 alternatives was chosen solely for the purpose of evaluating the proposed hierarchical decision model. By selecting an already analyzed subset of BPSS tools, the effectiveness of the developed decision model can be directly compared to the results from previously performed analysis.

Validation.

The results from the Gartner [20, 30] analysis are used as a reference. Since Gartner's results are presented in a form of so-called "magic quadrant", for comparison purposes, the obtained ranking results are presented in the same form as shown in Fig 4. The term magic quadrant comes from the Gartner's magic quadrants which use two-dimensional matrix that evaluates vendors based on their completeness of vision and ability to execute. In Fig 4, the values on the ordinate represents the ranking output of the DEX/QQ model. The abscissa is inversely proportional to the effort required for setting up the BPSS tool and performing simple simulation. This is a somewhat personal grade of the required computer skills in order to set up and use a particular BPSS tool, assessed by one of the authors while setting up the software tools.

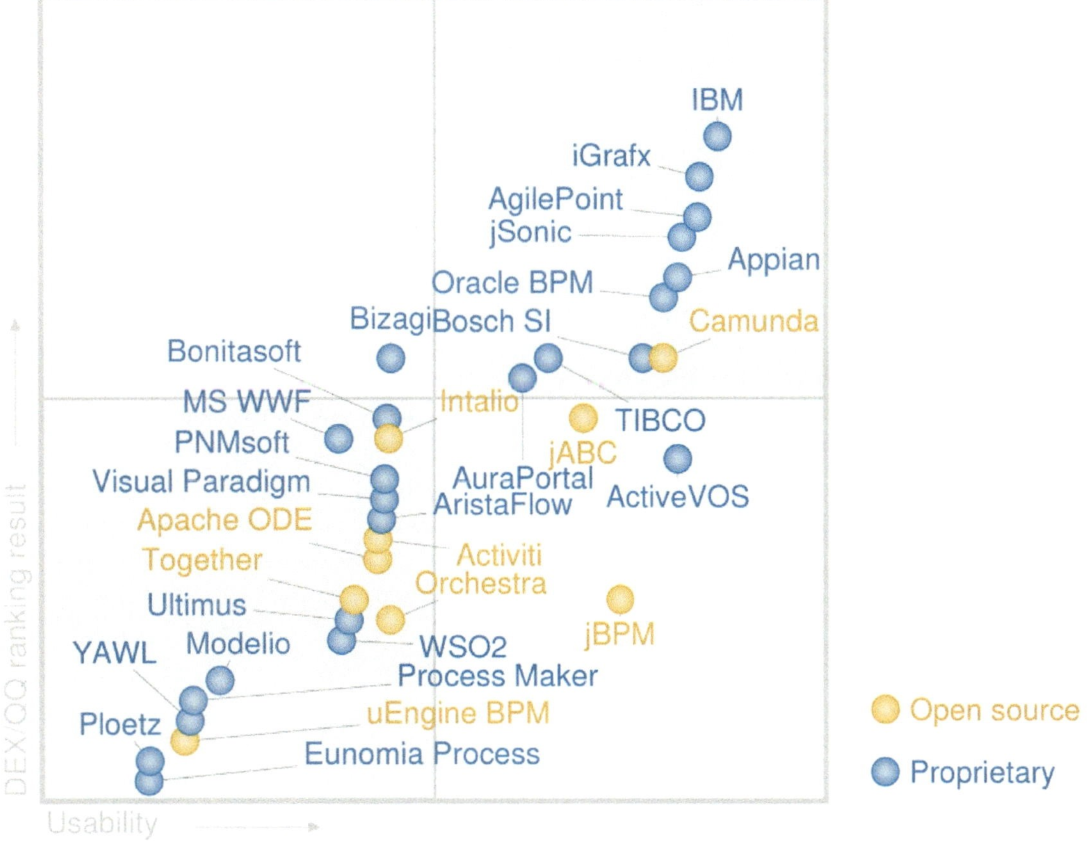

Figure 4. Magic quadrant for BPSS using the proposed hierarchical decision model.

It should be noted that the proposed DEX/QQ model uses different attributes than Gartner's. Consequently, the implemented decision rules differ. Nevertheless, the comparison of the locations of the proprietary business process simulations softwares (BPSSs) tools, presented in this as well as in Gartner's analysis [20, 30], shows that the proposed hierarchical decision model provides similar results. Minor discrepancies are present only in those BPSS tools that are near the borders between two quadrants. Therefore, despite the differences in the decision rules, the results show that the proposed hierarchical decision model provides viable results, compatible to the results from Gartner's analysis.

It can be noticed that the open source solutions are ranked quite high (values on the abscissa) predominantly due to the novelty and flexibility of the implemented features. However, in many cases, exploitation of the open-source solutions requires significant software skills making them unpopular for broad applicability, hence low values on the ordinate. However, there are cases, like the Camunda package, that despite being open-source, have high "Usability" value. This is mainly due to the support that is offered by the governing company.

Discussion on the Ranking Results.

The hierarchical decision model allows an in-depth analysis of the reasons for particular ranking values of a BPSS tool. As shown in Fig 5, there are three typical clusters of BPSS tools. The top ones, marked with green, have the highest marks for all segments. The middle ones, marked with yellow, have poor or none visual functionalities. The last ones, marked with red, lack advanced statistical tools. This clustering reflects the state on the BPSS tools market.

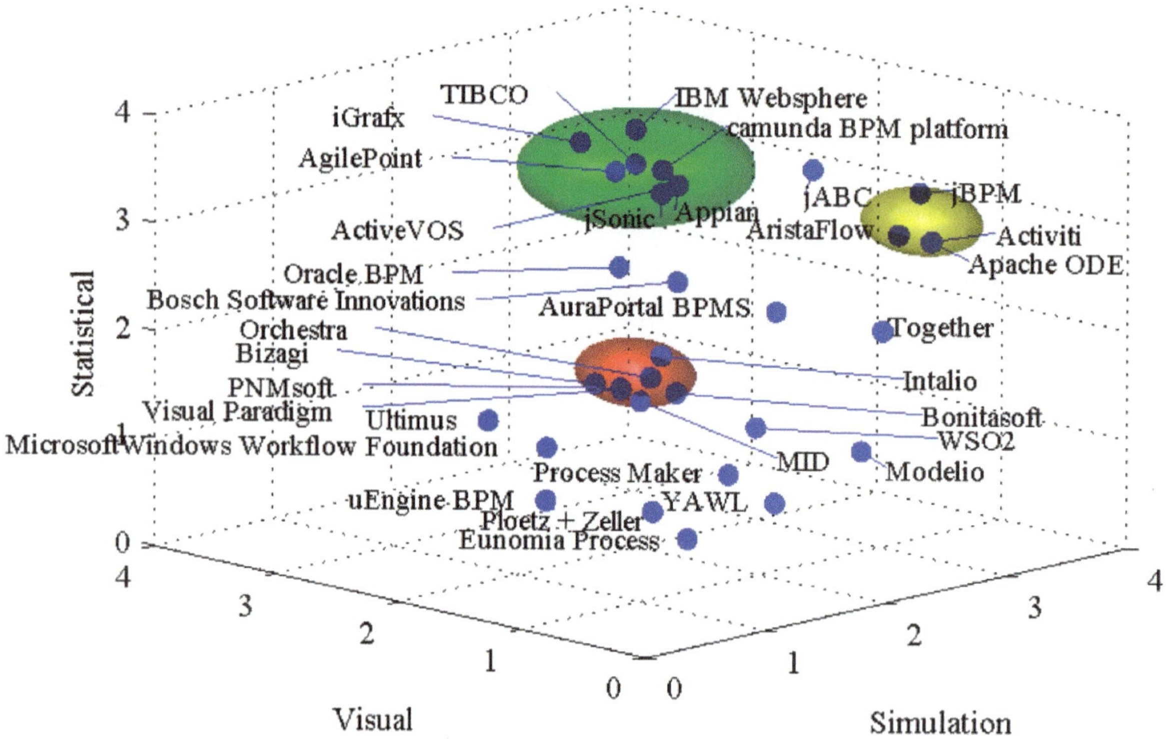

Figure 5. Multi-dimensional representation of the ranking results.

The tools in the yellow cluster are open-source BPSS tools. These business process simulations softwares (BPSSs), in many cases, have the most advanced capabilities for complex simulation and advanced statistical analysis that are even further enhanced with the possibility of adding custom extensions. On the other hand, open-source tools have poor or none visual (or user friendly) properties. In many cases substantial computer skills are required in order to utilize the offered capabilities.

The red cluster includes predominantly proprietary BPSS tools. These tools focus on the user friendly aspects. However, they typically fail to provide sufficiently powerful statistical analysis platforms. This is even further limited by the inability for adding 3rd party extensions.

Therefore, open-source tools tend to have the newest implemented algorithms while in the same time lacking appealing user interfaces. On the other hand, there are many proprietary tools that are user-friendly but offer suboptimal implementations of the crucial simulation capabilities.

Possible Extensions of the Model

The hierarchical structure, as shown in Fig 3, can be easily extended by either adding new attributes as leaves in the tree structure or by adding a complete new subtree. The addition of a new attribute would require an extension of the corresponding utility function, i.e., adding an additional attribute A_{n+1} in the Function (4).

The procedure for adding an additional subtree structure is somewhat more complicated and requires three steps:

- **Step 1**: Specify the new utility function in a form of Table 2.
- **Step 2**: Convert the qualitative table into a quantitative one using Algorithm 1.
- **Step 3**: Extend the utility functions that aggregate the new attributes by adding an additional argument A_{n+1} to the appropriate functions defined by Eq (4).

A typical extension would be adding a new subtree describing the economical impact of purchasing and running the BPSS tool.

CONCLUSION

This study provides a hierarchical decision support model for ranking and choosing of BPSS tools based on DEX/QQ methodology. Such a model enables systematic criteria management due to its capability for incorporating a large number of possibly conflicting criteria as well as fairly simple integration of new ones. Furthermore, the usage of hierarchical decision models leads to simple and focused utility functions thus allowing humans to achieve consistent decision making.

The proposed hierarchical model includes a set of criteria covering all aspects of a BPSS tools performance. The ranking results are inline with the publicly available results for BPSS tools ranking, thus justifying the applicability of the hierarchical decision model in combination with DEX/QQ methodology. Finally, the model is implemented as a freely accessible DSS tool.

AUTHOR CONTRIBUTIONS

Conceived and designed the experiments: ND PB MB BMB. Performed the experiments: ND PB MB BMB. Analyzed the data: ND PB MB BMB. Contributed reagents/materials/ analysis tools: ND PB MB BMB. Wrote the paper: ND PB MB BMB.

REFERENCES

1. Damij N, Damij T. A Multi-disciplinary Guide to Theory, Modeling, and Methodology. Progress in IS. Berlin Heidelberg: Springer; 2014.
2. Damij N, Damij T, Grad J, Jelenc F. A methodology for business process improvement and IS development. Information and software technology. 2008;50:1127–1141. doi: 10.1016/j.infsof.2007.11.004.
3. Laguna M, Marklund J. Business Process Modeling, Simulation, and Design. New Jersey: Pearson Education, Inc.; 2005.
4. Patig S, Stolz M. A pattern-based approach for the verification of business process descriptions. Information and Software Technology. 2013;55(1):58–87. Special section: Best papers from the 2nd International Symposium on Search Based Software Engineering 2010.
5. Savén R, Olhager J. Integration of product, process and functional orientations: principles and a case study. In: Jagdev H, Wortmann J, Pels H, editors. Collaborative Systems for Production Management. vol. 129 of IFIP—The International Federation for Information Processing. Springer US; 2003. p. 375–389.
6. Rücker B. Building an open source Business Process Simulation tool with JBoss jBPM. Stuttgart University of applied science; 2008.
7. Kellnera M, Madachyb RJ, Raffoc DM. Software process simulation modeling: Why? What? How? Journal of Systems and Software. 1999;46(2–3):91–105. doi: 10.1016/S0164-1212(99)00003-5.
8. Bosilj-Vuksic V, Ceric V, Hlupic V. Criteria for the Evaluation of Business Process. Interdisciplinary Journal of Information, Knowledge, and Management. 2007;2:73–88.
9. Pidd M, Carvalho A. Simulation software: Not the same yesterday, today or forever. Journal of Simulation. 2007;1:7–20. doi: 10.1057/palgrave.jos.4250004.
10. Tüzün E, Tekinerdogan B, Kalender ME, Bilgen S. Empirical evaluation of a decision support model for adopting software product line engineering. Information and Software Technology. 2015;60(0):77–101. doi: 10.1016/j.infsof.2014.12.007
11. Jadhav AS, Sonar RM. Evaluating and selecting software packages: A review. Information and Software Technology. 2009;51(3):555–563. Available from:http://www.sciencedirect.com/science/article/pii/S0950584908001262. doi: 10.1016/j.infsof.2008.09.003.
12. Lin HY, Hsu PY, Sheen GJ. A fuzzy-based decision-making procedure for data warehouse system selection. Expert Systems with Applications. 2007;32(3):939–953. Available from: http://www.sciencedirect.com/science/article/pii/S0957417406000509. doi: 10.1016/j.eswa.2006.01.031.
13. Azadeh A, Shirkouhi SN, Rezaie K. A robust decision-making methodology for evaluation and selection of simulation software package. The International Journal of Advanced Manufacturing Technology. 2010;47(1–4):381–393. Available from:http://dx.doi.org/10.1007/s00170-009-2205-6. doi: 10.1007/s00170-009-2205-6.
14. Jansen-Vullers M, Netjes M. Business process simulation–a tool survey. In: Workshop and Tutorial on Practical Use of Coloured Petri Nets and the CPN Tools; 2006.
15. Jahangirian M, Eldabi T, Naseer A, Stergioulas LK, Young T. Simulation in manufacturing and business: A review. European Journal of Operational Research. 2010;203(1):1–13. Available from:http://www.sciencedirect.com/science/article/pii/S0377221709004263. doi: 10.1016/j.ejor.2009.06.004.
16. Kaschek R, Pavlov R, Shekhovtsov VA, Zlatkin S. Characterization and Tool Supported Selection of Business Process Modeling Methodologies. In: Abramowicz W, Mayr H, editors. Technologies for Business Information Systems. Springer Netherlands; 2007. p. 25–37.
17. Ding S, Xia CY, Zhou KL, Yang SL, Shang JS. Decision Support for Personalized Cloud Service Selection through Multi-Attribute Trustworthiness Evaluation. PLoS ONE. 2014 06;9(6):e97762. Available from:http://dx.doi.org/10.1371%2Fjournal.pone.0097762. doi: 10.1371/journal.pone.0097762. pmid:24972237
18. Changyun L, Haiyan C, Gexin M, Zhibing W. A BPM Software Evaluation Method. In: Intelligent System Design and Engineering Application (ISDEA), 2012 Second International Conference on; 2012. p. 1–4.
19. Bohanec M, Rajkovic V. DEX: An expert system shell for decision support. Sistemica. 1990;1:145–157.
20. Norton D, Blechar M, Jones T. Magic Quadrant for Business Process Analysis Tools. Gartner RAS Core; 2010.
21. Bana e Costa CA, De Corte J, Vansnick J. MACBETH. In: Meskens N, Roubens M, editors. Advances in Decision Analysis, Book Series: Mathematical Modelling: Theory and Applications. Kluwer Academic Publishers; 1999. p. 131–157.
22. Larichev OI. Ranking multicriteria alternatives: The method ZAPROS III. European Journal of Operational Research 131. 2001;131:550–558. doi: 10.1016/S0377-2217(00)00096-5.
23. Jacquet-Lagreze E, Siskos Y. Preference disaggregation: 20 years of MCDA experience. European Journal of Operational Research. 2001;130:233–245. doi: 10.1016/S0377-2217(00)00035-7.
24. Greco S, Matarazzo B, Slowinski R. Rough sets theory for multicriteria decision analysis. European Journal of Operational Research. 2001;129:1–47. doi: 10.1016/S0377-2217(00)00167-3.
25. Baracskai Z, Dörfler V. Automated Fuzzy-Clustering for Doctus Expert System. In: Paper presented at

International Conference on Computational Cybernetics, Siófok, Hungary; 2003.

26. Bohanec M. DEXi: Program for Multi-Attribute Decision Making: User's manual: version 5.00. IJS Report DP-11897, Jožef Stefan Institute, Ljubljana; 2015.

27. Bohanec M, Urh B, Rajkovič V. Evaluation of options by combined qualitative and quantitative methods. Acta Psychologica. 1992;80:67–89. doi: 10.1016/0001-6918(92)90041-B.

28. Boshkoska BM. From Qualitative to Quantitative Evaluation Methods in Multi-Criteria Decission Models. Jožef Stefan International Postgraduate School; 2013.

29. Bohanec M. Statistical Analysis of Qualitative Multi Criteria Decision Models, Developed with Qualitative Hierarchical Method DEX. In: 23rd International Conference on Multiple Criteria Decision Making; 215.

30. Sinur J, Hill JB. Magic Quadrant for Business Process Management Suites. Gartner RAS Core; 2010.

CHAPTER 3

ALGORITHMIC OPTIMISATION METHOD FOR IMPROVING USE CASE POINTS ESTIMATION

Radek Silhavy, Petr Silhavy, Zdenka Prokopova

Faculty of Applied Informatics, Tomas Bata University in Zlin, Zlin, Czech Republic

ABSTRACT

This paper presents a new size estimation method that can be used to estimate size level for software engineering projects. The Algorithmic Optimisation Method is based on Use Case Points and on Multiple Least Square Regression. The method is derived into three phases. The first phase deals with calculation Use Case Points and correction coefficients values. Correction coefficients are obtained by using Multiple Least Square Regression. New project is estimated in the second and third phase. In the second phase Use Case Points parameters for new estimation are set up and in the third phase project estimation is performed. Final estimation is obtained by using newly developed estimation equation, which used two correction coefficients. The Algorithmic Optimisation Method performs approximately 43% better than the Use Case Points method, based on their magnitude of relative error score. All results were evaluated by standard approach: visual inspection, goodness of fit measure and statistical significance.

INTRODUCTION

Software development effort estimation plays an important role in the software engineering field. There are several approaches under investigation. The first is method-based Functional Points Analysis (FPA), which has an official technical standard [1] in ISO standardization. This method depends on the ability and experiences of an analyst, who is responsible for evaluating parameters. The system is descripted as set of functions, but the analyst must understand the system in great detail. A tendency of personal influence on the estimation can be described in the case of each individual analysis. Functional analysis considers a system as a black box. It is not important to describe the platform, the development method or any hardware used. The results of the calculation estimate only the effort of each individual system function or ability. The personal opinion of the analyst, which influences the estimation, makes this method unsuitable for comparing productivity in system or software development. However, if the same analyst prepares the calculation, the quality of the original estimation can be measured. If the results of the analysis in each development phase are compared and the error curve is flat, then the estimation is calculated accurately. This method is based on interactions between computer systems.

FPA considers external inputs or outputs. The boundary is the border between two systems from the user perspective.

Citation: Silhavy R, Silhavy P, Prokopova Z (2015) Algorithmic Optimisation Method for Improving Use Case Points Estimation. PLoS ONE 10(11): e0141887. doi:10.1371/journal.pone.0141887.

communication, plays a key role in the coordination between co-operating individuals. As a result, communication traces are commonly used to infer the social networks as the discrete spaces to study the dynamics of many other activities [7–9].

Sequence analysis, which has long history of being useful in molecular biology [10], has been, as of recently, also used in social science [11, 12], where researchers investigate life courses [13], and career trajectories [14]. Whereas DNA sequences are curled up in three-dimensional space, social events are arranged according to their time of occurrence. Due to our interest in social phenomena mostly local in time, the positions of social events in a sequence refer to relative, rather than absolute, time points. In bioinformatics, a number of global and local sequence alignment methods are used to compare the molecules' genetic similarity within and across different organisms, so as to elucidate their biological functions [15, 16]. Here we adopt a local alignment method to find and enumerate short patterns in work-talk (W-T) sequences of different people in online communities. We use these short W-T pattern counts as data points for modeling human behavior using hidden Markov models (HMMs) [17]. The goodness of fit of these models are established via their ability to predict the numbers of larger patterns in the sequences [15].

In collaborative communities there is interplay between work and talk activities, resulting in meaningful W-T sequence patterns that can be used to characterize different individuals. E.g., the simplest distinguishing W-T pattern for an individual is that they either tend to work continuously on the shared product, i.e. the sequence WWWW…, or talk continuously to co-ordinate work with others, and strengthen relationships, i.e. the sequence TTTTT…. More complex patterns are a combination of the two. If the W-T patterns are shared between people, then whole communities can also be characterized along those patterns as having a shared "community culture", in this case a work culture. This connotation of "culture" is consistent with Etzioni's notion [18]: "the set of assumptions shared by members of a societal unit which sets a context for its view of the world and itself". It is known that community culture plays an important role in innovation [19], the quality of work-products [20], and can facilitate the decision-making [21]. Recent studies on collaboration reveal that community size, team assembling mechanisms, and team structure have significant effects on team performance [22–24]. Thus, quantitatively characterizing the community culture is of much interest and provides novel insights for collaboration especially when it can be related to individual productivity and work efficiency.

To quantitatively study the emergence of work culture in online task-oriented groups we built an analytic framework for analysis of patterns jointly emerging along two basic collaborative dimensions, work and talk. Particularly, different from the previous studies mostly relied on talk activities to generate social networks [7–9], here we treat both activities equally as events sequenced over time, and use sequence analysis methods and stochastic models to reveal and contrast W-T patterns of individuals in online task-oriented communities. Here, we use OSS communities, where abundant data is publicly available [25–27], to study the W-T patterns of software developers for three main reasons. First, the work in OSS communities is easy to observe, and most of the talk activities are meaningfully related (because of community norms) to work activities; this simplifies the observation of functional W-T patterns. Second, the work and talk activities in OSS communities are always archived [28], so they are readily collected for analysis. Finally, performance properties, such as productivity, in terms of number of lines of code (LoC) written, can also be measured using the state of the produced software.

In this paper, we make the following specific contributions. We first propose two-state dynamic hidden Markov models (HMMs) as abstractions for software developers' work-talk behavior over time, and apply them on W-T sequences derived from Apache Software Foundation OSS projects. By characterizing each developer using their corresponding HMM parameters, we find evidence for community culture in OSS projects: developers in the same community tend to have more similar W-T patterns than those from different ones, and this pattern-affinity strengthens with time. We also observed that developers who have balanced W-T patterns are just as productive as those who work more continuously (fewer "talk" interruptions), but the former tend to stay active longer; this suggests that W-T balance is important to sustain OSS communities. Moreover, we create social and cooperation networks, and find that the convergence of W-T patterns between a given pair of developers appears to be re-enforced by both talk- and work-related interactions. This indicates that the emergence of a community W-T culture is apparently driven by both "work" and "talk" activities, and may offer a novel perspective on the co-evolving mechanisms of socio-technical, interdependent networks [29–31].

MATERIALS AND METHODS

We follow the definitions of work and talk in software engineering [28] and collected these activities from 31 OSS communities in the Apache Software Foundation on March 24th, 2012. In each community, there are several volunteer developers who contribute by committing to files, i.e., adding or removing software code; these activities are recorded in a Git repository and are our "work events", or "W"s. OSS developers use developer mailing lists to share programming knowledge and coordinate with others in the project. We record sent emails of a developer as "talk events", or "T"s (the received emails are included in the talk activities of others). Using this data, a W-T sequence of work and talk activities, as shown in Fig 1, can be recorded for each developer. Note that messages may be automatically posted to a mailing list in an OSS community to inform others when some work is completed. We exclude such trivial talk activities and only consider response emails [32, 33] which make up about 73% of all messages. We also use a semi-automatic approach to solve the problem of multiple aliases [32].

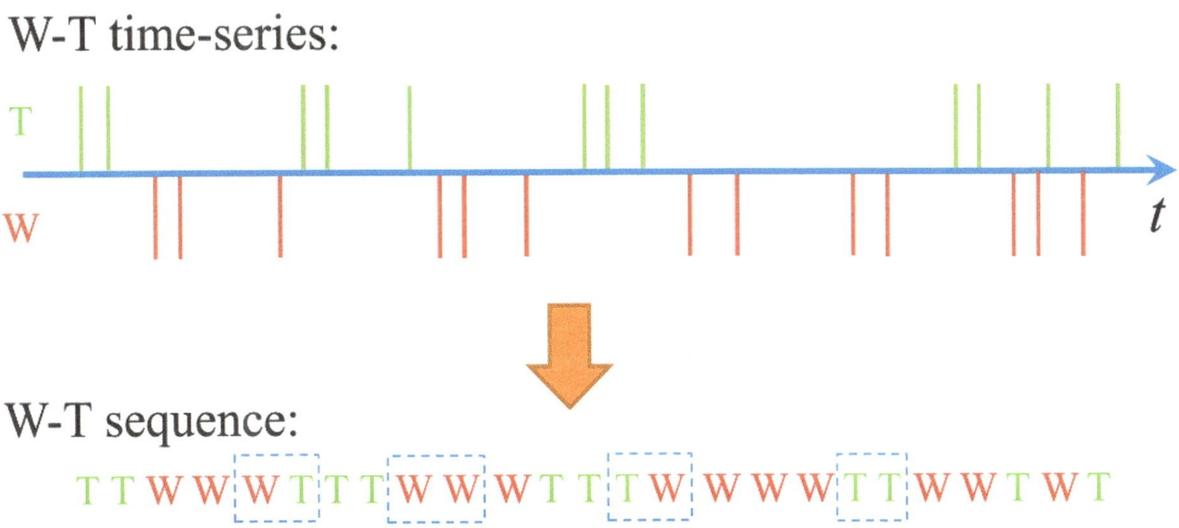

Figure 1. A multiple time-series of work and talk activities and the corresponding W-T sequence. The four different two-patterns, i.e., WW, WT, TW, and TT, are marked by the dashed rectangles.

We pre-process the W-T sequence data in several ways. To ensure a sufficient number of samples to reliably compare the W-T patterns between pairs of developers in the same or from different communities, we select a subset of "top developers" with sequences including at least 500 work and talk activities, and a subset of communities with at least 5 such developers. We acknowledge a risk of left-censorship of both work & talk activities, if any OSS communities did not archive their emails, or if they had used different version control systems before they moved to Git, some early data could be lost. Besides, it is known that many individuals need to first earn social capital in the OSS community by communicating with others before they are accepted as developers [34, 35]. As a result, we often observe long, pure work (resp. talk) subsequences before the first talk (resp. work) activity of a developer. In this study, we remove these trivial prefixes of pure work or talk activities, i.e., we only consider W-T sequences starting from the first work (resp. talk) activity if it occurred after a talk (resp. work) activity.

The above pre-processing of the data yielded 14 communities with 120 "top developers". The full data is available at: https://dx.doi.org/10.6084/m9.figshare.3181555. Some basic properties of those OSS projects are shown in Table 1. Besides developers, there we also list the number of active users (including developers) in each community. These users might not directly change files, but they may contribute to the communities by other ways, such as report bugs etc.

Table 1. Basic properties of the fourteen OSS communities

Communities	Description	Time frame	#Users	#Devs	#Top devs	#Files
Activemq	Integration patterns server	2005/12/12–2012/03/16	2012	28	6	16788
Ant	Build tool	2000/01/13–2012/03/16	1402	44	9	11620
Axis2_c	Web services engine	2004/02/03–2012/03/15	582	24	8	10262
Axis2_java	Web services engine	2001/01/30–2012/03/19	3738	72	15	129978
Camel	Integration framework	2007/03/19–2012/03/17	805	31	6	36965
Cxf	Web services framework	2005/07/22–2012/03/16	427	45	7	37867
Derby	Database management system	2004/08/10–2012/03/22	1118	35	16	6563
Lucene	Search software	2001/09/11–2012/03/23	2102	41	14	6674
Mahout	Machine learning library	2008/01/15–2012/03/23	533	15	6	5123
Nutch	Web search software	2005/01/25–2012/03/22	556	16	6	3072
Ode	Web services	2006/02/18–2012/03/22	365	17	6	11006
Openejb	Container system and server	2002/01/18–2012/03/22	169	38	5	43960
Solr	Enterprise search platform	2006/01/20–2011/03/01	825	19	8	8534
Wicket	Web application framework	2004/09/21–2012/03/21	539	24	8	48045

doi:10.1371/journal.pone.0154324.t001

Finding Surprising Sequence Patterns

A G-pattern in a sequence over the alphabet {W, T} is a subsequence of length G. There are total 2^G possible different G-patterns. Typically, the length of a pattern is much shorter than the length of the given sequence. In our study we focus on 2-patterns and 3-patterns. Given a sequence $\theta = \{s_1, s_2, \ldots, s_h\}$ over {W, T}, we count the occurrence of each of the 2^G patterns, by rolling a window of size G over the sequence, and incrementing the count for the pattern we find. For instance, in the W-T sequence shown in Fig 1, the four possible 2-patterns, WW, WT, TW, and TT, occur eight, five, five, and six times, respectively.

To assess the probability that a pattern occurs by chance, we create a null (baseline) model by randomizing the observed W-T sequence so as to preserve the proportion of work to talk activities. This can be achieved, e.g., by using the R's

[36] sample() function on the sequence indexes. Then, the preference for pattern P in the observed sequence, θ, over the randomized sequence, θ*, is calculated by the relative difference between the counts for that pattern, C_p and C^*_p, in the respective sequences,

$$\lambda_P = \frac{C_P - \langle C^*_P \rangle}{\langle C^*_P \rangle} \times 100\%. \tag{1}$$

For $< C^*_p >$, we generated 100 randomized sequences for each observed one. For each pattern P in a sequence, we also calculate its Z-score [37] as $Z = \lambda_P \langle C^*_P \rangle / \varsigma$, where ς is the standard deviation of the pattern counts in θ*. Larger |Z| values indicate more surprising observed counts.

Hidden Markov Model

A Hidden Markov Model, HMM, is a simple stochastic model used to abstract behavior involving several different states and transitions among them. To model developers and their work-talk behavior, we use an HMM with two states, "work", "W", and "talk", "T", and transitions between them corresponding to either continuing to perform the same activity, W followed by a W or T followed by a T, or switching activities, W followed by a T, and vice versa. The parameters αand β, representing the conditional transition probabilities P(W|W) and P(T|T), respectively. The HMM diagram is shown in Fig 2.

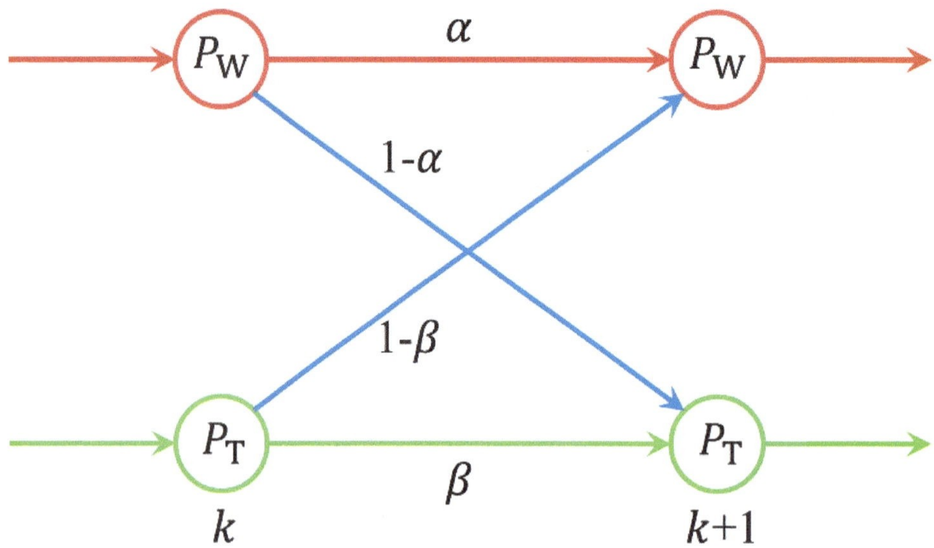

Figure 2. An HMM with two states, i.e., "work" and "talk", denoted by "W" and "T", respectively. The model is used to explain the W-T patterns of developers in different communities.

If we denote by $P_W(k)$ and $P_T(k)$ the probabilities that work, resp. talk, happen at time step k, then for the next time point we have

$$P_W(k+1) = \alpha P_W(k) + (1-\beta)P_T(k), \tag{2}$$

$$P_T(k+1) = (1-\alpha)P_W(k) + \beta P_T(k), \tag{3}$$

where α and β are the transition probabilities. We note here that while α and β could evolve with time, they don't change much between successive activities, therefore we can consider them as constants in the sequences with certain lengths. Thus, Eqs (2) and (3) can be approximated for continuous time, τ, and then transformed to the following more compact matrix form:

$$\dot{P}(\tau) = \begin{bmatrix} \alpha-1 & 1-\beta \\ 1-\alpha & \beta-1 \end{bmatrix} P(\tau), \tag{4}$$

with $P(\tau) = [P_W(\tau), P_T(\tau)]^T$. By solving Eq (4), we have

$$P(\tau) = D_1 \begin{bmatrix} 1-\beta \\ 1-\alpha \end{bmatrix} + D_2 \begin{bmatrix} 1 \\ -1 \end{bmatrix} e^{(\alpha+\beta-2)\tau}, \tag{5}$$

where D_1 and D_2 are some constants. The fractions of work and talk activities, P_W and P_T, in a sequence with length L can be estimated by

$$\begin{bmatrix} P_W \\ P_T \end{bmatrix} = \frac{1}{L}\int_0^L P(\tau)d\tau. \tag{6}$$

By substituting Eq (5) into Eq (6), we have

$$\begin{bmatrix} P_W \\ P_T \end{bmatrix} = \frac{D_1}{(2-\alpha-\beta)L} \begin{bmatrix} 1 \\ -1 \end{bmatrix} \left[1 - e^{(\alpha+\beta-2)L}\right] + D_2 \begin{bmatrix} 1-\beta \\ 1-\alpha \end{bmatrix}. \tag{7}$$

In the right side of Eq (7), the first term is negligible when the sequence is long enough, considering $\alpha + \beta < 2$. Since it is always satisfied $P_W + P_T = 1$, we have

$$P_W = \frac{1-\beta}{2-\alpha-\beta}, \quad P_T = \frac{1-\alpha}{2-\alpha-\beta}, \tag{8}$$

which are fully determined by the two parameters in the model. Then, the probabilities for the four different two-patterns in the sequence, in terms of α and β, are given by:

$$P_{WW} = \alpha P_W = \frac{\alpha(1-\beta)}{2-\alpha-\beta}, \tag{9}$$

$$P_{WT} = (1-\alpha)P_W = \frac{(1-\alpha)(1-\beta)}{2-\alpha-\beta}, \tag{10}$$

$$P_{TW} = (1-\beta)P_T = \frac{(1-\alpha)(1-\beta)}{2-\alpha-\beta}, \tag{11}$$

$$P_{TT} = \beta P_T = \frac{(1-\alpha)\beta}{2-\alpha-\beta}, \quad (12)$$

Intuitively, larger α and β means higher proportions of WW and TT patterns, respectively, in the sequence. Furthermore, the probabilities for longer patterns can be calculated similarly, once the model parameters α and β are estimated from Eqs (9) to (12). It is important to note that for the randomized W-T sequences generated by the null model, the current state is independent from the previous state, thus we have $\alpha = 1 - \beta$, i.e., $\alpha + \beta = 1$. In this case, α and β are equal to the fractions of work and talk activities, respectively.

Based on the above model, we have the following solutions for the parameters:

$$\alpha = \frac{P_{WW}}{P_{WW}+P_{WT}}, \quad \beta = \frac{P_{TT}}{P_{TT}+P_{TW}}, \quad (13)$$

where P_{WW}, P_{WT}, P_{TW}, and P_{TT} denote the probabilities of the four different two-patterns for each developer, and can be estimated from the counts of the four different two-patterns as long as the corresponding W-T sequence is sufficiently long. Thus, this HMM is fully determined by the numbers of the four different two-patterns.

Hazard Modeling

To study the tenure, or survival time, of developers in the projects (time from joining until leaving) in terms of the HMM parameters α and β, we use survival analysis, which enables modeling of outcomes in the presence of censored data. In our case the censoring is due to the uncertainty that long time periods without activities may or may not indicate that a developer has left the community. Generally, survival analysis involves calculating the Hazard rate [38], defined as the limit of the number of events per δt time divided by the number at risk, as $\delta t \to 0$. Supposing a developer does not leave the community until time Γ, the Hazard rate is given by

$$h(t) = \lim_{\delta t \to 0} \frac{P(t \le \Gamma < t + \delta t | t \le \Gamma)}{\delta t}. \quad (14)$$

Our primary interest is the survival function defined as $S(t) = P(t < \Gamma)$, which can be calculated from Eq (14) by

$$S(t) = e^{-\int_0^t h(\tau)d\tau}. \quad (15)$$

Suppose α or β can influence the survival time, then we adopt the Cox model [39] to define the Hazard rate h(t) by

$$h(t) = h_0(t)e^{bx}, \quad (16)$$

with $h_0(t)$ describing how the hazard changes over time at baseline level of covariate x, either αor β. Here we focus on the hazard ratio $h(t)/h_0(t)$ to see whether increasing the covariate will significantly increase or decrease the survival time, e.g., $b > 0$ means that the individuals of larger x will have statistically shorter survival times.

RESULTS

We begin by studying two-pattern preference in developer's behavior. Given an observed W-T sequence for each person, we count in it the occurrences of all four two-patterns, and derive the preference for each, denoted by λ_i, i = 1, 2, 3, 4, respectively, in the real sequences as compared to random ones as described above. We find that, on average, for all developers, $\lambda_1 = 148.9\%$ and $\lambda_4 = 40.5\%$, while $\lambda_2 = -38.0\%$ and $\lambda_3 = -38.6\%$, i.e., WW and TT are positively enriched, while WT and TW are negatively enriched. We find that $|Z| > 5$ in 462 out of 480 cases (120 developers times 4 two-patterns), indicating that most of the observed counts are surprising. These suggest that developers much prefer to persist with one activity-type, rather than switch frequently between activities.

It may be argued that two successive activities should not be considered as a two-pattern if the time interval between them is relatively long, e.g., longer than one month. To show that our method is robust with respect to time-scale, we also calculate the relative difference by varying the thresholds for the time-intervals over which we consider the two-patterns. We vary the thresholds, denoted by ξ = 1, 7, 30 (days), and only the patterns with intervals $\le \xi$ are considered. The results are shown in Fig 3, where we can see that WW and TT patterns are always much more preferred than WT and TW patterns in the real sequences under thresholds varying from one day to one month. Interestingly, we also find a slight trend that the WW pattern becomes more preferred, and the TT pattern less preferred, when we exclude more repeated activities with relatively shorter time intervals (and thus a smaller ξ). Since the number of these long time-interval patterns is relatively small (2.2% and 0.3% for ξ = 7 and ξ = 30, respectively), this slight trend still indicates that developers are more likely to start and end a repeated and relatively compressed work sequence with talk activities, viz., talk activities plays important role in enabling new tasks (work activities) in these online communities.

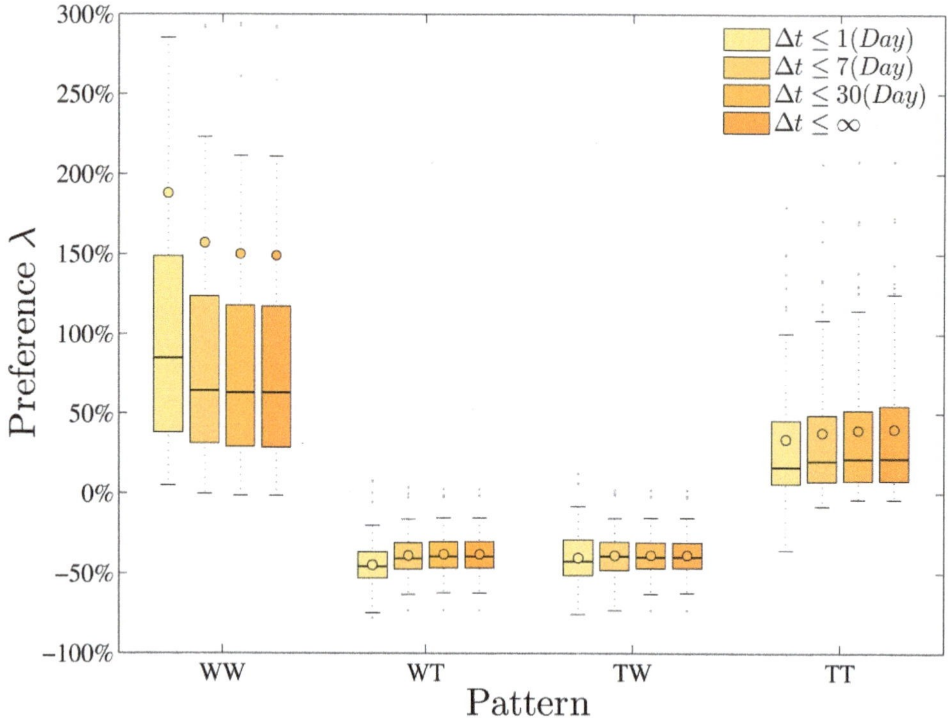

Figure 3. The box-and-whisker diagram for the preferences of the four different two-patterns in the real W-T sequences under the different time-interval conditions by comparing with the random ones.

Emergence of Community Culture

We use HMMs, described above, as two parameter, α and β, models of software developers' work-talk behavioral patterns. To validate the use of HMMs, we check their efficacy in predicting the counts of longer patterns, e.g., three-patterns. We find that the HMMs do predict the numbers of all the eight three-patterns with significantly smaller relative errors ($p = 1.8 \times 10^{-16}$on average) than the random mechanism for the developers we studied, i.e., 14.5% versus 67.4% on average. We characterize each developer with the parameters α and β coming out of the HMM fitted to their W-T sequence. Those α and β can, then, be compared across developers and communities. To study the work-talk behavior of developers within and between communities, we first visualize all (α, β) pairs in the α − β plane, as shown in Fig 4, where the developers of the same communities are marked by the same symbols. Evidence of clustering is visually apparent: the points representing the developers in the same communities are indeed closer to each other when compared with those from different communities. We further divided all the developers into three groups by the k-means method [40], and find that most developers in the same communities are centralized in one of three clusters, rather than uniformly distributed in all the three, which indicates different community cultures that emphasize continuous work (cluster #3), talk (cluster #1), or both (cluster #2), respectively. Here, we also provide the baseline formed by the HMM parameters of the W-T sequences that are generated by the random mechanism with different fractions of work activities. Since this baseline must satisfy α + β = 1, and almost all the points being above this based line validates again the preferred patterns WW and TT in all communities.

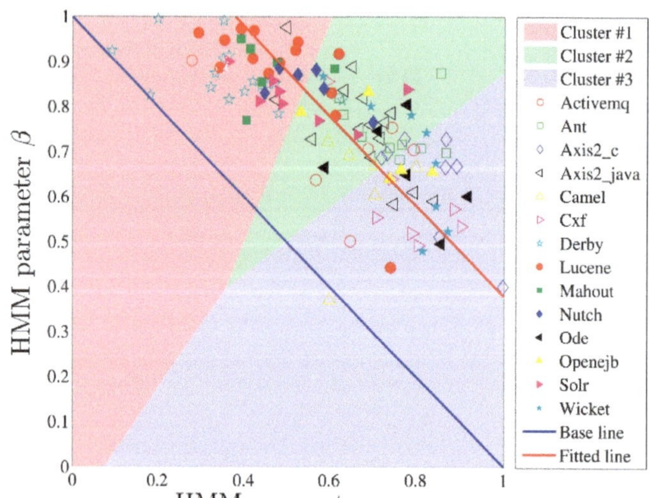

Figure 4. Visualization of developers on *α-β* plane by considering their whole sequences, where developers are points and those of the same communities are marked by the same symbols. The parameters are grouped into three clusters by the "K-means" method. The base line is

formed by the HMM parameters of the random W-T sequences with different fractions of work activities. The points are fitted by the linear function $\alpha + \beta = \varepsilon$, with $\varepsilon = 1.38$.

More specifically, most developers ($\geq$ 50%) in Derby, Lucene, Mahout, Nutch, and Solr belong to cluster #1, which corresponds to mostly talk activities (high β), while most of the developers in Axis2_c, Camel, Cxf, Ode, Openejb, and Wicket belong to cluster #3, corresponding to mostly work activities (high α). As a whole, we define the center of a community in $\alpha - \beta$ plane by the median of the HMM parameters of the developers in it, then calculate its diversity by the average distances of HMM parameters between the developers and the center, as shown inFig 5 for the above 11 communities. It is interesting to find that the communities sharing similar W-T patterns also belong to similar domains (description in Table 1). For example, Lucene, Nutch, and Solr are all about "search" and they are intrinsically related to each other, just like the introduction of Nutch on its web site: "Stemming from Apache Lucene, Apache Nutch now builds on Apache Solr adding web-specifics". Besides, Axis2_c, Cxf, and Ode are all about "services", while each of Camel, Cxf, and Wicket is a software framework that provides a shared architecture for class of applications.

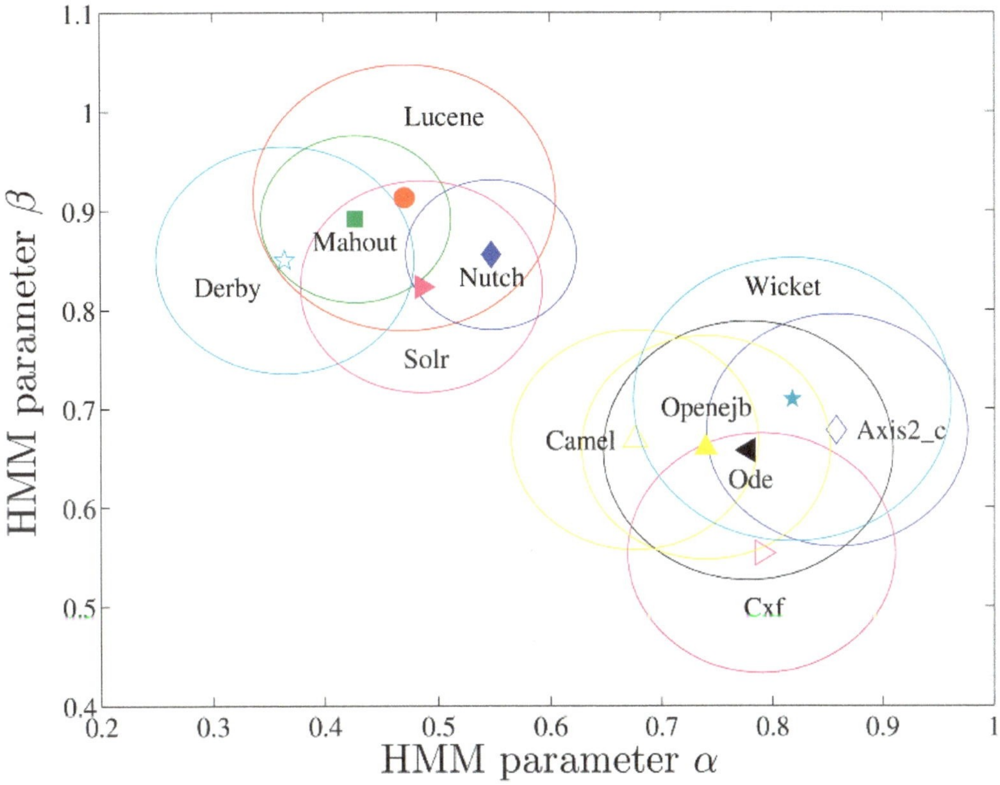

Figure 5. The centers and the respective diversities (the large circles) of the eleven communities on $\alpha - \beta$ plane, defined as the medians of the HMM parameters of their developers and the average distances of HMM parameters between the developers and the corresponding centers, respectively.

More formally, if we denote by α_i and β_i the HMM parameters of developer d_i, we can calculate the Euclidean distance of HMM parameters between two developers d_i and d_j by

$$\rho_{ij} = \sqrt{(\alpha_i - \alpha_j)^2 + (\beta_i - \beta_j)^2}, \quad \textbf{(17)}$$

as a quantitative metric for the similarity between the W-T patterns of developers, i.e., the shorter the distance between them, the more similar the W-T patterns of the two developers. Then, we compare the distances of HMM parameters between all pairs of developers in the same communities with those between pairs of developers from different communities, and find that the former list of distances are significantly shorter (p = 0) than the later ones. These qualitative and quantitative analysis lend support to using the HMM parameters as a reasonable proxy for the way the interplay of work and talk testify to community culture.

To study the clustering phenomenon of W-T patterns in more detail so as to answer whether developers choose to join communities with similar W-T patterns as theirs or the similarity emerges over time as developers participate and evolve with their communities, we do the same pattern analysis as above, using only the initial 100 activities in the W-T sequences. Based on the comparison, we find that:

1. The developers in the same community showed similar W-T patterns starting with their inception into the project. I.e., for their first 100 activities, the distances of HMM parameters between pairs of developers in the same communities are significantly shorter (p = 3.1e-13) than those from different communities.
2. In addition, the community cultures of different communities converge rather than diverge from each other, as time evolves. I.e., both the inner (within-community) and inter (between-community) distances decrease significantly (p = 0) with time, as shown in Fig 6. We also calculate the average inner distance

for all communities by considering their respective first ϱ activities with different values of ϱ, as shown in Fig 7, to study the converging process. We find that the inner distances decrease as ϱ increases, for most communities. As examples, the evolutions of the HMM parameters with time for the communities Axis2_java, Derby, and Lucene are shown in Fig 8.

3. The clustering of the HMM parameters within communities grows tighter with time. I.e., the convergence rates of the parameter distances from the first 100 activities to all activities within communities (the average distance decreases from 0.3381 to 0.1832) is significantly larger ($p = 1.7e\text{-}7$) than those between communities (it decreases from 0.4216 to 0.2861).

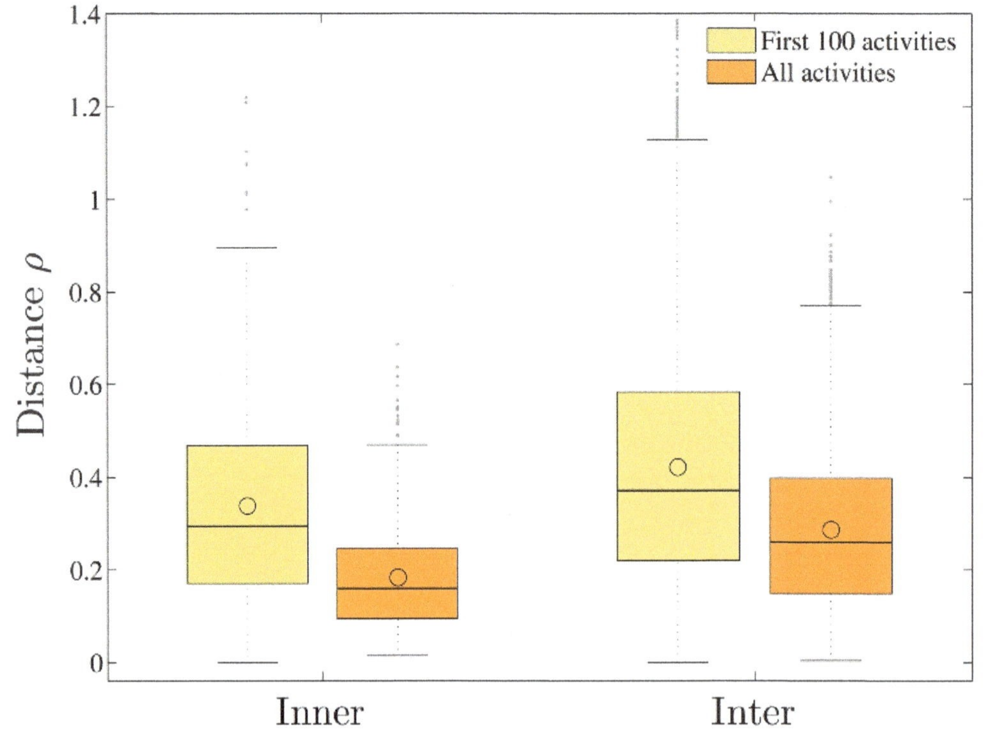

Figure 6. The box-and-whisker diagrams for the distances of the HMM parameters of the first 100 activities and those of the whole W-T sequences between pairs of developers inner and inter communities.

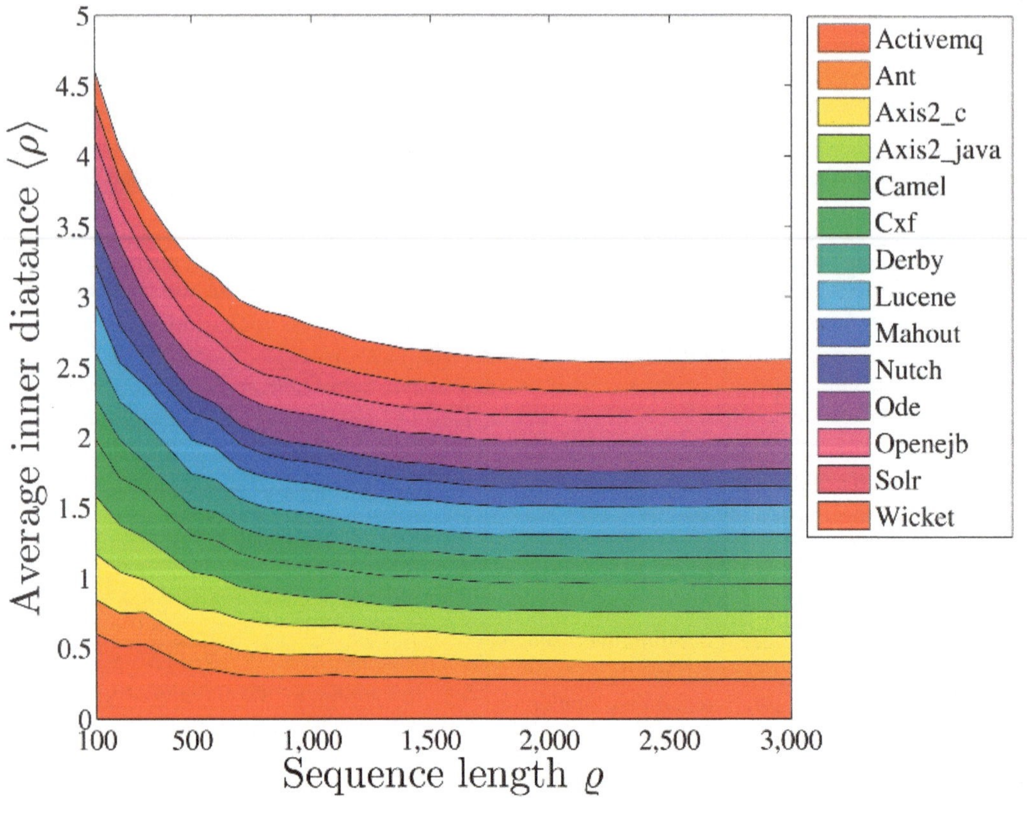

Figure 7. The average inner distances of HMM parameters between pairwise developers for the fourteen communities.

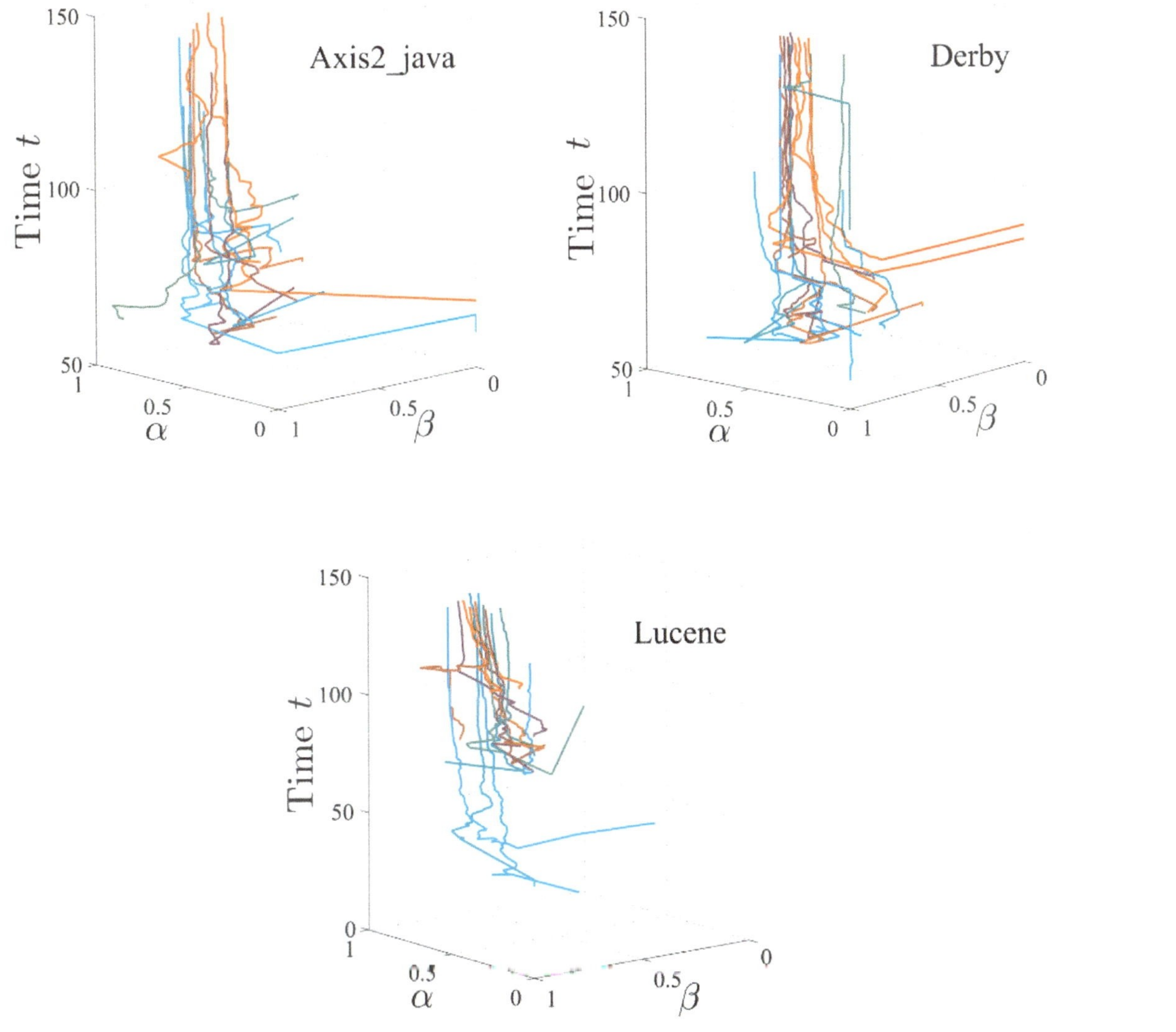

Figure 8. Developers' ***α*** **&** ***β*** monthly evolving curves, e.g., Axis2_java, Derby, and Lucene.

These findings suggest that developers with similar W-T patterns are indeed more likely to join in the same communities, and continue to harmonize their patterns as they work and talk as a team. In fact, since there are many online communities on similar topics, people can first experience the culture of these communities and then decide to join or not [41–43]. For OSS, it is clear that most developers do communicate a fair bit on the developer mailing list before actually contributing work [34, 44]; indeed, this type of "socialization" is a necessary prerequisite to having one's work contributions accepted. Thus, it is to be expected that the developers are more likely to join in the communities with harmonized work and talk patterns, in order to reduce co-ordination efforts.

In addition, we find that different community cultures will slightly converge rather than diverge from each other over time; this suggests that there may be an over-arching trend of the W-T patterns for all the developers (in all communities). To investigate this further, we compare the two parameters α and β separately for all developers, considering a) the first 100 activities andb) all activities. We find that both of them increase as time evolves, i.e., the HMMs in case a)have significantly smaller α ($p = 0.027$) and β ($p = 1.4e\text{-}5$) than those in b). In fact, the efficiency of overall work and talk activities may be measured by the sum α + β; larger values of this sum indicate less switching between activities and thus fewer interruptions. This arguably represents higher efficiency [45–47]. In other words, the HMM parameters (α_i, β_i) shown in Fig 4 can be fitted by the linear function:

$$\alpha + \beta = \varepsilon, \tag{18}$$

with a single parameter ε representing the average efficiency of all the developers. Using the least squares method, we get the average efficiency ε and the corresponding standard deviation σ from the regression line as

$$\varepsilon = \frac{\Sigma_{i=1}^{N}(\alpha_i + \beta_i)}{N}, \quad \sigma = \sqrt{\frac{\Sigma_{i=1}^{N}(\alpha_i + \beta_i - \varepsilon)^2}{2N}}, \tag{19}$$

respectively, for the N developers. We find that the average efficiency steadily increases, while the variance decreases, with time, which means that as time goes on developers tend to have longer bursts of pure work and pure talk, suggesting that their discussions are becoming more effective, and that the ensuing co-operative work proceeds relatively more uninterruptedly.

Looking at the change in the rate of talk activities for all developers, in terms of α and β, Eq (8), we find that the rate increases significantly ($p = 0.0046$) with time, indicating that most developers become more socialized in the process. This phenomenon is consistent with the fact that more discussions are always needed to further improve a mature product. Meanwhile, contributing to these online communities is social work, i.e., the contributions of developers are highly visible and will be checked by many other users [33], so it is not surprising that they need to reply to comments more frequently when contributing more.

Community Culture and Individual Performance

We then study the correlations with community culture of five measures of individual performance work rhythm (# work activities per day), thousands of lines of code added per unit time (KLoC per day), talk rhythm (# talk activities per day), newly established social links per week, and observed survival time (# year), resp., X_1 to X_5. The first four properties are calculated in the same time period of the person's W-T sequence. The survival time, X_5, of a developer is defined as the period of time from her first activity to the last one, which may be longer than the period of their W-T sequence, considering that the W-T sequences under study were preprocessed by removing prefixes of pure work or talk activities. The survival time of a developer is only observed when the developer has left the respective community. Here, as a reasonable estimation, we consider that a developer has left the community if they have not been active for a relatively long time, i.e., longer than some threshold T.

All developers are divided into three clusters by their HMM parameters, as shown in Fig 4. The developers in Cluster #1 emphasize "talk", those in Cluster #3 emphasize "work", while those in Cluster #2 seek balance between the two. For each property from X_1 to X_4, we have a list of their values for developers in each cluster, and the comparisons between the properties of developers in different clusters are visualized by the box-and-whisker diagrams shown in Fig 9(A), with the significance presented in Table 2. We find that the developers in Cluster #3 have the fastest working rhythms, those in Cluster #2 follow, while the developers in Cluster #1 work the slowest. The direction reverses for their talking rhythms. However, the situation is a little different when we compare the abilities of developers of different clusters in producing codes and earning social status. We find that the developers in Cluster #2 and Cluster #3 can produce similar KLoC per day, and both groups produce significantly more than the developers in Cluster #1, while the developers in Cluster #2 and Cluster #1 earn similar numbers of social links per week, and both groups earn significantly more than the developers in Cluster #3. Interestingly, balanced, and W-heavy W-T patterns are likelier among ASF members: the fractions of ASF members in Clusters #2 and #3 are 55.6% and 55.9%, respectively, while in Cluster #1 it is 46.3%. These indicate that extended discussion is always accompanied with the slowing down of work rhythms, but not always with decrease of productivity, and the developers seeking balance between work and talk behave competitively on both productivity and socialization as those who mostly work or mostly talk.

(A)
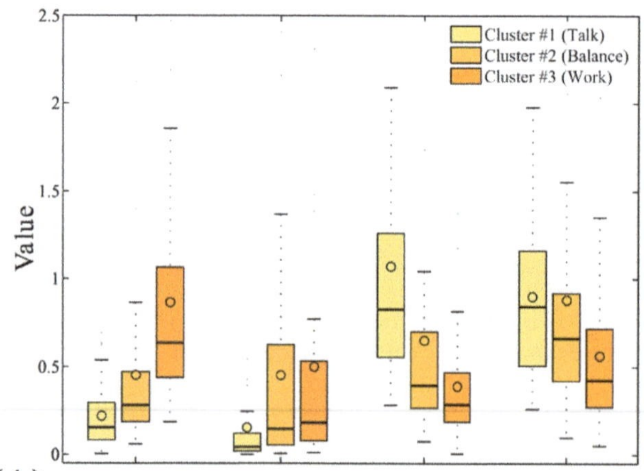

(B)
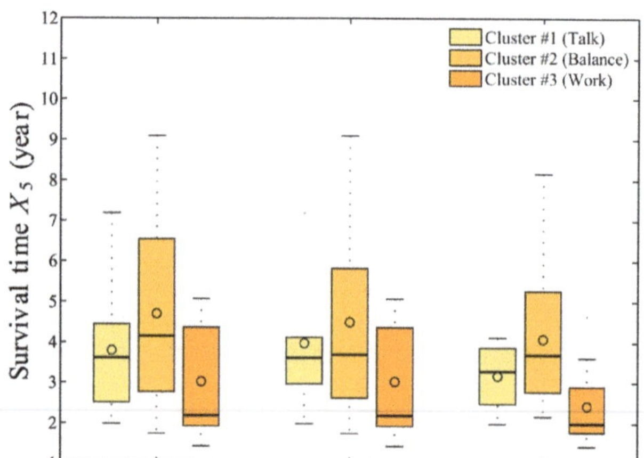

Figure 9. The effects of community culture on individual properties. The box-and-whisker diagrams for (A) the four individual properties X_1 to X_4, and (B) the observed survival time X_5 with different time thresholds T_1 (half year), T_2 (one year), and T_3 (two years), for the developers in the three clusters determined by their HMM parameters.

Table 2. The student's t-tests for five individual properties between different clusters. Here, p_{ij} denotes the significance of difference between the developers in Cluster #i and Cluster #j

Property	Mean value			Significance		
	#1	#2	#3	p_{12}	p_{23}	p_{13}
X_1	0.2173	0.4524	0.8664	0.0189	0.0054	1.23e-07
X_2	0.2099	0.7955	0.7930	0.0142	0.9939	0.0146
X_3	1.0696	0.6503	0.3878	0.0119	0.0576	6.63e-06
X_4	0.8988	0.8814	0.5626	0.9035	0.0365	0.0020
X_5	3.7974	4.6988	3.0243	0.3016	0.0368	0.2692

doi:10.1371/journal.pone.0154324.t002

Although it seems that the developers who mostly work have the fastest working rhythms and the highest productivity, on average, it doesn't mean that choice is the healthiest for them or for the overall community, since these developers are more likely to feel boring and then quit the communities. Based on the Hazard model to consider the censoring data, we find that developers with smaller α or larger β will have suggestively longer survival times (p = 0.077 andb = 1.7 for α and p = 0.042 and b = −2.4 for β), indicating that, by comparison, talk activities are more important than work activities for developer retention. Indeed, we find that developers with more balance between their work and talk stay active in the communities for suggestively longer periods of time than those who mostly work, as shown in Fig 9(B), i.e., the significance is equal to 0.037, 0.078, and 0.049 when the survival times of the developers with their last activities occurred half year, one year, and two years before are considered, respectively. The significance of comparison for the survival time among the three clusters of developers are presented in Table 2 when T = 0.5 (year). These findings suggest that developers with balanced W-T patterns are important to sustain OSS communities. Each of the communities we studied has at least one balanced developer, and there is also a natural trend that developers become more balanced, i.e., both α and β increase with time.

Role of Socio-Technical Links

Here, we study the extent to which developers with similar W-T patterns tend to be linked more in the email social network or the technical cooperation network. In social networks, social weight between two developers intuitively means the number of emails between them. In cooperation networks, a pair of developers are linked with an edge indicating the number of files on which they have both worked. In particular, denoting by ψ_i the list of files that developerd_i commits to, the cooperative weight between a pair of developers d_i and d_j, in terms of the files to which they have committed, is defined as

$$\omega_{ij} = \frac{\psi_i \cap \psi_j}{\psi_i \cup \psi_j}. \tag{20}$$

On the social side, for pairs of developers, we get Spearman correlations (Pearson correlations yield very similar results) between the distances of HMM parameters and the number of emails they have exchanged, shown in Table 3, in the Social weight columns. We find negative correlation in ten out of fourteen projects, with the significance $p < 0.1$ in six of them, includingAxis2_c, Camel, Derby, Lucene, Ode, and Solr, while we find positive correlation with the significance $p < 0.1$ in only one project called Mahout. The negative correlation means that the smaller the HMM parameter distance between two developers, the larger the number of emails they have exchanged.

Table 3. Spearman correlation of HMM parameters and social & cooperative weights for developer pairs in different projects

Project	Social weight		Cooperative weight	
	Correlation	Significance	Correlation	Significance
Activemq	−0.3058	0.2080	−0.5007	0.0323
Ant	0.0049	0.9774	−0.3704	0.0268
Axis2_c	−0.4667	0.0123	0.2474	0.2036
Axis2_java	−0.0442	0.6547	−0.1714	0.0805
Camel	−0.6000	0.0204	−0.3679	0.1779
Cxf	0.0651	0.7793	0.1948	0.3957
Derby	−0.1940	0.0337	−0.3232	3.41e-04
Lucene	−0.6046	2.20e-10	−0.2275	0.0303
Mahout	0.6685	0.0064	−0.3429	0.2110
Nutch	−0.2832	0.3065	0.4071	0.1333
Ode	−0.4866	0.0659	−0.1429	0.6114
Openejb	0.0667	0.8648	−0.3818	0.2790
Solr	−0.5083	0.0058	−0.5457	0.0031
Wicket	−0.1363	0.4876	−0.1795	0.3591
All	−0.2517	2.81e-09	−0.2037	1.84e-06

doi:10.1371/journal.pone.0154324.t003

On the technical end, we study the Spearman correlation between the distances of HMM parameters and the strength of file cooperation links between developers. We get the results in Table 3, under the Cooperative weight columns. In this case negative correlation is found in eleven out of fourteen projects, with the significance $p < 0.1$ in six of them, including Activemq,Ant, Axis2_java, Derby, Lucene, and Solr, while no project has positive correlation with significance $p < 0.1$. The negative correlation means that the smaller the HMM parameter distance between two developers, the larger the cooperation between them.

When considering all communities together, we obtain a significantly negative correlation in both cases (the last row of Table 3). Thus, developers with more emails between them or committing to more of the same files are more likely to have similar W-T patterns. The results also indicate that community culture may be either social or task (technical) oriented; the distances between HMM parameters are more likely to be correlated with social weights in some communities, and with cooperative weights in others. Note that such findings are reasonable, considering that developers who commit more to popular files or who communicate more are likelier to coordinate more with each other [48], which may require higher-level convergence between their W-T patterns.

DISCUSSION

In this paper, we demonstrate that work-talk patterns of software developers in a number of OSS communities can be effectively studied using sequence analysis methods on sequences arising from simple two-state behavior models of work and talk activities.

Our methods enabled us to learn about a series of interesting task-oriented community based phenomena: that developers in a community present similar W-T patterns, and this clustering of W-T patterns is enhanced with time, reflecting different work cultures in these communities, with emphasis on different proportions of continuous work to continuous talk activities; that social and technical interactions may play a role in synchronizing W-T patterns, since developers with stronger social or technical links in a community have more similar W-T patterns; and that although successful task-communities may have relatively different cultures, developers with balanced work-talk patterns seems to play critical roles in sustaining them, and, at least in the ones we studied, each has at least one such developer. These findings suggest that online individuals may synchronize their behaviors with others to better fit in the task communities and to improve coordinating efficiencies. We acknowledge that the talk activities we discussed here are meaningfully related to work activities, and thus can be considered also as being work activities, in a more general sense. But commits and email communications are still different kinds of activities [28, 33, 49] and thus it's reasonable to use HMM to describe the switching patterns between them. Moreover, it is because talk and work are related that the functional W-T patterns are meaningful.

In the future, the methods proposed in this paper can be further expanded and applied to analyze the switching pattern of more varied kinds of activities in more diverse online communities, such as GitHub [50], Wikipedia [51], and StackExchange [52]. Like other empirical research, our work is based on a sample of work and talk activities of developers, although commits [49, 53–55] and email communications [32, 56] have been extensively studied in the area of software engineering and were referred as work and talk [28], respectively. In reality, developers may have other kinds of work activities, e.g. consulting StackOverflow, which are relatively difficult to be captured. There are also talk activities that we do not capture, e.g., the discussion on issue tracking systems. Collecting more complete data sets will definitely help to derive more comprehensive results. To address this, we collected issue tracking data from Jira and Bugzilla [35], and arguably experimented with including them as talk activities (both opening issue as initializing the discussion and comments). Our result did not change significantly, indicating the revealed phenomena are quite robust. We use lines of code, LoC, to measure the productivity of a developer since it has been used extensively [27,49, 53]. This, while appropriate, is not the only such measure. Alternative metrics include the number of issues fixed [57], the development time of tasks [58], and the number of bugs [59]. Using them may offer additional insight into the benefits of balanced W-T patterns.

ACKNOWLEDGMENTS

The authors would like to thank all the members in the DECAL Lab in the Department of Computer Science, University of California in Davis, for the valuable discussion about the ideas and technical details presented in this paper. QX acknowledges support from the National Natural Science Foundation of China (Grant Nos. 61572439, 61273212).

AUTHOR CONTRIBUTIONS

Conceived and designed the experiments: QX PD VF. Performed the experiments: QX. Analyzed the data: QX. Wrote the paper: QX PD VF.

REFERENCES

1. Koerin B. Violent crime: Prediction and control. Crime & Delinquency. 1978;24:49–58. doi: 10.1177/001112877802400105.
2. Eck J, Chainey S, Cameron J, Leitner M, Wilson R. Mapping Crime: Understanding Hot Spots. Washington: National Institute of Justice; 2005.
3. Kitamura R, Chen C, Pendyala RM, Narayaran R. Micro-simulation of daily activity-travelpatterns fortraveldemandforecasting. Transportation. 2000;27:25–51. doi: 10.1023/A:1005259324588.
4. González MC, Hidalgo CA, Barabási AL. Understanding individual human mobility patterns. Nature. 2008;453:779–782. doi: 10.1038/nature06958. pmid:18528393
5. Bhatnagar A, Misra S, Rao HR. On risk, convenience, and Internet shopping behavior. Communications of the ACM. 2000;43:98–105. doi: 10.1145/353360.353371.
6. Bodapati AV. Recommendation systems with purchase data. Journal of Marketing Research. 2008;45:77–93. doi: 10.1509/jmkr.45.1.77.
7. Eagle N, Macy M, Claxton R. Network diversity and economic development. Science. 2010;328:1029–1031. doi: 10.1126/science.1186605. pmid:20489022
8. Onnela JP, Saramäki J, Hyvönen J, Szabó G, Lazer D, Kaski K, et al. Structure and tie strengths in mobile communication networks. Proceedings of the Natlional Academy of Sciences USA. 2007;104:7332–7336. doi: 10.1073/pnas.0610245104.
9. Newman MEJ, Forrest S, Balthrop J. Email networks and the spread of computer viruses. Physical Review E. 2002;66:035101. doi: 10.1103/PhysRevE.66.035101.
10. Watson JD, Crick FHC. The structure of DNA. Cold Spring Harbor Symposia on Quantitative Biology. 1953;18:123–131. doi: 10.1101/SQB.1953.018.01.020. pmid:13168976
11. Abbott A. Sequence analysis: New methods for old ideas. Annual Review of Sociology. 1995;21:93–113. Available: http://www.jstor.org/stable/2083405 doi: 10.1146/annurev.so.21.080195.000521.
12. Brzinsky-Fay C, Kohler U. Sequence analysis with Stata. The Stata Journal. 2006;6:435–460. Available: http://www.stata-journal.com/article.html?article=st0111
13. Aisenbrey S, Fasang AE. New life for old ideas: The "second wave" of sequence analysis bringing the "course" back into the life course. Sociological Methods & Research. 2010;38:420462. doi: 10.1177/0049124109357532

14. Abbott A, Hrycak A. Measuring resemblance in sequence data: An optimal matching analysis of musicians' careers. American Journal of Sociology. 1990;96:144–185. Available: http://www.jstor.org/stable/2780695 doi: 10.1086/229495.

15. Sharma KR. Bioinformatics: Sequence Alignment and Markov Models. New York: McGraw-Hill Professional; 2008.

16. Rosenberg MS. Sequence Alignment: Methods, Models, Concepts, and Strategies. Berkeley: University of California Press; 2009.

17. Eddy SR. Hidden Markov models. Current Opinion in Structural Biology. 1996;6:361–365. doi: 10.1016/S0959-440X(96)80056-X. pmid:8804822

18. Etzioni A. The Active Society. New York: Free Press; 1968.

19. Hurley RF. Group culture and its effect on innovative productivity. Journal of Engineering and Technology Management. 1995;12(1):57–75. doi: 10.1016/0923-4748(95)00004-6.

20. Astrachan JH. Family firm and community culture. Family Business Review. 1988;1(2):165–189. doi: 10.1111/j.1741-6248.1988.00165.x.

21. Chen AY, Sawyers RB, Williams PF. Reinforcing ethical decision making through corporate culture. Journal of Business Ethics. 1997;16(8):855–865. doi: 10.1023/A:1017953517947.

22. Wuchty S, Jones BF, Uzzi B. The increasing dominance of teams in production of knowledge. Science. 2007;316(5827):1036–1039. doi: 10.1126/sciencc.1136099. pmid:17431139

23. Guimerà R, Uzzi B, Spiro J, Amaral LAN. Team assembly mechanisms determine collaboration network structure and team performance. Science. 2005;308(5722):697–702. doi: 10.1126/science.1106340. pmid:15860629

24. Xuan Q, Fang H, Fu C, Filkov V. Temporal motifs reveal collaboration patterns in online task-oriented networks. Physical Review E. 2015;91(5):052813. doi: 10.1103/PhysRevE.91.052813.

25. Dempsey BJ, Weiss D, Jones P, Greenberg J. Who is an open source software developer? Communications of the ACM. 2002;45(2):67–72. doi: 10.1145/503124.503125.

26. Mockus A, Fielding RT, Herbsleb JD. Two case studies of open source software development: Apache and Mozilla. ACM Transactions on Software Engineering and Methodology. 2002;11(3):309–346. doi: 10.1145/567793.567795.

27. Weber S. The Success of Open Source. Cambridge, MA: Cambridge University Press; 2004. doi: 10.1145/567793.567795

28. Pattison DS, Bird CA, Devanbu PT. Talk and work: A preliminary report. In: Proceedings of the 2008 International Working Conference on Mining Software Repositories. New York; 2008. p. 113–116.

29. Buldyrev SV, Parshani R, Paul G, Stanley HE, Havlin S. Catastrophic cascade of failures in interdependent networks. Nature. 2010;464(7291):1025–1028. doi: 10.1038/nature08932. pmid:20393559

30. Brummitt CD, D'Souza RM, Leicht E. Suppressing cascades of load in interdependent networks. Proceedings of the National Academy of Sciences. 2012;109(12):E680–E689. doi: 10.1073/pnas.1110586109.

31. Xuan Q, Du F, Yu L, Chen G. Reaction-diffusion processes and metapopulation models on duplex networks. Physical Review E. 2013;87(3):032809. doi: 10.1103/PhysRevE.87.032809.

32. Bird C, Gourley A, Devanbu P, Gertz M, Swaminathan A. Mining email social networks. In: Proceedings of the 3th International Workshop on Mining Software Repositories. Shanghai, China: ACM; 2006. p. 137–143.

33. Xuan Q, Gharehyazie M, Devanbu PT, Filkov V. Measuring the effect of social communications on individual working rhythms: A case study of open source software. In: Proceedings of the 2012 International Conference on Social Informatics. Washington D.C.: IEEE; 2012. p. 78–85.

34. Bird C, Gourley A, Devanbu P, Swaminathan A, Hsu G. Open borders? Immigration in open source projects. In: Proceedings of the 4th International Workshop on Mining Software Repositories. IEEE; 2007. p. 6–6.

35. Gharehyazie M, Posnett D, Filkov V. Social activities rival patch submission for prediction of developer initiation in OSS projects. In: Proceedings of the 29th IEEE International Conference on Software Maintenance. IEEE; 2013. p. 340–349.

36. Team RC. R: A language and environment for statistical computing. R Foundation for Statistical Computing, Vienna, Austria. 2013. ISBN 3-900051-07-0; 2014.

37. Kashtan N, Alon U. Spontaneous evolution of modularity and network motifs. Proceedings of the National Academy of Sciences. 2005;102(39):13773–13778. doi: 10.1073/pnas.0503610102.

38. Elandt-Johnson RC, Johnson NL. Survival Models and Data Analysis. Wiley New York; 1980.

39. Cox DR. Regression models and life tables. JR stat soc B. 1972;34(2):187–220. Available: http://www.jstor.org/stable/2985181

40. Jain AK, Murty MN, Flynn PJ. Data clustering: A review. ACM Computing Surveys (CSUR). 1999;31(3):264–323. doi: 10.1145/331499.331504.

41. Cothrel JP. Measuring the success of an online community. Strategy & Leadership. 2000;28(2):17–21. doi: 10.1108/10878570010341609.

42. Preece J, Nonnecke B, Andrews D. The top five reasons for lurking: Improving community experiences for everyone. Computers in Human Behavior. 2004;20(2):201–223. doi: 10.1016/j.chb.2003.10.015.

43. Ridings CM, Gefen D. Virtual community attraction: Why people hang out online. Journal of Computer-Mediated Communication. 2004;10(1):00–00. doi: 10.1111/j.1083-6101.2004.tb00229.x.

44. Von Krogh G, Spaeth S, Lakhani KR. Community, joining, and specialization in open source software innovation: a case study. Research Policy. 2003;32(7):1217–1241. doi: 10.1016/S0048-7333(03)00050-7.

45. Adamczyk PD, Bailey BP. If not now, when?: The effects of interruption at different moments within task execution. In: Proceedings of the SIGCHI Conference on Human Factors in Computing Systems. Vienna, Austria: ACM; 2004. p. 271–278.

46. Basoglu KA, Fuller MA, Sweeney JT. Investigating the effects of computer mediated interruptions: An analysis of task characteristics and interruption frequency on financial performance. International Journal of Accounting Information Systems. 2009;10(4):177–189. doi: 10.1016/j.accinf.2009.10.003.

47. LaToza TD, Venolia G, DeLine R. Maintaining mental models: A study of developer work habits. In: Proceedings of the 28th International Conference on Software Engineering. Shanghai, China: ACM; 2006. p. 492–501. doi: 10.1016/j.accinf.2009.10.003

48. Cataldo M, Herbsleb JD. Coordination breakdowns and their impact on development productivity and software failures. IEEE Transactions on Software Engineering. 2013;39(3):343–360. doi: 10.1109/TSE.2012.32.

49. Xuan Q, Filkov V. Building it together: Synchronous development in OSS. In: Proceedings of the 36th International Conference on Software Engineering. Hyderabad, India: ACM; 2014. p. 222–233.

50. Dabbish L, Stuart C, Tsay J, Herbsleb J. Social coding in GitHub: transparency and collaboration in an open software repository. In: Proceedings of the ACM 2012 Conference on Computer Supported Cooperative Work. Seattle, WA: ACM; 2012. p. 1277–1286.

51. Giles J. Internet encyclopaedias go head to head. Nature. 2005;438(7070):900–901. doi: 10.1038/438900a. pmid:16355180

52. Vasilescu B, Filkov V, Serebrenik A. StackOverflow and GitHub: Associations between software development and crowdsourced knowledge. In: Proceedings of the 2013 International Conference on Social Computing. Alexandria, VA: IEEE; 2013. p. 188–195.

53. Xuan Q, Okano A, Devanbu PT, Filkov V. Focus-shifting patterns of OSS developers and their congruence with call graphs. In: Proceedings of the 22nd ACM SIGSOFT International Symposium on the Foundations of Software Engineering. Hong Kong, China: ACM; 2014.

54. Cataldo M, Mockus A, Roberts JA, James D Herbsleb Herbsleb JD. Software dependencies, work dependencies, and their impact on failures. IEEE Transactions on Software Engineering. 2009;35(6):864–878. doi: 10.1109/TSE.2009.42.

55. Bird C, Nagappan N, Gall H, Murphy B, Devanbu P. Putting it all together: Using socio-technical networks to predict failures. In: Proceedings of the 20th International Symposium on Software Reliability Engineering. Mysuru, Karnataka: IEEE; 2009. p. 109–119.

56. Wagstrom P, Herbsleb J, Carley K. A social network approach to free/open source software simulation. In: Proceedings of the 1st International Conference on Open Source Systems; 2005. p. 16–23. Available:http://alliance.casos.cs.cmu.edu/publications/papers/2005ASocialNetworkApproach.pdf

57. Zhou M, Mockus A. What make long term contributors: Willingness and opportunity in oss community. In: Proceedings of the 34th International Conference on Software Engineering. IEEE; 2012. p. 518–528.

58. Herbsleb JD, Roberts JA. Collaboration in software engineering projects: A theory of coordination. In: Proceedings of the 2006 International Conference on Information Systems. Milwaukee, Wisconsin; 2006. p. 38. Available:http://aisel.aisnet.org/icis2006/38

59. Aberdour M. Achieving quality in open-source software. IEEE Software. 2007;24(1):58–64. doi: 10.1109/MS.2007.2.

CHAPTER 4

ALGORITHMIC OPTIMISATION METHOD FOR IMPROVING USE CASE POINTS ESTIMATION

Radek Silhavy, Petr Silhavy, Zdenka Prokopova

Faculty of Applied Informatics, Tomas Bata University in Zlin, Zlin, Czech Republic

ABSTRACT

This paper presents a new size estimation method that can be used to estimate size level for software engineering projects. The Algorithmic Optimisation Method is based on Use Case Points and on Multiple Least Square Regression. The method is derived into three phases. The first phase deals with calculation Use Case Points and correction coefficients values. Correction coefficients are obtained by using Multiple Least Square Regression. New project is estimated in the second and third phase. In the second phase Use Case Points parameters for new estimation are set up and in the third phase project estimation is performed. Final estimation is obtained by using newly developed estimation equation, which used two correction coefficients. The Algorithmic Optimisation Method performs approximately 43% better than the Use Case Points method, based on their magnitude of relative error score. All results were evaluated by standard approach: visual inspection, goodness of fit measure and statistical significance.

INTRODUCTION

Software development effort estimation plays an important role in the software engineering field. There are several approaches under investigation. The first is method-based Functional Points Analysis (FPA), which has an official technical standard [1] in ISO standardization. This method depends on the ability and experiences of an analyst, who is responsible for evaluating parameters. The system is descripted as set of functions, but the analyst must understand the system in great detail. A tendency of personal influence on the estimation can be described in the case of each individual analysis. Functional analysis considers a system as a black box. It is not important to describe the platform, the development method or any hardware used. The results of the calculation estimate only the effort of each individual system function or ability. The personal opinion of the analyst, which influences the estimation, makes this method unsuitable for comparing productivity in system or software development. However, if the same analyst prepares the calculation, the quality of the original estimation can be measured. If the results of the analysis in each development phase are compared and the error curve is flat, then the estimation is calculated accurately. This method is based on interactions between computer systems.

FPA considers external inputs or outputs. The boundary is the border between two systems from the user perspective.

Citation: Silhavy R, Silhavy P, Prokopova Z (2015) Algorithmic Optimisation Method for Improving Use Case Points Estimation. PLoS ONE 10(11): e0141887. doi:10.1371/journal.pone.0141887.

External inputs are processes that send data into the boundary. This input can be the control input or data input. The data may be used to maintain one or more internal logical files and can be either control information or business information. External outputs consider data from one or more internal logical files (ILFs) and external interface files. The input process does not update the ILFs, and the output side does not contain derived data.

An estimation technique for early stage estimation is called Use Case Points (UCP) method, which was developed by Gustav Karner [2]. His perspective addresses object-oriented design and is thus widely used. The method is based on use case models, which are commonly used as functional descriptions of proposed systems or software. A number of use case steps were initially involved in the estimation process. There have been several modifications of the original principles, such as use case size points [3], extended use case points [4], use case points modified [5], adapted use case points [6], and transaction or path analysis [7].

Karner's basic method is based on assigning weights to clustered actors and use cases. Karner's UCP method identifies three clusters–simple, average and complex. The sum of weighted actors creates a value called unadjusted actor weights (UAW), and in the same sense, the unadjusted use case weights (UUCW) value is calculated. Two coefficients, technical factors and environmental factors, are used to describe the project, related information and development team experience. Summing UAW and UUCW and then multiplying this value by the technical and environmental factor coefficients obtain the number of UCP. Finally, Karner [2] works with the productivity factor, i.e., the number of man-hours per point. This factor is one of the greatest issues with the methodology, as this final operation can change the estimate considerably.

Use case size points is investigated in [3]. The authors emphasize the internal structure of the use case scenario in their method. The primary actors take roles and classifications based on the adjustment factor. Fuzzy sets are used for the estimation.

Several authors have presented improvements to Karner's method based on identifying transactions instead of steps in use cases. In [7], the number of stimuli is equal to the number of transactions. A stimulus is an activity of an actor in a use case. The authors of [1] and [7] improve transactions by calculating paths. The final complexity of the transaction is based on the number of binary or multiple conditions used in the scenarios.

The second modification described here is prepared by Wang [4] and is called extended UCP. This approach employs fuzzy sets and a Bayesian belief network, which is used to set unadjusted UCP. The result of this approach is a probabilistic effort estimation model.

Diev [5] notes that if the actors and use cases are precisely defined, then unadjusted UCP can be multiplied by technical factors. Technical factors are used to establish a coefficient of base system complexity. According to [5], the effort of further activities must be added. These further activities are supportive tasks, such as configuration management or testing.

The next interpretation is called adapted UCP [6]. UCP are adapted to incremental development for large-scale projects. In the first increment, all actors are classified as average and all use cases as complex. The authors also propose the decomposition of use cases to smaller ones, which are classified into the typical three categories.

Use case-based methods of estimation have certain well-known issues [8]. Use cases are written in natural language, and there is no rigorous approach to allow for a comparison of the use case quality or fragmentation. Therefore, the number of steps may vary, which affects the estimation accuracy. In a single individual use case, there can be more than one scenario, which can influence the accuracy of the estimation. Thus, the use case model is critical for system functional or behavioral modelling, but for the purpose of estimation, use cases can be used only if the estimation approach can be adjusted or calibrated for individual work conditions and writing style. Here, we propose an algorithm of calibrating the model by setting the productivity factor according to historical data.

METHODS

UCP Method Description

In the UCP method [1, 2, 4, 9], actors and use cases are classified as simple, average or complex [2]. A simple actor typically represents an application programming interface (API) or, more generally, a non-physical system user. A system interconnected by network protocol is classified as average, and finally, physical users interacting with the system through a graphical user interface are complex actors. These factors are summarized in Table 1.

Table 1. Actor Classification and Actor Weighting Factor

Actor Classification (AC)	Weighting Factor (WFa)
Simple	1
Average	2
Complex	3

doi:10.1371/journal.pone.0141887.t001

The total unadjusted actor weights (TUAW) are calculated according to the following formula:

$$TUAW = \sum AC \times WFa \quad (1)$$

Use cases are classified in a similar manner (see Table 2). The complexity of use cases is based on the number of steps, also called a transaction. However, a transaction typically refers to a path of activity, not a simple step in a structured scenario. Therefore, the term "step" is used here. The step counting process is not clear from the inline view. The original method counts steps in a primary scenario and in alternative scenarios. If the use case is extended (or included) by another use case, these steps are not counted: these use cases are counted as separate scenarios.

Table 2. Use Case Classification and Weighting Factor

Use Case Classification (UCC)	Number of Steps	Weighting Factor (WFb)
Simple	(0,4)	5
Average	<4,7>	10
Complex	(7, ∞)	15

doi:10.1371/journal.pone.0141887.t002

The unadjusted use case weights (UUCW) are calculated according to the following formula:

$$UUCW = \sum UCC \times WFb \tag{2}$$

Technical factors (first correction value) are then applied to the unadjusted UCP (UUCP). The technical complexity is already known in the FPA method. The second correction value is based on environmental factors. This factor describes non-functional requirements. Table 3presents the technical factors, and Table 4 presents the environmental factors, as they are known in UCP.

Table 3. Technical Factors

Factor ID	Description	Weight (WFc)	Significance (Sla)
T1	Distributed System	2	<0,5>
T2	Response adjectives	2	<0,5>
T3	End-User Efficiency	1	<0,5>
T4	Complex Processing	1	<0,5>
T5	Reusable Code	1	<0,5>
T6	Easy to Install	0.5	<0,5>
T7	Ease to Use	0.5	<0,5>
T8	Portable	2	<0,5>
T9	Easy to Change	1	<0,5>
T10	Concurrent	1	<0,5>
T11	Security Feature	1	<0,5>
T12	Access for Third Parties	1	<0,5>
T13	Special Training Required	1	<0,5>

doi:10.1371/journal.pone.0141887.t003

Table 4. Environmental Factors

Factor ID	Description	Weight (WFd)	Significance (Slb)
E1	Familiar with RUP	1.5	<0,5>
E2	Application Experience	0.5	<0,5>
E3	Object-oriented Experience	1	<0,5>
E4	Lead Analyst Capability	0.5	<0,5>
E5	Motivation	1	<0,5>
E6	Stable Requirements	2	<0,5>
E7	Part-Time Workers	-1	<0,5>
E8	Difficult Programming Language	2	<0,5>

doi:10.1371/journal.pone.0141887.t004

Factors T1-T13 and E1-E8 have fixed weights. Moreover, for each factor, the significance can be set in the interval from 0 to 5, where 0 indicates no impact, 3 indicates an average impact, and 5 indicates a strong impact. The technical complexity factor (TCF), that is, the first correction coefficient, can be calculated according to the following formula [7]:

$$TCF = 0.6 + (0.01 \times \sum_{T13}^{T1} WFc \times SIa) \tag{3}$$

The second correction coefficient is called the environmental complexity factor (ECF). The formula for calculation is similar to the above:

$$ECF = 1.4 + (-0.03 \times \sum_{E8}^{E1} WFd \times SIb) \tag{4}$$

The final result of the estimation is called adjusted UCP (AUCP) and represents the project (system or software) size in points. The unadjusted value of points from actors and points from use cases are summarized, and then, the TCF and ECF are applied. The following formula is used [1, 2, 4, 9]:

$$UCP = (TUAW + UUCW) \times TCF \times ECF \tag{5}$$

The UCP value represents a system size, but a man-hour value is used to measure the work effort. Therefore, UCP is typically multiplied by 20 (according to [2]) or, more generally, by 15–30 man-hours per point. This value is a productivity factor of the development team.

Transactions in a use case scenario have been investigated as a method of tuning the traditional UCP concepts. Robiolo et al. and Ochodek et al. [7, 10] introduce transaction-based methods. According to [7], a transaction is a part of a use case scenario that represents a stimulus. As an example, a scenario can be reduced to a set of pairs. If transactions are used, then the UUCW is different from that in an example with steps. Each use case scenario typically has more steps than transactions.

Algorithmic Optimisation Method Design

The proposed Algorithmic Optimisation Method (AOM) design is motivated by investigating the possibility of solving issues with the standard estimation process, which are described in the UCP method description section. Therefore, we have applied an optimization method based on increasing the correction coefficients accuracy by multiple least squares regression [11].

Furthermore, we simplify the estimation process itself and make it less sensitive to personal ability and experiences.

New approach indeed brings straightforward approach, which is based on historical data. This principal idea allows minimalizing an error as integral part of estimation process.

The AOM is based on a widely used version of the UCP method, which was previously described in the text.

AOM brings tree-phases design, as can be seen in Fig 1. The Preparation Phase (Phase I) is used for calculation of the (a_1, a_2) correction coefficients. Least Squares Regression (LSR), or, more precisely, multiple linear regression is used for obtaining these coefficients (a_1, a_2). Following formula is applying for calculation:

$$\begin{pmatrix} y_1 \\ \vdots \\ y_n \end{pmatrix} = \begin{pmatrix} x_{11} & x_{12} \\ \vdots & \vdots \\ x_{n1} & x_{n2} \end{pmatrix} \times \begin{pmatrix} a_1 \\ a_2 \end{pmatrix} \Rightarrow \begin{pmatrix} a_1 \\ a_2 \end{pmatrix} = (X^T \times X)^{-1} \times (X^T \times Y) \tag{6}$$

Where x_{i1} and x_{i2}, $i = 1\ldots n$, are as follows:

$$x_{i1} = (TUAW_i \times TCF_i \times ECF_i) \tag{7}$$

$$x_{i2} = (UUCW_i \times TCF_i \times ECF_i) \tag{8}$$

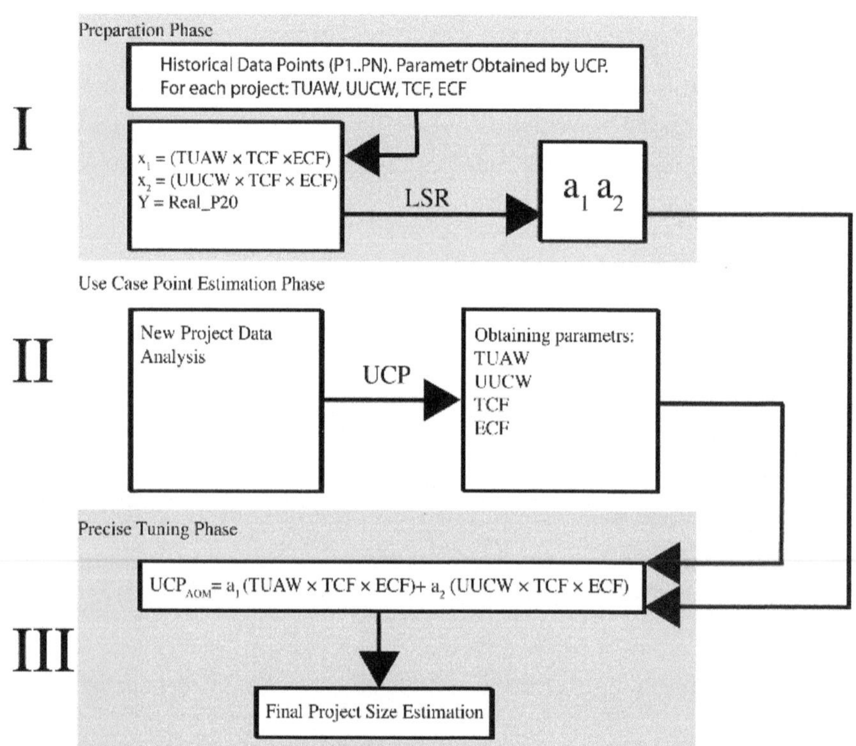

Figure 1. Algorithmic Optimisation Method Schema.

And y_i represents real size (Real_P20 values), which is real size of software projects form historical dataset (see Table 5). Therefore values of a_1, a_2 can be different for each individual dataset or generally for each project pool and developers. The values a_1, a_2 are not generally valid and their numerical values cannot be applied to other dataset or project. This method can be used only, if the historical data points exist. It is inevitable for correction functioning of AOM to perform Preparation Phase again, when historical dataset expands. New data points can be added to historical dataset only, if there is new finished project and its real size is known.

Table 5. Raw Project Data [9, 12]

Project No.	TUAW	UUCW	TCF	ECF	Est_P	Real_P20
1	12	375	0,92	0,78	277,7112	151,85
2	10	85	0,75	0,81	57,7125	95,85
3	6	115	0,9	1,05	114,345	58,65
4	9	205	0,85	0,89	161,891	37,1
5	12	160	0,82	0,79	111,4216	30,7
6	9	115	0,85	0,88	92,752	24,6
7	6	85	0,78	0,51	36,1998	13,85
8	14	515	0,94	1,02	507,2052	179,65
9	12	185	1,03	0,8	162,328	84,05
10	12	290	0,71	0,73	156,5266	67,2
11	9	150	1,05	0,95	158,6025	61
12	12	135	0,78	0,79	90,5814	36
13	4	60	0,96	0,96	58,9824	25,7
14	15	160	0,9	0,91	143,325	19,85
15	15	355	1,125	0,77	320,5125	184,2
16	18	145	1,08	0,77	135,5508	99
17	12	325	1,095	0,95	350,56425	197,5
18	6	90	1,02	1,085	106,2432	96,25
19	9	125	1,025	0,98	134,603	108,75
20	9	120	1,118	0,995	143,50089	111,3
21	12	200	1	0,92	195,04	132
22	9	175	0,95	0,92	160,816	128,4
23	12	245	0,89	1,19	272,1887	152,1
24	6	140	0,965	0,755	106,37195	84,8
25	7	180	0,81	0,84	127,2348	183,5
26	7	155	0,9	0,94	137,052	143
27	5	210	0,72	0,67	103,716	137
28	6	340	0,8	0,74	204,832	168

doi:10.1371/journal.pone.0141887.t005

Secondly the basic UCP parameters are calculated. Eqs (1–4) are used for obtaining of TUAW, UUCW, TCF and ECF parameters.

Adopting the part of UCP estimation methodology supports consistency early processes of estimation. These parameters can be obtained from various CASE tools.

Thirdly, Precise Tuning Phase is performing. UCP_{AOM} value represents final estimated project size, which should be used for project planning and later on for effort estimation. UCP_{AOM} is obtained according Eq (9).

$$UCP_{AOM} = a_1(TUAW \times TCF \times ECF) + a_2(UUCW \times TCF \times ECF) \quad (9)$$

Experiment Planning

The experiment in our study deals with evaluating AOM principles, which may significantly improve prediction model based on Use Case Points.

In order to validate effectiveness of AOM an empirical validation was conducted. The first model, which was evaluated, is a Use Case Points (UCP). UCP was used as simple base model for setting basic performance level.

The second model, which may be called, advanced is AOM. Finally, the accuracy of prediction of two presented models was compared.

Let assume, that the prediction error of AOM will be significantly lower, that error of UCP method and optimal values of correction coefficients a_1, a_2, will be set.

Our task is not to offer generally valid coefficients. This paper will demonstrate that AOM is applicable to several projects pool.

In order to decide whether the model is more capable for prediction, a statistical hypothesis was tested:

H_0: UCP = AOM, There is no difference in the capability of prediction between UCP and AOM models. No difference in estimation errors.

Alternative hypothesis:

H_1: UCP≠AOM, there is difference in prediction capability between UCP and AOM models. There is a difference in estimation errors.

This paper compares the accuracy of the AOM model with that of the UCP model using t-test. The t-test is used as a test of the null hypothesis that the means of two normally distributed populations are equal. The t-test will be used for evaluation of MRE.

Adopted Metrics for Performance Evaluation

Magnitude of Relative Error (MRE), Mean Magnitude of Relative Error (MMRE) and Percentage of Prediction (PRED(0.25)) is accepted as standard evaluation in size prediction and effort estimation techniques. In this paper are used this methods for purpose of future cross comparison to other approaches.

We also adopted Total Sum of Squares (TSS), which as metric for evaluation of the prediction models and median of errors. Following equations are used for obtaining this performance metrics:

$$\text{MRE} = \frac{|PredictedSize - Real\_P20|}{Real\_P20} \quad \textbf{(10)}$$

$$\text{MMRE} = \frac{\sum_i^N MRE}{N} \quad \textbf{(11)}$$

$$\text{PRED}(0.25) = \frac{A}{N} \quad \textbf{(12)}$$

$$\text{TSS} = \sum_{i=1}^{n} (Real\_P20 - PredictedSize)^2 \quad \textbf{(13)}$$

PredictedSize value stands for values of predicted project size. This value is a value of UCP or AOM. A "N" in Eqs (11) and (12) stands for number of observed projects. Next metric is a PRED(0.25). An "A" in Eq (12) stands for number of projects, which have MRE<0.25.

Goal for results is to keep MMRE and TSS minimalized and PRED(0.25) maximized. For purpose of our evaluation the most important criterion is minimal value of TSS, because it means that LSR algorithm achieved optimal performance.

RESULTS AND DISCUSSION

In this paper the UCP method [2] and our proposed method, called the Algorithmic Optimization Method (AOM) were compared.

Table 5 summarizes the raw project data. The TUAW, UUCW, TCF and ECF are known from UCP. Est_P is an estimation (in points) according UCP method (see Eqs (1–5)) a Real_P20 is a value, which represents real project size, which were measured in points, when project were finished.

The results were evaluated against three datasets, which take role as simulated software project pools. Each testing dataset were constructed as random selection of 10 projects for Phase I (see Table 6) from raw project data (see Table 5). These datasets takes role as historical dataset. For the evaluation we have used rest of dataset. Our evaluation will at $\alpha = 0.05$ significance level.

Table 6. Preparation Phase Datasets Characteristics

Test Case	Historical Data Points	Real-P20 (Min)	Real-P20 (Max)	Mean	Standard Deviation
Test1	P23,P6,P4,P26,P18,P3,P8,P16,P17,P2	24,6	197,5	108,37	55,76
Test2	P20,P1,P8,P2,P3,P24,P12,P9,P27,P18	36	179,65	103,54	40,9
Test3	P19,P1,P24,P27,P20,P22,P2,P11,P9,P5	30,7	151,85	99,37	34,48

doi:10.1371/journal.pone.0141887.t006

Results of evaluation are based on rest of the dataset. It means that for evaluation were used:

Test1: P1, P5, P7, P9, P10, P11, P12, P13, P14, P15, P19, P20, P21, P22, P24, P25, P27, P28

Test2: P4, P5, P6, P7, P10, P11, P13, P14, P15, P16, P17, P19, P21, P22, P23, P25, P26, P28

Test3: P3, P4, P6, P7, P8, P10, P12, P13, P14, P15, P16, P17, P18, P21, P23, P25, P26, P28

Projects, which were used during a Preparation Phase, were omitted. The obtained results are presented in Table 7. Real_P20 were obtained from Table 5 and estimated size was calculated according Eq (9) for AOM or according Eq (5) for UCP.

Table 7. Comparison of the Estimation Methods Performance

	Test1	Test2	Test3
MMRE-UCP	1,17	1,39	0,69
MMRE-AOM	0,69	0,83	0,69
PRED(0.25)-UCP	0,17	0,17	0,17
PRED(0.25)-AOM	0,39	0,34	0,34
TSS-UCP	97229,35	129109,46	224825,52
TSS-AOM	52041,24	51708,79	50679,76

doi:10.1371/journal.pone.0141887.t007

Fig 2 shows the Magnitude of Relative Error of the AOM for the Test1-3 datasets and compares them to UCP performance on same datasets. Table 7 and Fig 2 illustrate that AOM produces significantly better estimates than UCP. The mean MRE is 0.74 in the case of AOM, which is more than 43% better then result obtained UCP method. According to PRED(0.25) AOM is more then twice better.

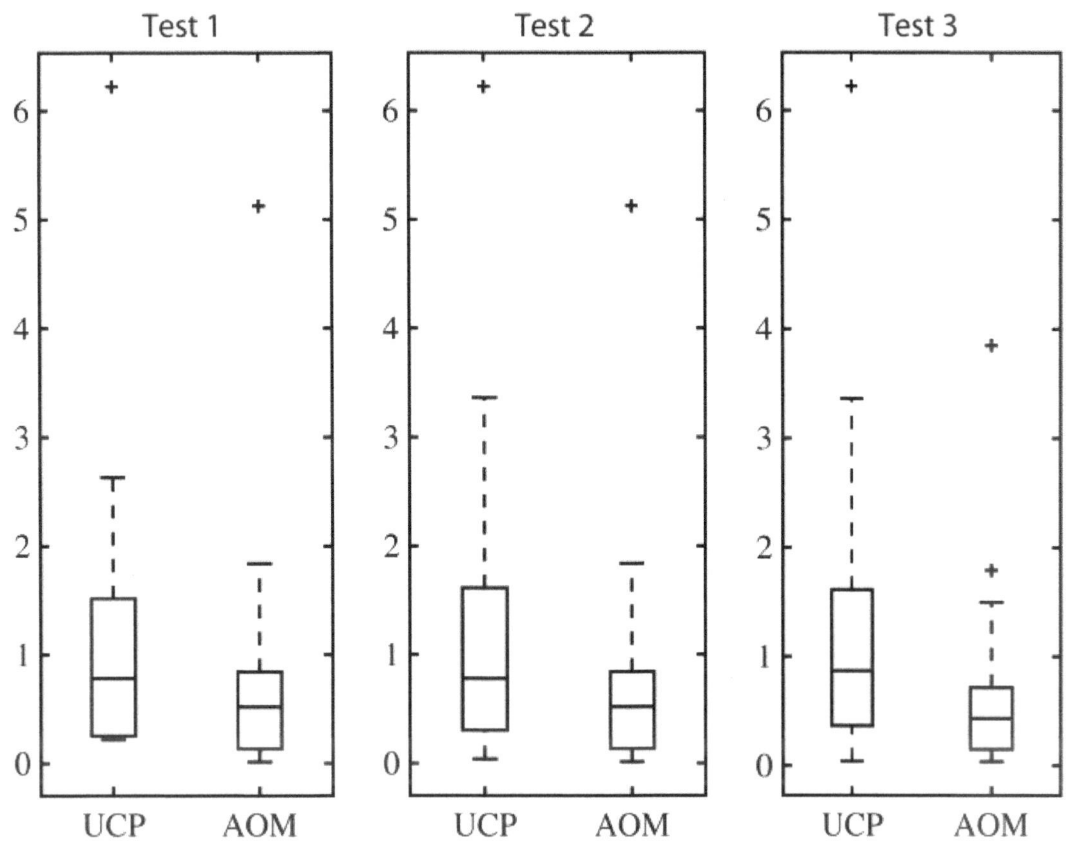

Figure 2. Box Plot on MRE Results obtained from testing datasets.

Fig 3 describes a low correlation between Error and AOM predicted Size. The AOM performs consistently better as can be seen from Fig 2 (MRE distribution) and from Fig 4, which shows a Total Sum of Squares.

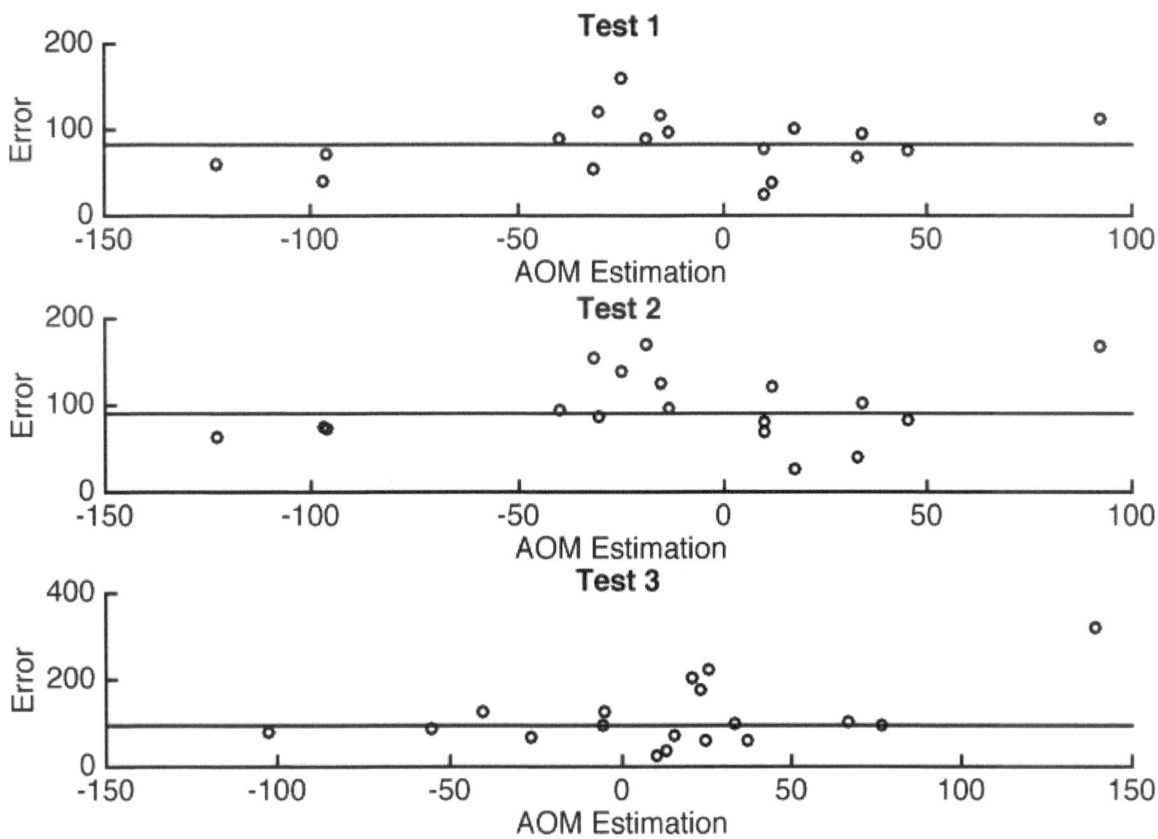

Figure 3. Error and AOM (PredictectSize) Correlation.

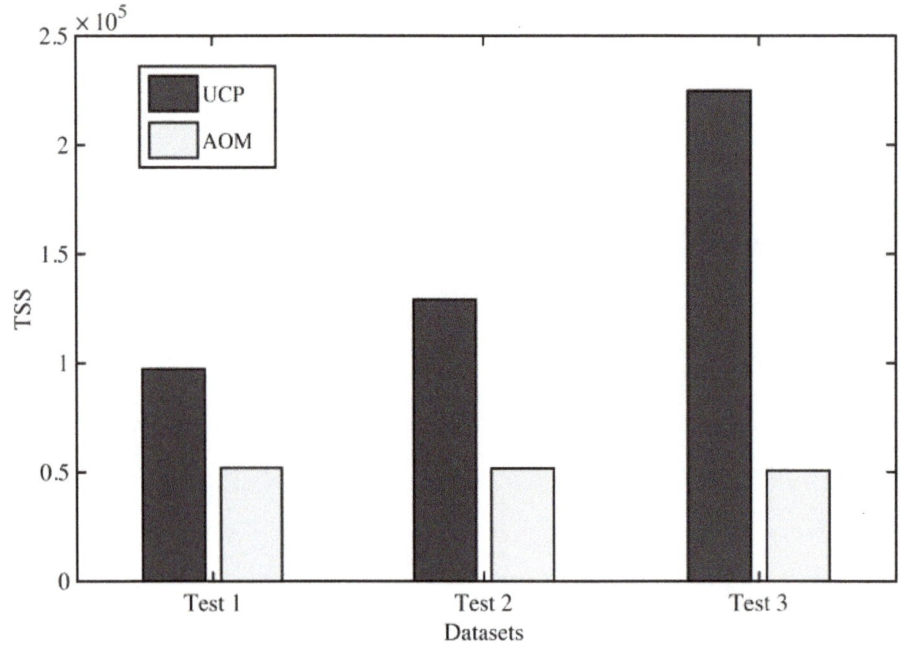

Figure 4. Total Sum of Squares.

Results Interpretation

Results, which are presented, in previous section show, that AOM model can produce significantly better estimations. AOM produce more reliable and more consistent results. The result of the t-test for MRE is given in Table 8. All datasets (Test1, Test 2 and Test3) were tested independently.

Table 8. Results of t-test for MRE

	Test 1	Test 2	Test 3
SD	0.5992	0.6373	0.6685
Degree of freedom	17	17	17
t value	-3.3393	-3.7059	-4.3011
p value	0.0039	0.0018	0,00048385
h value	1	1	1

doi:10.1371/journal.pone.0141887.t008

Results of t-test for MRE as a computational results (MRE, MMRE, PRED and TSS) show, that AOM performs significantly better. MRE was tested at significance level 0.05 and null hypothesis can be rejected. Performance of AOM and UCP is not equal.

Validity Treats

There is an issue connecting with size of dataset. Use Case points dataset is not broadly available and therefore all studies are perform on relatively small datasets. We have used 28 data points, which were divided into two parts randomly. Three (Test 1, Test 2 and Test 3) dataset were created.

Our data points represent small and medium projects and for this should be a limitation. Therefore further investigation based on broad project pool and for bigger projects will be needed. Whereas it becomes apparent, that project size and project size variance is important parameter for model construction.

The main aim of this paper was to show that AOM approach could lead to more precise and consistent prediction than UCP. UCP is used as valuable initial estimation, from which some parameters are used for AOM estimation.

Case Study

The following case study will illustrate real-life situation of using AOM. Case Study is descripted in phases according Fig 1.

Preparation Phase.

Lets assume that there are 10 projects in historical dataset. Table 9 illustrates historical project data.

Table 9. Case Study Historical Data Points

Project No.	TUAW	UUCW	TCF	ECF	Real_P20
P1	12	375	0,92	0,78	151,85
P2	10	85	0,75	0,81	95,85
P3	12	160	0,82	0,79	30,7
P4	9	115	0,85	0,88	24,6
P5	12	185	1,03	0,8	84,05
P6	9	125	1,025	0,98	108,75
P7	9	120	1,118	0,995	111,3
P8	9	175	0,95	0,92	128,4
P9	6	140	0,965	0,755	84,8
P10	5	210	0,72	0,67	137

doi:10.1371/journal.pone.0141887.t009

These data points are used for setting x_1 and x_2 as is declared in Eqs (7) and (8). Real_P20 represents know value of real project effort.

Next step is to obtain (a_1, a_2) values. These are calculated by using multiple linear regressions. Values are as follows: a_1 = 0.96737, a_2 = 0.64416.

Use Case Points Estimation Phase.

Values of TUAW, UUCW, TCF and ECF for the project, which is estimated, are obtained by UCP Eqs (1–4). Parameters values are: TUAW = 12, UUCW = 245, TCF = 0,89, ECF = 1,19.

Precise Tuning Phase.

Finally project size estimation can be obtained by using Eq (9). For our project Equation is UCP_{AOM} = 0,96737 × (12 × 0,89 × 1,19) + 0.64416 × (245 × 0,89 × 1,19). Therefore, new project estimation is 179 use case points.

CONCLUSIONS

In this article, we presented a new estimation approach based on a three-phase algorithm, called AOM. In the first phase, we applied a calculation based on UCP to obtain set of parameters (TUAW, UUCW, TCF, ECF) for each of historical project. Next we have obtain a correction values (a_1, a_2). These values were obtained via least squares regression. This approach employs historical project data to refine the estimation. By applying the least squares regression approach, the algorithm penalises errors in the estimation caused by human factors and company practice.

The AOM is significantly better than UCP estimation methods, with a mean MRE that is 43% better than that obtained with UCP.

Results of AOM are better and according Fig 4, results are significantly more consistent than those obtain by UCP.

The AOM represents an estimation workflow and describes approach how a size of software project could be estimated. AOM employs correction values (a_1, a_2), which are making a model less sensitive to introduction a personal errors.

As results clearly shows AOM produce consistent predictions. Ability of adaptation to individual project characteristics is improvement too.

A comparison drawn with regard to a number of descriptive characteristics has shown that datasets can influence the quality of the estimation. Therefore, in our future research, we will focus on dataset expansion and clustering projects into homogenized segments, which should improve the accuracy of the estimation.

AUTHOR CONTRIBUTIONS

Conceived and designed the experiments: RS PS ZP. Performed the experiments: RS PS ZP. Analyzed the data: RS. Contributed reagents/materials/analysis tools: RS PS ZP. Wrote the paper: RS.

REFERENCES

1. Robiolo G, Orosco R. Employing use cases to early estimate effort with simpler metrics. Innovations in
2. Karner G. Metrics for objectory', December 1993, Diploma, University of Linkoping, Sweden, No. LiTH-IDA-Ex-9344. 21.
3. Braz MR, Vergilio SR, editors. Software effort estimation based on use cases. Computer Software and Applications Conference, 2006 COMPSAC'06 30th Annual International; 2006: IEEE.
4. Wang F, Yang X, Zhu X, Chen L. Extended Use Case Points Method for Software Cost Estimation. 2009:1–5. doi: 10.1109/cise.2009.5364706.
5. Diev S. Use cases modeling and software estimation. ACM SIGSOFT Software Engineering Notes. 2006;31(6):1. doi: 10.1145/1218776.1218780.
6. Mohagheghi P, Anda B, Conradi R. Effort estimation of use cases for incremental large-scale software development. 2005:303–11. doi: 10.1109/icse.2005.1553573.
7. Robiolo G, Badano C, Orosco R. Transactions and paths: Two use case based metrics which improve the early effort estimation. 2009:422–5. doi: 10.1109/esem.2009.5316021.
8. Azevedo S, Machado RJ, Bragança A, Ribeiro H. On the refinement of use case models with variability support. Innovations in Systems and Software Engineering. 2011;8(1):51–64. doi: 10.1007/s11334-011-0177-9.

9. Ochodek M, Nawrocki J, Kwarciak K. Simplifying effort estimation based on Use Case Points. Information and Software Technology. 2011;53(3):200–13. doi: 10.1016/j.infsof.2010.10.005.

10. Ochodek M, Alchimowicz B, Jurkiewicz J, Nawrocki J. Improving the reliability of transaction identification in use cases. Information and Software Technology. 2011;53(8):885–97. doi: 10.1016/J.Infsof.2011.02.004 pmid:WOS:000292176300007.

11. Pindyck RS, Rubinfeld DL. Econometric models and economic forecasts: Irwin/McGraw-Hill Boston; 1998.

12. Subriadi A, Ningrum P. Critical review of the effort rate value in use case point method for estimating software development effort. Journal of Theroretical and Applied Information Technology. 2014;59(3):735–44.

CHAPTER 5 AN EFFICIENCY COMPARISON OF DOCUMENT PREPARATION SYSTEMS USED IN ACADEMIC RESEARCH AND DEVELOPMENT

Markus Knauff, Jelica Nejasmic

Department of Psychology, Experimental Psychology and Cognitive Science, University of Giessen, Giessen, Germany

ABSTRACT

The choice of an efficient document preparation system is an important decision for any academic researcher. To assist the research community, we report a software usability study in which 40 researchers across different disciplines prepared scholarly texts with either Microsoft Word or LaTeX. The probe texts included simple continuous text, text with tables and subheadings, and complex text with several mathematical equations. We show that LaTeX users were slower than Word users, wrote less text in the same amount of time, and produced more typesetting, orthographical, grammatical, and formatting errors. On most measures, expert LaTeX users performed even worse than novice Word users. LaTeX users, however, more often report enjoying using their respective software. We conclude that even experienced LaTeX users may suffer a loss in productivity when LaTeX is used, relative to other document preparation systems. Individuals, institutions, and journals should carefully consider the ramifications of this finding when choosing document preparation strategies, or requiring them of authors.

INTRODUCTION

The key communication of academic research and development is through diverse forms of publications. Most scholars spend many hours writing journal articles, books, or other forms of scholarly text. Virtually all researchers use one of two document preparation systems: Microsoft Word or LaTeX. Publishers often accept just one of the two text file formats [1]. Microsoft Word is based on a principle called "What you see is what you get" (WYSIWYG), which means that the user immediately sees the document on the screen as it will appear on the printed page. LaTeX, in contrast, embodies the principle of "What you get is what you mean" (WYGIWYM), which implies that the document is not directly displayed on the screen and changes, such as format settings, are not immediately visible. Microsoft Word requires little start-up time and provides easy and instantaneous control of textual input and output. Microsoft Word is the predominant document preparation system across many disciplines, including medicine, law, business, and the life sciences, and is also the dominant document preparation system for professional communications. LaTeX, in contrast, is a programming language that requires the use of an external editing interface to produce documents. LaTeX is frequently

Citation: Knauff M, Nejasmic J (2014) An Efficiency Comparison of Document Preparation Systems Used in Academic Research and Development. PLoS ONE 9(12): e115069. doi:10.1371/journal.pone.0115069.

used in mathematics, physics, computer science, and engineering because it provides the user unlimited flexibility and is particularly useful if the user needs to set complex mathematic equations in a professional layout. LaTeX is freely available as open-source software. In contrast, Microsoft Word is a commercial product licensed by the Microsoft Corporation.

In the "publish or perish" age of academic research, many senior researchers advise their students and junior researchers about how to create professional document layouts, which software system to use, and which system is more efficient or user-friendly. Many of these senior researchers will attempt to convince their students and junior researchers that one system is "better", "more elegant" "simpler", or "more flexible" than the other system. There are very few researchers, however, who can confirm empirically how one system is superior to the other and on what basis they have drawn this conclusion. To date, no empirical studies exist to identify which system is more efficient. The preference toward a particular document preparation system can be particularly obstructive to the progress of research if the research question requires interdisciplinary teams. For example, a brain computer interface project may require collaborations between medical scientists, psychologists, computer scientists, biologists, physicists, and engineers. Any researcher who has ever collaborated on such large interdisciplinary projects has experienced the difficulty with reaching a consensus about which document preparation system to use. Discussions about document preparation systems are often unproductive and driven by preconceived opinions, individual biases, and disciplinary traditions. A fair comparison of the efficiency and usability of the different document preparation systems based on empirical evidence rather than individual habits and biases may facilitate such discussions.

PARTICIPANTS, MATERIALS, AND METHODS

To assist the academic research community in the choice of an efficient document preparation system, we empirically compared the usability of LaTeX and Word under highly realistic working conditions. The volunteers for this study included 40 researchers and advanced graduate students from six German universities who wrote scholarly texts in either Microsoft Word or LaTeX (mean age 25.4 years; 14 female; Physics: 12; Psychology: 5; Computer Science: 4; Mathematics: 4; Electrical engineering: 3; MBA: 3; Sport Science: 4; others: 5). They were recruited from newsgroups, mailing lists, blogs, and other sources. Most participants were tested in their personal office setting, and all participants used their own computer, which ran either the Windows or Linux operating system. They were informed that the purpose of the study was to evaluate the quality of their document preparation system they use in their daily work.

All participants were properly instructed and have indicated that they consent to participate by signing the informed consent paperwork. The study has been conducted according to the principles expressed in the Declaration of Helsinki; the risks of the study were no higher than those experienced by people using their respective software (Word or LaTeX) on a day-to-day basis, participants could withdraw from the task at any time, and no identifiable data will be released about participants. For such studies the ethical guidelines of the Deutsche Gesellschaft für Psychologie (German Psychological Society, DGPs) and the Bund Deutscher Psychologen (German Psychological Association, BDP) revised on June 28, 2004 specify that approval from an Ethics Committee can be waived "if it can reasonably be assumed that participation in the research produces no damage or no discomfort that go beyond everyday experience, and if the research (a) refers to common education methods, curricula or teaching methods in education; ... or (c) refers to factors that affect work and organizational efficiency in organizations whose investigation can have no occupational disadvantages for individuals and for which confidentiality is guaranteed (p. 2, paragraph 6)". The present research belongs to this class of studies; thus, no further approval from an ethics committee was required.

The participants were divided into 4 groups with 10 participants in each group: Word novices, Word experts, LaTeX novices, and LaTeX experts. Participants were classified as "novices" if they had less than 500 hours of experience with the respective program and "experts" if they had more than 1000 hours of experience with the respective program. In the resulting groups, participants who were classified as "novices" had on average 234 hours (SD = 153) experience with the respective program, whereas "experts" had on average 1909 hours experience with the respective program (SD = 211).

The probe texts included three different text structures: (1) simple continuous text; (2) text with tables; and (3) mathematical text with several equations. The texts were selected based on a pilot study so that an expert could reproduce around 90% of the text in thirty minutes. All texts came from the Journal "Kognitionswissenschaft" which was the official Journal of the German Cognitive Science Society until the year 2002. The selected texts are presented in Fig. 1. Thecontinuous text consisted of a headline and headings with different font sizes, four paragraphs, and two footnotes (Fig. 1). The table text consisted of a headline, two paragraphs, and a table that was divided into several segments and surrounded by text (Fig. 2). The equation text_consisted of a headline, four paragraphs, and six equations (Fig. 3). Participants were allowed to use all tools, editors, plug-ins, and add-ons that they were accustomed to using with their respective software. For example, many LaTeX users produce documents with external text editors such as TeXnicCenter, LaTeX Editor, Kile, or WinEdit because LaTeX does not offer an internal text editor. All participants already had some experience with formatting tables and equations and were tested in the presence of the experimenter. The three text types were presented in a random order to each participant. The participants were instructed to reproduce the source text within thirty minutes. Each participant was given five minutes to familiarize themselves with the text. The performance of each participant was measured for each text sample by three variables: (1) the number of orthographic and grammatical mistakes; (2) the number of formatting errors and typos; and (3) the amount of written text (in symbols and words) produced within 30 minutes. Table 1 provides an overview of all possible errors in the three probe texts. To measure the user's opinions and satisfaction with their software system, each participant also completed an international standard questionnaire (ISO 9241–10) about usability engineering. To motivate the participants, the best three performers from each group received a monetary prize of 150, 100, or 50 euros, respectively. In the following section, we report the performance of the four groups of participants for the three types of probe text. Then, we report the results of the ISO 9241–10 questionnaire, which examines how well each document preparation system fulfilled the general ergonomic principles that apply to the design of dialogues between humans and information systems. In the final part of the article, we present some psychological explanations for the reported results and discuss some implications for academic research and development.

Kognitionswissenschaft (1998) 7: 95–100

Einleitung zum Themenheft „Ressourcenadaptive kognitive Prozesse“

Anthony Jameson, Kai Buchholz*

Sonderforschungsbereich 378, FB 14 Informatik und FR 5.1 Philosophie, Universität des Saarlandes, Postfach 151150, D-66041 Saarbrücken

In der Kognitionswissenschaft tritt der Begriff einer *beschränkten Ressource* in vielen Zusammenhängen auf. Insbesondere wird der Term *Ressource* auf sehr unterschiedliche Entitäten angewandt, unter anderem auf Zeit, (menschliches und maschinelles) Gedächtnis, Wissen und Information. Durch die breite Anwendung dieses Begriffs lassen sich einige weitere gemeinsame Begriffe – sowie damit zusammenhängende Fragestellungen – erkennen. Aus diesen Gemeinsamkeiten ergeben sich Möglichkeiten für eine fruchtbare interdisziplinäre Zusammenarbeit.

Anfang 1996 nahm in Saarbrücken der von der Deutschen Forschungsgemeinschaft unterstützte Sonderforschungsbereich „Ressourcenadaptive kognitive Prozesse“ seine Arbeit auf. Dieses Forschungsprogramm umfaßt 11 Projekte, deren Leiter in den Disziplinen Computerlinguistik, Informatik, Philosophie und Psychologie tätig sind; mehrere der Projekte werden von Vertretern verschiedener Disziplinen gemeinsam geleitet.

Das vorliegende Themenheft soll den Lesern eine repräsentative Stichprobe der Forschung in diesem SFB bieten. Während die Autoren und der Gastherausgeber aus dem SFB 378 stammen, wurden alle Gutachten (mindestens zwei für jede Einreichung) von Fachkollegen außerhalb Saarbrückens erstellt. Mit ihren fachkundigen und ausführlichen Kritiken haben die Gutachter das Themenheft entscheidend mitgestaltet. Aufgrund der Gutachten traf der Herausgeber der Zeitschrift *Kognitionswissenschaft*, Prof. Dr. Gerhard Weber, die Entscheidungen in bezug auf Annahme und Ablehnung von Manuskripten.

In dieser Einleitung wird zuerst der weitgefaßte Begriff einer *Ressource*, der im SFB 378 verwendet wird, kurz motiviert und skizziert. Dann werden die einzelnen Artikel im Themenheft in diesen Rahmen eingeordnet. Insbesondere wird am Schluß erörtert, welche Formen von *Ressourcenadaptivität* in den Projekten des SFB unterschieden werden.[1]

* Der erste Autor ist Gastherausgeber dieses Themenhefts. Der Beitrag des zweiten Autors zu dieser Einleitung wurde von der Deutschen Forschungsgemeinschaft im Rahmen des SFB 378 gefördert.

[1] Eine ausführlichere Besprechung und Einordnung der Artikel dieses Themenhefts ist über die WWW-Seite des SFB 378 verfügbar: `http://www.coli.uni-sb.de/sfb378/`.

Figure 1. The *continuous text* used in the present study. From: Jameson, A. & Buchholz, K. (1998). Einleitung zum Themenheft “Ressourcenadaptive kognitive Prozesse”, *Kognitionswissenschaft*, 7, 95.

B. Müller: Kompositionsbildung und Bediensequenzen

Die Anpassungsgüte für die Bedingung ohne zeitliche Differenzierung in beiden Experimentalphasen ist nach wie vor nicht akzeptabel. Um hier eine weitere Möglichkeit zu untersuchen, wurde die Entscheidungsfunktion so verändert, daß die Differenzwerte mit dem Faktor 2 verstärkt wurden. Dies führt zu einem deutlicheren Unterschied von Urteilswahrscheinlichkeiten im Bereich geringer Differenzen. Der Abszissenabschnitt des Indifferenzpunktes wurde auf die Hälfte reduziert, damit unter diesen veränderten Bedingungen die Urteilswahrscheinlichkeit bei einer Nulldifferenz nach wie vor die durchschnittliche empirische Urteilswahrscheinlichkeit reflektiert.

In Tabelle 6 sind für diese Simulation, die der Bedingung mit permanenter Verfügbarkeit in beiden Phasen entspricht, die Ablehnungsquoten, Parameterwerte sowie die Anpassungsgüte angegeben. Es zeigt sich, daß selbst bei dieser erhöhten Diskriminationsfähigkeit lediglich bei valider Kompositionsbildung Urteilshäufigkeiten simuliert werden können, die von den empirisch ermittelten nicht signifikant abweichen. Der Wert für den Vergessensparameter indiziert eine sehr hohe Vergessensquote, der Wert für den Wettbewerbsparameter weist auf eine etwas reduzierte Wahrscheinlichkeit der Kompositionsbildung bzw. des -abrufs hin.

Tabelle 7. Geschätzte Parameter des multinomialen Modells für empirische und simulierte Daten sowie geschätzte Wahrscheinlichkeiten der Kompositionsbildung bzw. des -abrufs für simulierte Daten.

Zeitliche Differenzierung innerhalb von Sequenzen		Parameterschätzungen				Wkt. von Kompositionsbildung bzw. -abruf	
		empirisch		simuliert			
Diskriminationsphase	Memorierphase	Parameter	Wert	Parameter	Wert	Wkt.	Wert
mit	mit	s	.049	s	.141	Satz	.181
		pw	.241	pw	.152	Phrase	.189
		pl	.273	pl	.440	Phrase-1-Prop.	.415
		r	.664	r	.671	p(ja | Diff = 0)	.640
	ohne	s	.161	s	.133	Satz	.174
		pw	.149	pw	.156	Phrase	.183
		pl	.208	pl	.463	Phrase-1-Prop.	.455
		r	.672	r	.648	p(ja | Diff = 0)	.620
ohne	mit	s	.180	s	.141	Satz	.155
		pw	.102	pw	.139	Phrase	.175
		pl	.625	pl	.478	Phrase-1-Prop.	.461
		r	.488	r	.472	p(ja | Diff = 0)	.480
	ohne	s	.456	s	.385	Satz	.283
		pw	.163	pw	.364	Phrase	.307
		pl	.412	pl	.488	Phrase-1-Prop.	.499
		r	.411	r	.400	p(ja | Diff = 0)	.420

Anmerkung. Phrase-1-Prop.: Anteil der Wahrscheinlichkeit, die erste Phrase abzurufen bzw. zu bilden an der Wahrscheinlichkeit, eine der beiden möglichen Phrasen abzurufen bzw. zu bilden; p(ja | Diff = 0): dem gewählten Indifferenzpunkt der Entscheidungsfunktion entsprechende Wahrscheinlichkeit, bei einer Nulldifferenz eine Sequenz als grammatisch zu beurteilen

Figure 2. The *table text* used in the present study. From: Müller, B. (1998). Kompositionsbildung bei Symbolfolgen und Bediensequenzen: Empirische Befunde und die Theorie des "Competitive Chunking", Kognitioswissenschaft, 7, 85.

M. Spies: Das Langzeitgedächtnis als Boltzmann-Maschine

Da sicherlich der Stichprobenwert für Kante i (nämlich $x(i)$) nicht mit dem Parameter $\phi_c(j)$ zusammenhängt, vereinfacht sich nach Gleichung 52 die rechte Seite weiter zu

$$\frac{\partial}{\partial \phi_c(j)} p_c(x(i)) = \frac{\partial}{\partial \phi_c(j)} \sum_{r \in \mathcal{R}} q_c(x_r) x_r(i) \qquad (61)$$

Da wieder $x_r(i)$ nicht mit $\phi_c(j)$ zusammenhängt, ergeben Summationsregel und Produktregel für partielle Ableitungen weiter

$$\frac{\partial}{\partial \phi_c(j)} p_c(x(i)) = \sum_{r \in \mathcal{R}} x_r(i) \frac{\partial}{\partial \phi_c(j)} q_c(x_r) \qquad (62)$$

Benutzen wir nun die Gleichung für die stationäre Verteilung (9), so läßt sich die partielle Ableitung in dieser Formel bestimmen:

$$\frac{\partial}{\partial \phi_c(j)} q_c(x_r) = \frac{\partial}{\partial \phi_c(j)} \left(\frac{1}{a(\phi_c)} \exp(x_r^T \phi_c) \right) \qquad (63)$$

Leiten wir jeden Term des Produktes einzeln ab:

$$\begin{aligned} \frac{\partial}{\partial \phi_c(j)} \frac{1}{a(\phi_c)} &= \frac{-1}{(a(\phi_c))^2} \frac{\partial}{\partial \phi_c(j)} a(\phi_c) \\ &= \frac{-1}{(a(\phi_c))^2} \sum_{r \in \mathcal{R}} \exp(C(r)/c) x_r(j)) \\ &= \frac{-1}{a(\phi_c)} p_c(x(j)) \qquad (64) \end{aligned}$$

Figure 3. The *equation text* used in the present study. From: Spies, M. (1999). Das Langzeitgedächtnis als Boltzmann-Maschine, *Kognitionswissenschaft*, 8, 71.

Table 1. Overview of possible mistakes in the three probe texts

		Continuous text	Table text	Equation text
Orthographic and grammatical mistakes	in words	X	X	X
	in formulas	—	—	X
Formatting errors and typos	header	X	X	X
	headline	X	—	—
	paragraph	X	X	X
	spacing	X	X	X
	font	X	X	X
	footnote	X	—	—
	columns	X	X	X
	lines	—	X	—
	justified text	X	X	X
Amount of written text	missing words	X	X	X
	missing signs	X	X	X

Note: X = possible;— = Not possible

doi:10.1371/journal.pone.0115069.t001

RESULTS

The performance of the four experimental groups (Word novices, Word experts, LaTeX novices, and LaTeX experts) on the three probe texts (continuous text, table text, and equation text) is summarized in Table 2 and Figs. 2, 3, and 4. The results of the usability questionnaire are presented in Table 3.

Table 2. Mean absolute frequencies of orthographic and grammatical mistakes, formatting errors and typos, and the amount of written text (i.e., number of words) across all four groups for the continuous text (a), the table text (b), and the equation text (c)

a. Continuous text

	Word						LaTeX					
	Novices		Experts		Overall		Novices		Experts		Overall	
	M	*SD*	*M*	*SD*	*M*	*SD*	*M*	*SD*	*M*	*SD*	*M*	*SD*
Orthographic and grammatical mistakes	5.9	3.5	7.9	6.7	6.9	5.3	7.0	6.6	11.3	9.5	9.2	8.2
Formatting errors and typos	10.0	3.9	9.3	4.1	9.7	3.9	17.3	4.1	16.1	4.0	17.1	4.0
Amount of written text	331	49.1	379	11, 7	355	42.4	250	104	308	99.4	279	103.3

b. Table text

	Word						LaTeX					
	Novices		Experts		Overall		Novices		Experts		Overall	
	M	*SD*	*M*	*SD*	*M*	*SD*	*M*	*SD*	*M*	*SD*	*M*	*SD*
Orthographic and grammatical mistakes	9.9	7.8	7.1	4.4	8.5	6.4	9.7	10.5	7.8	4.5	8.8	7.9
Formatting errors and typos	12.0	3.7	11.3	4.1	11.4	3.9	19.5	3.6	18.7	3.0	19.1	3.3
Amount of written text	353	82.9	395	78.7	374	81.6	191	118	260	137.8	226	130

c. Equation text

	Word						LaTeX					
	Novices		Experts		Overall		Novices		Experts		Overall	
	M	*SD*	*M*	*SD*	*M*	*SD*	*M*	*SD*	*M*	*SD*	*M*	*SD*
Orthographic and grammatical mistakes	5.2	4.1	3.9	3.5	4.6	3.8	11.4	8.2	9.3	7.9	10.4	7.9
Formatting errors and typos	24.4	6.4	19.3	11.8	21.9	9.6	14.9	5.5	12.5	4.9	13.7	5.2
Amount of written text	231	57.4	270	67.3	250	64.1	314	16.7	312	24.6	313	20.5

Note—Orthographic and grammatical mistakes were counted as one mistake per word, even if a participant made more than one mistakes in a word. Each formatting error and each typo was counted as one mistake. For instance, if a text contains three different font sizes each wrong formatted text section was counted as one mistake.

doi:10.1371/journal.pone.0115069.t002

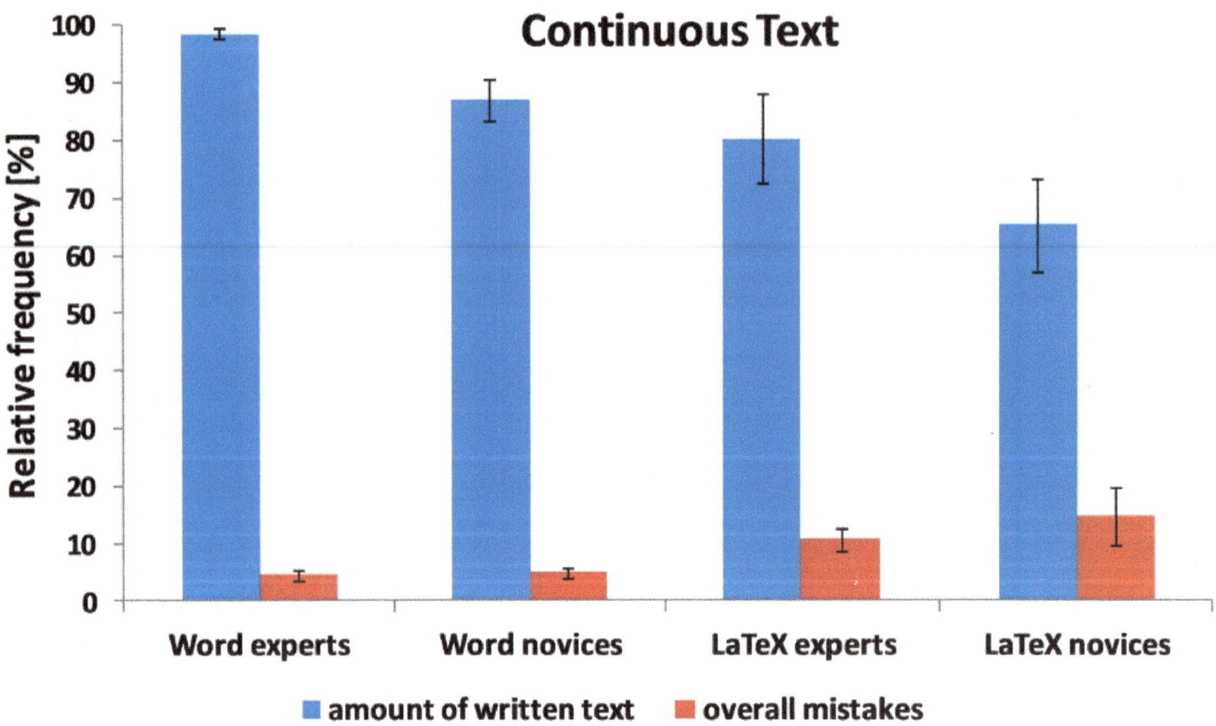

Figure 4. Mean amount of text written within 30 minutes and the overall number of mistakes for the *continuous text* for the four groups of participants (Word experts, Word novices, LaTeX experts, and LaTeX novices).

Error bars represent the standard error.

Table 3. Results from the usability questionnaire ISO 9241–10

	Software			
	Word		LaTeX	
Usability questionnaire	*M*	*SD*	*M*	*SD*
Tiredness	3.4	1.9	2.2	1.4
Frustration	3.3	2.0	2.1	1.5
Enjoyment	3.6	1.7	5.2	1.4
Suitability for the task	0.6	1.1	1.4	0.8
Self-descriptiveness	-0.2	0.9	-0.3	1.2
Controllability	1.6	1.0	1.7	0.9
Conformity with user expectations	1.3	0.7	1.3	0.9
Error tolerance	0.3	1.1	-0.6	1.2
Suitability for individualization	0.2	1.1	0.7	1.1
Suitability for learning	0.4	1.1	-0.3	0.8

doi:10.1371/journal.pone.0115069.t003

Continuous Text

As shown in Table 2a and Fig. 4, Word users (both novices and experts) made fewer formatting mistakes (t (37.97) = -5.94, p <. 001) and wrote significantly more text within 30 minutes (t (38) = 3.10, p <. 01) compared with LaTeX novice and expert users. The number of orthographic and grammatical errors did not differ significantly between Word and LaTeX users (t (38) = -1.02, p = .31). However, Word experts made significantly fewer formatting mistakes than LaTeX experts (t (18) = -4.15, p <. 01) and Word novices made significantly fewer formatting mistakes than LaTeX novices (t (17.92) = -4.05, p <. 01). Interestingly, Word novices also made significantly fewer formatting mistakes than LaTeX experts (t (17.98) = -3.84, p <. 01). Word experts wrote significantly more text than LaTeX experts (t (18) = 2.24, p <. 05) and Word novices wrote significantly more text than LaTeX novices (t (18) = 2.31, p <. 05).

Table Text

As shown in Table 2b and Fig. 5, Word users (both novices and experts) made significantly fewer formatting mistakes (t (36.78) = -6.72, p <. 001) and wrote more text within 30 minutes (t(31.73) = 4.31, p <. 001) compared with LaTeX novice and expert users. Word experts made significantly fewer formatting mistakes than LaTeX experts (t (16) = -4.40, p <. 001) and Word novices made significantly fewer mistakes than LaTeX novices (t (18) = -4.98, p <. 001). Word experts wrote significantly more text than LaTeX experts (t (14.19) = 2.68, p <. 05) and Word novices wrote significantly more text than LaTeX novices (t (15.99) = 3.52, p <. 01). Interestingly, Word novices made significantly fewer formatting mistakes (t (17.33) = -4.78, p <. 001) and produced more text than LaTeX experts (t (15.99) = 3.52, p <. 01).

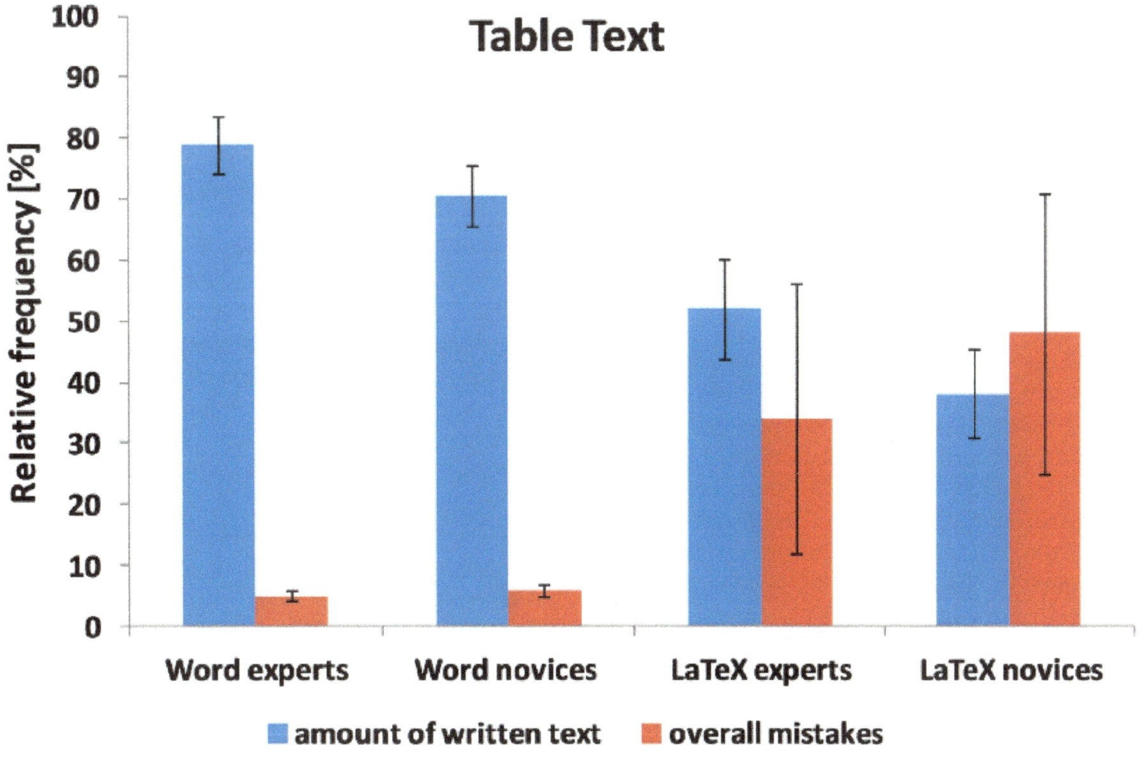

Figure 5. Mean amount of text written within 30 minutes and the overall number of mistakes for the, table text for the four groups of participants (Word experts, Word novices, LaTeX experts, and LaTeX novices). Error bars represent the standard error.

Equation Text

As shown in Table 2c and Fig. 6, LaTeX users (both novices and experts) made significantly fewer formatting mistakes (t (38) = 3.35, p <. 01) and wrote more text within 30 minutes (t (38) = -2.96, p <. 001) compared with Word novices and experts. However, LaTeX users made significantly more orthographic and grammatical errors than Word users (t (38) = -2.96, p <. 01). LaTeX novices made significantly fewer formatting mistakes (t (17.61) = 3.57, p <. 01) and also wrote more text (t (18) = -4.30, p <. 001) than Word novices. Overall, however, the performance of LaTeX experts and Word experts did not differ significantly.

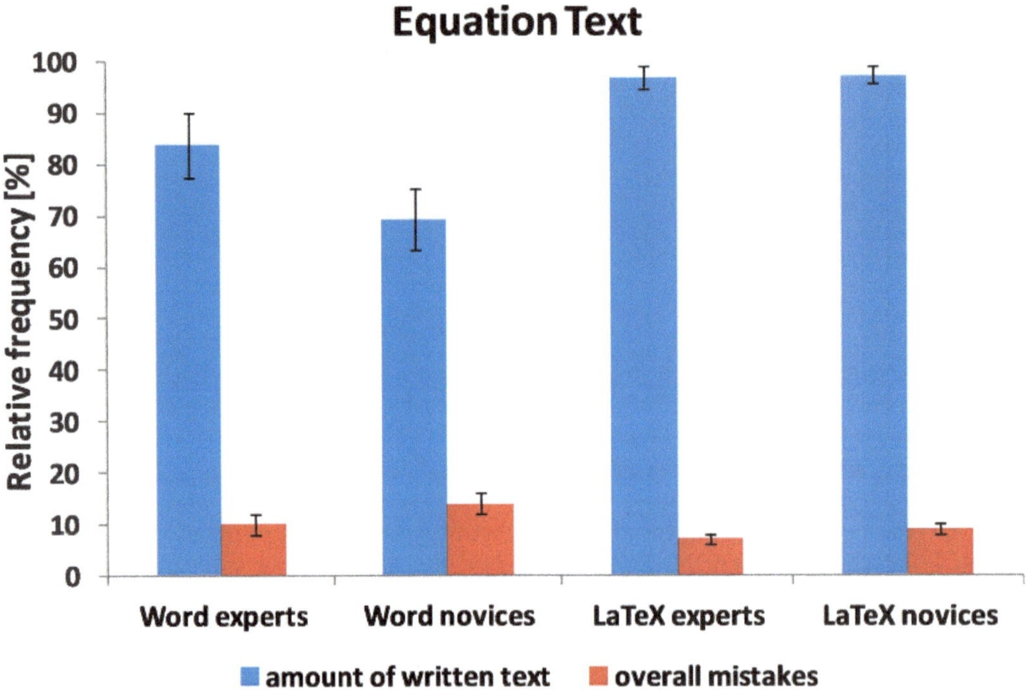

Figure 6. Mean amount of text written within 30 minutes and the overall number of mistakes for the equation text for the four groups of participants (Word experts, Word novices, LaTeX experts, and LaTeX novices). Error bars represent the standard error.

Usability Questionnaire

The international standard questionnaire ISO 9241–10 measures user's opinions and satisfaction with their software system. The questionnaire addresses general ergonomic principles that apply to the design of dialogues between humans and information systems, including suitability for the task, suitability for learning, suitability for individualization, conformity with user expectations, self-descriptiveness, controllability, and error tolerance. Furthermore, we asked whether users perceived their work with the respective software as tiresome, frustrating, or delightful. Participants rated their software on a seven-point scale from very bad (-3) to very good (3). As shown in Table 3, Word users rated their respective software as less efficient than LaTeX users (t (35.6) = -2.80, p <. 01), but LaTeX users rated the learnability of their respective software as poorer than Word users (t (33.6) = 2.13, p <. 05). However, LaTeX users assessed their work as less tiresome (t (35.38) = 2.16, p <. 05) and less frustrating than Word users (t (38) = 2.27, p <. 05). LaTeX users significantly more often reported to enjoy their work with their respective software than Word users (t (36.27) = -3.23, p <. 01).

DISCUSSION

Many academic authors believe that they have the right to design documents themselves and that each researcher should have the freedom to choose the software that he or she prefers. In fact, our study shows that each document preparation system has unique advantages and disadvantages, and there might be no "best" tool for all aspects of a highly complex task such as producing diverse scientific publications. For example, LaTeX users in our study attained better performance in the typesetting of mathematical equations, and it is not surprising that LaTeX users are typically in disciplines where mathematical formulas are frequent (e.g., mathematics, engineering, or computer science). Indeed these disciplinary preferences fit with the original motivation for the development of TeX (the basis of LaTeX) in the 1970s, which was to provide a powerful means to typeset complex mathematical formulas [2]. Some computer scientists may therefore think that mastering LaTeX is a "must" for any "true" expert in their discipline and that someone who already invested significant time and effort in learning LaTeX may not want to re-learn another tool. One may also argue that given a well-designed LaTeX document class file, document development speed and text and formatting accuracy are significantly improved. Another characteristic of our study is that it is practically impossible to evaluate LaTeX without also evaluating the used editors. In fact, our research measured the efficiency of Word against LaTeX in combination with some editor interfaces. However, recent research shows that it is possible to improve the interfaces to LaTeX by making them do more what the authors expect instead of what the programmers imagined [3].

However, our study suggests that LaTeX should be used as a document preparation system only in cases in which a document is heavily loaded with mathematical equations.

For all other types of documents, our results suggest that LaTeX reduces the user's productivity and results in more orthographical, grammatical, and formatting errors, more typos, and less written text than Microsoft Word over the same duration of time. LaTeX users may argue that the overall quality of the text that is created with LaTeX is better than the text that is created with Microsoft Word. Although this argument may be true, the differences between text produced in more recent editions of Microsoft Word and text produced in LaTeX may be less obvious than it was in the past. Moreover, we believe that the appearance of text matters less than the scientific content and impact to the field. In particular, LaTeX is also used frequently for text that does not contain a significant amount of mathematical symbols and formula. We believe that the use of LaTeX under these circumstances is highly problematic and that researchers should reflect on the criteria that drive their preferences to use LaTeX over Microsoft Word for text that does not require significant mathematical representations.

One decision criterion that factors into the choice to use a particular software system is the usability of the available systems for the given task. The usability of a software system is a measure of how easy it is to use the program to carry out a prescribed task. In human-computer interaction and cognitive ergonomics, the most central aspects of usability include the "efficiency" of the system (which refers to how quickly users can perform tasks once they have learned the design), "errors" (which refers to how many errors users make, the severity of these errors, and how easily users can recover from these errors), and "user satisfaction" (the overall pleasantness and feasibility of the design) [4,5]. Based on these criteria, our results show that no reasons exist to use LaTeX for documents that do not contain complex mathematical formula.

A second decision criterion that factors into the choice to use a particular software system is reflection about what drives certain preferences. A striking result of our study is that LaTeX users are highly satisfied with their system despite reduced usability and productivity. From a psychological perspective, this finding may be related to motivational factors, i.e., the driving forces that compel or reinforce individuals to act in a certain way to achieve a desired goal. A vital motivational factor is the tendency to reduce cognitive dissonance. According to the theory of cognitive dissonance, each individual has a motivational drive to seek consonance between their beliefs and their actual actions. If a belief set does not concur with the individual's actual behavior, then it is usually easier to change the belief rather than the behavior [6]. The results from many psychological studies in which people have been asked to choose between one of two items (e.g., products, objects, gifts, etc.) and then asked to rate the desirability, value, attractiveness, or usefulness of their choice, report that participants often reduce unpleasant feelings of cognitive dissonance by rationalizing the chosen alternative as more desirable than the unchosen alternative [6, 7]. This bias is usually unconscious and becomes stronger as the effort to reject the chosen alternative increases, which is similar in nature to the case of learning and using LaTeX.

A third decision criterion that should factor into a researcher's choice of a document preparation system is the cost of research and development to the public or industry. Researchers have a responsibility to act economically and efficiently to create new technologies and theories that benefit society, especially in cases in which research is publicly funded. In 2010, the 27 countries of the European Union invested approximately 247 billion euros into research and development, which represents approximately 1.9 percent of the EU's gross domestic product. In the same year, Germany invested 2.9% (75 billion euros) and the US invested 2.8% (370 billion dollars) of its gross domestic expenditures into research and development. A significant portion of these budgets is allocated to the salaries of researchers. According to the American Association for the Advancement of Science (AAAS), there are approximately 5.8 million science and engineering researchers worldwide [8]. No reliable data is available about how many of these researchers use LaTeX (or MS Word). However, a google search for LaTeX (together with TeX to avoid ambiguities) results in approximately 18 million hits. Brischoux and Legagneux found that approximately 26% of submissions to 54 randomly selected scholarly journals from 15 different scientific disciplines were written in LaTeX, with a significant difference between LaTeX-using and non-LaTeX-using disciplines [1]. We can only roughly estimate the average number of hours per day that a researcher spends on writing scholarly texts, such as internal technical reports, journal articles, and book publications. For researchers in the field of cognitive and brain science, researchers may spend approximately 10 to 30 percent of their time engaged in writing.

Given these numbers it remains an open question to determine the amount of taxpayer money that is spent worldwide for researchers to use LaTeX over a more efficient document preparation system, which would free up their time to advance their respective field. Some publishers may save a significant amount of money by requesting or allowing LaTeX submissions because a well-formed LaTeX document complying with a well-designed class file (template) is much easier to bring into their publication workflow. However, this is at the expense of the researchers' labor time and effort. We therefore suggest that leading scientific journals should consider accepting submissions in LaTeX only if this is justified by the level of mathematics presented in the paper. In all other cases, we think that scholarly journals should request authors to submit their documents in Word or PDF format. We believe that this would be a good policy for two reasons. First, we think that the appearance of the text is secondary to the scientific merit of an article and its impact to the field. And, second, preventing researchers from producing documents in LaTeX would save time and money to maximize the benefit of research and development for both the research team and the public.

ACKNOWLEDGMENTS

The text processing software Microsoft Word is licensed and traded by the Microsoft Corporation. The authors do not have any connection to this company, and the Microsoft Corporation had no role in the study design, data collection, data analysis, decision to publish, or preparation of the manuscript. We thank all participants for contributing to this study and Peter Flynn and Gerhard Strube for many helpful suggestions for improving the revision of this article.

AUTHOR CONTRIBUTIONS

Conceived and designed the experiments: MK JN. Performed the experiments: JN. Analyzed the data: JN. Contributed reagents/materials/analysis tools: JN. Wrote the paper: MK.

REFERENCES

1. Brischoux F Legagneux P (2009) Don't Format Manuscripts. *The Scientist*, 23: 24–24.
2. Knuth DE (1996) The TeXBook. München: Addison-Wesley.
3. Flynn P (2014) Human Interfaces to Structured Documents: The usability of software for authoring and editing". PhD Thesis, University College Cork, Ireland. Available:http://epu.ucc.ie/theses/pflynn/ Accessed 20 Nov. 2014.
4. Nielsen J (1993) Usability Engineering. San Diego: Academic Press.
5. Rubin J (1994) Handbook of Usability Testing. New York: John Wiley & Sons.
6. Festinger L (1985) A theory of cognitive dissonance. Stanford, CA: Stanford University Press (first published 1957).
7. Brehm JW (1956) Postdecision changes in the desirability of alternatives. J Abnorm Soc Psych 52: 384–389. doi: 10.1037/h0041006
8. OECD (2013) Gross domestic expenditure on R&D, Science and Technology. Available: doi: 10.1787/rdxp-table-2013-1-en. Calculated using full-time equivalents. Accessed 20 Nov 2014

CHAPTER 6

ORTHOGONALIZATION OF REGRESSORS IN FMRI MODELS

Jeanette A. Mumford[1], Jean-Baptiste Poline[2] , Russell A. Poldrack[3]

[1] Center for Investigating Healthy Minds at the Waisman Center, University of Wisconsin—Madison, Madison, WI, USA

[2] Helen Wills Neuroscience Institute, Brain Imaging Center, University of California, Berkeley, CA, USA

[3] Department of Psychology, Stanford University, Palo Alto, CA, USA

ABSTRACT

The occurrence of collinearity in fMRI-based GLMs (general linear models) may reduce power or produce unreliable parameter estimates. It is commonly believed that orthogonalizing collinear regressors in the model will solve this problem, and some software packages apply automatic orthogonalization. However, the effects of orthogonalization on the interpretation of the resulting parameter estimates is widely unappreciated or misunderstood. Here we discuss the nature and causes of collinearity in fMRI models, with a focus on the appropriate uses of orthogonalization. Special attention is given to how the two popular fMRI data analysis software packages, SPM and FSL, handle orthogonalization, and pitfalls that may be encountered in their usage. Strategies are discussed for reducing collinearity in fMRI designs and addressing their effects when they occur.

INTRODUCTION

When regressors in a general linear model (GLM) are orthogonal to each other, they do not share any descriptive variability and are completely uncorrelated. In contrast, collinearity occurs when there is pairwise correlation between either single regressors or linear combinations of multiple regressors. Eq 1 shows two examples of perfect collinearity.

$$\begin{bmatrix} 1 & 2 & 0 \\ 1 & 2 & 0 \\ 0 & 0 & 1 \\ 0 & 0 & 1 \end{bmatrix} : \quad c_2 = 2c_1$$
$$\begin{bmatrix} 1 & 0 & 2 \\ 1 & 0 & 2 \\ 0 & 1 & 4 \\ 0 & 1 & 4 \end{bmatrix} : c_3 = 2c_1 + 4c_2 \qquad (1)$$

Citation: Mumford JA, Poline J-B, Poldrack RA (2015) Orthogonalization of Regressors in fMRI Models. PLoS ONE 10(4): e0126255. doi:10.1371/journal.pone.0126255

On the top, the first regressor is perfectly correlated with the second and on the bottom the third regressor is perfectly correlated with a linear combination of the first two. Near-collinearity occurs when the correlation between linear combinations of regressors is high but not perfect. For example, in an fMRI experiment where a stimulus is always followed 2s later by feedback, the stimulus- and feedback-specific regressors will be highly correlated due to the blurring effect of the hemodynamic response. This can also occur when a set of trials has two sets of parametrically modulated values to be modeled. For example, when the model includes a regressor modeling response times (RT) along with a parametric regressor that has a direct effect on RT, such as stimulus intensity; because the onset times are identical for both regressors, the resulting parametric regressors will be correlated. Fig 1 shows how the parametrically modulated regressors are created and illustrates that when RT and the task parameter are highly correlated, the resulting parametrically modulated regressors will also be correlated, in this case the correlation is greater than 0.80. Correlation between regressors is also common in second level studies; for example, age and task performance regressors are likely to be correlated. It should also be noted that collinearity can impact contrasts of parameter estimates as well as individual model parameters [1]. One way to think of this is to re-parametrize the model such that the contrast of effects to be tested is coded with one regressor, and to consider how much correlation there is in the rest of the model with this regressor. Notably, the overall model fit is not impacted by the collinearity in the model, but the quality of the parameter estimates will suffer, in terms of variability.

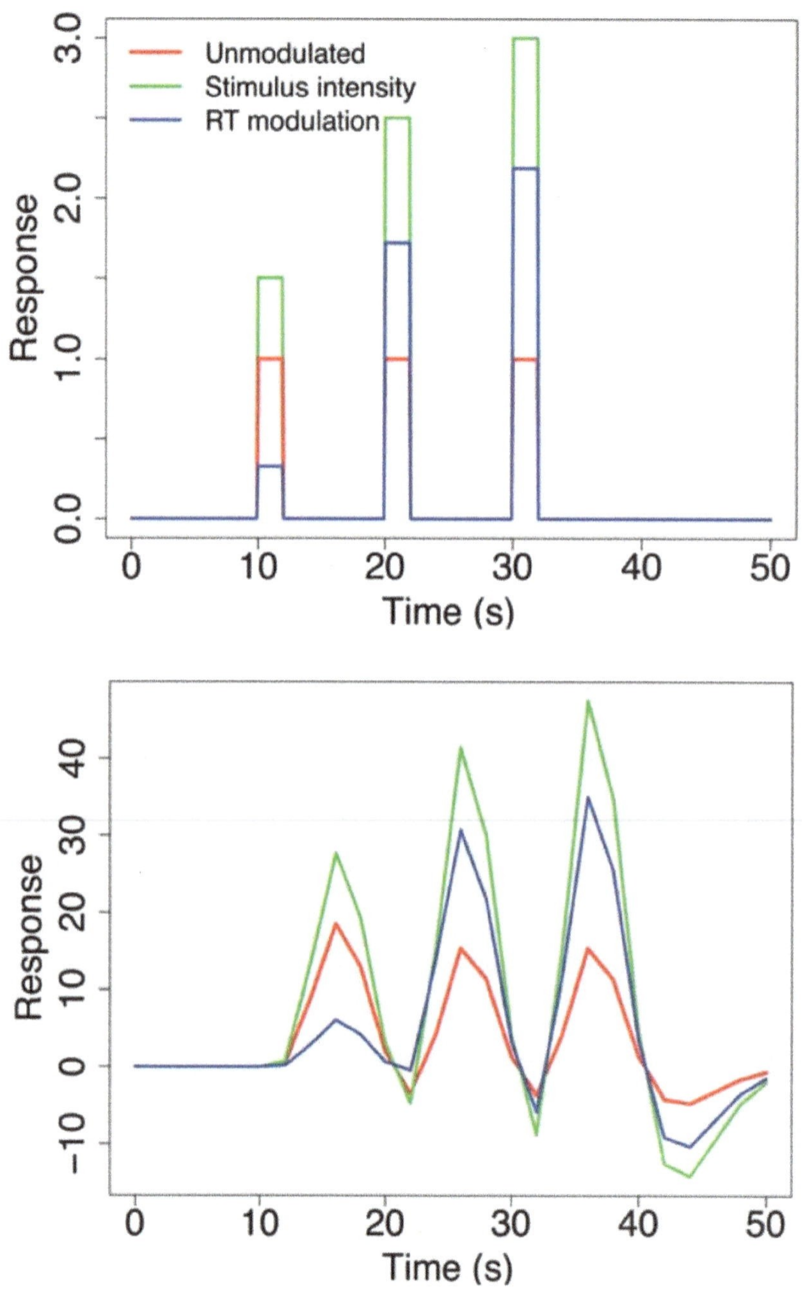

Figure 1. How parametrically modulated regressors are constructed. The left graph shows the unconvolved regressors for 3 trials, where each trial for stimulus intensity and RT is modulated by the appropriate value. The right graph shows the convolved regressors and all pairwise correlations of regressors are above 0.80, indicating possible collinearity.

Models with perfect collinearity are not estimable because there is an infinite number of solutions that could fit the data equally well. This is comparable to solving the problem of identifying 2 numbers that sum to 10 (5 and 5, -50 and 60, etc.). With near-collinearity, the model is estimable but the resulting parameter estimates are highly variable. Fig 2 shows three different modeling examples for the experiment with a 2s long stimulus followed by feedback for low collinearity (top), high collinearity (middle) and high collinearity with an orthogonalized regressor (bottom). Notice that often we are not concerned by identification of all parameters of the model, but rather with some (linear) combination of these. For now we will focus on individual parameters for simplicity. The orthogonalized case will be discussed shortly, but to understand the impact of collinearity, the current focus is on the top two rows of the figure. The Venn diagrams illustrate the descriptive variability of each regressor, or explanatory variable, in terms of which variance is unique (red and blue) versus shared between the two variables (purple). The rightmost plots show activation estimates for 20 simulated subjects for stimulus and feedback, where the solid lines indicate the true activation strengths. In the low collinearity case (top row, Fig 2), each covariate has a large portion of unique descriptive variability, which leads to activation estimates with a low variance across subjects. In the high collinearity case, with an ISI of 1s (middle, Fig 2), when one parameter estimate within subject is unusually high this is offset by an unusually low estimate for the other parameter, in order to maintain a good overall model fit. For example, the first subject's stimulus estimate is much higher than the true mean and the feedback estimate is much lower. What is crucial to recognize (and often misunderstood) is that general linear model parameter estimates are unbiased in the case of near-collinearity, but have inflated variance; the standard method of GLM parameter estimation automatically removes the effects of shared variability, so that each effect is adjusted for all others. In the example above, this would allow the stimulus parameter to be interpreted as unique stimulus activation adjusted for feedback activation and likewise the estimated feedback activation is adjusted for the stimulus-related effect. If one wishes to look at the common variance explained by either regressors, an F statistic should be employed.

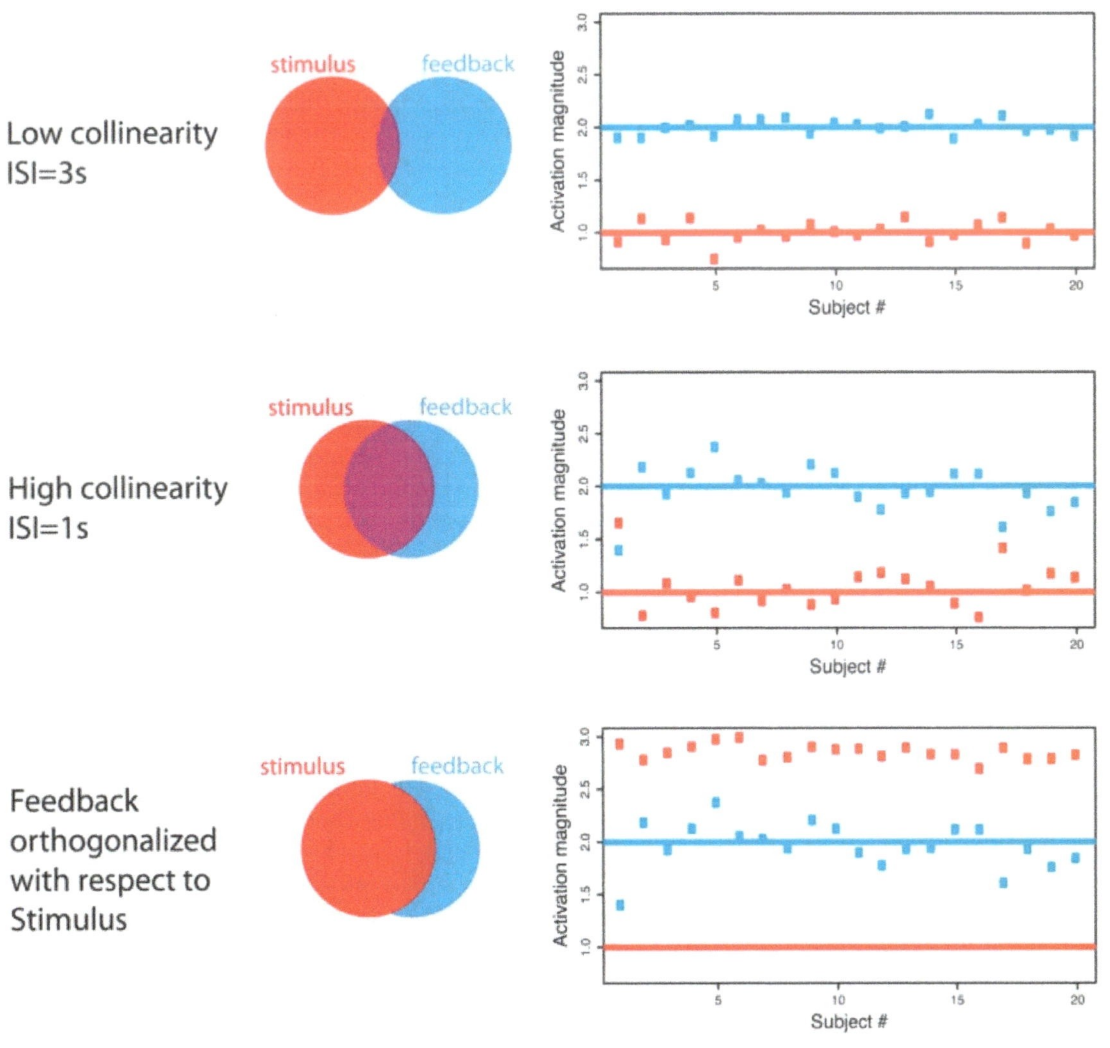

Figure 2. Illustration of parameter estimate behavior for 20 simulated subjects when model has low collinearity (top), high collinearity (middle) and high collinearity where the feedback regressor is orthogonalized with respect to the stimulus regressor (bottom). The Venn diagrams indicate how the variability is distributed across the 2 regressors where red is unique to stimulus, blue is unique to feedback and purple is shared. The rightmost column shows the parameter estimates for stimulus (red) and feedback (blue) across 20 subjects, where the solid lines indicate the true values. With low collinearity the variability of the parameter estimates is much smaller than the high collinearity case, although in both cases the estimates are unbiased on average. Orthogonalization does not change the feedback parameter estimates (middle and bottom blue data points are identical), but the stimulus feedback has lower variability and the estimate is much higher.

A common misconception is that orthogonalization is necessary and/or optimal to address the effects of collinearity. Whereas the standard GLM removes the shared variability from all of the individual regressors, orthogonalization instead assigns the shared variability to one of the regressors and is accomplished by regressing one covariate on the other and extracting the residual. In the example, in order to orthogonalize feedback with respect to stimulus, the feedback regressor would be replaced with the residual from the following GLM: feedback $=\beta_*$stimulus$+\epsilon$. The bottom row of Fig 2 illustrates the orthogonalized model and, importantly, the interpretation of the stimulus effect in this model is "stimulus unadjusted for feedback". In other words, the parameter estimate for stimulus is the same as what would be obtained if feedback was not even in the model (though the residual variance may differ between the model with orthogonalized feedback and feedback omitted). Since collinearity is high, the unadjusted stimulus effect is roughly the sum of the stimulus and feedback effect sizes (1+2 = 3). In addition, since more descriptive variability is assigned to the stimulus regressor, this regressor now explains both what is common to feedback and stimuli as well as what is specific to stimulus. In addition, the variance of the estimate is much smaller in this model, i.e., the subject-specific estimates are less variable across subjects. The overall goodness of fits for the models with and without orthogonalization are identical, as are the parameter estimates for the feedback covariate (blue points, middle and bottom rows, Fig 2). This occurs since the same descriptive variability is available for both models, in other words, the portion in the Venn diagrams unique to feedback (blue) is the same in both models. A related example written in Python illustrating orthogonalization using can be found inhttp://nbviewer.ipython.org/github/jmumford/orthogonalizaton_ipynb/blob/master/orthogonalization.ipynb.

Overall, the only effect of orthogonalization in the example is to change the interpretation of the parameter associated with the stimulus. This effect of orthogonalization is often overlooked and/or misunderstood when interpreting the parameters of the model, which produces a misleading result. The test statistic for a parameter estimate consists of the estimated mean divided by the estimated variance. As shown in this example, orthogonalization in the presence of collinearity may result in an increased mean estimate (subject-specific estimates in row 3 ofFig 2 are too high) and a decreased variance estimate (variance of subject-specific estimates in row 3 is smaller than row 2), resulting in a higher test statistic and smaller p-value. Although the p-value for the stimulus regressor in the orthogonalized model is not appropriate for the "stimulus activation adjusted for feedback", it is applicable to "stimulus, without adjusting for feedback activation". This crucial difference in the interpretation of the results is unfortunately often overlooked when researchers use orthogonalization in fMRI analyses.

The above example of orthogonalization demonstrates how misleading the model results can be when orthogonalization is performed. The purpose of the present paper is to clarify when and why orthogonalization is appropriate and highlight the ways in which it affects the interpretation of results. Additionally, fMRI software packages handle orthogonalization in different ways. SPM (Statistical Parametric Mapping) automatically applies orthogonalization in certain situations, which may result in misinterpretation if users are unaware of this procedure. FSL (FMRIB Software Library) allows the user to specify what regressors are orthogonalized and so it is up to the user to do this properly. Proper uses of orthogonalization in fMRI data analysis will be discussed next, followed by the software dependent issues. Some strategies for avoiding collinearity in study design will be discussed. Finally, the overall impact that collinearity will have on group-level inferences will be described.

METHODS

When Orthogonalization is Necessary

Orthogonalization is rarely warranted in fMRI analysis, but in a few special cases it is necessary in order to improve the interpretation of the model's inferences. The simplest case is in a group level model where the BOLD contrast across subjects is modeled as a function of some parameter (e.g., age) and the inferences of interest are for the overall group mean and the age effect. In other words, the model is

$$Y = \beta_0 + \beta_1 * \text{Age} + \epsilon, \quad (2)$$

where Y, the response or explained variable, is a vector of BOLD activation values for each subject (to be "explained" by the model), Age, the explanatory variable, is the vector of ages over subjects, β_0 and β_1 are the parameters of interest and ϵ is the error term. The $\beta_1$parameter describes how much the BOLD activation changes with a 1-unit change in Age, in other words, for two subjects who are 1 year apart, the difference in their BOLD activations isβ_1. The other parameter, β_0, is the value of the BOLD activation when Age is zero, which is not informative. However, if Age is orthogonalized with respect to the mean, this will change the interpretation of the intercept, β_0, to be the overall mean, as Age will be giving up any information about the mean of the response variable. Specifically, this orthogonalization is performed by mean centering the Age variable, since the residual from the model regressing the mean from Age is Age_{DM} = Age−mean(Age). Now the GLM is

$$Y = \beta_0^* + \beta_1^* * Age_{DM} + \epsilon.$$

Where Age_{DM} stands for "Age de-meaned". Although the Age regressor changed, this does not change the estimate of β*1β1* since if two subjects are 1 year apart in age, they are also 1 year apart in mean centered age, i.e. the slope parameter is unchanged. Instead, the estimate of β*0β0*now reflects the average BOLD activation, as Y=β*0Y=β0* when Age−mean(Age) = 0 or when Age= mean(Age). In many cases there may not be any interest in the overall mean of Y and the extra step of mean centering age could be skipped. We highlight again here the fact that orthogonalization of age against the mean changes the parameter estimate for the mean, i.e. the intercept, not for the Age variable.

Orthogonalization is also necessary in first level fMRI designs where the model includes a parametric modulation, as shown in Fig 1, or when different trial durations are modeled, which might occur if the stimulus was shown for different periods of time across trials. In these cases a constant duration, unmodulated regressor is required (Red regressor in Fig 1). Often this regressor is of interest for studying the overall mean activation across trials, but even if of no interest it is necessary to include it. If the constant duration regressor is omitted, the model assumes that when the modulation value (i.e. intensity) is 0, the BOLD activation is 0. This is often a strong assumption and adding an unmodulated regressor will improve the model's ability to fit the data. Using modulation by stimulus intensity as an example, the interpretation of the unmodulated regressor is the mean activation for an intensity of 0, but by orthogonalizing the modulated regressor with respect to the unmodulated regressor, the interpretation for the unmodulated regressor is the mean activation across trials. Again, the orthogonalized regressor's inferences remain exactly the same, but the p-values and interpretation of the unmodulated regressor will change.

Fig 3 extends this example to when there are 2 modulation values: RT and stimulus intensity. The top row illustrates how the descriptive variability is split across the 3 explanatory variables where there are 3 unique portions and 4 shared portions. The interpretations for the RT and intensity regressors are sensible, but the unmodulated regressor's interpretation is the mean activation when both RT and stimulus intensity are 0, which is not of interest. In this case both the RT and intensity modulated regressors would be orthogonalized with respect to the unmodulated regressor to assign all variability shared with the unmodulated regressor to it (second row, Fig 3). Now each parameter has the proper interpretation. The unmodulated regressor is the overall mean BOLD activation across trials, the RT effect is adjusted for intensity and the intensity effect is adjusted for RT.

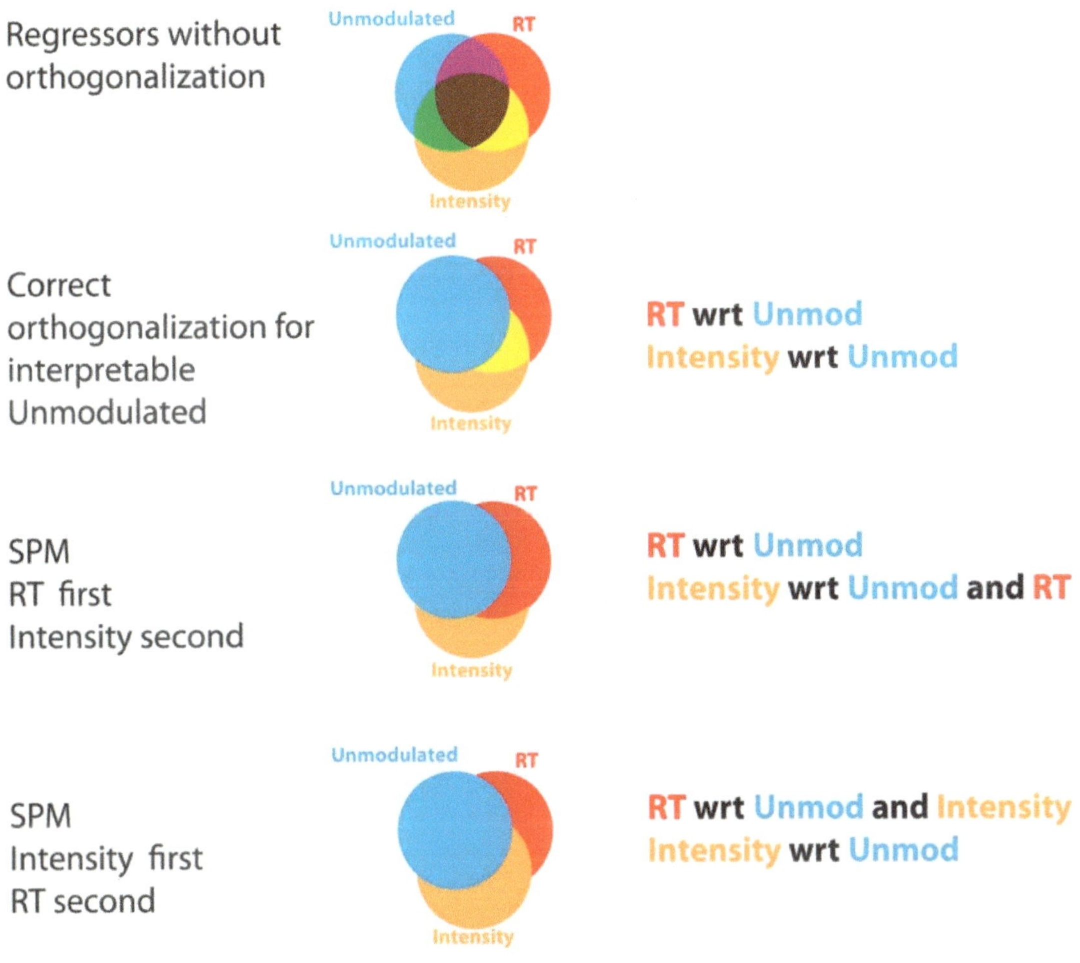

Figure 3. Distribution of descriptive variability with 2 sets of parametric modulators, RT and stimulus intensity. The top row shows how descriptive variability is shared when there is no orthogonalization. In this case the unmodulated regressor's interpretation is average BOLD when RT and intensity are 0. The second row shows the orthogonalization necessary to change the interpretation of the unmodulated regressor to the average activation. Note the shared variability between RT and intensity. The last two rows show how the variability is distributed when using the automated orthogonalization in SPM when RT is entered before intensity and vice versa. The modulation that is entered first is not adjusted for the second, which can lead to misleading results. SPM sequentially orthogonalizes a modulated regressor with the previous regressors, therefore two models may have to be run to obtain the specific variance of two modulations.

Orthogonalization in fMRI software

SPM.

The SPM software package automatically performs orthogonalization for parametrically modulated regressors in versions 8 and older. However, due to how orthogonalization is performed when more than one set of parametric modulation values is used for a set of trials, it is possible to misinterpret the resulting inferences. In the case of a single parametrically modulated value per trial, for example RT, SPM first creates the unmodulated regressor and next creates a regressor where each trial is modulated by the reaction time. In this case the modulated regressor is automatically orthogonalized with respect to the unmodulated regressor. As discussed above, this is an appropriate use of orthogonalization for improving the interpretation of the unmodulated regressor.

As described in the previous section (second row, Fig 3) both RT and stimulus intensity should be orthogonalized with respect to the unmodulated regressor to improve the interpretation of the unmodulated regressor. Instead, SPM (up to version 8) orthogonalizes each regressor with respect to the ones preceding it; thus, the results will vary depending upon the order in which the regressors are specified in the model. If the RT modulations are entered prior to the intensity modulations, RT is orthogonalized with respect to the unmodulated regressor and stimulus intensity is orthogonalized with respect to the unmodulated regressor and RT. As shown in the third row of Fig 3, RT is no longer adjusted for stimulus intensity. Since RT was given the shared descriptive variability (the yellow portion) it is likely that the p-value for RT in the 3rd row will be smaller than that of the correct model in the second row. This paired with the incorrect interpretation that the inference applies to RT adjusted for stimulus intensity can yield misleading results in publications. Likewise, if stimulus intensity is entered first, followed by RT, the intensity effect is no longer adjusted for RT (last row, Fig 3).

The solution to this problem is to circumvent the automated procedure. One possibility would be to run 2 models, one where RT was the second modulation entered and one where stimulus intensity amount was the second modulation, in order to obtain the appropriate statistics for the adjusted RT and stimulus intensity effects, respectively. Another solution is to create modulated regressors outside of the GUI and enter them as user-specific regressors in the SPM analysis. If using SPM12, there is now an option to orthogonalize within the graphical user interface.

One other instance in which orthogonalization is automatic in SPM is when derivatives of regressors are added to a model. This is typically done in an effort to adjust for minor misspecifications in the stimulus timing. In SPM the regressor corresponding to the first derivative of the regressor is orthogonalized with respect to the original regressor. As illustrated in [2], this can have a beneficial impact on the overall model fit and the estimate of the original regressor, which is typically the regressor of interest.

FSL.

The FSL package does not perform automatic orthogonalization, but it does allow for user-specified orthogonalization. It is up to the user to properly orthogonalize regressors when necessary. To do so, a button marked "Orthogonalise" would be clicked and then the regressors to orthogonalize with respect to would be checked. Note, the regressor for which "Orthogonalise" is selected is giving up its shared variability to the other checked regressor(s). The parameter estimates and inferences for the orthogonalized regressor will remain exactly the same while the regressors corresponding to the boxes that are checked in the GUI will change if they are correlated. Care must be taken in interpreting any regressor to which another has been orthogonalized, as it is no longer adjusted. For example, if the motion parameters are orthogonalized with respect to task, the task effect is no longer adjusted for motion, which can lead to inflated effect sizes due to artifact in the data if the convolved task is correlated with motion.

Of note, it is common practice to mean center the modulation values in the behavioral onset file that is fed into an FSL analysis and this will remove collinearity between the parametrically modulated regressor and the constant duration regressor. In this case, orthogonalization is not necessary. It is most commonly used in first level models where the duration of a trial varies across trials.

Similar to SPM, FSL also allows for the modeling of temporal derivatives of regressors to account for minor timing misspecifications. FSL uses a slightly different orthgonalization strategy where the derivative is orthogonalized with respect to both the original regressor and the overall mean. As shown in [2], this approach may still be beneficial in improving the estimate for the regressor of interest, the original regressor, but not as beneficial as only orthogonalizing with respect to the original regressor, as done in SPM.

AFNI.

The AFNI package does not appear to have specific tools for orthogonalization. It does include a tool (xmat_tool.py) that can display the correlation matrix for the model regressors.

Avoiding Collinearity

Collinearity in a study design can be avoided if, during the study planning phase, efficiency calculations are be used to identify the most efficient design and reduce any collinearity issues. Efficiency calculations can be used to compute a numeric value associated with the unique descriptive variability associated with each parameter estimate, as shown in the Venn diagrams above. Specifically, the efficiency for a specific contrast of parameters, say if the alternative hypothesis is whether $c\beta > 0$, for some contrast row-vector, c, the efficiency is given by

$$\text{eff}(c\beta) = 1/c(X'X)^{-1}c' \qquad (3)$$

[3]. For simplicity, assume there are only two regressors in the model, x_1 and x_2 with corresponding regression parameters β_1 and β_2 where the interest is maximizing the efficiency for β_1. Assuming the regressors are mean centered, it can be shown that the efficiency for β_1 is

$$\text{eff}(\beta_1) = (N-1)\text{Var}(x_1)(1 - cor^2(x_1, x_2)), \qquad (4)$$

where N is the number of observations. This equation illustrates that if the variance of x_1 is fixed, when the correlation between x_1 and x_2 increases, the efficiency decreases. This relationship is illustrated by the green line in Fig 4 of efficiency as a function of correlation Since a typical efficiency calculation fixes the number of trials, but simply randomizes trial order until the most efficient design is found, the variance for x_1 and x_2 will be fixed across all candidate designs, implying the most efficient design that is identified will be the design with the lowest correlation between x_1 and x_2. Also of interest may be the sum or difference of parameter and the red and blue lines in Fig 4 illustrate that these contrasts of parameter estimates are also negatively impacted by collinearity between the explanatory variables.

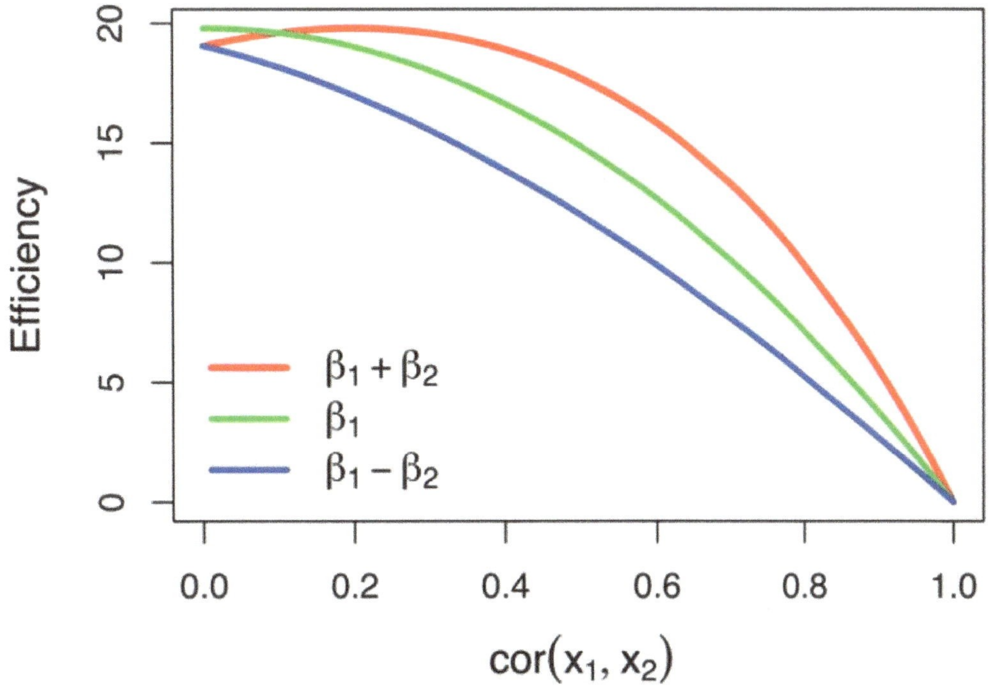

Figure 4. Efficiency as a function of correlation between two regressors for a single parameter (green), the sum of parameters (red) and their difference (blue). As collinearity increases, the efficiencies of all three of these contrasts of parameter estimates diminishes.

To reduce collinearity and increase efficiency the ISI can be increased. Varying the ISI (e.g., randomly drawing from a distribution such as the truncated exponential) will also help reduce collinearity between adjacent trials, as in the stimulus/feedback cue model discussed earlier. There will often be a slight tradeoff in obtaining a design with low collinearity while staying within a reasonable range of ISIs for psychological criteria to be met. For example, if a stimulus and feedback are very close, the separate BOLD signals cannot be determined, but if they are separated by a large ISI, this may impede learning. Given this information, it is also helpful if any behavioral studies run prior to the imaging portion of the study also take these stimulus timing issues into consideration in order to keep the initial behavioral results consistent with what will occur in the scanner. Even though these collinearity issues are not a problem in a strictly behavioral analysis, if behavior effects are diminished after optimizing a behavioral study for the scanner, the fMRI effects may also diminish.

Although efficiency can be used to find the best design within a subset of possible designs, the measure alone does not indicate the degree of collinearity. If the parameters set for the model search only include highly collinear designs, the search will find a most efficient design, but it is not guaranteed to be free of collinearity. In addition to traditional efficiency calculations, the variance inflation factor (VIF) can be used to study collinearity directly. The VIF for a regressor X_i is defined by $VIF_i=1/(1-R^2_i)$, where R^2_i is the R^2 from the model where the regressor of interest is modeled as a function of all other regressors ($X_i = \beta_1 X_1+\ldots+\beta_{i-1} X_{i-1}+\beta_{i+1} X_{i+1}+\ldots+\beta_N X_N+\epsilon$) (wikipedia.org/wiki/Variance_inflation_factor). If the R^2 value is high, the VIF will also be high, indicating the regressor of interest is a linear combination of the other regressors and a collinearity problem is present. Typically a cutoff of 5 or 10 is used as a threshold for problematic collinearity. This rule of thumb however is criticized by [4] who note that the VIF should be considered in the context of group sizes. In practice, it would be useful to record efficiency as well as VIF for the candidate designs in order to maximize efficiency while guaranteeing a low level of collinearity. In addition, if the study has already been carried out, the VIF can help assess the degree of the collinearity.

Impact of Collinearity on Inferences

Collinearity can be problematic when interpreting model results, and a common misunderstanding in fMRI analysis is that collinearity fully ruins any ability to interpret the results. In all cases of collinearity inferences are valid, meaning the type I error rate is controlled. The primary worry is that the highly variable parameter estimates may be much larger or smaller than the true magnitude, but when collinearity causes this to occur in the model the estimated variance is also large. Thus, although the parameter estimates are highly variable, they are unbiased and Type 1 error rate is preserved, so inferences remain valid in the presence of collinearity [5]. This means if multiple estimates from independent studies (or subjects) are averaged, the mean will converge on the true value. Most fMRI analysis software packages use a multistage approach to analyze data, otherwise known as the summary statistics approach to the mixed model [6, 7]. The first stage of analysis involves analyzing each run of data independently and, assuming there is a single run per subject, the second stage combines first level estimates in a group model. The impact of collinearity depends on what stage of modeling the collinearity occurred (single subject or in group model). If the collinearity occurs in the first level, say if two explanatory variables for two trial types are correlated and the interest is in the effect of the first trial type, the individual subject parameter estimates will be highly variable, but when averaged at the group level the estimates that are too large tend to balance out with those that are too small to arrive at an estimate that is closer to the true mean estimate. On the other hand, collinearity between age and gender would occur in the group model and in this case the parameter estimate with, say, age may be much larger or smaller than the true effect such that if the magnitude of the effect is of great interest, care should be taken in interpreting it. The confidence interval associated with the estimate will reflect the wide range of parameter values that are consistent with the data, so if a region of interest analysis is performed this should be included as well. Note that this would also be the case in analyses, such as VBM (voxel based morphometry), where there is only one stage in the analysis analyzing relationships between brain measures and sets of covariates that tend to be highly correlated. The inferences are valid, but in the presence of collinearity, the parameter estimates will be highly variable.

CONCLUSIONS AND DISCUSSION

Even the best planned studies can result in models with collinear regressors. Although the use of orthogonalization may be a tempting way to remove collinearity from the model, it does not change the overall fit of the model and in most cases it confuses the interpretation of the resulting inferences. When applying orthogonalization, if automated by data analysis software or manually done by a user, it is important to understand the impact this has on the inferences associated with that model when reporting results. Orthogonalization should only be used to improve the interpretation of regressors, such as in the case of mean centering a continuous covariate so that the mean regressor is interpreted as the overall mean.

AUTHOR CONTRIBUTIONS

Conceived and designed the experiments: JM RP JP. Performed the experiments: JM. Wrote the paper: JM RP JP.

REFERENCES

1. Poline JB, Kherif F, Pallier C, Penny W (2007) Contrasts and classical inference. elsevier: Amsterdam. In: Friston K, Ashburner J, Kiebel S, Nichols T, Penny W, editors, Statistical parametric mapping: the analysis of functional brain images., Amsterdam: Elsevier. pp. 126–139.
2. Pernet CR (2014) Misconceptions in the use of the General Linear Model applied to functional MRI: a tutorial for junior neuro-imagers. Front Neurosci 8: 1. doi: 10.3389/fnins.2014.00001. pmid:24478622
3. Dale AM (1999) Optimal experimental design for event-related fMRI. Hum Brain Mapp 8: 109–114. doi: 10.1002/(SICI)1097-0193(1999)8:2/3%3C109::AID-HBM7%3E3.3.CO;2-N. pmid:10524601
4. Obrien RM (2007) A caution regarding rules of thumb for variance inflation factors. Quality & Quantity 41: 673–690. doi: 10.1007/s11135-006-9018-6.
5. Neter J, Kutner M, Nachtsheim C, Wasserman W (1996) Applied Linear Statistical Models. WCB McGraw-Hill.
6. Holmes A, Friston K (1998) Generalisability, random effects and populations inference. Fourth international conference on functional mapping of the human brain, NeuroImage 7: S754.
7. Mumford JA, Nichols T (2006) Modeling and inference of multisubject fMRI data. IEEE Eng Med Biol Mag 25: 42–51. doi: 10.1109/MEMB.2006.1607668. pmid:16568936

CHAPTER 7

BEYOND SELF-REPORT: TOOLS TO COMPARE ESTIMATED AND REAL-WORLD SMARTPHONE USE

Sally Andrews[1], David A. Ellis[2,3], Heather Shaw[3], Lukasz Piwek[4]

[1] Division of Psychology, Nottingham Trent University, Nottingham, United Kingdom

[2] Department of Psychology, Lancaster University, Lancaster, United Kingdom

[3] School of Psychology, University of Lincoln, Lincoln, United Kingdom

[4] Faculty of Business and Law, University of the West of England, Bristol, United Kingdom

ABSTRACT

Psychologists typically rely on self-report data when quantifying mobile phone usage, despite little evidence of its validity. In this paper we explore the accuracy of using self-reported estimates when compared with actual smartphone use. We also include source code to process and visualize these data. We compared 23 participants' actual smartphone use over a two-week period with self-reported estimates and the Mobile Phone Problem Use Scale. Our results indicate that estimated time spent using a smartphone may be an adequate measure of use, unless a greater resolution of data are required. Estimates concerning the number of times an individual used their phone across a typical day did not correlate with actual smartphone use. Neither estimated duration nor number of uses correlated with the Mobile Phone Problem Use Scale. We conclude that estimated smartphone use should be interpreted with caution in psychological research.

INTRODUCTION

Around 2 billion people use smartphones across the globe, with over half the population in developed countries relying on them daily [1]. This ubiquity means that there is the potential for objective smartphone data to be used to address research questions in the real world [2]. Indeed, there has been a rapid increase in the number of publications examining the relationship between smartphone use, personality, cognition, health, and behavior e.g. [3–8]. Despite this, smartphones themselves have yet to become a standard item in the psychologist's research toolbox, and little is known about the validity of self-reported estimates of smartphone use.

Miller recently [9] highlighted how important it is for social science researchers to be current with new developments in smartphone research methods. Perhaps the biggest barrier to exploring the objective (actual) use of smartphone data includes developing suitable apps and the appropriate tools for processing, analyzing and visualizing big-data sets [10]. Whereas open source software to create *Android* apps is freely available for those with no programming experience [11], there remains no open source software for analyzing and visualizing the resulting data.

While self-report data can be collected successfully in situations where it is difficult to obtain objective data, this may not be an appropriate measure when it comes to

Citation: Andrews S, Ellis DA, Shaw H, Piwek L (2015) Beyond Self-Report: Tools to Compare Estimated and Real-World Smartphone Use. PLoS ONE 10(10): e0139004. doi:10.1371/journal.pone.0139004.

estimating smartphone use. It remains possible that estimates are sufficient for some research questions. but much of the cognitive literature on time-perception suggests we are poor at estimating such durations [12]. Any subjective estimate is also likely to ignore rapid, yet pervasive, checking behaviors [13].

Here we propose that a simple measure—recording when the phone is in use—can provide a vast array of information about an individual's daily routine. We describe and explore different metrics for objective evaluation of smartphone data, and what this can reveal about smartphone use. We include source code for processing, visualizing and analyzing objective smartphone data, which can be used by those with little to no programming knowledge. As an applied example, we then explore the claim that people engage in habitual smartphone checking behaviors, by correlating self-report smartphone use estimates with actual smartphone use and standardized measures of problem mobile phone use [14]. We finally consider other research questions that could be explored with this methodology.

METHOD

Participants

Twenty-nine participants were recruited (17 female, mean age = 22.52, range = 18–33). All participants owned *Android* smartphones and consisted of staff and students at the University of Lincoln. A priori calculations suggest this number to be adequate for finding a moderate correlation between actual and self-reported use, so we stopped collecting after this number was reached. The study conformed to the recommendations of the Declaration of Helsinki. All participants provided written and oral informed consent after being advised of the purpose of the study, and the type of data being collected. Approval for the project was obtained from the School of Psychology Research Ethics Committee at the University of Lincoln. All participants were reimbursed a small fee (£10) for their time. Two participants were excluded as they had technological problems partway through the study, while four additional participants were excluded from the analysis for not providing all self-report estimates.

Materials

Smartphone Application: We developed an *Android* smartphone app using *Funf in a Box* [11]. Apps collecting data from *Android* devices are generated by selecting sensors, and specifying sampling frequency. We selected the screen on/off option, resulting in a small app that records a timestamp when a use starts and ends. Data is encrypted and uploaded to a server over Wi-Fi (for more details see [11]). Our app simply recorded a timestamp when the phone became active, and a second when this interaction ended (typically screen use, although this also includes processor intensive activities including calls and playing music).

Mobile Phone Problem Use Scale (MPPUS): This questionnaire consists of 27 items, which have previously demonstrated positive correlations with self-reported mobile phone use [14]. The MPPUS remains a highly cited scale across health and psychological research [15–19], and has been used as an additional means of measuring mobile phone use more generally [6,20, 21]) (Cronbach's alpha = .89 for standardised items in our sample).

Procedure

On arrival at the lab, a smartphone application was installed on participants' smartphones. They were then sent a standardized SMS that they were asked to relay back to the experimenter, to determine the length of time taken to check a message. Time taken was recorded from the notification tone until the message had been relayed. Participants were asked to record an estimate each evening of how long they used their phone that day, for the next 14 consecutive days. We asked participants to only estimate their phone use during periods where their phone screen was switched on, as the *Funf* on-off sensor was advertised as measuring screen state. However, during testing, it was discovered that the on-off sensor actually measured whether the phone was in an interactive state, which included activities such as phone calls and listening to music, commonly done with the screen switched off. While we did not analyze the diary data further, it is possible that the process influenced participants' later estimations of their phone use. When participants returned to the lab after 14 days, they were asked to estimate how much they used their phone on average each day (including calls and listening to music). This measure was used in subsequent analyses of subjective estimates. They were then asked to estimate how many times they use their phone each day (number of uses), and finally were asked to complete the MPPUS. The app was then uninstalled from their device.

Data from the app were converted into a comma separate values file using *Funf* processing scripts. This file was further processed using source code to calculate descriptive statistics and barcode visualizations (as shown in Fig 1). The scripts allow the user to explore different times of day (morning, afternoon, evening, and night), and to explore different metrics associated with checking behaviors of different durations (N.B. the source code requires Matlab 2014b or later). These can be calculated separately for each day, or across the entire duration of a study. We use descriptive statistics for the first 14 days of the study throughout. Some timestamps showed very long single use durations (i.e. > 5 hours). Another limitation to the application is that when the phone switches off, the app does not record the screen turning off. When the phone is turned on again, it also does not record the screen turning on. This results in a seemingly long 'on' duration, when the phone itself was actually turned off. It was therefore unclear whether long durations during the day were as a result of the phone being in use (e.g. listening to music, or watching a film), or whether the phone was turned off. As it is impossible to be sure that all long durations were because of this, we retain these data in all analyses, and use median values when calculating an average values for each day, as this is a more accurate summary of the average use length. We then use these values to calculate the mean use length for each participant. We established that occasions when this occurred overnight were the result of the phone being turned off. The included source code (S1 Appendix) enables the visualization of the data for each participant across all days, or to create an 'average heatmap' of one day, seven days, or weekdays and weekends (not shown here).

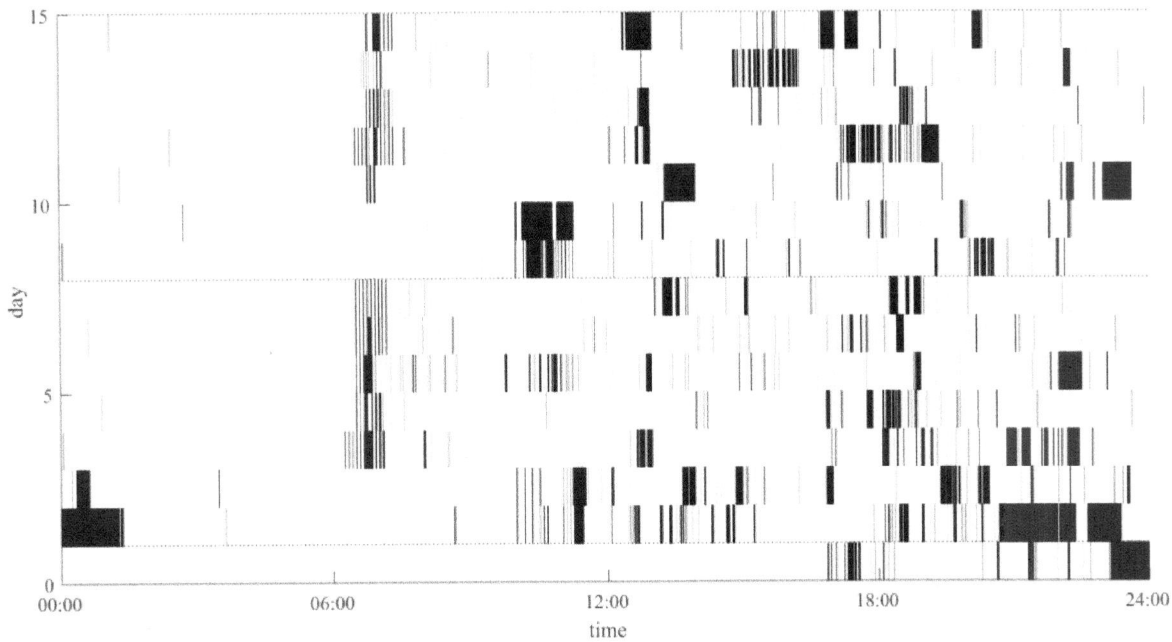

Figure 1. Barcode of smartphone use over two weeks. Black areas indicate times where the phone was in use and Saturdays are indicated with a red dashed line. Weekday alarm clock times (and snoozing) are clearly evident.

RESULTS

Objective Data

The mean daily number of uses and the mean length of these durations (including a median length for all the durations in a day) and a mean daily duration of phone use (total daily duration) were calculated for each participant. Participants used their phones a mean of 84.68 times each day (SD = 55.23) and spent 5.05 hours each day using their smartphone (SD = 2.73). Length of use was, unsurprisingly, highly skewed, with 55% of all uses less than 30 seconds in duration (see Fig 2).

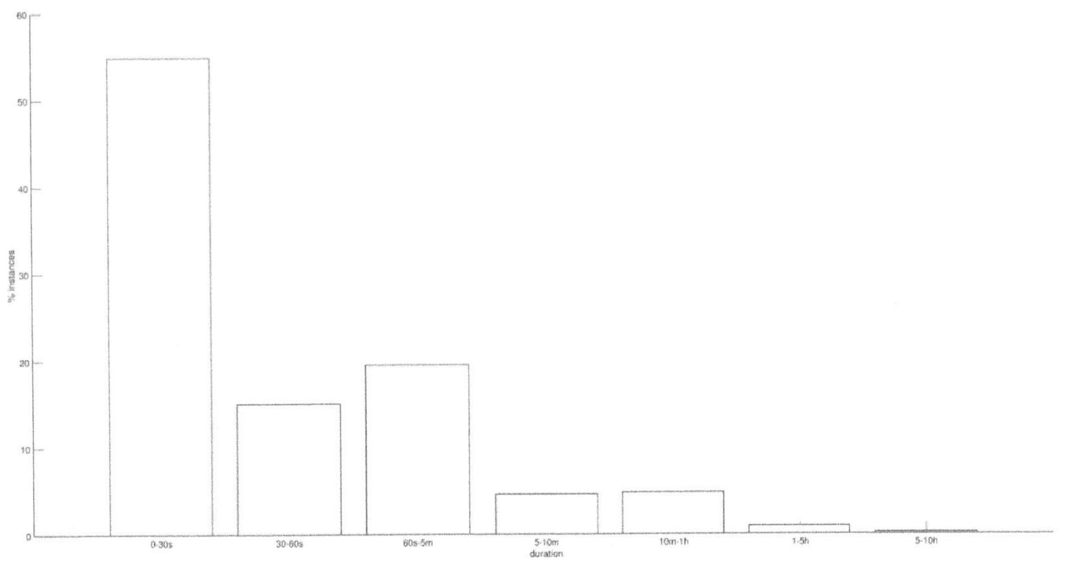

Figure 2. Percentage of uses categorized by duration. This illustrates the highly skewed nature of smartphone usage.

We classify 'checks' as uses up to 15 seconds in duration. To explore these behaviors more closely, we analyzed the percentage of phone interactions with durations under 15 seconds. These showed three distinct periods of increased use; from 1-3s, 5-6s, and 10–11 seconds. Fig 3 shows a histogram of such checks (in 0.5 second bins). In the lab, mean time taken to unlock the phone and read a short message was 8.42s (SD = 1.53). With added distractions outside the lab, the 10-11s time bin is likely to reflect the time taken to read a short message, check the time or other notifications. We explored whether any of these durations could result from the display turning itself off, after a period of being idle. However, results indicated that these default times did not explain any spike in use (default display off times: $mean_{LOCKED} = 274.88s$, $SD_{LOCKED} = 842.85s$; $mean_{UNLOCKED} = 282.06s$, $SD_{UNLOCKED} = 524.33s$).

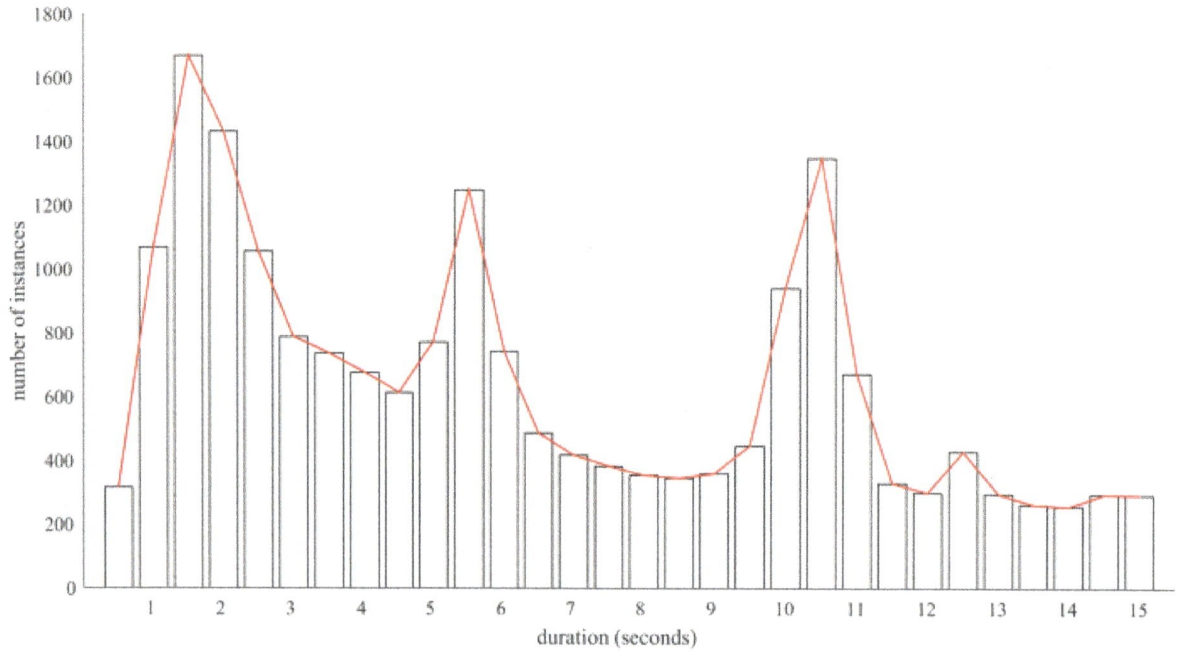

Figure 3. Number of checks in 0.5 second bins across all participants over a 15 second period. Three spikes of checking duration are visible.

We also compared phone use at different times of day; night (00:00–06:00), morning (06:00–12:00), afternoon (12:00–18:00), and evening (18:00–24:00), as shown in Fig 4. In this comparison we calculate median duration length—i.e. the median amount of time a user engaged with their phone before turning the display off—for each participant. Finally, we explored the total duration spent using the phone at each time of day. For the purposes of this analysis, phone uses that spanned two time windows (e.g. commencing in the morning and ending in the afternoon) was allocated to the time period in which it originated.

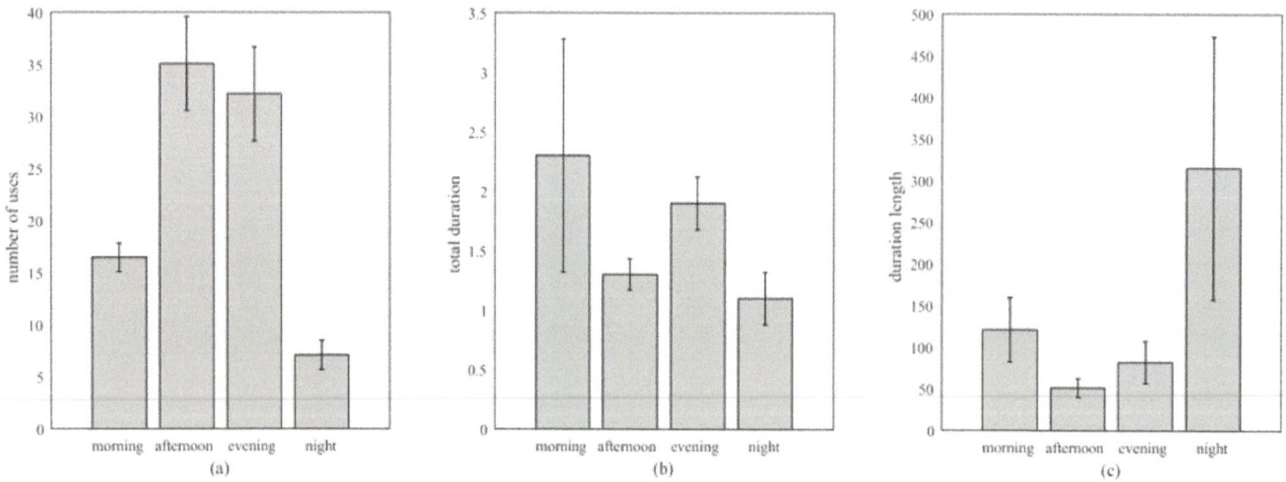

Figure 4. Participants' mean number of phone uses (a), mean total duration (b), and mean duration length (c) at different times of day. Error bars show 1 SE from the mean.

Three one-way repeated measures ANOVAs (Time of Day; morning, afternoon, evening, night) were calculated separately for total daily duration, use length, and number of uses. Data from one participant was removed from total daily duration and median use length analyses, as they had no data from the night time period. There was a significant difference in the number of phone uses at different times of day (F(3, 78) = 34.62, $p < .001$, $\eta_p^2 = .571$). Tukey's LSD comparisons revealed more individual uses in the afternoon and evening than in the morning and at night (all $ps < .001$), that there were more uses in the morning than at night ($p < .001$), but that there were no differences in the number of uses between afternoon and evening ($p = .083$). Fig 4a shows these differences. There were no significant differences in total daily duration at different times of day (F(3, 78) = .94, $p = .414$, $\eta_p^2 = .036$; see Fig 4b, nor in median use length (F(3, 78) = 2.33, $p = .081$, $\eta_p^2 = .082$; see Fig 4c).

Comparison of Objective and Subjective Measures of Smartphone Use

We conducted paired-samples t-tests and Pearson correlations to compare actual and estimated smartphone use (see Table 1). For number of phone uses, there were far more actual phone uses (84.68) than were estimated (37.20; t(23) = 3.93, $p <$ .001), and no significant correlation between the two (r(21)

= .11, p = .610) indicating that estimated number of phone uses does not reflect actual number of uses. For total daily duration there was no significant difference between actual (5.05 hours) and estimated use (4.12 hours; $t(22) = 1.78, p = .086$) and there was a moderate positive correlation between the two (p = .02). This suggests that estimated duration of use may have reasonable relative validity.

Table 1. Correlation matrix of MPPUS scores, and actual and estimated smartphone use

	Estimated uses	Actual uses	Estimated duration	Actual duration
Actual uses	0.11			
Estimated duration	0.02	-0.03		
Actual duration	0.23	0.12	0.47[a]	
MPPUS	0.03	0.29	0.17	0.30

[a] p = .02

doi:10.1371/journal.pone.0139004.t001

We finally compared scores on the MPPUS with objective and estimated smartphone use and checks using Pearson's correlations (see Table 1). None of these analyses revealed any significant relationships ($ps > .15$). Ten participants scored more than 2SD greater than Bianchi & Phillips' [14] mean, indicating problem use.

DISCUSSION

Estimated levels of smartphone use have previously been related to sleep, interpersonal relationships, driving safety, and personality [5, 7, 22, 23]. Here we observe that self-reported estimates of phone use relate moderately to actual behavior in such situations. Conversely, estimated number of checks showed no clear relationship with actual uses; indeed, actual uses amounted to more than double the estimated number. It is possible that our limited sample size obscured a larger effect size. Nevertheless, we suggest that estimated use may not be sufficient if a higher resolution of data are required, but that estimates of total use are likely to be adequate for many research designs. However, for exploring checking behaviors, estimated number of uses show little reliability for measuring actual uses.

The quantity of short checking behaviors we observed are comparable with those found by Oulasvirta and colleagues [24], who collected data in 2009. Smartphone use has become much more prevalent in the intervening six years, and it would be easy to assume that smartphone use would increase accordingly. However, our data indicate that checking behaviors are no more prevalent now than they were six years ago. It is interesting to note that people have little awareness of the frequency with which they check their phone. Oulasvirta and colleagues made this claim in 2012, however this is the first paper to demonstrate that rapid mobile phone interactions are habitual [25]. While phone interactions under thirty seconds have previously been classified as 'checking behaviors', our data suggest that habitual goal-and reward-based actions are likely to be less than 15 seconds in duration when it comes to checking the time or message notifications.

In our study, the MPPUS did not correlate with any measure of phone use—actual or estimated. The MPPUS is used not only as a measure of problem phone use, but also as an additional measure of phone use more generally. To determine validity of the MPPUS for this purpose, we correlated objective phone use with MPPUS scores. This is not to say that the MPPUS lacks validity, but rather that people use smartphones for a variety of reasons [26], and that increased use does not necessitate a problem in itself [27]. It may seem reasonable to assume that those who spend a long time on their phone have problem mobile phone use. However, heavy users are not necessarily the same as problem users. While it is easy to conflate heavy use with problem use, research into smartphone use should identify heavy use and problem use independently of one another (e.g. [8]).

Examining how much people actually use their smartphone can be useful for a variety of applications. For example, all except one of our participants used their phone as an alarm clock, and most reported that they always use their phone last thing before sleeping. These usage patterns therefore provide a non-invasive indication of sleep length, which has the potential to augment sleep diary data [28]. Furthermore, while we have considered usage patterns across the day, a further extension to this analysis would be to consider how these patterns across different days of the week. This is likely to have additional social and occupational consequences [29].

Trull and Ebner-Priemer [9] and Miller [10] argue that smartphone data have a great deal to offer as a research tool in psychology, yet comparatively little research utilizes objective smartphone data. Here we show that estimates of smartphone use have a place within current research, but we caution that its validity is limited and should be complimented by measurements of real behavior. We also provide the first method to automatically sample and easily visualize the frequency of smartphone use with a simple background app. We hope that methods described in this paper will help overcome some barriers to accessing smartphone data for research in psychology and that it will form a foundation to build upon in the coming years.

AUTHOR CONTRIBUTIONS

Conceived and designed the experiments: SA HS DAE. Performed the experiments: HS. Analyzed the data: SA. Contributed reagents/materials/analysis tools: SA. Wrote the paper: SA DAE HS LP.

REFERENCES

1. McIlroy T. Planet of the phones. The Economist. 2015. Available:http://www.economist.com/news/leaders/21645180-smartphone-ubiquitous-addictive-and-transformative-planet-phones

2. MacKerron G, Mourato S. Happiness is greater in natural environments. Global Environmental Change. 2013;23(5): 992–1000. doi: 10.1016/j.gloenvcha.2013.03.010

3. Clayton R, Leshner G, Almond A. The Extended iSelf: The Impact of iPhone Separation on Cognition, Emotion, and Physiology. J Comput-Mediat Comm. 2015;20(2): 119–135. doi: 10.1111/jcc4.12109

4. Dolev-Cohen M, Barak A. Adolescents' use of Instant Messaging as a means of emotional relief. Computers in Human Behavior. 2013;29(1): 58–63. doi: 10.1016/j.chb.2012.07.016

5. Feldman G, Greeson J, Renna M, Robbins-Monteith K. Mindfulness predicts less texting while driving among young adults: Examining attention- and emotion-regulation motives as potential mediators. Personality and Individual Differences. 2011;51(7): 856–861. pmid:22031789 doi: 10.1016/j.paid.2011.07.020

6. Walsh S, White K, Young R. Over-connected? A qualitative exploration of the relationship between Australian youth and their mobile phones. Journal of Adolescence. 2008;31(1): 77–92. pmid:17560644 doi: 10.1016/j.adolescence.2007.04.004

7. Walsh S, White K, Young RMcD. Needing to connect: The effect of self and others on young people's involvement with their mobile phones. Aus J of Psych. 2010;62(4): 194–203. doi: 10.1080/00049530903567229

8. White A, Buboltz W, Igou F. Mobile phone use and sleep quality and length in college students. International Journal of Humanities and Social Science. 2011;1(18): 51–58.

9. Miller G. The Smartphone Psychology Manifesto. Perspectives on Psychological Science. 2012;7(3): 221–237. doi: 10.1177/1745691612441215. pmid:26168460

10. Trull T, Ebner-Priemer U. The Role of Ambulatory Assessment in Psychological Science. Current Directions in Psychological Science. 2014;23(6): 466–470. pmid:25530686 doi: 10.1177/0963721414550706

11. Aharony N, Pan W, Ip C, Khayal I, Pentland A. Social fMRI: Investigating and shaping social mechanisms in the real world. Pervasive and Mobile Computing. 2011;7(6): 643–659. doi: 10.1016/j.pmcj.2011.09.004

12. Grondin S. Timing and time perception: A review of recent behavioral and neuroscience findings and theoretical directions. Attention, Perception, & Psychophysics. 2010;72(3): 561–582. doi: 10.3758/app.72.3.561

13. Rachman S. A cognitive theory of compulsive checking. Behavior Research and Therapy. 2002;40(6): 625–639. pmid:12051482 doi: 10.1016/s0005-7967(01)00028-6

14. Bianchi A, Phillips J. Psychological Predictors of Problem Mobile Phone Use. CyberPsychology & Behavior. 2005;8(1): 39–51. doi: 10.1089/cpb.2005.8.39

15. Hadlington LJ. Cognitive failures in daily life: Exploring the link with Internet addiction and problematic mobile phone use. Computers in Human Behavior. 2015;51: 75–81. doi: 10.1016/j.chb.2015.04.036

16. Leung L. Linking psychological attributes to addiction and improper use of the mobile phone among adolescents in Hong Kong. Journal of Children and Media. 2008;2(2): 93–113. doi: 10.1080/17482790802078565

17. Lin TTC, Chiang Y, Jiang C. Sociable people beware? Investigating smartphone vs non-smartphone dependency symptoms among young Singaporeans. Social Behavior and Personality. 2015;43 (7): 1209–1216. doi: 10.2224/sbp.2015.43.7.1209

18. Öz F, Arslantaş D, Buğrul N, Koyuncu T, Ünsal A. Evaluation of problematic use of mobile phones and quality of sleep among high school students. International Journal of Human Sciences. 2015;12(1): 226–235. doi: 10.14687/ijhs.v12i1.3122

19. Takao M, Takahashi S, and Kitamura M. Addictive personality and problematic mobile phone use. CyberPsychology & Behavior 12.5 (2009): 501–507. doi: 10.1089/cpb.2009.0022

20. Kalhori SM, Mohammadi MR, Alavi SS, Jannatifard F, Sepahbodi G, Reisi MB, et al. Validation and Psychometric Properties of Mobile Phone Problematic Use Scale (MPPUS) in University Students of Tehran. Iranian Journal of Psychiatry. 2015;10(1): 25–31. pmid:26005477

21. Lopez-Fernandez O, Honrubia-Serrans ML, Freixa-Blanxart M. Adapting the Mobile Phone Problem Use Scale for the Mobile Phone Problem Use Scale for adolescents: The English Version. Personality and Individual Differences. 2014;60: S24–S47. doi: 10.1016/j.paid.2013.07.024

22. Butt S, Phillips J. Personality and self reported mobile phone use. Computers in Human Behavior. 2008;24(2): 346–360. doi: 10.1016/j.chb.2007.01.019

23. Ehrenberg A, Juckes S, White K, Walsh S. Personality and Self-Esteem as Predictors of Young People›s Technology Use. CyberPsychology & Behavior. 2008;11(6):7 39–741. doi: 10.1089/cpb.2008.0030

24. Oulasvirta A, Rattenbury T, Ma L, Raita E. Habits make smartphone use more pervasive. Pers Ubiquit Comput. 2011;16(1): 105–114. doi: 10.1007/s00779-011-0412-2

25. Lally P, van Jaarsveld C, Potts H, Wardle J. How are habits formed: Modelling habit formation in the real world. Eur J Soc Psychol. 2009;40(6): 998–1009. doi: 10.1002/ejsp.674

26. Smith A. U.S. Smartphone Use in 2015. Pew Research Center: Internet, Science & Tech. 2015. Available: http://www.pewinternet.org/2015/04/01/us-smartphone-use-in-2015/

27. Billieux J. Problematic use of the mobile phone: a literature review and a pathways model. Current Psychiatry Reviews. 2012;8(4): 299–307. doi: 10.2174/157340012803520522

28. Vallières A, Moran C. Actigraphy in the assessment of insomnia. Journal of Sleep. 2003;26(7): 902–906. pmid:14655927

29. Ellis DA, Wiseman R, Jenkins R. Mental representations of weekdays. PLoS ONE. 2015;10(8): e0134555. doi: 10.1371/journal.pone.0134555. pmid:26288194

CHAPTER 8

GUIDOCK: USING DOCKER CONTAINERS WITH A COMMON GRAPHICS USER INTERFACE TO ADDRESS THE REPRODUCIBILITY OF RESEARCH

Ling-Hong Hung, Daniel Kristiyanto, Sung Bong Lee, Ka Yee Yeung

Institute of Technology, University of Washington, Tacoma, WA 98402, United States of America

ABSTRACT

Reproducibility is vital in science. For complex computational methods, it is often necessary, not just to recreate the code, but also the software and hardware environment to reproduce results. Virtual machines, and container software such as Docker, make it possible to reproduce the exact environment regardless of the underlying hardware and operating system. However, workflows that use Graphical User Interfaces (GUIs) remain difficult to replicate on different host systems as there is no high level graphical software layer common to all platforms. GUIdock allows for the facile distribution of a systems biology application along with its graphics environment. Complex graphics based workflows, ubiquitous in systems biology, can now be easily exported and reproduced on many different platforms. GUIdock uses Docker, an open source project that provides a container with only the absolutely necessary software dependencies and configures a common X Windows (X11) graphic interface on Linux, Macintosh and Windows platforms. As proof of concept, we present a Docker package that contains a Bioconductor application written in R and C++ called networkBMA for gene network inference. Our package also includes Cytoscape, a java-based platform with a graphical user interface for visualizing and analyzing gene networks, and the CyNetworkBMA app, a Cytoscape app that allows the use of networkBMA via the user-friendly Cytoscape interface.

Citation: Hung L-H, Kristiyanto D, Lee SB, Yeung KY (2016) GUIdock: Using Docker Containers with a Common Graphics User Interface to Address the Reproducibility of Research. PLoS ONE 11(4): e0152686. doi:10.1371/journal.pone.0152686

INTRODUCTION

Reproducibility is a vital feature in science [1, 2]. Recent articles in the June 26 issue of Science discussed how rarely published results can be reproduced across different disciplines [2, 3]. Nosek and colleagues proposed guidelines consisting of eight standards and three levels to promote transparency, openness and reproducibility in scientific publications [1]. These guidelines progress from level 0 to level 3 and become increasingly stringent for each standard (see "proposed standards and references" in the Supplementary Material of Nosek *et al.* [1] for details). Computational method development and data analyses have become integral to many disciplines, such as biomedical research. For data analyses and software implementations, level 2 of the Nosek *et al.* guidelines requires that the code must be posted to a trusted repository. In level 3, they propose the additional requirement that the reported analyzes be reproduced independently before publication.

These suggestions overlook the fact that modern biomedical workflows and pipelines consist of multiple applications and libraries, each with their own set of software dependencies. Hence, suites such as Bioconductor [4], BioPython [5], and BioPerl [6] where the user is assured that the dependencies for the components are properly installed have become increasingly popular. The obvious drawback to this approach is that one is limited to the components included in the suite. In addition, reproducing workflows that use interactive graphics remain problematic as each operating system uses their own graphical environment. Our solution to this problem is GUIdock, which allows for replication of the application, graphics and software environments that produced the analytic results reported in scientific publications.

GUIdock uses Docker https://www.docker.com/, an open source project that incorporates a light weight Linux wrapper (container) to ensure application portability and infrastructure flexibility. On a Linux host, Docker uses the host system. On Mac OS and Windows systems, a single Docker container consists of a Virtual Machine (VM) containing the guest software and its Linux environment. Containers differ from traditional VMs in that the resources of the operating system (OS) and not the hardware are shared transparently (virtualized). Multiple containers share a single OS kernel saving considerable resources. Docker also supports Dockerfiles that contain the instructions to build a Docker Image from scratch or another Docker Image. Images can be downloaded from repositories using git https://git-scm.com/ or bundled with the Dockerfile to form packages. Docker provides an easy, modular method to build, distribute and replicate complex pipelines and workflows across multiple platforms.

Although Docker provides a container with the original computational environment, the host system, where the container software is executed, is responsible for rendering graphics. GUIdock configures an additional X Windows software layer that allows for consistent graphics on a variety of host platforms. Thus a complex bioinformatics pipeline with GUI components originally running on a Linux machine can be replicated and tested on a Windows or Mac OS machine. This greatly facilitates the reproduction of scientific results arising from real-world workflows. Fig 1 shows an overview of GUIdock.

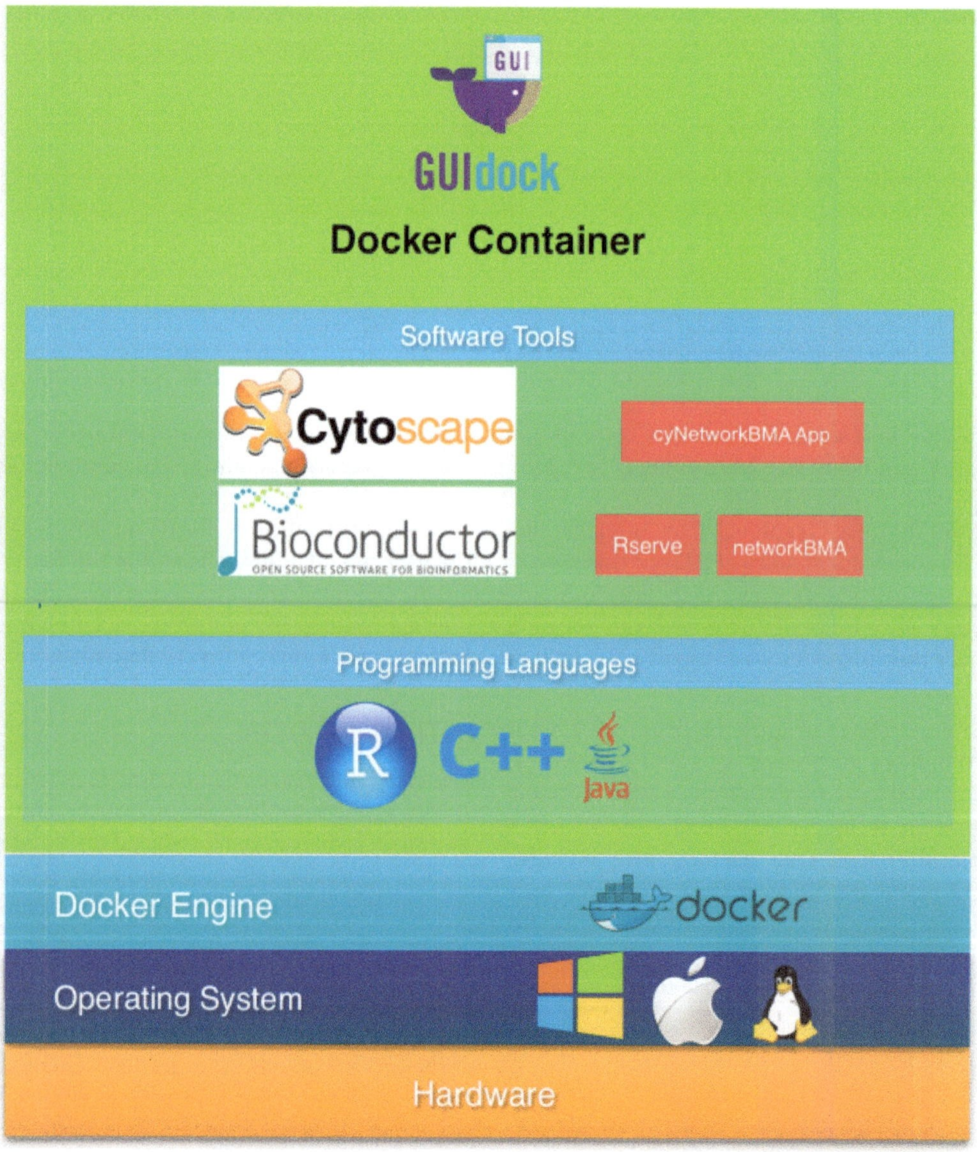

Figure 1. Overview of GUIdock.

Related Work

In this work, we showcase GUIdock, a method for deploying containers with a graphical user interface. As proof of concept, our GUIdock package includes our previously published software tools for gene network inference [7–11]. A gene network can be represented by a graph, in which nodes are genes and edges capture relationships between genes. There are many applications for these computationally derived gene networks, such as systems approaches to identify disease genes [12]. Therefore, many computational methods and software tools have been developed to infer gene networks from genome-wide data and subsequently to formulate hypotheses from these computationally derived networks. Excellent review articles have been written to cover these advances in methods and tools, for example, [12–14].

Inference of Gene Networks using Bayesian Model Averaging (BMA).

In regression-based network inference algorithms, we aim to search for candidate regulators (i.e. parent nodes) for each target gene. In other words, we model the target gene's expression levels as the response variable (y), and the candidate regulators' expression levels as independent variables ($x's$) in a regression framework. This problem is then reduced to a variable selection problem such that the goal is to identify variables (parent nodes) that can be used to predict the expression levels of the target gene. Many regression-based gene network inference methods have been developed, such as [15–17].

BMA is an ensemble method that accounts for model uncertainty by averaging over the predictions of multiple models [18, 19]. In the context of gene network inference, a model is a set of candidate regulators. We previously showed the effectiveness of using variants of BMA as multivariate variable selection methods in the context of time series gene expression data [7–9].

networkBMA.

We implemented these BMA network inference methods in R and C++. Our networkBMA package [10] is publicly available from the Bioconductor repositoryhttp://bioconductor.org/packages/release/bioc/html/networkBMA.html. The main functionnetworkBMA takes gene expression data as one of the input arguments, allows the specification of prior probabilities to guide the search of optimal parent nodes for each target gene, and outputs an edge list consisting of edges in the form of (parent, child, posterior probabilities) relationships. The user can also specify a posterior probability threshold to filter out edges below the given threshold.

In addition to gene network inference, the networkBMA package also features functions for the assessment of gene networks. Specifically, the contabs.netwBMA function compares the edges in the inferred network to a given set of known regulatory relationships using a contingency table approach, and the scores function computes assessment statistics corresponding to the contingency table, including sensitivity, precision, specificity, recall etc. There are also functions to plot and compute the area under the receiver operating characteristic (ROC) and precision recall (PR) curves.

Cytoscape.

Visualization and analyses of networks are integral to systems biology research. Cytoscape is a well-established Java-based stand-alone application for analyzing and visualizing networks [20–22]. Cytoscape offers a user-friendly graphical user interface (GUI) for visualizing a given network, and provides an app store at http://apps.cytoscape.org/ from which apps for various systems biology applications can be downloaded [23]. In addition, software developers can submit new apps to be made available from the Cytoscape App Store, such as [11, 24–26]. As an example, cyREST is a RESTful API module for Cytoscape [24], and the Ideker Lab has demonstrated the use of Cytoscape, cyREST and Docker in a meeting focused on visualizing biological data (VIZBI 2015 [27]).

CyNetworkBMA app.

CyNetworkBMA [11] is available on the Cytoscape App Store athttp://apps.cytoscape.org/apps/cynetworkbma. It is an easy-to-use tool that integrates our networkBMA Bioconductor package into Cytoscape, thus allowing the user to directly visualize the resulting gene networks using the Cytoscape utilities. In particular, CyNetworkBMA uses Rserve to integrate with R over a binary protocol on top of TCP/IP [28]. This means Cytoscape and R run in separate processes, potentially on different machines and platforms.

While the CyNetworkBMA app adds an easy-to-use graphical interface and visualization utilities to the BMA-based gene network inference methods implemented in the networkBMA Bioconductor package, there are many steps involved in installing CyNetworkBMA. In addition to Cytoscape and R, CyNetworkBMA depends on multiple R and Bioconductor packages, including networkBMA for network inference and assessment, igraph [29] for algorithms used in removing potential cycles from networks, and Rserve for exposing R services over TCP/IP.

Docker for bioinformatics applications.

Docker is an emerging platform that is gaining traction in the scientific community [30]. In particular, Rocker is a project containing pre-built Docker images and Dockerfiles to run R using Docker containers [31], and the Bioconductor project has deposited Docker Images in Docker Hub and source Dockerfiles in GitHub [32]. As another example, the BioDocker and BioBoxes project has a GitHub repositories for pre-configured containers with bioinformatics tools [33]. As of September 2015, there are about 15 containers in the BioDocker repository, and most of these containers are built for proteomics and mass spectrometry data analyses. In addition, the Genouest group in France has begun hosting a repository for Docker containers called Bioshadock [34]. Galaxy has an easy-to-use interface and provides a browser-based infrastructure for workflow management. Users can build a workflow in Galaxy and export the workflow to Docker [35, 36].

Our Contributions

Docker containers have largely been used for non-graphical applications. Containers have *not*been used to distribute the normal GUI based workflows that users are accustomed to.

This is due to the difference in high level APIs used for the different windowing environments by the major operating systems. GUIdock addresses this deficiency by configuring a common X11 windowing interface on Linux, Mac OS and Windows. A GUI workflow using X Windows can now be duplicated on most platforms.

We demonstrate the feasibility of using Docker for applications with a GUI, and hence containers that support software tools and data analytic pipelines with a graphical user interface. In particular, we illustrate the use of containers for systems biology applications, including Bioconductor packages written in R and C++, and Cytoscape, a stand-alone java-based application with a graphical user interface. The Docker package we present is a proof-of-concept example that containers can enhance the reproducibility of analytic results produced using applications with graphical interfaces. Our Docker image and Dockerfile are publicly available at https://github.com/WebDataScience/GUIdock.

Previous to GUIdock, the workaround when graphics interaction is required has been to distribute WebAPIs that provide a consistent GUI. An example is cyREST [24] which is also available as a Docker package. cyREST provides a RESTful API to Cytoscape and uses a jquery library (cytoscape.js) to render graphics on the different host systems. However, some knowledge of programming is needed to use the API and the result is dependent on the browser and operating system. In contrast, our GUIdock package exports the native Cytoscape GUI into a more consistent X Windows environment. A user simply double-clicks on an icon and the application pops up and is used exactly as it would be when run in its native environment. Fig 2 compares GUIdock to virtual machines and Fig 3 shows the software components added by GUIdock.

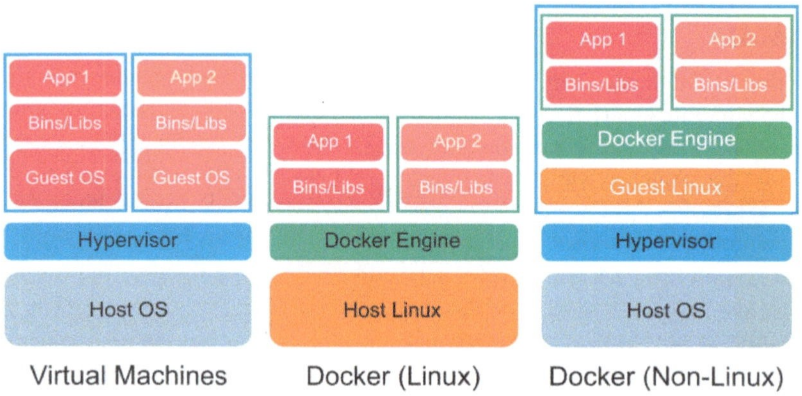

Figure 2. A comparison of the architecture of virtual machines and Docker software containers. Virtual machines are denoted by cyan boxes and software containers are denoted by green boxes. The left stack is a Type-2 virtual machine (VM) which uses a hypervisor to emulate the guest OS. The application software, dependences, and the guest OS are all contained inside the VM. A separate VM, dependencies and guest OS are required for each application stack that is to be deployed. The middle stack depicts Docker container software on a Linux host. Docker uses the host Linux system and packages the application and dependencies into modular containers. No VM is necessary and the OS resources for the two application stacks are shared between different containers. The right stack depicts Docker on a non-Linux system. Because Docker requires Linux, a lightweight VM with a mini-Linux Guest OS is necessary to run Docker and encapsulate the software containers. This still has the advantage that only a single VM and Guest Linux system is required regardless of the number of containers.

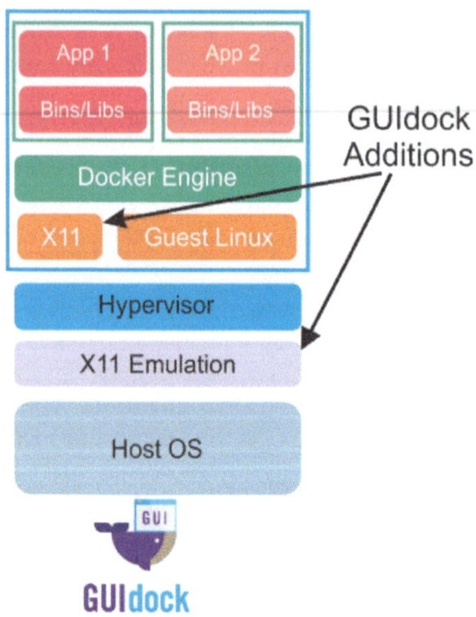

Figure 3. Software components added by GUIdock. Our GUIdock package ensures that the X11 libraries are present in the Linux OS that runs Docker. In the case of a Linux host, this is the host OS. For Windows and Mac OS, this is a guest OS inside a VM. An additional X Windows emulation layer is configured for Windows and Mac OS which allows for GUI commands to be exported from the container software and rendered on the host.

MATERIALS AND METHODS

A Docker container is essentially a barebones wrapper providing a Linux environment for a set of user applications. Linux distributions use X Windows (X11) as their native GUI. The challenge is to produce the same GUI on hosts that run other operating systems. The solution adopted by GUIdock is to pass the container X Windows commands to a host X Window emulator which renders the GUI. No additional software needs to be included within the container. Everything is done by scripts that are easily modified to install, configure and run any Dockerfile or Docker Image. GUIdock is a truly portable approach that is independent of the contents of the container. Fig 3 summarizes the relationship between various layers, including host operating system, Docker engine, X11 and software applications included in GUIdock.

Building the CyNetworkBMA GUIdock Package

Docker images are reproducible, and it is possible to build a new image from previously established image. Since we have chosen gene network inference as our proof-of-concept example, the Bioconductor Base Image is chosen as the starting point. This image contains R and basic Bioconductor packages. The Dockerfile starts with this image. We then added all the other tools needed to run the CyNetworkBMA app to our Docker image, including R Packages such as Rserve [28], igraph [29], BMA [37], Bioconductor package networkBMA [10], and additional software like java and Cytoscape. We also configured our Docker image to run Rserve in the background before launching Cytoscape.

CyNetworkBMA uses the Cytoscape GUI for user interaction. After the Docker package is created, additional steps are needed to forward the GUI information and render the graphics on the local host. These steps are dependent on the operating system that the local host is running and is automated by GUIdock.

GUIdock: on Linux Operating Systems

The simplest case is when containers are deployed on Linux systems which use X Windows natively. Since the containers use the same OS as the host, a virtual machine is unnecessary. Instead, the host OS and resources are used and only the necessary supporting libraries and binaries are included in the container. The guest software in the container can also export GUI information and let the host X Windows system render the GUI. These facilities are already provided by Docker. GUIdock uses a simple configurable bash script to automate the installation.

GUIdock: on Mac OS

Mac OS, like Linux, is a form of UNIX but differs sufficiently that the host OS is not used and a VM is required to encapsulate a guest Linux OS in the container. The creators of Docker have provided Docker machine which uses VirtualBox to create the necessary VM. However, the guest OS cannot directly export GUI commands to the host Mac OS as support for X Windows was dropped in OS X 10.8 (Mountain Lion). Therefore, we use XQuartz [38], an open source project, to provide X11 support on the host. We use socat [39] to bind XQuartz services to an open port and make XQuartz reachable by the Docker container. Socat is a command line based utility that establishes two bidirectional byte streams and transfers data between them. The DISPLAY environment variable in the Docker container is also set to the IP address of the local host running OS X. In this way, the internal X Windows commands are exported to XQuartz which renders the graphics on the host computer. GUIdock provides a set of bash scripts to automate the entire installation, configuration and run process.

GUIdock: on Microsoft Windows Operating Systems

The Microsoft Windows operating systems are very different from Linux and use several different proprietary APIs to implement their native GUI. The Windows version of Docker machine, using VirtualBox, provides a VM with Linux for the container. The current Docker toolbox also provides Kitematic, a GUI based manager to deploy containers but not for rendering the GUI from software within containers. We use a lightweight application, MobaXterm [40] for this purpose. Although MobaXterm is proprietary, a full-featured free version is available for download at http://mobaxterm.mobatek.net/download.html. MobaXterm, provides X Windows support and supports ssh (secure shell) tunneling. Ssh is a widely-used UNIX-based command interface and protocol for securely accessing a remote computer. Using MobaXterm, we set up X11 forwarding using ssh to connect the Docker container with a MobaXterm terminal. The GUI commands pass through the ssh tunnel to the MobaXterm X Windows emulator which renders the GUI on the host system. GUIdock provides a double-clickable script to initialize, configure the environment, and run the Docker container.

Availability and Requirements

- Project name: GUIdock
- Project home page: https://github.com/WebDataScience/GUIdock
- Contents available for download: Docker Images, Dockerfiles, installation scripts and execution scripts.
- Operating system(s): Linux, Mac OS X, Microsoft Windows. Specifically, we tested GUIdock on
  - Linux: Fedora, Ubuntu 15.04
  - Mac OS X: 10.9, 10.10
  - Microsoft Windows: 7, 8.1, 10
- Demo video (S1 Video): https://youtu.be/k1WkIx0EENo

RESULTS

We deployed the CyNetworkBMA GUIdock package and applied it to three different datasets of biological relevance: RNAseq data across human cancer cell lines [41], yeast time series gene expression data [7] and DREAM4 simulated time series data [42]. Note that our demos cover static (non-time series) RNAseq gene expression data in human, time series microarray data in a simple model organism (yeast), and simulated time series data.

We show that we get identical results after deploying the package on Linux, Mac OS and Windows. We added these test data and results to the GUIdock image. We encourage the readers to download our image and reproduce the results shown in Fig 4.

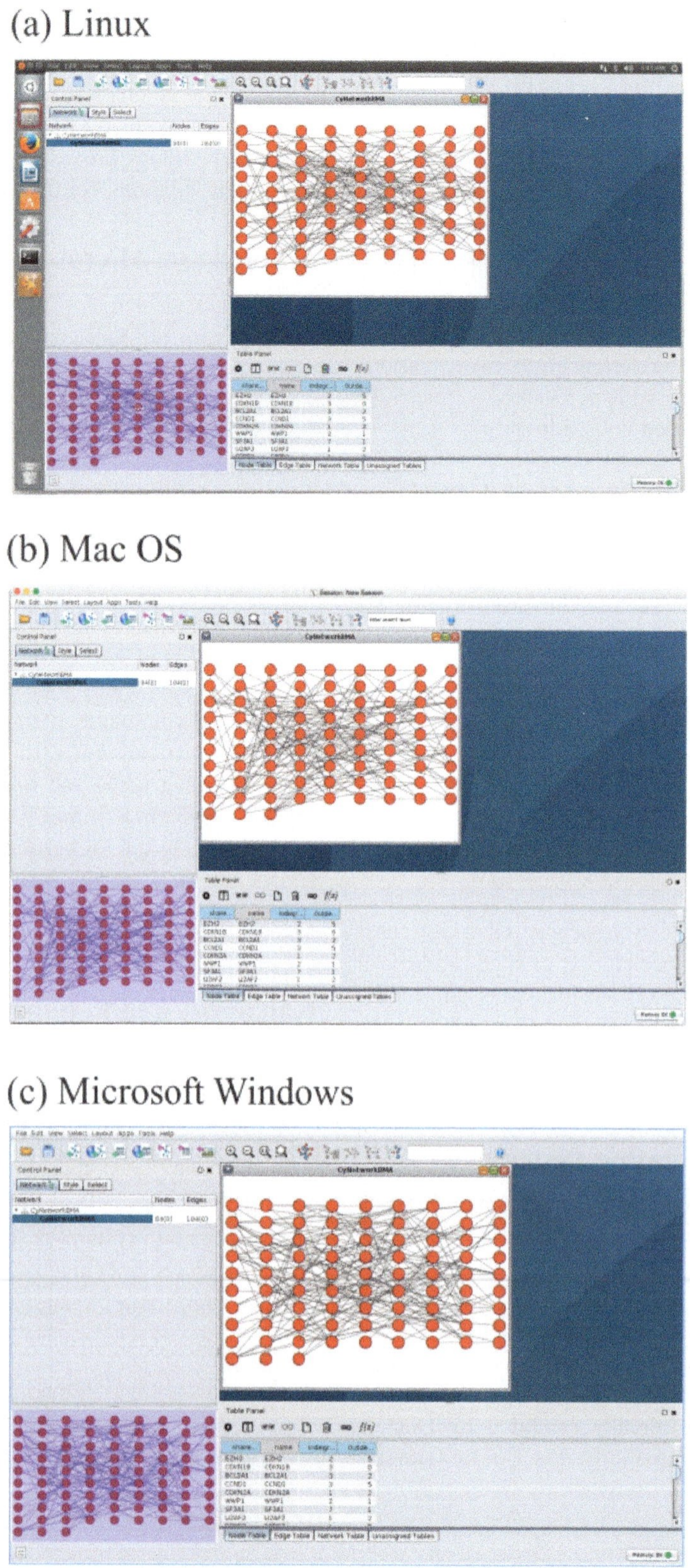

Figure 4. Screen shot of gene networks generated by GUIdock on (a) Linux, (b) Mac OS, (c) Microsoft Windows using the human cancer RNAseq data from Klijn *et al.* Our goal is to demonstrate the reproducibility of analytical results when GUIdock is deployed on computers running different operating systems.

Scenario 1: Human Cancer RNAseq Data

Klijn *et al.* generated an extensive RNAseq gene expression data across 675 frequently used human cancer cell lines [41]. We downloaded the variance stabilized version of the normalized RNAseq data produced by the DESeq Bioconductor package [43] from http://research-pub.gene.com/KlijnEtAl2014/. We then extracted a subset of 84 genes that belong to 21 cancer-related pathways that are known to be functionally altered in cancer (see Supplementary Table 12 in Klijn *et al.* [41]). This is a steady-state (non-time series) dataset. We applied the ScanBMA [9] gene network inference algorithm as implemented in the CyNetworkBMA app from within the GUIdock container.

Fig 4 show the identical results generated by the GUIdock package when installed on a computer running the Linux, Mac OS X and Windows operating systems respectively, after applying CyNetworkBMA to the same Klijn *et al.* cancer cell line RNAseq data. We demonstrate the reproducibility of analytical results when GUIdock is deployed on local hosts running different operating systems. Fig 5 shows a zoomed in sub-graph of the same network. From Fig 5, we observe inferred edges among nodes (CDKN2A, CDKN2B, CCNE1, CCND1) that are part of the cell cycle pathway as indicated in Supplementary Table 12 in Klijn *et al.* [41]. Similarly, we also observe inferred edges among nodes (ZRSR2, U2AF1, U2AF2, SRSF2, and SF3A1) that belong to the splicing pathway.

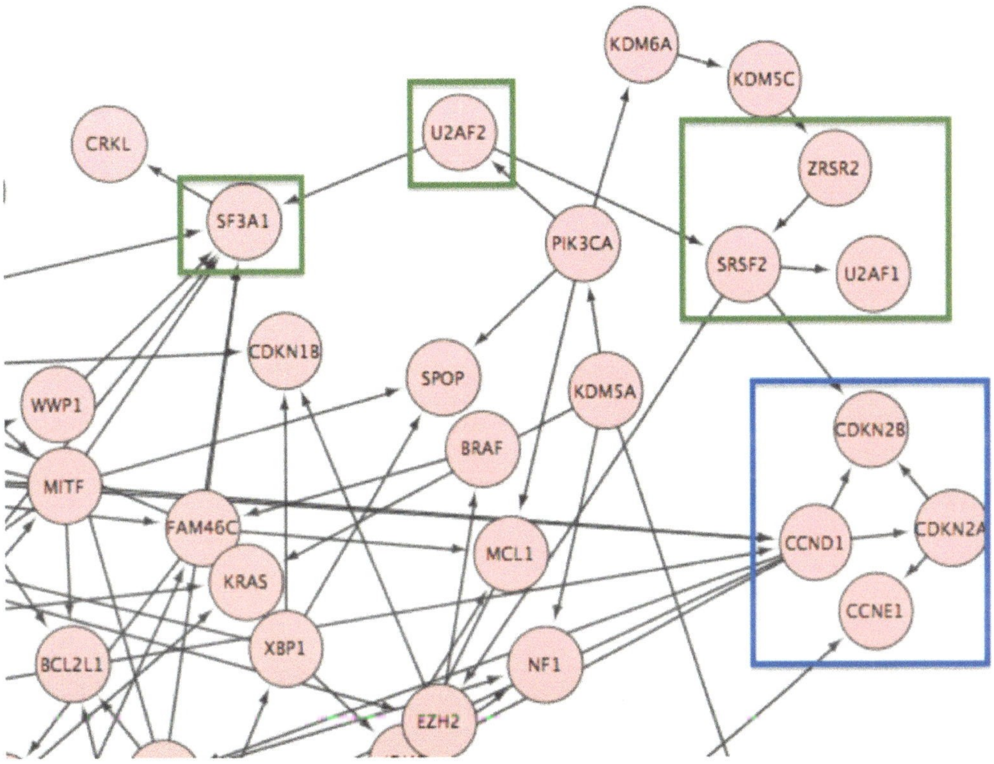

Figure 5. A zoomed-in version of the screen shot of gene network generated by GUIdock using the human cancer RNAseq data from Klijn *et al.* Nodes (CDKN2A, CDKN2B, CCNE1, CCND1) that are part of the cell cycle pathway are highlighted in blue. Nodes (ZRSR2, U2AF1, U2AF2, SRSF2, and SF3A1) that belong to the splicing pathway are highlighted in green.

Scenario 2: Yeast Time Series Microarray Data

We also deployed the GUIdock package and applied CyNetworkBMA to a subset of the yeast time series data [7]. Yeung *et al.* profiled the response of 97 yeast segregants over six time points subjected to rapamycin perturbation using microarrays. We extracted a 100-gene subset and applied CyNetworkBMA using all default settings. Similar to the previous subsection, we deployed GUIdock on both Windows and mac.

Scenario 3: DREAM 4 Simulated Data

The DREAM4 simulated time series data consist of 100 genes over 21 time points [42]. We deployed the GUIdock package on Linux, Mac and Windows.

DISCUSSION

In academic bioinformatics research, data is usually collected and analyzed using a suite of multiple software tools, implemented by different developers using different languages. Most workflows are not completely command-line based and have a GUI component. Gathering and compiling the software components is not a trivial task and is *not* always sufficient to reproduce identical results as reported in the scientific literature. GUIdock uses Docker containers to replicate and distribute the original workflow.

We used gene network inference as a proof-of-concept example. Distribution of the CyNetworkBMA app was non-trivial because the user is required to install and set up dependencies such as Rserve, even though the app itself was written in portable java and Cytoscape runs natively on different platforms. In our figures and demo videos, we show that by using GUIdock, the user only has to run a provided script to replicate the original environment and reproduce the results.

Bioinformatics often have to deal with big data that are stored in the cloud. The modular Docker container repository paradigm is particularly well suited for building cloud based applications. In the future, we plan to extend GUIdock to work with Docker containers deployed in the cloud and have done some preliminary work on configuring Microsoft Azure instances and with multiple containers. We also plan to study the performance impact of adding the X11 layer to GUIdock in various operating systems.

The primary purpose of this manuscript is to provide a proof of concept for using the GUIdock methodology to reproduce bioinformatics results. The choice of software was primarily driven by robustness and the ease of installation and use by the end user. Another obvious application for container methods is the construction and deployment of custom pipelines from individual modules rather than from downloading an entire application suite. In this case, performance becomes a consideration and we may need to reconsider some design choices such the X-emulator used and the use of a ssh tunnel to transfer X Windows information.

To summarize, we have developed GUIdock, a new container based workflow to deploy GUI based pipelines. We have demonstrated the effectiveness of GUIdock by using it to deploy our Cytoscape based CyNetworkBMA app on Linux, Mac OS and Windows host systems. We have provided scripts to automate the installation and deployment of GUIdock packages. We anticipate that GUIdock will be an important step in solving the problem of testing and reproducing scientific results that come from ever-increasingly complicated multi-component software.

ACKNOWLEDGMENTS

We thank Sina Khankhajeh and Migao Wu for testing the Docker package. We also thank Chris Fraley, Adrian Raftery and William Chad Young for their contributions to the networkBMA package, and Maciej Fronczuk for his contributions to the CyNetworkBMA app.

AUTHOR CONTRIBUTIONS

Conceived and designed the experiments: KYY. Performed the experiments: LHH DK SBL. Analyzed the data: DK SBL. Contributed reagents/materials/analysis tools: LHH DK SBL. Wrote the paper: LHH DK SBL KYY. Developed the Docker package: LHH DK SBL. Tested the Docker package: LHH DK SBL. Developed GUIdock workflow: SBL DK LHH. GUIdock scripts: LHH DK. Created supporting information: DK SBL LHH.

REFERENCES

1. Nosek BA, Alter G, Banks GC, Borsboom D, Bowman SD, Breckler SJ, et al. Promoting an open research culture: Author guidelines for journals could help to promote transparency, openness and reproducibility. Science. 2015;348(6242):1422–1425. doi: 10.1126/science.aab2374.
2. Buck S. Solving reproducibility. Science. 2015;348:1403. doi: 10.1126/science.aac8041. pmid:26113692
3. Kaiser J. The cancer test. Science. 2015;348:1411–1413. doi: 10.1126/science.348.6242.1411. pmid:26113698
4. Gentleman RC, Carey VJ, Bates DM, Bolstad B, Dettling M, Dudoit S, et al. Bioconductor: open software development for computational biology and bioinformatics. Genome Biology. 2004;5(10):R80. doi: 10.1186/gb-2004-5-10-r80. pmid:15461798
5. Biopython;. Available from: http://biopython.org/wiki/Main_Page.
6. BioPerl;. Available from: http://www.bioperl.org/wiki/Main_Page.
7. Yeung KY, Dombek KM, Lo K, Mittler JE, Zhu J, Schadt EE, et al. Construction of regulatory networks using expression time-series data of a genotyped population. Proceedings of the National Academy of Sciences. 2011;108(48):1943–19441. doi: 10.1073/pnas.1116442108.
8. Lo K, Raftery A, Dombek K, Zhu J, Schadt E, Bumgarner R, et al. Integrating external biological knowledge in the construction of regulatory networks from time-series expression data. BMC Systems Biology. 2012;6(1):101. doi: 10.1186/1752-0509-6-101. pmid:22898396
9. Young WC, Raftery AE, Yeung KY. Fast Bayesian inference for gene regulatory networks using ScanBMA. BMC Systems Biology. 2014;8(1):47. doi: 10.1186/1752-0509-8-47. pmid:24742092
10. Yeung KY, Fraley C, Young WC, Bumgarner R, Raftery AE. Bayesian Model Averaging methods and R package for gene network construction. In: Big Data Analytic Technology For Bioinformatics and Health Informatics (KDDBHI), workshop at the 20th ACM SIGKDD Conference on Knowledge Discovery and Data Mining (KDD); 2014.
11. Fronczuk M, Raftery AE, Yeung KY. CyNetworkBMA: a Cytoscape app for inferring gene regulatory networks. Under revision;.
12. Chuang HY, Hofree M, Ideker T. A decade of systems biology. Annual Review of Cell and Developmental Biology. 2010;26:721–744. doi: 10.1146/annurev-cellbio-100109-104122. pmid:20604711
13. Novere NL. Quantitative and logic modelling of molecular and gene networks. Nature Reviews Genetics. 2015;16:146–158. doi: 10.1038/nrg3885. pmid:25645874
14. Emmert-Streib F, Glazko GV, Altay G, de Matos Simoes R. Statistical inference and reverse engineering of gene regulatory networks from observational expression data. Frontiers in Genetics. 2012;3:8. doi: 10.3389/fgene.2012.00008. pmid:22408642
15. Zhang SQ, Ching WK, Tsing NK, Leung HY, Guo D. A new multiple regression approach for the construction of genetic regulatory networks. Artificial Intelligence in Medicine. 2010;48:153–160. doi: 10.1016/j.artmed.2009.11.001. pmid:19963359
16. Charbonnier C, Chiquet J, Ambroise C. Weighted-LASSO for structured network inference from time course data. Statistical Applications in Genetics and Molecular Biology. 2010;9:15. doi: 10.2202/1544-6115.1519.
17. Liu LZ, Wu FX, Zhang WJ. A group LASSO-based method for robustly inferring gene regulatory networks from multiple time-course datasets. BMC Systems Biology. 2014;8 (Suppl 3):S1. doi: 10.1186/1752-0509-8-S3-S1.
18. Raftery AE. Bayesian model selection in social research (with Discussion). Sociological Methodology;25:111–196. doi: 10.2307/271063.
19. Hoeting JA, Madigan D, Raftery AE, Volinsky CT. Bayesian model averaging: A tutorial (with Discussion). Statistical Science;14:382–401. doi: 10.1214/ss/1009212814

20. Shannon P, Markiel A, Ozier O, Baliga NS, Wang JT, Ramage D, et al. Cytoscape: a software environment for integrated models of biomolecular interaction networks. Genome Research. 2003;13(11):2498–2504. doi: 10.1101/gr.1239303. pmid:14597658
21. Christmas R, Avila-Campillo I, Bolouri H, Schwikowski B, Anderson M, Kelley R, et al. Cytoscape: A Software Environment for Integrated Models of Biomolecular Interaction Networks; 2005. Available from:http://educationbook.aacrjournals.org/cgi/content/full/2005/1/12.
22. Cline MS, Smoot M, Cerami E, Kuchinsky A, Landys N, Workman C, et al. Integration of biological networks and gene expression data using Cytoscape. Nature Protocols. 2007; p. 2366–2382. doi: 10.1038/nprot.2007.324. pmid:17947979
23. Pico AR, Bader GD, Demchak B, Pla OG, Hull T, Longabaugh W, et al. The Cytoscape app article collection. F1000 Research. 2014;3:138. doi: 10.12688/f1000research.4642.1. pmid:25580224
24. Ono K, Muetze T, Kolishovski G, Shannon P, Demchak B. CyREST: Turbocharging Cytoscape Access for External Tools via a RESTful API. F1000 Research. 2015;4:478. doi: 10.12688/f1000research.6767.1. pmid:26672762
25. Cumbo F, Paci P, Santoni D, Paola LD, Giuliani A. GIANT: A Cytoscape Plugin for Modular Networks. PLoS ONE;9:e105001. doi: 10.1371/journal.pone.0105001. pmid:25275465
26. Kutmon M, Kelder T, Mandaviya P, Evelo CTA, Coort SL. CyTargetLinker: A Cytoscape App to Integrate Regulatory Interactions in Network Analysis. PLoS ONE;8:e82160. doi: 10.1371/journal.pone.0082160. pmid:24340000
27. Ono K. VIZBI 2015 Tutorial: Cytoscape, iPython, Docker, and reproducible workflow;. Available from: https://github.com/idekerlab/cyREST/wiki/VIZBI-2015-Tutorial.
28. Urbanek S. A Fast Way to Provide R Functionality to Applications. In: Proceedings of DSC; 2003. p. 2.
29. Csardi G, Nepusz T. The igraph Software Package for Complex Network Research. InterJournal. 2006;Complex Systems:1695.
30. Boettiger C. An introduction to Docker for reproducible research, with examples from the R environment. ACM SIGOPS Operating Systems Review, Special Issue on Repeatability and Sharing of Experimental Artifacts. 2015;49(1):71–79. doi: 10.1145/2723872.2723882.
31. Introducing Rocker: Docker for R;. Available from:http://dirk.eddelbuettel.com/blog/2014/10/23/.
32. Docker containers for Bioconductor;. Available from:https://www.bioconductor.org/help/docker/.
33. Bio Docker: Docker for Bioinformatics;. Available from: http://biodocker.org/.
34. Moreews F, Sallou O, Ménager H, Le Bras Y, Monjeaud C, Blanchet C, et al. BioShaDock: a community driven bioinformatics shared Docker-based tools registry. F1000Research. 2015;4:1443. doi: 10.12688/f1000research.7536.1. pmid:26913191
35. Goecks J, Nekrutenko A, Taylor J, et al. Galaxy: a comprehensive approach for supporting accessible, reproducible, and transparent computational research in the life sciences. Genome Biol. 2010;11(8):R86. doi: 10.1186/gb-2010-11-8-r86. pmid:20738864
36. Aranguren ME, Wilkinson MD. Enhanced reproducibility of SADI web service workflows with Galaxy and Docker. GigaScience. 2015;4(1):1–9. doi: 10.1186/s13742-015-0092-3.
37. BMA: Bayesian Model Averaging. Package for Bayesian model averaging for linear models, generalizable linear models and survival models (cox regression);. Available from: https://cran.r-project.org/web/packages/BMA/index.html.
38. XQuartz: A version of the X Window System that runs on OS X;. Available from:http://xquartz.macosforge.org/landing/.
39. socat: Multipurpose relay (SOcket CAT);. Available from: http://www.dest-unreach.org/socat/doc/socat.html.
40. MobaXterm: Enhanced terminal for Windows with X11 server, tabbed SSH client, network tools and much more;. Available from: http://mobaxterm.mobatek.net/.
41. Klijn C, Durinck S, Stawiski EW, Haverty PM, Jiang Z, Liu H, et al. A comprehensive transcriptional portrait of human cancer cell lines. Nature Biotechnology. 2015;33:306–312. doi: 10.1038/nbt.3080. pmid:25485619
42. Marbach D, Schaffter T, Mattiussi C, Floreano D. Generating Realistic In Silico Gene Networks for Performance Assessment of Reverse Engineering Methods. Journal of Computational Biology. 2009;16(2):229–239. doi: 10.1089/cmb.2008.09TT. pmid:19183003
43. Anders S, Huber W. Differential expression analysis for sequence count data. Genome Biology. 2010;11:R106. doi: 10.1186/gb-2010-11-10-r106. pmid:20979621

CHAPTER 9

INEQUALITIES IN OPEN SOURCE SOFTWARE DEVELOPMENT: ANALYSIS OF CONTRIBUTOR'S COMMITS IN APACHE SOFTWARE FOUNDATION PROJECTS

Tadeusz Chełkowski[1], Peter Gloor[2], Dariusz Jemielniak[3]

[1] Kozminski University, Warsaw, Poland

[2] Massachusetts Institute of Technology, Center for Cognitive Intelligence, Cambridge, Massachusetts, United States of America

[3] Kozminski University, New Research on Digital Societies (NeRDS) group, Warsaw, Poland

ABSTRACT

While researchers are becoming increasingly interested in studying OSS phenomenon, there is still a small number of studies analyzing larger samples of projects investigating the structure of activities among OSS developers. The significant amount of information that has been gathered in the publicly available open-source software repositories and mailing-list archives offers an opportunity to analyze projects structures and participant involvement. In this article, using on commits data from 263 Apache projects repositories (nearly all), we show that although OSS development is often described as collaborative, but it in fact predominantly relies on radically solitary input and individual, non-collaborative contributions. We also show, in the first published study of this magnitude, that the engagement of contributors is based on a power-law distribution.

INTRODUCTION

Open collaboration communities have been in the limelight of organization and information studies for the last decade [1]. Open collaboration, in principle, is a way of developing a product collectively, by the use of bottom-up collective intelligence [2] relying on self-organizing communities [3] "open" for anyone to join (or quit), and thus lacking the traditional thresholds of employment and the traditional fears of being fired.

Citation: Chełkowski T, Gloor P, Jemielniak D (2016) Inequalities in Open Source Software Development: Analysis of Contributor's Commits in Apache Software Foundation Projects. PLoS ONE 11(4): e0152976. doi:10.1371/journal.pone.0152976.

In a famous metaphor introduced by Eric S. Raymond [4], the traditional model can be compared to a medieval cathedral building with top-down management and hierarchy, while the open-collaboration model resembles a bazaar with an a-hierarchical structure without a coordinating center, which still is very successful. Even though not they are not physically present in the same place, software developers involved in Open Source Software (OSS) can create large-scale software [5].

"Open source can be seen as a movement, where communities of highly skilled programmers collectively develop software, often of a quality that outperforms commercial proprietary software" [6]. Indeed, the triumphs of Linux, MySQL, Firefox, and Wordpress speak for themselves. One of the most prominent examples of successful open-software projects is also Apache—absolutely dominating as web server software (running nearly half of all servers worldwide). Open collaboration is sometimes called peer production [7,8,9]. This perspective also emphasizes the equal and a-hierarchical character of open-source development [10,11].

While some authors criticize open-collaboration and peer-production phenomenon as leading to deterioration of quality [12,13], or as resulting in exploitation of participants and creating new inequalities [14,15,16], many others see its great promise [17]. According to Yochai Benkler [18,19], peer production has the potential to redefine capitalism and create a new mode of goods development and consumption with an anti-bureaucratic and a-hierarchical organization of work.

Whether these revolutionary results can in fact be initiated by open collaboration projects remains to be seen [9]. Yet, it is clear that these approaches, at least, rhetorically assume that the phenomenon they are describing relies, in fact, on "collaboration" and "peers". While some authors are critical of such newspeak [20], it is generally assumed that "collaboration generally happens within the context of a particular production goal; in other words, open collaboration is about people trying to make something together" [1]. As we will show in this article, this presumption is not necessarily valid. From the perspective of code commitment, the processes covered by terms of "open collaboration" or "peer production" are mostly not, in fact, collaborative at all. Instead of a network of peers, they rely on a collection of separate individuals focused on their own goals and ambitions.

Moreover, the participation of contributors is following a steep power law distribution. It is worth noting that open collaboration communities in general follow the "1-9-90 rule" [21,22], under which only 1% of community members actively produce content, 9% are generally somewhat active, and the remaining 90% are passive lurkers. This rule has been widely accepted as valid in open-software projects based on smaller studies. Our findings show that even among the professional and committed contributors, participation is similarly unequal. This finding is significant as we are able to confirm a wide assumption using on an analysis conducted on unprecedented scale (virtually all projects of a major, leading open-source initiative are taken into account). We are able to further ground this finding in an analysis if Gini indexes (counting disparities of commitments) between projects.

OPEN-SOURCE CONTRIBUTORS

Open-source contributors can be divided into five groups based on the nature of their involvement. Core developers are responsible for technical concepts and key code commitment. Maintainers are responsible for keeping the project up to date, including porting and compatibility. Patchers actively respond to problems, fixing the product issues. Bug reporters provide issue descriptions. Finally, documenters play the role of power users, supporting others with documentation and instructions [23,24]. Researchers have also examined that, in terms of active participation, North America and Europe are the top regions for Open-Source developers [25]. Self-report studies have measured individual developers' time commitments, discovering differences in time spent between project leaders (14.13 hours/week), developers (11.10 hours/week) and bug fixers (5.6 hours/week) [26]. In addition to the time spent on development, researchers studied the amount of time community members spent on supporting forums, finding that it may take up 1.5 hours per week [27], and that helping other members is a significant part of software development [28]. On the other hand, Robles and Gonzalez-Barahona have explored the commits distribution in project MONO characterizing commits vs. time and authorship attribution [29], finding high inequalities in the level of commits between different participants. Some researchers have advanced an understanding of the commits distribution on the single-project level (project Ximian Evolution), providing another interesting example of the high inequalities among developers' commits. "From a total of 196 developers, 5 account for 47% of the MRs, while 20 account for 81% of the MRs, and 55 have done 95% of them" [30], where As defined by German and Mockus, "MR is a logical change of software". High inequalities have been also confirmed by the GNOME project studies where "[t]he number of checkins performed by a programmer was in the mean 731 with a standard deviation of 1 857 and a maximum of 23 000" [31]–a checkin is an equivalent of a commit.

The Apache Software Foundation has been the subject of a number of academic studies. Researchers have been mostly interested in individual projects such as the Apache HTTP Server [32,33], Apache Lucene [34], or Apache Ant [35]. MacLean, Knutson have provided a Neo4J graph representation of the commit behavior (Apache Software Foundation developers for 2010 and 2011) [36], and in a study of the Apache community, Gala-Pérez, Robles, González-Barahona, and Herraiz [37] analyzed the ratio of mailing list activity to the total number of commits.

Yet, surprisingly, little research has examined commits distribution among the larger group of the Apache Foundation Open Source projects [38], even though studying one of the most successful peer production projects using a large dataset should allow for the most accurate analysis of the studied phenomenon. Our article presents the first analysis of this sort using data from nearly all Apache projects.

MOTIVATION, RESEARCH QUESTIONS, AND HYPOTHESIS

The goal of this article is to improve our understanding of the OSS participation distribution by analyzing user commits frequency using a large group of the Apache Foundation Open Source projects.

Research Question:

What is the structure of the Apache Software Foundation projects commits distribution?

Hypothesis:

The contributions in the analyzed Apache Software Foundation projects measured in commits are highly unequal, the vast majority of projects are created by a minor but very active part of the open-source community.

RESEARCH METHOD

In this section, we discuss the methodology used to analyze the collected data. In order to achieve the aims of this study, this work uses the quantification of the individual contributors' activity on the project level. For the basic picture and the relationship between commits and contributors we use contingency tables. A contingency table is an widely used scientific research standard developed as a unified analytic approach for the multivariate frequency distribution [39]. For the close examination of open source commits distribution, we measure the statistical dispersion using the Gini coefficient. The Gini coefficient is a well-established single measure of inequalities [40] and a popular method supporting studies such as wealth empirical studies. Like most of the inequalities measures, the Gini index might be derived from the Lorenz curve "Gini is a 1 minus twice the area under the Lorenz curve" [41]. For the purpose of the Gini calculation, however, we use the Gini index relationship to covariance proved by Lerman and Yitzhaki [42]: $G = 2cov[y/F(y)]/\bar{y}$

The advantage of the Gini index is that it's an easy-to-interpret ratio analysis method. Gini coefficients range between 0 and 1, where 0 represents complete equality and 1 represents complete inequality. It's worth mentioning that Gini index limitation—since it's a relative and not absolute measure—might be misleading (e.g. the Gini index will remain the same for the population of developers where 50% of the participants have no activity and the remaining 50% of the population contributes equally, and the population where 75% of the developers contributes in 25% in the overall project activity, and the remaining 25% contributes the remaining 75%) [43].

Sample Selection

The open-source software "movement" is represented by the network of collaborating programmers. However, there is no single place integrating all existing open-source projects. Open-source projects exist in a wide variety of social, technical, and licensing structures. Cloud-versioning software and repository services like GitHub integrates 26.9M repositories and 10.9M people (see https://github.com/about/press).

For further analysis we've selected only projects from the Apache Software Foundation. The Apache Foundation is one of the oldest open-source development organizations. Since 1999, the Apache Foundation has provided technical governance, including collaboration, licensing, and technical policies, for the project committers (a committer is a developer granted access to an Apache Project). For the purpose of collaborative-code development, Apache committers use the subversion revision control system. The Apache Foundation was sampled for the following reasons: firstly, it contains more than 350 projects (see http://apache.org/foundation/), mostly stable and well-established projects with a unified governance model. Secondly, the vast majority of projects are developed over the years, which gives us an opportunity to analyze the structure over time (e.g. the Apache HTTP Server was founded in 1995). Thirdly, the Apache Foundation supported the development of some of the most well-known open-source projects such as Apache HTTP Server and Apache Open Office. Regardless of the Apache Software Foundation's long history and significant size, the results of this study should not be generalized beyond the Apache Software Foundation community.

What qualifies as an Apache project is, to some extent, open to debate. Even the Apache Foundation lists 262 projects, in some documents 350, or simply "300+ initiatives" elsewhere (on the very same page they also refer to 278 projects). This includes projects in the incubation phase, as well as defunct ones that may cause obvious distortions in the results. Similarly, we have decided against counting the projects that have merged separately or projects that have just one commit, as in our best judgment they should not qualify. Our approach is typical for this kind of research [44].

Commit

To analyze the contributor activity distribution, we measure the number of commits submitted by the individual contributors. The collective open-software development process consists of commits submitted by the programmers to the unified project repository supported by the source code versioning software. A commit represents a synchronization/exchange of local changes with a remote project repository and is a submission of the individual programmer's changes. A source-code modification, such as adding, modifying, or removing lines of code, adding or removing files, changes in the documentation files, are typical examples of commits. Because of the open nature of software repositories and their accessibility, commits have been a subject of numerous software development studies [32,45]. Although many researchers tried to classify the value of commits using their size or a number of received comments, we intend to measure only the contributor's activity, not the value of their work. [45,46,47].

Data Source

We use data collected by OpenHub.net (formerly Ohloh)—the open-source projects registry. This article is based on the June 2014 snapshot of the OpenHub database, which contains more than 664 thousand open-source projects. In particular, OpenHub provides descriptive information about projects, including name, main programming language, date of creation. Additionally, the registry provides information about the individual contributors and commits. OpenHub retrieves the project data directly from open-source project repositories using connectors to the most popular source versioning systems such as Git, SubVersion, CVS, Mercurial, and Bazaar. OpenHub integrates project information with a user's feedback, managing the open-source project contributors' feedback and community. For the purposes of this article, however, we use only raw commit data without information added by the OpenHub community. The Apache Foundation references OpenHub as the historical raw data source.

Data Collection

In order to collect the Apache Software Foundation project commits data, we developed a Java-based program that crawls the OpenHub database using the REST-based API provided. Our program queries the OpenHub registry using "Apache" as a project identification key word, then iterates over the result table, searching for the unique project ID. Using the project ID, the program executes additional queries and collects project details such as individual contributors' commits. The initial query returned not only the open-source project originating from the Apache Foundation, but all related projects that extend, use, or integrate Apache projects. Therefore, for the final analysis we have decided to create unified filtering criteria to prepare a clean dataset.

Filtering criteria:

- The project must be listed as an official Apache foundation project athttp://projects.apache.org/. Only projects registered and listed are qualified by the Apache Foundation as the "Apache project".
- The project must not be qualified as "incubating" by the Apache Software Foundation and its homepage must not be listed under the incubator.apache.org domain. The incubation program has been created for the projects wishing to become a part of the Apache Foundation. Typically, it's a place to verify external organization donation, making sure that it follows the Apache Software Foundation legal standards. A donated project contains existing code with limited and unverified commits information. Thus, projects listed as a part of the incubation are not considered valid date entries for this study. Additionally, the incubation process can lead to project rejection, and a project may not be established as a full Apache member.
- The project must not be qualified by the Apache Software Foundation as discontinued ("moved to attic"). The Apache Software Foundation has created an "attic" project category to manage issues with project life end. It is intended to provide a controlled process to close the project without the active committers or committers that are unable to fulfill their duties. It is common that projects classified as "attic" are merged and integrated with other projects, therefore their commits might be included in other projects.
- Additionally, we have removed 77 records without a proper user name. For selected cases, a detailed review of the removed cases indicated that it belongs to "anonymous", "none", "user name", "unknown", "root" users, e.g. representing the technical accounts used for the project's migration process.

Finally, the collected data encompasses 1,348,405 individual commits. The selected 263 Apache Projects represent 10, 045,099 lines of the source code, which have been created by the 4,661 unique committer accounts (one contributor can commit to multiple projects—see Table 1 and Fig 1).

Table 1. Sample commit record retrieved from OpenHub

Project name	Contributor	Commits
Apache Jackrabbit	Angela Schreiber	1,499

doi:10.1371/journal.pone.0152976.t001

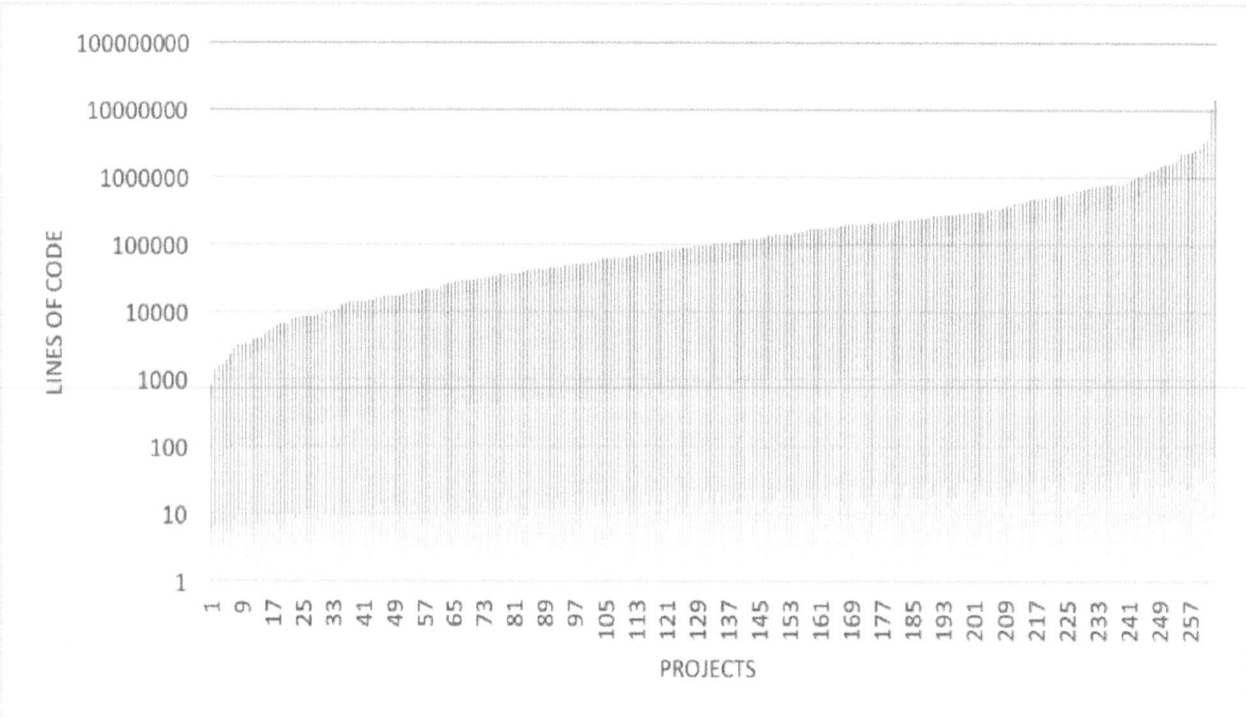

Figure 1. Projects sizes measured as lines of code

The analyzed projects vary in commits size and contributors amount (Table 2).

Table 2. Basic statistics of the analyzed dataset

Attribute	Total code lines	Total Commits	Contributors
Minimum	822	16	3
Mean	399,411.02	5,127.02	38.30
Median	97,753	1,993	19
1 Quartile	28,459	639	11
3 Quartile	300,162	5,509	35
Maximum	14,625,904	94,585	527
Standard deviation	1,237,915.25	9,710,75	35

doi:10.1371/journal.pone.0152976.t002

DATA AND RESULTS VERIFICATION

In order to verify the data source (Open Hub), we have selected a set of projects and conducted a manual verification of the OpenHub data with the projects repositories. Data collected automatically has been compared to the commit records inside the projects repository. The only inconsistency we found was that the code collection by OpenHub was delayed compared to the data inside the project repositories.

Additionally, for the project-list validation we reviewed the official Apache project list, making sure that only the Apache projects and its version have been selected for the analysis.

Finally, we matched the individual data records against selected contributors to validate the accuracy of the collected data. We interviewed three developers, and during the interview we presented the commits records and asked for confirmation of the data accuracy. All of the interviewed developers confirmed their commits records.

RESULTS

The descriptive analysis (Table 3) of the analyzed projects shows a highly unequal distribution of commits among contributors. Additionally, skewness, a metric of asymmetry, confirms that the mass of the distribution is concentrated on the left with a long right tail (Fig 2).

Table 3. Descriptive analysis of commits among contributors

N	4,661
Minimum	1
Maximum	19,053
Sum	1,348,405
Mean	289.295
Std. Deviation	968.641
Skewness	8.428

doi:10.1371/journal.pone.0152976.t003

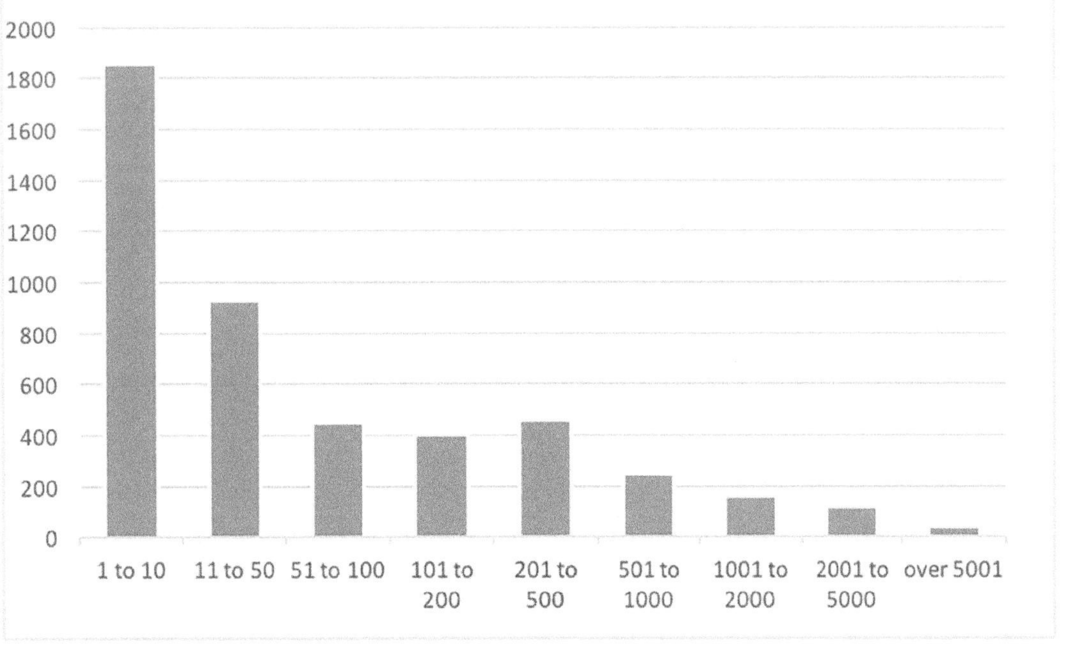

Figure 2. Histogram commits distribution among contributors.

To better understand the data distribution and identify similar data groups in an unsupervised way, we have conducted a cluster analysis using k-means clustering and the JENKS algorithm. Both methods provide similar results. As noted in Table 4, in the nine cluster commit frequency distribution list, significant numbers of committers (85.82%) have been aggregated around the lowest cluster center value (56).

Table 4. Commits aggregation using k-means clustering classification

Cluster no.	Cluster center	Committers	%Committers
1	56	4,000	85.82%
2	737	424	9.10%
3	1,921	131	2.81%
4	3,560.8	65	1.39%
5	6,199.8	30	0.64%
6	9,336	3	0.06%
7	12,269	2	0.04%
8	14,230	5	0.11%
9	19,053	1	0.02%

doi:10.1371/journal.pone.0152976.t004

For better clarity, we used the expert method (interviews with open-source contributors) to classify nine commit-contribution categories. As presented in Table 5 and Fig 3, 156 committers (the sum of the two top contributing categories), representing only 3.35% of the total analyzed committer's population, contribute 50.13% of all commits. On the other hand, 2,786 contributors (the sum of the two bottom categories 1–50), representing 59.77% of the population, contribute only 2.27% of the total commits. Fig 4 presents exponential decrease of the committer number for the selected categories and the increase of the commits for the selected categories.

Table 5. Commits aggregation using expert method

Category	Commits	Committers	%Commits	%Committers
1 to 10	5,942	1,858	0.441%	39.863%
11 to 50	24,085	928	1.786%	19.910%
51 to 100	33,018	449	2.449%	9.633%
101 to 200	58,829	405	4.363%	8.689%
201 to 500	146,814	460	10.888%	9.869%
501 to 1000	178,262	246	13.220%	5.278%
1001 to 2000	225,521	159	16.725%	3.411%
2001 to 5000	357,141	117	26.486%	2.510%
over 5001	318,793	39	23.642%	0.837%

doi:10.1371/journal.pone.0152976.t005

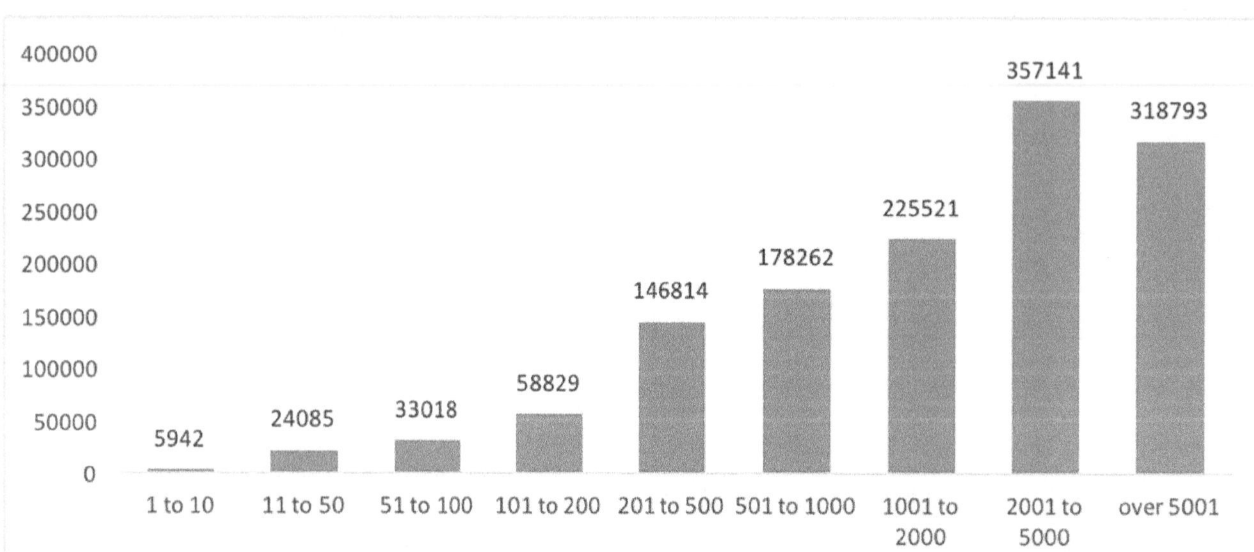

Figure 3. Commits aggregation using expert method.

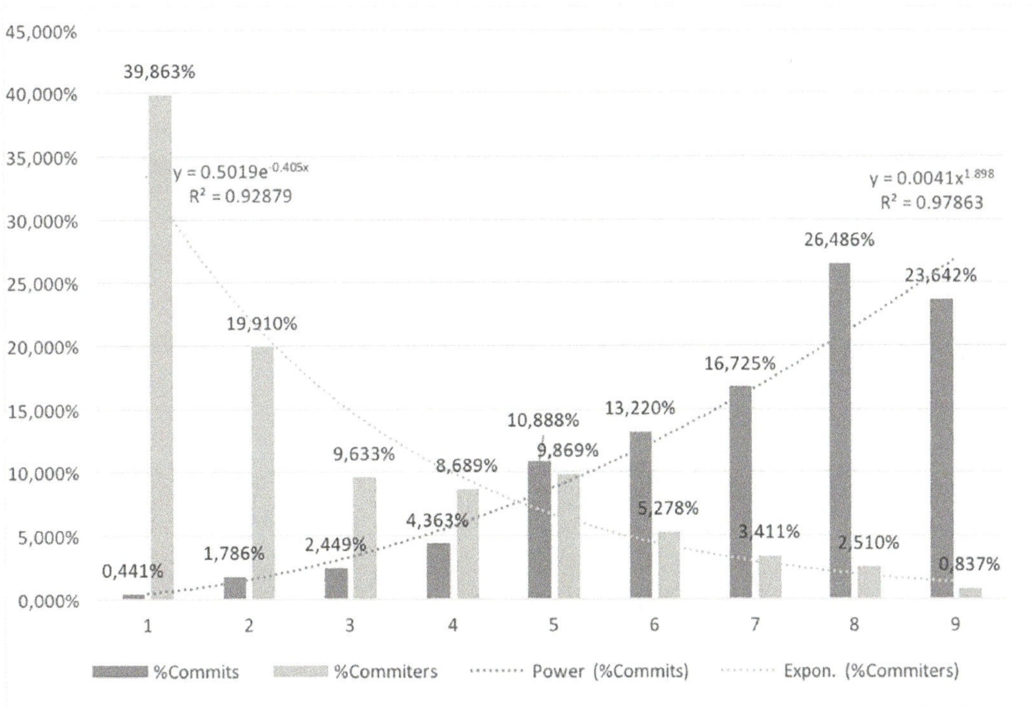

Figure 4. Commits and committers distribution in categories.

Gini Index Analysis

We observe (Fig 5, Tables 6 and 7) high inequalities among the committers' activities on the project level, measured as Gini index values. Among the 263 analyzed cases, 100 (38.02%) cases are in the range of 0.7–0.8, while 234 (88.97%) of the analyzed population is between 0.6 and 0.9. Additionally, only 9.51% of projects have a Gini value lower than 0.6, and 1.52% are in the range of 0.9 to 1.0. It should be noted that analyzed Gini indexes values are highly concentrated around the mean value. Apache Camel (Gini index 0.919) is the project with the highest level of commit inequality, while Portal JSF Bridge with Gini index = 0.301 has the most equally distributed commits among all of the analyzed projects. Gini-indexes analysis confirms the findings in the contingency-tables analysis. We were unable to find any particular correlation between Gini index value and project size measured as the total lines of code (r = 0.1189), Gini index and project size measured as the number of participating contributors (r = 0.1255), as well as Gini index and project size measured as the number of commits (r = 0.1658). The distribution of Gini indexes and the relationship to project sizes is presented in Figs 6, 7 and 8.

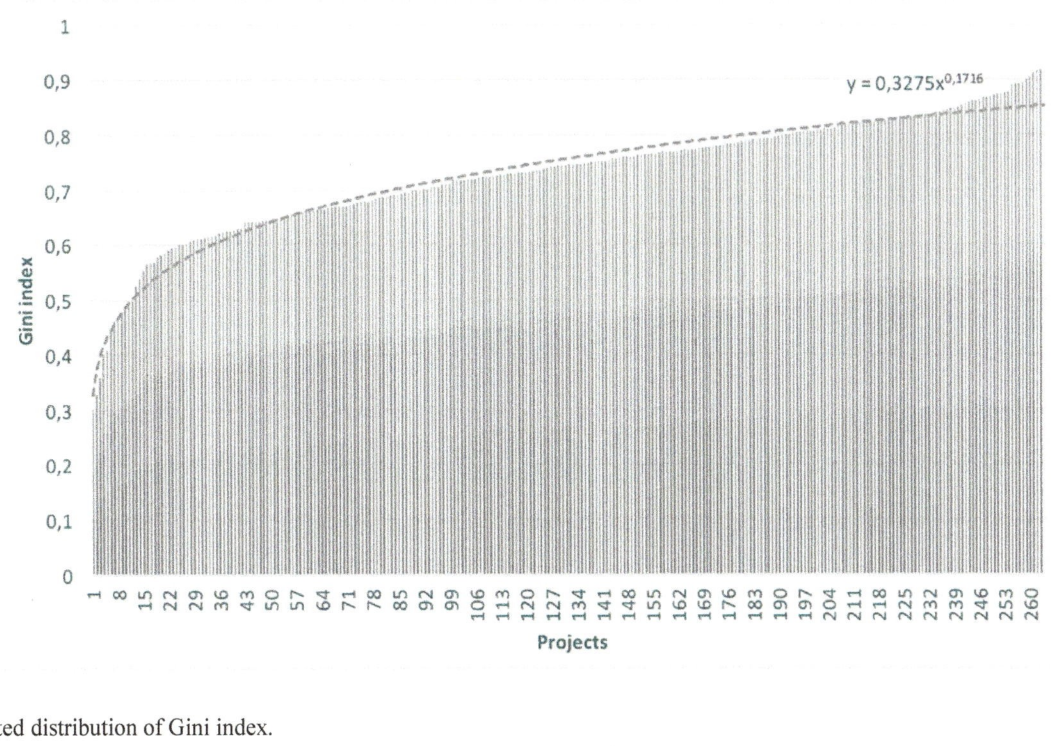

Figure 5. Sorted distribution of Gini index.

Table 6. Properties of the projects Gini Indexes

Attribute	Gini index of the analyzed 263 projects
Minimum	0.301587302
Mean	0.728541383
Median	0.745753403
1 quartile	0.667293233
3 quartile	0.805603143
Maximum	0.919309711
Standard deviation	0.106680995
Variance	0.013348064

doi:10.1371/journal.pone.0152976.t006

Table 7. Distribution of the Gini Indexes

Gini index value	Number of projects	# of the projects	Accumulated number of the project	Accumulated % of the projects
0.0 <x< = 0.4	3	1.14%	3	1.141%
0.4 <x< = 0.5	9	3.42%	12	4.563%
0.5 <x< = 0.6	13	4.94%	25	9.506%
0.6 <x< = 0.7	66	25.10%	91	34.601%
0.7 <x< = 0.8	100	38.02%	191	72.624%
0.8 <x< = 0.9	68	25.86%	259	98.479%
0.9 <x< = 1.0	4	1.52%	263	100.000%

doi:10.1371/journal.pone.0152976.t007

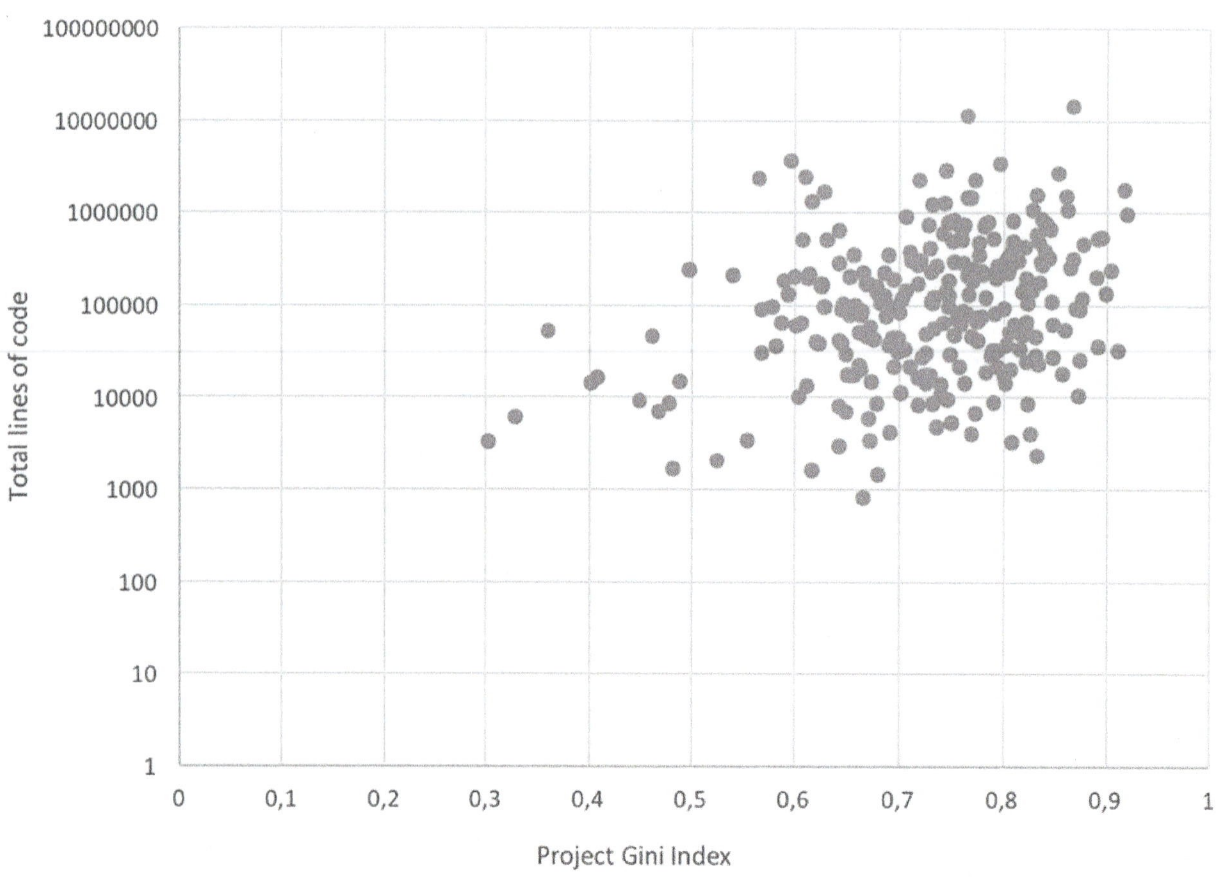

Figure 6. Gini indexes and project size.

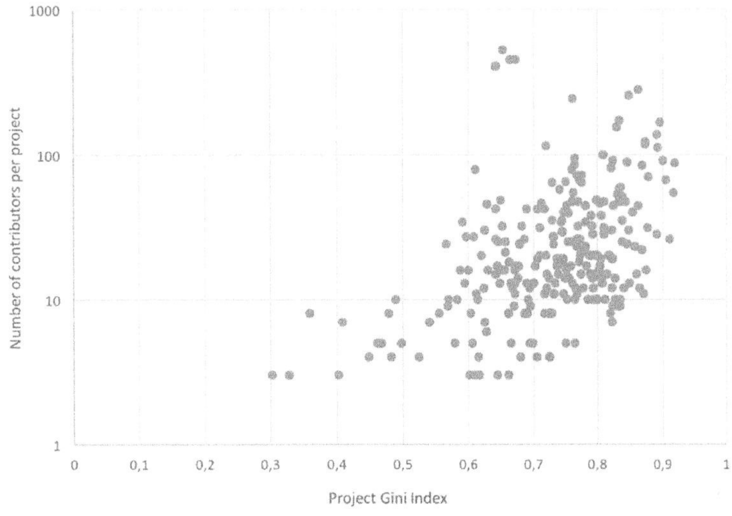

Figure 7. Gini indexes and committers population.

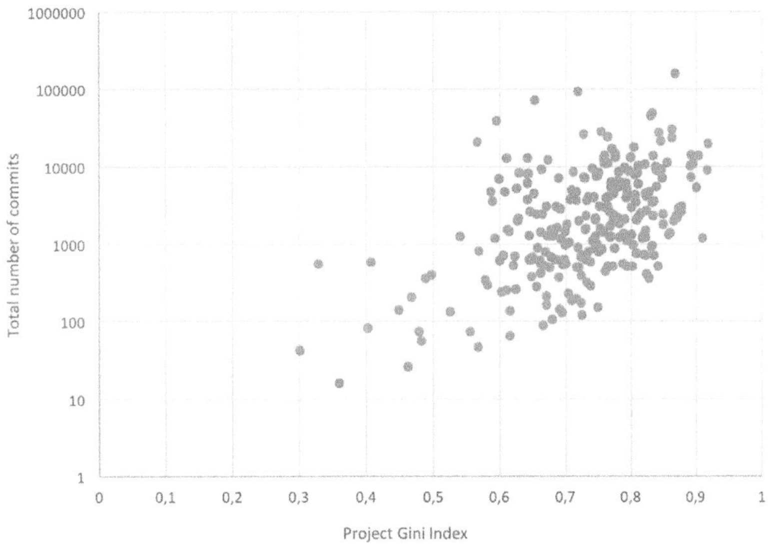

Figure 8. Gini indexes and commits number.

SOCIAL NETWORK ANALYSIS

We also conducted a social network analysis of the contributor and project networks by constructing a bipartite graph (Fig 9). The network has been constructed by showing all links between the 4,661 developers and the 263 projects on which they are working. In this bipartite graph we calculate betweenness centrality (Freeman 1977) as a proxy for importance of the developers, as well as a proxy for the importance of the projects. We find that Apache Taglibs has the highest betweenness centrality among the analyzed cases (see Tables 8 and 9). It's a mature and well-established open-source project, the first code contribution was committed over 15 years ago in September 2000. Over the years, 527 contributors have developed it. Apache Taglibs supports Java Server Pages (JSP). JSP it's a popular technology simplifying the web application development in Java programming language, and in recent years has became a standard for Java-based web applications. Apache Taglibs is a custom JSP tags library project, which makes it easier for other developers to join the collaborative development effort since their commitments can be easily separated and are more modular than in other projects. We believe that a combination of the three above-mentioned characteristics—mature and well-established project, popular technology, and the modular nature of the Apache Taglibs—are the reasons behind the highest number of contributors, and also indirectly the reason for the highest betweenness centrality among the analyzed projects. When correlating betweenness centrality of projects in the network graph with number of lines, number of committers, and number of commits of the project, we find significant correlation between number of developers and betweenness of a project in the graph ($r = 0.907$, $p<0.001$, $N = 263$). The correlation between commits and project betweenness is $r = 0.471$ ($p<0.001$), while the correlation between number of lines and betweenness of the project is $r = 0.168$ ($p = 0.005$). This result is not surprising, as we are constructing our network based on the number of people simultaneously working on more than one network, and the more people that work on a project, the more central it becomes. If there is one insight from this short analysis, it is that it is quality of the code matters more than the quantity measured through number of lines or number of commits. It seems that having many eyeballs involved is the best way to increase the influence of a project.

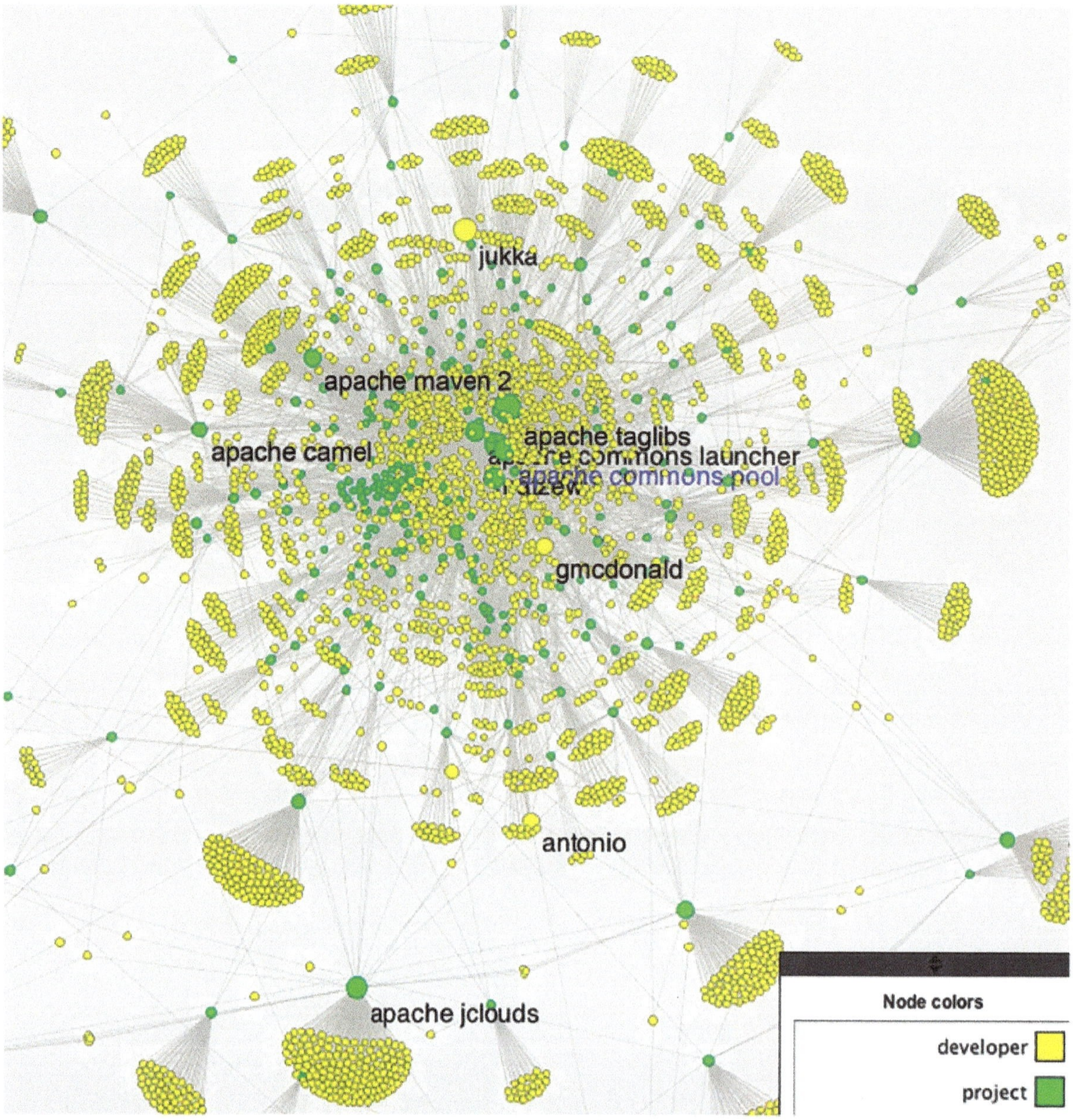

Figure 9. Bipartite graph illustrating the contributor and project network (4924 actors, 4661 developers, 263 projects).

Table 8. The top 15 projects by betweenness. We also looked at project size and number of collaborators

Betweenness centrality	Project name	# of lines	#Commits	#Committers
1,734,235.578	Apache Taglibs	77,397	68,179	527
1,333,166.445	Apache Shale Framework	85,645	9,163	451
1,239,350.732	Apache Cloudstack	1,540,264	23,520	279
1,223,937.202	Apache Spark	109,532	7,055	255
1,156,618.107	Apache Commons Pool	14,702	12,173	447
1,134,737.378	Apache Jclouds	546,572	11,012	166
1,089,733.276	Cordova-Android	25,617	2,552	122
1,075,281.033	Apache Commons Launcher	2,992	7,954	406
1,073,539.122	Apache Commons Modeler	7,981	7,945	405
790,400.008	Apache Maven 2	1,065,693	46,020	155
763,373.662	Apache Libcloud	133,591	5,446	91
761,588.927	Apache Subversion	592,060	49,995	170
626791,9109	Apache Camel	959,655	19,945	87
593164,5311	Apache Gump	36,250	14,181	137
566926,3238	Apache Traffic Server	536,615	7,408	111

doi:10.1371/journal.pone.0152976.t008

Table 9. Top 15 committers by betweenness. We also compared their number of commits and number of lines of code they contributed

Project name	Betweenness centrality	Commits
jukka	1,386,508.632	6,345
joes	919,986.125	1,562
gmcdonald	823,993.580	474
antonio	682,878.895	2,947
joe schaefer	611,604.685	49
gavin mcdonald	527,732,533	39
bdelacretaz	470,439.078	2,476
carlos	372815.024	1,461
niq	358,758.946	1,735
jim	317,239.08	4,972
ashutosh	269,789.440	13
bayard	252,713.137	2,720
sebb	226,232.766	14,447
jesse	223,974.211	1,091
tomwhite	221,081.369	642

doi:10.1371/journal.pone.0152976.t009

As for the Social Network Analysis of the developer, we found that user "jukka", with 6,345 commits, is the developer with the highest betweenness centrality. Real user "jukka" is a combined record of the accounts "jukka" with 3,208 commits, "Jukka Zitting" with 3,133 commits, and "Jukka Lauri Zitting" with 4 commits, which we have identified as accounts all represented by the same person. A close examination of the project commit logs revealed that "jukka" contributed to 20 projects, including Apache Jackrabbit, Apache Sling, Apache Taglibs, and a number of Apache Commons projects that developers commonly use as a foundational component of other projects. The correlation between the number of commits of a developer and their betweenness centrality is $r = 0.222$ ($p<0.001$, $N = 4660$), which means there is a significant—but not strong—correlation. For instance, user sebb, with 14,447 commits, was well above jukka but has a much lower betweenness. Taking the number of commits as a metric of activity of a developer, we find that the most active developers are not necessarily the most central ones. Rather, we find that there are developers in the core of the social network who, with comparatively few commits, are highly central.

DISCUSSION

Our study findings undermine the widespread idealistic belief that open-source development is a wide collaborative movement. Rather, we show that in the analyzed Apache Software foundation projects were created by a small, but very active, group of individual, separate contributors.

We conclude that the analyzed Apache Foundation projects experience high levels of inequalities in contributors' activities measured as commits. The contingency table analysis shows that a small group of contributors is responsible for the majority of commits, which is reinforced by the high levels of the Gini indices among the analyzed projects regardless of project size and committer population.

One main advantage of our research is the analyzed group of projects. The selected 263 cases represent a homogenous group of Apache Software Foundation projects developed under the highly respected Apache Foundation brand. Apache Foundation projects are considered to be among the best organized and the most reliable projects among all OSS projects.

One of the potential issues of our methodology is the semantic association of the commit with the individual programmer's project contribution. Although commits have been widely used in similar analysis and represent a fundamental element of open-source development, commits are not the only type of open-source collaboration. Community members contribute to open-source development by a number of supporting activities such as reading and answering users' support questions, preparing technical documentation, or speaking at conferences. Additionally it could be argued that commits might not represent the actual project contribution of a developer. However, the other well-known alternative method of measuring the project contribution by calculating lines of codes has serious flaws and gives no information about the value of the contribution—adding hundreds of lines into a project's documentation branch is treated identical to a small but essential modification of a project's core component [48,49]. Therefore, a more effective way of calculating a programmer's contribution—not only activity as presented in this paper—is an issue that merits further investigation.

Our findings confirm the hypothesis that activities of contributors measured as commits (committers) are unequal. In the analyzed 263 Apache projects, a small but very active core group of developers submitted the majority of commits. Similar power law distributions have been observed in online communities, for example in relation to users' popularity [50] and for user-content generation [51].

CONCLUSIONS

Our results are not that surprising in the larger context of open-software development. While in other non-professional contexts [52,53] of open collaboration, the benefits of participation are much less clear in economic terms, in open-source software, while not payment-related, they are quite obvious [10,54]. A developer participates in a gift culture, develops one's network, gets recognition for one's skills, and also can often combine work with some commercial endeavor. This combined model is increasing in popularity [55,56]. Thus, reputation may be a major factor driving people to develop open source [57,58,59]. To build such a reputation, one does not necessarily have to prove one's teamwork or leadership skills.

In fact, being a lone hero may be an optimal strategy for portfolio building. Also, while there are methodologies for cyber-teams allowing people to work collectively [60,61], open-collaboration communities in general, and open-software development in particular, attract people who avoid hierarchy and prefer individual work [62,63,64].

Our findings support this perspective. Additionally, our results help problematize the overly simplistic view of open-software development as a mainly collaborative endeavor, as described in our introduction. Open collaboration may well be the best thing since sliced bread, but calling it "collaboration" is an over-emphasis. Peer production is mainly a solitary endeavor and relies much less on peers than enthusiasts of open collaboration would like it to believe.

AUTHOR CONTRIBUTIONS

Analyzed the data: TC PG DJ. Wrote the paper: TC PG DJ.

REFERENCES

1. Forte A, Lampe C (2013) Defining, understanding, and supporting open collaboration lessons from the literature. American Behavioral Scientist 57: 535–547. doi: 10.1177/0002764212469362
2. Riehle D, Ellenberger J, Menahem T, Mikhailovski B, Natchetoi Y, Naveh B, et al. (2009) Open collaboration within corporations using software forges. Software, IEEE 26: 52–58. doi: 10.1109/ms.2009.44
3. Ostrom E (2000) Collective action and the evolution of social norms. The Journal of Economic Perspectives 14: 137–158. doi: 10.1257/jep.14.3.137
4. Raymond ES (1999) The cathedral and the bazaar. Knowledge, Technology & Policy 12: 23–49. doi: 10.1007/s12130-999-1026-0
5. Ciesielska M, Petersen G (2013) Boundary object as a trust buffer. The study of an open source code repository. Tamara Journal for Critical Organization Inquiry 11: 5–14.
6. Ljungberg J (2000) Open source movements as a model for organising. European Journal of Information Systems 9: 208–216. doi: 10.1057/palgrave.ejis.3000373
7. Benkler Y, Nissenbaum H (2006) Commons-based Peer Production and Virtue*. Journal of Political Philosophy 14: 394–419. doi: 10.1111/j.1467-9760.2006.00235.x
8. Bauwens M (2009) Class and capital in peer production. Capital & Class 33: 121–141. doi: 10.1177/030981680909700107
9. Kreiss D, Finn M, Turner F (2011) The limits of peer production: Some reminders from Max Weber for the network society. New Media & Society 13: 243–259. doi: 10.1177/1461444810370951
10. Baytiyeh H, Pfaffman J (2010) Open source software: A community of altruists. Computers in Human Behavior 26: 1345–1354. doi: 10.1016/j.chb.2010.04.008
11. Bergquist M, Ljungberg J (2001) The power of gifts: organizing social relationships in open source communities. Information Systems Journal 11: 305–320. doi: 10.1046/j.1365-2575.2001.00111.x
12. Lanier J (2006) Digital Maoism. The Hazards of the New Online Collectivism. The Edge org: retrieved on 6 April 2012.
13. Keen A (2007) The cult of the amateur: how today's internet is killing our culture. New York: Broadway Business.
14. Ritzer G, Jurgenson N (2010) Production, Consumption, Prosumption The nature of capitalism in the age of the digital 'prosumer'. Journal of Consumer Culture 10: 13–36. doi: 10.1177/1469540509354673
15. O'Neil M (2010) Shirky and Sanger, or the costs of crowdsourcing. Journal of Science Communication 9: 1–6.
16. O'Neil M (2011) The sociology of critique in Wikipedia. Critical Studies in Peer Production 1: 1–11.
17. Pouwelse JA, Garbacki P, Epema D, Sips H (2008) Pirates and Samaritans: A decade of measurements on peer production and their implications for net neutrality and copyright. Telecommunications Policy 32: 701–712. doi: 10.1016/j.telpol.2008.09.004
18. Benkler Y (2002) Coase's Penguin, or, Linux and" The Nature of the Firm". Yale Law Journal 112: 369–446. doi: 10.2307/1562247
19. Benkler Y (2006) The wealth of networks: how social production transforms markets and freedom. New Haven: Yale University Press. xii, 515 p. p.
20. Van Dijck J, Nieborg D (2009) Wikinomics and its discontents: a critical analysis of Web 2.0 business manifestos. New Media & Society 11: 855–874. doi: 10.1177/1461444809105356
21. Gabbiadini A, Mari S, Volpato C (2013) Virtual users support forum: do community members really want to help you? Cyberpsychology, Behavior, and Social Networking 16: 285–292. doi: 10.1089/cyber.2012.0412
22. Roth S, Kaivo-Oja J, Hirschmann T (2013) Smart regions: Two cases of crowdsourcing for regional development. International Journal of Entrepreneurship and Small Business 20: 272–285. doi: 10.1504/ijesb.2013.056890
23. Ducheneaut N (2005) Socialization in an open source software community: A socio-technical analysis. Computer Supported Cooperative Work (CSCW) 14: 323–368. doi: 10.1007/s10606-005-9000-1
24. Moon JY, Sproull L (2002) Essence of distributed work: The case of the Linux kernel. First Monday 5. Available:http://firstmonday.org/ojs/index.php/fm/article/viewArticle/801/710.
25. Gonzalez-Barahona JM, Robles G, Andradas-Izquierdo R, Ghosh RA (2008) Geographic origin of libre software developers. Information Economics and Policy 20: 356–

363. doi: 10.1016/j.infoecopol.2008.07.001

26. Luthiger B (2005) Fun and software development. Proceedings of the First International Conference on Open Source Systems 273–278.
27. Lakhani KR, Von Hippel E (2003) How open source software works. Research policy 32: 923–943. doi: 10.1016/s0048-7333(02)00095-1
28. Jemielniak D (2009) Time as symbolic currency in knowledge work. Information and Organization 19: 277–293. doi: 10.1016/j.infoandorg.2009.08.002
29. Matellán Olivera V (2003) Studying the evolution of libre software projects using publicly available data. 3rd Workshop on Open Source Software Engineering. Available: http://buleria.unileon.es/xmlui/handle/10612/1796: 111–115.
30. German D, Mockus A (2003) Automating the measurement of open source projects. Proceedings of the 3rd workshop on open source software engineering 63–67.
31. Koch S, Schneider G (2000) Results from software engineering research into open source development projects using public data. Diskussionspapiere zum Tätigkeitsfeld Informationsverarbeitung und Informationswirtschaft.
32. Fielding RT (1999) Shared leadership in the Apache project. Communications of the ACM 42: 42–43. doi: 10.1145/299157.299167
33. Mockus A, Fielding RT, Herbsleb JD (2002) Two case studies of open source software development: Apache and Mozilla. ACM Transactions on Software Engineering and Methodology (TOSEM) 11: 309–346. doi: 10.1145/567793.567795
34. McCandless M, Hatcher E, Gospodnetic O (2010) Lucene in Action: Covers Apache Lucene 3.0. Greenwich, CT: Manning Publications Co.
35. Oliva GA, Santana FW, de Oliveira KC, de Souza CR, Gerosa MA (2012) Characterizing key developers: a case study with apache ant. Collaboration and Technology: Springer. pp. 97–112.
36. MacLean AC, Knutson CD (2013) Apache Commit History in Neo4J Representation.
37. Gala-Pérez S, Robles G, González-Barahona JM, Herraiz I (2013) Intensive metrics for the study of the evolution of open source projects: Case studies from Apache Software Foundation projects. MSR '13 Proceedings of the 10th Working Conference on Mining Software Repositories 159–168.
38. Crowston K, Wei K, Howison J, Wiggins A (2012) Free/Libre open-source software development: What we know and what we do not know. ACM Computing Surveys (CSUR) 44: 1–35. doi: 10.1145/2089125.2089127
39. Bishop YM, Fienberg SE, Holland PW (1975) Discrete multivariate analysis: theory and practice. Cambridge, MA: MIT Press.
40. Cheong K (2000) A new interpretation and derivation of the Gini coefficient. Seoul Journal of Economics 13: 391–406.
41. Shalit H (1985) PRACTITIONERS'CORNER* Calculating the Gini Index of inequality for Individual Data. Oxford Bulletin of Economics and Statistics 47: 185–189. doi: 10.1111/j.1468-0084.1985.mp47002006.x
42. Lerman RI, Yitzhaki S (1989) Improving the accuracy of estimates of Gini coefficients. Journal of econometrics 42: 43–47. doi: 10.1016/0304-4076(89)90074-2
43. De Maio FG (2007) Income inequality measures. Journal of epidemiology and community health 61: 849–852. pmid:17873219 doi: 10.1136/jech.2006.052969
44. Howison J, Crowston K (2004) The perils and pitfalls of mining SourceForge. Proceedings of the International Workshop on Mining Software Repositories (MSR 2004). Available:http://floss.syr.edu/sites/crowston.syr.edu/files/The%20perils%20and%20pitfalls%20of%20mining%20SourceForge.pdf: 7–11.
45. Arafat O, Riehle D (2009) The commit size distribution of open source software. HICSS'09 42nd Hawaii International Conference on System Sciences 1–8.
46. Hebb DO (1946) On the nature of fear. Psychological Review 53: 259. pmid:20285975 doi: 10.1037/h0061690
47. Hahsler M, Koch S (2005) Discussion of a large-scale open source data collection methodology. HICSS'05 Proceedings of the 38th Annual Hawaii International Conference on System Sciences
48. Krishnamurthy S (2002) Cave or community?: An empirical examination of 100 mature open source projects. First Monday 2.
49. Bird C, Nagappan N (2012) Who? where? what?: examining distributed development in two large open source projects. Proceedings of the 9th IEEE Working Conference on Mining Software Repositories 237–246.
50. Johnson SL, Faraj S, Kudaravalli S (2014) Emergence of Power Laws in Online Communities: The Role of Social Mechanisms and Preferential Attachment. MIS Quarterly 38: 795–808.
51. Hargittai E, Walejko G (2008) The Participation Divide: Content creation and sharing in the digital age. Information, Community and Society 11: 239–256. doi: 10.1080/13691180801946150
52. Jemielniak D (2014) Common knowledge? An ethnography of Wikipedia. Stanford, CA: Stanford University Press.
53. Hill BM, Monroy-Hernández A (2013) The Remixing Dilemma The Trade-Off Between Generativity and Originality. American Behavioral Scientist 57: 643–663. doi: 10.1177/0002764212469359
54. Bitzer J, Schrettl W, Schröder PJ (2007) Intrinsic motivation in open source software development. Journal of Comparative Economics 35: 160–169. doi: 10.1016/j.jce.2006.10.001
55. Fitzgerald B (2006) The transformation of open source software. MIS Quarterly 30: 587–598.
56. Riehle D (2012) The single-vendor commercial open course business model. Information Systems and e-Business Management 10: 5–17. doi: 10.1007/s10257-010-0149-x

57. Wasko MM, Faraj S (2005) Why should I share? Examining social capital and knowledge contribution in electronic networks of practice. MIS Quarterly 29: 35–57.

58. Von Hippel E, Von Krogh G (2003) Open source software and the" private-collective" innovation model: Issues for organization science. Organization Science: 209–223. doi: 10.1287/orsc.14.2.209.14992

59. Weber S (2004) The Success of Open Source. Cambridge: Harvard University Press.

60. Gloor PA (2005) Swarm creativity: Competitive advantage through collaborative innovation networks. Oxford: Oxford University Press.

61. Gloor PA, Cooper SM (2007) The new principles of a swarm business. MIT Sloan Management Review 48: 81–84.

62. Jemielniak D (2015) Naturally emerging regulation and the danger of delegitimizing conventional leadership: Drawing on the example of Wikipedia. In: Bradbury H, editor. The SAGE Handbook of Action Research. London, UK—New Delphi, India—Thousand Oaks, CA: Sage.

63. Crowston K, Howison J (2006) Hierarchy and centralization in free and open source software team communications. Knowledge, Technology & Policy 18: 65–85. doi: 10.1007/s12130-006-1004-8

64. Demil B, Lecocq X (2006) Neither market nor hierarchy nor network: The emergence of bazaar governance. Organization Studies 27: 1447–1466. doi: 10.1177/0170840606067250

CHAPTER 10

MEASURING SOFTWARE TIMING ERRORS IN THE PRESENTATION OF VISUAL STIMULI IN COGNITIVE NEUROSCIENCE EXPERIMENTS

Pablo Garaizar[1], Miguel A. Vadillo[2], Diego López-de-Ipiña[1], Helena Matute[3]

[1] Deusto Institute of Technology, DeustoTech, Universidad de Deusto, Bilbao, Spain

[2] Cognitive, Perceptual and Brain Sciences, University College London, London, United Kingdom

[3] Faculty of Psychology and Education, Universidad de Deusto, Bilbao, Spain

ABSTRACT

Because of the features provided by an abundance of specialized experimental software packages, personal computers have become prominent and powerful tools in cognitive research. Most of these programs have mechanisms to control the precision and accuracy with which visual stimuli are presented as well as the response times. However, external factors, often related to the technology used to display the visual information, can have a noticeable impact on the actual performance and may be easily overlooked by researchers. The aim of this study is to measure the precision and accuracy of the timing mechanisms of some of the most popular software packages used in a typical laboratory scenario in order to assess whether presentation times configured by researchers do not differ from measured times more than what is expected due to the hardware limitations. Despite the apparent precision and accuracy of the results, important issues related to timing setups in the presentation of visual stimuli were found, and they should be taken into account by researchers in their experiments.

INTRODUCTION

Since the days of Wilhelm Wundt, experimental psychologists have studied the temporal dynamics of the cognitive processes involved in perception and attention. Experimental apparatus that allow researchers to present visual stimuli for very short periods of time, such as tachistoscopes, quickly became popular in most experimental psychology laboratories. Since the 1980s, these complex and delicate devices have been replaced by personal computers and standard monitors, which are cheaper and easier to use. Moreover, experimental psychologists and cognitive neuroscientists now have several software alternatives that accurately present visual stimuli [1]. However, most of these tools run on standard personal computers (PCs), and this type of hardware is not optimized for the accurate presentation of visual stimuli. There are many limitations related to stimuli presentation durations caused by the underlying technologies of CRT and LCD displays and the timing mechanisms provided by non-real-time operating systems (e.g., Microsoft Windows on a PC). Both factors can have a significant impact on the accuracy and precision of the visual stimuli presentation, particularly in experimental paradigms that have very short Stimulus Onset Asynchrony (SOA) [2] [3] [4].

Citation: Garaizar P, Vadillo MA, López-de-Ipiña D, Matute H (2014) Measuring Software Timing Errors in the Presentation of Visual Stimuli in Cognitive Neuroscience Experiments. PLoS ONE 9(1): e85108. doi:10.1371/journal.pone.0085108

The goal of this research was to assess the potential discrepancies between the timing conditions defined by the researchers when using a subset of specialized software for the presentation of visual stimuli on common-use hardware and software (i.e., low-refresh-rate displays and non-real-time operating systems) and the actual onset and offset times of the visual stimuli detected using external photodetectors. Assessing the size of these potential timing errors is a first and necessary step in order to minimize and correct them. Whenever possible, we will also describe the way in which we were able to compensate these errors.

CRT and LCD Displays

The widespread success of displays based on the cathode ray tube (CRT) established this type of monitor as the standard in computer-based experimental laboratories. A CRT monitor has an electron gun at the back that points to a glass screen covered with phosphors located at the front of the monitor. To display an image, the electron gun points to the top left corner of the screen and shoots a beam at the phosphors, briefly lighting them up. Once the image displaying process has started, the gun moves rapidly, and the beam energizes the entire screen, line by line down to the lower right corner. Once there, the electron gun turns off, points again to the top left corner, and the painting process starts again. The last step is controlled by the VSYNC (vertical synchronization) signal, and the refresh rate of the CRT monitor depends on how fast this signal is triggered (see Figure 1). The period between two VSYNC signals is known as a "tick," and its duration depends on the refresh rate (e.g., 16.667 ms at 60 Hz and 10 ms at 100 Hz).

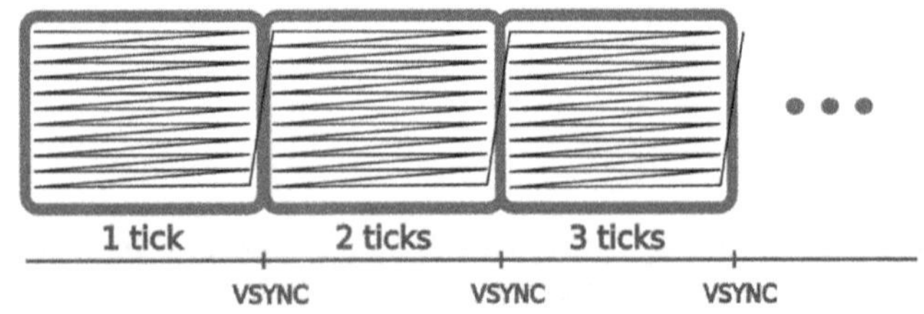

Figure 1. Representation of the path followed by the electron gun for a CRT monitor. At the end of each frame, the electron gun returns to the top left corner and starts again (VSYNC signal).

It is important to notice that the luminance of each dot of the image displayed by a CRT monitor is not constant but dependent on two factors: the refresh rate (i.e., the time the electron gun needs to energize it again) and the decay time, which depends on the phosphor type (1.5 to 6 ms for the frequently used P-22 phosphor). Therefore, researchers conducting experiments with CRT monitors should not assume a rectangular-shaped signal of the configured number of ticks of duration in their visual stimuli presentations, but a set of discrete pulses separated by the duration of a tick and the decay time.

Despite the continuous advances in liquid crystal display (LCD) technology, CRT monitors have been considered more suitable for the precise and accurate presentation of visual stimuli [5]. Their higher frame rates (typically around 85–100 Hz, but some models can achieve 240 Hz), greater number of frames per second (FPS), and shorter rise and decay times enable abrupt changes from one frame to another.

Nevertheless, because of their small size and low weight, LCDs are becoming more popular. Moreover, they offer some characteristics that increase visibility, such as the absence of flickering when displaying static images, and the poor temporal characteristics typically associated with LCD screens are based on studies of older LCD technology. Using current LCD displays, Lagroix, Yanko, and Spalek [6] found photometric estimates of the rise time that are far shorter (1–6 ms) than earlier estimates (20–150 ms) and approach those of CRTs (<1 ms). In addition, Wang and Nikolic [7] tested an inexpensive 120 Hz LCD display that was shown to have timing and stability characteristics at least as good as a CRT monitor. These findings suggest that LCD displays are suitable for studies that require high accuracy in the timing of visual presentations, but the truth is that both display technologies are affected by different limitations that make them inappropriate for brief stimuli presentations [8] [9].

The luminance of each dot of an LCD display is defined by the orientation of the liquid crystal molecules placed between two polarized glasses and two electrodes. To display an image, the array of electrodes modifies the amount of visible light emitted from the back of the display. Although this backlight is often assumed to be constant, its luminance level is pulse-width modulated. Instead of varying its intensity to adjust the luminance, it is switched off for brief periods of time (the higher the amplitude of the modulation, the lower the backlight luminance). The backlight modulation frequencies are far from the critical flicker frequency [10] and usually neglected, but might introduce undesirable effects in the visualization of stimuli (e.g., steady-state evoked visual potentials). The time needed to switch a dot of an LCD display from one luminance level to another is known as response time (RT). Instead of calculating the RT as the time needed to switch from full black to white as suggested by ISO 9241–305, most manufacturers provide the RT as the time needed to perform a grey-to-grey transition which is significantly shorter due to Response Time Compensation (RTC) mechanisms. RTC, also known as overdrive, is based on applying an over-voltage to accelerate the orientation change of the liquid crystals. This relation between luminance levels and response time in LCD displays hinders synchronous presentations of stimuli formed by different luminance levels [8].

Although there are significant differences between the underlying technologies of CRTs and LCDs, some mechanisms are similar [11] and they are operated in the same way from the operating system due to compatibility issues. Even in LCD monitors, the refresh rate configurations affect the monitor's performance. In order to minimize flicker, tearing, and other artifacts, most programs use a technique called double-buffer (or multiple-buffer for cases with more than 2 buffers). While the graphics card is rastering one buffer on the screen, the software is preparing the next frame in the other buffer. At VSYNC signal, both buffers are flipped, and the process starts again. Therefore, different images cannot be shown on the screen at a rate faster than the refresh rate.

Because CRT monitors are decreasing in popularity with consumers, fewer are being produced, and it is becoming difficult for experimental laboratories to find CRT monitors through conventional supply channels. Some researchers fight this trend by buying and storing CRT monitors for future use or purchasing them through nonconventional supply channels (e.g., eBay) or even repairing them when they malfunction. However, these strategies do not seem viable in the long term. Therefore, we use a computer equipped with an LCD display to perform tests of software specialized for the presentation of visual stimuli.

General Purpose and Real-Time Operating Systems

To evaluate the influence of the real-time nature of an operating system in these experiments, some of the tests conducted in our study were run under a real-time operating system (Linux 2.6.33–29-realtime). It is important to recall how a real-time operating system differs from a general-purpose operating system. Contrary to popular belief, real-time operating systems are not necessarily faster, but they are predictable. Their schedulers work like traffic lights on a road. The schedulers' main goal is not to maximize the overall throughput but, rather, to meet the predictability and fairness requirements. By contrast, the goal of general-purpose operating systems is usually the opposite. Throughput is maximized, even if background tasks are starved for long periods. As a result of their scheduling policies, the length of these periods is unpredictable. These non-real-time scheduling policies manage multitasking concurrency similar to a yield sign on a road (i.e., no task will wait unnecessarily if it can be attended to instantly, but the maximum running delay for a task when the system is overloaded is unpredictable). In general, a real-time and low-latency operating system is recommended for experiments that have high accuracy requirements. Unfortunately, nearly every specialized software package used in experimental psychology and neuroscience research runs on a general-purpose operating system (e.g., Microsoft Windows) and might be affected by the unpredictability of the task scheduling process. The good news is that specialized software eliminates eventual delays by implementing several optimizations (e.g., priority boosting and frame precomputation). However, optimizing twice (i.e., using a low-latency operating system and specialized software with built-in performance boosts) may lead to suboptimal resource allocation, which will result in poorer overall performance. Therefore, we tested whether the combination of a real-time operating system and the specialized software is optimal compared with the same software running on a general-purpose operating system. As will be explained further in the Results section, not all tests run using a real-time operating system were better than tests run using a general-purpose operating system in all conditions.

MATERIALS AND METHODS

We used Black Box Toolkit (BBTK) [12] to test the accuracy and precision of the timing mechanisms used to present visual stimuli by several specialized software packages on PCs: E-Prime 2.0.8.90 [13], DMDX 4.0.4.8 [14] and PsychoPy 1.64.00 [15]. All were tested on Microsoft Windows 7 32-bit Professional Edition. Because PsychoPy 1.64.00 can run natively on both operating systems, it was also tested on Ubuntu Linux 10.04 with the Linux 2.6.33-29-realtime kernel.

This subset of software packages is not aimed to be exhaustive but to serve as an example of the type of errors that can be found in their underlying timing mechanisms and the type of corrections that should be applied for time-sensitive experiments' configurations. The selection of the investigated software packages has been done with the following criteria: select a popular commercial software package, a popular free software package, and a multiplatform software package. Regarding popularity, E-Prime is one of the most popular experimental software packages worldwide. Its combination of a graphical authoring tool and custom programming language to configure the experiments, its licensing model, and its underlying mechanisms to schedule and present stimuli make it a representative instance of this class (without detriment or other popular software packages such as DirectRT, NBS Presentation, etc.). DMDX is representative of a long tradition of experimental software, starting at 1975 with DMASTR and ending with its recent port to Microsoft DirectX libraries. In fact, these libraries are used by other software packages (e.g., NBS Presentation), therefore their limitations might affect all of them in a similar way. PsychoPy is a multiplatform software package that can run natively in Microsoft Windows, GNU/Linux and Apple Mac OS X. It is based on Python, like many other alternatives available (e.g., Experiment Builder, PyEPL, OpenSesame, Vision Egg), and provides a graphical authoring tool and a set of Python libraries to set up the experiments. All software tests were conducted using the same hardware: an Apple Macbook Pro with an Intel Core 2 Duo T7600 processor and an ATI Radeon Mobility X1600 graphics card. The native resolution of the display was 1440×900 pixels at 60 Hz. The suitability of the display was confirmed using the 6-hour *RefreshClockTest* of E-Prime (available at:http://www.pstnet.com/support/kb.asp?TopicID=3003) and an analysis of the results provided by the *timeByFrames* test of PsychoPy.

The BBTK photodetectors were used to measure the timing under all conditions. The BBTK was designed for this type of measurement [12] [16] and is able to transfer detected changes in luminance from the photodetector to the parallel port in less than 100 ns.

A well-known procedure was used to test the precision and accuracy of the visual stimuli presentations [17] [18]. For each of the experimental software packages examined, the photodetector, placed in the middle of the screen, was programmed to detect black to white and white to black screen transitions in the presentation display. In five independent series of 60 seconds, a continuous alternation of white and black screens was scheduled to be repeated with interval durations of 16.667, 50, 100, 200, 500, and 1000 ms (i.e., 1, 3, 6, 12, 30 and 60 ticks at 60 Hz, respectively). To compute the amount of missed frames, the whole set of measurements for each testing condition was used (i.e., approximately 300, 600, 1500, 3000, 6000, and 18000 for 1000, 500, 200, 100, 50, and 16.667 ms, respectively).

As in previous studies using this measurement procedure [17] [18], the presentation and measurement equipment used for all timing conditions are independent in order to avoid undesired interferences between the timing mechanisms used to generate the black to white and white to black transitions of the specialized software and the real-time application used to gather the data provided by the photodetector. The Apple MacBook Pro runs the experimental software independently (as it would be run in a real experiment with human participants), and the BBTK detects all changes in luminance from the Macbook's display and sends them, via a parallel-port connection, to an auxiliary computer (AMD Sempron 2200 running the BBTK's capture data software under Microsoft Windows XP 32-bit Professional edition).

RESULTS

After considering all the previously mentioned details regarding displays, we expected that the difference between the interval configured by the experimenter for a visual stimulus presentation and the actual interval displayed by the software would be a multiple of the duration of a tick (see Figure 2a). However, we observed that all measured timing errors (MTEs) were concentrated around two peaks: one slightly before the VSYNC signal, the other slightly later. Figure 2b shows an ideal representation, and Figure 2c shows an example of the measurements collected by our photodetectors during the analysis of a 1000-ms interval animation performed using E-Prime.

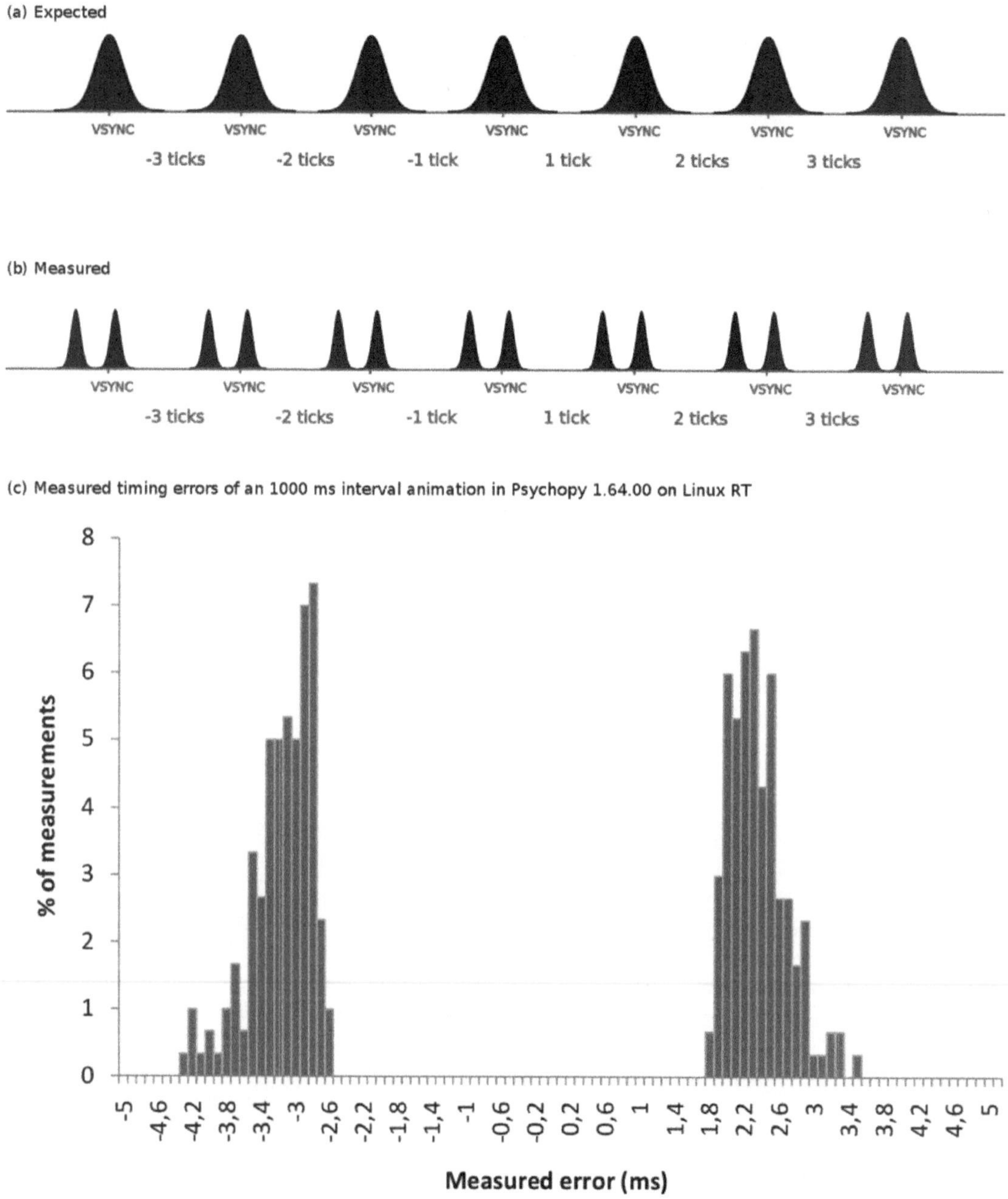

Figure 2. Measured timing errors distribution. Measured timing errors distribution: (a) Expected distribution of measured timing errors. (b) Actual distribution of measured timing errors. (c) Distribution of measured timing errors (in ms) of the PsychoPy 1.64.00 software displaying an animation from black to white every 1000 ms onLinux 2.6.33-29-realtime.

The discrepancy between our expectations and the actual measurements can be explained by considering the rise and decay times of the LCD display. Because the response time is greater than 0 ms, these times are slightly longer for black-to-white transitions and slightly shorter for white-to-black transitions. Further technical details about rise and decay times of LCD displays and their implications in the duration of the stimuli are explained by Elze [8] [9] and Elze and Tanner [10]. Moreover, the BBTK photosensors do not provide a continuous analog value but a discrete digital one based on an adjustable threshold. This MTE is attributed to the technology used to show and measure the visual stimuli and not to the experimental software. Therefore, we decided to convert the MTE to full missed frames using the formula:

$$Missed\,frames = \begin{cases} \left\lfloor MTE - \frac{tick}{2} \right\rfloor, MTE < 0 \\ \left\lfloor MTE + \frac{tick}{2} \right\rfloor, MTE \geq 0 \end{cases} \quad (1)$$

where $\lfloor\,\rfloor$ denotes the floor function.

Even with this conversion, we found discrepancies between stipulated and measured intervals in most of the setups we configured in DMDX, E-Prime and PsychoPy. These discrepancies were so consistent across all tests (each test was repeated 5 times per interval and software) that we decided to identify ways to compensate for them, as described below. We then repeated the measurements to assess the optimal precision and accuracy of the presentation of visual stimuli using the tested software. The results shown in Table 1 are the final measurements, once all adjustments and corrections had been made (the complete dataset can be found in https://opensciencefram ework.org/project/F2gBN.).

Table 1. Missed frames for each testing condition

Software /OS	Interval (ms)	Expectancy (frames)	Missed frames					
			−2	**−1**	**0**	**1**	**2**	**>2**
DMDX	1000	300	0	0	300	0	0	0
/Windows 7	500	600	0	0	600	0	0	0
	200	1500	0	0	1500	0	0	0
	100	3000	0	0	2999	1	0	0
	50	6000	0	0	6000	0	0	0
	16.667	18000	0	0	17998	1	0	0
			−2	**−1**	**0**	**1**	**2**	**>2**
E-Prime	1000	300	0	0	299	1	0	0
/Windows 7	500	600	0	0	600	0	0	0
	200	1500	0	0	300	0	0	0
	100	3000	0	0	3000	0	0	0
	50	6000	0	0	5997	1	1	0
	16.667	18000	0	0	17857	28	20	12*
			−2	**−1**	**0**	**1**	**2**	**>2**
PsychoPy	1000	300	0	0	300	0	0	0
/Windows 7	500	600	0	0	600	0	0	0
	200	1500	0	2	1496	2	0	0
	100	3000	0	1179	634	1187	0	0
	50	6000	0	0	2572	2573	0	0
	16.667	18000	0	0	5981	5980	0	0
			−2	**−1**	**0**	**1**	**2**	**>2**
PsychoPy	1000	300	0	0	300	0	0	0
/Linux RT	500	600	0	9	582	9	0	0
	200	1500	2	13	1447	13	0	0
	100	3000	2	25	2889	32	2	0
	50	6000	0	0	5113	575	0	0
	16.667	18000	0	0	17908	14	3	10**

*E-Prime, 16.667 ms interval, >2 missed frames distribution: 3 missed frames: 8; 4 missed frames: 3; 11 missed frames: 1.
**PsychoPy under Linux RT, 16.667 ms interval, >2 missed frames distribution: 3 missed frames: 10.
doi:10.1371/journal.pone.0085108.t001

In our initial DMDX configurations, we could not attain transition intervals shorter than three ticks (i.e., 50 ms at 60 Hz), even if the delay between trials was set to 0 ticks. In a personal communication, K. I. Forster confirmed that fast sequences of different items should not be presented as separate items but as a single item with multiple frames. This advice should be heeded by DMDX users when very short transitions between different trials are needed. Researchers should adjust related aspects of the experiment (e.g., non-visual stimuli presentations, reaction time measurement, or external apparatus synchronization) to compensate for this change.

We faced a different problem with E-Prime. Because durations in E-Prime are configured in milliseconds and not ticks, the duration of each interval was defined as a multiple of the number of milliseconds in one tick (i.e., 1000 ms for 60 ticks, 500 ms for 30 ticks, 200 ms for 12 ticks, etc.), and we requested VSYNC synchronization. After analyzing our initial measurements, we found that E-Prime was consistently missing a frame in each interval. Fortunately, information about these timing errors was provided in E-Prime's log files, and they are related to the preparation time of the following stimulus (configured via the PreRelease value, which allows the current stimulus to release a portion of its execution time to a following stimulus in order to allow the following stimulus to perform setup activities) and E-Prime's timing modes (i.e., Cumulative Mode and Event Mode). After testing several configurations, we concluded that the best way to optimize the precision and accuracy of visual stimuli presentations using E-Prime for this simple animation is to use E-Prime's Event Mode timing (i.e., delays in the onset of an event will not affect the specified duration of the event), to subtract the duration of one tick from the interval duration in each transition (e.g., 1000 ms–16.667 ms=983.333 ms) and to force the synchronization with VSYNC signal at the onset and offset of the stimulus. This adjustment is coherent with the "rule of thumb" provided by vendors in the user manual, according to which the stimulus duration should be set to 10ms below the expected total duration of the stimulus ("A good rule of thumb is to set the stimulus duration to 10 ms below the expected total duration of all refresh cycles desired for the stimulus. Since the visual duration is always rounded up to the next refresh, the display duration must be specified as some portion of one refresh below the targeted refresh duration plus the expected measurement error for when to look for the vertical blanking signal indicating the time of a refresh." [13]). But instead of using an arbitrary correction value, we decided to follow a more detailed suggestion provided in the E-Prime users' manual and make this correction value dependent on the refresh rate of the monitor and the time needed to prepare the next frame of the animation (i.e., a non-zero but negligible value in our simple animation).

Our tests using PsychoPy also required adjustments. We found that a black frame lasting 1 tick was introduced in every frame transition, which increased the duration of the black intervals by two ticks (one before the beginning of the interval and another after the end) and had no effect in the duration of white intervals. To compensate for this, we subtracted two ticks from the duration of the black intervals (e.g., 1000 ms–2×16.667 ms=966.667 ms). For intervals lasting 1 tick, a continuous white to white transition 1 tick in length was configured because PsychoPy automatically inserted one black frame 1 tick in duration between them.

As mentioned previously, the results shown in Table 1 represent the missed frames (i.e., the number of frames away from the target) for intervals lasting 1000, 500, 200, 100, 50, and 16.667 ms, respectively once all adjustments were performed. Note that the number of missed frames in each row do not necessarily add up to the expected number of frames. This happens because exactly 5 minutes of black-to-white and white-to-black transitions were recorded. If any of the frames happened to be presented later than scheduled, then the 5 minute-interval might not suffice to present the whole sequence of programmed transitions. Positive values represent intervals longer than the configured interval, negative values represent shorter intervals, and zero means the interval lasted the stipulated duration. Quite interestingly, the number of missed frames is noticeably higher when the shortest intervals were tested with PsychoPy, both in Microsoft Windows and Linux. Figure 3 depicts the mean number of missed frames when using PsychoPy under both OS. To improve the comparability across time intervals, we computed these means using only the first 50 transitions in each round (250 transitions in each condition). As can be seen, the performance of PsychoPy is worse under very brief intervals, but this effect is somewhat ameliorated when PsychoPy operates under realtime-Linux.

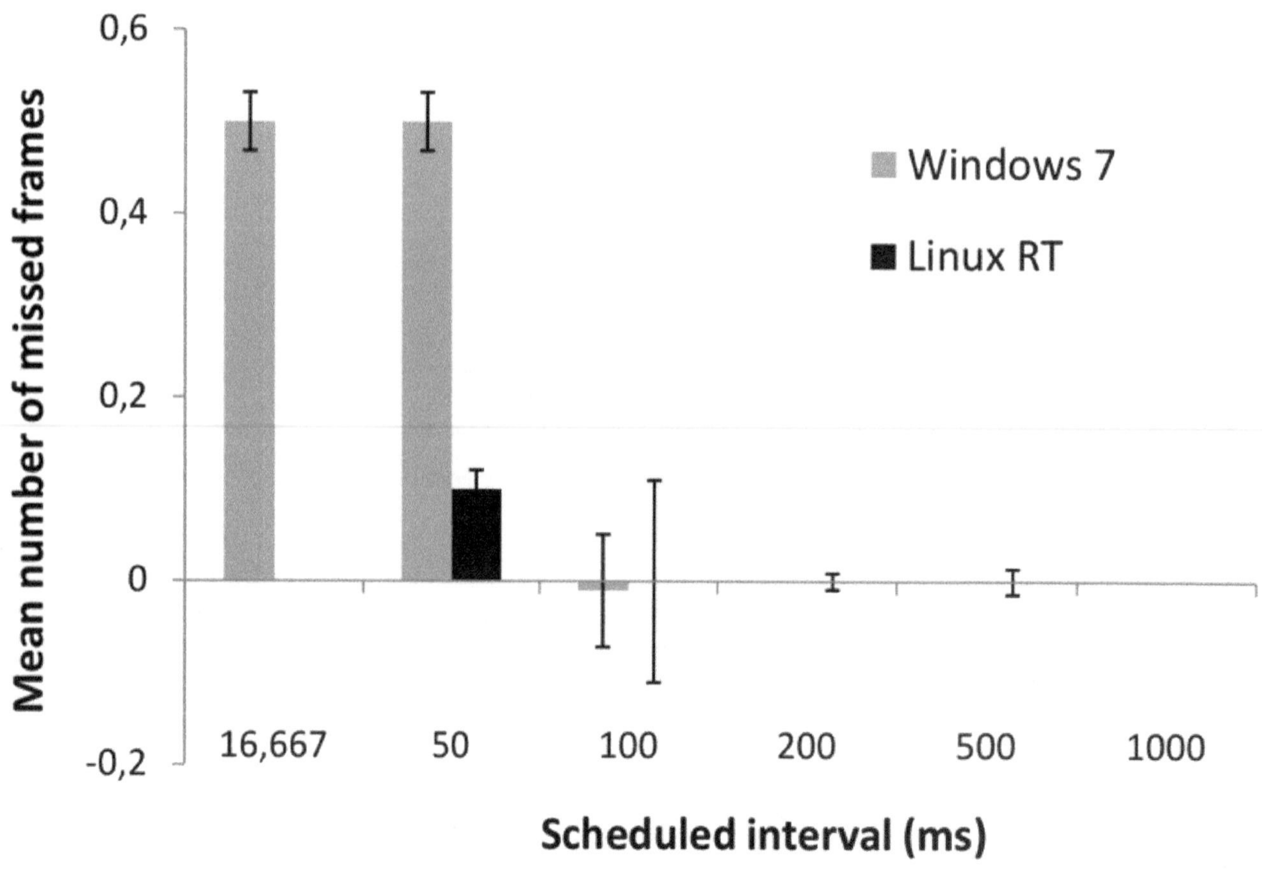

Figure 3. Absolute number of missed frames in PsychoPy tests. Absolute number of missed frames for each testing condition of PsychoPy running on Microsoft Windows 7 Professional 32-bit edition and Ubuntu 10.04 LTS with Linux 2.6.33–29-realtime.

DISCUSSION

In all of our tests, DMDX presented visual stimuli with high precision and accuracy. Were it not for the difficulty in programming experiments using the DMASTR syntax, it would be a perfect tool. DMDX allows defining time intervals both in ticks and in milliseconds. Although defining stimuli durations in ticks can be tricky, it is closer to the actual implementation of the experiment and makes the limitations of the hardware explicit to researchers, which discourages them from setting intervals that are impossible to meet (i.e., those that are not a multiple of the tick duration). In fact, as Forster explains in the DMDX Online Help page [19], millisecond-oriented keywords are only provided for one of two situations: (1) when researchers do not care about precise tachistoscopic presentations, or (2) when the item file is needed to work on multiple machines regardless of their refresh rates. Moreover, very short stimuli presentations have to be aggregated as different frames of the same trial to eliminate inter-trial delays. This change can interfere with other aspects of the experimental design (e.g., non-visual stimuli presentations, reaction time measurements, etc.) or be overlooked by experimenters.

We conclude that E-Prime is a highly precise software package for the presentation of visual stimuli. However, setting the stimuli durations in milliseconds (and not in ticks) might introduce a source of error. On the one hand, it is much easier for researchers to use. They are accustomed to thinking in terms of seconds or milliseconds and may not be aware of the concept of a tick. On the other hand, using presentation times that are not multiple of the refresh rate may lead to timing errors. These errors can be smaller than the duration of one tick, but will still increase the measured error. According to our tests, even visual stimuli with a duration that is a multiple of the refresh rate may have to wait to be synchronized with the VSYNC signal of the display. This delay results in larger presentation times for the previous stimulus. As mentioned previously, correcting this deviation is straightforward. However, if a researcher focuses on the reaction times in the E-Prime logs and does not analyze the registered timing errors during the presentation of stimuli, this error can be overlooked. We recommend that researchers set the VSYNC signal synchronization and subtract the duration of one tick when defining stimuli intervals, and ensure that the pre-computation time needed to prepare stimuli does not exceed on that subtracted tick plus the amount of time configured in the PreRelease value of the stimulus.

Both PsychoPy and E-Prime provide the experimenter with a user-friendly interface for setting up experiments and the ability to define arbitrary times for the duration of the stimuli. Therefore, similar recommendations apply. In addition, PsychoPy automatically includes a black frame lasting 1 tick in every stimuli transition. This inclusion should be taken into account in experimental paradigms with high precision and accuracy requirements, and the frame duration should be corrected by subtracting the black frames when possible. Moreover, PsychoPy is able to eliminate the limitations of the Graphical User Interface (GUI) by providing an Application Programming Interface (API) from which experiments can be easily developed in Python. Combining both high-level (i.e., GUI) and low-level (i.e., Python API) approaches, experimenters are able to generate experimental setups that are as accurate as the underlying platform (e.g., using frame refresh periods to control presentation timing accurately). Therefore, PsychoPy is an attractive alternative for designing and running cognitive experiments with some very interesting characteristics. For example, it is published under a Free Software license. In addition, it runs under the most popular general-purpose operating systems (i.e., Microsoft Windows, GNU/Linux and Mac OS X) and is even able to take advantage of the reliability provided by real-time operating systems (e.g., Linux 2.6.33–29-realtime).

The significant differences between a multi-platform software package such as PsychoPy and single-platform alternatives like E-Prime or DMDX are related to the software abstraction layers involved in each case. DMDX uses a multimedia library specifically designed for the development of real-time applications (i.e., DirectX) and requires pre-configuration of display equipment to achieve the maximum accuracy and precision. E-Prime is not as close to the hardware as DMDX, but leverages best timing APIs in Microsoft Windows (i.e., QueryPerformanceCounters and Multimedia Timers) to maximize the accuracy and precision of stimulus presentations. PsychoPy, by contrast, relies on a high-level and multi-platform interpreted language (i.e., Python). The benefits of this approach are clear: any PsychoPy-based experiment can run smoothly on all major operating systems. However, the transition from PsychoPy experiment setup files (i.e., XML-based psyexp files) to the control of the display hardware might be performed sub-optimally if not tuned manually. The good news is that PsychoPy gives advanced users the ability to maximize the accuracy and precision of stimulus presentation when used as a Python library through the use of a non-slip (global) clock timing mechanism. This functionality is also available from the Experiment Builder of PsychoPy since version 1.74.00. Moreover, Python scripts generated by PsychoPy could improve their performance if compiled to native executable code or used an optimized Python interpreter.

There may be several causes that explain the differences between the results gathered using PsychoPy on Microsoft Windows and on Linux real-time. The best-effort policy of a non-real-time operating system like Microsoft Windows is able to provide a better throughput than a real-time operating system in non demanding cases (i.e., tests with larger intervals), while performs worse in demanding situations (i.e., tests with shorter intervals). Moreover, the software architecture of each operating system is significantly different regarding the graphical layer (i.e., it runs as a user process in Linux, whereas it is integrated in the kernel in Microsoft Windows), and might be the cause of a slightly poorer performance in Linux in tests where the stress of the system is not an issue.

Further research is needed to extend these conclusions to a wider range of experimental software. Providing sub-millisecond accuracy is a typical claim of vision-related experimental software, but the validity of these claims should be tested by third-party researchers. Nevertheless, although some parameters (e.g., the refresh rate of the LCD display) were not optimal, the overall performance of the tested operating systems and experimental software combinations were sufficient to fulfill the requirements of most of the experimental tasks performed by researchers. This is good news for researchers who need to present stimuli with high accuracy. Provided that the recommendations explained in the present work are taken into account by researchers, we consider DMDX, E-Prime and PsychoPy suitable for most of the experimental paradigms used in cognitive research that require high levels of precision and accuracy.

AUTHOR CONTRIBUTIONS

Conceived and designed the experiments: PG MAV DLI HM. Performed the experiments: PG. Analyzed the data: PG MAV. Contributed reagents/materials/analysis tools: HM. Wrote the paper: PG MAV DLI HM.

REFERENCES

1. Mathôt S, Schreij D, Theeuwes J (2011) OpenSesame: An open-source, graphical experiment builder for the social sciences. Beh Res Methods, 44, 314–324.
2. Neely JH (1977) Semantic priming and retrieval from lexical memory: Roles of inhibitionless spreading activation and limited-capacity attention. J Exp Psychol-Gen, 106, 225–254.
3. Ratcliff R, McKoon G (1978) Priming in item recognition: Evidence for the prepositional structure of sentences. J Verbal Learn Verb Beh, 17, 403–417.
4. Fazio RH, Sanbonmatsu DM, Powell MC, Kardes FR (1986) On the automatic activation of attitudes. J Pers Soc Psychol, 50, 229–238.
5. Cowan WB (1995) Displays for vision research. In M. Bass (Ed.), Handbook of optics, Vol. 1: Fundamentals, techniques, and design (pp. 27.21–27.44). New York: McGraw-Hill.
6. Lagroix H, Yanko M, Spalek T (2012) LCDs are better: Psychophysical and photometric estimates of the temporal characteristics of CRT and LCD monitors. Atten Percep Psychophys., 74, 1033–41.
7. Wang P, Nikolic D (2011) An LCD monitor with sufficiently precise timing for research in vision. Front Hum Neurosci, 5, 85.
8. Elze T (2010) Achieving precise display timing in visual neuroscience experiments. J Neurosci Methods, 191, 171–179.
9. Elze T (2010) Misspecifications of Stimulus Presentation Durations in Experimental Psychology: A Systematic Review of the Psychophysics Literature. PLoS ONE, 5, e12792.
10. Elze T, Tanner T (2009) Liquid crystal display response times estimation for medical applications. Med Phys, 36, 4984–4990.
11. Castellano JA (1992) Handbook of display technology. New York: Academic Press.
12. Plant RR, Hammond N, Turner G (2004) Self-validating presentation and response timing in cognitive paradigms: How and why? Beh Res Meth Instr C, 36, 291–303.
13. Schneider W, Eschman A, Zuccolotto A (2002) E-Prime user's guide. Pittsburgh, PA: Psychology Software Tools.
14. Forster KI, Forster JC (2003) DMDX: A Windows display program with millisecond accuracy. Beh Res Methods, 35, 116–124.
15. Peirce JW (2007) PsychoPy: Psychophysics software in Python. J Neurosci Methods, 162, 8–13.
16. Plant RR, Turner G (2009) Millisecond precision psychological research in a world of commodity computers: New hardware, new problems? Beh Res Methods, 41, 598–614.
17. Schmidt WC (2001) Presentation accuracy of Web animation methods. Beh Res Meth Instr C, 33, 187–200.
18. Stewart N (2006) Millisecond accuracy video display using OpenGL under Linux. Beh Res Methods, 8, 142–145.
19. Foster K (2012) DMDX Display Software. Retrieved 18 November 2013, fromhttp://www.u.arizona.edu/~kforster/dmdx/dmdx.htm.

CHAPTER 11 ACCURACY AND PRECISION OF VISUAL STIMULUS TIMING IN PSYCHOPY: NO TIMING ERRORS IN STANDARD USAGE

Pablo Garaizar[1], Miguel A. Vadillo[2,3]

[1] Deusto Institute of Technology, DeustoTech, Universidad de Deusto, Bilbao, Spain

[2] Department of Experimental Psychology, University College London, London, United Kingdom

[3] Primary Care and Public Health Sciences, King's College London, London, United Kingdom

ABSTRACT

In a recent report published in PLoS ONE, we found that the performance of PsychoPy degraded with very short timing intervals, suggesting that it might not be perfectly suitable for experiments requiring the presentation of very brief stimuli. The present study aims to provide an updated performance assessment for the most recent version of PsychoPy (v1.80) under different hardware/software conditions. Overall, the results show that PsychoPy can achieve high levels of precision and accuracy in the presentation of brief visual stimuli. Although occasional timing errors were found in very demanding benchmarking tests, there is no reason to think that they can pose any problem for standard experiments developed by researchers.

During the last decades, computers have become an essential tool in psychological and neuroscientific research. Thanks to them, it is possible to present participants stimuli in different audiovisual formats and register different aspects of their reaction to those materials, including verbal judgments or response latencies. However, not all combinations of software and hardware are able to comply with the strict requirements of some experimental paradigms. For instance, researchers often need to present stimuli for very brief periods of time. Experiments on subliminal priming typically involve the presentation of words or images for intervals no longer than 16–50 ms [1], [2]. In these experiments, even small deviations from programmed durations (e.g., from 16 to 33 ms) can make a substantial difference in participants' ability to perceive stimuli. Similarly, some experimental paradigms require very accurate measurement of reaction times. Many of these experiments explore effects in the range of just 30–100 ms [3],[4]. Problems in the presentation of stimuli or in the logging of responses can affect the results of these kinds of experiments. Although measurement errors usually have a minimal impact on data when researchers average reaction times collected across many trials [5], [6], they can compromise more sophisticated analyses like, for example, fitting models to the distribution of reaction-times [7]–[9].

Fortunately for researchers, there is a wide variety of software packages available that have been carefully designed to comply with these strict requirements. In addition to proprietary software (e.g., E-Prime, Presentations), some outstanding open and free access alternatives are also available [10]–[13].

Citation: Garaizar P, Vadillo MA (2014) Accuracy and Precision of Visual Stimulus Timing in PsychoPy: No Timing Errors in Standard Usage. PLoS ONE 9(11): e112033. doi:10.1371/journal.pone.0112033

Among them, PsychoPy is quickly becoming a popular choice [14]. PsychoPy is a multiplatform software package for designing and conducting cognitive experiments that can run natively in Microsoft Windows, GNU/Linux and Apple Mac OS X. It is coded in Python, like many other alternatives available (e.g., Experiment Builder, PyEPL, OpenSesame, Vision Egg), and provides a graphical authoring tool (PsychoPy experiment builder) and a set of Python libraries for building experiments.

Unfortunately, in a recent report published in PLoS ONE, we found that the performance of PsychoPy degraded with very short timing intervals, suggesting that it might not be perfectly suitable for experiments requiring the presentation of very brief stimuli [15]. Although the performance of PsychoPy improved noticeably when running under a real-time operative system, important timing errors still remained for stimuli durations of 100 ms or less. However, there are reasons to suspect that the results of our previous tests might underestimate the potential accuracy of PsychoPy. Firstly, as noted by the author of PsychoPy himself [16], our study on the accuracy of PsychoPy was conducted with an early version of the software package that was almost 3 years old at the time the study was finally published. Our report ignored any improvements introduced in PsychoPy during that time. Secondly, the scripts used in our tests were generated using the experiment builder interface, which was not fully operative in that version. Furthermore, the experiment builder of the tested version did not allow defining stimulus durations in terms of ticks (i.e., display refreshes). Therefore, in our benchmark tests stimulus durations were defined in time units. This might have given rise to problems in the translation from the millisecond definition of stimuli to the corresponding number of ticks. Finally, given that the original study used a single computer for all tests, it is impossible to discard the possibility that the poor performance of PsychoPy reflected limitations of hardware, rather than genuine problems of software. The present study aims at providing an update of the performance of the more recent version of PsychoPy under ideal conditions.

METHODS

The main differences with respect to the previous study [15] are the version of PsychoPy being tested (1.80 instead of 1.64) and the specific scripts used to assess its accuracy. In the present study, the scripts were not created with PsychoPy's experiment builder. Instead, we adapted a benchmarking program developed by Jeremy Gray [17]. In addition, we have conducted our tests on updated operative systems.

Methodology and Apparatus

Tests were conducted on two different computers: 1) Apple MacBook Pro 11,1 "Core i5" 2.4 13″ Late 2013 with 8 GB of RAM, a 13.3″ retina display (2560×1600 px), and an integrated Intel Iris 5100 graphics processor that shares memory with the system; and 2) Apple MacBook Pro 5,5 "Core 2 Duo" 2.26 13″ (SD/FW) Mid 2009 with 2 GB of RAM, a 13.3″ display (1280×800 px), and a NVIDIA GeForce 9400M graphics processor with 256 MB of DDR3 SDRAM shared with main memory. Three operative systems were installed on these machines: 1) MacOS X "Mavericks"; 2) Windows 7 64-bit Ultimate edition; y 3) Ubuntu Linux 13.10 "Saucy Salamander". All tests were conducted in full screen mode, with the Bluetooth and the network connection (WiFi/Ethernet) disabled. The accuracy and precision of stimulus presentation was assessed using the Black Box Toolkit (BBTK), a set of photodetectors specifically designed to conduct benchmarking studies like the one reported here [18]. The BBTK detects changes in luminance from the photodetector and sends this information to the parallel port of an auxiliary computer, different from the one whose performance is being tested. This avoids any interference between the timing mechanisms used to generate the black to white and white to black transitions and the real-time application used to gather the data provided by the BBTK photodetector.

Design and Procedure

For each combination of hardware and operative system we developed several full-screen animations with non-gradual, repeated white-black transitions. The duration of each keyframe was manipulated with values 1000, 500, 200, 100, 50, and 16.667 ms (60, 30, 12, 6, 3, and 1 display refreshes at 60 Hz, respectively), although, as explained below, not all durations were included in all tests. For each of these conditions, we collected data from 5 independent series of 60 seconds each. We limited our study to repeated white-black transitions because many studies about accuracy and precision in visual stimuli presentation use similar procedures[19]–[22] and because it is safe to assume that preparation times of this kind of simple stimuli will not affect their presentation times. Trying to measure the presentation times of complex or real-time generated stimuli from luminance changes usually gives rise to spurious errors that can be avoided by resorting to simple black-and-white transitions.

As mentioned above, to avoid any potential error in our PsychoPy code, we adapted a script previously published by Jeremy Gray, one of PsychoPy's developers, in a comment to our previous study [17]. We only modified the number of iterations in the trial loop (depending on the duration of each keyframe we needed more or less trials to complete the 60 seconds of measurement) and the number of durations of each experiments (we tested only one duration in each test, instead of 6). Apart from these two changes, the rest of the scripts were a verbatim copy of Gray's original.

RESULTS

Detailed data for all the tests reported below are available at the Open Science Framework public repository (https://osf.io/9dkgz/). The main goal of our tests was to find the threshold where PsychoPy started to show timing errors. For this reason, we did not test all stimulus durations (1000, 500, 200, 100, 50, and 16.667 ms) for all combinations of hardware and software. We started our analyses by testing the 1000, 500, 200, 100, and 50 ms conditions on MacOS X running on the MacBook Pro Late 2013. The results of these tests are shown inTable 1. As can be seen, the performance of PsychoPy was perfect for this range of stimulus durations. However, we did find timing errors when we proceeded to test the 16.667 ms interval. Upon further exploration of the benchmarking scripts, we found that the number of trials per loop was a key determinant of these timing errors. Specifically, we observed that errors were somewhat decreased when the number of trials per loop was reduced from 960 to 800. Following this observation, we further adjusted the number of trials per loop to 640 and observed that timing errors virtually disappeared under these conditions. These results have important consequences. Firstly, they confirm that PsychoPy is perfectly able to reach maximal precision even with the briefest stimulus presentation (16.667 ms). Secondly, they show that the number of trials per loop somehow affects the performance of PsychoPy. As a result, this parameter was also manipulated in the following tests.

Table 1. PsychoPy 1.80 timing tests on MacBook Pro Late 2013 under MacOS X "Mavericks"

Duration (ms)	*Trials per loop*	*Test*	*Missed frames*
1000	60	1	0
	60	2	0
	60	3	0
	60	4	0
	60	5	0
500	120	1	0
	120	2	0
	120	3	0
	120	4	0
	120	5	0
200	300	1	0
	300	2	0
	300	3	0
	300	4	0
	300	5	0
100	600	1	0
	600	2	0
	600	3	0
	600	4	0
	600	5	0
50	1200	1	0
	1200	2	0
	1200	3	0
	1200	4	0
	1200	5	0
16.667	2400	1	1199
	2400	2	1198
	2400	3	1199
	2400	4	1200
	2400	5	1198
	2000	1	61
	2000	2	1173
	2000	3	1164
	2000	4	50
	2000	5	1173
	1600	1	0
	1600	2	1
	1600	3	0
	1600	4	0
	1600	5	0

doi:10.1371/journal.pone.0112033.t001

We then explored the performance of PsychoPy under Windows 7 using the same computer. Table 2 shows the results of these tests. As can be seen, these tests yielded very poor results even for the less demanding conditions (1000 ms). This made us suspect that the timing errors observed in this condition could not be attributed to a problem in PsychoPy. Instead, these results are likely to be due to the deficient performance of the driver for the integrated Intel Iris 5100 graphics processor running on Windows 7, to the lack of precision and accuracy in Microsoft's latest operative systems [9], or to a combination of both. As shown below, PsychoPy shows a good performance under Windows 7 when a different graphics card and different drivers are used.

Table 2. PsychoPy 1.80 timing tests on MacBook Pro Late 2013 under Windows 7 64-bit Ultimate

Duration (ms)	*Trials per loop*	*Test*	*Missed frames*
1000	60	1	130
	60	2	123
	60	3	123
	60	4	125
	60	5	124

doi:10.1371/journal.pone.0112033.t002

We also tested PsychoPy on Ubuntu Linux running on the same computer. The results of these tests are summarized in Table 3. After checking that no timing errors were observed with 200 ms, we proceeded to test the 100 and the 50 ms conditions. Preliminary examination of the 50 ms interval did yield some timing errors. Therefore, we decided to adjust the number of trials per loop to 300. With this change, timing errors were no longer observed for the 50 ms interval. However, we did still observe timing errors in the 16.667 ms condition and we decided to further reduce the number of trials per loop to 150, which eliminated all timing errors in 4 out of the 5 tests conducted.

Table 3. PsychoPy 1.80 timing tests on MacBook Pro Late 2013 under Ubuntu Linux 13.10 "Saucy Salamander"

Duration (ms)	*Trials per loop*	*Test*	*Missed frames*
200	300	1	0
	300	2	0
	300	3	0
	300	4	0
	300	5	0
100	600	1	0
	600	2	0
	600	3	0
	600	4	0
	600	5	0
50	300	1	0
	300	2	1
	300	3	0
	300	4	0
	300	5	0
16.667	300	1	15
	300	2	15
	300	3	2
	300	4	40
	300	5	26
	150	1	0
	150	2	15
	150	3	0
	150	4	0
	150	5	0

doi:10.1371/journal.pone.0112033.t003

We took a similar approach to explore the performance of PsychoPy in the second computer, a MacBook Pro Mid 2009. Table 4 shows the results of the tests conducted with MacOS X running on this machine. In this case, we started by testing the 200 ms condition, which yielded no errors. We proceeded to conduct the tests in the 100 ms condition, where we did observe numerous timing errors. As in our previous tests, we followed up these tests changing the number of trials per loop from 1200 to 600. After this modification, timing errors were no longer observed in the 100 ms condition. Bearing this in mind, we tested the 50 ms condition with 600 trials per loop and we also found no timing errors. The same happened when testing the 16.667 ms interval. However, when we increased again the number of trials per loop in the 16.667 ms condition, we found again timing errors. This confirms that the timing errors that we found in PsychoPy so far should not be attributed to its ability to present very brief stimuli, but to the large number of trials per loop included in each test. Note that this large number of trials, although common for benchmarking studies, is rather unusual in the typical experiments designed by researchers.

Table 4. PsychoPy 1.80 timing tests on MacBook Pro Mid 2009 under MacOS X "Mavericks"

Duration (ms)	*Trials per loop*	*Test*	*Missed frames*
100	600	1	0
	600	2	0
	600	3	0
	600	4	0
	600	5	0
50	1200	1	573
	1200	2	572
	1200	3	573
	1200	4	573
	1200	5	576
	600	1	0
	600	2	0
	600	3	0
	600	4	0
	600	5	0
16.667	1200	1	600
	1200	2	600
	1200	3	600
	1200	4	600
	1200	5	600
	600	1	0
	600	2	0
	600	3	0
	600	4	0
	600	5	0

doi:10.1371/journal.pone.0112033.t004

The results obtained with Windows 7 running on the MacBook Pro Mid 2009 are shown inTable 5. In contrast with the results obtained with the MacBook Pro Late 2013, no timing errors were observed in the 100 ms condition. Isolated errors took place in the 50 ms condition, all of them conveniently reported in the PsychoPy log file. Surprisingly, only 1 out of the 5 tests conducted in the 16.667 ms condition yielded timing errors, even when the number of trials per loop was set to 1200. The outstanding performance of PsychoPy on Windows 7 even on adverse conditions is in stark contrast with its poor performance on the same operative system running on the MacBook Pro Late 2013. As explained above, everything suggests that these timing errors should not be attributed to a poor performance of PsychoPy. We found, however, that timing errors could still be observed if the number of trials per loop was set to 2400.

Table 5. PsychoPy 1.80 timing tests on MacBook Pro Mid 2009 under Windows 7 64-bit Ultimate

Duration (ms)	*Trials per loop*	*Test*	*Missed frames*
100	600	1	0
	600	2	0
	600	3	0
	600	4	0
	600	5	0
50	1200	1	0
	1200	2	15
	1200	3	0
	1200	4	0
	1200	5	2
16.667	2400	1	600
	2400	2	600
	2400	3	600
	2400	4	600
	2400	5	599
	1200	1	0
	1200	2	0
	1200	3	1
	1200	4	0
	1200	5	0

doi:10.1371/journal.pone.0112033.t005

Finally, Table 6 shows the results of the tests conducted with Ubuntu Linux running on the MacBook Pro Mid 2009. Before gathering these data, we found a problem in the execution of our tests: Preliminary tests showed that the stimulus durations registered by the BBTK photosensors doubled the expected values (e.g., white and black frames lasted 200 ms in the 100 ms condition). Surprisingly, this error was not reported in the PsychoPy log file. After commenting these results with the developers of PsychoPy, they informed us that in some configurations of Linux the graphics card is being told twice to wait for a vertical blank before proceeding, so every frame actually takes two frames. Because the frame time remains consistent, PsychoPy assumes that the frame rate of the monitor is 30 Hz (and not 60 Hz). Therefore, it does not report any missed frames (all frames look like the expected period by this measure). Fortunately, there was a simple solution. PsychoPy includes a property option to disable the wait for the next vertical blank (win.waitBanking=False). After implementing this change, we tested the 200 ms condition and found no timing errors. We also found no errors for the 100, 50, and 16.667 ms conditions when 600 trials per loop were requested. However, errors were found when the number of trials per loop was set to 1200.

Table 6. PsychoPy 1.80 timing tests on MacBook Pro Mid 2009 under Ubuntu Linux 13.10 "Saucy Salamander"

Duration (ms)	*Trials per loop*	*Test*	*Missed frames*
200	600	1	0
	600	2	0
	600	3	0
	600	4	0
	600	5	0
100	1200	1	94
	1200	2	97
	1200	3	86
	1200	4	99
	1200	5	97
	600	1	0
	600	2	0
	600	3	0
	600	4	0
	600	5	0
50	1200	1	184
	1200	2	157
	1200	3	166
	1200	4	163
	1200	5	142
	600	1	0
	600	2	0
	600	3	0
	600	4	0
	600	5	0
16.667	1200	1	35
	1200	2	28
	1200	3	27
	1200	4	29
	1200	5	37
	600	1	0
	600	2	0
	600	3	0
	600	4	0
	600	5	0

doi:10.1371/journal.pone.0112033.t006

DISCUSSION

When our previous study on the accuracy and precision of PsychoPy and other experimental software was originally published [15], the developers of PsychoPy [16] suggested that the timing errors that we detected could be due either to the fact that those tests were based on an earlier version of PsychoPy (1.64) or to the definition of stimulus durations in terms of time units instead of ticks (display refreshes). Actually, the latter problem was related to the former, given that the experiment builder of PsychoPy 1.64 did not allow defining durations in terms of ticks. It is very likely that the timing errors found in the previous study can be attributed to this feature of the testing procedure. Timing visual events based on timing intervals is known to be prone to artifacts, because those intervals often do not synchronize precisely with the hardware screen refresh interval, leading to uncertainties in the actual achieved display times.

In light of the present results it appears that an additional factor played a determinant role: The number of trials per loop implemented in each test. Although testing large numbers of trials per loop is common practice in software benchmarking, the parameters used in this kind of studies are rather unusual in psychological experiments. The divergence between the procedures used in cognitive research and the methods used in benchmarking has already been highlighted by Plant. As he mentioned in his comment to our original study, "flashing a bitmap over and over on idealized equipment is not representative of what real researchers do in the field! Their equipment is never ideal, their coding never as good as yours, their experiment is more complicated, they link to different equipment to yours… Or they are using a different version of the software to you" [23]. We might add that the divergence sometimes runs in the opposite direction: As the present study illustrates, sometimes the requirements of the software used to benchmark timing errors can be much more demanding than those of standard programs designed by experimenters. Given our results, a practical recommendation for cognitive researchers is that large numbers of trials per loop should be avoided by all means whenever it is possible.

The negative impact of this factor might be due to the large amount of information that PsychoPy has to log in relatively little time. Even though we disabled XLSX and CSV outputs, we still found errors with large numbers of trials per loop. Fortunately, this is more of a technical than a practical problem, because it only poses timing problems in highly unusual conditions. However, in light of the present results, it seems advisable to avoid complex data output formats, such as XLSX, when timing errors can be an issue, particularly for experimental programs requiring multiple loops.

It is also important to note that the performance of PsychoPy was also affected by details of the hardware and software used to run the experiment. Severe timing errors were observed in Windows 7 in one of the computers, possibly due to problems of the graphic card driver. Similarly, the configuration of the graphic card in Ubuntu Linux gave rise to unexpected timing errors that, fortunately, could be fixed using the appropriate property options in PsychoPy. These two examples illustrate that researchers can never take for granted that their software will reach the highest precision and accuracy levels under all circumstances. If a series of experiments demands compliance with strict timing requirements, the precision and accuracy of the experimental software should always be tested first.

Based on the results of our studies, we can offer some guidelines for researchers that are planning to use PsychoPy to conduct experiments with strict timing requirements. First, it is important to use suitable hardware equipment (i.e., a computer provided with a fast CPU, enough RAM, a dedicated graphics processor, and a display with low refresh rate) with the appropriate configuration (i.e., Bluetooth, Ethernet. Wi-Fi, Mobile and other kind of connections disabled; desktop visual effects disabled; antivirus, software updates, background programs, and other kind of asynchronous events sources disabled). Second, any configuration problem of the graphics processor should be detected and fixed (i.e., updating display's and graphics processor's drivers and using vendor's test utilities to benchmark them, if available). Third, it is advisable to use the last version of PsychoPy. It is free, and every update comes with new interesting features. Fourth, visual stimuli should be defined in durations in ticks (screen refreshes) and not in milliseconds. Fifth, it is preferable to avoid defining too many trials per loop in experiments. For experimental paradigms with large numbers of trials (i.e., experimental paradigms with several hundreds of trials, such as priming or contextual cueing [1], [3]), splitting the whole set of trials in several blocks is an easy way to avoid potential problems. Sixth, it is recommendable to analyze and reduce the impact of logging processes during the experiment (e.g., using XLSX log format is more demanding than TXT log format). In addition to these general recommendations, the precision and accuracy of the experimental setup should be tested prior to conducting the experiment. In most cases, PsychoPy's logging information should be enough to detect timing inaccuracies. In our study, all the timing errors except the one caused by the Nvidia graphics configuration in Linux were correctly reported by PsychoPy. To make sure that such faulty configuration is not being used unknowingly, researchers can define a human-measurable stimulus duration (e.g., 120 ticks=2000 ms at 60 Hz) and check that the duration is not doubled (i.e., 4000 ms). If that is the case, there is a simple workaround in PsychoPy: Disabling waitBlank feature and defining stimuli durations in milliseconds and not in ticks (contrary to the previous recommendation).

To sum up, the present study shows that the most recent versions of PsychoPy can achieve the highest levels of precision and accuracy in the presentation of brief visual stimuli. There is no reason to think that occasional timing errors found in benchmarking tests with many trials per loop can pose any problem for standard experiments developed by researchers. Properly used, PsychoPy is an excellent tool for psychological research even under the most demanding conditions.

ACKNOWLEDGMENTS

The authors would like to thank Gorka Urkiola and Gorka Gorrotxategi for granting us access to their MacBook Pro for the present study, Tom Hardwicke for his corrections of a previous draft, and Jonathan Peirce, Jeremy Gray, and Michael MacAskill for their help and support.

AUTHOR CONTRIBUTIONS

Conceived and designed the experiments: PG MAV. Performed the experiments: PG. Analyzed the data: PG. Contributed reagents/materials/analysis tools: PG MAV. Wrote the paper: PG MAV.

REFERENCES

1. Dehaene S, Naccache L, Le Clec'H G, Koechlin E, Mueller M, et al. (1998) Imaging unconscious semantic priming. Nature 395: 597–600. doi: 10.1038/26967
2. Hassin RR, Ferguson MJ, Shidlovski D, Gross T (2007) Subliminal exposure to national flags affects political thought and behavior. PNAS 104: 19757–19761. doi: 10.1073/pnas.0704679104
3. Chun MM, Jiang Y (1998) Contextual cueing: Implicit learning and memory of visual context guides spatial attention. Cognitive Psychol 36: 28–71. doi: 10.1006/cogp.1998.0681

4. Ratcliff R, McKoon G (1978) Priming in item recognition: Evidence for the prepositional structure of sentences. J Verbal Learn Verb Beh 17: 403–417. doi: 10.1016/s0022-5371(78)90238-4
5. Brand A, Bradley MT (2012) Assessing the effect of technical variance on the statistical outcomes of web experiments measuring response times. Soc Sci Comput Rev 30: 350–357. doi: 10.1177/0894439311415604
6. Damian MF (2010) Does variability in human performance outweigh imprecision in response devices such as computer keyboards? Behav Res Methods 42: 205–211. doi: 10.3758/brm.42.1.205
7. Donkin C, Averell L, Brown S, Heathcote A (2009) Getting more from accuracy and response time data: Methods for fitting the linear ballistic accumulator. Behav Res Methods 41: 1095–1110. doi: 10.3758/brm.41.4.1095
8. Wagenmakers EJ (2009) Methodological and empirical developments for the Ratcliff diffusion model of response times and accuracy. Eur J Cogn Psychol 21: 641–671. doi: 10.1080/09541440802205067
9. Plant RR, Quinlan PT (2013) Could millisecond timing errors in commonly used equipment be a cause of replication failure in some neuroscience studies? Cogn Affect Behav Ne 13: 598–614. doi: 10.3758/s13415-013-0166-6
10. Brainard DH (1997) The Psychophysics Toolbox. Spatial Vision 10: 433–436. doi: 10.1163/156856897x00357
11. Forster KI, Forster JC (2003) DMDX: A Windows display program with millisecond accuracy. Beh Res Methods 35: 116–124. doi: 10.3758/bf03195503
12. Mathôt S, Schreij D, Theeuwes J (2011) OpenSesame: An open-source, graphical experiment builder for the social sciences. Beh Res Methods 44: 314–324. doi: 10.3758/s13428-011-0168-7
13. Pelli DG (1997) The VideoToolbox software for visual psychophysics: Transforming numbers into movies. Spatial Vision 10: 437–442. doi: 10.1163/156856897x00366
14. Peirce JW (2007) PsychoPy—psychophysics software in Python. J Neurosci Methods 162: 8–13. doi: 10.1016/j.jneumeth.2006.11.017
15. Garaizar P, Vadillo MA, López-de-Ipiña D, Matute H (2014) Measuring software timing errors in the presentation of visual stimuli in cognitive neuroscience experiments. PLOS ONE 9: e85108. doi: 10.1371/journal.pone.0085108
16. Peirce JW (2014) PsychoPy can provide precise stimulus timing. Available:http://www.plosone.org/annotation/listThread.action?root=78527. Accessed 2014 Oct 14.
17. Gray J (2014) PsychoPy timing test script. Available:https://gist.github.com/jeremygray/9062586. Accessed 2014 Oct 14.
18. Plant RR, Turner G (2004) Self-validating presentation and response timing in cognitive paradigms: How and why? Behav Res Meth Ins C 36: 291–303. doi: 10.3758/bf03195575
19. Schmidt W (2001) Presentation accuracy of Web animation methods. Behav Res Methods 33: 187–200. doi: 10.3758/bf03195365
20. Stewart N (2006) Millisecond accuracy video display using OpenGL under Linux. Behav Res Methods 38: 142–145. doi: 10.3758/bf03192759
21. Reingold EM (2014) Eye tracking research and technology: Towards objective measurement of data quality,. Vis Cogn 22: 635–652. doi: 10.1080/13506285.2013.876481
22. Reimers S, Stewart N (in press) Presentation and response timing accuracy in Adobe Flash and HTML5/JavaScript Web experiments. Behav Res Methods doi: 10.3758/s13428-014-0471-1
23. Plant RR (2014) Do these results generalise to what researchers really do? Available:http://www.plosone.org/annotation/listThread.action?root=78527. Accessed 2014 Oct 14.

CHAPTER 12

MARMAP: A PACKAGE FOR IMPORTING, PLOTTING AND ANALYZING BATHYMETRIC AND TOPOGRAPHIC DATA IN R

Eric Pante, Benoit Simon-Bouhet.

Littoral, Environnement et Socie´te´s Joint Research Unit 7266 Centre National de la Recherche Scientifique, Universite´ de La Rochelle, La Rochelle, France

ABSTRACT

In this communication we introduce marmap, a package designed for downloading, plotting and manipulating bathymetric and topographic data in R. marmap can query the ETOPO1 bathymetry and topography database hosted by the NOAA, use simple latitude-longitude-depth data in ascii format, and take advantage of the advanced plotting tools available in R to build publication-quality bathymetric maps. Functions to query data (bathymetry, sampling information...) are available interactively by clicking on marmap maps. Bathymetric and topographic data can also be used to calculate projected surface areas within specified depth/altitude intervals, and constrain the calculation of realistic shortest path distances. Such information can be used in molecular ecology, for example, to evaluate genetic isolation by distance in a spatially-explicit framework.

INTRODUCTION

Marine ecologists still lack simple, highly-customizable tools for building and using marine charts, open-source tools being particularly lacking. Currently, apart from commercial solutions, marine ecologists can use GIS tools such as GRASS GIS [1], or the graphical user interface provided by GeoMapApp [2] and Google Earth [3] to prepare publication-quality bathymetric charts, but these tools either require knowledge in the field of GIS, or are limited in the number of functions, datasets, and analyses available. The R environment [4] is a convenient platform for generating maps, thanks to its built-in functions for data matrix manipulation and advanced graphics. The package marmap [5], introduced herein, takes advantage of these built-in functions, as well as packages for spatial analysis developed by others, to provide a simple and flexible tool for importing, manipulating, plotting and exporting bathymetric data. It provides a simple platform for bathymetric data analysis and plotting even with limited experience with R, and allows production of publication-quality maps. The entirety of the marmap package was coded in the R language, providing advanced R users with the opportunity to fine-tune or expand any function. Also, because all bathymetric data are imported as R objects, the arsenal of R tools can be utilized for analyses not implemented in the marmap package.

Citation: Pante E, Simon-Bouhet B (2013) marmap: A Package for Importing, Plotting and Analyzing Bathymetric and Topographic Data in R. PLoS ONE 8(9): e73051. doi:10.1371/journal.pone.0073051

DESCRIPTION OF THE MARMAP PACKAGE

Portability

Binaries and source code for the marmap package are freely available on the Comprehensive R Archive Network (CRAN [6]), along with a tutorial (also called "R vignette"). marmap contains R code exclusively, which maximizes its portability across platforms. CRAN makes the source code and binaries available for Unix-like and Windows operating systems [5].

Importing and Plotting Bathymetric Data

marmap offers different ways to upload bathymetric information, which should provide flexible data preparation, depending on need and access to online resources. First, bathymetric data can be downloaded directly from within R by querying the ETOPO1 database [7] hosted by the NOAA. Second, three-column data frames (with longitude, latitude, and depth data) can be imported from different sources, such as the US National Ocean and Atmospheric Administration (NOAA) [8]. Third, marmap has functions to prepare and use a local SQL database, stored on the user›s hard drive. Use of a personalized SQL bathymetry database is convenient for querying subsets of very large bathymetric datasets such as the 5Go ETOPO1. Finally, data can be imported like any other dataset into R, and converted using marmap functions. While marmap was originally designed for marine ecologists, it is fully compatible with topographical data, which can be treated along with bathymetric data, or analyzed on their own.

Once loaded into R, bathymetric data are re-organized as a matrix that is used for manipulation, plotting and exporting. These data are represented as an R class called "bathy", valid within a marmap session. The creation of a custom R class allows the use of generic functions such as plot and summary. Bathymetric data of class "bathy" can be plotted with the streamlined marmap plotting tools, or used with other geographic analysis packages (e.g. "maps" [9]). Bathymetric data can be plotted as simple contour plots, with control over the range, density and look of isobaths, or with automatic isobath choice and placement. Contour plots can be coupled with heat maps with built-in and customizable color ramps (Figure 1A,E). Sampling data (GPS points, tracks, polygons, etc...) and text (legends, labels, scales, etc...) can simply be added to marmap maps using R low-level functions.

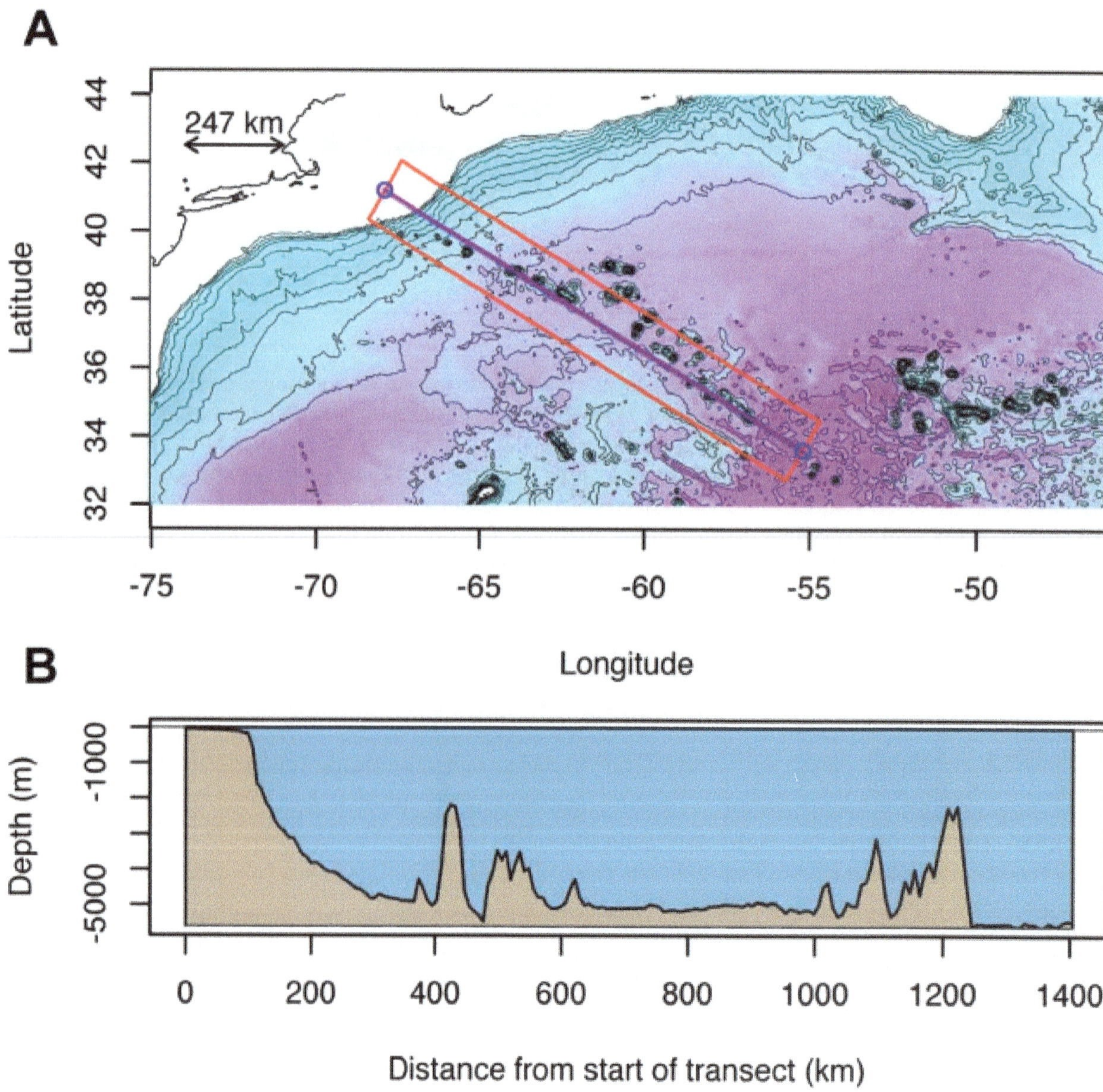

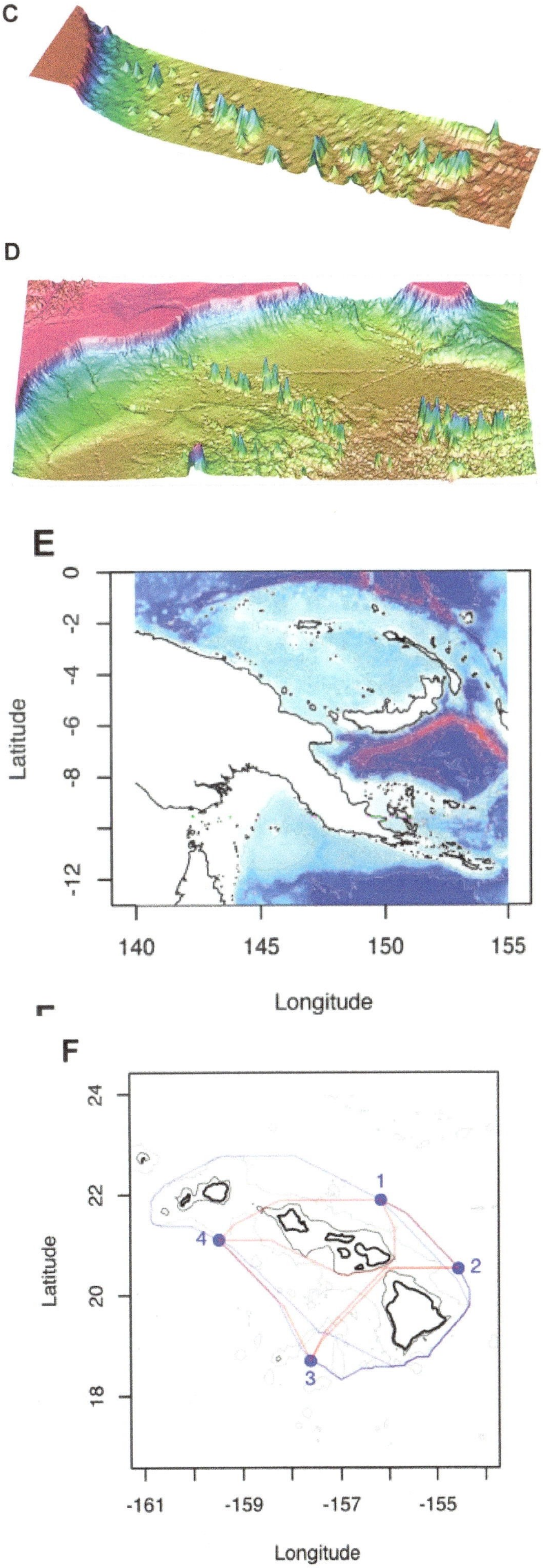
C
D
E
0
-2
-4
-6
-8
-12
Latitude
140
145
150
155
Longitude
F
24
22
20
18
Latitude
1
2
3
4
-161
-159
-157
-155
Longitude

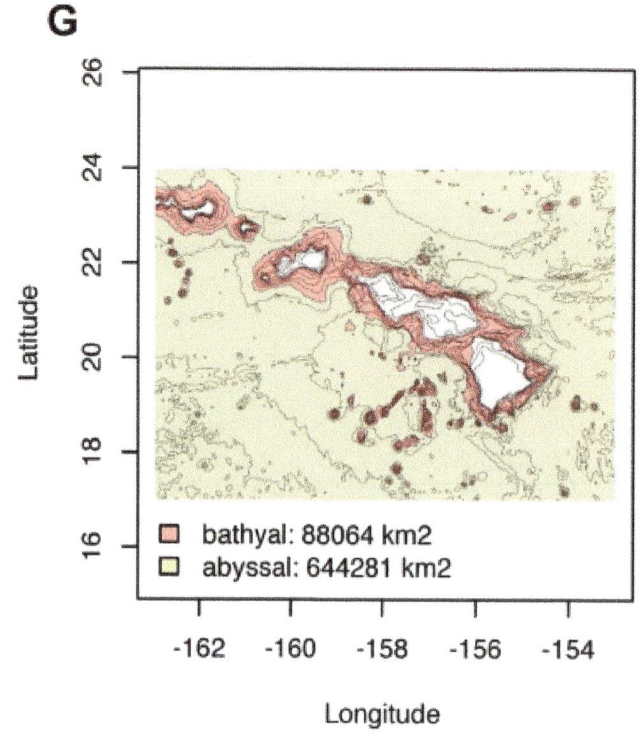

Figure 1. Examples of two and three dimensional plots created using marmap tools. Left panel (A): data from the NW Atlantic Ocean, showing the NE coast of the USA and the New England and Corner Rise seamounts chains. The blue line represents the position of two- (B) and three- (C) dimensional cross sections, the red rectangle delimiting the area covered by the belt transect. The bottom left figure (D) represents the NW Atlantic data as plotted with the wireframe function from package lattice [21], based on data imported with marmap. Right panel: map of Papua New Guinea and satellite islands (**E**; see text). The middle figure (**F**) represents the results of a least-cost path analysis around the Hawaiian islands (coastline in thick black, dark grey: 1000 m isobath, light grey 4000 m isobath; red line: path avoiding waters shallower than 1000 m, blue line: path avoiding waters shallower than 4000 m). The bottom figure (**G**) represents the results of projected surface area calculations for the bathyal and abyssal areas around the Hawaiian islands. R code is available in File S1.

For example, creating a map of Papua New Guinea can be done in three lines of code, in a new R session:

- > library(marmap)
- > getNOAA.bathy(lon1 = 140,lon2 = 155,lat1 = -13,lat2 = 0, resolution=1) ->papoue
- >plot(papoue, image=TRUE)

The first line loads marmap, the second queries bathymetric data (resolution of 1 minute) and stores the result in a variable of class "bathy," and the third line creates a map with automatic isobath choice and built-in color ramp. The upper right map on Figure 1, plotted with isobaths of different widths and colors as well as a custom color ramp was produced with these two lines (the first creating and storing a custom palette, and the second creating the map; details on commands and their arguments are available in the marmap documentation on CRAN):

- > colorRampPalette(c("red","purple","blue","cadetblue1","white")) -> blues
- >plot(papoue, image=T, bpal=blues(100),
- deep=c(−9000, −3000,0), shallow=c(−3000, −10, 0), step=c(1000, 1000, 0),
- col = c("lightgrey","darkgrey","black"), lwd=c(0.3,0.3,0.6), lty=c(1,1,1),
- drawlabel=c(F,F,F))

Using Bathymetric for Further Ecological Analysis

By interactively clicking on a map, the user can retrieve bathymetric data (either from a point or an area), sampling information (e.g. list of specimens sampled within a particular geographic area), or two- and three-dimensional depth cross-sections (Figure 1B–C). Projected surface areas can also be estimated for specified depth ranges, such as the bathyal and abyssal zones around Hawaii (Figure 1G).

Based on functions developed by Jacob van Etten in the raster and gdistance packages [10],[11], marmap facilitates analysis of geographically-explicit ecological data, by allowing least-cost path calculation constrained by bathymetry and/or topography. Shortest great-circle (haversine) distance between pairs of sites, avoiding land masses or depth layers, are calculated. Outputs of least-cost path analysis can be in the form of great-circle distance, taking into account the curvature of the Earth, and in the form of geographical paths that can be plotted on marmap maps, and used to compute two- and three-dimensional depth cross-sections. Distance data can be easily exported for direct use in landscape genetics software such as TESS [12]. Data can also be used directly from within R to perform Mantel tests or other analyses [13]–[15].

Interactions with other Packages

marmap interacts with multiple existing R packages for visualization and analysis, such as lattice for building three-dimensional plots (Figure 1C–D), and gdistance for least-cost path calculations (see above). marmap also contains functions to ease interactions with other packages dedicated to the analysis of spatial data. Data from class bathy can be transformed into raster objets for use in the raster package [10] (functions trans.mat and as.raster). Bathy objects can also be converted into the class SpatialGridDataFrame for use in the sp package[16], [17] (function as.SpatialGridDataFrame). These transformed objects can be converted back into objects of class bathy using the as.bathy function. In the example below, the package raster is used to change the projection of a dataset extracted from ETOPO1. The first line creates a raster object from a bathy object, the second defines the target projection (PROJ.4 format), the third creates a new projected raster object, and the last converts the new raster projection into a bathy object for plotting with marmap. Figure 2 provides an example of such transformed data.

- > r1<- as.raster(original.marmap.data)
- > new.projection <- "+proj=ortho"
- > r2<- projectRaster(r1,crs=new.projection)
- >projected.marmap.data <- as.bathy(r2)

Figure 2. Exemple of ETOPO1 data downloaded with the marmap package, transformed with the raster package, and plotted with marmap. Orthographic projection, resolution of 10 minutes.

CONCLUSIONS

marmap was designed to provide easy-to-use tools for importing and using bathymetric and topographic data in R. While marmap has been primarily designed for research, and the rapid production of publication-quality maps (examples: [18]–[20]), its simplicity of use should make it interesting as a teaching tool as well.

ACKNOWLEDGMENTS

The authors thank Mikael Guichard for his help with remote data accession, as well as Amélia Viricel and two anonymous reviewers for constructive criticism of the manuscript.

AUTHOR CONTRIBUTIONS

Conceived and designed the experiments: EGP BSB. Performed the experiments: EGP BSB. Analyzed the data: EGP BSB. Contributed reagents/materials/analysis tools: EGP BSB. Wrote the paper: EGP BSB.

REFERENCES

1. GRASS Development Team (2012) Geographic Resources Analysis Support System (GRASS GIS) Software. Open Source Geospatial Foundation, USA. Available:http://grass.osgeo.org. Accessed: 2013 Apr 5.
2. Ryan W, Carbotte S, Coplan J, O'Hara S, Melkonian A, et al. (2009) Global multi-resolution topography synthesis. Geochemistry, Geophysics, Geosystems 10: Q03014. doi: 10.1029/2008gc002332
3. Google (2013) Google Earth. Available: http://www.google.fr/earth/. Accessed: 2013 Mar 27.
4. R Development Core Team (2012) R: A Language and Environment for Statistical Computing R Foundation for Statistical Computing, Vienna, Austria. ISBN 3-900051-07-0. Available: http://www.R-project.org. Accessed: 2013 Apr 5.
5. Pante E, Simon-Bouhet B (2013) marmap: Import, plot and analyze bathymetric and topographic data. R package version 0.5 Available: http://CRAN.R-project.org/package=marmap. Accessed: 2013 Apr 10.
6. CRAN (2013) The Comprehensive R Archive Network. Available: http://cran.r-project.org/. Accessed: 2013 Apr 5.
7. Amante C, Eakins BW (2009) Etopol 1 arc-minute global relief model: Procedures, data sources and analysis. NOAA Technical Memorandum NESDIS NGDC-24 1–19.
8. NOAA National Geophysical Data Center (2013) GEODAS Grid Translator - Design a grid. Available: http://www.ngdc.noaa.gov/mgg/gdas/gd_designagrid.html. Accessed: 2013 Apr 5.
9. Original S code by Richard A Becker and Allan R Wilks R version by Ray Brown-rigg Enhancements by Thomas P Minka (2013) maps: Draw Geographical Maps. Available:http://CRAN.R-project.org/package=maps. R package version 2.3–2. Accessed: 2013 Apr 10.
10. van Etten RJHJ (2012) raster: Geographic data analysis and modeling. Available:http://CRAN.R-project.org/package=raster. R package version 2.0–41. Accessed: 2013 Apr 10.
11. van Etten J (2012) gdistance: Distances and routes on geographical grids. R package version 1.1–4. Available: http://CRAN.R-project.org/package=gdistance. Accessed: 2013 Apr 10.
12. Durand E, Jay F, Gaggiotti O, François O (2009) Spatial inference of admixture proportions and secondary contact zones. Molecular Biology and Evolution 26: 1963–1973. doi: 10.1093/molbev/msp106
13. Dray S, Dufour A, Chessel D (2007) The ade4 package-II: Two-table and K-table methods. R News 7: 47–52.
14. Dray S, Dufour A (2007) The ade4 package: implementing the duality diagram for ecologists. Journal of Statistical Software 22: 1–20.
15. Chessel D, Dufour A, Thioulouse J (2004) The ade4 package -I- One-table methods. R News 4: 5–10.

16. Pebesma EJ, Bivand RS (2005) Classes and methods for spatial data in R. R News. 5: 9–13. doi: 10.1007/978-1-4614-7618-4_2

17. Bivand RS, Pebesma EJ, Gomez-Rubio V (2008) Applied spatial data analysis with R. Springer, NY. Available: http://www.asdar-book.org/.

18. Thoma JN, Pante E, Brugler MR, France SC (2009) Deep-sea octocorals and antipatharians show no evidence of seamount-scale endemism in the NW Atlantic. Marine Ecology Progress Series 397: 25–35. doi: 10.3354/meps08318

19. Pante E, Corbari L, Thubaut J, Chan TY, Mana R, et al. (2012) Exploration of the deep-sea fauna of Papua New Guinea. Oceanography 25: 214–225. doi: 10.5670/oceanog.2012.65

20. Pante E, Watling L (2012) *Chrysogorgia* from the New England and Corner Seamounts: Atlantic – Pacific connections. Journal of the Marine Biological Association of the United Kingdom 92: 911–927. doi: 10.1017/s0025315411001354

21. Sarkar D (2008) Lattice: Multivariate Data Visualization with R. New York: Springer. ISBN 978-0-387-75968-5. Available: http://lmdvr.r-forge.r-project.org. Accessed: 2013 Apr 10.

CHAPTER 13

MODELING THE INTERNET OF THINGS, SELF-ORGANIZING AND OTHER COMPLEX ADAPTIVE COMMUNICATION NETWORKS: A COGNITIVE AGENT-BASED COMPUTING APPROACH

Samreen Laghari[1], Muaz A. Niazi[2]

[1] Computer Science Department, Islamabad Model College for Girls, Street #25, F-6/2, Islamabad, Pakistan

[2] Computer Science Department, COMSATS Institute of IT, Park Road, Islamabad, Pakistan

ABSTRACT

Background

Computer Networks have a tendency to grow at an unprecedented scale. Modern networks involve not only computers but also a wide variety of other interconnected devices ranging from mobile phones to other household items fitted with sensors. This vision of the "Internet of Things" (IoT) implies an inherent difficulty in modeling problems.

Purpose

It is practically impossible to implement and test all scenarios for large-scale and complex adaptive communication networks as part of Complex Adaptive Communication Networks and Environments (CACOONS). The goal of this study is to explore the use of Agent-based Modeling as part of the Cognitive Agent-based Computing (CABC) framework to model a Complex communication network problem.

Method

We use Exploratory Agent-based Modeling (EABM), as part of the CABC framework, to develop an autonomous multi-agent architecture for managing carbon footprint in a corporate network. To evaluate the application of complexity in practical scenarios, we have also introduced a company-defined computer usage policy.

Citation: Laghari S, Niazi MA (2016) Modeling the Internet of Things, Self-Organizing and Other Complex Adaptive Communication Networks: A Cognitive Agent-Based Computing Approach. PLoS ONE 11(1): e0146760. doi:10.1371/journal.pone.0146760.

Results

The conducted experiments demonstrated two important results: Primarily CABC-based modeling approach such as using Agent-based Modeling can be an effective approach to modeling complex problems in the domain of IoT. Secondly, the specific problem of managing the Carbon footprint can be solved using a multiagent system approach.

INTRODUCTION

Modern technological supply chains offer a rapid channel for consumer technology creation and adoption. As new types of technology enters the everyday lives globally, these newer concepts offer new challenges [1]. Practical examples of concepts becoming reality include "PhoneBloks" a phone based on highly modular connected components [2], the Internet of Things (IoT) [3] and cloud computing [4, 5]. These technologies have all become not just commonplace in the Information Technology industry but also in various fields of scientific research. Researchers from fields as diverse as Bioinformatics [6] and astronomy [7] have started to use technology to solve scientific problems in a better way.

As technology becomes commonplace, unfortunately, the human race is expanding its use without completely realizing its implications. We live in a consumer-centric society where manufacturers focus on building devices which sell. The actual implications of the technology, its impact on the environment, the planet and its inhabitants seems to be the least of the concerns. The key problem here is that to be able to understand complex systems, we need to be able to model and simulate them [8].

Electronics in general, and personal computers, in particular, are well-known for their long-term detrimental effects on the environment [9]. Not only do computers significantly add to an ever-increasing pile of waste, yearly usage of a single desktop personal computer can produce around *220* kilos of carbon dioxide (CO_2) [10]. Industrial whitepapers, such as by the International Data Corporation (IDC) [11] have noted that the environmental damage due to personal computers is of the same order as the environmental impact of the entire airline industry. Likewise, the Australian Computer Society (ACS) [12] has reported that the use of ICT by Australian businesses generates close to 8 million tons (Mt) of carbon emissions yearly. Besides the environmental impact of 20 million tons of carbon emissions, it has been estimated that US businesses spend an extra 2.8 billion USD for keeping computers operational (Including power usage and air conditioning) even in off hours due to reasons such as for the installation of overnight patches [13].

A deceptively simple solution for solving this management problem of power utilization has been proposed by Munzi [14]. Munzi analyzes three projects and notes that simply turning computers off can actually be one of the most effective policies for saving power in the corporate world. Likewise, a similar solution has been proposed by Gartner [15] and others such as the US Department of Energy [16].

While turning computers off could be an effective strategy, unfortunately it is impractical in the corporate world. Any new policy should not cause more problems for an already struggling corporation in the recession-hit global economy. While, in theory at least, it may be easy to control and cut the use of some residential computers by this means, it is not enforceable globally. This is especially true in active corporations with various segments of the workforce in crunch at all times.

Problem STATEMENT

In previous work, we have proposed the use of modeling and simulation to reduce power usage and to model corporate footprint [17, 18]. However, to the best of our knowledge, previous work has not been performed on modeling the Carbon footprint usage for networks of an entire corporation using Cognitive Agent-based Computing approach [19].

Research Contributions

In this paper, we model a self-adaptive architecture for managing the Carbon footprint in a corporate environment using a heterogeneous multiagent system. Our key contribution is to model this system using Cognitive Agent-based Computing (CABC). We also illustrate how the Exploratory Agent-based Modeling (EABM) level of the CABC framework helps in modeling complex systems. This modeling exercise demonstrates the modeling of an autonomous system. The proposed system monitors and controls carbon footprint use in a complex network. The system architecture of the proposed Multiagent System for Managing Carbon Footprint (MASMINC) is also presented. MASMINC can be implemented by using a set of cooperative software agents in any corporate network. We show how MASMINC can be useful in management and minimization of corporate Carbon footprint.

Research Scope and Validation Details

To summarize, the key goal of the paper is to present the modeling exercise for MASMINC using EABM of the CABC framework. MASMINC agents work to reduce the carbon footprint utilization by a mix of following measures:

- Acquire corporate rules policy from a centralized server.
- Report individual computer usage to a central server (Allowing for a real-time analysis of the network measured in terms of depletion of allocated Carbon footprint)
- Identify idle computers on the network by monitoring human interactions.
- Perform analysis of all computers by making inferences based on rules in light of the usage by the computer user.
- Decide between different types of computer shutdown policies such as stand-by, hibernation and power off, using assigned policies by the network administrator or the local computer user.
- In case of a complete or partial exhaustion of assigned corporate footprint for a given network, agents can also be appropriately engineered to notify the network

administrator to make further contingency decisions based on the usage.

For an effective validation of the architecture, we develop an agent-based simulation model based on typical personal computer usage platforms in corporate environments (Such as lunch times, schedule of people arriving and leaving offices etc.). The simulation is conducted for networks up to *1000* computers for a number of different scenarios. In all cases, the results demonstrate the effectiveness and scalability of the MASMINC approach in reducing carbon footprint usage–as compared with existing approaches such as the Energy-Star.

Outline

The rest of the paper is structured as follows:

In the next section, we present necessary background and introduce terms as well as discuss relevant literature. Next, we present the architecture of the proposed multiagent system and the design of the Exploratory agent-based model used for validation of the architecture. This is followed by a detailed discussion of results including suggestions for a practical implementation of the work. Finally, we conclude the paper giving proposals for future directions.

BACKGROUND

In this section, we present background for developing a better understanding of the proposed architecture.

Carbon Footprint

The notion of a carbon footprint is a commonly comprehensible term in relation to the role of emission of Carbon-related gases in the environment. Wiedmann et al. [20] notes that while the term itself is in common usage starting from the concept of ecological footprint by Wackernagel and Rees [21], there is considerable confusion regarding its exact nature. Keeping this in mind, they have introduced a systematic definition of "carbon footprint" to sort out practical questions such as system boundaries, completeness, comprehensiveness, units and robustness of the indicator given as follows:

Definition: "The carbon footprint is a measure of the exclusive total amount of carbon dioxide emissions that is directly and indirectly caused by an activity or is accumulated over the life stages of a product."

Weber et al. [22] have investigated the global and distributional facets of American household carbon footprint using consumer expenditure surveys and multi-country life cycle assessment techniques. It is pertinent to mention here that Murugesan [23] has noted that a single personal computer can produce a ton of Carbon dioxide yearly.

Agent-based Computing

Agent-based computing involves the use of agents in different computing scenarios. The use of Agent-based computing ranges from (software) multiagent systems, which are software systems consisting of several agents in a network, to agent-based models [24, 25]. Furthermore, as part of a recent Special Issue of the journal Simulation, Niazi and Hussain have collected papers on the use of agent-based computing in Complex Adaptive COmmunicatiOn Networks and environmentS (CACOONS) [26, 27]. These papers demonstrate the utility of agent-based models to model various systems ranging from distributed computing systems to multiagent systems and sensor networks [28]. Agents in a multiagent system are often classified according to various criteria and attributes such as being intelligent, autonomous, mobile [29], reactive or rational [30].

Cognitive Agent-based Computing

Cognitive Agent-based Computing Framework was presented by Niazi and Hussain in [19]. The idea is to be able to take any real-world complex system and convert it into a suitable model by choosing a particular modeling level [31]. A particularly notable use of Agent-based Modeling (ABM) and the CABC framework is to allow for the validation of large-scale multiagent systems, which would perhaps otherwise have been impossible to validate before construction [32]. This particular problem arises because during building software agents, it is difficult to foresee the exact nature of interactions of agents as the number of agents grows considerably large. Several case study examples of use of CABC have been presented in literature such as in [31, 33–35].

ABM has been formally discussed in detail by Miller and Page in [36] in the domain of Complex Adaptive Systems (CAS). Furthermore, North and Macal present ABM in the context of businesses [37]. Likewise, Railsback and Grimm, have presented a practical approach to ABM using NetLogo in [38]. Gilbert and Troitzsch present the use of NetLogo and other tools for developing ABM for social simulation [39]. Modeling and simulation is an important part of modern science tools because it allows for prediction and explanation of phenomena which would otherwise not have been possible. Recent examples of such uses include work by Kiparsky et al. [40].

MODEL DEVELOPMENT

This section first presents the proposed multiagent architecture including various possible mechanisms for the allocation of the distributed Carbon Footprint Allowance (CFPA). Here, it is pertinent to note that the term CFPA has been used to refer to the total usable amount of carbon footprint allocated to a given network. This is followed by the design of the Exploratory agent-based model design using CABC framework.

Architecture Goal

The proposed MASMINC multiagent architecture is demonstrated in Fig 1. MASMINC has been designed specifically to autonomously monitor carbon footprint usage by turning idle computers off by using shutdown, sleep or hibernation modes intelligently according to company policy. While, an architecture is typically not associated with internal details, here we do present some possible implementation scenarios in the subsequent sections.

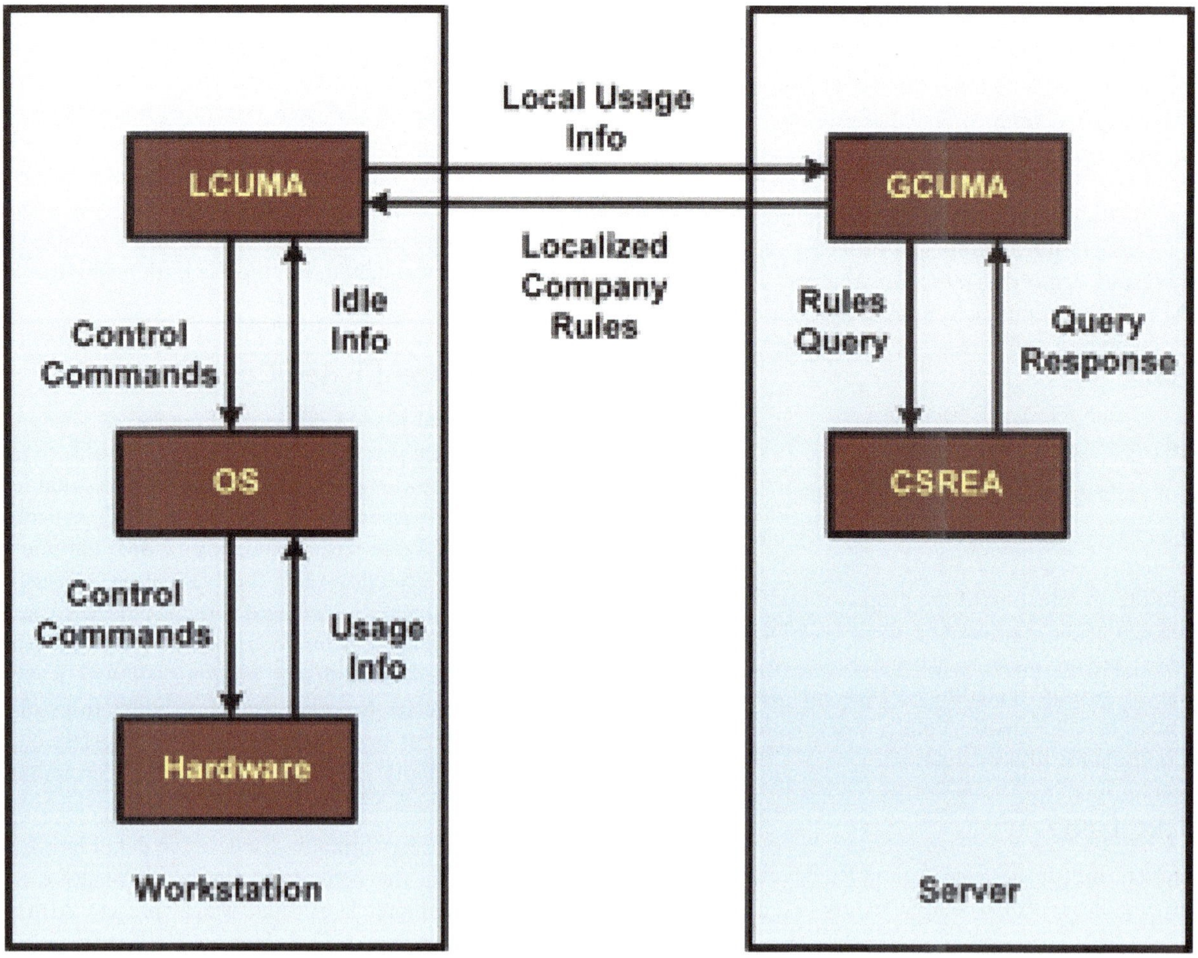

Figure 1. MASMINC Architeture.

Overview

Traditional green approaches focus on minimizing Carbon footprint by turning computers off but do not give ideas on how to do it in an automated manner. MASMINC allows for an ability to control computer usage on a corporate network using autonomous software agents while still allowing users to publish and enforce policies at the company level.

MASMINC is made up of heterogeneous agents that observe and act based on inputs from the network. A simple example could be if agents were to monitor the idle time processing of a system and compare it with any assigned threshold. Subsequently, specific agents can be asked to power off any given computer based on the corporate policy. It is important to also note here that the exact level of idle processing required by agents and similar minor implementation details are left for customization up to the company implementing MASMINC. E.g. Idle time processing can be either simply based on CPU usage or else it can be based on office timing such that during the office time, MASMINC agents would not shut computers down but during off hours, idle processing could be used to power them off. The intent of the specific approach taken in this paper is to present a generalized architecture rather than focusing only on a single implementation which would have required giving specific details pertinent only to a specific Operating System (OS) or a multiagent toolkit–thereby limiting practical implementations in the corporate world. This is important because in the corporate world, what works for one OS may certainly be unsuitable for another. This is also true for different versions of the same OS. Besides, there is no guarantee that a specific OS or a toolkit will be suitable for the needs of every company aiming to implement MASMINC in their environment.

While these software agents are intrinsically simple in design, it is commonly known that simple agents can interact to exhibit collective intelligence in the form of an artificial CAS which can exhibit emergent behavior at the global level. Emergence is a phenomenon also prevalent in nature where simple agents such as cells interact based on sensors and actuators using chemical flow passing through the cell walls. Still, these simple agents form massively complex dynamic systems i.e. complex multi-cellular life. Likewise, depending upon the implementation details and company requirements for MASMINC, the agents may be used to act as intelligently as required by choosing between different outcomes.

To summarize, goals of the agents can include (but are not restricted to) the follows:

- Dissemination of company policy from network administrators to individual computers via servers on the network.
- Enforce and propagate company policy to computers allowing for the emergent minimization of carbon footprint usage over the network.
- Allowing for programmable approaches to minimize loss of user data based on company timings and policy while reducing the carbon footprint. Timed

shutdowns can also be configured using MASMINC to minimize hardware damage or data loss. Furthermore, MASMINC agents can be programmed to use decision support to minimize false positives and also give automated recommendations for shutting computers down. The program can be designed to differentiate between various types and reasons for invoking a shutdown. Specified rules can govern invoking specific actions on a particular computer autonomously in various ways and any operation can be executed either at a specific time "t", after a certain time duration "Δt" or else immediately.

Modeling Exercise

In this subsection, we formally present the design of the MASMINC architecture. Here, we first define a MASMINC Scenario.

Definition: MASMINC Scenario. A MASMINC scenario S_i is formally defined as a vector of operation O and urgency U as follows:

$$S_i = < o, u > \quad (1)$$

Where

$$O = \{Shutdown, Restart, Standby, Hibernate\},\ o \in O$$

$$U = \{t_n, t_f, t_d\},\ u \in U \text{ with}$$

$$t_n = \text{Now}$$

$$t_f = \text{At a fixed time}$$

$$t_d = \text{After a duration}$$

A list of possible scenarios of MASMINC is summarized in tabular form in Table 1. Here, we can note that all four possible operations can be coupled with three types of urgencies to create a total of 12 possible cases:

Table 1. MASMINC Scenario.

Scenario	Operation	Urgency
1.	Shutdown	Right Now
2.	Shutdown	At a Specific Time
3.	Shutdown	After a Specific Time Duration
4.	Restart	Right Now
5.	Restart	At a Specific Time
6.	Restart	After a Specific Time Duration
7.	Standby	Right Now
8.	Standby	At a Specific Time
9.	Standby	After a Specific Time Duration
10.	Hibernate	Right Now
11.	Hibernate	At a Specific Time
12.	Hibernate	After a Specific Time Duration

doi:10.1371/journal.pone.0146760.t001

Agent Design

As discussed earlier, while architecture does not focus on implementation details, our goal here is to assist the readers in implementing the concept of MASMINC. As such, here we also give some details of the agent-design. The exact number of these agents in a particular network is customizable. This allows for different implementation strategies and may vary based on each instance of the operational environment. However, in general, MASMINC agents are of the following three basic types and will be discussed in more details in the subsequent sections:

- Global Carbon Usage Monitoring Agent (GCUMA),
- Local Carbon Usage Monitoring Agent (LCUMA),
- Company Specific Rules Enforcement Agent (CSREA).

Next, we discuss some of the key architectural details of MASMINC:

Customizability by Design.

MASMINC has intrinsically been designed as a customizable architecture that may be implemented in any suitable corporate environment. All MASMINC rules can be placed in the form of a text file which can be maintained by the network administrator. The rule file is loaded by the CSREA. By decoupling the rules from the agent code in the form of a separate file, we have eliminated the requirement to re-compile agents if rules are to be changed. A new rule file may simply be placed in a particular folder under observation by the CSREA. CSREA will load updated rules and propagate them to other agents across the network. As such, in this paper, while we do not focus on a particular rule file or format, we do however give proposals for developing a suitable customized implementation of the rule file.

Autonomous Checking

MASMINC can be used to provide autonomous checking of system statistics such as idle time, number of processes, CPU usage, interactive input from user etc. The LCUMAs that reside on the machines can be implemented on a particular system to periodically check system statistics automatically in order to take appropriate decisions based on the company and user rules.

Central Logging of Energy Saving Data

It is proposed that a centralized "Energy Consumption" log be maintained at the server machine. This log can be a text file or it can be in the form of a database. The idea is to use GCUMA to perform centralized logging based on status updates from LCUMAs. The LCUMAs themselves can also be designed as stateless considering that there may not be any need to save localized information. If required, Computer usage history can also be saved in separate tables in addition to the current status of each system in the log.

Agent Communication

Agents coordinate with each other using message passing. It is proposed that messages be designed to be of at least two key types: The first type is logging messages–messages which emanate whenever a computer is about to take some action. In addition, a second message type can be "control" messages–messages which can be used to advise agents to perform shutdown/standby or hibernation on the local machine. Fig 2 and Fig 3 represent the flow of messages between the agents of MASMINC. Table 2 shows the nature of messages that are exchanged between the agents of MASMINC.

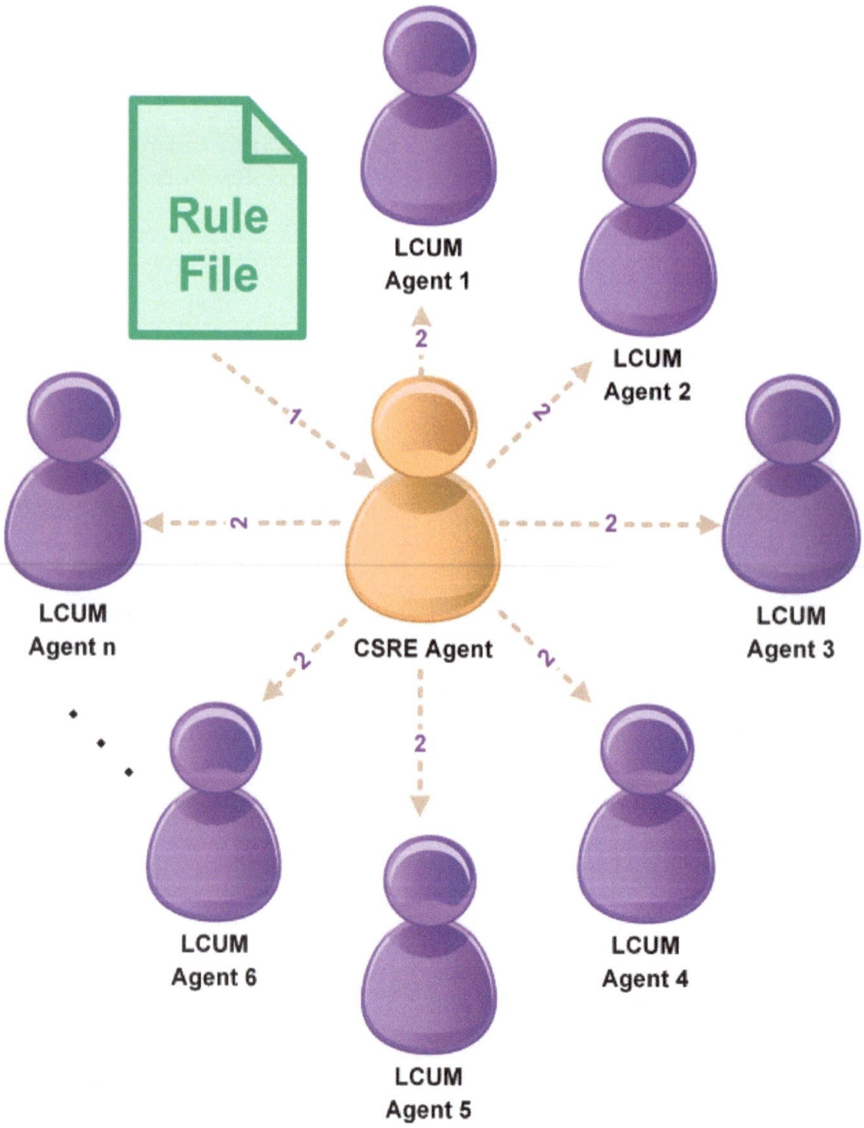

Figure 2. Communication between Agents of MASMINC and CSRE Agent.

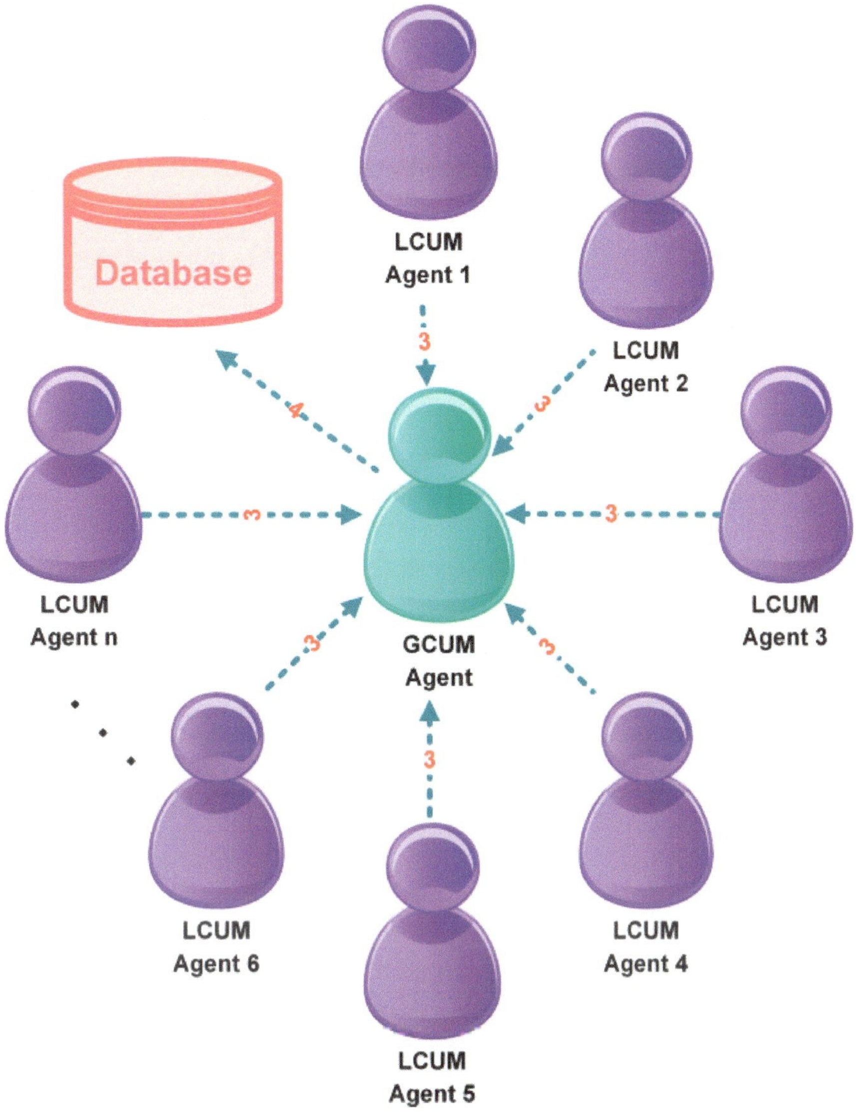

Figure 3. Communication between Agents of MASMINC and GCUM Agent.

Table 2. Types of Messages that are exchanged between MASMINC Agents.

Agent name	Send message to	Message Content
CSRE Agent	-	(1) Get rule file
CSRE Agent	LCUM Agent	(2) A rule file is sent
LCUM Agent	GCUM Agent	(3) Status update of corresponding machines is sent.
GCUM Agent	-	(4) Log information to the database

doi:10.1371/journal.pone.0146760.t002

As can be noted here, GCUMA monitors the status of all other agents. Centralized logging allows the GCUMA to observe and 1maintain a complete status log of all computers. LCUMAs keep track of idle time and also periodically report machine status to GCUMA to ensure smooth network operation based on publicized rules. The CSREA loads administrative rules from the server machine and subsequently communicates these rules to various LCUMAs. As an example, rules may be designed such that a computer's idle time may be used in conjunction with a threshold metric to make decisions in terms of the exact procedure to adopt for turning off the computer. While performing any local operation, a LCUMA also updates GCUMA about the status of the system. Thus, a GCUMA also serves as a bookkeeper for all machines managed by the MASMINC environment.

A detailed description of the working of MASMINC is as follows:

- Initially, the GCUMA and CSREA are created on the server machine (at boot up).
- Likewise, each machine managed by MASMINC creates LCUMAs at boot time.
- After boot, each LCUMA connects with the GCUMA and informs about the system.
- The CSREA extracts rules from the rule file. Subsequently these rules are sent to all LCUMAs.

- After the initialization of the system, i.e., the creation of GCUMA, CSREA and the LCUMAs, the LCUMAs start monitoring local resources by observing and keeping a short-term utilization record in the respective machines.
- The LCUMAs also periodically send status information back to the GCUMA regarding the energy usage, which includes system information such as system idle time, the system boot time, keyboard/mouse status etc.
- The GCUMA periodically updates this information to determine if the computer is idle or in use by a current active user in a database.

Fig 4 depicts the detailed working of the system as described above. Here, we note that MASMINC can be implemented using any multiagent run-time. However, just to give an example, we present some ideas for using a popular toolkit such as Java Agent Development Framework (JADE) [41]. In this figure, we note that initially different agents are created at startup on various machines. Although client machines only execute LCUMAs, the server machine(s) execute GCUMA and CSREA.

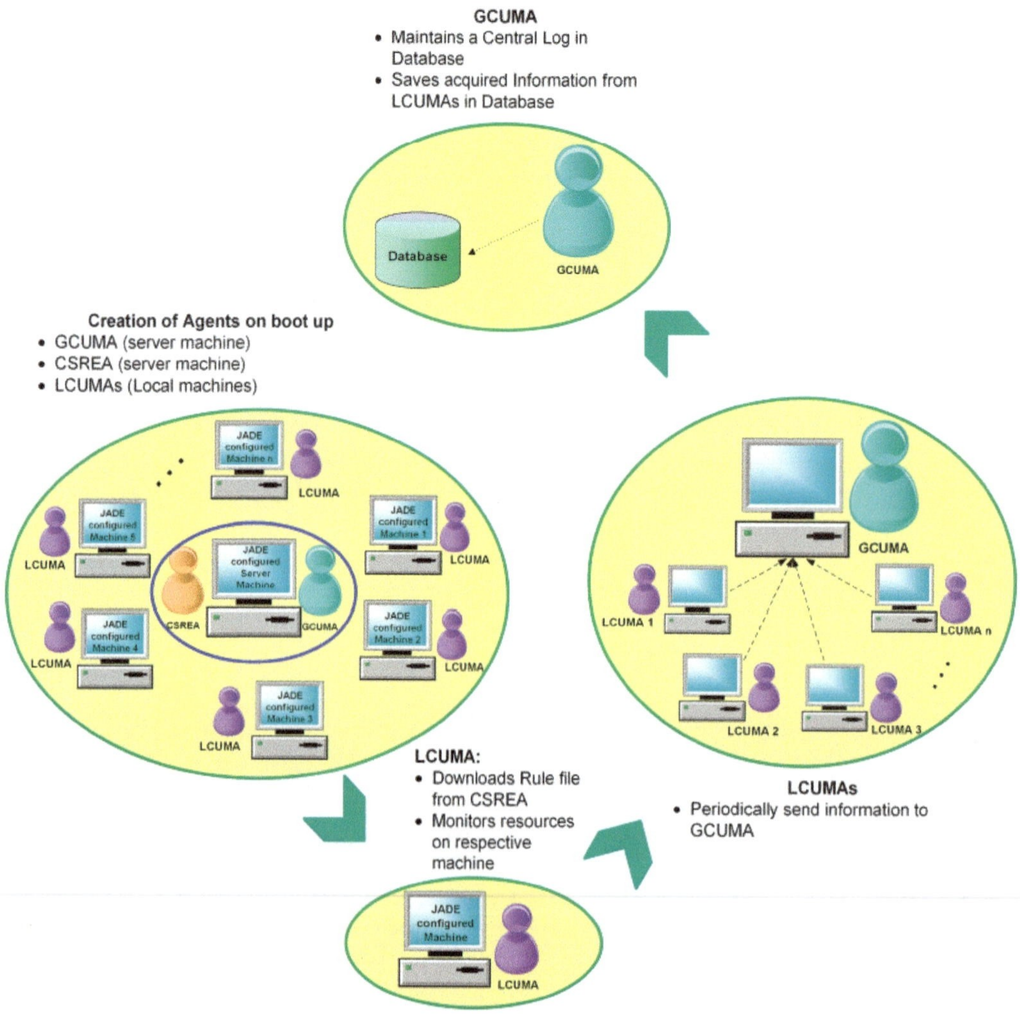

Figure 4. Illustration of the working of MASMINC (assuming JADE run-time).

Agent Environment

The concepts of the Agent Environment of MASMINC have been adapted from Russell and Norvig [42]. The dimensions along which task environments are categorized are given as follows:

- Fully Observable vs. Partially Observable
- Deterministic vs. Stochastic
- Episodic vs. Sequential
- Static vs. Dynamic
- Discrete vs. Continuous
- Single agent vs. Multiagent

The specific properties of MASMINC agents' environment can thus be noted as follows:

Partially Observable

The environment itself is not fully observable. Besides, since other agents do not keep a state of their own; the GCUMA must keep an internal state to keep track of its environment.

Deterministic

The agent environment is deterministic, as the next state of the environment is completely determined by the current state and the action executed by the agent in a particular scenario is already specified in the rule file. The behavior of the agents is also predictable and is based on the inferences made using the rules file. The rules file provided by the CSREA agent can contain explicit sequence of actions that need to be accomplished in any particular course of events or they can instead actually contain rules which are usable for inference making using an appropriate expert system such as JESS [43].

Here, we would also clarify that the definition of "Deterministic" according to AIMA book by Russell and Norvig [42] entails that an environment is deterministic if the previous states completely determine the outcome of the next states. In other words, while the actions of the users may themselves be considered stochastic in nature, since the output state of the system is completely dictated by the previous state, hence we have labeled the task environment as deterministic.

Episodic

MASMINC agents have an episodic task environment as in each episode; the agent perceives the environment and then performs an appropriate action.

Static

The environment is static because the environment does not change its state except for the situation when any agent performs one of the expected actions.

Discrete

The environment is discrete in terms of the number of computers.

Multiagent

Since MASMINC involves sets of agents that cooperate to accomplish a common goal of managing carbon footprint, the environment is formally noted to be a multiagent environment as per the definition given in the above standard reference for intelligent agents.

Distributed Staggered CFPA Allocation Mechanisms

Now that we have talked about various agents, we now present strategies which may be used to allocate carbon footprint to individual computers. Once an amount of carbon footprint to a particular corporate environment has been allocated, five types of CFPA distribution schemes are proposed here as examples for usage in particular implementation–described as follows:

- Constant Distribution of Carbon Footprint Allowance
- Uniform Distribution of Carbon Footprint Allowance
- Customized Distribution of Carbon Footprint Allowance
- Triangular Distribution of Carbon Footprint Allowance
- Hybrid Distribution of Carbon Footprint Allowance

A graphical representation of four types of CFPA allocation schemes is given in. It should be noted here that the graphical representations of the CFPA allocation schemes are provided to Fig 5 give a general idea of the distribution schemes, thus figures are not drawn to scale.

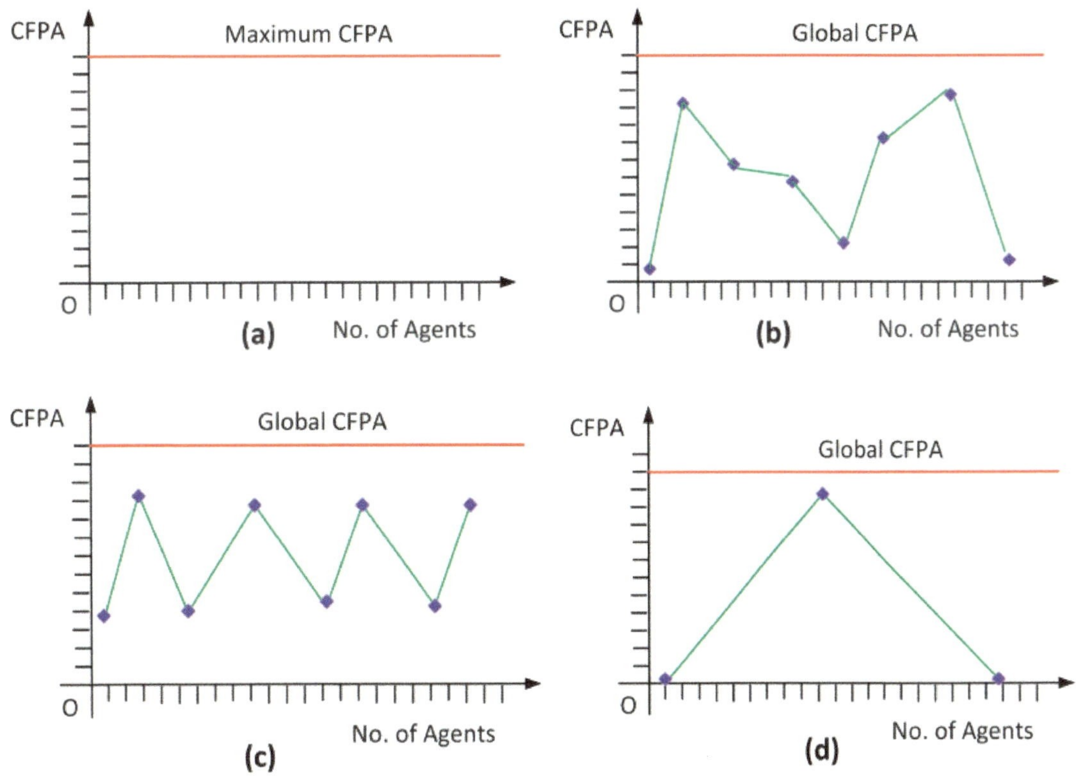

Figure 5. Different CFPA Distribution Schemes. (a) Constant Distribution of CFPA–All agents get the same amount of CFPA (b) Uniform Distribution of CFPA–Distribution of CFPA to agents is variable but all local values of CFPA should add up to the Global CFPA limit of the company (c) Customized Distribution of CFPA–Some random agents are assigned very higher values of CFPA (d) Triangular Distribution of CFPA–distribution of CFPA to agents follows Triangular distribution.

The details of the above-mentioned distributions are given as follows:

Constant Distribution of Carbon Footprint Allowance

In this type of distribution, a constant amount of CFPA is apportioned to each computer. Fig 5(A) represents Constant Distribution of CFPA.

Uniform Distribution of Carbon Footprint Allowance

In uniform distribution of CFPA, a random amount of CFPA is allotted to each agent. However, there is a constraint on the distribution of random CFPA to the agents, i.e., the total random CFPA allocated to all the agents must be equal to the Global CFPA as specified by the company. Let LCFPA denote the Local Carbon Foot Print Allowance, GCFPA denotes the Global Carbon Foot Print Allowance with k denoting the total number of agents residing on the machines in a network then we can note that

$$GCFPA = \sum_{n=1}^{k} LCFPA_n \quad \textbf{(2)}$$

This type of distribution is illustrated in Fig 5(B).

Customized Distribution of Carbon Foot Print Allowance

The Customized distribution is convenient in the sense that the desired amount of CFPA can be allocated to a specific machine. For example, a company might want to provide a relatively larger amount of CFPA to a server machine and smaller amounts of CFPA to the nodes. Thus, through this distribution, the CFPA allocation can be customized as desired by company policy. Customized Distribution is shown in Fig 5(C).

Triangular Distribution of Carbon Foot Print Allowance

In the Triangular distribution, there are three parameters that define the allocation: a maximum value, a minimum value and a mode value for CFPA allocation, giving rise to a triangular distribution. The mode value of CFPA is the most likely value. As an example, let's say if we have a maximum CFPA value of 100, a minimum CFPA value of 10 and a mode CFPA value of 50, then this type of distribution will generate random samples with a minimum value of 10, most likely value of 50, and maximum value of 100 as shown in Fig 5(D).

Hybrid Distribution of Carbon Foot Print Allowance

As the name suggests, this type of distribution can be used based on a combination of other distributions. In particular, the possible usage of hybrid distribution of the CFPA could be based on a mixture of the triangular distribution and customized distribution.

Rule-based Administration

The idea of using rules developed from the actual MASMINC system can be realized by means of a text file (e.g., an XML file) that contains the rules for autonomous execution. The file is thus an imperative part of the system. Agents dynamically evaluate the state of machines using these rules specified in the file allowing them to take decisions in order to save carbon footprint usage without causing disruptions to working users.

There are clearly two distinct possibilities of hosting the administrative rule file. The first and more traditional approach to disseminating a rule file is to host it on each machine where it could be loaded by the agents at startup of the system. However, this approach has several inherent problems. Firstly, every time, the rule file changes, the administrator would have to manually upload the rule file to all machines. Secondly, there is a risk of manual editing by the user, which might end up inadvertently destroying important files by causing unnecessary shutdowns. Therefore, to minimize user errors as well as to provide a common interface for the autonomously execution of rules, we propose that the corporations implementing MASMINC may host the rule file on the server. After hosting, an agent can parse the rules from this file and the same may subsequently be propagated to other agents on the rest of the network computers.

Technically, this heterogeneous agent environment collectively forms a cooperative multiagent system [44]. In a cooperative multiagent environment, agents cooperate with each other towards a common goal. In the present system, this common goal is to autonomously limit the usage of Carbon footprint while minimizing any delays or data loss in personal computer usage on the network.

Fig 6 proposes example semantics of a rule file.

```
If (Certain Condition 1)
    Then (Rule Outcome 1)
   Else
If (Certain Condition 2)
    Then (Rule Outcome 2)
   Else
          •
          •
          •
   Else
If (Certain Condition n)
    Then (Rule Outcome n)
```

Figure 6. Examples of rule in a Rule File.

Fig 7 presents a set of examples of rules for turning off or hibernating machines.

If (No. of Programs Running == 0)

Then (Turn Off the Machine)

Else

If (No. of Programs Running > 0)
Then (Hibernate the Machine)

If (User has not used system for t > 20 mins)

Then (Hibernate the Machine)

Figure 7. Example rules for turning off or hibernating a particular machine.

Experimental Setup for Validation

This section presents two experimental setups. In the first case, simulation experiments are presented for large-scale corporate networks using an ABM. Whereas subsequently, we give details on how an actual multiagent system may be practically implemented for the proposed MASMINC architecture. It is important to note here once again that our focus is on presenting an architecture which requires being platform and toolkit agnostic. Based on our previous experience in developing software multiagent systems, we believe that experienced software developers, should be able to use this detailed guidance to easily develop implementations of the MASMINC architecture, using any standard multiagent toolkit on a given version of an OS.

Agent-based Model Design

In this section we present an experimental setup for a large number of computers, i.e., up to 1000 computers, using the NetLogo Simulation Environment [45]. It is important to note here the importance of the simulation because it is impractical to actually perform experiments on corporate networks having more than 100 computers on physical hardware–thereby demonstrating the effectiveness of the agent-directed simulation approach.

NetLogo, An Introduction

NetLogo is a suitable candidate for multiagent simulation and has already been used in the multiagent literature for similar use. Choosing NetLogo to simulate MASMINC is backed by several reasons. Wilensky [46] notes that NetLogo is particularly well suited for modeling complex systems over time, making it a suitable choice as a simulator for MASMINC. In addition, considerable work has previously been published on the use of NetLogo and similar agent-based simulation toolkits for developing simulations of multiagent systems including[44, 47–49].

Implementation Details of Netlogo Model

The agents are created in NetLogo with the "breed" keyword. After defining the breeds, different breeds can be made to behave differently using NetLogo functions. The function "make-agents" is used to create and place all agents in the environment.

Here personal computers are modeled as agents and thus follow the state chart as noted inFig 8. A machine can turn on and off. It can also go to the standby state if idle. Likewise, the computer can be hibernated or restarted.

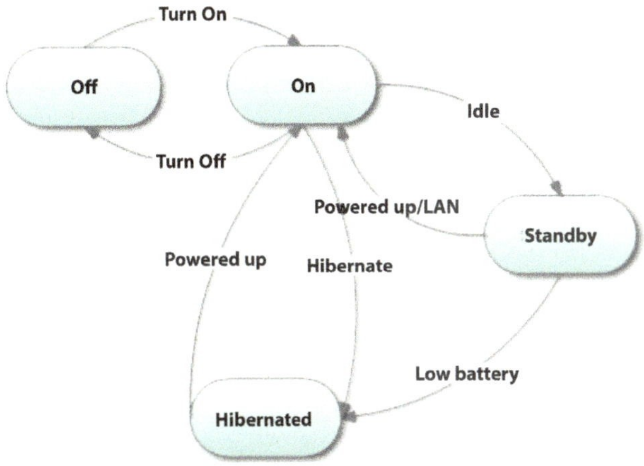

Figure 8. State transition model of a typical personal computer.

Example of Using a Software MAS Toolbox

In this section, we present an example setup for MASMINC which multiagent researchers can easily develop for practical application in networks. While, as noted earlier, the basic design goal of MASMINC is to be platform and toolkit-agnostic, this setup is intended to be an example for researchers who develop their own practical solutions.

The agents in MASMINC may be implemented physically using a toolkit such as JADE. JADE is a software environment to build agent systems for the management of networked information resources. The JADE toolkit has been developed to model agents which comply with the Foundation for Intelligent Physical Agents (FIPA 2000) specifications for interoperable multi-agent systems [50].

Messaging among the MASMINC Agents

Here we present example messages for MASMINC agents using JADE. As an example of sending messages from GCUMA to a particular LCUMA, example code is given as follows:

ACLMessage msg = new ACLMessage (ACLMessage. INFORM);

msg.setContent("Send the list of computer activity according to rule 1 of rule file");

AID LCUMA1 =...;

Msg.addReceiver(LCUMA1);

Send msg;

An example of receiving message from GCUMA to a particular LCUMA is given as:

ACLMessage msg = receive();

if (msg! = null)

<.... Report computer activities to the GCUMA...>

else

<... Monitor computer activities on the designated computer...>

Likewise, other important features of MASMINC can also be easily implemented in JADE or any other multiagent toolkit.

SIMULATION RESULTS

In this section, we present the simulation results using the agent-based model described earlier for validating MASMINC. A key goal of the simulation experiments was firstly to validate the benefits of MASMINC. Secondly, we wanted to evaluate if the benefits offered by MASMINC would hold with a variation in the number of managed computers. The simulation data is available online from the Dryad Digital Repository [51].

Metrics

In this section, we describe the metrics followed by the experimental setup and a detailed discussion of the results. The key metric used for performance evaluation in this model is the Maximal Carbon Footprint Allowance (MCFPA). It is defined as *"The maximum carbon footprint of a computer if it were turned on for the entire day"–thereby representing the greenhouse gases for a single computer remaining in power-up state for a day.*

Having this metric is important because of several reasons:

- In its absence, it is difficult to generalize how a single computer would behave.
- There are no other known metrics of a maximum allowance for a single computer in a given corporate network.
- Having a maximum allowance allows us to ensure that we evaluate and compare the performance of any appropriate scheme with the maximum. In other words, we can measure how much of the allowance is left over after each day for each scheme.

The maximum carbon footprint allowance (MCFPA) and its relationship with the daily carbon footprint allowance (DCFPA) can thus be expressed formally as given in the following set of equations:

$$CFPA_{max} = 24 \times CFPA_{Single} \tag{3}$$

Here $CFPA_{max}$ is the MCFPA, N is the total number of computers in the network and $CFPA_{Single}$ is the allowance for one computer for 1 hour.

Assuming a unit value for $CFPA_{Single}$ and using 3, we can express the "Daily Carbon Footprint Allowance" (DCFPA) as follows:

$$DCFPA = CFPA_{max} - \sum_{t=0}^{t=23} n_t \tag{4}$$

It follows from 4 that

$$DCFPA = 24 \times N - \sum_{t=0}^{t=23} n_t \tag{5}$$

Where

n_t represents the average number of computers which remained on in the hour t.

Next, we can calculate the hourly change in Carbon Footprint Allowance as follows:

$$\Delta Allowance_h = (Allowance)_{h-1} - (Allowance)_h \tag{6}$$

$$Hourly\ Change\ in\ Allowance = \Delta Allowance_h \tag{7}$$

Next, we present description of different experiments for the validation of the proposed MASMINC architecture.

Modeling a typical Office Network

The first set of simulation experiments was to simulate the CFPA consumption in relation to the usage of computers in a typical corporate working environment. This experiment demonstrates how the simulation screen varies over a simulated typical day as can be seen in Fig 9. In the figure, the X-axis represents time in hours and the Y-axis represents the Carbon Foot Print Allowance. The numbers 0 and 24 on the x-axis represent 24 hours of a day whereas the numbers 2640, 13200, 26400 on the Y-axis is the maximum Carbon Foot Print Allowance that is associated with a specific company. Here we can notice that at the start of the day, computers are almost all turned off so leftover allowance is constant, i.e., the usage of CFPA amount is nearly negligible. As time passes, gradually some computers are on and some are turned off during office hours, resulting in lowering of the allowance, i.e., the usage of the allowed CFPA amount. During peak hours, almost all of the computers are in use, resulting in usage of a significant amount of the CFPA allowance. During breaks such as lunchtime, few computers may be in active use. This data has been simulated based on a typical office environment in the corporate world. However, it should be noted here that this particular setup has only been used as an example–other office cultures can also be easily modeled in the same simulation model.

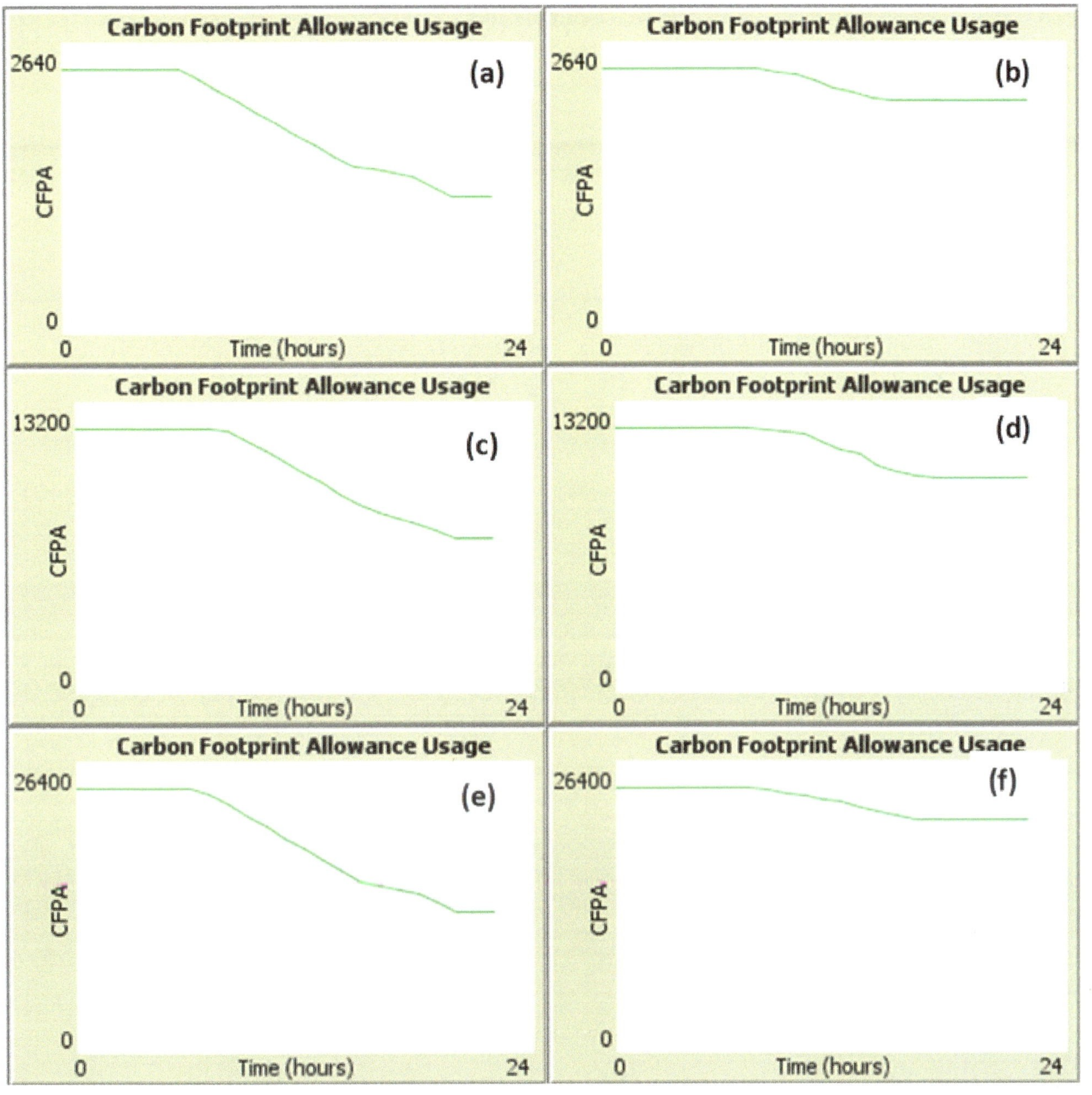

Figure 9. NetLogo Simulation plot showing the normal workplace carbon footprint Allowance usage in 24 hours of a day. (a) with n = 100 without MASMINC (b) with n = 100 with MASMINC (c) with n = 500 without MASMINC (d) with n = 500 with MASMINC (e) with n = 1000 without MASMINC and (f) with n = 1000 with MASMINC.

Variation of Carbon Footprint Allowance Usage with Number of computers

The objective of the second set of experiments was to discover how CFPA consumption varied with the number of computers in a company. To minimize the stochastic effects of simulation, each simulation experiment was repeated *50* times. Subsequently, results obtained from the simulation have been plotted on the plot. It is pertinent to note here that parameter sweeping has also been used. Fig 10, Fig 11 and Fig 12 illustrate the results of simulation experiments by varying the number of computers in the system. On the x-axis, we see the 24 hours while the y-axis shows the CFPA consumed by the computers. Initially, the maximum CFPA remains constant. This can be seen by the appearance of the initial straight line. The usage of computers increases with the passage of time. This usage causes a gradual decrease in the CFPA. The CFPA approaches zero, representing a scenario when a computer has used up the allowed CFPA. In other words, this situation now calls for action to be taken based on heuristics. This action could be a shut down or hibernation either immediately or after some time. The details of this shutdown are dictated by the company rules as can be publicized via the rule file. As can be seen in the three scenarios, the emergent patterns are almost the same for the number of computers ranging from N = 100, N = 500 and N = 1000. In all cases, MASMINC outperforms computers without MASMINC and a significant amount of leftover allowance is also available in all cases.

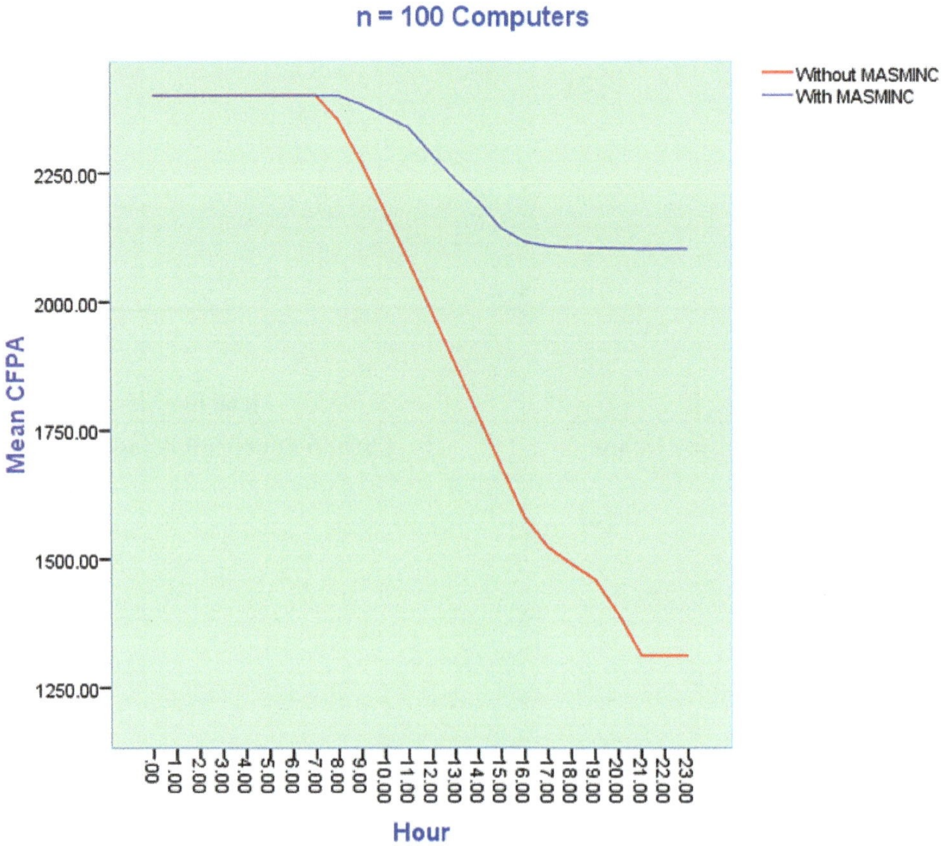

Figure 10. Results of 50 Simulation experiments with n = 100 computers during a day before and after applying the proposed MASMINC Approach.

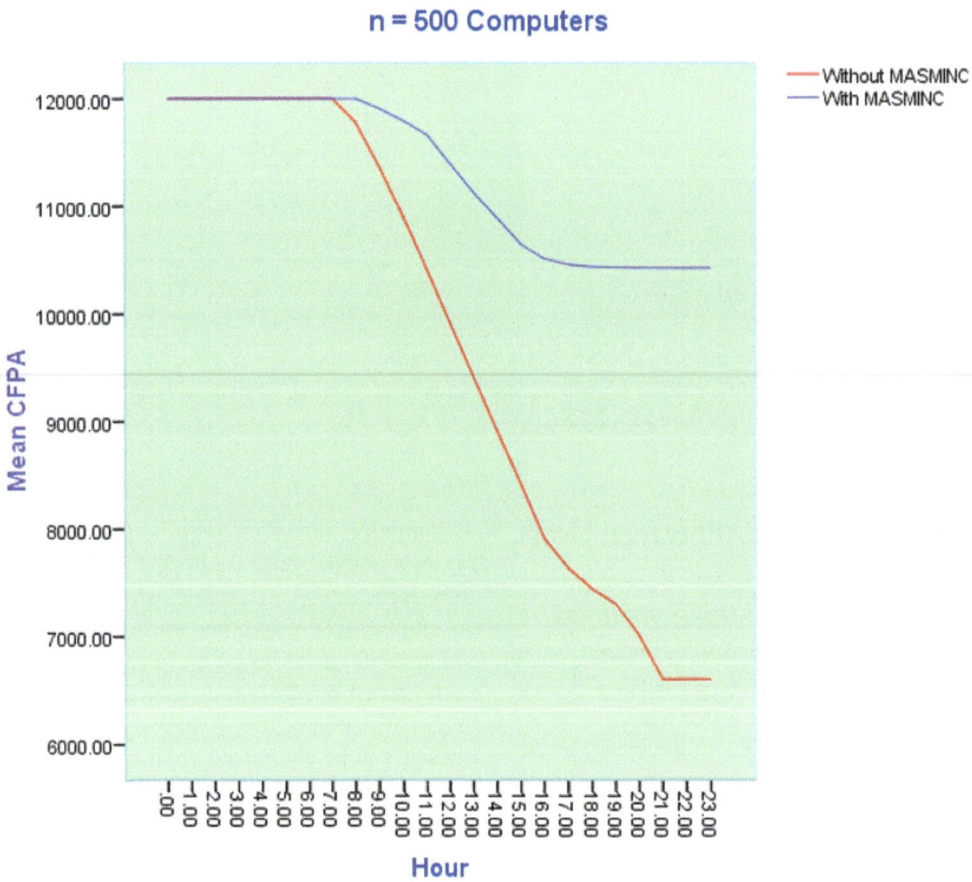

Figure 11. Results of 50 Simulation experiments with n = 500 computers during a day before and after applying the proposed MASMINC Approach.

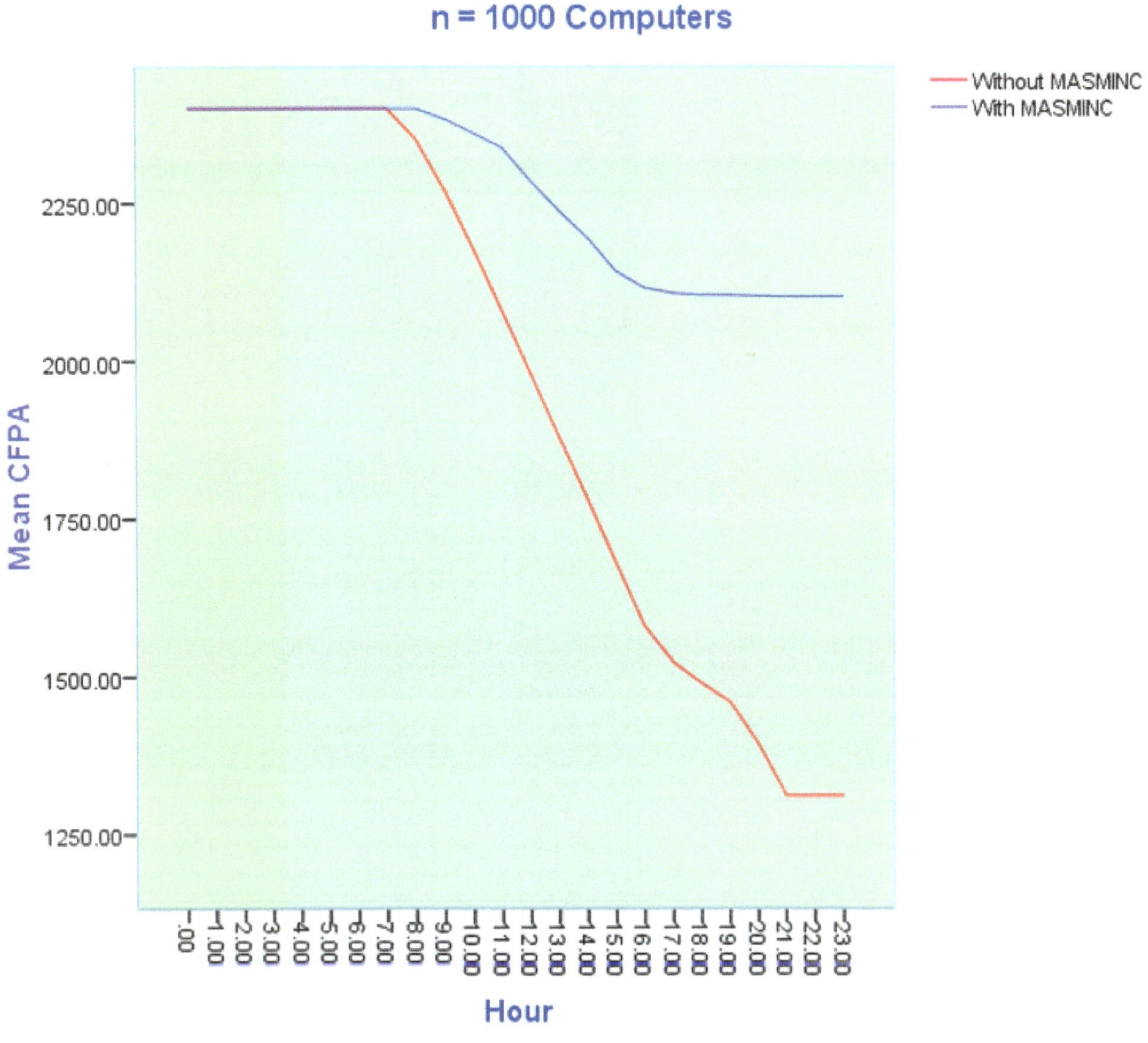

Figure 12. Results of 50 Simulation experiments with n = 1000 computers during a day before and after applying the proposed MASMINC Approach.

Comparative Evaluation of MASMINC with Energy Star Approach with Change in the Number of Computers

The Energy Star program was introduced by the Environmental Protection Agency (EPA) of the United States for the promotion and identification of energy efficient products. The computer manufacturers focused on high performance keeping in view the energy efficiency constraint [52].

In this section, we compare MASMINC with the Energy Star Model. Energy Star Model saves the energy of the system by simply shutting down the computers that are sitting idle without the consideration of the loss of user data. On the other hand, the MASMINC approach decides rationally which computers should be turned off. Here, we compare the effects of the Energy-Star approach to the MASMINC approach by means of varying the number of computers. We perform extensive simulation experiments by varying the number of computers from 100 to 1000. Each simulation was repeated 50 times and results were plotted using a 95% confidence interval as can be seen in Fig 13. Here it is pertinent to mention that if we examine the plots, we note a higher variance in the case of MASMINC. The variance is high because computers are being shutdown as per need. In the case of regular usage, the computers are kept turned on resulting in low variance. This however is actually besides the point; the important point to be noted here is actually that the Carbon footprint allocated in the case of MASMINC is saved more than without MASMINC even in extreme cases.

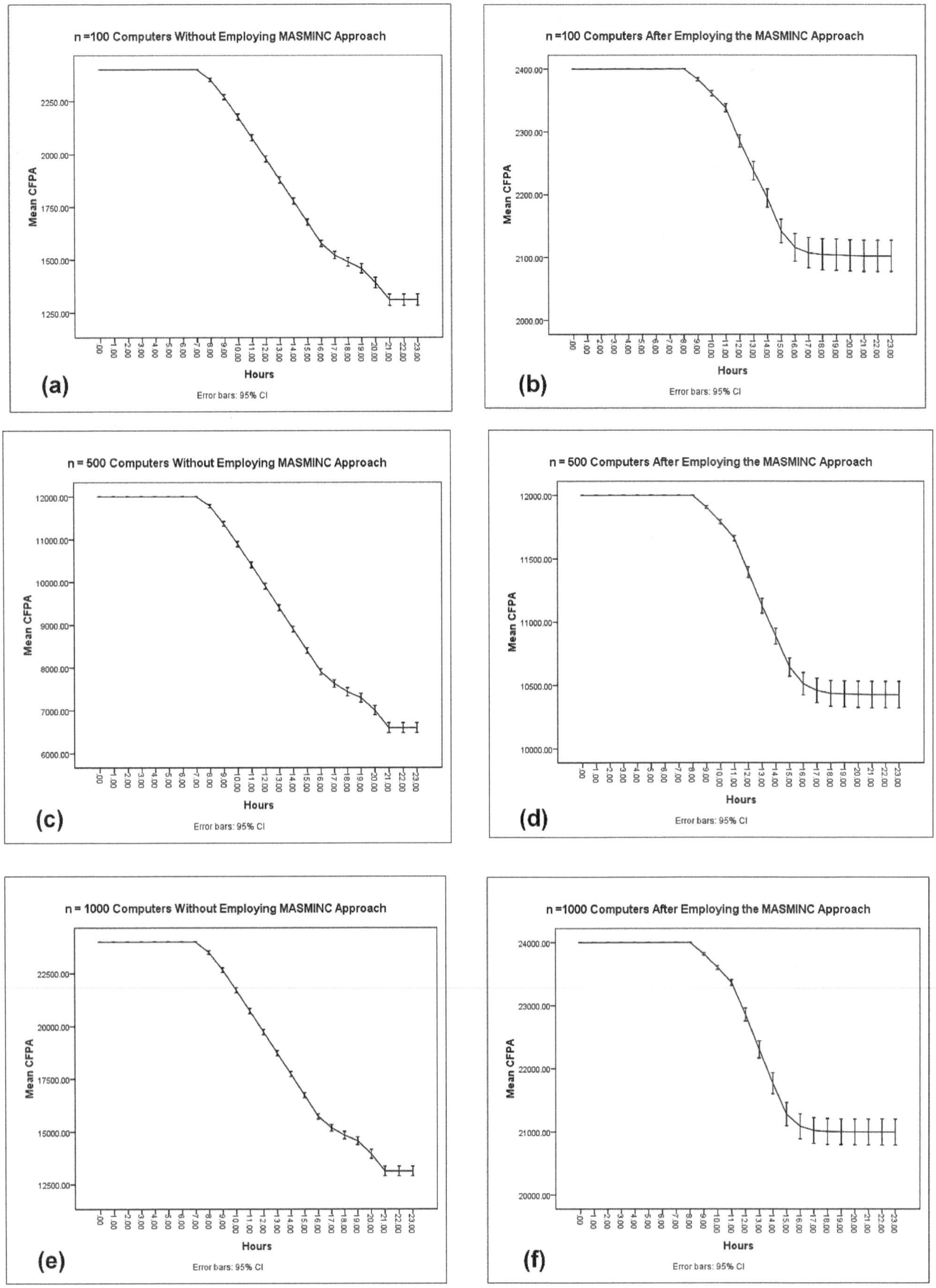

Figure 13. Results of 50 simulation experiments of daily Carbon Footprint Allowance Usage of computers ranging from 100 to 1000 during a day showing error bars with 95% Confidence Interval with Energy Star (Left) and with MASMINC (right).

On the left side, the allowance is plotted with the use of Energy Star and on the right side, it is plotted using MASMINC. As can be seen, the number of computers that remain consuming power is significantly lower in the case of MASMINC as compared with the Energy Star approach.

Discussion on why the MASMINC Approach Performs Better than Energy*

It is clearly apparent that a blanket policy of shutting down computers is not a viable approach in a corporate environment. Now, let us examine the Energy Star approach which is mostly used for home computers and does not cater for corporate networks as seen in the simulation experiments in the previous section:

- Firstly, Energy Star is an approach designed primarily for residential computers. By default, it does not offer a mechanism for a medium to large-sized company to enforce and implement a complex computer usage policy. Simple policies such as Energy star are thus not effective in this domain [53]. Complex situations can include employees being given short and hard deadlines. In these situations, the company would probably be more interested in accepting the extra usage of computers rather than forcing users to shut computers down to save the environment. Besides, in practice, this policy would anyway be impractical because system administrators cannot easily enforce such type of policies on large networks.
- Secondly, suppose for a moment, even if there was a way of updating the Energy Star settings in a distributed manner, the user can simply change the times of shutting down or standby of the computer, thereby nullifying the effects of the company policy.
- Thirdly, it is common experience that hibernation and standby procedures of personal computers are error-prone and can cause data loss or even cause significant disruption of work.

Thus, we can note here that while computers may be manually configured for Energy star to follow good energy usage practices–the approach is impractical from the standpoint of the corporate world and the larger a company network, the more visible this problem would be.

Why an Agent-based Approach?

Here, in this section, we would like to elaborate exactly why an agent-based approach is more appropriate for the presented solution. The primary reason for using agents instead of simple software is that in any typical large corporation, rules governing the use of Computing resources can actually be extremely complex. If these rules were to be implemented in an architecture then of course such software agents can physically be implemented as software services. However, if we examine the design of such software, technically these are rational agents as per the definitions of Russell and Norvig in their renowned book on Artificial Intelligence [42]. Therefore, these rational agents can be designed for a particular corporation to use complex rules such as "only hibernate a computer if the user is not a Manager" or "turn off if the time is after regular work hours and the user has not used the computer for 20+ minutes and the company mode is currently "regular" in contrast to "Crunchtime" mode in which case the computer should not be hibernated" etc. It is following of these complex rules which requires these pieces of software to be termed specifically as agents as is norm in the research of this area.

CONCLUSIONS AND FUTURE WORK

In this paper, we have presented, we believe for the first time, the demonstration of Cognitive Agent-based Computing to model a Multiagent system for managing and minimizing Carbon-footprint in corporate networks. We have demonstrated how Exploratory Agent-based Modeling can help in modeling complex systems and scenarios in Communication Network architectures. MASMINC has been designed to autonomously monitor and limit Carbon footprint usage without causing a significant degradation of the user experience. Autonomous agents running on different computers perform various system maintenance tasks using rule files loaded on the server machine. We present the Exploratory Agent-based model demonstrating various simulation experiments using realistic data for a large variation of computers. Extensive simulation experiments demonstrated the effectiveness and scalable nature of the MASMINC approach in a variety of scenarios. The proposed MASMINC architecture is particularly useful for implementation in large corporate offices.

A limitation of our current work is that we have not evaluated the effects of MASMINC on the quality of service to the end users–being out of scope of this work. As such, a future direction could be to study an implementation of MASMINC in a particular environment to subsequently evaluate it in terms of how to better design MASMINC rules causing minimal disruption to end-users users or a loss of grade of quality of service experience. Another possible extension of the work could be to evaluate the use of MASMINC on the "Internet of Things" and "cloud computing" since visions of these areas envisage possibly extensive usage of data centers. Additionally, we believe that the use of autonomous architectures such as MASMINC on cloud computing is imperative for two key reasons. Firstly, the movement away from traditional desktop environments to mobile devices and servers to the cloud makes it an important case study. Secondly, the use of virtualization in cloud computing results in diverse energy patterns on physical servers. Prevailing trends also require servers to move to using low-power architectures like ARM that also have better (lower carbon emission) cooling requirements. Finally, more work needs to be performed to evaluate the effects of Carbon footprint allocation inside data centers to minimize "hot spots" due to localized allocation of work units to physically-close CPUs in data centers.

AUTHOR CONTRIBUTIONS

Conceived and designed the experiments: MN. Performed the experiments: SL MN. Analyzed the data: SL MN. Contributed reagents/materials/analysis tools: SL MN. Wrote the paper: SL MN.

REFERENCES

1. Niazi MA, Hussain A. Social Network Analysis of trends in the consumer electronics domain. Consumer Electronics (ICCE), 2011 IEEE International Conference on; 9–12 Jan. 20112011. p. 219–20.
2. Niazi MA, Laghari S. Highly Modular Electronics: Self-Organized Power Hotspot Management in Components. 2015 IEEE International Conference on Consumer

Electronics (ICCE); 9–12 January, 2015; Las Vegas, USA: IEEE; 2015. p. 464–5.

3. Ashton K. That Internet of Things Thing. RFID Journal. 2009.
4. Armbrust M, Fox A, Griffith R, Joseph AD, Katz R, Konwinski A, et al. A view of cloud computing. Communications of the ACM. 2010;53(4):50–8. doi: 10. 1145/1721654. 1721672
5. Habiba U, Masood R, Shibli MA, Niazi MA. Cloud identity management security issues & solutions: a taxonomy. Complex Adaptive Systems Modeling. 2014;2(1):1–37. doi: 10. 1186/s40294-014-0005-9
6. Angiuoli SV, Matalka M, Gussman A, Galens K, Vangala M, Riley DR, et al. CloVR: a virtual machine for automated and portable sequence analysis from the desktop using cloud computing. BMC bioinformatics. 2011;12(1):356. doi: 10. 1186/1471-2105-12-356
7. Berriman GB, Juve G, Deelman E, Regelson M, Plavchan P, editors. The application of cloud computing to astronomy: A study of cost and performance. e-Science Workshops, 2010 Sixth IEEE International Conference on; 2010: IEEE.
8. Holland JH. Signals and boundaries: Building blocks for complex adaptive systems: Mit Press; 2012.
9. Moore S. Gartner Says Environmental Sustainability is Becoming a More Important Criterion in PC Brand Selection in Asia Pacific. Gartner. 2010.
10. Habib SJ, Marimuthu PN, editors. Carbon offsetting through computer network redesign. Information Networking (ICOIN), 2012 International Conference on; 2012: IEEE.
11. "IDC Launches Green IT and Digital Marketplace Research Practices as part of its New Emerging Technology Advisory Services (ETAS) Program" North Sydney: PC World, IDG Communications, accessed January, 2013, http://tinyurl. com/q4oh6y6; [cited 2013 January, 2013]. Available from: http://tinyurl. com/q4oh6y6.
12. Campbell P, Tate N, Jackson A. Queensland ICT Industry Launches Green IT Initiatives. ACS News. 2008
13. Swartz J. Leaving PCs on overnight costs companies $2. 8B a year. USA Today. 2009.
14. Munzi A. Computers: turn them off or leave them on? Bothell: University of Washington; 2011.
15. Mingay S. 10 Key Elements of a 'Green IT' Strategy. Gartner, 2007 Contract No. : G00154085.
16. USGov. When to turn off computers. US Department of Energy, 2011.
17. Niazi MA, Laghari S, editors. An Intelligent Self-Organizing Power-Saving Architecture: An Agent-Based Approach. Computational Intelligence, Modelling and Simulation (CIMSiM), 2012 Fourth International Conference on; 2012: IEEE.
18. Laghari S, Niazi MA. Modeling for a Greener Internet of Things: Carbon Footprint Planning and Allocation. Frontiers of Information Technology; Islamabad, Pakistan: IEEE; 2015.
19. Niazi MA, Hussain A. Cognitive Agent-based Computing-I: A Unified Framework for Modeling Complex Adaptive Systems Using Agent-based & Complex Network-based Methods. Hussain A, editor. Dordrecht: Springer Netherlands; 2013. 75 p.
20. Wiedmann T, Minx J. A definition of 'Carbon Footprint'. ISA Research Report. 2007;1.
21. Wackernagel M, Rees W. Our ecological footprint: reducing human impact on the earth: New Society Publishers; 1996.
22. Weber CL, Matthews HS. Quantifying the global and distributional aspects of American household carbon footprint. Ecological Economics. 2008;66(2–3):379–91. doi: 10. 1016/j. ecolecon. 2007. 09. 021
23. Murugesan S. Harnessing green IT: Principles and practices. IT professional. 2008;10(1):24–33. doi: 10. 1109/mitp. 2008. 10
24. Niazi M, Hussain A. Agent-based computing from multi-agent systems to agent-based models: a visual survey. Scientometrics. 2011;89(2):479–99. doi: 10. 1007/ s11192-011-0468-9.
25. Hui C, Goldberg M, Magdon-Ismail M, Wallace WA. Simulating the diffusion of information: An agent-based modeling approach. International Journal of Agent Technologies and Systems (IJATS). 2010;2(3):31–46. doi: 10. 4018/jats. 2010070103
26. Niazi MA, Hussain A. Complex adaptive communication networks and environments: Part 2. SIMULATION. 2013;89(7):787–9. doi: 10. 1177/0037549713497714.
27. Niazi MA, Hussain A. Complex adaptive communication networks and environments: Part 1. SIMULATION. 2013;89(5):559–61. doi: 10. 1177/0037549713492122.
28. Hosseingholizadeh A, Abhari A, editors. A new agent-based solution for wireless sensor networks management. Proceedings of the 2009 Spring Simulation Multiconference; 2009: Society for Computer Simulation International.
29. Ilarri S, Mena E, Illarramendi A. A system based on mobile agents to test mobile computing applications. Journal of Network and Computer Applications. 2009;32(4):846–65. doi: 10. 1016/j. jnca. 2009. 01. 003.
30. Russell S, Norvig P. Artificial Intelligence A Modern Approach. Second ed: Prentice Hall; 2003.
31. Niazi MAK. Towards A Novel Unified Framework for Developing Formal, Network and Validated Agent-Based Simulation Models of Complex Adaptive Systems. Stirling: University of Stirling; 2011.
32. Fortino G, Garro A, Russo W. From Modeling to Simulation of Multi-Agent Systems: An Integrated Approach and a Case Study. Multiagent System Technologies, LNAI 3187: Springer-Verlag; 2004. p. 213–27.
33. Niazi M, Siddiqa A, Fortino G. Modeling AIDS Spread in Social Networks. In: Klusch M, Thimm M, Paprzycki M, editors. Multiagent System Technologies. Lecture Notes in Computer Science. 8076: Springer Berlin Heidelberg; 2013. p. 361–71.

34. Laghari S, Niazi MA. Carbon and Hot-spot Management in Green Data-Centric Networks: Self-Organization, Cellular Automata and Agents. USA: Healthy Mind Media; 2013.
35. Hussain A, Niazi M. Toward a Formal, Visual Framework of Emergent Cognitive Development of Scholars. Cognitive Computation. 2013:1–12. doi: 10. 1007/s12559-013-9219-y.
36. Miller JH, Page SE. Complex Adaptive Systems: An Introduction to Computational Models of Social Life: Princeton University Press; 2007.
37. North MJ, Macal CM. Managing business complexity: discovering strategic solutions with agent-based modeling and simulation: Oxford University Press, USA; 2007.
38. Railsback SF, Grimm V. Agent-based and Individual-based Modeling: A Practical Introduction: Princeton University Press; 2011.
39. Gilbert N, Troitzsch KG. Simulation for the social Scientist. Second ed: McGraw Hill Education; 2005.
40. Kiparsky M, Joyce B, Purkey D, Young C. Potential Impacts of Climate Warming on Water Supply Reliability in the Tuolumne and Merced River Basins, California. PLoS ONE. 2014;9(1):e84946. doi: 10. 1371/journal. pone. 0084946. pmid:24465455
41. Bellifemine F, Poggi A, Rimassa G, editors. JADE–A FIPA-compliant agent framework. Proceedings of PAAM; 1999: London.
42. Russell SJ, Norvig P. Artificial intelligence: a modern approach: Prentice hall; 2010.
43. Friedman-Hill EJ. Jess, the java expert system shell. Distributed Computing Systems, Sandia National Laboratories, USA. 1997.
44. Panait L, Luke S. Cooperative multi-agent learning: The state of the art. Autonomous Agents and Multi-Agent Systems. 2005;11(3):387–434. doi: 10. 1007/s10458-005-2631-2
45. Wilensky U. {NetLogo}. 1999.
46. Wilensky U. NetLogo 4. 0. 2 User Manual. Center for Connected Learning and Computer-Based Modeling, Northwestern University, Evanston, Illinois, USA. 2007.
47. Huynh N, Vidal JM. An agent-based approach to modeling yard cranes at seaport container terminals. Proceedings of the 2010 Spring Simulation Multiconference; Orlando, Florida. 1878663: ACM; 2010. p. 1–8.
48. Vidal JM. Fundamentals of Multiagent Systems: Using NetLogo Models: University of South Carolina; 2006.
49. Vidal JM, Buhler P, Goradia H. The Past and Future of Multiagent Systems. AAMAS Workshop on Teaching Multi-Agent Systems. 2004.
50. Bellifemine F, Poggi A, Rimassa G, editors. JADE–A FIPA-compliant agent framework1999.
51. Laghari S, Niazi MA. Data from: Modeling the internet of things, self-organizing and other complex adaptive communication networks: a cognitive agent-based computing approach http://dx. doi. org/10. 5061/dryad. mq793. Dryad Digial Repository; 2016.
52. Johnson BJ, Zoi CR, editors. EPA energy star computers: the next generation of office equipment. Proceedings of the 1992 ACEEE Summer Study on Energy Efficiency in Buildings; 1992.
53. Lim SR, Schoenung JM. Measurement and analysis of product energy efficiency to assist energy star criteria development: An example for desktop computers. Energy Policy. 2011. doi: 10. 1016/j. enpol. 2011. 09. 055

CHAPTER 14

A RE-ANALYSIS OF THE COCHRANE LIBRARY DATA: THE DANGERS OF UNOBSERVED HETEROGENEITY IN META-ANALYSES

Evangelos Kontopantelis[1,2,3], David A. Springate[1,2], David Reeves[1,2]

[1] Centre for Primary Care, NIHR School for Primary Care Research, Institute of Population Health, University of Manchester, Manchester, United Kingdom

[2] Centre for Biostatistics, Institute of Population Health, University of Manchester, Manchester, United Kingdom

[3] Centre for Health Informatics, Institute of Population Health, University of Manchester, Manchester, United Kingdom

ABSTRACT

Background

Heterogeneity has a key role in meta-analysis methods and can greatly affect conclusions. However, true levels of heterogeneity are unknown and often researchers assume homogeneity. We aim to: a) investigate the prevalence of unobserved heterogeneity and the validity of the assumption of homogeneity; b) assess the performance of various meta-analysis methods; c) apply the findings to published meta-analyses.

Methods and Findings

We accessed 57,397 meta-analyses, available in the Cochrane Library in August 2012. Using simulated data we assessed the performance of various meta-analysis methods in different scenarios. The prevalence of a zero heterogeneity estimate in the simulated scenarios was compared with that in the Cochrane data, to estimate the degree of unobserved heterogeneity in the latter. We re-analysed all meta-analyses using all methods and assessed the sensitivity of the statistical conclusions. Levels of unobserved heterogeneity in the Cochrane data appeared to be high, especially for small meta-analyses. A bootstrapped version of the DerSimonian-Laird approach performed best in both detecting heterogeneity and in returning more accurate overall effect estimates. Re-analysing all meta-analyses with this new method we found that in cases where heterogeneity had originally been detected but ignored, 17–20% of the statistical conclusions changed. Rates were much lower where the original analysis did not detect heterogeneity or took it into account, between 1% and 3%.

Citation: Kontopantelis E, Springate DA, Reeves D (2013) A Re-Analysis of the Cochrane Library Data: The Dangers of Unobserved Heterogeneity in Meta-Analyses. PLoS ONE 8(7): e69930. doi:10.1371/journal.pone.0069930.

Conclusions

When evidence for heterogeneity is lacking, standard practice is to assume homogeneity and apply a simpler fixed-effect meta-analysis. We find that assuming homogeneity often results in a misleading analysis, since heterogeneity is very likely present but undetected. Our new method represents a small improvement but the problem largely remains, especially for very small meta-analyses. One solution is to test the sensitivity of the meta-analysis conclusions to assumed moderate and large degrees of heterogeneity. Equally, whenever heterogeneity is detected, it should not be ignored.

INTRODUCTION

Meta-analysis (MA), the methodologies of synthesising existing evidence to answer a clinical or other research question, is a relatively young and dynamic area of research. The furore of methodological activity reflects the clinical importance of meta-analysis and its potential to provide conclusive answers, rather than incremental knowledge contributions, much more cheaply than a new large Randomised Clinical Trial (RCT).

The best analysis approach is an Individual Patient Data (IPD) meta-analysis, which requires access to patient level data and considerably more effort (to obtain the datasets mainly). However, with IPD data, clinical and methodological heterogeneity, arguably the biggest concern for meta-analysts, can be addressed through patient-level covariate controlling or subgroup analyses when covariate data are not available across all studies.

When the original data are unavailable, researchers have to combine the evidence in a two stage process, retrieving the relevant summary effects statistics from publications and using a suitable meta-analysis model to calculate an overall effect estimate $\hat{\mu}$. Model selection depends on the estimated heterogeneity, or between-study variance, and its presence usually leads to the adoption of a random-effects (RE) model. The alternative, the fixed-effects model (FE), is used when meta-analysts, for theoretical or practical reasons, decide not to adjust for heterogeneity, or have assumed or estimated the between-study variability to be zero. Different approaches exist for combining individual study results into an overall estimate of effect under the fixed- or random-effects assumptions: inverse variance, Mantel-Haenszel and Peto [1].

Inverse variance approaches are the most flexible and are suitable for continuous or dichotomous data through a fixed-effect or one of numerous random-effects methods. The DerSimonian and Laird [2] method (DL), a moment-based estimator, is the oldest and most widely used random-effects model and justifiably so since it has proven to be remarkably robust in various scenarios [3] including skew-normal and extreme distributions for the effects [4]. Numerous other inverse variance-based approaches to meta-analysis have also been developed: Biggerstaff and Tweedie [5], Follmann and Proschan [6], Sidik and Jonkman [7], maximum likelihood, restricted maximum likelihood and profile likelihood [8]. Most of these are computationally expensive methods and for some convergence to a solution is not guaranteed, but the added complexity does not seem to lead to better overall performance. Although some of the methods perform better on coverage, this is achieved at the expense of power and wider confidence intervals on the effect estimate, especially for meta-analyses of small numbers of studies (with the possible exception of restricted maximum likelihood and profile likelihood) [4], [9], [10].

Mantel-Haenszel [11] methods are suitable for dichotomous data and use a different weighting scheme that depends on the selected effect measure, which can be an odds ratio, a risk ratio or a risk difference. These fixed-effects methods have been shown to have better statistical properties than inverse variance methods when events numbers are low or studies are small [12]. Another fixed-effect alternative is the Peto method which is only suitable for dichotomous outcomes and calculates each study effect as a Peto odds ratio before combining [13]. The method performs well when intervention effects are small or when events are very rare. However, in the presence of heterogeneity, meta-analysts have to revert to inverse variance weighting to use a random-effects model.

For all random-effects models, an accurate estimate of the true between-study variance τ^2 is an important driver of performance. A large $\hat{\tau}^2$ results in wider confidence intervals around the effect estimate with the models taking into account the variability of the effect across studies, while a zero $\hat{\tau}^2$ reduces the DL, Sidik-Jonkman, Follmann- Proschan, maximum likelihood and restricted maximum likelihood methods to a fixed-effect model; effectively assuming there is study homogeneity. Although the Biggerstaff-Tweedie and profile likelihood methods take into account the uncertainty in the between-study variance estimate and adjust the confidence intervals accordingly (while all other methods treat the estimate as fixed), their performance is still dependent on an accurate $\hat{\tau}^2$.

The between-study variance can be estimated using a number of different approaches. The three mainstream approaches stem from the DL ($\hat{\tau}^2_{DL}$), maximum likelihood ($\hat{\tau}^2_{ML}$) and restricted maximum likelihood ($\hat{\tau}^2_{REML}$) methods and are inherent in them. All the other meta-analysis methods discussed above use $\hat{\tau}^2_{DL}$, $\hat{\tau}^2_{ML}$ or $\hat{\tau}^2_{REML}$ but vary their approach in estimating the effect μ. Other methods include the variance component (VC) type estimator[14], [15] and the newer two-step VC and DL [16], model error variance (MV) estimators [17],[18] and Bayes estimators [19].

In practice, $\hat{\tau}^2_{DL}$ is computed for most meta-analyses and used to quantify heterogeneity in a more interpretable way through Cochran's Q statistic [20] or I^2 [21]. Although these measures are not without flaws [22], [23], they inform the decision between a fixed-effect and a random-effects meta-analysis model (usually DL). In our experience, researchers are reassured (and reviewers are less critical) when the between study variance estimate is zero, not having to interpret study heterogeneity or deal with model selection dilemmas. Sometimes, researchers opt to use a fixed-effect model even when a small amount of heterogeneity is detected, despite recommendations for the more conservative nature of the random-effects approach and its better performance [3], [4], [23].

The Cochrane Database of Systematic Reviews is the richest resource of meta-analyses in the world with fifty-four active groups responsible for organising, advising on and publishing systematic reviews. Authors are obliged to use RevMan [24], software that has been developed by the Nordic Cochrane Centre and submit the data and analyses file along with the review, contributing to the creation of a vast data resource. Although RevMan offers quite a few fixed-effect choices, only the DerSimonian-Laird random-effects method has been implemented to quantify and account for heterogeneity.

In this paper, following our investigation of effect estimation methods [4], we assess the performance of heterogeneity estimation methods, aiming to bring researchers' attention to the potential bias from assuming between-study variance is zero. More specifically, we:

- Compare the performance of between- study variance estimators in various scenarios, through simulations, focusing on non-normal distributions and small numbers of meta-analysed studies. The distributions of the estimates and bias will be compared against the hypothetical distribution used in the simulations. We will also estimate the rates of under- and over-estimation and zero $\hat{\tau}^2$, when heterogeneity is present.
- Investigate the performance of alternative methods, focusing on the $\hat{\tau}^2=0$ case.
- Present the distribution of $\hat{\tau}^2$ derived from using all meta-analyses in the Cochrane Library (Aug 2012, up to and including CD009888), overall and by method type, as well as details on the number of meta-analysed studies, model selection and zero $\hat{\tau}^2$. We will also assess the sensitivity of the results and conclusions using alternative models.

METHODS

Between-study Variance Estimators

Let us consider a group of k studies with effect size estimates $Y_1, Y_2, \ldots, Y_k$ from which we wish to estimate the overall true mean effect θ. Under the random-effects model, the effect size will vary across studies due to error attributed to within- and between-study variability:

$$Y_i = \theta_i + e_i,\ e_i \sim N(0,\sigma_i^2) \tag{1}$$

$$\theta_i = \theta + \varepsilon_i,\ \varepsilon_i \sim N(0,\tau^2)$$

Where σ_i^2 is the within study variance for study i and τ^2 the between-study variance. All variance components are empirically estimated from the available data and the within-study variance estimates $\hat{\sigma}_i^2$ are assumed to equate to their true values, a potentially problematic approach due to the ignored uncertainty [3]. For the between-variance estimate, a plethora of methods exist, frequentist and Bayesian. Again, the estimate uncertainty is almost always ignored and only the point-estimate is incorporated in the random-effects model, while most methods can return a negative estimate and have to be constrained (in which case $\hat{\tau}^2$ is set to zero). All the methods we assess have been presented in detail by Deeks et al [25], Sidik and Jonkman [18], DerSimonian and Kacker [16] and Rukhin [19] and we are providing a simplified overview. In terms of a-priori assumptions regarding heterogeneity, methods can be categorised in two groups: a) methods which allow heterogeneity to be either zero or positive ($\hat{\tau}^2 \geq 0$); and b) methods that assume heterogeneity is strictly positive, i.e. always greater than zero ($\hat{\tau}^2 > 0$). For convenience, we refer to the first group as zero-or-positive (heterogeneity) methods and the second group as positive-only methods.

DerSimonian-Laird estimators.

The most commonly used approach is the non-iterative method of moments estimator proposed by DerSimonian and Laird [2]:

$$\hat{\tau}_{DL}^2 = \frac{Q_{\hat{W}} - (k-1)}{\sum_{i=1}^{k} \hat{w}_i - \sum_{i=1}^{k} \hat{w}_i^2 \Big/ \sum_{i=1}^{k} \hat{w}_i} \tag{2}$$

Where $\hat{w}_i = 1/\hat{\sigma}_i^2,\ Q_{\hat{W}} = \sum_{i=1}^{K} \hat{w}_i (Y_i - \bar{Y})^2$ the Cochran heterogeneity statistic [15] and $\bar{Y}$ the overall effect estimate using the respective fixed-effects model (i.e. inverse variance, Mantel-Haenszel or Peto).

More recently, DerSimonian and Kacker [16] suggested a two-step approach:

$$\hat{\tau}_{DL2}^2 = \frac{\sum_{i=1}^{k} \hat{w}_i (Y_i - \hat{\theta}_{DL}) - \left(\sum_{i=1}^{k} \hat{w}_i \hat{\sigma}_i^2 - \sum_{i=1}^{k} \hat{w}_i^2 \hat{\sigma}_i^2 \Big/ \sum_{i=1}^{k} \hat{w}_i \right)}{\sum_{i=1}^{k} \hat{w}_i - \sum_{i=1}^{k} \hat{w}_i^2 \Big/ \sum_{i=1}^{k} \hat{w}_i} \tag{3}$$

Where $\hat{w}_i = 1/\left(\hat{\sigma}_i^2 + \hat{\tau}_{DL}^2\right)$ and $\hat{\theta}_{DL}$ is the effect estimate obtained from the one-step DL method. When equations (2), (3) provide a negative estimate, it is truncated to zero in practice.

We also generated a non-parametric bootstrap [26] version of the DL estimator by randomly sampling studies with replacement 10,000 times and selecting the mean of the truncated estimates. Under this process, for each selected random sample (e.g. for four studies a sample might include studies 1, 1, 2 and 4), between-study variance is estimated using (2) and truncated if negative. The mean of these 10,000 estimates we called $\hat{\tau}_{DLb}^2$.

For a fairer comparison between the DerSimonian-Laird estimator and the Sidik-Jonkman and Rukhin estimators that arbitrarily assume heterogeneity a-priori, we generated estimator $\hat{\tau}_{DLi}^2$ which assumes a between study variance of 0.01 if a zero or negative $\hat{\tau}_{DLi}^2$ is obtained:

$$\hat{\tau}_{DLi}^2 = \begin{cases} \hat{\tau}_{DL}^2 & when\ \ \hat{\tau}_{DL}^2 > 0 \\ 0.01 & when\ \ \hat{\tau}_{DL}^2 \leq 0 \end{cases} \tag{4}$$

Variance component estimators.

Another method of moments estimator was proposed by Hedges [27]:

$$\hat{\tau}^2_{VC} = \frac{1}{k-1}\sum_{i=1}^{k}(Y_i - \bar{Y}) - \frac{1}{k}\sum_{i=1}^{k}\hat{\sigma}_i^2 \qquad (5)$$

This simple approach partitions the overall variance estimate into within- and between-variance components and solves for the latter.

A two-step approach has also been suggested [16]:

$$\hat{\tau}^2_{VC2} = \frac{\sum_{i=1}^{k}\hat{w}_i(Y_i - \hat{\theta}_{VC}) - \left(\sum_{i=1}^{k}\hat{w}_i\hat{\sigma}_i^2 - \sum_{i=1}^{k}\hat{w}_i^2\hat{\sigma}_i^2 \Big/ \sum_{i=1}^{k}\hat{w}_i\right)}{\sum_{i=1}^{k}\hat{w}_i - \sum_{i=1}^{k}\hat{w}_i^2 \Big/ \sum_{i=1}^{k}\hat{w}_i} \qquad (6)$$

The estimates from the one-step variance component method are fed into the formula with $\hat{w}_i = 1/(\hat{\sigma}_i^2 + \hat{\tau}^2_{VC})$ and $\hat{\theta}_{VC}$ the effect estimate.

In practice, as with the DL estimators, variance components estimators are truncated to zero.

Iterative estimators.

Maximum-likelihood (ML) is a more computationally demanding iterative approach, assuming within-study variances are known, solves the log likelihood function [8], [18]:

$$\log L(\theta,\tau^2) = -\frac{k}{2}\log(2\pi) - \frac{1}{2}\sum_{i=1}^{k}\log(\hat{\sigma}_i^2 + \tau^2) - \frac{1}{2}\sum_{i=1}^{k}\frac{(Y_i - \theta)^2}{\hat{\sigma}_i^2 + \tau^2} \qquad (7)$$

And the estimate can be obtained from the iteratively solved equation:

$$\hat{\tau}^2_{ML} = \frac{\sum_{i=1}^{k}\hat{w}_i^2\left[\left(Y_i - \sum_{i=1}^{k}\hat{w}_iY_i \Big/ \sum_{i=1}^{k}\hat{w}_i\right) - \hat{\sigma}_i^2\right]}{\sum_{i=1}^{k}\hat{w}_i^2} \qquad (8)$$

Where $\hat{w}_i = 1/(\hat{\sigma}_i^2 + \hat{\tau}^2_{ML})$

Restricted Maximum Likelihood (REML) estimator is another iterative approach, assuming within-study variances are known, solves the restricted log likelihood function [8], [18]:

$$\log L'(\theta,\tau^2) = -\frac{1}{2}\left[\sum_{i=1}^{k}\log\{2\pi(\hat{\sigma}_i^2 + \tau^2)\} + \sum_{i=1}^{k}\frac{Y_i - \hat{\theta}_W}{\hat{\sigma}_i^2 + \tau^2}\right] - \frac{1}{2}\log\sum_{i=1}^{k}\frac{1}{\hat{\sigma}_i^2 + \tau^2} \qquad (9)$$

Where

$$\hat{\theta}_W = \sum_{i=1}^{k}w_iY_i / \sum_{i=1}^{k}w_i \text{ and } \hat{w}_i = 1/(\hat{\sigma}_i^2 + \tau^2)$$

The iterative solution to the equation is the restricted maximum likelihood estimate:

$$\hat{\tau}^2_{REML} = \frac{\sum_{i=1}^{k}\hat{w}_i^2\left[\left(Y_i - \sum_{i=1}^{k}\hat{w}_iY_i \Big/ \sum_{i=1}^{k}\hat{w}_i\right) + 1 \Big/ \sum_{i=1}^{k}\hat{w}_i - \hat{\sigma}_i^2\right]}{\sum_{i=1}^{k}\hat{w}_i^2} \qquad (10)$$

Where $\hat{w}_i = 1/(\hat{\sigma}_i^2 + \hat{\tau}^2_{REML})$

For both ML and REML, truncation to zero at each iteration prevents the estimate from having a negative value. Convergence to a solution is not always successful.

Sidik and Jonkman Model Error Variance Estimators

Sidik and Jonkman [17] proposed a non-iterative estimator under a different parameterisation of the overall study variability, assuming a positive a-priori value for the between-study variance:

$$\hat{\tau}^2_{MV} = \frac{1}{k-1}\sum_{i=1}^{k}\frac{1}{\hat{r}_i+1}\left(Y_i - \frac{\sum_{i=1}^{k}[(1/\hat{r}_i+1)Y_i]}{\sum_{i=1}^{k}(1/\hat{r}_i+1)}\right) \qquad (11)$$

Where r_i is the within- to between-study variance ratio for study i $(r_i = \sigma_i^2/\tau^2)$. When crude ratio estimates are used as a-priori values, with $\hat{r}_i = \hat{\sigma}_i^2 / \frac{1}{k}\sum_{i=1}^{k}(Y_i - \bar{Y})$ truncation at zero is not necessary since $\hat{\tau}^2_{MV}$ is always positive – we call this estimator $\hat{\tau}^2_{MVa}$. An alternative approach was suggested in which the VC estimator is used to inform on the a-priori values of the ratios, with $\hat{r}_i = \hat{\sigma}_i^2/\hat{\tau}^2_{VC}$. Since the denominator can be zero, an arbitrary value has to be added to it when $\hat{\tau}^2_{VC} = 0$. We used 0.01 in compliance with the method's authors and call this estimator $\hat{\tau}^2_{MVb}$. Note that we do not discuss the empirical Bayes estimator proposed by Morris [28], due to its practical similarity to the model error variance estimators[18].

Rukhin Bayes Estimators

More recently, Rukhin [19] proposed a Bayes estimator that can be reduced to the following when the prior between-study variance is set to zero:

$$\hat{\tau}^2_{B0} = \frac{1}{k+1}\sum_{i=1}^{k}(Y_i - \bar{Y})^2 - \frac{\left(\sum_{i=1}^{k}n_i - k\right)(k+1)\sum_{i=1}^{k}\hat{\sigma}_i^2}{k(k+1)\sum_{i=1}^{k}(n_i - k + 2)} \qquad (12)$$

Where n_i the number of subjects in study i. Truncation to zero is necessary since negative estimates are a possibility. Assuming the between-study variance prior is $0.5(k-1)\sum_{i=1}^{k}(\hat{\sigma}_i^2/k)$ a simpler and always positive estimator can be obtained:

$$\hat{\tau}_{BP}^2 = \frac{1}{k+1}\sum_{i=1}^{k}(Y_i - \bar{Y})^2 \quad (13)$$

Simulations

Our approach was similar to Brockwell's and Gordon's [3], generating effect size estimates Y_i and within study variance estimates $\hat{\sigma}_i^2$ for each simulated meta-analysis study. The distribution of the $\hat{\sigma}_i^2$ was based on the χ_1^2 distribution, divided by four and restricted to the (0.009, 0.6) interval, with a mean of 0.173. For the $Y_i = \theta_i + e_i$, we assumed that $e_i \sim N(0, \hat{\sigma}_i^2)$. but we simulated various distribution scenarios for θ_i with a mean of 0.5 and variance τ^2 normal skewness = 0, kurtosis = 3), moderate skew-normal (skewness = 1, kurtosis = 4), extreme skew-normal (skewness = 2, kurtosis = 9), uniform, bimodal and double-spike (designed to simulate a situation where study effects take one of two values, a possibility when testing an intervention under two experimental designs). We used three τ^2values in an attempt to capture low, medium and large levels of heterogeneity: 0.01, 0.03 and 0.10. These correspond to H^2 values of 1.18, 1.54 and 2.78 [23] and I^2 values of approximately, since the measure is not entirely independent of the number of studies in the meta-analysis, 15.1%, 34.9% and 64.1% [21]. To be able to assess $\hat{\tau}_{B0}^2$ we also independently simulated study sizes n_i uniformly distributed in the [50,500] range, since estimated study mean Y_i and variance $\hat{\sigma}_i^2$ are independent of sample size. For each distributional assumption, τ^2. value, and meta-analysis size (which varied from 2 to 30 studies), 10,000 meta-analyses cases were simulated. The full details of the simulation methods have been provided elsewhere [4]. All methods were implemented and analysed in Stata v12.1 for Windows [29].

Assessment Criteria

The performance of the estimators was assessed using four measures: a) the average bias in the heterogeneity estimate; b) the percentage of zero heterogeneity estimates; c) the coverage probability for the effect estimate; and d) the point and error-interval estimation for the effect.

Average Bias in the Heterogeneity Estimate

This is the simplest measure, an aggregate of the bias in the estimate provided by each method (compared to the known τ^2 value), across the 10,000 meta-analysis cases in each simulation scenario. This will give us a picture of under-or over-estimation for each method, but not of the overall level of bias (since negative and positive biases will cancel each other out). Therefore, we also calculate and report the average absolute bias.

Percentage of Zero Heterogeneity Estimates

We can get a better understanding of a method's performance by summarising the percentage of cases for which between-study variance is estimated to be zero. Erroneously assuming homogeneity is potentially a big problem for all estimators that do not always return a positive τ^2.

Coverage Probability and Error-interval Estimation for The Effect

The accuracy of the between-study variance estimate is just one, albeit very important, parameter for obtaining a precise overall effect estimate, the main goal of all meta-analysis methods. The overall random-effects estimate is usually provided by:

$$\hat{\theta} = \sum_{i=1}^{k} \hat{w}_i Y_i / \sum_{i=1}^{k} \hat{w}_i \quad (14)$$

Where $\hat{w}_i = 1/(\hat{\sigma}_i^2 + \hat{\tau}^2)$ However, the approach is different for the iterative likelihood methods, i.e. maximum, restricted maximum and profile likelihood [8], while variants of (14) have been proposed by Biggerstaff and Tweedie [5] and Sidik and Jonkman [7]. Profile likelihood, which has be shown to be an accurate method [3], [4], uses the $\hat{\tau}_{ML}^2$ point estimate but also calculates a confidence interval for the estimator and incorporates the uncertainty in the overall effect estimate calculation. The Biggerstaff-Tweedie and Sidik-Jonkman variants provide similar or worse estimates to (14) with $\hat{\tau}_{DL}^2$ [4] and for convenience we only use the last approach.

The coverage probability is the proportion of 95% confidence intervals for the overall effect estimate that contain the true overall effect θ, in the 10,000 meta-analysis cases for each simulation scenario. Theoretically, this should be close to 95% but heterogeneity, the number of studies in the meta-analysis and, to a lesser extent, the distribution of the true effects, can affect coverage levels [3], [4].

However, a method can provide high coverage probability rates by overestimating the standard error for the overall effect estimate and thus providing confidence intervals that are overly wide. To better assess the methods we constructed a measure of the accuracy of estimation of the error-interval around the point estimate, computed as the ratio of the estimated confidence interval for the effect, compared to the interval based on the true τ^2:

$$EI = \frac{upperCI(\hat{\theta}) - lowerCI(\hat{\theta})}{3.92\sqrt{1\Big/\sum_{i=1}^{k}\frac{1}{\tau^2+\hat{\sigma}_i^2}}} \quad (15)$$

Where $upperCI(\hat{\theta})$ and $lowerCI(\hat{\theta})$ are the upper and lower bounds of the 95% confidence interval for the estimated effect, respectively. The main advantage of this measure is that it allows a straightforward comparison across very different methods [4]. We used the median and the 25th and 75th percentiles of the EI metric, to assess its performance more effectively.

Cochrane Data

All Cochrane library systematic reviews are constrained to use RevMan [24] and the data for each review, if any relevant studies are identified, are available on the Wiley Group website[30]. Institutional or personal access is required and we developed crawling code in Python[31] to automate the procedure. We were able to access the Wiley website and all Cochrane systematic reviews available in August 2012 (CD000004 to CD009888), downloaded the relevant RevMan files and exported them as *.csv files, before importing in

Stata. A total of 3,984 files were available and 3,845 were successfully downloaded (139 files were corrupt). The code has been made available as two supplementary python script files.

Each RevMan file is a systematic review (e.g. olanzapine for schizophrenia). Within a review, various research questions might have been posed (e.g. olanzapine vs placebo, olanzapine vs typical antipsychotics, olanzapine vs atypical antipsychotics) and each question might be investigated across various relevant outcomes, (e.g. global effect: no important clinical response by 6 weeks, adverse events: other). In each of these, an overall meta-analysis is performed on all identified studies, if more than one. However, there might exist a further break-down due to variability in the intervention or the outcome (e.g. drug dosage, or types of other adverse events) and sub-group meta-analyses are then performed. In these cases, an overall meta-analysis which summarises across all studies in the sub-groups can also be executed, if deemed reasonable by the researchers, but this is rarely the case.

From each file, available data for all meta-analyses (e.g. study sizes, event and non-event counts, effect sizes and their variances, alpha level used), overall or subgroup, were collected including the meta-analysis method used and the RevMan output. Method choice in the software is limited to: a) inverse variance fixed-effect or random-effects with DL for continuous or dichotomous outcomes; b) Mantel-Haenszel fixed-effect or Mantel-Haenszel random-effects with DL for dichotomous outcomes; c) Peto fixed-effect for dichotomous outcomes; and d) Peto "O-E" (observed minus expected) fixed-effect time-to-event data. Next, we re-analysed all meta-analyses using the methods implemented in the software [32] and all the random-effects methods described in section 2.1 above, in Stata. This allowed us to identify and report potential bugs in RevMan, assess the sensitivity of the meta-analyses results to the method choice and compare the distributions of the between-study variance estimates obtained by the various methods.

RESULTS

Simulations

We present results for just two of the effect-size distributions we simulated, since results for the assessment measures we used were consistent across all distributions: normal and extreme skew-normal. For the iterative methods, non-convergence varied by meta-analysis size and heterogeneity level from 0.1% to 3.5%. Bias assessment is presented in Table S1 in File S1, coverage and zero between-study variance estimate rates in Table S2 and error intervals in Table S3 in File S1.

Bias assessment

For low levels of heterogeneity ($\tau^2=0.01$; $H^2=1.18$; $I^2=15.1\%$), all estimators displayed positive mean bias with ML having the smaller mean and mean absolute bias across all meta-analysis sizes, followed by B0 (for $k<5$) and REML (for $k\geq5$). The worst performers were MVa and BP, for $k\geq3$ and DLb for $k=2$. The picture was similar for moderate heterogeneity ($\tau^2=0.03$; $H^2=1.54$; $I^2=34.9\%$) with ML being the best performer and, overall, only slightly underestimating the between-study variance for larger meta-analyses. For considerable heterogeneity ($\tau^2=0.10$; $H^2=2.78$; $I^2=64.1\%$), ML still displays the smallest absolute bias levels for all meta-analyses sizes except when $k=2$, in which case B0 performs slightly better. When it comes to mean bias levels, however, ML consistently underestimates heterogeneity, especially when k is small. DL and REML seem to be the best performers for large meta-analyses and B0 for very small ones. Levels of DLb bias were the highest for meta-analyses of two studies but acceptable for five or more studies. Across all three heterogeneity levels, observed levels of mean bias and mean absolute bias decreased as the number of studies increased except for the B0 and BP estimators. Interestingly, BP bias was higher for larger meta-analyses (Table S1 in File S1).

Coverage and Erroneous Homogeneity Assumption

When heterogeneity was low, DLb, MVb and DLi provided coverage rates close to 95%, while DL, REML and, for larger meta-analyses only, PL also performed well. Amongst the zero-or-positive heterogeneity methods, DLb was the best in terms of detecting any heterogeneity, especially for larger meta-analyses. For moderate heterogeneity levels, DLi and MVb, both of which are positive-only heterogeneity methods, were the best performers overall. In the zero-or-positive estimator group, DLb performed the best in terms of heterogeneity detection while providing good coverage and PL was the best in coverage. For large heterogeneity, MVa had the most accurate coverage levels overall, with BP performing well only for small meta-analyses. Methods DLb and PL also performed well, with the former outperforming all other zero-or-positive methods and the latter providing the best coverage levels. The higher heterogeneity detection rates for DLb are not surprising considering its high bias for small meta-analyses. However, for larger meta-analyses of 5 or more studies, when DLb bias is comparable or even lower to bias observed for other $\hat{\tau}^2\geq0$ methods, DLb is still the best performer in heterogeneity detection. Note that across all methods, levels of coverage decreased as heterogeneity increased (Table S2 in File S1).

Error Interval Estimation

For low levels of heterogeneity, the positive-only heterogeneity methods DLi and MVb did particularly well, since the assumed minimum degree of positive heterogeneity matched the mean value in the simulation. Amongst the zero-or-positive heterogeneity methods, DLb was the best overall performer in terms of median performance, only slightly over-estimating the error interval for larger meta-analysis. Other good performers were DL, REML and B0 (especially for small study numbers), while MVa, BP and PL provided error intervals that were too wide (PL for smaller and MVa, BP for larger meta-analyses). In terms of the variability in the estimate, B0 was more consistent in providing an accurate estimate for $k<5$ and DL and REML for $k\geq5$. When heterogeneity was moderate, the picture did not change much with the only noticeable differences being the slight improvement in the DLb median estimate and the small performance deterioration for DLi and MVb (since the a-priori assumption is now an under-estimate). For large level of heterogeneity, most methods underestimated the error interval by more than 10% when $k \leq 3$. For very small meta-analyses, the positive-only methods BP and MVa methods performed well. DLb was the best overall performer and scored particularly well when $k > 3$ (Table S3 in File S1).

Cochrane Data

Of the 3,845 downloaded files (systematic reviews) only 2,801 had identified relevant studies and contained any data. A total of 98,615 analyses were extracted, 57,397 of which were meta-analyses (i.e. combined results across more than one study). Of these, 32,005 were overall meta-analyses and 25,392 were subgroup meta-analyses. Figure 1 provides the analyses counts by Cochrane Group. In these meta-analyses, the estimation of an overall effect was obtained with a Peto method in 4,340 (7.6%) cases, a Mantel-Haenszel method in 33,184 (57.8%) cases and an inverse variance method in 19,873 (34.6%) cases. For the Peto meta-analyses, 585 of these used the "O-E" method. Choice of fixed- or a random-effects model varied by meta-analysis size and method; random-effects models were more prevalent in inverse variance methods and larger meta-analyses (Figure 2).

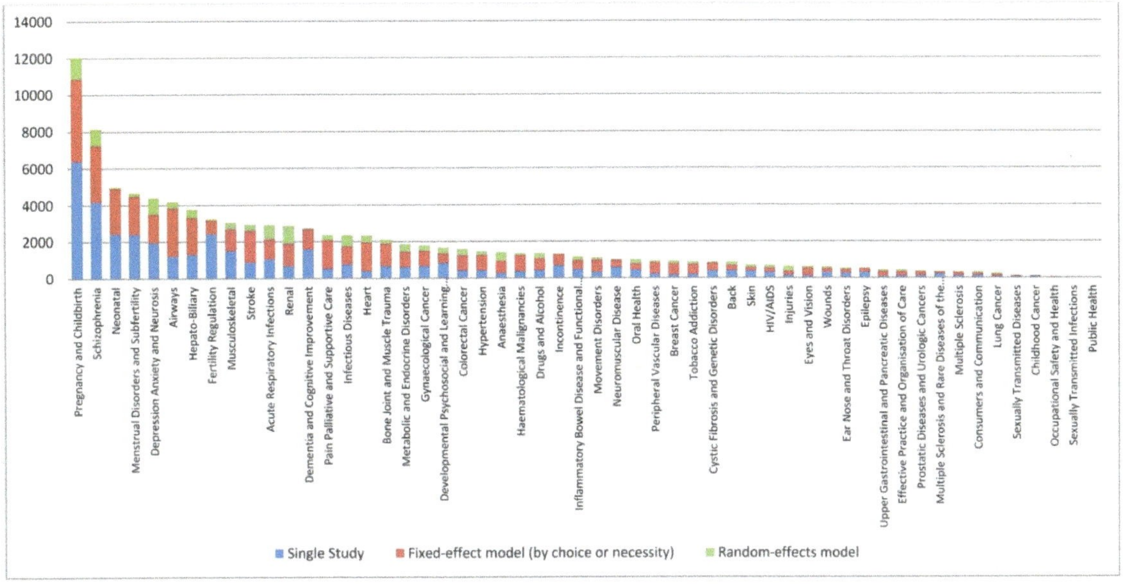

Figure 1. All meta-analyses, including single-study and subgroup meta-analyses.

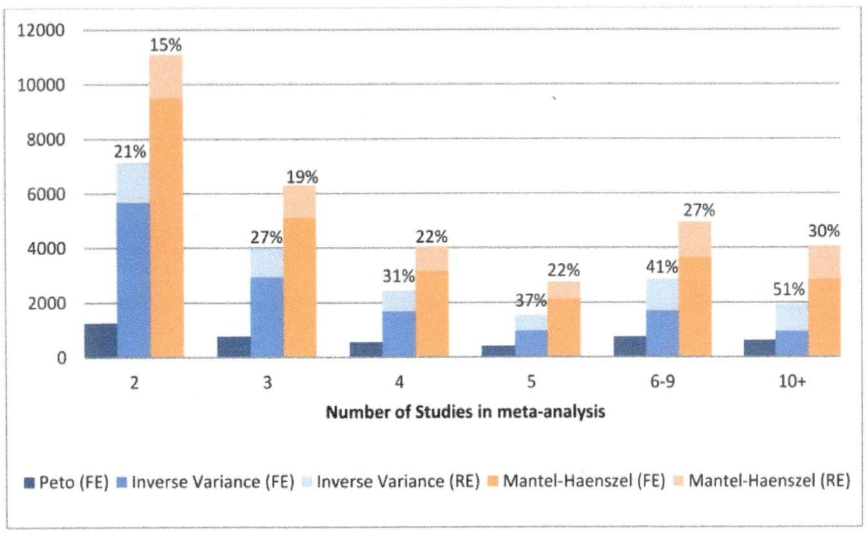

*note that in many cases fixed-effect models were used when heterogeneity was detected

Figure 2. Model selection by number of available studies (and % of random-effects meta-analyses)*.

To assess the validity of a homogeneity assumption and, thus, a fixed-effect model choice in Cochrane data meta-analyses, we compared the percentage of zero between-study variance estimates under the DerSimonian-Laird method, in the real and simulated data (Figure 3). To proceed with the comparison we calculated the between-study variance estimate for all Cochrane meta-analyses, since the measure is not reported in RevMan when a fixed-effect method is used. We observed that the percentage of zero between-study variance estimates was lower in the real data than in the low and moderate heterogeneity simulated data. This suggests that the mean true between-study variance is higher than generally assumed but fails to be detected, especially when the number of studies meta-analyses is small.

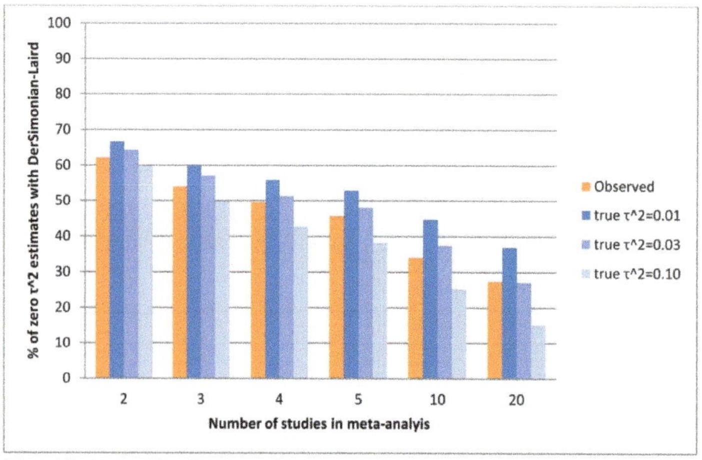

*Normal distribution of the effects assumed in the simulations (more extreme distributions produced similar results).

Figure 3. Comparison of zero between-study variance estimates rates in the Cochrane library data and in simulations, using the DerSimonian-Laird method*.

RevMan Issues

For the Mantel-Haenszel methods, we encountered some problems, when events or non-events were very rare. When study event or non-event cells were empty, calculations for risk ratios and risk differences (in RevMan v5.2.3) were not in complete agreement with the documentation [32], potentially affecting overall effect estimates. The issues were reported to the Nordic Cochrane Centre.

Prior to version 5.0.17 (1 Dec 2008) the Peto method was not using the correct study (Peto) odds ratio estimates and we encountered a few meta-analyses that had not been updated with the corrections.

Method Comparison

We applied the methods described in section 2.1 to all 57,397 meta-analyses to assess the distributions of $\hat{\tau}^2$ and the sensitivity of the results and conclusions. All comparisons are presented in Tables 1, 2 and 3 but for simplicity we only discuss differences between the standard methods and the bootstrapped DerSimonian Laird (not a perfect method, but one that performs well overall, despite its larger heterogeneity bias for small meta-analyses).

Table 1. Variation in terms of statistical conclusion for inverse variance meta-analyses.

		RevMan method					
		Fixed-effect ($\hat{\tau}^2_{DL}=0$)		Fixed-effect ($\hat{\tau}^2_{DL}>0$)		Random-effects DL ($\hat{\tau}^2_{DL}>0$)	
		Counts (cell percentages)		Counts (cell percentages)		Counts (cell percentages)	
Stata method		**NS**	**Sig**	**NS**	**Sig**	**NS**	**Sig**
FE	NS	4494(50.3%)*	0(0.0%)†	1743(35.3%)	0(0.0%)	1622(27.0%)	17(0.3%)
	Sig	0(0.0%)‡	4438(49.7%)§	0(0.0%)	3194(64.7%)	1161(19.3%)	3204(53.4%)
DL	NS	4494(50.3%)	0(0.0%)	1737(35.2%)	831(16.8%)	2783(46.4%)	0(0.0%)
	Sig	0(0.0%)	4438(49.7%)	6(0.1%)	2363(47.9%)	0(0.0%)	3221(53.6%)
DLb	NS	4494(50.3%)	84(0.9%)	1737(35.2%)	936(19.0%)	2777(46.3%)	140(2.3%)
	Sig	0(0.0%)	4354(48.7%)	6(0.1%)	2258(45.7%)	6(0.1%)	3081(51.3%)
VC	NS	4494(50.3%)	38(0.4%)	1739(35.2%)	857(17.4%)	2646(44.1%)	207(3.4%)
	Sig	0(0.0%)	4400(49.3%)	4(0.1%)	2337(47.3%)	137(2.3%)	3014(50.2%)
MVa	NS	4415(49.4%)	309(3.5%)	1738(35.2%)	1021(20.7%)	2733(45.5%)	277(4.6%)
	Sig	0(0.0%)	4069(45.6%)	5(0.1%)	2173(44.0%)	50(0.8%)	2944(49.0%)
MVb	NS	4494(50.3%)	117(1.3%)	1739(35.2%)	878(17.8%)	2680(44.6%)	178(3.0%)
	Sig	0(0.0%)	4321(48.4%)	4(0.1%)	2316(46.9%)	103(1.7%)	3043(50.7%)
BP	NS	4494(50.3%)	532(6.0%)	1737(35.2%)	952(19.3%)	2579(43.0%)	303(5.0%)
	Sig	0(0.0%)	3906(43.7%)	6(0.1%)	2242(45.4%)	204(3.4%)	2918(48.6%)
B0	NS	4494(50.3%)	31(0.3%)	1736(35.2%)	601(12.2%)	2381(39.7%)	120(2.0%)
	Sig	0(0.0%)	4407(49.3%)	7(0.1%)	2593(52.5%)	402(6.7%)	3101(51.6%)
VC2	NS	4494(50.3%)	13(0.1%)	1737(35.2%)	898(18.2%)	2754(45.9%)	167(2.8%)
	Sig	0(0.0%)	4425(49.5%)	6(0.1%)	2296(46.5%)	29(0.5%)	3054(50.9%)
DL2	NS	4494(50.3%)	0(0.0%)	1736(35.2%)	844(17.1%)	2717(45.3%)	117(1.9%)
	Sig	0(0.0%)	4438(49.7%)	7(0.1%)	2350(47.6%)	66(1.1%)	3104(51.7%)
ML	NS	4468(50.0%)	1(0.0%)	1725(34.9%)	442(9.0%)	2272(37.8%)	44(0.7%)
	Sig	0(0.0%)	4404(49.3%)	8(0.2%)	2721(55.1%)	499(8.3%)	3141(52.3%)
	No conv‖	26(0.3%)	33(0.4%)	10(0.2%)	31(0.6%)	12(0.2%)	36(0.6%)
REML	NS	4365(48.9%)	14(0.2%)	1730(35.0%)	852(17.3%)	2713(45.2%)	108(1.8%)
	Sig	0(0.0%)	4314(48.3%)	6(0.1%)	2332(47.2%)	66(1.1%)	3103(51.7%)
	No conv‖	129(1.4%)	110(1.2%)	7(0.1%)	10(0.2%)	4(0.1%)	10(0.2%)
PL	NS	4440(49.7%)	514(5.8%)	1716(34.8%)	1006(20.4%)	2709(45.1%)	300(5.0%)
	Sig	1(0.0%)	3862(43.2%)	4(0.1%)	2133(43.2%)	50(0.8%)	2881(48.0%)
	No conv‖	53(0.6%)	62(0.7%)	23(0.5%)	55(1.1%)	24(0.4%)	40(0.7%)

*Agreement in statistical conclusion (non-significant effect) between RevMan and Stata methods.
†Non agreement in statistical conclusion between RevMan (significant effect) and Stata methods (non-significant effect).
‡Non agreement in statistical conclusion between RevMan (significant effect) and Stata methods (non-significant effect).
§Agreement in statistical conclusion (significant effect) between RevMan and Stata methods.
‖Iterative method failed to convergence to a solution.
doi:10.1371/journal.pone.0069930.t001

Table 2. Variation in terms of statistical conclusion for Mantel-Haenszel meta-analyses*.

		RevMan method					
		Fixed-effect ($\hat{\tau}^2_{DL}=0$)		Fixed-effect ($\hat{\tau}^2_{DL}>0$)		Random-effects DL ($\hat{\tau}^2_{DL}>0$)	
		Counts (cell percentages)		Counts (cell percentages)		Counts (cell percentages)	
Stata method		**NS**	**Sig**	**NS**	**Sig**	**NS**	**Sig**
FE (MH fixed)	NS	8929(70.8%)	0(0.0%)	4311(51.7%)	2(0.0%)	6422(52.5%)	51(0.4%)
	Sig	11(0.1%)	3678(29.1%)	8(0.1%)	3983(47.7%)	1666(13.6%)	4067(33.3%)
	No comp†	0(0.0%)	0(0.0%)	37(0.4%)	3(0.0%)	16(0.1%)	0(0.0%)
DL (MH random)	NS	8882(70.4%)	196(1.6%)	4304(51.6%)	1539(18.4%)	8033(65.7%)	33(0.3%)
	Sig	58(0.5%)	3482(27.6%)	15(0.2%)	2446(29.3%)	55(0.5%)	4085(33.4%)
	No comp†	0(0.0%)	0(0.0%)	37(0.4%)	3(0.0%)	16(0.1%)	0(0.0%)
DLb	NS	8890(70.5%)	336(2.7%)	4306(51.6%)	1676(20.1%)	8023(65.6%)	265(2.2%)
	Sig	50(0.4%)	3342(26.5%)	13(0.2%)	2309(27.7%)	65(0.5%)	3853(31.5%)
	No comp†	0(0.0%)	0(0.0%)	37(0.4%)	3(0.0%)	16(0.1%)	0(0.0%)
VC	NS	8889(70.4%)	282(2.2%)	4298(51.5%)	1601(19.2%)	7844(64.2%)	316(2.6%)
	Sig	51(0.4%)	3396(26.9%)	21(0.3%)	2384(28.6%)	244(2.0%)	3802(31.1%)
	No comp†	0(0.0%)	0(0.0%)	37(0.4%)	3(0.0%)	16(0.1%)	0(0.0%)
MVa‡	NS	8863(70.2%)	787(6.2%)	4303(51.6%)	1882(22.6%)	7982(65.3%)	683(5.6%)
	Sig	19(0.2%)	2876(22.8%)	16(0.2%)	2103(25.2%)	84(0.7%)	3433(28.1%)
	No comp†	58(0.5%)	15(0.1%)	37(0.4%)	3(0.0%)	38(0.3%)	2(0.0%)
MVb	NS	8917(70.7%)	399(3.2%)	4303(51.6%)	1603(19.2%)	7912(64.7%)	374(3.1%)
	Sig	23(0.2%)	3279(26.0%)	16(0.2%)	2382(28.5%)	176(1.4%)	3744(30.6%)
	No comp†	0(0.0%)	0(0.0%)	37(0.4%)	3(0.0%)	16(0.1%)	0(0.0%)
BP	NS	8933(70.8%)	1111(8.8%)	4305(51.6%)	1944(23.3%)	7908(64.7%)	964(7.9%)
	Sig	7(0.1%)	2567(20.3%)	14(0.2%)	2041(24.5%)	180(1.5%)	3154(25.8%)
	No comp†	0(0.0%)	0(0.0%)	37(0.4%)	3(0.0%)	16(0.1%)	0(0.0%)
B0	NS	8887(70.4%)	267(2.1%)	4301(51.5%)	1290(15.5%)	7624(62.4%)	217(1.8%)
	Sig	53(0.4%)	3411(27.0%)	18(0.2%)	2695(32.3%)	464(3.8%)	3901(31.9%)
	No comp†	0(0.0%)	0(0.0%)	37(0.4%)	3(0.0%)	16(0.1%)	0(0.0%)
VC2	NS	8887(70.4%)	222(1.8%)	4301(51.5%)	1622(19.4%)	7978(65.3%)	202(1.7%)
	Sig	53(0.4%)	3456(27.4%)	18(0.2%)	2363(28.3%)	110(0.9%)	3916(32.0%)
	No comp†	0(0.0%)	0(0.0%)	37(0.4%)	3(0.0%)	16(0.1%)	0(0.0%)
DL2	NS	8884(70.4%)	196(1.6%)	4299(51.5%)	1504(18.0%)	7922(64.8%)	116(0.9%)
	Sig	56(0.4%)	3482(27.6%)	20(0.2%)	2481(29.7%)	166(1.4%)	4002(32.7%)
	No comp†	0(0.0%)	0(0.0%)	37(0.4%)	3(0.0%)	16(0.1%)	0(0.0%)
ML	NS	8831(70.0%)	63(0.5%)	4204(50.4%)	679(8.1%)	7113(58.2%)	64(0.5%)
	Sig	42(0.3%)	3571(28.3%)	70(0.8%)	3241(38.8%)	894(7.3%)	3985(32.6%)
	No conv/comp†	67(0.5%)	44(0.3%)	82(1.0%)	68(0.8%)	97(0.8%)	69(0.6%)
REML	NS	8629(68.4%)	212(1.7%)	4271(51.2%)	1423(17.1%)	7792(63.8%)	98(0.8%)
	Sig	56(0.4%)	3374(26.7%)	26(0.3%)	2538(30.4%)	189(1.5%)	3954(32.4%)
	No conv/comp†	255(2.0%)	92(0.7%)	59(0.7%)	27(0.3%)	123(1.0%)	66(0.5%)
PL	NS	8803(69.8%)	846(6.7%)	4260(51.1%)	1679(20.1%)	7876(64.4%)	576(4.7%)
	Sig	15(0.1%)	2766(21.9%)	14(0.2%)	2238(26.8%)	114(0.9%)	3463(28.3%)
	No conv/comp†	122(1.0%)	66(0.5%)	82(1.0%)	71(0.9%)	114(0.9%)	79(0.6%)

*Following the RevMan documentation we did not compute effects for some very rare events or non-events studies (although RevMan v5.2.3 does calculate effects for them) and hence some meta-analyses were not computable; i.e. when the remaining number of eligible studies was one or zero.

†Not computable (see above) or iterative method failed to convergence to a solution.

‡MVa fails to produce an estimate when all effects are equal, a scenario not unheard of when meta-analysing dichotomous data.

doi:10.1371/journal.pone.0069930.t002

Table 3. Variation in terms of statistical conclusion for Peto fixed-effect meta-analyses.

		RevMan method			
		Fixed-effect ($\hat{\tau}^2_{DL}=0$)		Fixed-effect ($\hat{\tau}^2_{DL}>0$)	
		Counts (cell percentages)		Counts (cell percentages)	
Stata method		**NS**	**Sig**	**NS**	**Sig**
FE (Peto)	NS	1367(62.0%)	0(0.0%)	1184(55.5%)	0(0.0%)
	Sig	4(0.2%)	835(37.9%)	0(0.0%)	950(44.5%)
DL	NS	1367(62.0%)	0(0.0%)	1178(55.2%)	318(14.9%)
	Sig	4(0.2%)	835(37.9%)	6(0.3%)	632(29.6%)
DLb	NS	1367(62.0%)	36(1.6%)	1177(55.2%)	359(16.8%)
	Sig	4(0.2%)	799(36.2%)	7(0.3%)	591(27.7%)
VC	NS	1367(62.0%)	17(0.8%)	1181(55.3%)	343(16.1%)
	Sig	4(0.2%)	818(37.1%)	3(0.1%)	607(28.4%)
MVa	NS	1366(61.9%)	117(5.3%)	1178(55.2%)	448(21.0%)
	Sig	4(0.2%)	718(32.5%)	6(0.3%)	502(23.5%)
	No comp*	1(0.0%)	0 (0.0%)	0(0.0%)	0 (0.0%)
MVb	NS	1367(62.0%)	39(1.8%)	1180(55.3%)	344(16.1%)
	Sig	4(0.2%)	796(36.1%)	4(0.2%)	606(28.4%)
BP	NS	1369(62.1%)	179(8.1%)	1178(55.2%)	462(21.6%)
	Sig	2(0.1%)	656(29.7%)	6(0.3%)	488(22.9%)
B0	NS	1367(62.0%)	13(0.6%)	1182(55.4%)	266(12.5%)
	Sig	4(0.2%)	822(37.3%)	2(0.1%)	684(32.1%)
VC2	NS	1367(62.0%)	4(0.2%)	1177(55.2%)	362(17.0%)
	Sig	4(0.2%)	831(37.7%)	7(0.3%)	588(27.6%)
DL2	NS	1367(62.0%)	0(0.0%)	1180(55.3%)	333(15.6%)
	Sig	4(0.2%)	835(37.9%)	4(0.2%)	617(28.9%)
ML	NS	1362(61.7%)	1(0.0%)	1174(55.0%)	156(7.3%)
	Sig	4(0.2%)	826(37.4%)	2(0.1%)	790(37.0%)
	No conv†	5(0.2%)	8(0.4%)	8(0.4%)	4(0.2%)
REML	NS	1343(60.9%)	3(0.1%)	1177(55.2%)	293(13.7%)
	Sig	4(0.2%)	819(37.1%)	6(0.3%)	653(30.6%)
	No conv†	24(1.1%)	13(0.6%)	1(0.0%)	4(0.2%)
PL	NS	1364(61.8%)	135(6.1%)	1174(55.0%)	382(17.9%)
	Sig	2(0.1%)	690(31.3%)	1(0.0%)	564(26.4%)
	No conv†	5(0.2%)	10(0.5%)	9(0.4%)	4(0.2%)

*MVa fails to produce an estimate when all effects are equal, a scenario not unheard of when meta-analysing dichotomous data.
†Iterative method failed to convergence to a solution.
doi:10.1371/journal.pone.0069930.t003

The distributions of the estimators that do not assume always present heterogeneity are provided in Figure 4 and cumulative distributions for all methods in Figure 5 (by approach type and overall). For inverse variance and Mantel-Haenszel methods, they are similar and in agreement with the hypothesised χ^2_1 distribution we used for the simulations. For Peto methods, the observed distributions are flatter although the much smaller number of studies might be a factor. As in the simulations, the bootstrapped DerSimonian-Laird method identifies more heterogeneous meta-analyses: overall, $\hat{\tau}^2=0$ for 31.2% of analyses with DLb and 50.7% with the standard DL. This 'success' is partly attributed to the higher positive bias rates for very small meta-analyses. The findings are similar when only focusing on the 32,005 'overall' meta-analyses (Figure S1 in File S1). The better performance of the bootstrap approach in identifying heterogeneity, compared to the standard approach, is consistent across various meta-analysis sizes (Figure S2 in File S1) but more profound when the number of studies is small (Figure S3 in File S1).

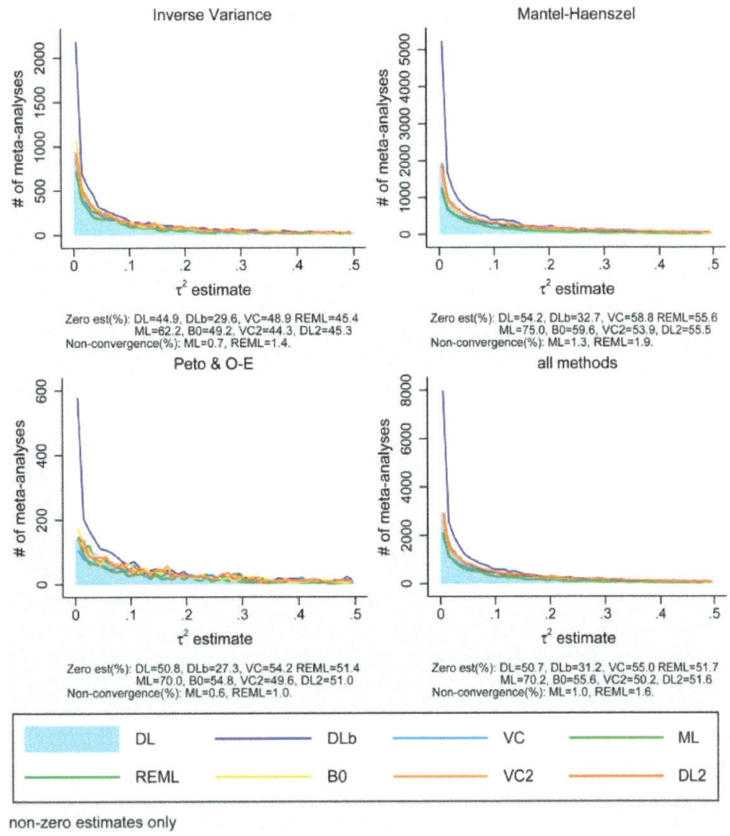

Figure 4. Distribution of between-study variance estimates by method type (including main and subgroup meta-analyses and truncated to 0.5 for better visualisation).

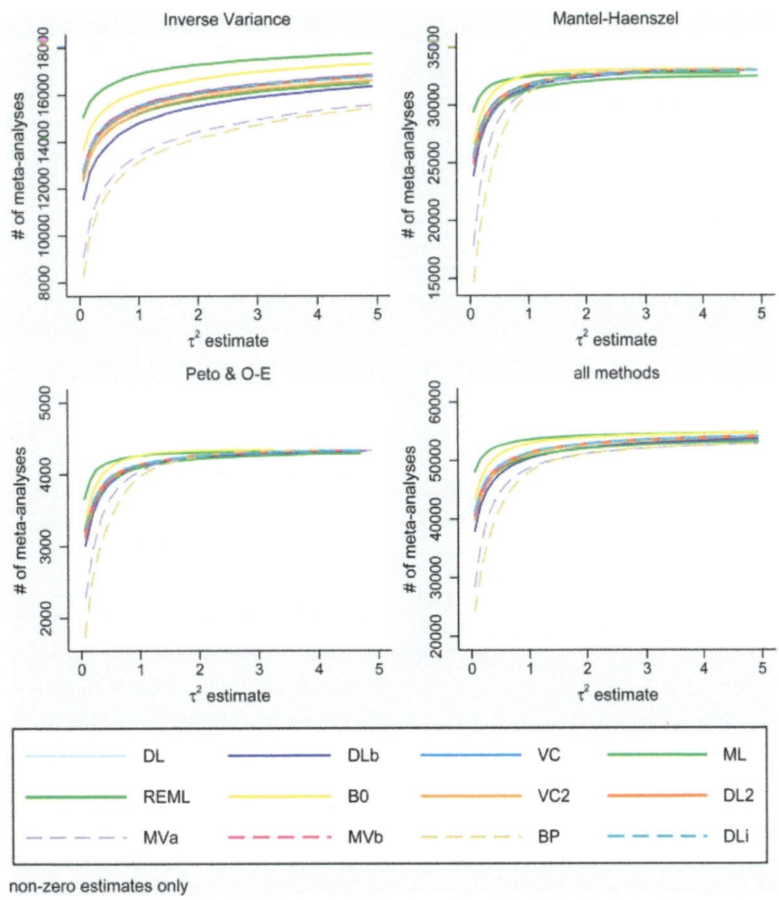

Figure 5. Cumulative distribution of between-study variance estimates by method type (including main and subgroup meta-analyses and truncated to 5 for better visualisation).

For inverse variance methods, the sensitivity of the results to the method choice, in terms of the statistical conclusion, is summarised in Table 1. When $\hat{\tau}^2_{DL}=0$, the fixed-effect method is necessarily used in RevMan and, as expected, the conclusions agree completely with what we obtained in Stata when using the same method (DL is reduced to fixed-effect in the absence of heterogeneity). However, the better at detecting heterogeneity DLb method identified heterogeneity for some of these studies, leading to the use of the respective random-effects model and a change in the conclusion to non-significant effect for 84 meta-analyses, approximately 0.9% of the analyses in the group. When $\hat{\tau}^2_{DL}>0$, the authors are given a choice between a fixed-effect and a DL random-effects model. Ignoring heterogeneity and proceeding with the former is not prudent, if the authors wish to their findings to be generalizable. In that scenario we identified 6 statistically non-significant effect analyses (0.1%) and 936 significant effect analyses (19.0%) for which the conclusions changed with DLb. When authors more appropriately used the DL random-effects approach, our calculations in Stata agree for the method but with DLb we also identified 6 non-significant effect analyses (0.1%) and 140 significant effect analyses (2.3%) for which the conclusions changed.

For Mantel-Haenszel approaches, we summarise the sensitivity of the conclusions to the method choice in Table 2. When $\hat{\tau}^2_{DL}=0$, the MH fixed-effect method is used in RevMan and as before, the DLb method identified heterogeneity for some of these analyses and the respective random-effects model produced overall effects for which the conclusion changed from non-significant in 50 cases (0.4%) and from significant in 336 cases (2.7%). When $\hat{\tau}^2_{DL}>0$ and heterogeneity is ignored through the MH fixed-effect approach, we identified 13 statistically non-significant effect analyses (0.2%) and 1,676 significant effect analyses (20.1%) for which the results changed with DLb. When authors took heterogeneity into account with a DL random-effects approach, we identified 65 non-significant effect analyses (0.5%) and 265 significant effect analyses (2.2%) for which the conclusions changed. The computational issues for the non-iterative methods and some of the changes in statistical conclusions are due to the very rare events (or non-events) disagreement with RevMan.

Table 3 summarises the differences in the statistical conclusions across methods when a Peto fixed-effect approach has been used in RevMan, irrespective of the estimated heterogeneity. When $\hat{\tau}^2_{DL}=0$, the DLb method identified heterogeneity for some of these analyses and the respective random-effects model produced overall effects for which the conclusion changed from non-significant in 4 cases (0.2%) and from significant in 36 cases (1.6%). When $\hat{\tau}^2_{DL}>0$, DLb identified 7 (0.3%) and 359 (16.8%) analyses for which the statistical conclusion changed from non-significant and significant respectively. A very few of the changes in the statistical conclusions are attributed to the unapplied Peto odds-ratio corrections in analyses executed in RevMan versions prior to 5.017.

The differences in the statistical conclusions between the standard methods and the DerSimonian-Laird bootstrap, by meta-analysis size, are presented in Tables S4 to S6 inFile S1. For inverse variance approaches, differences are more common for smaller meta-analyses and the methods agree more often in meta-analyses of 10 or more studies. For the Mantel-Haenszel and Peto approaches, differences are more consistent across meta-analysis sizes.

DISCUSSION

The importance of meta-analysis in medical research and its great influence in clinical practice are unquestionable. However, researchers and clinicians alike need to be aware of the potential issues with the current methods and, in particular, the likely fallacy of a homogeneity assumption. A zero between-study variance estimate, which is often observed when the number of studies to be meta-analyses is small, should be a cause for concern and further investigation.

Strengths and Limitations

The study used a vast resource to meet its goals, all available Cochrane Database of Systematic Reviews data in August 2012, a total of 57,397 meta-analyses. Nevertheless, there are a few limitations that need to be highlighted. Firstly, although the Cochrane library is the biggest resource for systematic reviews and meta-analysis it is not the only one. However, we have no reason to believe that our findings would not be applicable to other resources. Secondly, we used all reported meta-analyses, including 25,392 subgroup meta-analyses, and therefore there are instances where the same study is used in numerous analyses. Although this could potentially affect the distributions of the heterogeneity estimates (but this does not seem to be the case) we felt that it was more important to be inclusive and assess the sensitivity of all meta-analysis, especially since some overall analyses are not performed and only the subgroup ones are reported. Thirdly, for dichotomous outcomes, we did not compare across inverse variance, Mantel-Haenszel and Peto methods, but re-analysed using the same approach for simplicity. Fourth, the true heterogeneity distribution will very likely vary by outcome type or other study characteristics[33] but looking into these sub-categories is beyond the scope of this study.

Findings

In simulated data with specified degrees of non-zero heterogeneity, we demonstrated that most methods that allow the heterogeneity estimator to be zero, including the common DerSimonian-Laird approach, perform well on average, even for extreme distributions of the effects. However, these methods quite often fail to detect heterogeneity and thus produce biased estimates and conclusions, especially for small meta-analyses. The best method, overall, in particular in terms of detecting heterogeneity when it is present, appeared to be a non-parametric bootstrap of the DerSimonian-Laird, which we have implemented in Stata[34]. Although the method often produces positively biased heterogeneity estimates, especially for small meta-analyses, it performs very well on coverage, error-interval estimation and heterogeneity detection.

Not surprisingly, positive-only heterogeneity methods had high levels of bias which led to error intervals that were very wide, especially for larger meta-analyses. The best balance across all three measures of assessment was achieved by Sidik and Jonkman's MVb [17]. However, by arbitrarily assuming a minimum level of $\hat{\tau}^2=0.01$ with the standard DerSimonian-

Laird model, the same level MVb uses as a starting point, we obtained better results compared to MVb.

Using the Cochrane Database of Systematic Reviews we gained access to data for thousands of meta-analysis and using that resource we were able to further compare the performance of difference meta-analysis methods. The distribution of the between-study variance estimates was found to be consistent across inverse variance, Mantel-Haenszel and Peto approaches and similar to a χ_1^2 distribution as hypothesised in previous work [3].

A comparison between real and simulated data using the DerSimonian-Laird method suggested that mean true heterogeneity is higher than assumed or estimated in practice (higher than moderate) but the standard method fails to detect it, especially for meta-analyses of few studies. Thus we observed that random-effects methods are much more common in larger meta-analyses. This finding agrees with the conclusion of Turner et al, who found that meta-analysis size had a small effect on heterogeneity [33]. We found that to be true on average, but also that the risk of undetected heterogeneity is much higher when the number of studies to be meta-analysed is small. This reduced likelihood in identifying true underlying heterogeneity in small meta-analyses appears to be compensated for by the relatively larger positive bias in the bootstrap method, for those cases.

Even when heterogeneity is detected, it is not uncommon for researchers to ignore it and use a fixed-effect method. Such an approach has implications for the generalisability of the conclusions beyond the specific conditions and locations pertaining to the included studies. For full generalisability, a random-effects approach is required. The distributions of the between-study variance estimates from the various methods we used demonstrated that the bootstrap approach was better at detecting low heterogeneity levels in the real data, as in the simulations. Re-analysing all meta-analyses with this method we found that 19 to 21% of the statistical conclusions change, when heterogeneity is detected and ignored. The rates were much lower when the standard DerSimonian-Laird method did not detect heterogeneity, between approximately 1% (inverse variance) and 3% (Mantel-Haenszel), depending on the approach. When heterogeneity was detected and the random-effects model was used, we found that the statistical conclusions changed for approximately 2.5% of analyses, under the bootstrap.

Amongst the methods that permitted a zero-heterogeneity estimate, the bootstrapped DerSimonian-Laird performed best on the basis of our simulations – despite its higher bias for small meta-analyses. Even so, the high rate of failure to detect existing heterogeneity indicates that positive-only heterogeneity methods may be preferred, depending on the setting. MVa and BP, the Bayesian estimators proposed by Sidik and Jonkman [17] and Ruhkin [19] respectively, performed very well when two or three studies were meta-analysed and should be considered.

CONCLUSIONS

Not surprisingly, detecting heterogeneity and accurately estimating it when the number of studies being meta-analysed is very small is difficult, if not impossible, yet more than half of all the meta-analyses in the Cochrane database include just two or three studies.

Current practice assumes that a zero between-study variance estimate leads to a more reliable meta-analysis, while high levels of estimated heterogeneity are alarming and potentially prohibitive for an analysis. However, our results indicate that estimates of zero (or even low) heterogeneity should also be a concern since heterogeneity is very likely present but undetected (or underestimated). Although the bootstrapped DerSimonian-Laird leads to a small improvement over the standard random-effects model, the problem largely remains, especially for very small meta-analyses. One possible solution in these cases is to arbitrarily assume moderate or large levels of heterogeneity and to test the sensitivity of the conclusions to these degrees of unobserved heterogeneity. This sensitivity-analysis approach, along with the bootstrapped DerSimonian-Laird have been included in an update for *metaan* [34]. Alternatively, confidence intervals for the bootstrapped DerSimonian-Laird estimate can easily be obtained and considered for sensitivity-analyses, but we found them to be of little value when the number of studies was small.

Finally, we must caution researchers against ignoring heterogeneity when detected. The narrower confidence intervals for the estimate and the fact that results are more likely to be statistically significant under the fixed-effect approach, should not influence their decision. Perhaps software developers should not offer a choice and sensitivity analyses should be reported as standard.

SUPPORTING INFORMATION

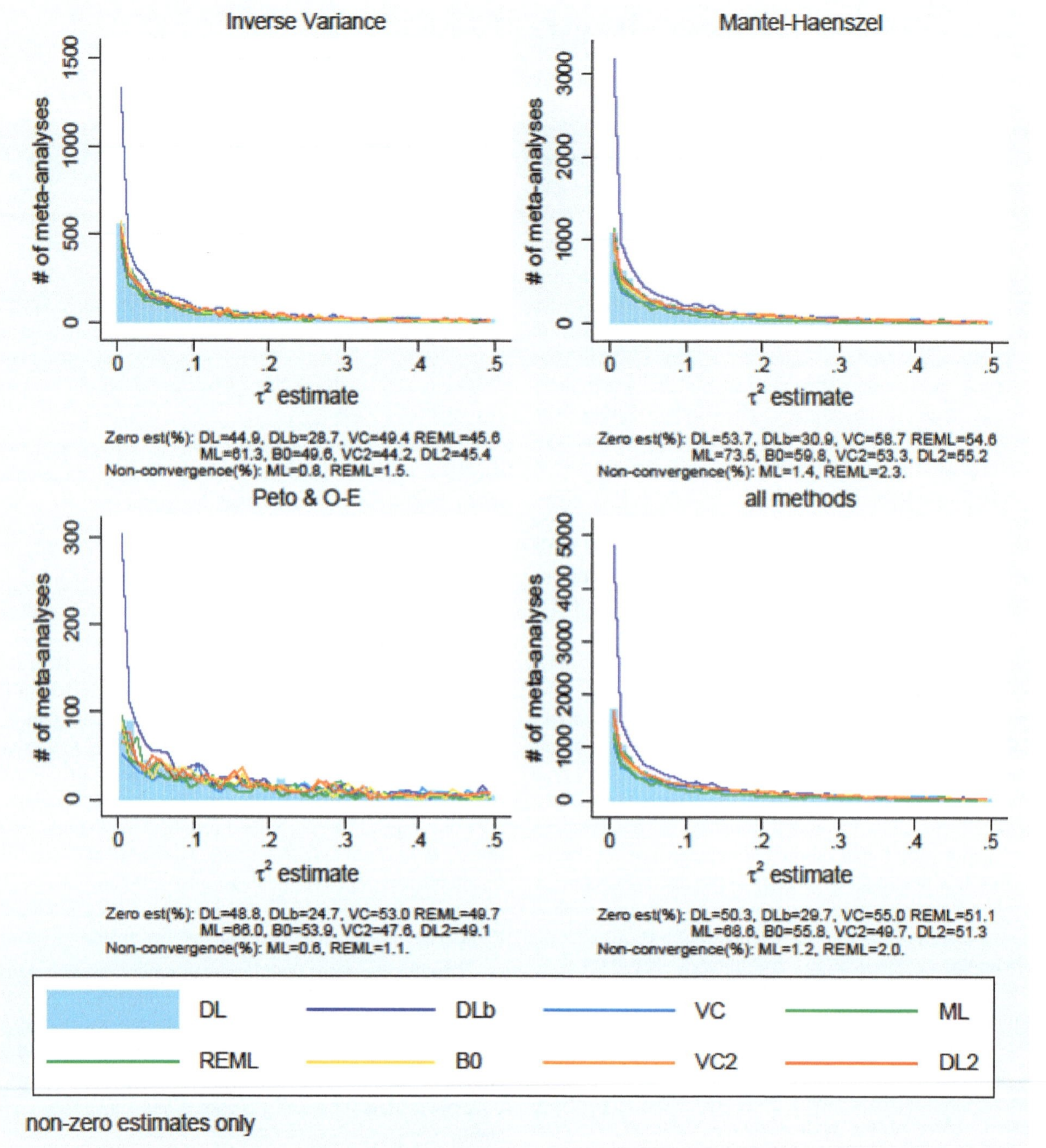

File S1. - doi:10.1371/journal.pone.0069930.s001

ACKNOWLEDGMENTS

We greatly appreciate all the hard work behind the Cochrane Collaboration and the wealth of information it creates, which made this study possible.

EK is the guarantor of this work and, as such, had full access to all the data in the study and takes responsibility for the integrity of the data and the accuracy of the data analysis.

Data sharing

Although we do not have permission to re-distribute the Cochrane library data, we can provide python code to users with institutional or personal access to the Wiley website to help them download all available RevMan files and convert them to csv format.

AUTHOR CONTRIBUTIONS

Conceived and designed the experiments: EK DR. Analyzed the data: EK. Wrote the paper: EK. Extracted the data: EK DS. Performed the statistical analyses: EK. Edited the manuscript: DR DS.

REFERENCES

1. Egger M, Smith GD, Altman DG, NetLibrary I (2001) Systematic reviews in health care : meta-analysis in context: London : BMJ Books.

2. DerSimonian R, Laird N (1986) Meta-analysis in clinical trials. Control ClinTrials 7: 177–188. doi: 10. 1016/0197-2456(86)90046-2

3. Brockwell SE, Gordon IR (2001) A comparison of statistical methods for meta-analysis. StatMed 20: 825–840. doi: 10. 1002/sim. 650

4. Kontopantelis E, Reeves D (2012) Performance of statistical methods for meta-analysis when true study effects are non-normally distributed: A simulation study. Statistical Methods in Medical Research 21: 409–426. doi: 10. 1177/0962280210392008

5. Biggerstaff BJ, Tweedie RL (1997) Incorporating variability in estimates of heterogeneity in the random effects model in meta-analysis. Statistics in Medicine 16: 753–768. doi: 10. 1002/(sici)1097-0258(19970415)16:7<753::aid-sim494>3. 0. co;2-g

6. Follmann DA, Proschan MA (1999) Valid inference in random effects meta-analysis. Biometrics 55: 732–737. doi: 10. 1111/j. 0006-341x. 1999. 00732. x

7. Sidik K, Jonkman JN (2002) A simple confidence interval for meta-analysis. Statistics in Medicine 21: 3153–3159. doi: 10. 1002/sim. 1262

8. Hardy RJ, Thompson SG (1996) A likelihood approach to meta-analysis with random effects. StatMed 15: 619–629. doi: 10. 1002/(sici)1097-0258(19960330)15:6<619::aid-sim188>3. 0. co;2-a

9. Jackson D, Bowden J, Baker R (2010) How does the DerSimonian and Laird procedure for random effects meta-analysis compare with its more efficient but harder to compute counterparts? Journal of Statistical Planning and Inference 140: 961 970. doi: 10. 1016/j. jspi. 2009. 09. 017

10. Kontopantelis E, Reeves D (2012) Letter: Performance of statistical methods for meta-analysis when true study effects are non-normally distributed: a comparison between DerSimonian-Laird and Restricted Maximum Likelihood. Statistical Methods in Medical Research 21.

11. Mantel N, Haenszel W (1959) Statistical Aspects of the Analysis of Data from Retrospective Studies of Disease. Biometrics 15: 639–640.

12. Greenland S, Robins JM (1985) Estimation of a Common Effect Parameter from Sparse Follow-up Data. Biometrics 41: 55–68. doi: 10. 2307/2530643

13. Yusuf S, Peto R, Lewis J, Collins R, Sleight P (1985) Beta-Blockade during and after Myocardial-Infarction - an Overview of the Randomized Trials. Progress in Cardiovascular Diseases 27: 335–371. doi: 10. 1016/s0033-0620(85)80003-7

14. Hedges LV (1983) A random effects model for effect sizes. Psychological Bulletin 93: 388. doi: 10. 1037/0033-2909. 93. 2. 388

15. Cochran WG (1954) The combination of estimates from different experiments. Biometrics 10: 101–129. doi: 10. 2307/3001666

16. DerSimonian R, Kacker R (2007) Random-effects model for meta-analysis of clinical trials: An update. Contemporary Clinical Trials 28: 105–114. doi: 10. 1016/j. cct. 2006. 04. 004

17. Sidik K, Jonkman JN (2005) Simple heterogeneity variance estimation for meta-analysis. Journal of the Royal Statistical Society Series C-Applied Statistics 54: 367–384. doi: 10. 1111/j. 1467-9876. 2005. 00489. x

18. Sidik K, Jonkman JN (2007) A comparison of heterogeneity variance estimators in combining results of studies. Statistics in Medicine 26: 1964–1981. doi: 10. 1002/sim. 2688

19. Rukhin AL (2012) Estimating heterogeneity variance in meta-analysis. Journal of the Royal Statistical Society: Series B (Statistical Methodology).

20. Cochran WG (1937) Problems arising in the analysis of a series of similar experiments. Supplement to the Journal of the Royal Statistical Society 4: 102–118. doi: 10. 2307/2984123

21. Higgins JP, Thompson SG (2002) Quantifying heterogeneity in a meta-analysis. StatMed 21: 1539–1558. doi: 10. 1002/sim. 1186

22. Hardy RJ, Thompson SG (1998) Detecting and describing heterogeneity in meta-analysis. Statistics in Medicine 17: 841–856. doi: 10. 1002/(sici)1097-0258(19980430)17:8<841::aid-sim781>3. 0. co;2-d

23. Mittlbock M, Heinzl H (2006) A simulation study comparing properties of heterogeneity measures in meta-analyses. StatMed 25: 4321–4333. doi: 10. 1002/sim. 2692

24. The Nordic Cochrane Centre (2011) Review Manager (RevMan). 5. 1 ed. Copenhagen: The Cochrane Collaboration.

25. Deeks JJ, Altman DG, Bradburn MJ (2008) Statistical Methods for Examining Heterogeneity and Combining Results from Several Studies in Meta-Analysis. Systematic Reviews in Health Care: BMJ Publishing Group. 285–312.

26. Efron B (1981) Nonparametric Estimates of Standard Error - the Jackknife, the Bootstrap and Other Methods. Biometrika 68: 589–599. doi: 10. 2307/2335441

27. Hedges LV (1983) A Random Effects Model for Effect Sizes. Psychological Bulletin 93: 388–395. doi: 10. 1037/0033-2909. 93. 2. 388

28. Morris CN (1983) Parametric Empirical Bayes Inference - Theory and Applications. Journal of the American Statistical Association 78: 47–55. doi: 10. 2307/2287098

29. StataCorp L P. (2011) Stata Statistical software for Windows. 12. 1 ed.

30. Wiley (2012) The Cochrane Library.

31. GNU General Public Licence (2012) Python(x,y).

32. Deeks JJ, Higgins JP (2010) Statistical algorithms in Review Manager 5. Statistical Methods Group of The Cochrane Collaboration. 1–11.

33. Turner RM, Davey J, Clarke MJ, Thompson SG, Higgins JPT (2012) Predicting the extent of heterogeneity in meta-analysis, using empirical data from the Cochrane Database of Systematic Reviews. International Journal of Epidemiology 41: 818–827. doi: 10. 1093/ije/dys041

34. Kontopantelis E, Reeves D (2010) metaan: Random-effects meta-analysis. Stata Journal 10: 395–407.

CHAPTER 15

ANALYTIC PROGRAMMING WITH FMRI DATA: A QUICK-START GUIDE FOR STATISTICIANS USING R

Ani Eloyan[1], Shanshan Li[2] , John Muschelli[1] , Jim J. Pekar[3,4], Stewart H. Mostofsky[3,5], Brian S. Caffo[1]

[1] Department of Biostatistics, Bloomberg School of Public Health, Johns Hopkins University, Baltimore, Maryland, United States of America

[2] Department of Biostatistics, Indiana University Fairbanks School of Public Health, Indianapolis, Indiana, United States of America

[3] F. M. Kirby Research Center for Functional Brain Imaging, Kennedy Krieger Institute, Baltimore, Maryland, United States of America

[4] Department of Radiology, The Johns Hopkins School of Medicine, Baltimore, Maryland, United States of America

[5] Department of Neurology and Psychiatry, The Johns Hopkins School of Medicine, Baltimore, Maryland, United States of America

ABSTRACT

Functional magnetic resonance imaging (fMRI) is a thriving field that plays an important role in medical imaging analysis, biological and neuroscience research and practice. This manuscript gives a didactic introduction to the statistical analysis of fMRI data using the R project, along with the relevant R code. The goal is to give statisticians who would like to pursue research in this area a quick tutorial for programming with fMRI data. References of relevant packages and papers are provided for those interested in more advanced analysis.

INTRODUCTION

This primer was created to give statisticians who are new to the field of imaging data analysis a quick overview of functional magnetic resonance imaging (fMRI) data and to describe tools for programming their own analyses of fMRI. It is targeted at those who would like to pursue programming using the R project [1]. The key benefit of programming on one's own is the ability to extend analyses and build and create new tools. Of course, the key benefits of using the R project are that it is open source, cross-platform, free (as in cost), and is an award-winning lingua franca of statisticians. Matlab (www.mathworks.com) is the standard scripting language in neuroimaging and signal processing, and has a widely used integrated development environment and GUI creation software. Both R and Matlab are cross-platform and have excellent graphics capabilities. Both are high level scripting languages that are easy to learn and have a large collection of add-ons and subroutines.

For those wanting more automated methods for the analysis of fMRI data, several programs exist to perform most standard analyses. In addition, power users should learn these programs for comparison purposes to avoid reinventing existing and well established tools. We give a nonexhaustive list of some of our favorite freely available software below.

SPM SPM (http://www.fil.ion.ucl.ac.uk/spm/) is a collection of open source Matlab scripts, often calling compiled code. SPM is arguably the most popular software for the analysis of fMRI data, in no small part due to a well-developed GUI. It has methods for single-subject and multi-subject analyses and tools for displaying the results and data visualization. It can perform all of the basic preprocessing

Citation: Eloyan A, Li S, Muschelli J, Pekar JJ, Mostofsky SH, Caffo BS (2014) Analytic Programming with fMRI Data: A Quick-Start Guide for Statisticians Using R. PLoS ONE 9(2): e89470. doi:10.1371/journal.pone.0089470.

procedures of the imaging data. Moreover, it has an active user community with several user contributed add-ons. The SPM scripts are well documented, and are easily understood.

FSL FSL (http://www.fmrib.ox.ac.uk/fsl/) is a UNIX-based software that performs single- and multi-subject analyses, preprocessing and visualization of results. It has a graphical user interface, though is most effectively used at the command line, tying routines together using shell scripts. FSL is open source and can be compiled from scratch. In addition, pre-compiled binaries are available, notably for OSX. For Windows, FSL can be run in a virtual machine.

MIPAV MIPAV (http://mipav.cit.nih.gov/) is a JAVA software created by the US National Institutes of Health. It has very broad functionality for preprocessing, analysis and visualization of imaging data. However, it is most useful through an active collection of modules.

AFNI AFNI (http://afni.nimh.nih.gov/afni/) is a UNIX-based software. It offers a full analysis and processing suite. We often use it in conjunction with FSL and BASH scripting.

FreeSurfer FreeSurfer (http://surfer.nmr.mgh.harvard.edu/) is a UNIX-based software for registration (often atlas based) and analysis of medical imaging data. It is often discussed as having excellent registration and visualization tools.

ANTS ANTS [3] is a UNIX-based software for preprocessing of imaging data. It provides methods for linear and nonlinear registration of images.

In addition to the above tools for analysis and processing of fMRI data, there are R packages related to fMRI. We list a few packages here primarily focused on analysis postregistration.

AnalyzeFMRI [3] Analysis package for reading and writing of fMRI including a graphical user interface. It can also be used for performing temporal and spatial ICA.

oro.nifti [4] Package for reading in NIfTI files, a common fMRI imaging format. It can be used for reading compressed files.

oro.dicom [5] Package for reading in DICOM files, another common fMRI imaging format.

fmri [6] Package for reading in and analyzing fMRI data. Includes graphical user interface for fMRI analysis and adaptive smoothing for fMRI along with inference.

neuRosim [7] Package for simulating fMRI data. As a consequence, has tools for creating and investigating designs with HRF convolution models.

arf3DS4 [8] Package for activated region fitting for fMRI data in NIfTI format.

Rniftilib [9] Package for loading and writing the 3D or 4D images.

RNiftyReg [10] Package for 2D or 3D image registration.

brainwaver [11] Package for functional connectivity analysis.

tractor.base [12] Package for reading, writing, and graphical representation of images.

waveslim [13] Package for wavelet analysis of 1D, 2D and 3D images.

cudaBayesreg [14] Package for Compute Unified Device Architecture (CUDA) based Bayesian multilevel analysis of fMRI data.

We will use some of the packages above in the examples in this manuscript. In addition, a frequently updated more exhaustive list on CRAN of packages for medical image analysis can be found here:

http://cran.r-project.org/web/views/MedicalImaging.html.

The remainder of the manuscript is organized as follows. Sections 1, 2 and 3 describe the structure of the fMRI data, discuss ways of obtaining the data and give a brief overview of the preprocessing steps. Section 4 describes the different formats that can be used for viewing the fMRI data in R along with examples of obtaining a Gaussian smoother of the data matrix and the mask of the three dimensional image. A discussion of the hemodynamic response (HR) function and the role of the design matrix in task-based fMRI studies is presented in Section 5. The between-subject random effect models are discussed in Section 6. Section 7 gives an overview of the connectivity based analysis of fMRI data including methods based on seed-voxel analysis, singular value decomposition and independent component analysis. As the main goal of the manuscript is centered on the statistical analysis of fMRI data via R, we do not present visualization tools in detail, however, we briefly discuss a few of the visualization tools in R or other software in Section 8. Finally, the last section completes the article by pointing out useful further reading material.

MATERIALS AND METHODS

fMRI

FMRI is a modern brain imaging measurement technology. As its name suggests, the technology is used to explore brain function (activity) by obtaining several images of the brain over time using an MRI machine. Standard fMRI images the so-called blood oxygen level dependent (BOLD) signal, described further below. An extensive overview of the statistical methods developed for the analysis of fMRI data is presented by [15], [16], [17]and [18]. Herein, we will discuss the implementation of some of these commonly used techniques in R, while providing brief discussions as to the methods and the interpretation of the results. BOLD fMRI is not the only functional brain imaging technology available using an MRI scanner (see [19] for an overview). For example, arterial spin labeling [20] is a closely related functional MRI technology. However, the term fMRI, when used without qualifying statements, refers to BOLD fMRI. We note that positron emissions tomography (PET), single photon emissions computed tomography, electroencephalograms (EEG), magnetoencephalograms (MEG) and other non-magnetic resonance based measurement devices can be used for functional brain imaging, each with different goals, limitations, strengths and scientific interpretations.

We will not thoroughly discuss the details of the methods by which the MRI scanners use the principles of magnetic resonance to achieve different images. However, newcomers to the area may be surprised to find the amazing variety of biological signals that one can visualize using MRI. These include separate modalities to study white matter, gray matter, overall structure, white matter tracts, tracers injected into the body and lesions in the brain. There are multiple types of structural and functional images, all acquired using the principles of MR. See [19] and [21] for a general introduction to MR imaging.

The BOLD signal ([22], [23]) measures the cerebral hemodynamic changes concomitant to neuronal activation of the brain. A localized increase in neural activity results in an increase in blood flow ("reactive hyperemia" [24],[25]) to the activated region when excess of oxygenated hemoglobin is delivered to the region. Consequently, a reduction in deoxyhemoglobin concentration follows, resulting in an increase in magnetic field homogeneity. The gradient echo EPI sequence ([26], [27]) allows to study the activation of specific regions of the brain during a task. Deoxyhemoglobin serves as an endogenous susceptibility contrast agent allowing MRI to report on local hemodynamic changes. Hence, the BOLD signal in response to a stimulus is given a name - the hemodynamic response.Figure 1 shows an example hemodynamic response function (HRF). In Figure 1, an initial delay of the response can be observed since it takes time for the vasculature of the brain to respond to the need for oxygen after the stimulus. This is followed by a subsequent brief undershoot [28]. The origin of the undershoot is controversial. One explanation of the undershoot is that there is ongoing oxygen consumption after reaching the point of origin. The other is that the excess volume of deoxygenated blood results in delayed vascular compliance.

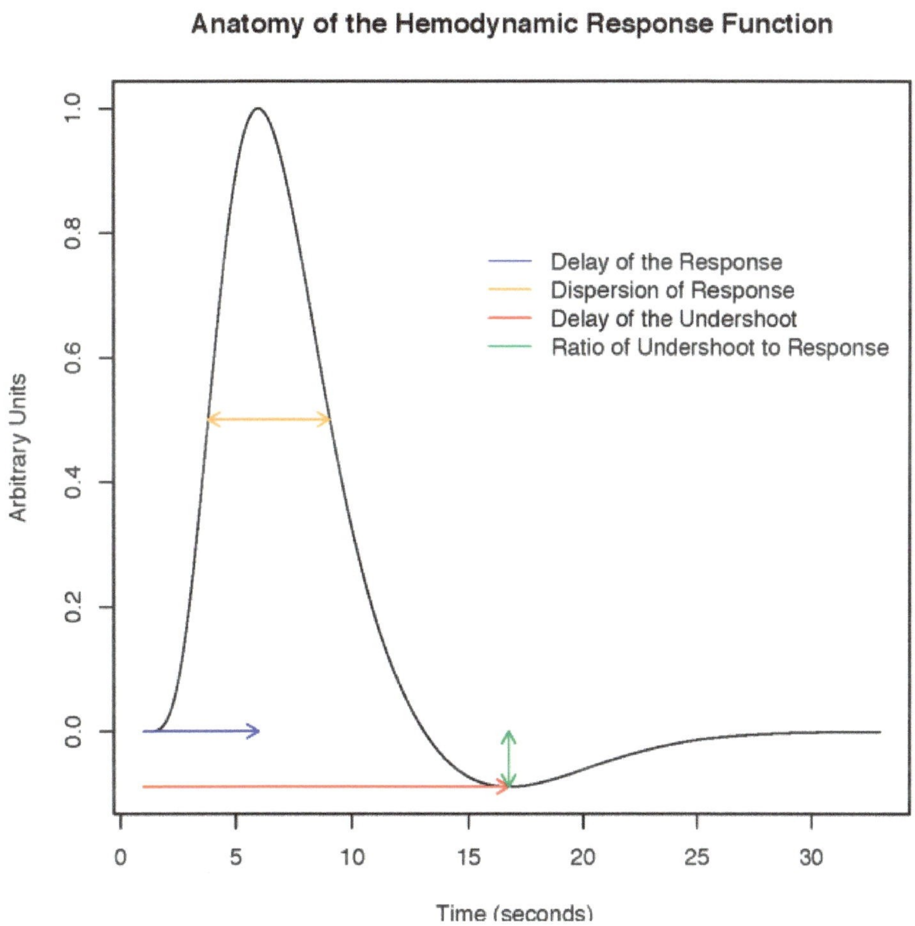

Figure 1. Anatomy of the HRF.

In BOLD fMRI the scanner records images approximately every second (the so-called TR or time of repetition). At each time point, a 3D image of the brain is obtained. Often, in BOLD fMRI, the image is collected one slice at a time for each time point instead of scanning the 3D image immediately. Hence, a slice time correction (e.g., by Fourier transformation [28]) is applied to the resulting images as part of the preprocessing. Empirical face validity of the methodology can be demonstrated by simple motor or visual tasks. For example, consider a "finger tapping" task where a subject is asked to tap their finger while in the scanner and then rest, repeating this sequence for a certain time interval. When the images are averaged over the times at rest and compared to the times when tapping the finger, and appropriate statistical tests are performed, motor areas of the brain are clearly activated (see [29] for overview of finger tapping task-related analysis in the literature). By virtue of the well-defined motor area of activation and ease of performing the task, finger tapping tasks are commonly used for scanner and methodological validation. They are also of intrinsic interest in the study of motor areas. Various other tasks can be designed depending on the goals of the study. More recently, resting state fMRI has been used to explore the brain function when the subject is at rest. Section

Provides Details on How the Experimental Design Can Inform the Statistical Analysis of the Data

The development of the BOLD fMRI technology facilitated research in the analysis of cognitive function of the brain [15]. For instance, one may be interested in identifying which regions are involved in performing a mental operation or a cognitive task, how active is a brain region during a task, what is the shape of the time course of activation or quantifying the extent of connectivity between brain regions during tasks. Since there are several sources of variability introduced during data collection, statistical methods are required in order to accurately obtain the regions of interest. For instance, in Section 5.1 we discuss two types of experimental designs used frequently in fMRI analysis: block design and event-related design. It can be shown that the block designs have high detection power (i.e., the ability of the method to detect activation), whereas the event related designs have better estimation efficiency in that they can be used to estimate the shape of the HRF [30]. In Section 5.1, we show several statistical methods that can be used to answer the questions posed above.

For the purpose of statistical analysis the observed fMRI dataset contains a 3D array of intensities for each time point. The number of timepoints can vary depending on the length of the scan and is usually in hundreds. Axial slices of the 3D images at each time point for a subject at rest are shown in Figure 2 top panel. A voxel (or volumetric pixel) is defined as a 3D unit element in the image. The background of the image is generally removed and the voxels in the brain are used for analysis. Depending on the research question one may choose to organize the data differently. For instance, the time courses of each voxel (as shown in Figure 2 bottom panel) may be analyzed (voxel-wise) to identify the voxels that are activated during a task. The 3D images at each time point may be vectorized and concatenated to obtain a $time \times space$ matrix that can be further analyzed to discover brain networks. The correlations of time courses for each pair of voxels in the brain are often used in connectivity analysis, that is in identifying areas of the brain that activate and deactivate together.

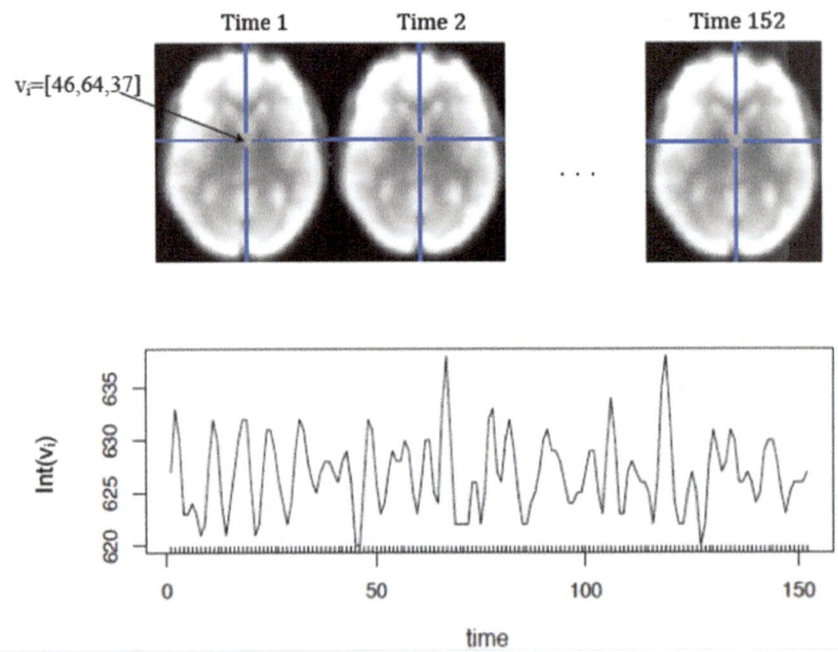

Figure 2. Resting state fMRI image for 1 subject. The top panel shows one axial slice from the 3D image acquared at each of the 152 time points. v_i denotes a voxel in the brain with coordinates [46, 64, 37]. The plot below shows the intensity of the image at voxel v_i (on the y-axis) at each time point (the x-axis corresponds to time).

Obtaining Data

As many neuroscience researchers are joining open science initiatives promoting public access for data, numerous websites offer datasets that can be downloaded freely. However, we have a few favorite canonical datasets that are good starting points for analysis. The first are SPM's example datasets that can be used for single-subject and inter-subject analyses. The second dataset of interest is the 1000 Functional Connectomes Project (FCP)/INDI [31]resting-state data. Most of the SPM datasets are preprocessed and ready for analysis; however, the FCP data need extensive preprocessing. UNIX shell scripts using FSL and AFNI can be found on their website for those who are interested in preprocessing.

The SPM example datasets can be downloaded at

http://www.fil.ion.ucl.ac.uk/spm/data/

The 1,000 FCP dataset can be downloaded at

http://www.nitrc.org/projects/fcon_1000/

As mentioned above, the 1,000 FCP data involves the most preprocessing. We therefore put a processed image in .nii format along with the corresponding 2D matrix in an R data file format with the extension .rda (the .rda files can be loaded by using the load() function in R) for download on our servers at

www.biostat.jhsph.edu/~bcaffo/downloads/rest_res2standard.nii.gzwww.biostat.jhsph.edu/~bcaffo/downloads/imageDataMatrix.rda

For illustrating the analysis in this manuscript, we choose images from the Kennedy Kreiger Institute (the home institution of some of the coauthors of this manuscript).

We also note that FSL has an evaluation suite, the FEEDS dataset, that we have found very useful, both for learning FSL as well as debugging new methods. The FSL example dataset can be downloaded at:

http://www.fmrib.ox.ac.uk/fsl/feeds/doc/index.html

Preprocessing

Preprocessing is an essential component in the analysis of fMRI data. Standard preprocessing requires, for example, skull stripping, evaluation and corrections for motion, coregistering, spatial smoothing and registration to a template. We discuss two preprocessing steps in particular: spatial smoothing and registration to a template. However, for newcomers to the area, we suggest leaving all the steps, except for possibly the spatial smoothing to standard software, or acquiring data where preprocessing has already been completed in an acceptable manner. For those readers interested in pursuing preprocessing as a research endeavor, good theoretical foundations are given by [32], [33]and [34].

Warping the images of a subject to a template, often called spatial registration or spatial normalization, is the key step of attempting to put subject images into a common space. That is, each registered image is transformed to the same space and hence the spatial locations of the voxels in the brain are ideally interpretable across subjects, in other words, voxel 1 for subject 1 is the same as voxel 1 for subject 2. In functional neuroimaging, this process relies on numerous assumptions. For example, it presumes anatomical similarity across subjects at the functional resolution of interest. This assumption becomes especially problematic when studying diseased brains, where anatomy can be drastically different than the healthy control template brain. Also, it presumes localization of the brain function of interest to common anatomical locales across subjects.

Setting these issues aside, registration is accomplished by mathematically warping each subject's collection of images over time to a so-called "template". A template is typically a highly detailed structural image obtained by imaging a subject repeatedly or warping several subjects into one common image. The template is useful for overlaying results on top of it which then helps in contextualizing the results. It is important to know what template was used to warp the images one is analyzing. Because it is often a highly accurate structural image (or there is an associated image in the same space), it is useful for interpretation, as neuroscientists can visually relate findings to important structural landmarks. Moreover, some templates are in wide use and key regions have been tabulated (see [35] for more details). We normally use templates created by the Montreal Neurological Institute (MNI) at:

http://imaging.mrc-cbu.cam.ac.uk/imaging/MniTalairach

The International Consortium for Brain Mapping (http://www.loni.ucla.edu/ICBM/) releases labeled brain atlases. We should also mention the famous Talairach Atlas, which is a coordinate system created before MR imaging was in place. Relating results to Talairach coordinates is often done to put results in a historical perspective familiar to neuroscientists. Some templates have conversion utilities to convert their coordinates to Talairach coordinates.

Finally, spatial smoothing using a filter is a step that can be easily done in R. The choice of whether spatial smoothing is necessary to perform is generally a designed component of a statistician's analysis plan. Hence, of all the preprocessing steps, this is the one we suggest to be performed in R if deemed necessary.

Loading data and structures

Array format

Two key data representations are the array format and the matrix format. The first is the more natural format for the data. Suppose I is an array representing a 3D image of the brain, where I[i,j,k] is the intensity of voxel i,j,k. If the image is collected repeatedly over time (as in fMRI), then 4D arrays (I[i,j,k,t]) are useful, though often are very large.

Medical images in neuroimaging are usually saved in one of a few available formats. However, all formats have common properties, for instance, they are binary and the data are stored as a long floating point vector. Header information includes descriptive features of the image such as the physical dimensions of a voxel and the size of each of the three dimensions, as well as other information.

DICOM Digital Imaging and Communications in Medicine (DICOM) is a standard image format from National Electrical Manufacturers Association often used as scanner output. DICOM images have the header information built into the binary file. 3D DICOM files are sometimes split into several files of 2D slices, but can be combined into a single file.

Analyze The Analyze format includes two files for each 3D image: a header file with the extension .hdr and an image file with the extension .img. The header and image files have to have the same filename and have to be saved in the same folder. The 4D fMRI images are often stored as separate files, where the 3D image for each time point is saved as a separate file. In Analyze 7.5 format, the 4D images can be saved using one .img and one .hdr file.

NIfTI NIfTI files typically have the extension .nii and are a current standard for the analysis of fMRI data. NIfTI files can have more than 3 dimensions. Often NIfTI files are compressed using gzip and so the file extension is .nii.gz. If your analysis program cannot gunzip the file, simply uncompress it using any of the standard compression software tools and the result will be a standard (uncompressed) NIfTI file. The R package oro.nifti can be used to read in the gzipped files directly.

In this example, we read in a sample 3D so-called contrast image and smooth it using a 3D Gaussian filter [36] included in the package AnalyzeFMRI. For illustration, we are using one of the SPM datasets (see [37], for more information about the dataset) described in Section 2. First we read in the data.

```
library(AnalyzeFMRI)
imageFileName <- "pathToImageFile/imageFile.img"
img <- f.read.analyze.volume(imageFileName)[,,,1]
```

Here we assume that imageFile.img is an Analyze image file with a header and image pair: imageFile.hdr and imageFile.img. Notice this data is 3D, yet the program reads it in as 4D, where the first three dimensions correspond to the size of the

3D image and the fourth dimension is set to 1. Hence the array subscripting drops the dimension by 1. It is often useful to read in the header information.

```
headerFileName <- "pathToImageFile/imageFile.hdr"
hdr <- f.read.analyze.header(headerFileName)
```

We can visualize this image using the image function.

```
# visualize the image
templmg <- img
templmg[is.na(templmg)] <- min(img, na.rm = TRUE)
for(k in 1: dim(img)[3])
image(templmg[,,k], axes = FALSE)
```

Note that the creation of the temporary image templmg in this example is only useful as the background of the raw image is stored as NA. Note also by default the image command does not scale the image relative to the actual voxel dimensions. The parameter asp can be used to specify the aspect ratio y/x which would result in the correct voxel dimensions. The following code smooths the image using the function GaussSmoothArray.

```
simg <- GaussSmoothArray(templmg,
voxdim =c(3, 3, 3),
ksize =5,
sigma = diag(4, 3),
mask = as.integer(!is.na(img)))
for(k in 1: dim(img)[3])
image(simg[,,k], axes = FALSE)
```

Here the mask statement contains the smoother to the non-background areas, i.e., the smoother is applied to the non-background voxels which have the value of 1 in the mask. The voxdim variable contains the voxel dimensions, in this case three millimeters cubed. The voxel dimensions can be found using visualization programs or inspecting the hdr variable. The ksize and sigma parameters are smoothing parameters. The sigma parameter is the standard deviation of the Gaussian kernel (specified in mm) while ksize is the truncation width. See the documentation for GaussSmoothArray for more information.Figure 3 shows an axial slice of the original image along with the corresponding smoothed image (see Section 8 for more details on displaying images).

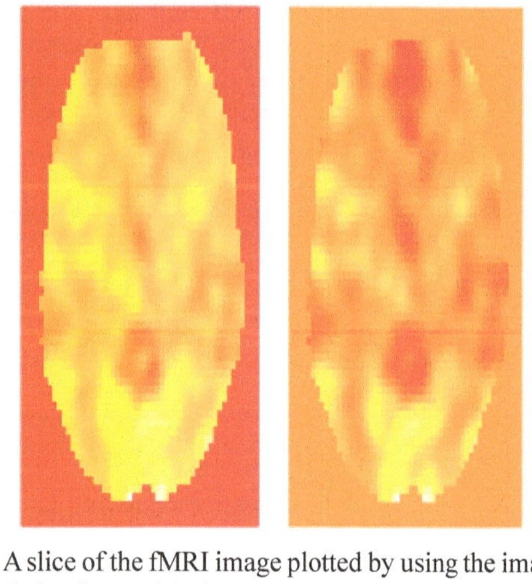

Figure 3. A slice of the fMRI image plotted by using the image() function in R (left) along with the corresponding smoothed slice (right). Here the red color corresponds to high intensity values, followed by yellow and white as the values decrease.

Matrix format

The array format, while useful for smoothing, is not a convenient data structure for most other analyses. Most importantly, it is not a parsimonious structure, since it includes all of the voxels outside of the brain, i.e., the background of the image. In some fMRI analysis, where the spatial structure of the voxels is disregarded, a common **mask** is applied to the 3D data and the data are then saved in a long 1D vector. In fMRI, if there is one vector per time or subject, these can be stacked into a matrix for analysis. Under this structure, any analysis of the resulting matrix must be invariant to spatial location. The spatial location information can be kept elsewhere for back reconstruction of the image. For example, if there are 30,000 nonbackground voxels, one could retain the 3×30,000 matrix of location indices for those voxels. Masks can be created in a variety of ways. They can be obtained from the template or from the data itself. The mask is an important structure to retain, as it can map a vector back to an array format for display.

Here, we will take a collection of 3D images for one subject (one 3D image per time point) and create a mask. Using the mask, we will then create the data matrix. First, we read in the list of the files (with absolute paths).

```
library(AnalyzeFMRI)
# the directory where the images are stored
fileDir <- "pathToImageFile"
# the collection of images
files <- dir(fileDir, pattern = "*.img", full.names= TRUE)
```

It is useful to have the image dimensions assigned to an object. We are assuming that all images are registered and have the same dimensions.

```
# obtain the image dimensions by loading the first image
imageDim <- f.read.analyze.header(files[1])$dim[2: 4]
```

Now we loop over the time courses and collect them into a matrix by grabbing the relevant indices across the time courses. We then find the corresponding non-background indices and place them in a vector called mask.

```
mask3D <- array(1, imageDim)
for (file in files) {
img <- f.read.analyze.volume(file)[,,,1]
mask3D <- mask3D * (!is.na(img))
}
# the mask is a list of indices
mask <- which(mask3D ==1)
```

Next, we loop over scans and collect them into a matrix by grabbing the relevant indices across scans.

```
# now cycle through the data and get the data into a matrix format
dataMatrix <- NULL
for (file in files) {
# load file and make 3D
img <- f.read.analyze.volume(file)[,,,1]
dataMatrix <- rbind(dataMatrix, img[mask])
}
```

```
noScans <- nrow(dataMatrix)
noVoxels <- ncol(dataMatrix)
```

Within Subject Paradigm Analysis

Discussion on Designs

When designing the experiment in task-based fMRI the aim is to maximize the statistical power in detecting activation during the task while assuring the validity of the psychological results. In task-based fMRI, there are two common designs: event-related and block design. Event-related refers to multiple stimuli that are assumed to occur instantaneously and have randomized time between events. A simple task would be to have the participant push a button approximately every 20 seconds to look at motor cortex activation though the events do not have to be equidistant. If a "continuous" task is performed, such as sequential finger tapping, for a certain time interval followed by a short block of rest, the design is referred to as block design. Examples of stimulus functions in each design are presented in Figure 4. The choice of event-related design versus a block design depends on the final goal of the experiment. The block designs lead to higher detection power, however, the subjects may learn the patterns of the experiment which may affect the interpretation of the results. Event-related designs reduce the effects of learning, boredom and other events unrelated to the task while exhibiting loss in detection power (see [17] for more discussion on designs and[38] on optimization of design parameters).

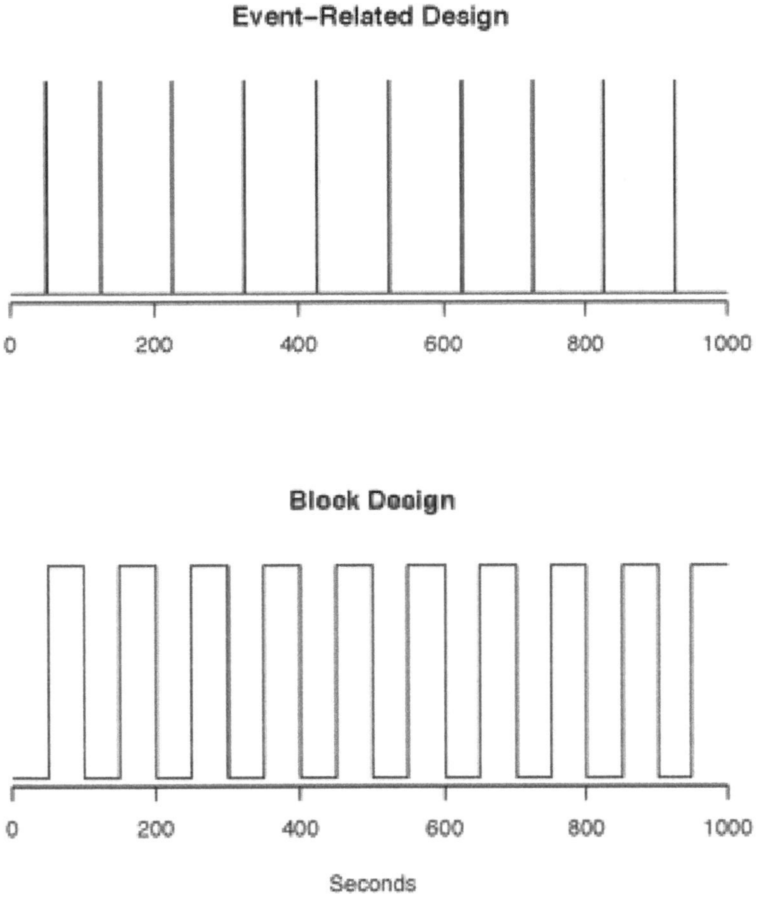

Figure 4. Stimulus vectors for an event-related design (top) and a block design (bottom). The spikes correspond to the onsets of stimuli. There is a sustained period of activity/task in the block design. In both cases, the spacings between events can be unequal.

Suppose we have fMRI data for one subject during a task. The goal is to identify the area of the brain that activates during the task, which is performed by the subject. Typically, the fMRI data can be modeled as a sum of response, drift and noise:$data = response + drift + noise$.

The response (i.e., the BOLD response) is often modeled using a linear time invariant system (see [17] for other ways of modeling the BOLD response). Assume the response is a linear combination of responses from K different stimuli. That is, the response for voxel i, $i=1,\ldots,V$ at time t, $t=1,\ldots,T$, can be written as $x_{i1}(t)\beta_{i1}+\ldots+x_{iK}(t)\beta_{iK}$, where $x_{ik}(t)$ is the response from stimulus k at time t in voxel i, K is the number of stimuli, T is the number of scans and V is the number of non-background voxels in each scan. The response from each stimulus depends on the stimulus function and the HRF, often modeled as a convolution of the two functions $\int h_i(u)s_k(t-u)du$, where $h_i(\cdot)$ is the HRF at voxel $i$and $s_k(\cdot)$ is the stimulus function corresponding to stimulus k. The modeling of the HRF function is an important part of the analysis and is discussed in more detail in Section 5.2.

In addition to the random variability, periodic noise may be present in fMRI data unrelated to the true BOLD response. This can result, for example, from the patient's heartbeat or other systematic effects. As a result, some voxels in the brain may show considerable drifts over time. The drift can be linear or nonlinear, hence a flexible polynomial model is often employed to allow for nonlinear effects in the drift. For example, a polynomial drift of order q for scan t at voxel i can be written as $\sum_{l=0}^{q} z_l \gamma_{il}$, where $z_l = t^{l-1}$. Finally, a random error $\epsilon_i(t)$ is added to the observed data, $Y_i(t)$, at voxel i scan t yielding

$$Y_i(t) = \sum_{k=1}^{K} x_{ik}(t)\beta_{ik} + \sum_{l=1}^{q} z_l \gamma_{il} + \epsilon_i(t).$$

In Section 4.2, we discussed how to construct a matrix from the 4D fMRI array. The resulting matrix is $T \times V$ dimensional: the columns of which correspond to time courses in each voxel and the rows are the spacial images for each scan. We define the vectorized 3D image for each time point t as Y_t and $Y = [Y_1, Y_2, ..., Y_T]^T$,

$$X = \begin{bmatrix} x_{11} & \cdots & x_{1K} & 1 & \cdots & 1 \\ x_{21} & \cdots & x_{2K} & 1 & \cdots & 2^q \\ \vdots & \vdots & \vdots & \vdots & \vdots & \vdots \\ x_{T1} & \cdots & x_{TK} & 1 & \cdots & T^q \end{bmatrix},$$

and

$$\beta = [\beta_1, ..., \beta_K, \gamma_0, ..., \gamma_q]^T, \epsilon = [\epsilon_1, \epsilon_2, ..., \epsilon_T]^T.$$

The general linear model (GLM) can be written in matrix notation as $Y = X\beta + \epsilon$.

Note that, in the above equation, X is derived based on specific hemodynamic assumptions, and β is interpreted as the size of the hemodynamic response (see [39] for more details). The random errors ϵ_t are generally not independent in time. The correlation structure can be specified based on assumptions one is willing to make about the dependence structure over time. Misspecification of the correlation structure in GLM can lead to biased estimation of coefficients. For example, the temporal correlations can be modeled using a first order autoregressive model [40], that is, $\epsilon_t = \rho\epsilon_{t-1} + \xi_i$, where $|\rho| < 1$ and ξ_i are independent and identically distributed. After estimating the parameters in the GLM model, the p-value maps of the β coefficients are thresholded to find the voxels where the corresponding β_{ik} is significantly different from 0.

HRF Modeling.

In Section 1 we discussed the HRF function, an example of which is shown in Figure 1. The estimation of the HRF function is often of interest in fMRI analysis. The HRF model in SPM implies that the HRF is a discretized difference of two gamma functions (see [15], [40])

$$f(u) = f_1(u) - f_2(u)/p_5$$

$$= \frac{\left(\frac{T}{p_3}\right)^{p_1/p_3} u^{p_1/p_3 - 1} \exp(-Tu/p_3)}{\Gamma(p_1/p_3)} - \frac{\left(\frac{T}{p_4}\right)^{p_2/p_4} u^{p_2/p_4 - 1} \exp(-Tu/p_4)}{\Gamma(p_2/p_4)p_5},$$

for $u > 0$. Typically, it is also normalized, either divided by its integral or maximum, to have an average or peak value of 1 respectively. The logic behind this specification of the HRF is that the initial post-stimulus increase in blood oxygenation is represented by f_1, with the subsequent depletion represented by f_2.

Notice that f_1 is a gamma density with shape p_1/p_3 and rate T/p_3, and f_2 is a gamma density with shape p_2/p_4 and rate T/p_5. The SPM documentation defines T as the TR, p_1 as the delay of the response to the onset, p_2 as the delay of the undershoot relative to the onset, p_3 as the dispersion of the response, p_4 as the dispersion of the undershoot and p_5 as the ratio of the response to the undershoot. Conceptually, these are illustrated in Figure 1. We briefly give motivation for these parameters. Note, the mean of density f_1 is p_1/T while the mean of density f_2 is p_2/T. Hence, if p_1 and p_2 are given in seconds and T is seconds per scan, p_1/T can be thought of as the delay to the mean (not modal) response in TR units while p_2/T is the delay to the mean undershoot in TR units. Given that the gamma variance is $p_1 p_3/T^2$, and the mean is p_1/T, p_3/T is the factor by which the response gamma distribution mean is scaled to obtain its variance. Similarly, p_4/T is the factor by which the undershoot gamma distribution mean is scaled to obtain its variance. Since the integral of f_1 and f_2 are 1, p_5 is the ratio of the two functions comprising the HRF. Note, it is not, as its name suggests, the ratio of the peak value of f_1 to the peak value of f_2.

The following example illustrates the use of the fmri. stimulus function in R to create the expected HRF as described by [40] and [6]. More appropriate choices of an HRF, such as spatially varying HRF and dynamic sets of basis functions may also be used [41]. For instance, finite impulse response models and Fourier basis sets are more flexible alternatives to the canonical HRF.

The R package fmri can be used to analyze fMRI data from one subject and identify activation during a task. In the following example, suppose imageFile.nii is a NIfTI data file. We first extract the 4D numeric array using the function read. NIFTI. The onset times of the stimulus (5.25, 21.45, 100.12, 223.5) and the durations of ON stimuli in scans (5, 5, 10, 10) are known from the experimental design. Next, we create the expected response for each stimulus (defined by $x_k(t)$ above, assuming that the HRF is the same in each voxel) using the function fmri.stimulus. The function fmri.design is invoked to create the design matrix. Finally, the coefficients of the hemodynamic response to the stimulus are evaluated in the GLM [42].

```
library(fmri)
imageFileName <- "pathToImageFile/imageFile.nii"
img <- read.NIFTI(imageFileName) onsets <- c(5.25, 21.45, 100.12, 223.5)
dur <- c(5, 5, 10, 10)
hrf <- fmri.stimulus(scans = img$dim0[4],
onsets = onsets,
durations = dur)
x <- fmri.design(hrf, order =2)
```

For event-related designs, the durations of the events would be considered instantaneous. Hence, the duration in the function fmri.stimulus would be 0. The example above is an example of a block design. The argument order in the function fmri.design is the order of the polynomial drift term of the design matrix, the default value of the order of the polynomial is 2. If there are K experimental stimuli, there will be k expected BOLD responses $hrf_1, hrf_2,...,hrf_K$. Note that in this example K=1. The design matrix can be created as follows

```
x <- fmri.design(cbind(hrf_1, …, hrf_K), order =2)
```

Given the design matrix, we may conduct voxel-wise analysis of the brain using regression models to identify the areas activated during the task. Suppose Y is the $voxel \times time$ matrix. Then we can use the following code for the analysis with the design matrix above via the fmri.lm function in fmri package.

```
model <- fmri.lm(img, x, keep = "all")
```

The argument keep in the function fmri.lm describes the parts of the output returned by the function. The default is keep="all", where residuals are included in the returned object. Alternatively, we can perform similar analysis via the lm function as follows. First, extract the data array and construct the data matrix as discussed in Section 4.2.

```
ttt <- extract.data(img)
mask <- img$mask
dataMatrix <- NULL
noScans <- img$dim[4]
for(t in 1:noScans) –
scan <- ttt[,,,t]
dataMatrix <- rbind(dataMatrix, scan[mask])
}
```

We can now run the lm function for each voxel and extract the coefficients and p-values. Note, we only use the lm function for didactic reasons, as the calculations can be done more efficiently using other approaches.

```
lms <- apply(dataMatrix, 2, function(y) lm(y~x))
# obtain the summary statistics for each voxel
summaries <- lapply(lms, summary)
# Coefficients
coefs <- lapply(summaries, function(x) x$coefficients)
# Intercept map
int_vals <- sapply(coefs, function(x) x[" (Intercept)", ])
int_est <- int_vals["Estimate",]
int_pvals <- int_vals["Pr(>|t|)",]
# Slope map
beta_vals <- sapply( coefs, function(x) x[2,])
beta_est <- beta_vals["Estimate",]
beta_pvals <- beta_vals["Pr(>|t|)",]
```

As a result of fitting the linear model, we obtain coefficients and their p-values for each voxel. The resulting p-values can be thresholded using a multiple comparisons correction procedure. Finally, the map can be saved in an image format to visualize the areas that are significantly associated with the task.

Between-Subjects Random Effect Models

In the fMRI literature, "random effect analysis" refers to an inter-subject analysis of paradigm-related contrast images. Specifically, in the first stage, subject-specific regression models are fit, relating the HRF-convolved design matrix to the fMRI time series at each voxel separately. Coefficients or estimable linear combinations of coefficients (so-called contrasts) are obtained from the fit. For each subject, as there is one contrast per voxel (one coefficient per voxel), the resulting collection of voxel-specific contrast values is referred to as the subject specific contrast image, and is usually stored as a 3D image. Random effect models then analyze these images across subjects. That is, they compare inter-subject variation in estimated hemodynamic response to the paradigm to variation in covariates, diagnoses, treatments, and so on. The name "random effect analysis" is given as the process is an approximation of formal random effects.

Example: Group Activation

Below, we consider a simple form of random effect analysis. We take the subject-specific contrasts and test whether their voxel specific mean is different from 0. One of the SPM datasets discussed in Section 4.1 is used to illustrate the results. We will assume that the following steps have been completed using the code provided in Section 4.2:1) a mask containing nonbackground voxels has been created, 2) the mask has been applied to every subject's contrast map resulting in a vectorized map, 3) the data have been concatenated into a matrix containing noSubjects (number of subjects) rows and noVoxels (number of voxels) columns, 4) the data matrix is assigned to the variable dataMatrix. In our case, there are 12 subjects and roughly 50,000 non-background voxels. As a first test, consider a test of 0 mean applied at each voxel.

```
# apply the function t.test to every column (voxel)
ttest.out <- apply(dataMatrix, 2,
function(x) {
temp <- t.test(x)
c(temp$statistic, temp$p.value)})
# label the rows
rownames(ttest.out) <- c("statistic", "pvalue")
```

Figure 5 displays the p-value histogram. Next, we threshold these p-values using the false discovery rate (FDR) threshold in AnalyzeFMRI package.

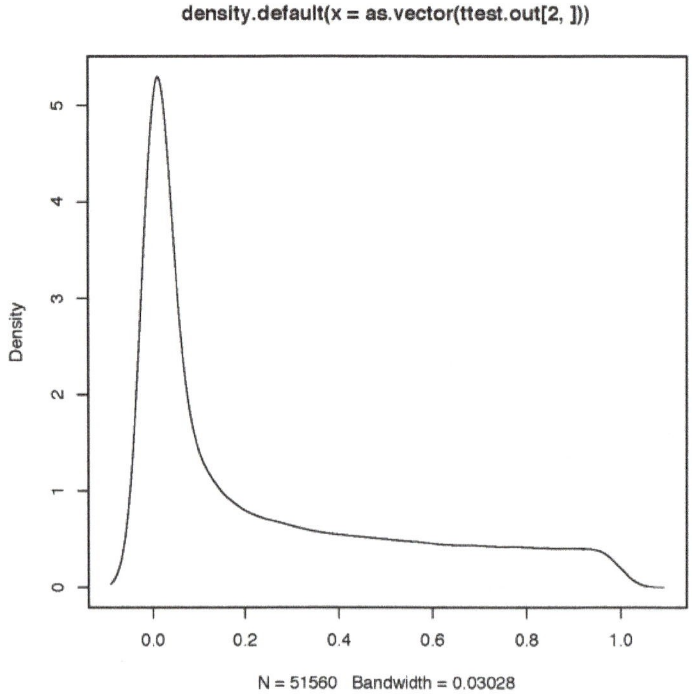

Figure 5. P-value histogram from a group-level test.

Threshold <- Threshold.FDR(ttest.out[1,],

q =.05,

cV.type =2,

type = "t",

df1 = noScans - 1)

Now we can create an image where we plot the thresholded p-values overlaid on a template brain. The resulting image can be plotted using the image function in R as described in Section 8. A slice from the resulting image overlaid on a template brain is shown in Figure 6.

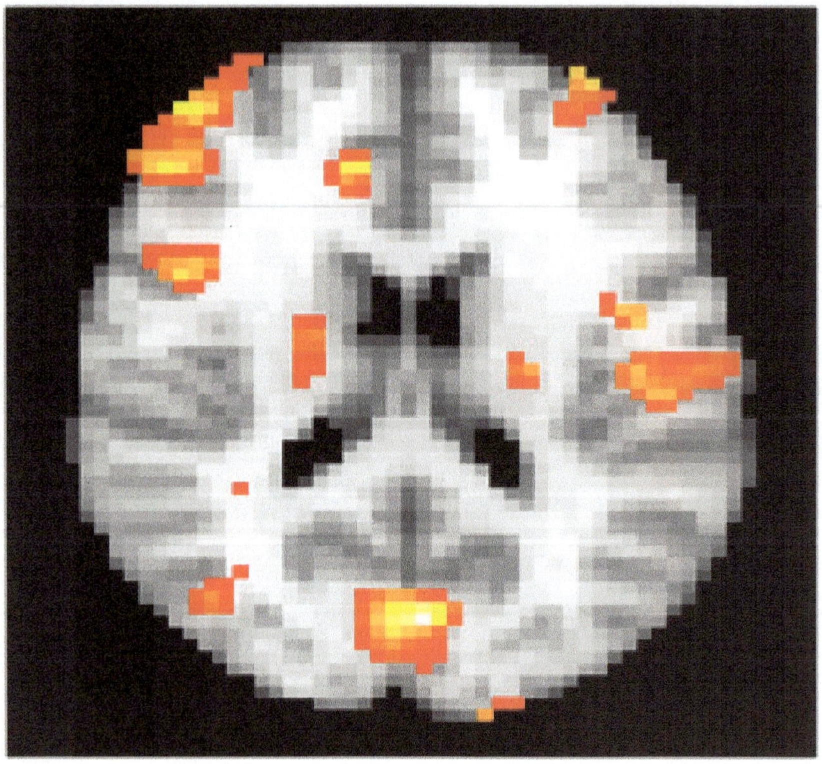

Figure 6. A slice of the thresholded output map overlaid on a template brain using the image() function.

```
outputImage <- array(0, imageDim)
toSave <- ttest.out[1,] >= Threshold
outputImage[mask[toSave]] <- ttest.out[1, toSave]
```

Example: Permutation Testing

Permutation testing [53] is often used to identify changes in activation in a group of subjects based on a covariate, such as disease diagnoses. As in example 6.1, suppose the mask has been created and the images have been vectorized and saved in the matrix dataMatrix. In addition, each subject's disease status is given as 0 for control or 1 for disease group. For any non-background voxel, if there is no difference in the experimental effect between the control and disease groups, then the labeling of each subject as 0 or 1 should be arbitrary. The labels can be permuted to obtain the t-statistic (e.g., mean difference between the two groups) for that voxel corresponding to each permutation. The distribution of the resulting test statistics for all permutations is often referred to as the permutation distribution.

```
# Number of subjects
n.s <- 12
n<- 2^n.s
# Matrix of all possible combinations of 1 and 0 for each subject
perm.mat <- matrix(1,n.s,n)
for(i in 1:n.s){
p<- n/(2^i)
j<- 1
while(j<(2^i)){
perm.mat[i,(p*j+1):(p*(j+1))] <- 0
j<- j+2
}}
```

The R function expand.grid() can also be used to obtain the grid for the permutation test above. For illustration purposes, we compute permutation distributions for two randomly selected voxels.

```
# Randomly select two voxels
perm.noVoxels =2
sub.dataMatrix = dataMatrix[,sample(noVoxels, size = perm.noVoxels)]
# Find the distribution of the t-statistic for each permutation
permutation.dist <- matrix(0, n, perm.noVoxels)
for(i in 1:n){
data.temp <- perm.mat[,i]*sub.dataMatrix
ttest.out <- apply(data.temp, 2,
function(x) {
temp <- t.test(x)
temp$statistic
})
permutation.dist[i,] <- ttest.out
}
```

The permutation distributions of the t-statistics for the two randomly selected voxels are shown in Figure 7. Using the permutation distribution, one can compute the p-value of observing the true labeling of disease status and make a decision about whether to reject the null hypothesis or not.

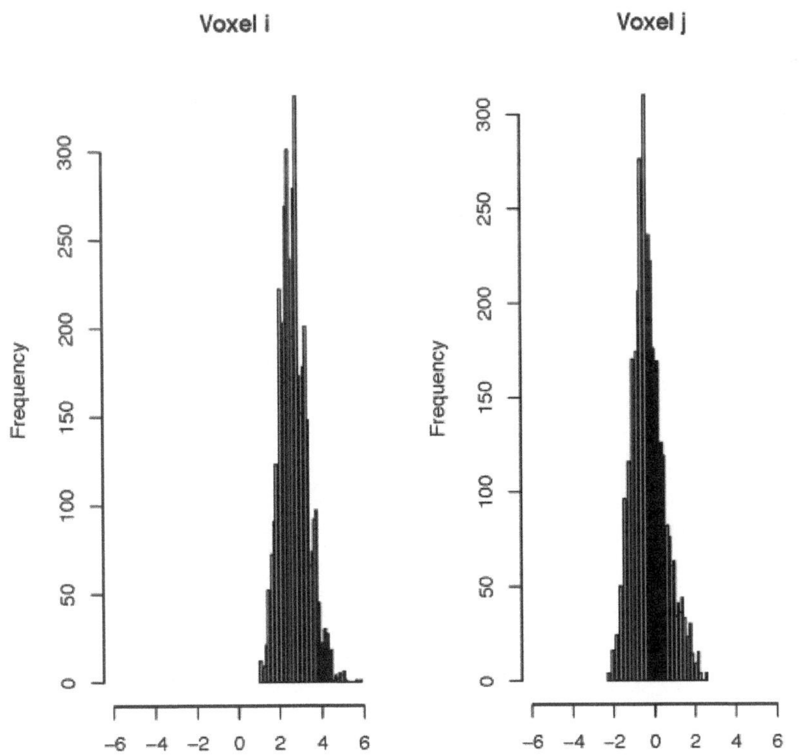

Figure 7. Permutation histograms of t-statistics for two voxels.

Connectivity Analysis

Functional connectivity refers to the analysis of correlations of measured brain function between potentially remote areas of the brain [15]. In fMRI, this translates to evaluating correlations, or perhaps other forms of associations between voxels or regions. We emphasize that fMRI represents only one modality to investigate functional connectivity. Others include: EEG, MEG and PET. When investigating connectivity, it is important to consider the goals of the analysis and the spatial/temporal resolution of the technology under study [15]. Such analyses have become so influential in fMRI, that they have been abbreviated as fc-fMRI (for functional connectivity fMRI). A subset of such analyses considers functional connectivity while a subject is at rest in the scanner, and is often referred to as resting state functional connectivity (rs-fc-fMRI). Much of the analysis of rs-fc-fMRI centers around the so-called "default mode network", a hypothesized brain network that is activated in subjects at rest [44].

Connectivity and Preprocessing

The analysis of brain connectivity data requires special preprocessing that may be useful for paradigm-related studies, but is crucial for the study of connectivity. Most notably it is addressing background nuisance signals. These include signals related to cardiac function and respiration. Because one is concerned with correlations between voxels, such background effects can create spurious relationships that are not of interest. In contrast, they are less crucial in a paradigm-related study, since the paradigm is likely not aliased with the nuisance signal, though to the contrary, they are probably not orthogonal to the paradigm. In event-related designs where events are presented randomly, the randomization mechanism helps ensure a lack of relationship with nuisance signals.

There are several methods for addressing nuisance signals in fc-fMRI. These include a connectivity analysis of the ventricles, the spaces in the brain filled with cerebrospinal fluid. There should be no measured connectivity of interest in the ventricles, hence any correlations found here and elsewhere likely represent nuisance signals. A similar approach would look at white matter, though such analyses would be highly dependent on very accurate registration. These issues should be taken into account when preprocessing the data.

Seed Voxel Approaches

Assuming that there are no nuisance signals in the brain, the correlations of the fMRI time courses can be computed for each pair of voxels. The number of these pairs is often very large and the brute force computation of the correlations may be computationally expensive. Instead, one can analyze regions of interest (ROI), which can be obtained, for example, by using the anatomy of the brain or by independent component analysis as described in Section 7.3. For each ROI, a seed voxel can be chosen as one of the voxels in the ROI or as the average time course of all voxels in the ROI. The correlation map of the seed voxel with the remaining voxels in the brain is called the connectivity map. The obtained connectivity maps may be used, for instance, to compare the connectivity of an ROI between subjects in two disease groups.

Generally, after calculating the raw correlation values, a Fisher R to Z transform is performed before analyzing the correlation map. The transform is defined as

$$z = \frac{1}{2}\frac{log(1+r)}{log(1-r)},$$

where r is a correlation value. The resulting connectivity maps should have approximately normally distributed values. Standardizing this matrix by the standard error $\frac{1}{\sqrt{T-3}}$, where T is the number of time points used to compute the correlation, is frequently used, especially when different participants have different lengths of scans. These maps then can be analyzed using random Markov field corrections for multiple comparisons, using t-tests or the nonparametric rank-sum test, or other methods for testing differences across groups[15].

Singular Value Decomposition and Independent Component Analysis

Since the fMRI data are very large and complex, dimension reduction techniques are often used to identify important signals in the data as well as help with visualization. For example, singular value decomposition, a well-known statistical dimension reduction technique, is often used for preprocessing the data before testing or inference.

Another commonly used dimension reduction method is independent component analysis (ICA, see [45] for an extensive overview). It is mainly used in fMRI to obtain functional networks in the brain. It has been implemented both for resting-state and task-related fMRI experiments. Here we show the use of ICA for an attention task using one of the SPM example datasets [46]. Four different conditions were explored: fixation, attention, no attention and stationary.

There are several methods one can use for applying ICA. For instance, the R package AnalyzeFMRI has a function f.ica.fmri that is based on the fastICA algorithm [45]. If the data are in Analyze format, where each 3D scan is saved in a separate file, the individual scans per time point have to be combined into one 4D image in order to use f.ica.fmri. Here, the 4D image is saved as fullimg.img, where one of the dimensions is time and the other three are the image dimensions.

```
library(AnalyzeFMRI)
# Specify the number of components that should be estimated
m<-10
f<- f.ica.fmri("fullimg.img", n.comp =m)
```

The fastICA package in R can be used directly for ICA analysis as follows. We create a matrix dataMatrix that is a 2D ($time \times voxel$) version of the fMRI data as described in Section 4.2, and apply the fastICA function to obtain m independent components.

```
library(fastICA)
f<- fastICA(t(dataMatrix), n.comp =m)
```

The variable $f\$S$ contains the collection of the independent components. Next, we back-reconstruct each of the components as an image. The networks are identified as the regions that are highly activated in the corresponding independent component. In other words, to obtain the brain networks we can threshold the values of each column in $f\$S$. We will use a simple thresholding tool here by including the values greater than a threshold θ. We also save the arrays in image format for visualization. Note, we assume imageDim constains the image dimensions as computed in Section 4.2.

```
theta <- 2
S <- f$S
S[S <= theta] <- 0
imageDimComp <- c(imageDim, m)
img <- array( 0, dim = imageDimComp)
for(i in 1:m){
temp2 <- array(0, imageDim)
temp2[mask] <- S[,i]
img[,,,i] <- temp2[,,]
}
f.write.analyze(img,
file = "fica",
size = "float",
pixdim = c(3, 3, 3, 1, 0, 0, 0),
originator = c(27, 38, 18, 0, 0))
```

Figure 8 shows a slice of the default brain network obtained by the above fastICA algorithm thresholded and overlaid on a template brain.

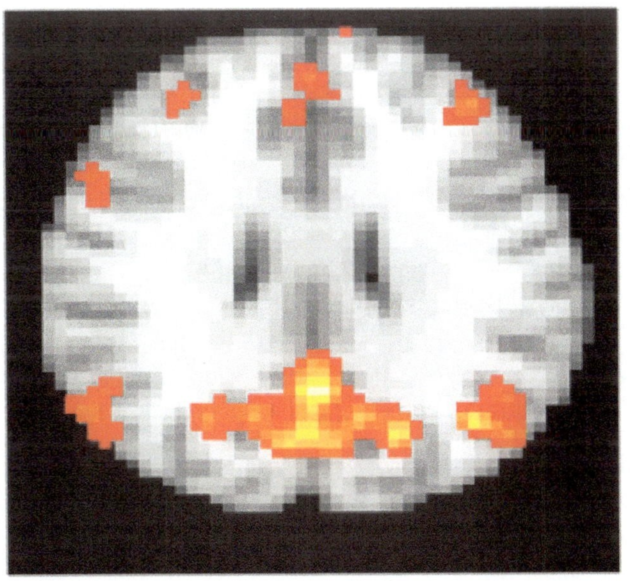

Figure 8. The default brain network obtained via fastICA and overlaid on a template brain.

Group ICA

Group ICA is the extension of the ICA method used to obtain brain networks from fMRI datasets in a population. The method was first introduced by [47] and has since been widely used in the neuroimaging literature [48], [49]. The method is based on concatenating the two-dimensional $time \times voxel$ matrices observed for each subject and applying principal component analysis to reduce the dimension to the desired number of components. Then the single subject ICA algorithm is applied to the resulting matrix to obtain the common independent components for the group.

There are two different choices for matrix concatenation: one assumes that the spatial brain networks are statistically independent (spatial group ICA), the other assumes that the time courses are statistically independent (temporal group ICA). Spatial group ICA, which assumes common spatial networks across subjects yet different temporal mixing matrices is more frequently used. By assuming common spatial maps, one can concatenate all subjects' data in the temporal domain, and apply ICA to the aggregated data matrix. Below is an example for spatial group ICA:

```
fileDir <- "pathToImageFile"
files <- dir(fileDir, pattern = "*.img", full.names= TRUE)
groupDataMatrix <- NULL
for (file in files) {
img <- f.read.analyze.volume(file)
imageDataMatrix <- t(apply(img, 4, function(imgi) imgi[mask]))
rmeans <- rowMeans(imageDataMatrix)
cmeans <- colMeans(imageDataMatrix)
imageDataMatrix <- sweep(imageDataMatrix, 2, cmeans, "-")
imageDataMatrix <- sweep(imageDataMatrix, 1, rmeans, "-")
groupDataMatrix <- rbind(groupDataMatrix, imageDataMatrix)
}
m <- 20
f <- fastICA(t(groupDataMatrix), n.comp = m)
```

Displaying Results

Different modalities can be used for displaying the results obtained by the analysis of fMRI data. In most cases, a group of voxels in the brain is found by the analyses and can be visualized by overlaying the voxels on a template brain. For instance, in the case of ICA, the functional networks obtained can be displayed by overlaying the networks on a template brain. In this section, we will discuss only a few of the functions that can be used for visualization in R or other software.

Within R

The function image () in R can be used for plotting the 2D images for each value of the third dimension to display the images for each slice of the brain. The rgl and misc3d packages have tools for creating 3D renderings and isosurfaces directly in R. We have found that images generally need to be slightly downsampled to avoid memory issues. Usually, this does not impact the appearance of the graphics dramatically. The misc3d package has some functions for plotting images and rendering in 3D activation maps for fMRI (http://www.tandfonline.com/doi/abs/10.1198/jcgs.2010.191ed). Contour3d and image3d are useful functions for displaying results and embedding 3D objects into PDFs or RGL objects.

When plotting images in R, a few important points should be taken into consideration. When overlaying selected voxels on a template brain, note that the template brain and the statistical image results: 1) may not have the same array dimensions, 2) voxels may not correspond to the same real world dimensions, such as the voxels in the template being 1 mm^3 while the voxels in the statistical image being 3 mm^3, 3) the images may not have the same origin. This information is contained in the raw and template image's header files. The origin is the point that is used to match images. Hence, when overlaying images if one appears shifted, it is probably due to incorrectly set values of the image origins. Another problem that can occur is that the voxels are not square. For example, the Z physical dimension (in the direction from the feet to the head), is often different than that of the other two. If this is not accounted for, the images will appear strange, not unlike a geographical map with an incorrect contrast ratio. These issues can all be handled in R.

Finally, when plotting the image via the image function, the number of colors used in plotting is 12 by default. That number can be increased by changing the parameter col (e.g., col = heat.colors(100)) to obtain a smoother image. In addition, it is common to plot fMRI data in greyscale as shown in Figure 2, hence the color spectrum can be changed to col = grey.colors(100) in the image function to achieve that.

Third Party Software

There are several visualization software platforms that can be used for examining fMRI data. They vary from software for quick visualization to 3D renderings of the brain with complicated visualizations of slices and cross-sections. For instance, 3D Slicer and Mipav can be used to obtain 3D renderings of the brain overlaid on template brains. These software platforms can also be used for masking the brain or cropping regions of interest as well as registration. The videos at http://www.youtube.com/watch?v=GNsWRnm7gQw show a step-by-step illustration of 3D Slicer or Mipav for visualization and analyses.

FURTHER READING

Below we give an incomplete list of papers in the area.

- A good starting point for fMRI is the SPM book [15]
- Nicole Lazar's introduction to fMRI [50] and book [18]
- Martin Lindquist's manuscript on fMRI [17]
- Thomas Nichol's overview paper on permutation testing in fMRI [43]
- Vincent Calhoun's introductions to ICA and group ICA in fMRI [51], [47]
- Jonathan Taylor's manuscript about the HRF [52]
- Technical papers about random field theory are [53], [54]
- An accessible discussion including permutation testing can be found in [55] and[56]
- A somewhat dated but still very relevant, overview of the analysis of fMRI data [57]
- A more recent tutorial can be found here [58]
- An expository article on R and neuroimaging [59]
- Our work on singular value decomposition for fMRI [60]

This manuscript gives an admittedly very brief introduction and quick start guide for fMRI. For those interested in pursuing further development in the area, we recommend investigating processing pipelines as a next important step.

Author Contributions

Analyzed the data: AE SL JM BC. Contributed reagents/materials/analysis tools: JJP SHM. Wrote the paper: AE SL JM BC.

REFERENCES

1. R Development Core Team (2011) R: a language and environment for statistical computing. R Foundation for Statistical Computing, Vienna, Austria. Available:http:// www. R-project. org/. ISBN 3-900051-07-0.
2. Avants BB, Tustison N, Song G (2009) Advanced normalization tools (ANTS). Insight J.
3. Bordier C, Dojat M, Lafayede Micheaux P (2009) AnalyzeFMRI: an R package to perform statistical analysis on fMRI datasets. Software: R Package, AnalyzeFMRI, version: 1–1.
4. Whitcher B, Schmid V, Thornton A (2011) oro. nifti: Rigorous-NIfTI input/output. R package version 02 6.
5. Whitcher B (2010) oro. dicom: Rigorous-DICOM input/output. R package version 02 7.
6. Polzehl J, Tabelow K (2007) fmri: A package for analyzing fMRI data. R News 7: 13–17. doi: 10. 1016/j. neuroimage. 2006. 06. 029
7. Welvaert M, Durnez J, Moerkerke B, Verdoolaege G, Rosseel Y (2011) neurosim: an R package for generating fMRI data. Journal of Statistical Software 44: 1–18.
8. Weeda W (2010) arf3ds4: Activated region fitting, fMRI data analysis (3d). R package version: 2–4.
9. Granert O (2010) Rniftilib: R interface to nifticlib (v1. 1. 0). R package version: 00–29.
10. Clayden J (2011) RNiftyReg: Medical image registration using the NiftyReg library. R package version 03 1.
11. Achard S (2010). brainwaver: basic wavelet analysis of multivariate time series with visualization and parameratization using graph theory. R package version 1. 5.
12. Clayden JD, Maniega SM, Storkey AJ, King MD, Bastin ME, et al. (2011) Tractor: Magnetic resonance imaging and tractography with R. Journal of Statistical Software. 44: 1–18.
13. Whitcher B (2007) Waveslim: basic wavelet routines for one-, two-and threedimensional signal processing. R package version 1.
14. da Silva AF (2010) cudabayesreg: Bayesian computation in CUDA. The R Journal 2: 48–55.
15. Friston KJ, Ashburner J, Stefan K, Nichols TE, Penny W, editors (2007) Statistical Parametric Mapping The Analysis of Functional Brain Images. Academic Press.
16. Tabelow K, Whitcher B (2011) Special volume on magnetic resonance imaging in R. Journal of Statistical Software 44: 1–6.
17. Lindquist MA (2008) The statistical analysis of fMRI data. Statistical Science 23: 439–464. doi: 10. 1214/09-sts282

18. Lazar NA (2008) The statistical analysis of functional MRI data. Springer Verlag.

19. Callaghan P (1991) Principles of nuclear magnetic resonance microscopy. Oxford University Press.

20. Zhou J, Wilson DA, Ulatowski JA, Traystman RJ, van Zijl PCM (2001) Two-compartment exchange model for perfusion quantification using arterial spin tagging. Journal of Cerebral Blood Flow & Metabolism 21: 440–455. doi: 10. 1097/00004647-200104000-00013

21. Prince JL, Links JM (2006) Medical imaging signals and systems. Pearson Prentice Hall.

22. Logothetis N, Pauls J, Augath M, Trinath T, Oeltermann A, et al. (2001) Neurophysiological investigation of the basis of the fMRI signal. Nature 412: 150–157. doi: 10. 1038/35084005

23. Logothetis NK, Wandell BA (2004) Interpreting the BOLD signal. Annual Review Physiology 66: 735–769. doi: 10. 1146/annurev. physiol. 66. 082602. 092845

24. Ogawa S, Lee T, Nayak A, Glynn P (1990) Oxygenation-sensitive contrast in magnetic resonance image of rodent brain at high magnetic fields. Magnetic Resonance in Medicine 14: 68–78. doi: 10. 1002/mrm. 1910140108

25. Ogawa S, Tank D, Menon R, Ellermann J, Kim S, et al. (1992) Intrinsic signal changes accompanying sensory stimulation: functional brain mapping with magnetic resonance imaging. Proceedings of the National Academy of Sciences 89: 5951. doi: 10. 1073/pnas. 89. 13. 5951

26. Turner R, Bihan D, Moonen C, Despres D, Frank J (1991) Echo-planar time course MRI of cat brain oxygenation changes. Magnetic Resonance in Medicine 22: 159–166. doi: 10. 1002/mrm. 1910220117

27. Turner R, Jezzard P, Wen H, Kwong K, Le Bihan D, et al. (1993) Functional mapping of the human visual cortex at 4 and 1. 5 tesla using deoxygenation contrast EPI. Magnetic resonance in medicine 29: 277–279. doi: 10. 1002/mrm. 1910290221

28. Aguirre GK, Zarahn E, D'Esposito M (1998) The variability of human, BOLD hemodynamic responses. Neuroimage 8: 360–369. doi: 10. 1006/nimg. 1998. 0369

29. Witt ST, Laird AR, Meyeranda ME (2008) Functional neuroimaging correlates of finger-tapping task variations: An ALE meta-analysis. NeuroImage 42: 343–356. doi: 10. 1016/j. neuroimage. 2008. 04. 025

30. Liu T, Frank L, Wong E, Buxton R (2001) Detection power, estimation efficiency, and predictability in event-related fMRI. NeuroImage 13: 759–773. doi: 10. 1006/nimg. 2000. 0728

31. Mennes M, Biswal B, Castellanos F, Milham M (2013) Making data sharing work: The FCP/INDI experience. NeuroImage 82: 683–91. doi: 10. 1016/j. neuroimage. 2012. 10. 064

32. Miller MI, Christensen GE, Amit Y, Grenander U (1993) Mathematical textbook of deformable neuroanatomies. Proceedings of the National Academy of Sciences 90: 11944–11948. doi: 10. 1073/pnas. 90. 24. 11944

33. Frackowiak R (2004) Human brain function. Academic Press.

34. Younes L (2010) Shapes and Di_eomorphisms. Springer Verlag.

35. Chialvo DR (2010) Emergent complex neural dynamics. Nature Physics 6: 744–750. doi: 10. 1038/nphys1803

36. Tabelow K, Polzehl J, Voss H, Spokoiny V (2006) Analyzing fMRI experiments with structural adaptive smoothing procedures. NeuroImage 33: 55–62. doi: 10. 1016/j. neuroimage. 2006. 06. 029

37. Henson R, Shallice T, Gorno-Tempini ML, Dolan R (2002) Face repetition effects in implicit and explicit memory tests as measured by fMRI. Cerebral Cortex 12: 178–186. doi: 10. 1093/cercor/12. 2. 178

38. Wager TD, Nichols TE (2003) Optimization of experimental design in fMRI: a general framework using a genetic algorithm. Neuroimage 18: 293–309. doi: 10. 1016/s1053-8119(02)00046-0

39. Lu Y, Bagshaw AP, Grova C, Kobayashi E, Dubeau F, et al. (2006) Using voxel-specific hemodynamic response function in EEG-fMRI data analysis. NeuroImage 32: 238–247. doi: 10. 1016/j. neuroimage. 2005. 11. 040

40. Worsley KJ, Liao CH, Aston J, Petre V, Duncan GH, et al. (2002) A general statistical analysis for fMRI data. NeuroImage 15: 1–15. doi: 10. 1006/nimg. 2001. 0933

41. Friston K, Frith C, Turner R, Frackowiak R (1995) Characterizing evoked hemodynamics with fMRI. Neuroimage 2: 157–165. doi: 10. 1006/nimg. 1995. 1018

42. Tabelow K, Polzehl J (2011) Statistical parametric maps for functional MRI experiments in R: The package fmri. Journal of Statistical Software 44: 1–21.

43. Nichols TE, Holmes AP (2002) Nonparametric permutation tests for functional neuroimaging: a primer with examples. Human Brain Mapping 15: 1–25. doi: 10. 1002/hbm. 1058

44. Buckner RL, Andrews-Hanna JR, Schacter DL (2008) The brain's default network: Anatomy, function, and relevance to disease. Ann NY Acad Sci 1124: 1–38. doi: 10. 1196/annals. 1440. 011

45. Hyvärinen A, Karhunen J, Oja E (2001) Independent Component Analysis. Wiley Inter-Science.

46. Büchel C, Friston K (1997) Modulation of connectivity in visual pathways by attention: cortical interactions evaluated with structural equation modelling and fMRI. Cerebral Cortex 7: 768–778. doi: 10. 1093/cercor/7. 8. 768

47. Calhoun VD, Adali T, Pearlson GD, Pekar JJ (2001) A method for making group inferences from functional MRI data using independent component analysis. Human Brain Mapping 14: 140–151. doi: 10. 1002/hbm. 1048

48. Beckmann C, DeLuca M, Devlin J, Smith S (2005) Investigations into resting-state connectivity using independent component analysis. Philosophical Transactions of the Royal Society B: Biological Sciences 360: 1001–1013. doi: 10. 1098/rstb. 2005. 1634

49. Guo Y, Pagnoni G (2008) A unified framework for group independent component analysis for multi-subject fMRI data. NeuroImage 42: 1078–1093. doi: 10. 1016/j. neuroimage. 2008. 05. 008

50. Lazar NA, Eddy WF, Genovese CR, Welling J (2001) Statistical issues in fMRI for brain imaging. International Statistical Review 69: 105–127. doi: 10. 1111/j. 1751-5823. 2001. tb00482. x

51. Calhoun VD, Adali T, Hansen LK, Larsen J, Pekar JJ (2003) ICA of functional MRI data: an overview. In: Fourth International Symposium on Independent Component Analysis and Blind Source Separation. pp. 281–288.

52. Worsley KJ, Taylor JE (2006) Detecting fMRI activation allowing for unknown latency of the hemodynamic response. Neuroimage 29: 649–654. doi: 10. 1016/j. neuroimage. 2005. 07. 032

53. Siegmund DO, Worsley KJ (1995) Testing for a signal with unknown location and scale in a stationary gaussian random field. The Annals of Statistics 23: 608–639. doi: 10. 1214/aos/1176324539

54. Worsley KJ (1995) Estimating the number of peaks in a random field using the Hadwiger characteristic of excursion sets, with applications to medical images. The Annals of Statistics 23: 640–669. doi: 10. 1214/aos/1176324540

55. Hayasaka S, Phan KL, Liberzon I, Worsley KJ, Nichols TE (2004) Nonstationary cluster-size inference with random field and permutation methods. Neuroimage 22: 676–687. doi: 10. 1016/j. neuroimage. 2004. 01. 041

56. Worsley KJ, Marrett S, Neelin P, Vandal AC, Friston KJ, et al. (1996) A unified statistical approach for determining significant signals in images of cerebral activation. Human Brain Mapping 4: 58–73. doi: 10. 1002/(sici)1097-0193(1996)4:1<58::aid-hbm4>3. 3. co;2-l

57. Worsley KJ (1997) An overview and some new developments in the statistical analysis of PET and fMRI data. Human Brain Mapping 5: 254–258. doi: 10. 1002/(sici)1097-0193(1997)5:4<254::aid-hbm9>3. 0. co;2-2

58. Smith SM (2004) Overview of fMRI analysis. British Journal of Radiology 77: S167. doi: 10. 1259/bjr/33553595

59. Tabelow K, Clayden JD, Lafaye de Micheaux P, Polzehl J, Schmid VJ, et al. (2011) Image analysis and statistical inference in neuroimaging with R. Neuroimage 55: 1686–93. doi: 10. 1016/j. neuroimage. 2011. 01. 013

60. Caffo BS, Crainiceanu CM, Verduzco G, Joel S, Mostofsky SH, et al. (2010) Two-stage decompositions for the analysis of functional connectivity for fMRI with application to Alzheimer's disease risk. NeuroImage 51: 1140–1149. doi: 10. 1016/j. neuroimage. 2010. 02. 081

CHAPTER 16 FLUCTUATING MINDS: SPONTANEOUS PSYCHOPHYSICAL VARIABILITY DURING MIND-WANDERING

Rodrigo A. Henríquez[1,2,3,4], Ana B. Chica[5] , Pablo Billeke[6] , Paolo Bartolomeo[1,2,3,4,7]

[1] Inserm U 1127, F-75013, Paris, France

[2] Sorbonne Universités, UPMC Univ Paris 06, UMR S 1127, F- 75013, Paris, France

[3] CNRS, UMR 7225, F-75013, Paris, France

[4] Institut du Cerveau et de la Moelle épinière, ICM, F-75013, Paris, France

[5] Department of Experimental Psychology, and Brain, Mind, and Behaviour Research Center, University of Granada, Granada, Spain

[6] Research Center for Social Complexity, Faculty of Government, University of Desarrollo, Santiago, Chile

[7] Department of Psychology, Catholic University Milan, Milan, Italy

ABSTRACT

Mind-wandering is the occasional distraction we experience while performing a cognitive task. It arises without any external precedent, varies over time, and interferes with the processing of sensory information. Here, we asked whether the transition from the on-task state to mind-wandering is a gradual process or an abrupt event. We developed a new experimental approach, based on the continuous, online assessment of individual psychophysical performance. Probe questions were asked whenever response times (RTs) exceeded 2 standard deviations from the participant's average RT. Results showed that mind-wandering reports were generally preceded by slower RTs, as compared to trials preceding on-task reports. Mind-wandering episodes could be reliably predicted from the response time difference between the last and the second-to-last trials. Thus, mind-wandering reports follow an abrupt increase in behavioral variability, lasting between 2.5 and 10 seconds.

INTRODUCTION

Mind-wandering, the occasional distraction we often experience while performing a cognitive task, is a self-generated condition, because it arises without any external precedent, varies over time spontaneously, and often interferes with the online processing of sensory information [1,2,3]. The very existence of mind-wandering supports the view that perception depends not only on its inputs, but also on the internal variability of the system.

Citation: Henríquez RA, Chica AB, Billeke P, Bartolomeo P (2016) Fluctuating Minds: Spontaneous Psychophysical Variability during Mind-Wandering. PLoS ONE 11(2): e0147174. doi:10.1371/journal.pone.0147174.

Studies have addressed mind-wandering using different experimental definitions, e.g. task-unrelated thoughts [4,5], stimulus-independent thoughts [6], incidental self-processing [7], inner speech [8] momentary attentional lapses [9], or spontaneous thoughts [10,11]. Patterns of performance related to mind-wandering include variations in response times (RTs) during a sustained attention task [12], and increased response variability on a metronome response task [13,14]. Studies on the neural bases of mind wandering have described reduced amplitude of event-related potentials (ERPs) such as P300, MMN, and P2 components [1,15,16], as well as the activation of the brain default network [10,11]. A causal role of the dorsolateral prefrontal cortex has also been proposed [17].

Mind wandering is often explored by asking participants thought sampling questions (TSQs) on their state of mind, while they perform a sustained attention task [18]. However, this method is not optimal to assess whether the transition to mind-wandering is a process that develops gradually, or it is a unique event that triggers a global cognitive change. Moreover, the temporal rate of presentation of the TSQs can affect the likelihood of mind-wandering reports, because people are more likely to report mind-wandering as the time between TSQs increases [14].

In the present study, we aimed at defining some of the psychophysical conditions necessary for mind-wandering to occur. We used a new experimental approach, inspired by the classic sustained attention to response task (SART) [19]. We identified online RT outliers exceeding 2 SD from the participant's mean RT. After each RT outlier, a TSQ was automatically asked. In comparison to traditional methods, this procedure allowed us to fit the behavioral variability associated with mind-wandering to the online statement of its occurrence in a more dynamic and ecological way.

MATERIALS AND METHODS

Participants

Thirty-three healthy undergraduates (3 males) from the University of Granada participated in this study for course credit. A further participant was not considered in the analysis because he did not produce consistent responses, by often changing the response key assignment for targets and nontarget. All participants were right-handed, with their age ranging from 18 to 30 years (M = 23.71). Participants had normal or corrected to normal vision. They had no history of neurological disease and were free from psychoactive medication use. All participants provided their written informed consent prior to participating in the study. The local ethics committee from the University of Granada approved the experimental protocol.

Stimuli

E-Prime® software (version 2.1, Psychology Software Tools Inc., http://www.pstnet.com) was used to control stimuli presentation and response collection. Stimuli were displayed on a 21" monitor with a refresh rate of 60 Hz, situated at approximately 57 cm from the participants' eyes. Ten randomly chosen upper-case letters were presented in rapid visual serial presentation. All the letters appeared inside an empty central white rectangle on a grey background. Each letter was presented for 100 ms, with an inter-stimulus interval varying randomly between 2,500 and 4,000 ms. There were three blocks of trials, each composed of 329 letters, and lasting for about 30 minutes. Participants were allowed to rest as much as they wanted between blocks.

Procedure

A keyboard with numeric keypad on the right side was used to provide responses. Participants were instructed to press as fast as possible a colored key (either a red "7" or a green "8", in different participants) on the numeric keypad each time they saw the target (letter F) appearing. This condition occurred in 10% of the trials (Fig 1). In the remaining trials, when letters different from F appeared, they had to press the other colored key. The key assignment to target and nontarget letters was counterbalanced across participants. All participants used their right hand to respond. Mean RTs for nontargets were calculated online based on the last 5 responses. Whenever a RT exceeded 2 SDs from each participant's RT mean within the last 5 trials (see below), the response was defined as an outlier RT, and a thought sampling question (TSQ) automatically appeared on the test display. Thus, average RTs before the TSQ were calculated on a number of consecutive trials, which could range from a minimum of 5 trials to a maximum of 10 trials (if no RT outlier was detected before trial 10). If no outlier RTs were produced during trials 6 to 9, after trial 10 a control TSQ appeared ("Standard TSQ").

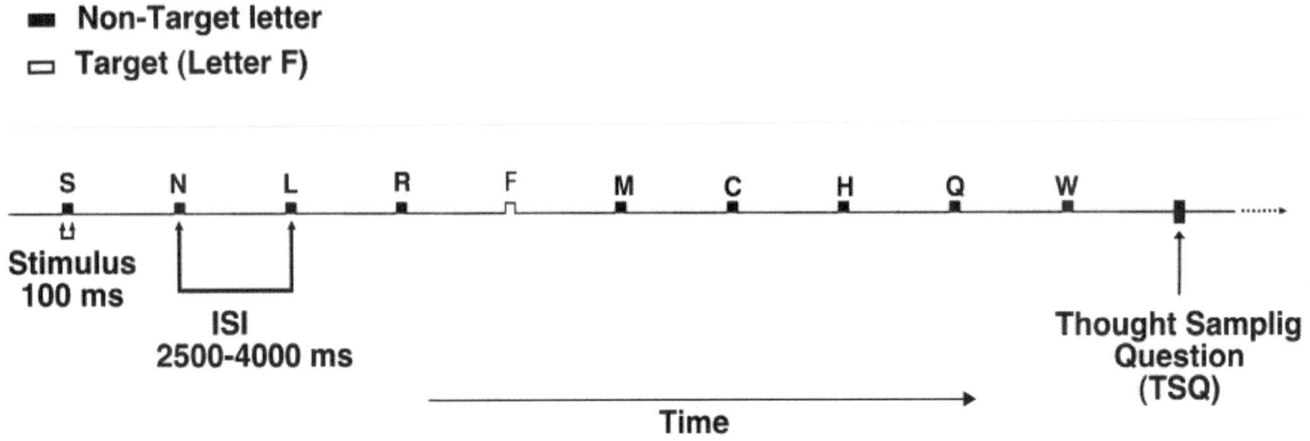

Figure 1. Schematic depiction of the experimental paradigm.

Each participant received an average of 48 TSQs per block. TSQs were formulated as follows: "Just before this question, your attention was distracted by." Five possible responses were then proposed: (1) My attention was not distracted. (2) External distraction (e.g., uncomfortable posture, itches, sneezing, coughing). (3) Internal distraction (memories, imagination, thoughts). (4) Loosing vigilance (feeling of falling asleep). (5) Others. Participants had to respond by pressing a button corresponding to the number of the chosen alternative over the numeric keypad (respectively, keys 1, 2, 3, 4, or 5) (Fig 1). Response 1 (no perceived distraction) was considered as evidence that participants were on-task, while response 3 (internal distraction) defined mind-wandering (off-task condition).

RESULTS

The level of statistical significance was set at alpha = .05. Bonferroni correction was used to correct for multiple comparisons. Performance was generally accurate, with 86% correct performance for nontarget stimuli (which constituted 90% of the total stimuli), and 81% correct responses to target stimuli (10% of the total stimuli). Participants chose response 1 (on-task) 55.5% of the time, and response 3 (mind-wandering) 18.6% of the time (Table 1). A t-test performed on the arcsin-transformed response rates demonstrated that on-task responses were more frequent than off-task responses, t (32) = 6.87, p <0.001, d = 1.19, 95% CIs [.18, .34]. The vast majority (67.3%) of these on-task responses followed standard RTs (within 2 SD around the mean, see Procedure); 23.4% of all on-task responses were given after slow RTs (>2SD above the mean), and 9.4% were given for faster responses (>2SD below the mean).

Table 1. Percentages of response types.

On-task	55.5%
External distraction	14.5%
Internal distraction (Off-task)	18.6%
Falling asleep	8.8%
Other	2.6%

doi:10.1371/journal.pone.0147174.t001

Responses to TSQs fell into two categories: responses related to outlier RTs (slow or fast), and responses related to standard (non-outlier) RTs. Based on previous evidence that RT variability is maximal in the trials just before mind-wandering episodes [13,20,21], we analyzed the 5 trials preceding on-task or off-task responses to TSQs (remember that 5 trials was the minimal possible interval between two TSQs).

Fig 2 shows the distribution of "slow" RTs (> 2 SD above the mean) across blocks. Each line represents a subject; red Xs represent median percentages per block. Slow RTs were not uniformly distributed among blocks (Block 1, 10%; Block 2, 14.5%, Block 3, 12%; Friedman chi-squared = 12.28, df = 2, p = 0.002), because they increased in Block 2 compared with Block 1 (Friedman test, p = 0.007; Bonferroni correction for 3 comparisons yields an alpha value of 0.017). There was no significant difference between Block 2 and Block 3 (p = 0.7) or between Block 1 and Block 3 (p = 0.045). However, the percentage of off-task responses did not vary across blocks (Block 1, 13%; Block 2, 16%, Block 3, 15%; Friedman chi-squared = 4.06, df = 2, p = 0.13). Thus, while there may be some general tendency to an RT increase across blocks, perhaps resulting from fatigue, the rate of mind-wandering reports did not significantly vary along the experimental session.

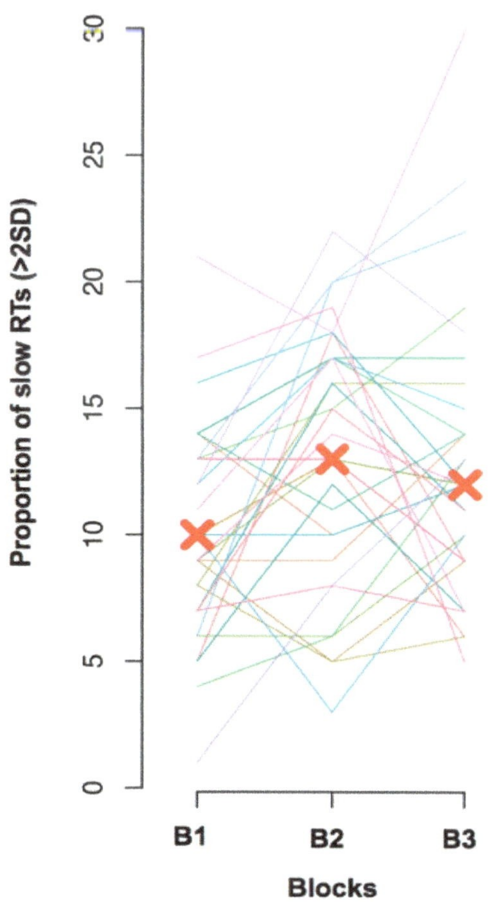

Figure 2. Distribution of slow RTs (> 2SD) across blocks. Each line represents a subject. Red Xs represent median percentages per block.

Fig 3 shows the evolution of RT during the last 5 trials before the TSQ. A 2x5 repeated measures ANOVA with condition (on-task and off-task) and trial position before the TSQ (N-1, N-2, N-3, N-4 and N-5) as within-participant factors revealed a main effect of trial position, F (4,128) = 44.00, p< .01, η_p^2 = .57, which interacted with condition, F (4,128) = 16.49, p < .01, η_p^2 = .34.

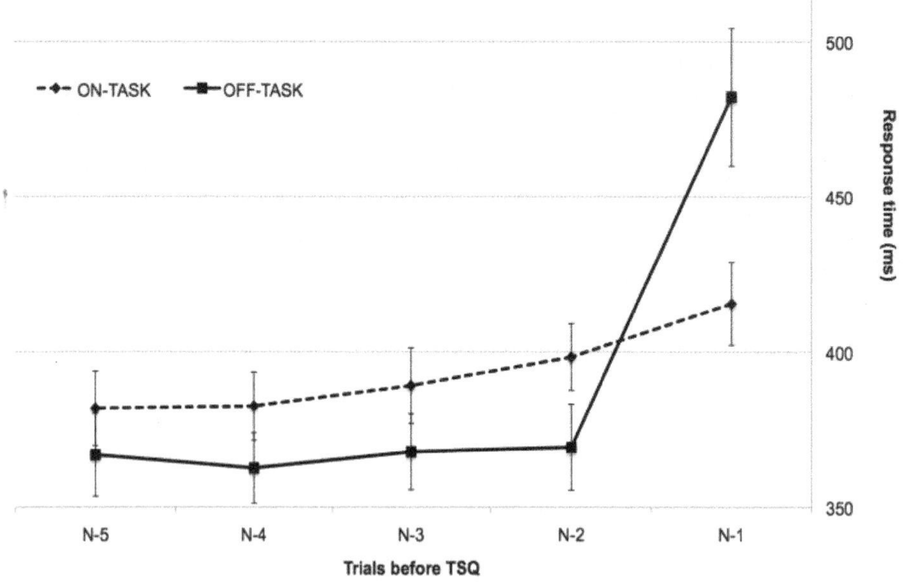

Figure 3. Distribution of mean RTs for the five trials before TSQ. Continuous line, off-task episodes related to mind-wandering; dashed line, on-task episodes. Error bars represent 1 standard error of the mean.

On-task and off-task conditions in trial N-5 led to similar RTs (Fig 3), $t(32)$ = 1.86, p >.05, d = .32, 95% CIs [-1.39, 31.36]. In the following three trials (N-4 to N-2), RTs were on average 23-ms faster in the off-task condition compared with the on-task condition (all $ts(32)$ > 2.84, allps < .01, d = .49, 95% CIs [14.02, 44.05; 6.04, 36.52; 6.89, 32.98], for all comparisons). However, this pattern reversed in trial N-1 (just before the TSQ), which elicited 66-ms slower RTs on the off-task condition than on the on-task condition, $t(32)$ = -3.53, p = 0.001, d = -.61, 95% CIs [-104.94, -28.18] (all these comparisons were Bonferroni corrected for 5 comparisons, with alpha = 0.01).

Although our aim was to explore internal distraction (mind wandering), we also assessed the RT profile of external distraction responses. We performed a 3x5 repeated measures ANOVA with response type (on-task, off-task task, and external distraction) and trial position before the TSQ (N-1, N-2, N-3, N-4 and N-5) as factors. The within-participant factors revealed a main effect of trial position, F (4, 128) = 96.22, p < .01, ηp2 = .75, which interacted with the response, F (4, 128) = 11.02, p < .01, ηp2 = .25. As shown in Table 2 , this interaction stemmed from the fact that on-task and external distraction RTs were similar for trials N-2 to N-5 (all ts(32) < .56, all ps > .57, d = -.09, 95% CIs [-18.31, 29.18; -15.06, 26.44; 6.89, 32.98; −23.88, 16.17]; Bonferroni correction for 5 comparisons, alpha = 0.01); however, similar to off-task responses, external distraction responses differed sharply from on-task responses for trial N-1, which elicited 108-ms slower RTs for external distraction responses than for on-task responses, t(32) = -6.09, p < .001, d = -1.05, 95% CIs [-145.47, -72.27]. Thus, off-task and external distraction responses gave rise to a similar RT profile.

Table 2. Mean RT and standard deviation for trials N-1 to N-5 before the TSQ for each possible response (on-task, off-task, external distraction, falling asleep, and other).

	N-1	N-2	N-3	N-4	N-5
On-task					
Mean	415.61	398.33	389.16	382.57	381.87
SD	77.55	62.34	70.33	63.25	69.44
External distraction					
Mean	524.48	392.89	383.47	387.65	385.72
SD	114.92	90.12	86.97	77.17	69.39
Off-task					
Mean	482.16	369.29	367.88	362.63	366.89
SD	128.51	80.21	70.89	65.74	76.55
Falling asleep					
Mean	323.79	362.67	371.73	368.24	360.16
SD	76.78	111.58	107.95	92.98	93.83
Other					
Mean	363.56	494.26	391.20	417.65	405.72
SD	154.13	310.48	112.57	223.81	135.61

doi:10.1371/journal.pone.0147174.t002

We also assessed whether the mean RT for each of the five trials preceding a TSQ could predict the participant's response ("on-task" or "off-task"), by performing a logistic regression analysis on the mean RT of each preceding trial (from N-1 to N-5). Results showed that increasing RTs significantly predicted reports of mind-wandering. The test of model coefficients was statistically significant, indicating that the predictors as a set reliably distinguished between trial position N-1 and N-2 (chi square = 34.09, $p < .01$ with df = 2). The Wald criterion demonstrated that trial N-2 and N-1 made a significant contribution to the prediction ($p < .01$). This is confirmed by Nagelkerke R square of .54 on second step that indicated a strong relationship between on- and off-task prediction and the position trials N-2 and N-1. Overall prediction success was 75.8% for the second step compared with less than 57.6% for the first step, which included only trial N-1 (Table 3).

Table 3. Logistic regression analysis of off-task and on-task condition for the last five trials before the TSQ.

	Variables	β	S.E	Wald	df	Sig.	Exp(β)
Step 1.	N-1	.006	.003	5.44	1	.020	1.0
	Constant	-2.79	1.21	5.26	1	.022	.06
Step 2.	N-1	.035	.010	12.30	1	.000	1.03
	N-2	-.045	.013	12.73	1	.000	.95
	Constant	2.06	1.76	1.37	1	.24	7.88

doi:10.1371/journal.pone.0147174.t003

RTs for the other tested trial positions (from N-3 to N-5) failed to predict the participant's response (all *ps* > .1). Finally, the RT difference between N-1 and N-2 trial significantly predicted participants' responses to the TSQ (paired Wilcoxon signed rank test, Z = -4.51, $p < .01$, r = -0.57). Thus, not only was mind-wandering indexed by slow RTs to the last trial before the TSQ, but also, and more accurately, by the RT difference between the last and the last-but-one trial.

In order to assess for long-range variations in RTs, we carried out a Fast Fourier Transform (FFT) to explore the variation of RTs through the task for each participant [22]. Then, we compared the resulting power spectrum with random distributions of the same data (2,000 permutations). RTs followed a 1/f distribution. Long-range variations (oscillations slower than one cycle per 6-minute period, Fig 4) were significantly greater that the random distribution. These oscillations represent variations longer than the maximum time interval between two TQS (41s). Finally, we assessed the possible relationship between these slow RT oscillations and the rate of off-task responses. We carried out correlation analyses between the rate of off-task responses and the power of these oscillations in 0.2-min bandwidth windows around the three fastest peaks in the FFT (11.1 min, 7.8 min, 6.0 min, see Fig 4). Results showed that subjects with greater power in the 5-min oscillation tended to produce less off-task responses (Spearman Correlation, 5.9–6.1. min, rho = -0.38, p = 0.02), while no correlation emerged for the other oscillations (7.9–7.7 min, rho = 0.08, p = 0.6; 11.0–11.2 min, rho = 0.27, p = 0.2).

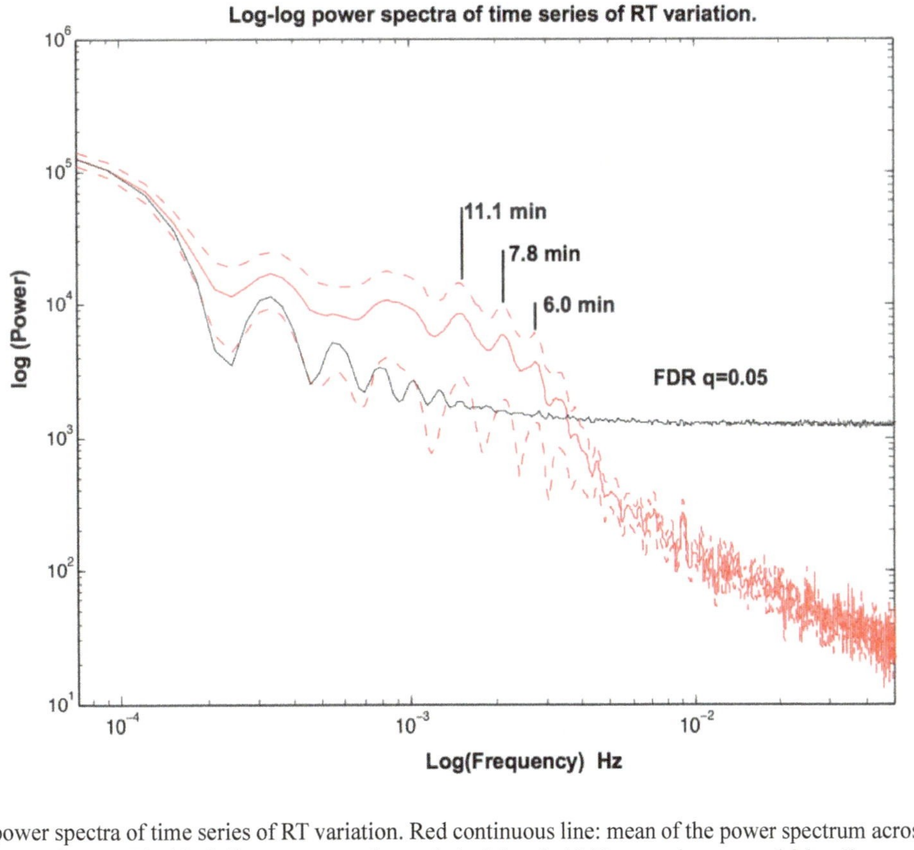

Figure 4. Log-log power spectra of time series of RT variation. Red continuous line: mean of the power spectrum across participants. Red dotted lines: standard error of mean. The black line represents the statistical threshold (Permutation test and false discovery rate (FDR), q = 0.05). The figure also shows the three only significant peaks at 11.1, 7.8, and 6.0 min.

DISCUSSION

A novel experimental procedure allowed us to identify episodes of mind-wandering based on the on-line assessment of RT fluctuations during a sustained attention task. Our procedure automatically detected outlier RTs and consequently triggered a TSQ during task performance. We explored different sources of mind-wandering based on individual responses to the five trials preceding the TSQ in both on- and off-task conditions. We observed that off-task reports were generally preceded by slower RTs as compared with trials before on-task responses. Note, however, that a substantial proportion of slow RTs (23%) occurred before "on-task" reports. Moreover, RTs tended to increase across blocks, without significant variation of the percentage of off-task responses. Thus, RTs alone are not to be considered as a reliable index of mind wandering. We also observed a clear difference between RTs in N-1 and N-2 trials compared to the remaining trials. This suggests that mind-wandering is not an attentional *state* in itself, characterized by a global slowing of responses. Rather, mind-wandering seems best characterized in a more dynamical way as a *transition* between different attentional states. Assessment of 1/f patterns showed the presence of slow oscillations (over several minutes) in RT performance. However, these oscillations either had no correlation or were negatively correlated with the rate of off-task responses. Thus, mind-wandering states seemed to interrupt these slow oscillations, rather than being part of them. Thus, our results suggest that mind-wandering is a local phenomenon lasting between 2.5 and 10 seconds, presumably driven by specific cognitive processes such as spontaneous fluctuations in the alertness system [23].

Previous studies have adjusted the presentation of evaluations of mind-wandering by using a pre-established rate of TSQs [18]. Our online method allowed us to automatically detect and assess different mind-wandering states continuously, and presumably in a more ecological way. Our psychophysical evidence demonstrates how dynamical local changes in the attentional system level can trigger global cognitive changes [24], and supports the hypothesis that changes of the attentional state not only depend on the nature of the stimuli, such as their physical properties, but also on the variability of the system itself [25–27]. Our approach could therefore inspire strategies to prevent inattention when mind-wandering can negatively impact cognitive performance [28].

Despite its clear and straightforward findings, this study has limitations. First, the observed RT profile was not able to clearly distinguish between internal and external distraction. Second, as compared to other methods our samples are presumably more specific, but also reduced in number. Third, it is difficult to estimate the potentially disruptive effects of the TSQs on the sustained attention task. Finally, the dichotomy between on- and off-task conditions might not be subtle enough to capture the richness of phenomenological experience. Thus, it is possible that this first attempt to make an online estimation of mind-wandering did not fully capture the richness of mind-wandering content, because our approach did not make any a priori assumptions about the cognitive definition of this phenomenon. Further experiments including a more precise evaluation of the cognitive content of mind-wandering should address these issues. To conclude, our new approach allowed us to identify mind-wandering as a dynamic transition between attentional states, which results in abruptly decoupling the attentional system from the external world.

ACKNOWLEDGMENTS

We are grateful to the participants for their patience and good will and to Dr. Julià Amengual for useful discussion.

AUTHOR CONTRIBUTIONS

Conceived and designed the experiments: RAH ABC. Performed the experiments: RAH. Analyzed the data: RAH. Contributed reagents/materials/analysis tools: RAH P. Billeke. Wrote the paper: RAH. Provided critical revisions: ABC P. Bartolomeo.

REFERENCES

1. Braboszcz C, Delorme A. Lost in thoughts: Neural markers of low alertness during mind wandering. Neuroimage. 2011;54:3040–7. doi: 10. 1016/j. neuroimage. 2010. 10. 008. pmid:20946963
2. Schooler JW, Smallwood J, Christoff K, Handy TC, Reichle ED,Sayette M a. . Meta-awareness, perceptual decoupling and the wandering mind. Trends Cogn Sci; 2011;15(7):319–26. doi: 10. 1016/j. tics. 2011. 05. 006. pmid:21684189
3. Smallwood J, Schooler JW. The restless mind. Psychol Bull. 2006;132(6):946–58. pmid:17073528 doi: 10. 1037/0033-2909. 132. 6. 946
4. Giambra LM. Task-Unrelated-Thought Frequency as a Function of Age: A Laboratory Study. 1989;4(2):136–43. doi: 10. 1037/0882-7974. 4. 2. 136
5. Smallwood JM, Baracaia SF, Lowe M, Obonsawin M. Task unrelated thought whilst encoding information. Conscious Cogn; 2003 Sep 1;12(3):452–84. pmid:12941287 doi: 10. 1016/s1053-8100(03)00018-7
6. Teasdale JD, Dritschel BH, Taylor MJ, Proctor L, Lloyd C a, Nimmo-Smith I, et al. Stimulus-independent thought depends on central executive resources. Mem Cognit. 1995;23(5):551–9. pmid:7476241 doi: 10. 3758/bf03197257
7. Gilbert SJ, Frith CD, Burgess PW. Involvement of rostral prefrontal cortex in selection between stimulus-oriented and stimulus-independent thought. Eur J Neurosci. 2005;21:1423–31. pmid:15813952 doi: 10. 1111/j. 1460-9568. 2005. 03981. x
8. Morin A. Inner Speech and Consciousness. In: Banks William P, (Editor), Encyclopedia of Consciousness volume 1, pp 389–402 Oxford: Elsevier; 2009. p. 1159–66.
9. Weissman DH, Roberts KC, Visscher KM, Woldorff MG. The neural bases of momentary lapses in attention. Nat Neurosci. 2006;9(7):971–8. pmid:16767087 doi: 10. 1038/nn1727
10. Christoff K, Gordon AM, Smallwood J, Smith R, Schooler JW. Experience sampling during fMRI reveals default network and executive system contributions to mind wandering. Proc Natl Acad Sci U S A. 2009;106:8719–24. doi: 10. 1073/pnas. 0900234106. pmid:19433790

11. Mason MF, Norton MI, Van Horn JD, Wegner DM, Grafton ST, Macrae CN. Wandering minds: the default network and stimulus-independent thought. Science (80-); 2007 Jan 19;315(5810):393–5. doi: 10. 1126/science. 1131295

12. Smallwood J, Davies JB, Heim D, Finnigan F, Sudberry M, O'Connor R, et al. Subjective experience and the attentional lapse: task engagement and disengagement during sustained attention. Conscious Cogn; 2004 Dec 1;13(4):657–90. pmid:15522626 doi: 10. 1016/j. concog. 2004. 06. 003

13. Seli P, Cheyne JA, Smilek D. Wandering minds and wavering rhythms: linking mind wandering and behavioral variability. J Exp Psychol Hum Percept Perform; 2013;39(1):1–5. doi: 10. 1037/a0030954. pmid:23244046

14. Seli P, Carriere JS a, Levene M, Smilek D. How few and far between? Examining the effects of probe rate on self-reported mind wandering. Front Psychol. 2013;4(July):1–5. doi: 10. 3389/fpsyg. 2013. 00430

15. Laufs H, Krakow K, Sterzer P, Eger E, Beyerle A, Salek-Haddadi A, et al. Electroencephalographic signatures of attentional and cognitive default modes in spontaneous brain activity fluctuations at rest. Proc Natl Acad Sci U S A; 2003 Sep 16;100(19):11053–8. pmid:12958209 doi: 10. 1073/pnas. 1831638100

16. Smallwood J, Beach E, Schooler JW, Handy TC. Going AWOL in the brain: mind wandering reduces cortical analysis of external events. J Cogn Neurosci. 2008;20:458–69. pmid:18004943 doi: 10. 1162/jocn. 2008. 20037

17. Axelrod V, Rees G, Lavidor M, Bar M. Increasing propensity to mind-wander with transcranial direct current stimulation. Proc Natl Acad Sci. ;2015;201421435. doi: 10. 1073/pnas. 1421435112

18. Smallwood J, McSpadden M, Luus B, Schooler J. Segmenting the stream of consciousness: the psychological correlates of temporal structures in the time series data of a continuous performance task. Brain Cogn; 2008 Feb 1;66(1):50–6. pmid:17614178 doi: 10. 1016/j. bandc. 2007. 05. 004

19. Robertson IH, Manly T, Andrade J, Baddeley BT, Yiend J. "Oops!": performance correlates of everyday attentional failures in traumatic brain injured and normal subjects. Neuropsychologia; 1997 Jun 1;35(6):747–58. pmid:9204482 doi: 10. 1016/s0028-3932(97)00015-8

20. Allan Cheyne J, Solman GJF, Carriere JS a, Smilek D. Anatomy of an error: A bidirectional state model of task engagement/disengagement and attention-related errors. Cognition; 2009;111(1):98–113. doi: 10. 1016/j. cognition. 2008. 12. 009. pmid:19215913

21. Bastian M, Sackur J. Mind wandering at the fingertips: Automatic parsing of subjective states based on response time variability. Front Psychol. 2013;4(September):1–11. doi: 10. 3389/fpsyg. 2013. 00573

22. Castellanos FX, Sonuga-Barke EJS, Scheres A, Di Martino A, Hyde C, Walters JR. Varieties of Attention-Deficit/Hyperactivity Disorder-related intra-individual variability. Biological Psychiatry. 2005;57(11):1416–1423. pmid:15950016 doi: 10. 1016/j. biopsych. 2004. 12. 005

23. Sadaghiani S, Scheeringa R, Lehongre K, Morillon B, Giraud A-L, Kleinschmidt A. Intrinsic connectivity networks, alpha oscillations, and tonic alertness: a simultaneous electroencephalography/functional magnetic resonance imaging study. J Neurosci. 2010;30(30):10243–50. doi: 10. 1523/JNEUROSCI. 1004-10. 2010. pmid:20668207

24. Le Van Quyen M. The brainweb of cross-scale interactions. New Ideas Psychol; 2011;29(2):57–63. doi: 10. 1016/j. newideapsych. 2010. 11. 001

25. Feldman H, Friston K. Attention, uncertainty, and free-energy. Front Hum Neurosci; 2010 Jan 1;4:215. doi: 10. 3389/fnhum. 2010. 00215. pmid:21160551

26. Friston K, Daunizeau J, Kilner J, Kiebel SJ. Action and behavior: a free-energy formulation. Biol Cybern; 2010 Mar 1;102(3):227–60. doi: 10. 1007/s00422-010-0364-z. pmid:20148260

27. Rastelli F, Tallon-Baudry C, Migliaccio R, Toba MN, Ducorps A, Pradat-Diehl P, et al. Neural dynamics of neglected targets in patients with right hemisphere damage. Cortex. 2013;49(7):1989–96. doi: 10. 1016/j. cortex. 2013. 04. 001. pmid:23664670

28. Killingsworth M a, Gilbert DT. A wandering mind is an unhappy mind. Science. 2010;330:932. doi: 10. 1126/ science. 1192439. pmid:21071660

CHAPTER 17

TOPOLOGY ANALYSIS OF SOCIAL NETWORKS EXTRACTED FROM LITERATURE

Michaël C. Waumans, Thibaut Nicodème , Hugues Bersini

École polytechnique de Bruxelles CoDE-IRIDIA, ULB, Brussels, Belgium

ABSTRACT

In a world where complex networks are an increasingly important part of science, it is interesting to question how the new reading of social realities they provide applies to our cultural background and in particular, popular culture. Are authors of successful novels able to reproduce social networks faithful to the ones found in reality? Is there any common trend connecting an author's oeuvre, or a genre of fiction? Such an analysis could provide new insight on how we, as a culture, perceive human interactions and consume media. The purpose of the work presented in this paper is to define the signature of a novel's story based on the topological analysis of its social network of characters. For this purpose, an automated tool was built that analyses the dialogs in novels, identifies characters and computes their relationships in a time-dependent manner in order to assess the network's evolution over the course of the story.

INTRODUCTION

The recipe of the Harry Potter saga's [1–7] success might reside in part in the very unique way its author has installed a familiar kind of social network in a fantasy world. In order for the reader to be seduced by the story of any novel, the social network narrated in the book must not be too distinct from the ones typically found in real life. Interestingly enough, a novel respectful of the social reality of its time also constitutes an interesting temporal compression (many years of the life of many characters held in but one, or a few, books) that allows clever text mining and natural language algorithms to more easily catch the main features of the social network depicted in the novel: its topology (i.e. its degree distribution: is Harry Potter social network scale-free?), its clustering degree (are the friends of Harry friends themselves?) [48] and the way it is being constructed in time (does the social network grow in a random way or does it follow some form of preferential attachment? [49]). Not only is it possible at the end of a book (or the series) to extract and analyse the complete topology of the characters relationship, but it is as well possible to follow the way new characters enter this social network and connect to the existing nodes. Accordingly, a first investigation described in this paper is the study of the various social networks (both their static features and their dynamic nature) found in several popular series and one classic: The seven "Harry Potter" books

Citation: Waumans MC, Nicodème T, Bersini H (2015) Topology Analysis of Social Networks Extracted from Literature. PLoS ONE 10(6): e0126470. doi:10.1371/journal.pone.0126470.

by J.K. Rowling, the (presently) five "A Song of Ice and Fire" [8–12] books by George R. R. Martin, the three "His Dark Materials" [13–15] books by Philip Pullman, the (presently) three "Lunar Chronicles" books by Marissa Meyer [16–18], the six "The Mortal Instruments" books by Cassandra Clare [19–24], the three "Liveship Traders" [25–27] and four "Rain Wild Chronicles" [28–31] books by Robin Hobb, the fifteen "The Wheel of Time" books by Robert Jordan [32–46], and "Les Misérables" [47] by Victor Hugo.

Our approach starts with an automated construction of the social networks, based on the processing of dialogs in the text. The characters intervening in each conversations are identified, and a network is formed between them based on these interactions. For instance, if in a given part of the text Harry speaks to Hermione, a new link will connect Harry to Hermione in the evolving social network if there were none. Similarly, the first time Jean Valjean addresses Cosette, both the new node "Cosette" and its new link to "Valjean" will be added. The temporal evolution of the network is assumed to follow the succession of dialogs in the books, meaning that new characters appear in a network as soon as they are involved in a conversation. However, we do not believe such an assumption has a major impact on the presented results.

The various steps leading to the creation of this network, as well as the finished social network, provide with a series of key features that form what appears to be a signature of each story, characterizing important elements relating to it, such as the scope, the number of protagonists, and even the author's style and reading level (for instance, whether or not an author assumes that the reader can keep track of the speakers in a conversation, or the relative proportion of narration within a conversation). This series of attributes leads to a way to characterize each book, and even draw parallels between several of them.

The rest of the article first summarizes the main assumptions and key decisions taken to automatically construct and follow in time the social networks out of the several books. Then, a more complete and sufficiently detailed technological description of the algorithmic steps will be presented in order for any interested reader to easily perform a very similar analysis of their favourite books or series. Finally, the results will be presented and discussed for the forty-seven best-selling books in terms of typical network measures (size, clustering and degree distribution) and the way these networks evolve in time (preferential attachment).

THE MAIN ASSUMPTIONS AND ALGORITHMIC IDEAS

First of all, the software technologies presented in this paper should be as automated and user-friendly as possible for anyone interested to easily extract the final social network and its time evolution out of their favourite book. All the software tools and the way to use them will be made available in the bibliography of the paper. The full extraction starts with a text version of the complete book or the complete series. We have arbitrarily restricted our analysis to forty-seven books, but nothing prevents to easily move ahead and enlarge our statistic samples to any size.

The key assumption to construct social networks lies in the exploitation of dialogs and successions of dialogs to automate the extraction in time of the nodes and the links. It is far from surprising to base a social network analysis upon communication among the nodes, since the most common interactive mode between people remains verbal communication. Dialogs are also generally easy to detect and to separate; however, indirect speech will be ignored as a result, as it is syntactically impossible to distinguish from regular narration.

An important algorithmic step of the full protocol is to first isolate one single dialog and insert it in a larger piece of text (including some surrounding narration) referred to as its context. The following key step is to identify the speaker in this context. Then this speaker is connected to the characters he speaks to, and possibly to some others not directly present but mentioned during this dialog. The connectivity pattern to associate with this dialog will be described next but could be: the speakers with all the others, or a fully connected sub-graph (all characters with all).

Incorporated in the algorithm is the possibility to weight or colour the links (as can be seen in the network Fig 1) as a result of a sentimental analysis performed on the basis of the words found in the context. In this paper, this additional description will be of no use as our focus is primarily on topology, while for a further characterization of the author's style or a study extended to weighted graphs, this additional data could be very profitable.

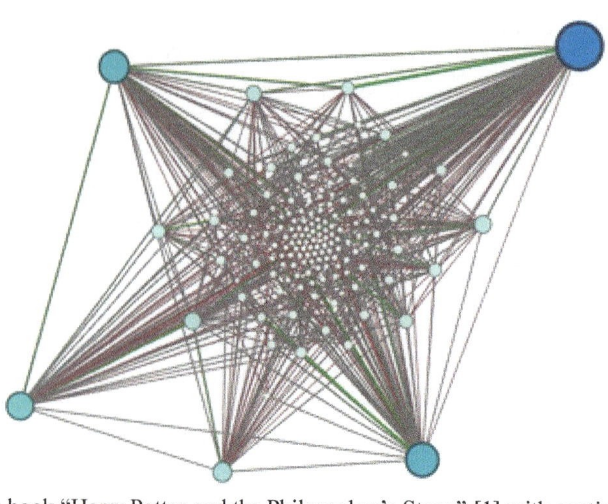

Figure 1. Network Extracted from the book "Harry Potter and the Philosopher's Stone" [1] with sentiment scores (Produced with NetworkX [50]).

One last assumption is to follow the network construction in time as a succession of the contexts just described above. This is a simplification: the events in a novel are not always told in chronological order. A classical figure of style is the use of flash-backs such as, for instance, at the heart of the narration in "les Misérables"; similarly, temporal inconsistencies may occur with shifting points of view, as are employed in "A Song of Ice and Fire". Nonetheless, our interest lies mainly in at what point in the story each new character is introduced, and who they are originally attached to when introduced, to verify that a preferential attachment occurs; with this objective and restrictive frame of analysis (the social network's evolution is only considered over the course of the book's story, ignoring all backstory and previously-established continuity), this first-order approximation is expected to hold.

IMPLEMENTATION

The principle of social network extraction from literature may seem simple in theory but is a very complex task in practice that involves many disciplines such as Natural Language Processing, Named-entity recognition, Co-references resolution, Aliases association, etc. Different steps are required to tackle the task properly, they are reviewed in detail in the following sections but an introduction of the important notions is first required.

An author tells a story by switching between descriptions of the events occurring during the story (i.e. the narration) and descriptions of the conversations happening between the different ***characters*** involved. Both are important as they provide information about the characters intervening in the action, but the identification and analysis of the conversations provide a more precise description of the way social links are built through the storytelling.

Each ***conversation*** depicted by the author consists in a succession of ***dialogs*** usually indicated in the text by double quotes (See Figs 2 and 3 for examples). As in real life, when someone speaks (the ***speaker***), he addresses himself to one or more persons; ***the audience*** (See Fig 2).

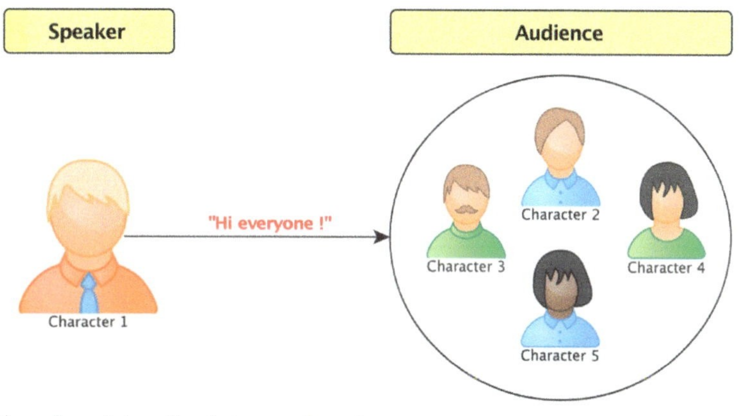

Figure 2. Schematic representation of one interaction between characters.

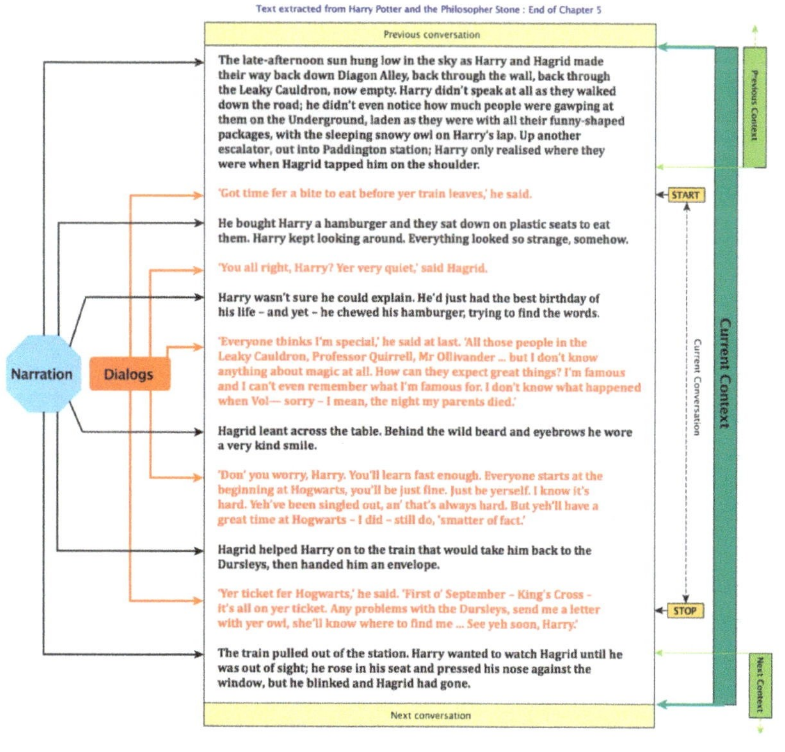

Figure 3. Text extract of a conversation from "Harry Potter and The Philosopher's Stone" [1] displaying the different elements manipulated (i.e. Narration, dialogs, context, conversation,…) and their relation with each other.

One last notion must be introduced, the ***context*** in which a conversation takes place. As explained before, the author switches between conversation and narration all trough the storytelling and even during a conversation to provide the reader with more information about the context in which it takes place (i.e. the location, who is involved, who they are… See Fig 3 for a practical example). The analysis of the context is necessary to differentiate between the characters participating in a conversation from those who are just mentioned in it (e.g. "I saw Ronald this morning": Ronald is not actually participating to the conversation but is mentioned nonetheless), and to identify the speakers even though their actual last name, first name or alias is not being used.

The speaker is usually identifiable (subject identification inside a dialog by means of grammatical analysis. See section) as well as the characters to whom he talks by analysing the entire conversion with all the dialogs it contains. The challenge resides in the identification of all the names that refer to each character, and building a network dynamically using the information extracted from the conversations.

To summarize, a novel is composed of many conversations that describe the social interactions between all the characters involved in the action at the specific point in time. Building a network by extracting those information is a complex succession of operations necessary to identify those characters and the way they relate to each other (i.e. who talks to whom).

Lexicon:

- ***Character:*** Person that participates to the story.
- ***Speaker:*** Character that speaks to other characters involved.
- ***Audience:*** Characters that listen to a speaker.
- ***Dialog:*** Line of text occurring in a novel denoted by double quotes to indicate that someone is speaking.
- ***Conversation:*** Succession of dialogs representing a conversation between two or more characters.
- ***Context:*** Before, during as well as after a conversation, the author may tell us more about the context in which a conversation takes place. This is what we call the context.

To reach this goal an algorithm composed of four consecutive steps was developed: Pre-processing, Extraction of dialogs and conversations, Characters identification and Network building. They are composed of multiple sub operations as depicted in Fig 4 that are detailed in the following sections.

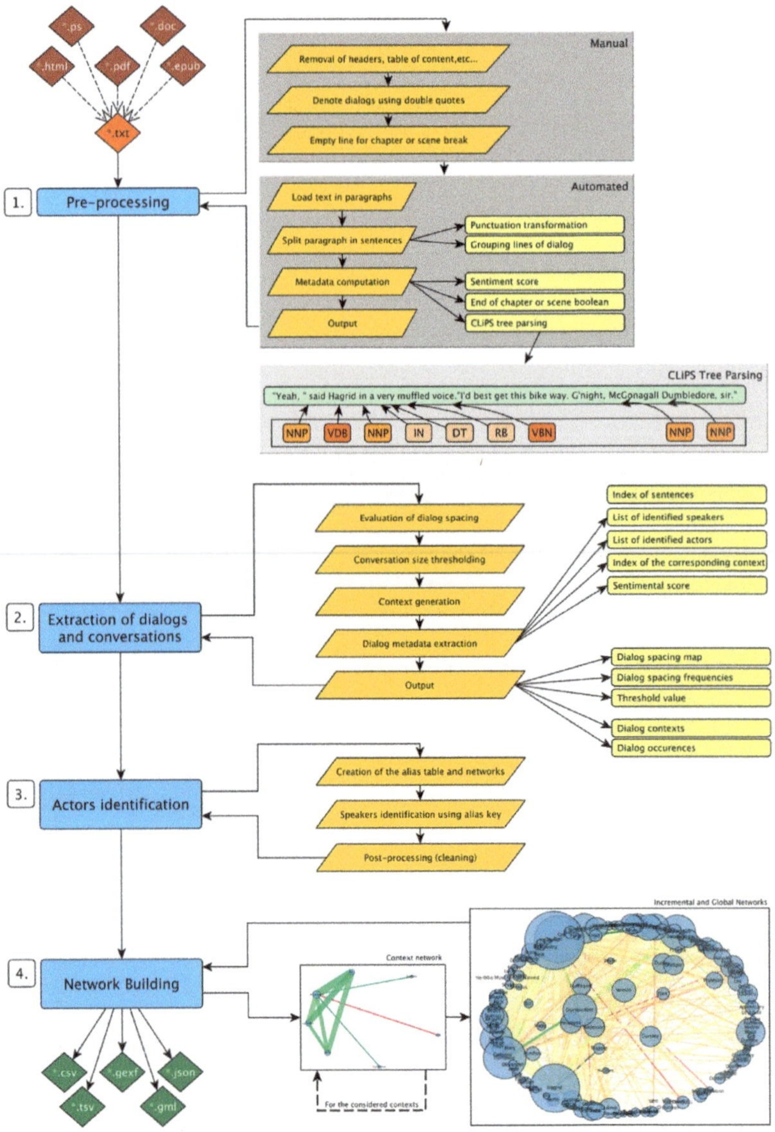

Figure 4. Schematic view of the entire algorithm's process.

Pre-processing

The text to analyse has to respect a specific format to be processable by the algorithm, formatting it properly is the goal of this step. The pre-processing involves manual intervention on the raw text for some aspects (i.e. Removal of headers, table of content,...) and the application of automated procedures to extract the necessary information from the novel.

Manual pre-processing The manual step consists in the acquisition of a proper raw text file. The actual text to analyse may be found in different file formats (i.e. HTML, DOC, EPUB, PS, PDF,...) that need to be converted to TXT. (The software Calibre [51] was used for this purpose). The books may also be formatted in different ways (i.e. Use of double quotes or simple quotes to indicate dialogs, use of multiple spacing or specific formatting to indicate the chapters,...) that are not appropriate for an automated processing to take place. At the end of this manual step, whatever the way chosen to apply those modifications, the text must answer only two requirements:

- *Use double quotes to denote dialogs (single quotes for apostrophes).*
- *Indicate chapter or scene breaks using empty lines with all other empty lines removed.*

Automated pre-processing The next step is fully automated. It takes the cleaned raw TXT file as input to compute various information detailed here:

- Split the text in sentences using the CLiPS Pattern [52] tree parser with two modifications applied to the content. First, some punctuation marks are transformed into others that are recognizable by the tree parser function. Then, the multiple lines forming one dialog are grouped in a same entity (by forcing an even number of quotation marks in a single entity).
- A sentiment score is computed for each line of text using the built-in opinion mining tool of CLiPS. (Other libraries like NLTK [52, 53, 60] with SentiWordNet [54–57] or CoreNLP [58] were considered, but CLiPS was retained as final solution for this implementation as it suited best the needs of this algorithm). Also, if a scene break or chapter break is found, it is indicated by a boolean value.
- Produce a parse tree using the CLiPS Tree parser for each sentence and do a division into chunks (i.e: Chunking consists in the division of a text in parts of word that are syntactically correlated. For examples, see Fig 3 in the section 'CLiPS Tree Parsing' and the section 'Characters identification and alias resolution'). This will also allow the determination of the grammatical roles of the words composing the sentences. (i.e. Subject, verb, complement,...).
- Save the metadata computed on files for later use.

To sum up, this part of the algorithm is concerned with the cleaning of the text as well as the preparation of numerous metadata used for the next steps of the program. Those metadata do include, for each line of text, the sentiment score, the parse tree, the identification of scene or chapter break and the index. (i.e. Each line of text is identified by its index, the number of the line inside the entire novel)

Extraction of Dialogs and Conversations

A novel tells us a story in which characters interact at different moments in time. While reading a book, we are able to differentiate the contexts that take place easily, as well as the different dialogs and members of the audience. This is much harder for a program to tackle without a perfect knowledge of the language used. This step tackles the task of solving this aspect of the problematic, it identifies the dialogs and conversations in each dialog and also extracts the context of a conversation. The algorithm proceeds as follows:

- **Evaluating dialog spacing:** This consists in a simple counting operation of the number of sentences present between two lines of dialog.

  To allow a proper division of the story into conversations using an automated process, the values of dialog spacing are analysed during the next step to compute a threshold indicating when one conversation must start and end. Drawing the distribution of those values yields histograms presented in Figs 5, 6 and 7.

  A few general conclusions can be derived from these results. First, the overall shape of the distribution (zeroes excluded since they represent chapter or scene breaks) remains the same and shows a rapidly decreasing profile. Second, each author appears to have a different typical profile as it was observed during the analysis of other series like "Game of Thrones" ([8–12]). This dialog spacing is a distinctive mark of the author's style. Indeed some authors are more prone to write long sequences of narration, whereas others tend to do the opposite, showing respectively higher or lower value of dialog spacing. Third, the author is more important to the profile than the length of the novel is, even though we reach higher values of spacing in longer novels regardless of the author.

- **Conversation size thresholding:** Using the values of dialog spacing, a threshold is computed to evaluate the maximum distance between two lines of dialog belonging to the same conversation.

  Unsurprisingly, the frequency distribution heavily favours small numbers since lines of dialog tend to be clustered in conversations. Such observation indicates that it is possible to extract most conversations automatically by relying on a threshold value of dialog spacing. This threshold corresponds to the usual number of spacing (i.e. Sentences of story telling) found between two dialogs. After the analysis of a few books, an empirical formula was derived. Namely, the threshold is the highest possible value of spacing, such that its frequency is higher than both 10 and double the frequency of the spacing one unit above, and such that all lower values of spacing have higher frequencies. However, if there is a higher value of spacing with a frequency above 100, this value is used as a threshold instead. This is summarized in the formula that follows:

$$
\begin{aligned}
threshold \;=\; \max\{s|s \in spacing \;\wedge \\
[\,(\,frequency(s) \;\geq\; 10\,)\;\wedge \\
(\,frequency(s) \;\geq\; (2 \,*\, frequency(s+1))\,)\;\wedge \\
(\forall\, t \;\in\; spacing \;: frequency(t) \;>\; frequency(s))\,] \\
\vee frequency(s) \;>\; 100\}
\end{aligned}
\tag{1}
$$

For "Harry Potter and the Philosopher's Stone" [1], the computed value is 8 (i.e. If more than eight lines do separate two dialogs, they do belong to two different conversations), as shown on Fig 8. It is then used to group the dialogs and to single out the successive conversations appearing in the novel.

- **Context generation:** To improve the process of speaker identification coming later on during the process, the conversation is being extended to a context. (i.e. The named entities found inside the corresponding context are used to enrich the information already extracted from the dialogs forming a conversation) It is built by listing every sentence from the end of the previous conversation up to the start of the next one. (See Fig 3)
- **Dialog metadata extraction:** For each dialog found inside the novel some metadata are computed and grouped to facilitate further processing. The result is a map of every dialog associated with the index of the dialog (i.e. the index of the corresponding line inside the novel, indicating the time at which the dialog occurs) as well as two fields, 'from' and 'to', containing the names identified and corresponding respectively to the speaker and the audience. Here they are explained with an example in Fig 9.

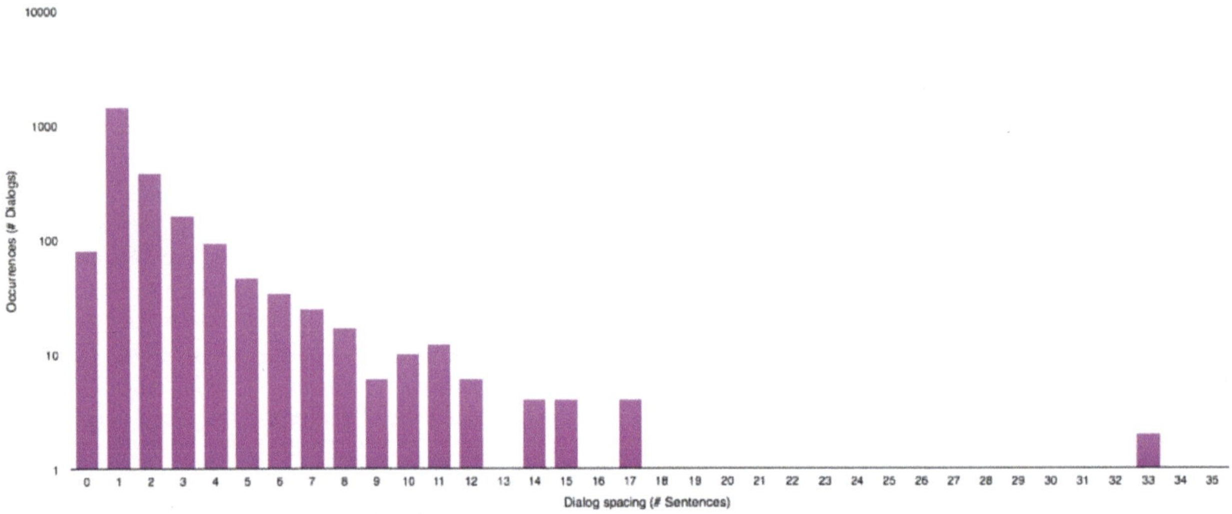

Figure 5. Dialog spacing distribution in "Harry Potter and the Philosopher's Stone" [1].

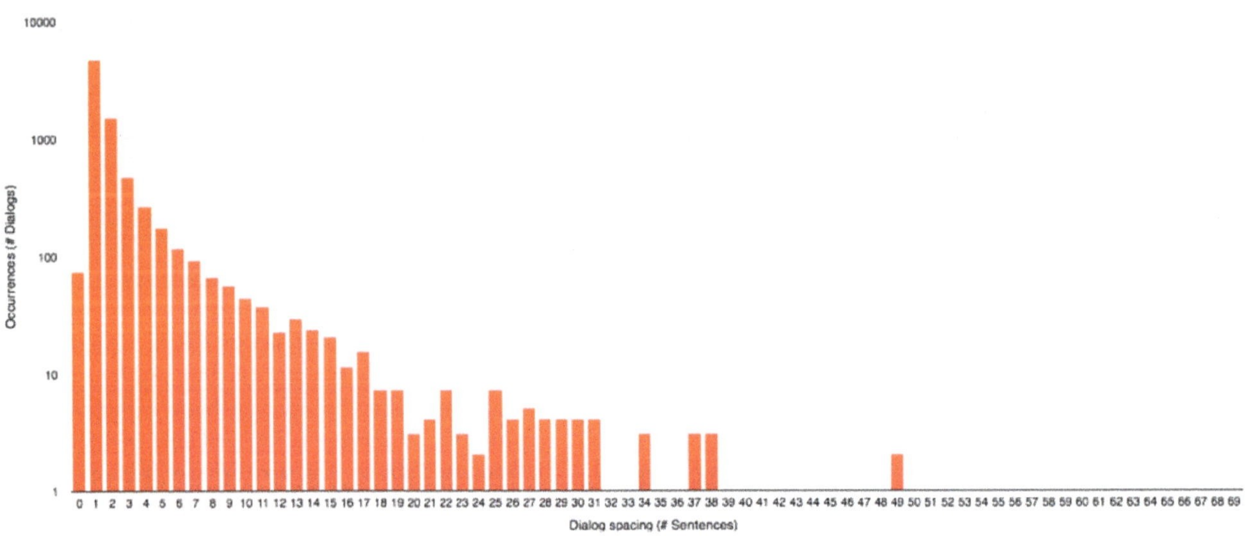

Figure 6. Dialog spacing distribution in "A Game of Thrones" [8].

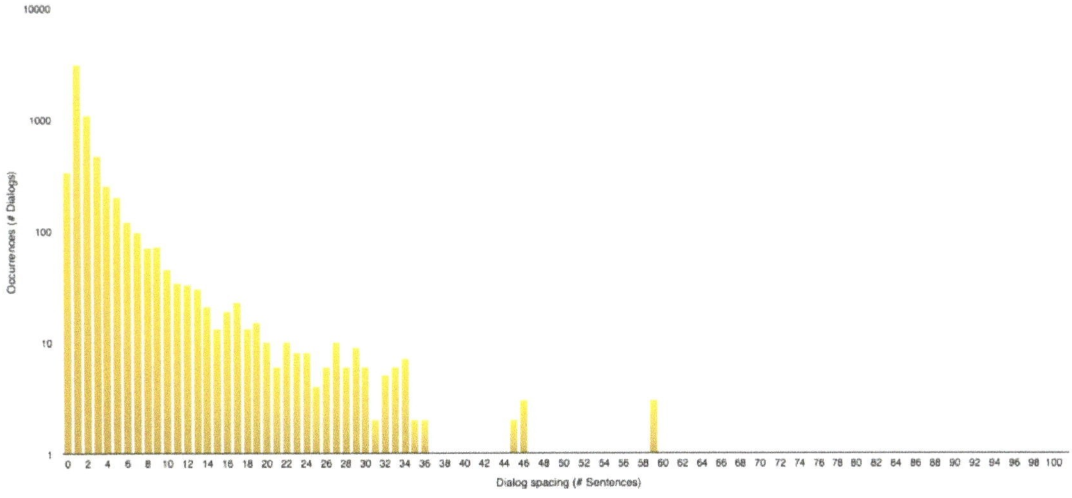

Figure 7. Dialog spacing distribution in "Les Misérables" [47].

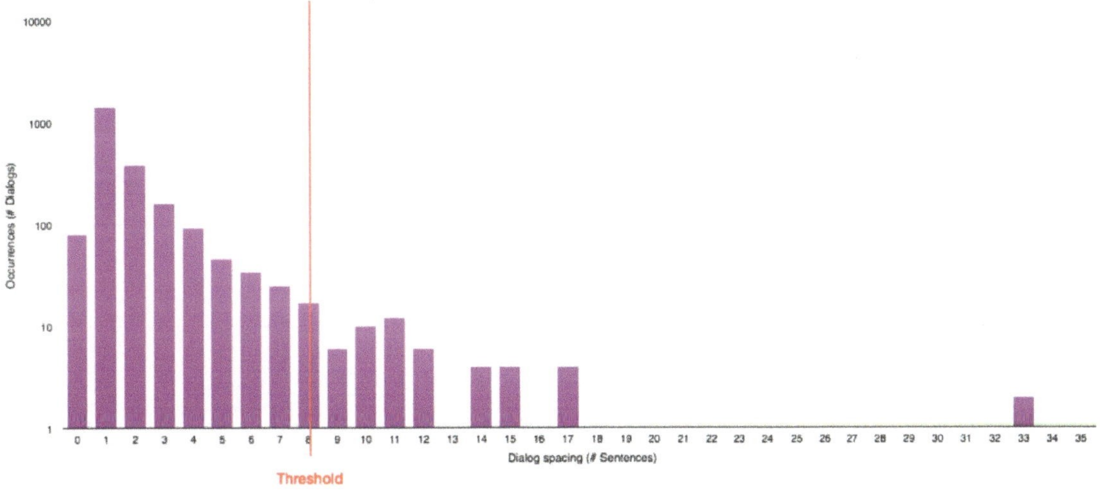

Figure 8. Dialog spacing distribution in "Harry Potter and the Philosopher's Stone" [1] with the computed threshold.

Input sentence	"Little tyke," chortled Mr. Dursley as he left the house.
Occurrence components	`sentence`
	"Little tyke," chortled Mr. Dursley as he left the house.
	`index`
	20
	`context`
	0
	`from`
	[Chunk ("he"), Chunk("Mr. Dursley")]
	`to`
	[]
	`sentiment`
	-0.09375

Figure 9. Example of input sentence and it's related metadata.

Metadata:

- **Index of the sentence:** Position of the line of dialog inside the entire text.
- **Identified speakers ('from'):** Character that speaks at that moment.
- **List of the identified characters within the dialog ('to'):** Characters mentioned in the dialog. This list contains all the NNPs (proper nouns) identified in it.
- **Index of the context to which that dialog belongs:** Corresponding to the number of the context (i.e. enriched conversation) in which the dialog falls after the conversation thresholding.

At the end of this step, dialogs are grouped into conversations, each of which has an associated context, and each dialog is enriched with metadata that serves as the basis to build a social network.

Characters Identification and Alias Resolution

Another problem occurring while reading a novel is the speaker and characters identification. "Who talks to whom?" illustrates the problem perfectly. Once again, this task is easy for a human but may be more difficult for a program depending on the writing style of the author (Namely, whether the book is intended for a young or an adult readership). Identifying the characters involved in the action and more specifically distinguishing the speaker from the audience is another difficult problem to solve.

This part of the algorithm runs in two steps and relies on the metadata previously computed (i.e. the parse tree and chunks already provide the information about the NNPs that are looked for) (See Table 1).

- **First**, the program takes each dialog of the novel and checks its grammatical structure computed while pre-processing the novel. During the metadata extraction in the previous step, the program already checked for the presence of dialog tags (bits of narration interspersed within the dialog to indicate a speaker, e.g. "he said") and extracted a speaker if the subject of that dialog tag was a proper noun (NNP tag), or a succession of proper nouns and stores it as the "from" field of the dialog occurrence. Otherwise, the speaker is not yet clearly identified, and that field is blank. (See Fig 10for an example and section for more information).
- **Second**, the problem of aliases is handled. Almost every characters possesses one or more aliases used through the story telling by the author at different moments (i.e. name, diminutive, title, full name,...) This step handles this problem by building an alias network which provides an association of the different names with their aliases and replaces their occurrences by the same name; the key of the character. Doing so, instead of risking to create a network full of characters different in appearance but actually identical, the algorithm is able to reduce the size of the resulting network by properly identifying the characters.

Table 1. Part-of-speech tags.

Tag	Meaning
CC	Conjunction, Coordination
CD	Cardinal number
DT	Determiner
EC	Existential there
FW	Foreign word
IN	Conjunction, subordinating proposition
JJ, JJR, JJS	Adjective (regular, comparative and superlative)
LS	List item marker
MD	Verb, modal auxiliary
NN, NNS, NNP, NNPS	Noun (singular or mass, plural, proper singular, proper plural)
PDT	Predeterminer
POS	Possessive ending
PRP, PRP$	Pronoun (personal, possessive)
RB,RBR,RBS,RP	Adverb (regular, comparative, superlative, particle)
SYM	Symbol
TO	Infinitival to
UH	Interjection
VB, VBZ, VBP, VBD, VBN, VBG	Verb (base form, 3rd person singular present, non-3rd person singular present, past tense, past participle, gerund or present participle)
WDT, WP, WP$, WRB	Wh-words (determiner, personal pronoun, possessive pronoun, adverb)
. ,: ()	Punctuation marks

doi:10.1371/journal.pone.0126470.t001

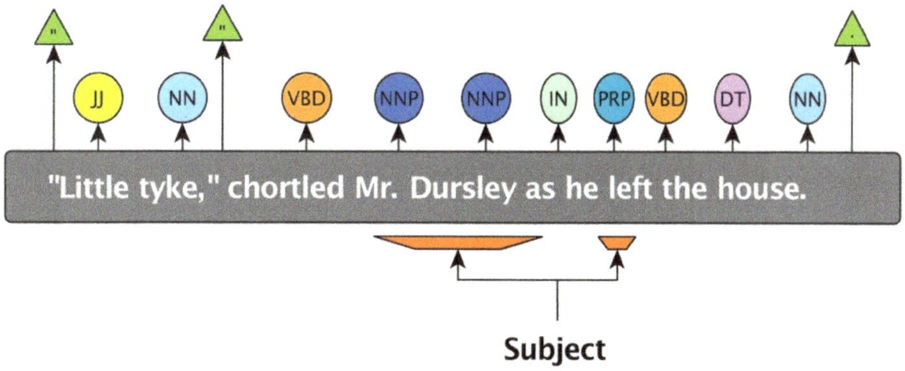

Figure 10. Example of the first step of the speaker's identification process. Locating the subject of the sentence.

Two main flaws arise from the use of the alias table however: the inability to identify characters from other proper nouns, and the handling of NNP tags that are applied to several characters, such as titles and family names.

The part-of-speech tags are based on the Brown Corpus [59] reduced in size to fit the orientation of the Penn Treebank [61, 62] used. It eliminates redundancy by taking into account lexical as well as syntactic information. Most NLP tools use those.

The former problem derives from the use of the Pen Treebank [61, 62]) tag set as the primary identifier of character names. Indeed, a variety of proper nouns are tagged as NNPs (Example: Gryffindor) with no regard to what they refer to. Because of this, we are unable to differentiate capitalized neologisms or named locations from character names.

The second error comes from titles and family names when several characters share them. It is impossible to fully solve those aliases, but a workaround (the alias table) was implemented to prevent those names from being referred to as mush as possible (e.g. "Professor McGonagall" would be included in the entry "McGonagall" but not professor, but if the author refers to her used only her title then the node "Professor" would still appear).

It should also be noted that the algorithm is incapable of differentiating between two characters who would have the same name. This could be corrected by employing a disambiguation algorithm; however, that only results to minor errors: characters in a fictional narrative, especially in writing, are rarely named the same way [63], as that could cause confusion even for a normal reader. This is consistent with other research in stylistic analysis over works of fiction, such as Argamon et al. [64]. It should be noted that a disambiguation algorithm may help the second error mentioned above; this may thus be the subject of future research.

Speaker identification. During the metadata extraction step, speakers are identified locally for each dialog (i.e. within the dialog itself), using dialog tags as announced. This means that the resulting speaker identification rate is highly dependent on the author's style; namely, whether or not they frequently remind the reader of who is speaking, and whether or not they use the character's name or pronouns to do so.

The resulting rate of speaker identification (SIR), averaged over all analysed books, is close to 50%, but with a high variance (standard deviation of about 10%). A breakdown by author, however, shows the expected result: the average rate of identification is very different depending on the writer. (See Table 2)

Table 2. Rate of speaker identification (SIR).

Author	Average SIR	Std dev
C. Clare	50.04%	3.2%
R. Hobb	50.46%	3.5%
V. Hugo	37.85%	N/A
R. Jordan	64.65%	5.5%
R. J. & B. Sanderson	52.95%	1.01%
G.R.R Martin	48.08%	4.41%
M. Meyer	33.81%	0.86%
P.Pullman	40.91%	4.84%
J.K. Rowling	57.27%	3.55%

For V. Hugo the standard deviation could not be computed since only one book was considered.

For B. Sanderson, due to the last three *Wheel of Time* books being written by a different author, they have to be considered separately.

doi:10.1371/journal.pone.0126470.t002

This leads to an acceptable rate of speakers identification. To improve the results obtained, some assumptions are made. For example, in a conversation where only two characters were identified as speakers, the algorithm infers that the characters speak in turn, and fits that pattern to the dialogs where no speaker has been identified yet as best as possible. The same happens when more than two characters are involved in a conversation: the algorithm takes into account the speakers identified for the neighboring dialogs to propose the best possible inferences. Doing so, the average rate of speaker identification reaches over 98%.

One question arises though: what about the accuracy of this identification? At this stage of development the accuracy cannot be measured for a simple reason: the correct speakers should be identified manually to assess the precision of the classifier. As an example, in *Harry Potter and the Philosopher's Stone* [1], the correct speaker was identified for 56.9% of individual occurrences.

However, the bulk of the analysis does not rely on individual occurrences, but on networks built from entire conversations. Within each conversation, all the identified speakers are interconnected; thus, as long as a speaker was identified within a conversation, it matters little whether or not it was assigned the correct specific lines of dialog, as it will result in the same network. This is measured by comparing the list of speakers appearing in each context of the extracted network to the same list in each context of a manually-generated correct graph, and counting how many are present in both lists. For the example of *Philosopher's Stone*, the proportion of speakers that were correctly found goes up to 82.4% when performing this bulk analysis. To get a better sense of what this represents, a differential between the extracted graph and the correct graph is shown in Fig 11. 73.3% of the edges from the extracted are present in the correct graphs.

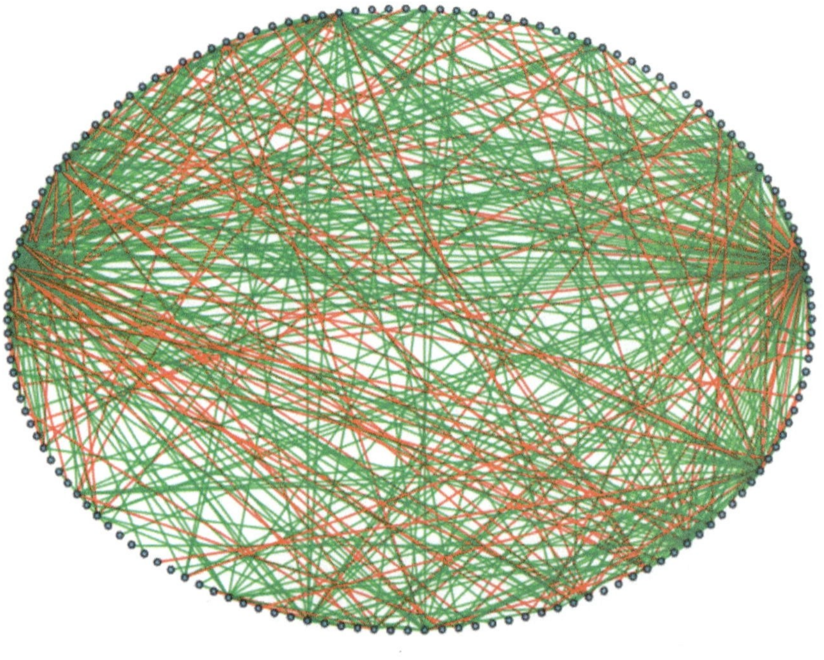

Figure 11. Differential between the extracted and correct networks in "Harry Potter and the Philosopher's Stone" [1]. Red edges are incorrect edges, green edges were identified correctly.

The discrepancy can be explained by some of the assumptions made, especially when assuming a strict order in which characters speak within a conversation. This means that any error propagates quickly within a conversation, for instance by "flipping" the speakers, whereas the characters identified for that conversation might remain correct.

To synthesize, this step is the most important. It tries to identify all the characters as well as their aliases and allows the identification of a speaker for a majority of the dialogs encountered. However, the interest of the speaker identification may seem useless at first glance. Indeed, building a social network should lead in a first approximation to an undirected network in which all the characters that do present social links are linked together. The speaker identification allows the algorithm to go further by giving a direction to each link, providing for a directed, dynamic network with an edge weight corresponding, for example, to the sentiment transmitted by the speaker. This aspect goes however out of the bounds of this paper and will be the object of later analysis. Here, the capabilities of the algorithm are just demonstrated.

Network Building

The final step of the process consists in the creation of the network. It is the simplest part in principle, but the potential outputs are numerous. Do we want a simple social network (undirected, unweighted, atemporal), do we want the network to be extracted from only one chapter, one context, one book or even an entire series? Do we want it to be dynamic? With sentiment scores? Do we want the scores obtained to be adapted over time or not? Many other networks can also be extracted such as the alias networks, dialog networks... However, for this paper, only social networks are used. Two types of social networks are extracted during the processing, each giving a different characteristic: the "Context Networks" and the "Incremental Networks".

The **"Context Networks"** are built using only the dialogs corresponding to a single conversation, for which the network is built. The resulting graph is undirected, since the interactions are considered to be reciprocal between two characters. All characters appearing in the context are interconnected. This is not mandatory: we could identify the speaker and the audience for each dialog and build a directed graph based on that information. Those networks can be used to analyse a precise sequence of storytelling, but are not the ones on which the following results are based; they will be the subject of further research. An example is given in Fig 12 for the context number 64 in the first book of Harry Potter.

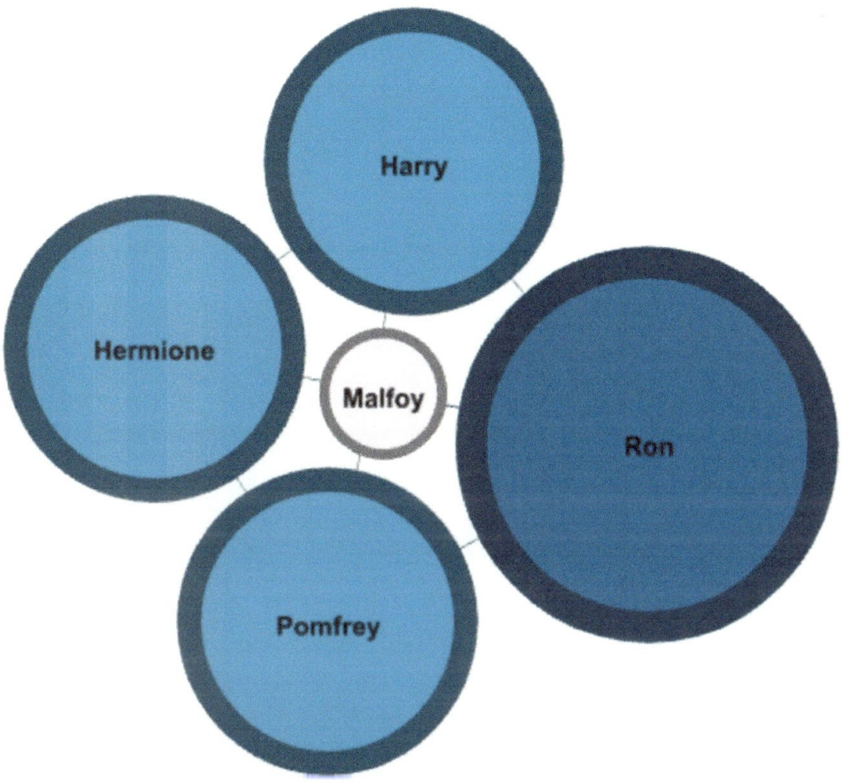

Figure 12. Context network #64 in "Harry Potter and the Philosopher's Stone" [1].

The **"Incremental Networks"**, on the other hand, are built iteratively from the context networks by merging all the context network until some point in the story; in other words, by taking all context networks from the first conversation to a given conversation, and merging them together. An example is given in Fig 13 with 498 contexts considered on the left side (Fig 13 left), roughly corresponding to a specific period of the novel in which only the family members of the main character, Harry, are interacting, as well as a few professors; and the global network on the right side (Fig 13 right), built using the 1670 dialogs available.

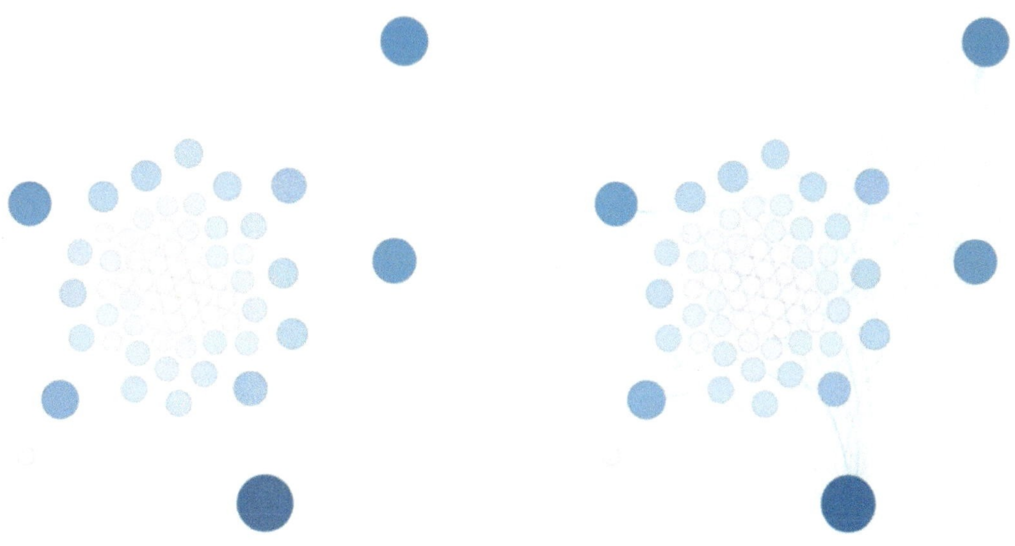

Figure 13. Example of incremental networks for "Harry Potter and the Philosopher's Stone" [1]. On the left, context 0 to 498. On the right, context 0 to 1670.

Every network is exported to the CSV format and drawn as a PNG image, while the final incremental graph, representing the social network at the end of the story, is written to the additional formats GEXF and JSON. The possibilities of outputs are obviously numerous and will undergo additional research in the future. Fig 14 shows an example of such a final graph from the Harry Potter series.

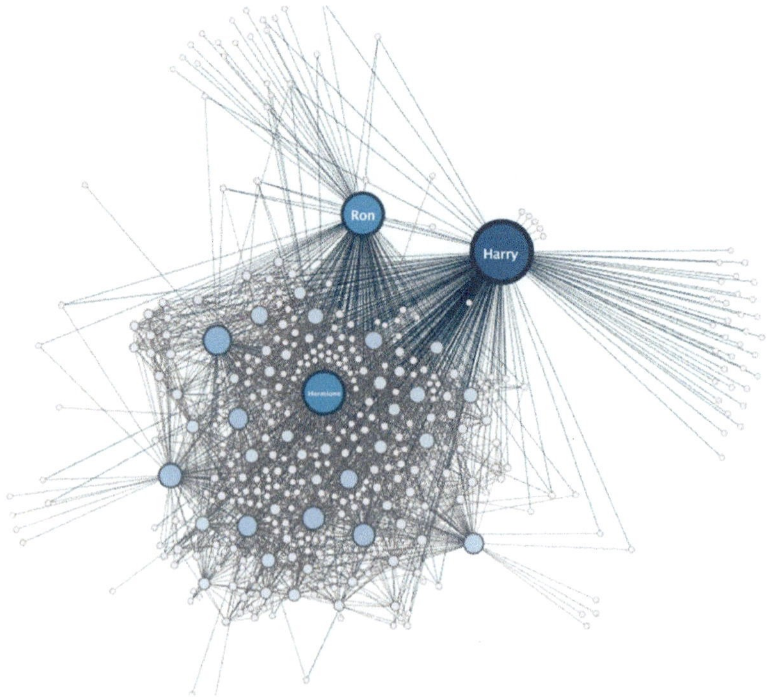

Figure 14. Network Extracted from the book "Harry Potter and the Order of the Phoenix" [5].

In summary, the algorithmic steps just described are able to generate many different types of networks all answering to specific questions. In this paper, we have decided to restrict our analysis on one main aspect: the topology and the time evolution of the characters social network (preferential attachment or not) as well as how they do compare with their real counterparts.

RESULTS

As outcome of the execution of the algorithm many results can be obtained. For the purpose of this article, mainly one example resulting from the social network extraction on "Harry Potter" is examined more deeply, even though the other books and series were analyzed.

Degree Distribution

The degree distributions for each book (See Fig 15 for the distributions of the book from the Harry Potter series) show similar profile and appear similar to the typical distribution of a scale-free network.

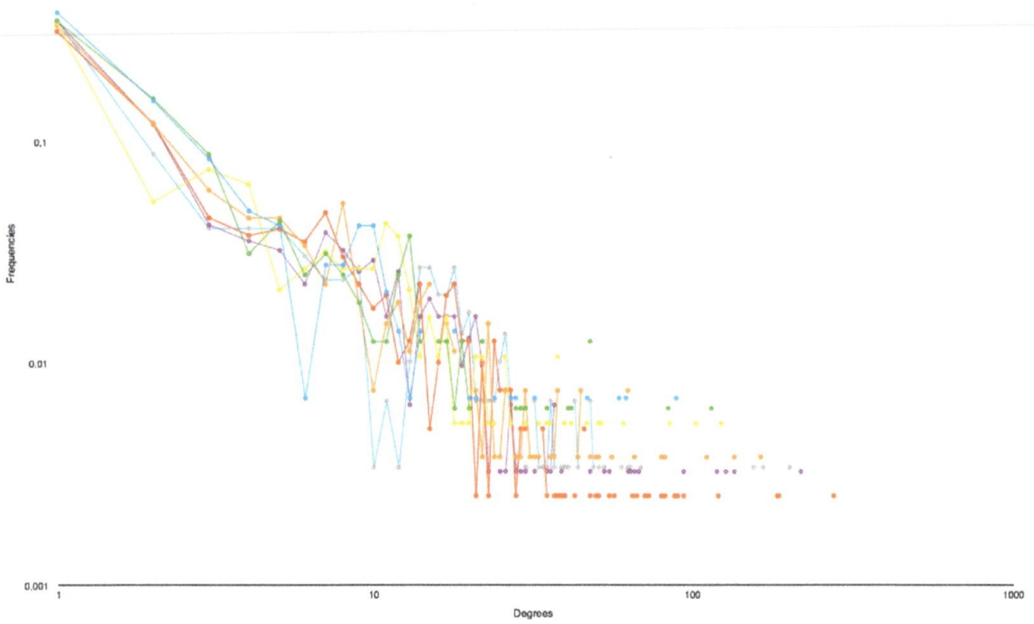

Figure 15. Degree distribution for all Harry Potter books.

It should be noted that, while there is a discrepancy with an ideal power law, it is fairly small (as indicated by the R^2 of the power function fitted to each distribuion) and mostly due to the small size of the networks, meaning that low frequencies for the highest degrees cannot effectively be reached. (See Table 3) The exponent of the power approximation falls in the [−1, −2] range, which is outside of the [−2, −3] predicted by theory [49] or shown by large, scale-free networks, such as the Web graph [65]. However, social networks do show exponents falling in that range ([66–69]). That the networks extracted from novels fall into the lower end of that range can be attributed to two factors that contribute to increasing the probabilities of higher degrees:

- Conversations tend to involve several people at once, either due to several people participating in a conversation or because another character is mentioned during the exchange.
- The specificities of fiction, in particular the so-called "Law of Conservation of Detail" [70], which dictates that any element mentioned in a work of fiction should be relevant (and thus be brought back up again).

Table 3. Exponent of the power approximation.

Book	Equation	R^2
Harry Potter 1	$y = 0.3166x^{-1.2492}$	0.8463
Harry Potter 2	$y = 0.2785x^{-1.1547}$	0.8888
Harry Potter 3	$y = 0.2320x^{-1.0662}$	0.8586
Harry Potter 4	$y = 0.2668x^{-1.1720}$	0.8722
Harry Potter 5	$y = 0.3177x^{-1.2498}$	0.8836
Harry Potter 6	$y = 0.3088x^{-1.2306}$	0.8816
Harry Potter 7	$y = 0.1994x^{-1.0549}$	0.7682
A Game of Thrones	$y = 0.3585x^{-1.2720}$	0.8723
A Clash of Kings	$y = 0.3032x^{-1.2195}$	0.8455
A Storm of Swords	$y = 0.3985x^{-1.3360}$	0.9123
A Feast of Crows	$y = 0.2713x^{-1.1743}$	0.8289
A Dance with Dragons	$y = 0.3207x^{-1.2020}$	0.8607
Nothern Lights	$y = 0.3685x^{-1.3620}$	0.8951
The Subtle Knife	$y = 0.4106x^{-1.4232}$	0.8952
The Amber Spyglass	$y = 0.2782x^{-1.1661}$	0.8238
Les Misérables	$y = 0.3441x^{-1.5805}$	0.9291

doi:10.1371/journal.pone.0126470.t003

These factors, added to the networks' small size, contribute to increasing the real frequencies for higher degrees. This is true, even when considering a series as a single entity, as shown on Fig 16.

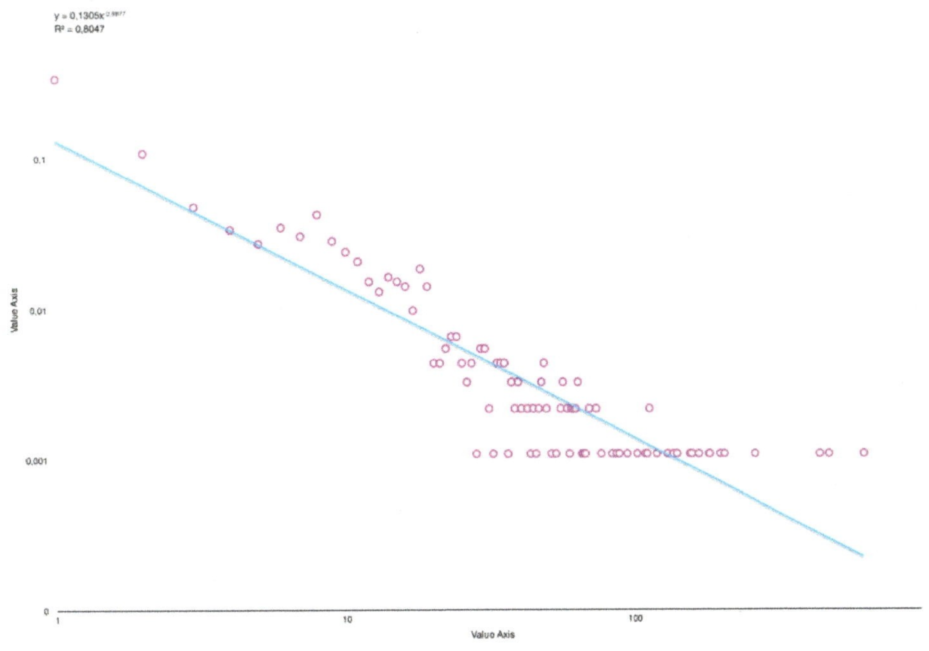

Figure 16. Degree distribution in the full "Harry Potter" series plus the power approximation.

Clustering Coefficient

The clustering coefficients of the incremental networks produced were also computed (See Figs 17 and 18). It shows a clear common trend for all the books: the clustering coefficient starts at a value which is heavily dependent on the first few contexts occurring in the book to quickly stabilize at a value close to its final one. The values then converges slowly.

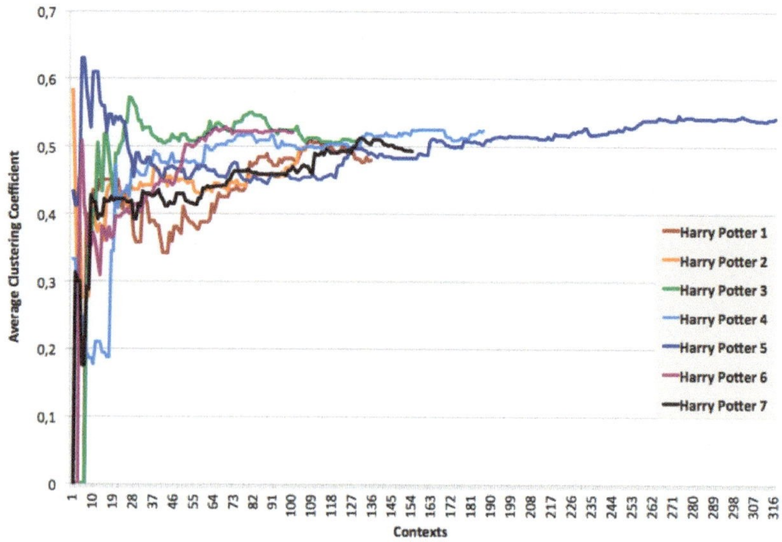

Figure 17. Clustering coefficient in the Harry Potter books.

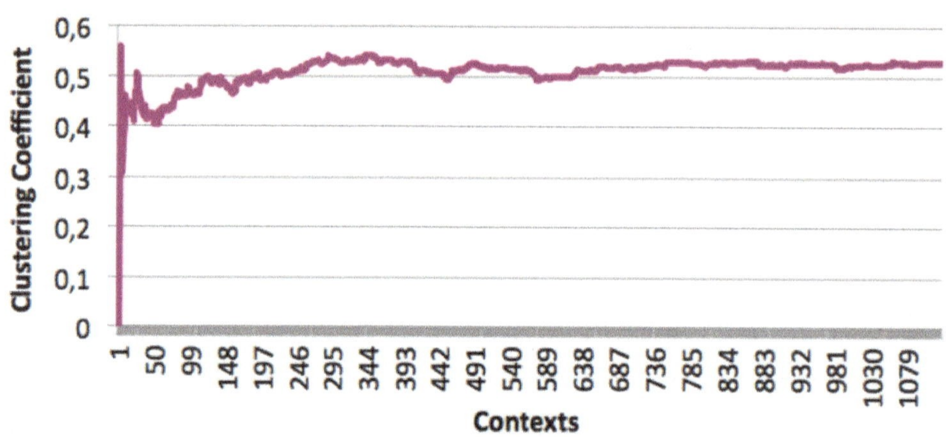

Figure 18. Average clustering coefficient for the seven "Harry Potter" books processed as a single entity.

To assess the significance of the clustering coefficient in a rigorous way, the best point of comparison to use is a similar random graph, whose clustering coefficient is given by $C_{rand} = \langle k \rangle / N$. The same values are computed for the extracted social networks, i.e. their **average clustering coefficient** [48]. The coefficient of a random graph is the proportion of two neighbouring nodes that are connected, equivalent to the probability that two random nodes are connected. The comparison is presented in the table from Fig 4.

The order of magnitude of the coefficient is greater for all the books considered, the same type of results that characterizes scale-free networks, as shown for instance in [48, 66, 67]: one of the common characteristic of social networks [73] is a high ratio of their clustering coefficient to that of a random graph with similar properties (average degree and size).

Going further in the analysis, the clustering coefficient can be explained with more detail by studying the type of narration of each book. For instance, a book that focuses on a single character or group of characters will present a higher clustering than stories focused on several characters. Similarly, extending the scope of the story across time or space will have a tendency to reduce the resulting social network's clustering.

For instance, compare two very different series: *Harry Potter* and *A Song of Ice and Fire*. The former, focused on a single protagonist, features a much higher clustering coefficient than the latter, in which the story follows several protagonist, often very separated in-universe. Another example is within a single series itself, *The Wheel of Time*: the clustering coefficient changes greatly from books where the protagonists are few and/or gathered for a single event ("New Spring", "The Eye of the World", "Winter's Heart") to when the characters are very separated ("The Dragon Reborn", "The Gathering Storm"). (See Table 4)

Table 4. Average clustering coefficient for each book & clustering coefficient for a similar random network.

Book	Clustering	Random
Harry Potter 1	48.00%	4.47%
Harry Potter 2	49.43%	4.75%
Harry Potter 3	50.80%	5.39%
Harry Potter 4	52.37%	3.92%
Harry Potter 5	54.19%	2.92%
Harry Potter 6	52.07%	3.32%
Harry Potter 7	49.40%	3.92%
A Game of Thrones	48.35%	2.95%
A Clash of Kings	47.48%	2.58%
A Storm of Swords	45.23%	1.82%
A Feast of Crows	51.51%	2.29%
A Dance with Dragons	53.24%	2.62%
Nothern Lights	35.41%	3.48%
The Subtle Knife	43.29%	4.07%
The Amber Spyglass	34.55%	4.74%
Les Misérables	20.55%	0.61%
Cinder	33.16%	6.43%
Scarlet	52.38%	5.93%
Cress	42.16%	5.65%
Ship of Magic	46.17%	2.69%
The Mad Ship	35.22%	2.99%
Ship of Destiny	45.82%	4.29%
The Dragon Keeper	33.44%	4.43%
Dragon Haven	36.5%	4.83%
City of Dragons	25.14%	3.35%
Blood of Dragons	33.29%	4.98%
City of Bones	47.76%	4.01%
City of Ashes	45.81%	4.93%
City of Glass	42.85%	4.74%
City of Fallen Angels	43.16%	3.80%
City of Lost Souls	42.61%	3.04%
City of Heavenly Fire	42.78%	3.88%
New Spring	49.62%	4.54%
The Eye of the World	49.35%	2.80%
The Great Hunt	41.08%	2.67%
The Dragon Reborn	37.23%	2.22%
The Shadow Rising	45.16%	2.34%
The Fires of Heaven	38.9%	2.29%
Lord of Chaos	38.87%	1.67%
A Crown of Swords	38.21%	1.79%
The Path of Daggers	35.32%	1.74%
Winter's Heart	42.10%	2.29%
Crossroads of Twilight	44.4%	2.21%
Knife of Dreams	39.11%	1.35%
The Gathering Storm	34.36%	1.80%
Towers of Midnight	37.04%	1.49%
A Memory of Light	42.37%	2.17%

doi:10.1371/journal.pone.0126470.t004

Preferential attachment

Preferential attachment has also been measured and evaluated. The plots in Figs 19 and20 represents the probability that a new node be attached to a node of a given degree, with those degrees being taken a posteriori from the global graph. Those profiles are tested by comparing them to a fitted linear function.

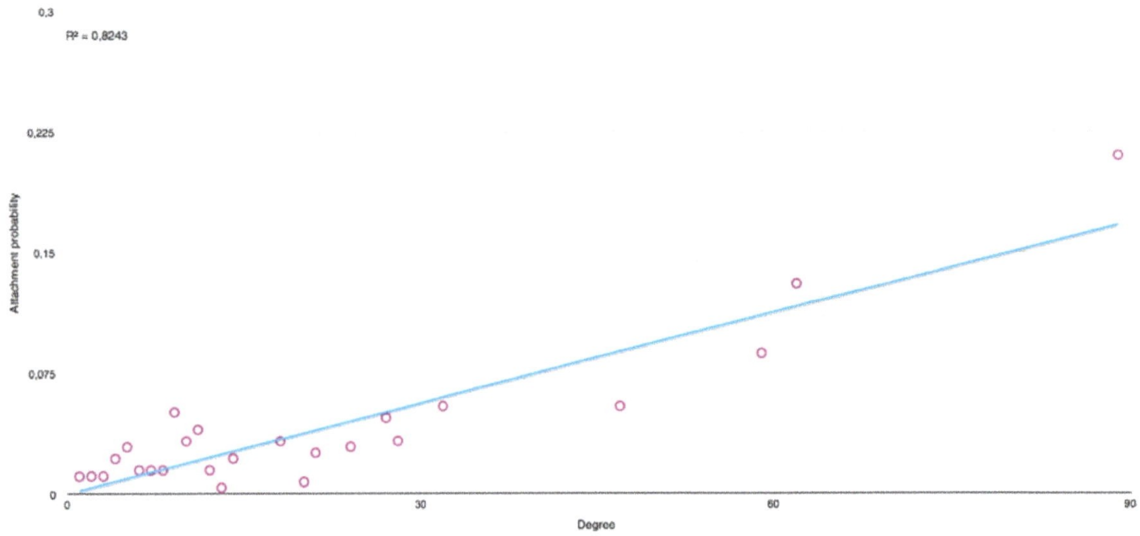

Figure 19. Preferential attachment in "Harry Potter and The Philosopher's Stone" [1]. This plot represents the probability, given the degree of a given node at a given time, that a new node being added to the social network will have a connection to that node.

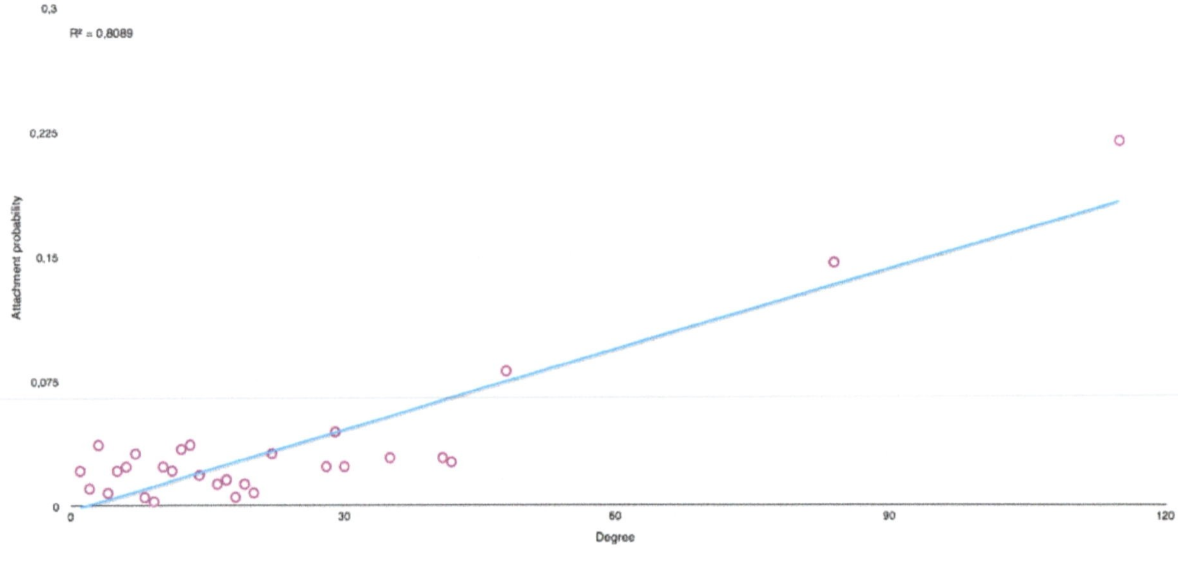

Figure 20. Preferential attachment in "Harry Potter and The Chamber of Secrets" [2].

From those graphs, we can observe that books with a single protagonist have a much higher tendency towards preferential attachment. Indeed, we can verify that in other series like "His Dark Materials", the R^2 values goes down tremendously due to the introduction of a new protagonist in every new book, where the value of R^2 remains similar in the series of "Harry Potter" as well as in the other books.

Clustering of the Books

During the extraction of each book's social network, a number of signature features were identified: the conversation size threshold, the speaker identification rate, the degree distribution's exponent, and the average clustering coefficient in the final network. Two methods of clustering were implemented to test these four features: hierarchical clustering, using the Ward variance minimization algorithm, on Fig 21, and a K-means classification, shown in Table 5.

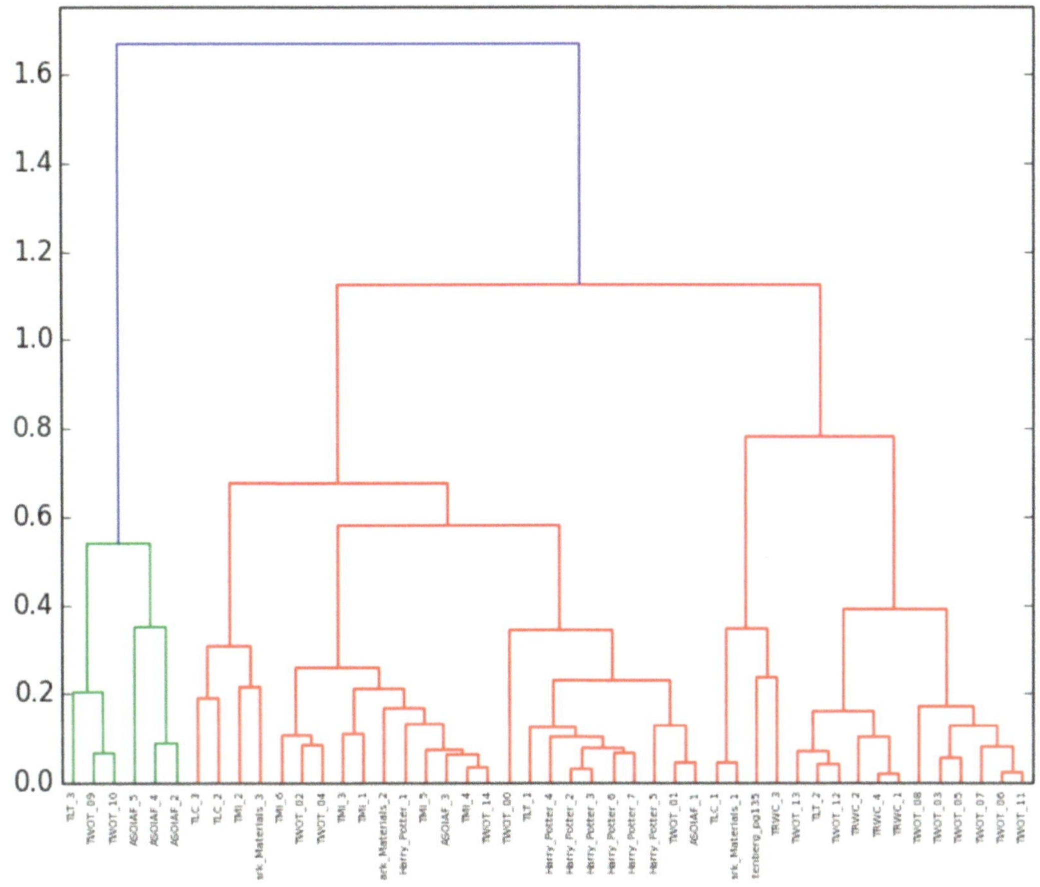

Figure 21. Dendrogram for the hierarchical clustering of the books using the Ward variance minimization algorithm.

Table 5. Clusters generated with K-Means, K = 10.

1	'His Dark Materials 3'
2	'TLT 2', 'TRWC 4', 'TRWC 3', 'TRWC 2', 'TRWC 1', 'TWOT 13', 'TWOT 12'
3	'Les Miserables', 'TLC 1', 'His Dark Materials 1'
4	'TLC 3', 'TLC 2', 'TMI 2'
5	'TWOT 01', 'TWOT 04', 'ASOIAF 1', 'TLT 1', 'Harry Potter 1', 'Harry Potter 2', 'Harry Potter 3', 'Harry Potter 4', 'Harry Potter 5', 'Harry Potter 6', 'Harry Potter 7'
6	'ASOIAF 4', 'ASOIAF 5', 'ASOIAF 2', 'TLT 3'
7	'ASOIAF 3', 'TMI 4', 'TMI 5', 'TMI 3', 'TMI 1', 'His Dark Materials 2', 'TWOT 14'
8	'TWOT 08', 'TWOT 02', 'TWOT 03', 'TWOT 06', 'TWOT 07', 'TWOT 05', 'TMI 6', 'TWOT 11'
9	'TWOT 09', 'TWOT 00', 'TWOT 10'

doi:10.1371/journal.pone.0126470.t005

The dendrogram shows a good clustering of certain series: "Harry Potter", "The Rain Wild Chronicles", "The Lunar Chronicles" and "The Mortal Instruments", for instance, appear to be clustered. Other series are more scattered, which can be attributed to a fluctuation of style: for instance, "The Wheel of Time" is separated in three sub-clusters, gathering similar books within the series together.

The K-means classification yields better results: although some series are still split across several clusters, they are much less numerous than before. With the clustering computed inTable 5, any pair of book is either in the same cluster and part of the same series, or part of different series and in different clusters, with a probability of 83.35%.

These are preliminary results for a proof of concept, and can be improved further.

- We cannot yet suggest a systematic way of pruning the dendrograms to obtain optimal clusters using this method.
- The number of clusters on the K-means analysis was assumed to be the number of distinct authors (10, counting that some books from "The Wheel of Time" were written by a different author). The K-means

clustering was tested with other numbers of clusters (from 2 to 15 clusters), and that value did provide an optimum in the separation of the books. This is a weakness of the K-means algorithm, since it assumes that the number of clusters is known in advance

CONCLUSION AND FUTURE WORK

This paper attempted to replicate the type of network analysis that sociologists perform in their daily studies. Is it important for literature to be respectful of social realities, or are the authors of successful novels imaginative enough in imposing in the same social topology of their history the same fantasy as they create in the fictional worlds in which their characters act?

We proposed a novel algorithm capable of generating multiple types of networks (directed, undirected, weighted, weighted using a sentiment analysis, dynamic) built from novels. Doing so, social networks, alias network, conversation networks now can be generated and analysed. A first social network analysis was also proposed and indicates similarities in the way the social network is presented in novels compared to real life social networks with explanation concerning the differences that might be observed (observation of a power-law degree distribution, high clustering coefficient and an a posteriori preferential attachment verification). Finally, some features were identified that might be relevant in the identification of the author's style like the dialog spacing and alias network topology.

Moreover, this network analysis provided with a number of characteristics related to the book's story and the author's style:

- The dialog spacing frequency (and the resulting threshold value), indicating the relative presence of narration within conversations
- The speaker identification rate, specifically after the metadata extraction step, indicating how much the author reminds their readers of the speakers' identity
- The degree distribution in the final network
- The average clustering coefficient in the final network, indicating the scope (in time, space and number of protagonists) as well as its relation to the clustering coefficient of a similar random network and its temporal evolution

Once further refined, these features will be combined with other method of stylistic analysis, such as the frequency of function words [64, 71], and the stylistic genome ("stylome") introduced by van Halteren et al. [72].

As the algorithm is still under development, there are many different ways to improve it and other further analyses are yet to be made considering the vast number of networks that can be generated. A few tasks seem to be most interesting to tackle quickly though. Those concern the formal verification of the character's identification process as well as the alias table accuracy, solving the coreferences to avoid relying too much on inferences based on the ordering of the dialogs, as well as a sentiment analysis of the dynamic network produced.

With those objectives as a priority, we hope to refine the algorithm further and apply it to other novels as well as other media and try to verify that those novels are built following the same schema of social network.

AUTHOR CONTRIBUTIONS

Conceived and designed the experiments: MCW TN. Performed the experiments: MCW TN. Analyzed the data: MCW TN. Contributed reagents/materials/analysis tools: MCW TN. Wrote the paper: MCW TN HB.

REFERENCES

1. Rowling JK. Harry Potter and the Philosopher's Stone. Bloomsbury Publishing; 1997.
2. Rowling JK. Harry Potter and the Chamber of Secrets. Bloomsbury Publishing; 1998.
3. Rowling JK. Harry Potter and the Prisoner of Azkaban. Bloomsbury Publishing; 1999.
4. Rowling JK. Harry Potter and the Goblet of Fire. Bloomsbury Publishing; 2000.
5. Rowling JK. Harry Potter and the Order of the Phoenix. Bloomsbury Publishing; 2003.
6. Rowling JK. Harry Potter and the Half-Blood Prince. Bloomsbury Publishing; 2005.
7. Rowling JK. Harry Potter and the Deathly Hallows. Bloomsbury Publishing; 2007.
8. Martin GRR. A Game of Thrones. Bantam; 1996.
9. Martin GRR. A Clash of Kings. Bantam; 1998.
10. Martin GRR. A Storm of Swords. Bantam; 1999.
11. Martin GRR. A Feast For Crows. Bantam; 2005.
12. Martin GRR. A Dance With Dragons. Bantam; 2011.
13. Pullman P. Northern Lights. Alfred A. Knopf; 1995.
14. Pullman P. The Subtle Knife. Alfred A. Knopf; 1996.
15. Pullman P. The Amber Spyglass. Alfred A. Knopf; 1999.
16. Meyer M. Cinder. Feiwel & Friends; 2012.
17. Meyer M. Scarlet. Feiwel & Friends; 2013.
18. Meyer M. Cress. Feiwel & Friends; 2014.
19. Clare C. City of Bones. Margaret K. McElderry Books; 2007.
20. Clare C. City of Ashes. Margaret K. McElderry Books; 2008.
21. Clare C. City of Glass. Margaret K. McElderry Books; 2009.
22. Clare C. City of Fallen Angels. Margaret K. McElderry Books; 2011.
23. Clare C. City of Lost Souls. Margaret K. McElderry Books; 2012.
24. Clare C. City of Heavenly Fire. Margaret K. McElderry Books; 2014.
25. Hobb R. Ship of Magic. Voyager; 1998.
26. Hobb R. The Mad Ship. Voyager; 1999.
27. Hobb R. Ship of Destiny. Voyager; 2000.
28. Hobb R. The Dragon Keeper. Voyager; 2009.
29. Hobb R. Dragon Haven. Voyager; 2010.
30. Hobb R. City of Dragons. Voyager; 2012.
31. Hobb R. Blood of Dragons. Voyager; 2013.
32. Jordan R. New Spring. Tor; 2004.
33. Jordan R. The Eye of the World. Tor; 1990.

34. Jordan R. The Great Hunt. Tor; 1990.
35. Jordan R. The Dragin Reborn. Tor; 1991.
36. Jordan R. The Shadow Rising. Tor; 1992.
37. Jordan R. The Fires of Heaven. Tor; 1993.
38. Jordan R. Lord of Chaos. Tor; 1994.
39. Jordan R. A Crown of Swords. Tor; 1996.
40. Jordan R. The Path of Daggers. Tor; 1998.
41. Jordan R. Winter's Heart. Tor; 2000.
42. Jordan R. Crossroads of Twilight. Tor; 2003.
43. Jordan R. Knife of Dreams. Tor; 2005.
44. Jordan R, Sanderson B. The Gathering Storm. Tor; 2009.
45. Jordan R, Sanderson B. Towers of Midnight. Tor; 2010.
46. Jordan R, Sanderson B. A Memory of Light. Tor; 2013.
47. Hugo V. Les Misérables. Project Gutenberg; 2008.
48. Watts DJ, Strogatz SH. Collective dynamics of 'small-world' networks. Nature 1998; 393:440–2. pmid:9623998 doi: 10. 1038/30918
49. Barabási AL, Albert R. Emergence of scaling in random networks. Science 1999 Oct; 286:509–12. doi: 10. 1126/science. 286. 5439. 509. pmid:10521342
50. NetworkX [Internet]. NetworkX developer team; c2014 May. Available from:http://networkx. github. io.
51. Calibre Ebook Management [Internet], Kovid Goyal; c2014 May. Available from:http://calibre-ebook. com.
52. CLiPS Pattern[Internet]. Computational Linguistics & Psycholinguistics Research Center; c2014 May. Available from: http://www. clips. ua. ac. be/pattern.
53. Bird S, Loper E. NLTK: The Natural Language Toolkit. Association for Computational Linguistics; Proceedings of the ACL demonstration session; Barcelona; 2004 Jul; p. 214–17.
54. Miller GA. WordNet: A Lexical Database for English. Communications of the ACM; 1995; 38(11):39–41. doi: 10. 1145/219717. 219748.
55. Fellbaum C. WordNet: An Electronic Lexical Database. Cambridge; MA: MIT Press; 1998.
56. WordNet [Internet]. Princeton WordNet; c2014 May. Available from:http://wordnet. princeton. edu/wordnet/,
57. Baccianella S, Esuli A, Sebastiani F. SENTIWORDNET 3. 0: An Enhanced Lexical Resource for Sentiment Analysis and Opinion Mining. LREC European Language Resources Association; 2010 Oct.
58. Stanford Core NLP [Internet]. The Stanford Natural Language Processing Group; c2014 May. Available from: http://nlp. stanford. edu/software/corenlp. shtml.
59. Francis WN, Kucera H. A Standard Corpus of Present-Day Edited American English, for use with Digital Computers. Department of Linguistics; Brown University; 1964.
60. NLTK. The Natural Language Toolkit; c2014 May. Available from: http://www. nltk. org/.
61. Penn Treebank [Internet]. University of Pennsylvania—Penn Treebank; c2014 May. Available from: http://www. cis. upenn. edu/~treebank/.
62. CLiPS Penn Treebank [Internet]. Computational Linguistics & Psycholinguistics Research Center; c2014 May. Available from: http://www. clips. ua. ac. be/pages/mbsp-tags.
63. TV Tropes—One Steve Limit [Internet]. TV Tropes; c2015 Mar. Available from:http://tvtropes. org/pmwiki/pmwiki. php/Main/OneSteveLimit.
64. Argamon S, Whitelaw C, Chase P, Dhawle S, Hota SR, Garg N, et al. Stylistic text classification using functional lexical features. Journal of the American Society for Information Science and Technology; 2007; 58(6):802822. doi: 10. 1002/asi. 20553.
65. Broder A, Kumar J, Maghoul F, Raghavan P, Rajagopalan S, Stata R et al. Graph structure in the Web. Computer Networks; 2000 Jun; 33(1?6):309–20. doi: 10. 1016/S1389-1286(00)00083-9.
66. Barabási AL, Jeong H, Néda Z, Ravasz E, Schubert A, Vicsek T. Evolution of the social network of scientific collaborations. Physical A: Statistical mechanics and its applications; 2002; 311(3):590–614. doi: 10. 1016/s0378-4371(02)00736-7
67. Mislove A, Marcon M, Gummadi KP, Druschel P, Bhattacharjee B, Measurement and analysis of online social networks. Proceedings of the 7th ACM SIGCOMM conference on Internet measurement; ACM; 2007.
68. Stephen AT, Toubia O, Explaining the power-law degree distribution in a social commerce network. Social Networks; 2009 Oct; 31(4):262–70. doi: 10. 1016/j socnet. 2009. 07. 002.
69. Muchnik L, Pei S, Parra LC, Reis SDS, Andrade JS Jr, Havlin S et al. Origins of power-law degree distribution in the heterogeneity of human activity in social networks. Scientific Reports; 2013; 3:1783. doi: 10. 1038/srep01783. pmid:23648793
70. TV Tropes, The Law of Conservation of Detail [Internet]. TV Tropes; c2014 May. Available from:http://tvtropes. org/pmwiki/pmwiki. php/Main/TheLawOfConservationOfDetail.
71. Mosteller F, Wallace D. Inference and disputed authorship: The Federalist. American Statistical Association Journal; 1963 Jun. doi: 10. 2307/2282943
72. van Halteren H, Baayen H, Tweedie F, Haverkort M, Neijt A. New machine learning methods demonstrate the existence of a human stylome. Journal of Quantitative Linguistics; 2005; 12(1):65–77. doi: 10. 1080/09296170500055350.
73. Kossinets G, Watts DJ. Empirical Analysis of an Evolving Social Network. Science; 2006; 311:88. doi: 10. 1126/science. 1116869. pmid:16400149

CHAPTER 18 DETERMINANTS OF UNLAWFUL FILE SHARING: A SCOPING REVIEW

Steven James Watson[1], Daniel John Zizzo[2], Piers Fleming[3]

[1] Department of Psychology, Lancaster University, Lancaster, Lancashire, United Kingdom

[2] BENC and Newcastle University Business School, Newcastle University, Newcastle Upon Tyne, Tyne and Wear, United Kingdom

[3] School of Psychology, University of East Anglia, Norwich, Norfolk, United Kingdom

ABSTRACT

We employ a scoping review methodology to consider and assess the existing evidence on the determinants of unlawful file sharing (UFS) transparently and systematically. Based on the evidence, we build a simple conceptual framework to model the psychological decision to engage in UFS, purchase legally or do nothing. We identify social, moral, experiential, technical, legal and financial utility sources of the decision to purchase or to file share. They interact in complex ways. We consider the strength of evidence within these areas and note patterns of results. There is good evidence for influences on UFS within each of the identified determinants, particularly for self-reported measures, with more behavioral research needed. There are also indications that the reasons for UFS differ across media; more studies exploring media other than music are required.

INTRODUCTION

This paper presents a simple conceptual framework to map out the existing available evidence regarding unlawful file sharing behavior (referred to as UFS hereafter) and models the decision to engage in the unauthorized consumption of copyright protected goods or to purchase those goods. We employ a *scoping review* that aims to be as systematic and transparent as possible, and which we borrow from areas such as public health and social policy research (e.g. [1, 2]). The application of a scoping review methodology to our context is novel within this field. We are also able to identify areas which require further empirical support in terms of the quantity and quality of available evidence.

The creative industries are worth £36.3 billion, and support 5% of employment and 270,000 businesses in the UK alone [3, 4]. However, these industries are purportedly at risk from unlawful distribution of creative works over the internet. The use of file sharing networks to acquire content for free is extremely common. One in six UK internet users consumes at least some content unlawfully online, or almost one in three of those that consume any content online [5]. Furthermore, peer-to-peer (p2p) file sharing networks are said to account for up to a third of all internet traffic [6]. Therefore, it is important to determine what research exists to explain why consumers

Citation: Watson SJ, Zizzo DJ, Fleming P (2015) Determinants of Unlawful File Sharing: A Scoping Review. PLoS ONE 10(6): e0127921. doi:10.1371/journal.pone.0127921.

choose to file share, or else choose to purchase when UFS is possible, and what are the limitations of that research. If we understand the mechanisms of user choice, this raises the possibility of developing strategies that can compete with UFS more effectively by targeting services to the needs of particular user groups [7].

Existing reviews on UFS are narrative summaries of the existing evidence. However, these are subject to various biases which do not allow them to be replicated or independently verified [8, 9]. The methods of study selection are not described and it is difficult for any one expert to remain up to date with the entire literature available on any one topic [10].

In order to investigate a broad research question, to determine the extent and nature of the research into the determinants of UFS and to provide an associated conceptual framework, the most appropriate method is a scoping review [11]. Scoping reviews specify the search strategy, inclusion and exclusion criteria, and principles of charting and coding data. The specific scope of the review as well as the inclusion criteria are refined iteratively during the data collection process as knowledge of the available evidence increases [1, 11]. It is not necessary to collect every available study on the topic. Instead, scoping reviews aim to cover the conceptual breadth of the available literature and identify the different types of evidence that have been put forward to answer relevant research questions [12]. The identified literature is then coded so that the variables and factors associated with UFS across a diverse array of literature can be meaningfully compared [1, 11, 13]. The net result of this process is a largely narrative account of the current state of play in a research area allowing for identification of research gaps and, potentially, the generation of theory for future empirical testing.

METHOD

These results come from a scoping review on the determinants and implications of UFS of digital media consumed for entertainment, initially defined as music, film, television, electronic games, books and pornography. Our search strategy maximised the breadth of literature regarding UFS from English language academic and grey literature. "Grey literature" refers to any research not published in academic journals. For example government or industry reports, as well as academic research that has not been published. Keywords were developed that combined a range of methods of sharing with relevant types of content that could be shared. Additional keywords were excluded which introduced only irrelevant articles into the search. To ensure the search was comprehensive, identified articles were checked against those from the reference lists of previous literature reviews [14], specifically [15], [16] and [17]. The search string was refined until identified results indicated that the included articles were as comprehensive as possible, i.e. the search prioritizes sensitivity over specificity [12]. The search strategy is summarized in Table 1. To encompass a range of disciplines and perspectives the search string was utilized in five academic databases; Web of Knowledge, EconLit, Communication and Mass Media, PsychInfo, and LexisNexis.

Table 1. Search strategy for academic databases.

Modes of sharing:
(File sharing OR file-sharing OR DRM OR Digital rights manag* OR digital medi* OR File upload* OR File download* OR Torrent file* OR peer-to-peer OR peer to peer OR p2p OR usenet OR freenet OR Newsgroup OR File transfer protocol OR ftp OR shared directory OR Piracy OR pirat* OR online piracy OR copywrit* OR intellectual property OR forum OR digital economy OR kazaa OR Limewire OR bittorrent OR Pirate Bay OR Napster OR isohunt OR eDonkey OR gnutella OR megaupload)
AND: Content shared
(video game OR video-game OR game OR gamer OR gaming OR electronic games OR digital game* OR digital music OR Music OR iTunes OR Album OR sound record* OR Music record* OR artist OR record sales OR DVD sales OR music purchas* OR DVD purchas* OR DVD OR film upload* OR film download* OR movie upload*OR movie download* OR motion picture* OR ebook OR e-book OR e book OR digital book* OR TV OR television OR tele vision OR tele-vision OR tele OR pornography OR porn OR xxx OR adult entertainment OR adult movie OR creativ* OR creator OR artist* OR entertain* OR attitude* OR intention OR social norm*)
NOT: Noise inducing keywords
(Medical OR medicine OR medieval OR Navy OR naval OR maritime)

Note: * refers to the wildcard character in the academic databases that accounts for words that may have multiple endings. E.g. 'Download*' would return 'download', 'downloading' and 'downloaded' *etc*.

doi:10.1371/journal.pone.0127921.t001

Due to search string incompatibility a reduced search was performed in the Westlaw database. It was "(piracy OR file sharing) AND (music OR books OR video games OR film OR television OR pornography)". To capture pre-publication articles, the database of working papers "Social Science Research Network" was searched for the past four full years (2009–2013) using the keywords "file sharing" and "piracy". This database does not support Boolean operators and the two searches were run separately and manually combined. Searches were performed and articles extracted from the 20th to 27th of February 2013.

Grey literature was sought on the websites of key stakeholders and research centers that investigate UFS. Where necessary, the organizations were contacted and access to any research requested. Table 2 lists organizations from which grey literature was sought.

Table 2. Attempted sources of grey literature.

Organizations from which literature was sought
Intellectual Property Office (IPO)
Ofcom
The European Commission
Federal Trade Commission (FTC)
Consumer Focus
Organisation for Economic Co-operation and Development (OECD)
Performing Right Society for Music (PRS)
International Federation of the Phonographic Industry (IFPI)
UK Music
Federation Against Copyright Theft (FACT)
Creative Coalition Campaign (CCC)
Alliance for Intellectual Property
British Phonographic Industry (BPI)
Association for United Kingdom Interactive Entertainment (UKIE)
Institute for Information Law (IVIR)

doi:10.1371/journal.pone.0127921.t002

Relevance Screening

One author (SJW) screened the titles of all identified articles. After excluding obviously irrelevant articles, two authors (SJW and PF) independently screened a random sample of 100 abstracts for inclusion. The decision to include the selected articles was discussed between the two authors to refine inclusion and exclusion criteria and the scope of the review. This promotes consistency in screening and limits single author bias. All remaining abstracts were screened by one author (SJW). Articles were retained for full text review where the abstract indicated that inclusion criteria may be met. Full text review was conducted by one author (SJW).

Inclusion and Exclusion Criteria and Data Extraction

Scoping reviews develop inclusion and exclusion criteria iteratively during the process of screening articles [1]. It became clear that it would be necessary to include unlawful acquisition of software not intended for entertainment use as well as entertainment media to fully explore motivations for UFS. Similarly, for practical reasons, the scope of the review was narrowed to cover the last 10 years of UFS research in the period between January 2003 and February 2013.

This analysis and the identified research focus upon individuals choosing to download copyrighted materials, though we recognize the growing importance of streaming. Only unlawful sharing of otherwise legal content is considered, i.e. studies exploring materials such as child pornography were excluded. Similarly, we focus upon the informal transfer of files between peers without financial transaction.

Only empirical studies were included. The included studies were limited to those including human participants, i.e. not theoretical models without primary observation. Only reports published in the English language are included. Table 3 has a summary of inclusion and exclusion criteria.

Table 3. Summary of inclusion and exclusion criteria.

Inclusion Criteria
To be included research must:
Explore the causes or consequences of UFS of digital media—Digital media is restricted to: Music, movies, software, TV shows, videogames, e-books, and pornography
Be published after January 1st 2003 inclusive
Be published in the English language
Exclusion criteria
Research is excluded where:
Media files are acquired via a financial transaction
Media files contain illegal material (e.g. child pornography)
No novel data is presented (e.g. reviews, opinion pieces, dual publications)
No empirical testing on human participants is performed (e.g. pure economic models)
The article is not written in the English language

doi:10.1371/journal.pone.0127921.t003

Outcome Measure

Data was extracted and categorized iteratively. The type of evidence was characterized in terms of the *distance of the unit of measurement from actual behavior*, which is what ultimately we are interested in when considering UFS and its welfare implications. Most distant from actual behavior, we have *stated preferences and attitudes* on how good or bad, right or wrong, an action is perceived to be, and *stated intentions to perform behavior*, i.e. to engage in UFS behavior. Closer to actual behavior are *willingness to pay (WTP)* measuring the amount of money that people state they are willing to pay to obtain a good and *stated behavior*, which is a participant's report of behavior that has occurred in the past, typically as stated in a survey. We classify a study as looking at *observed behavior* if it is behavior directly observed either at an individual or population level: behavioral experimental data and sales data fit into this category. Qualitative data is considered somewhat separate from this hierarchy as this can examine reports of stated behavior and preferences in a holistic manner. Table 4 summarizes the hierarchy of outcome measures.

Table 4. Definition of outcome measures for unlawful file sharing.

Outcome Measure	Definition
Qualitative research	Explorations of perceptions of or engagement in behaviors without quantitative assessment.
Stated preferences and attitudes	Outcome is at the level of how good or bad, right or wrong, or preferable an action is perceived to be
Intentions to perform behavior	Outcome described participants reports of behavior that they plan to engage in in the future
Willingness to pay (WTP)	Outcome represents the amount of money that a participant states they are willing to pay in order to obtain a good
Stated behavior	Outcome represents a participant's report of behavior that has been engaged in in the past, such as from a survey
Observed behavior	Outcome represents behavior that is either directly observed at the level of the individual, such as in an experiment, or else at the population level, such as from sales data

doi:10.1371/journal.pone.0127921.t004

Data Analysis

Data analysis was based upon thematic framework analysis [13, 18, 19]. Data were initially coded during extraction according to relatively *ad hoc* groups of similar variables. These were developed and refined into a framework in which the proposed correlates of UFS could be incorporated. The results within each subtheme were divided according to level of outcome measurement, and medium type (music, movies, TV, videogames, software, books or pornography). This allows comparison of the relative impacts of variables across different measures of outcome and media. A summary of the key points from each theme is presented. The supplements contain the full list of references (S1 File).

Selection of Studies

A large majority of the initially identified studies were excluded, this is common when searches are highly sensitive [12]. Fig 1 summarizes the inclusion and exclusion process for all articles identified through electronic databases. Reasons for excluding 134 articles at full text review were, not being an empirical study (46), not being relevant (43), being a duplicate publication (37), only examining exchanges which included a financial transfer (7), and one study was excluded for being in a foreign language. This left 195 articles to be included in the review, though only 192 were useable. Three studies did not provide data that could be synthesized into any of the categories of our conceptual framework and so were not used further. They only compared UFS attitudes and behavior depending upon occupation [20], provided a typology of those that UFS but without presenting sufficient information for the individual factors that determined this typology to be extracted and combined with similar studies [21], or else provided insufficient description of the variables included in their model to permit accurate classification of included factors [22]. One hundred and twenty-two reports were identified from the grey literature, of which 108 were excluded. The reasons for exclusion were not being empirical (48), not being relevant (43), being a duplicate publication of an already identified article (13), only examining exchanges of media which included a financial transfer (2), and being published in a foreign language (2). This included an additional 14 articles in the review. Therefore the final number of studies included in the review is 192 + 14 = 206. Only one article made any reference to pornography as a media [23], and in this case no predictors of unlawful pornography downloading were identified. Therefore this media was not analyzed further.

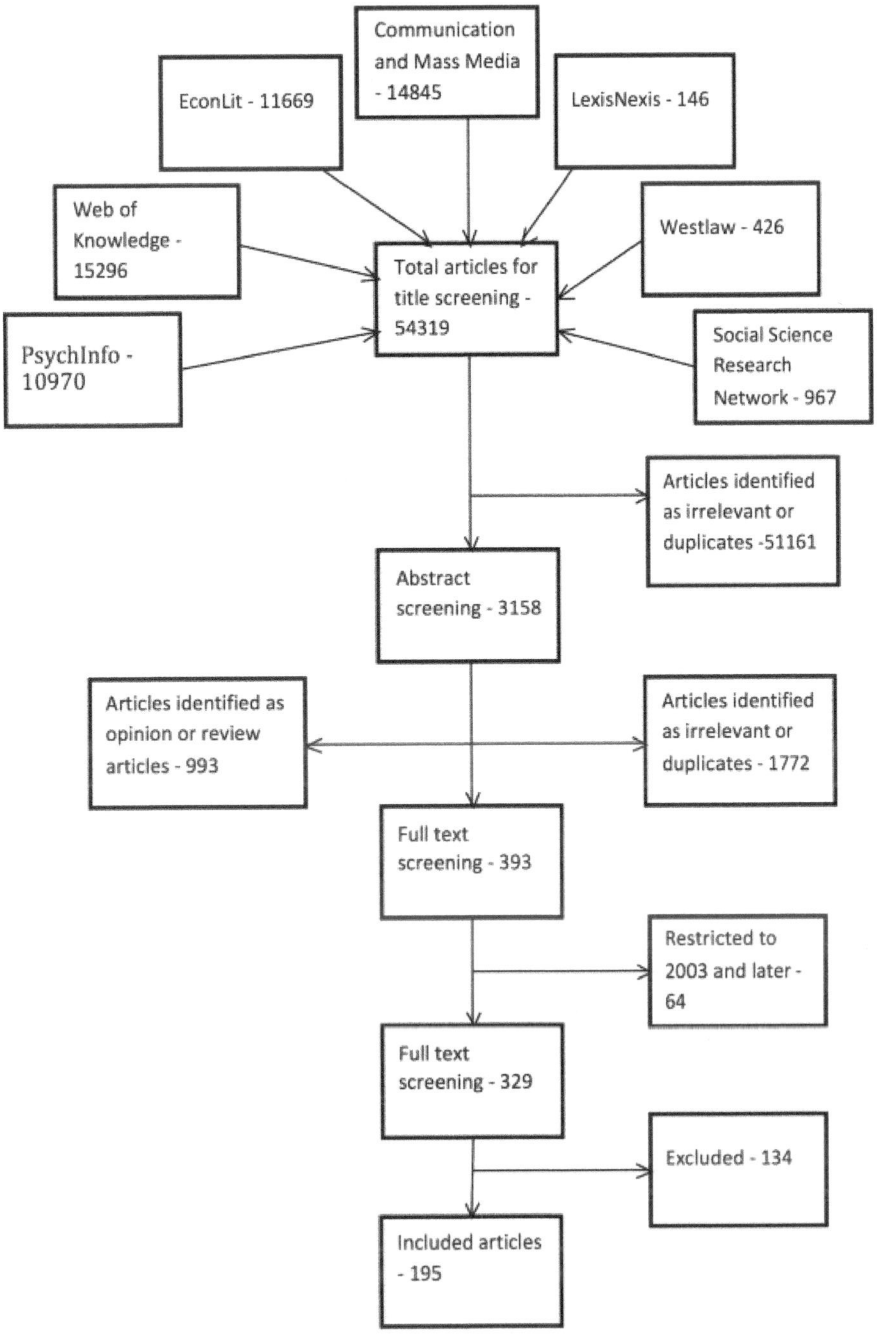

Figure 1. Flow diagram of academic articles included in the review (in addition to 14 grey literature articles).

RESULTS

In considering the evidence, it became clear that we could classify it depending on the type of factors affecting whether or not to engage in unlawful file sharing. To anticipate the conceptual framework presented later in the paper, we can consider legal and financial sources, experiential sources, technical sources, social sources and moral sources of utility. What we are going to label a *total net utility* judgment, i.e. one that takes into account (possibly in a interacting and non-linear way, as will be shown) all utility sources, then determines whether or not to engage in UFS, buy the product or do nothing, depending on which action leads the highest utility.

We can classify data from 186 of the 206 included studies from our scoping review according to the net utility source. Some studies (also) refer to total net utility estimates regarding how beneficial or otherwise UFS is perceived to be when compared to the options of legal purchase or no action; they are classified as providing information on total net utility.

We provide a conceptual representation of the available literature along three dimensions: (1) the net utility source or total net utility, as discussed; (2) the market medium (music, software, movies, TV, books and videogames); and (3) the outcome measure (qualitative, stated preferences, intentions, willingness to pay WTP, stated behavior, observed behavior). We illustrate this in Fig 2 and in Table 5. Note that Individual studies may be counted in multiple cells, e.g. a single study may cover both music and movies.

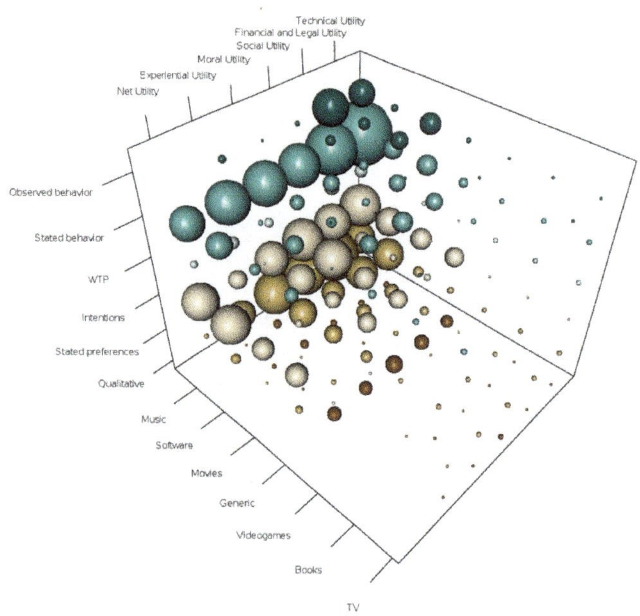

Figure 2. A Cubic Space of Available Evidence on Unlawful File Sharing. Note: the size of the sphere in the cube represents the amount of evidence available for each combination.

Table 5. Number of observations for each utility level, market medium and outcome measure.

Utility	Medium	Qualitative	Stated preferences	Intentions	WTP	Stated behavior	Observed behavior	Total
Financial and Legal Utility	Videogames	0	1	0	0	2	1	4
	Books	1	2	0	0	0	0	3
	TV	1	2	0	0	0	1	4
	Movies	0	7	3	0	7	7	24
	Software	3	16	7	1	4	5	36
	Music	3	26	18	7	24	16	94
	Generic	7	4	3	1	7	0	22
	Total	15	58	31	9	44	30	187
Experiential Utility	Videogames	0	0	1	0	3	0	4
	Books	0	1	0	0	2	1	4
	TV	1	1	0	0	2	0	4
	Movies	1	1	3	0	7	1	13
	Software	2	0	1	1	2	0	6
	Music	1	12	8	5	18	3	47
	Generic	6	2	0	0	1	1	10
	Total	11	17	13	6	35	6	88
Technical Utility	Videogames	0	2	1	2	2	1	8
	Books	1	2	1	2	2	1	9
	TV	1	2	1	2	2	1	9
	Movies	0	5	10	2	9	9	35
	Software	3	16	14	1	9	3	46
	Music	1	16	21	6	30	12	86
	Generic	6	3	9	1	4	2	25
	Total	12	46	57	16	58	29	218
Social Utility	Videogames	0	1	0	0	0	0	1
	Books	1	2	0	0	0	0	3
	TV	2	2	0	0	0	0	4
	Movies	1	7	10	0	3	1	22
	Software	3	11	18	1	7	4	44
	Music	4	21	20	1	19	2	67
	Generic	8	2	8	0	8	1	27
	Total	19	46	56	2	37	8	168
Moral Utility	Videogames	0	2	0	0	0	1	3
	Books	1	2	0	0	0	0	3
	TV	1	2	0	0	0	0	3
	Movies	0	8	7	0	4	0	19
	Software	4	13	13	0	6	0	36
	Music	4	20	16	4	19	1	64
	Generic	6	5	8	0	7	0	26
	Total	16	52	44	4	36	2	154
Total Net Utility	Videogames	0	0	1	0	0	0	1
	Books	0	0	0	0	0	0	0
	TV	0	0	0	0	0	0	0
	Movies	0	1	9	0	4	0	14
	Software	0	4	16	0	10	0	30
	Music	0	2	16	3	14	0	35
	Generic	0	3	9	0	5	0	17
	Total	0	10	51	3	33	0	97

doi:10.1371/journal.pone.0127921.t005

It is clear from Fig 2 and Table 5 that books, videogames, and TV have received very little attention. There is some literature represented that explores software and movie UFS, but by far the most common medium explored is music. A number also ask participants to report on "digital piracy", "p2p use" or "downloading of digital media" generally. The reliance on a generic description of behavior seems likely to generate measurement error. To prove an association between a proposed cause of a behavior and the behavior itself, it is important to be specific about the target behavior. Motives to download music unlawfully may differ from motives to download movies or software; this review finds potentially different financial and experiential effects for software compared to other media (see below). Asking participants for reasons they download media in general, leaves participants and researchers unable to specify which behaviors are being considered and thus introduces noise into estimates of association. Furthermore, estimates of behavior using actual observation are rare when compared to outcomes based upon perceptions of UFS, stated intentions to file share or purchase, or stated behaviors. Almost all of the studies of observed behavior concern financial and legal net utility and technical net utility, and even then are mostly restricted to music and movies. Most observations look at attitudes (stated preferences) and intentions, and it is unclear whether these would result in actual behavior, or where there is a relationship, whether they may reflect reverse causality (from behavior to statements made congruent to the behavior).

We now consider the existing evidence with respect to total net utility and each net utility source in detail.

Total Net Utility

Using global attitude assessments or reported cost-benefit assessments as a proxy for a net utility assessment provided evidence that these measures reflect consumer preferences regarding UFS.

There is overwhelming evidence for a relationship between *attitudes regarding UFS and intentions to file share* or purchase; only one study from 32 failed to find a relationship between the two variables [24]. Furthermore, all nine studies which estimated the *impact of attitudes upon stated UFS behavior* identified a relationship regardless of medium. One study explored the relationship between attitudes and legal purchases, and failed to identify a relationship between attitudes regarding UFS and legal purchases of digital music [25]. Intent to file share or purchase was similarly found to be associated with stated purchasing and UFS behaviors regardless of medium.

Hsu and Shiue [26] found participants with a higher WTP for software preferred legal over unlawful software, had higher legal purchase intentions, and were more likely to report having purchased legal software. There is also evidence from a further nine studies that those that engage in UFS have a lower WTP for content than those that do not, and that unlawfully downloaded content was valued less than purchased content [27]. It is clear overall that *WTP is related to UFS.*

The evidence base for net utility assessments comprised 97 outcomes, skewed towards music (36%), and software (31%). About half as many were relevant to movie UFS (14%), and only one was relevant to videogames. No studies utilized net utility estimates to investigate e-book or TV series UFS. 61 (63%) of the available outcome estimates utilized stated preferences or intentions as an outcome measure. While 33 outcomes (34%) referred to estimates of stated behavior, no study utilized observed behavior for total net utility.

Legal and Financial Utility

Nine studies compared the intellectual property (IP) *law strength* in different nations to estimate rates of UFS or legal sales. Overall, indicators of legal strength such as membership of international treaties, and legal enforcement costs and efficiency were associated with more legal sales and lower rates of UFS. The studies utilized estimates of UFS exclusively from the producers' side of the IP rights debates, such as the International Federation of the Phonographic Industry, Business Software Alliance, and the International Intellectual Property Alliance. A more fundamental problem is that correlation is not causation. For example, different cultural factors or economic development levels may be correlated with particular IP regimes and with particular levels of UFS. Relatedly, IP law strength was also correlated with national wealth which may confound the extent to which the two effects can be disentangled; although Walls [28] model implies that for unlawful movie file sharing legal strength may be the more important factor. The role of national income may not be linear, with some evidence that when income is high sales of "inferior goods" such as music may drop [29]. For software, four studies consistently found that higher national income was associated with less UFS, suggesting that conversely software is not an inferior good.

There is evidence for a *temporary effect of new laws* protecting IP. Adermon and Liang [30] monitored internet traffic after a new IP law was introduced in Sweden, and compared this to Norway and Finland where no new law was introduced. Internet traffic immediately after the introduction of the new law reduced by 18%, but had recovered within 6 months of the law being passed, implying the new law acted only as a short term deterrent. Blackburn [31] similarly found that, when the Recording Industry Association of America (RIAA) announced lawsuits against individual file sharers, the availability of files on five torrent sites dropped. However, by the time lawsuits were actually being filed, overall availability of files had actually increased. Danaher *et al.* [32] (This paper has since been accepted for publication in the Journal of Industrial Economics after peer review) found that iTunes sales increased when the French public became widely aware of the incoming HADOPI law, which suggests that legal disutilities from unlawful sharing had increased legal sales. However, when the law was actually passed, no effect was observed. This may be because the French public had already fully adjusted to the policy change. Bhattacharjee *et al.* [33] found that the RIAA lawsuits reduced the number of files available for UFS, but a significant proportion remained available.

An alternative approach is to examine the impact of deterrents upon individual attitudes and behavior. Three groups of variables were considered: those that examined the *legal risk*(that is, the probability of capture), those that examined the severity of the consequences of capture, and those that did not distinguish between the two effects (22 studies). Of the latter 22 studies, eight estimated the impact upon actual behavior, four of which found deterrents reduced behavior, and four did not. Evidence was more convincing that a legal deterrent lowers intent to UFS, with four of five studies finding an effect.

Participants also stated that they did perceive laws to be a deterrent against UFS [34], but in most cases *perception of laws* as a deterrent was seen as a concern to a minority and more participants were concerned by technical risks of UFS such as catching computer viruses [35, 36]. Qualitative research also emphasized that participants thought that UFS "did not feel like a crime" [37], and that participants were often unaware of what was or was not unlawful [38].

Studies on the role of probability and severity of consequences specifically, found conflicting evidence. Two out of six studies examining the role of severity upon stated behaviors found a relationship, but four out of five studies on attitudes found a relationship. Conversely, evidence linking attitudes to the probability of capture were less clearly related (three of seven studies found a relationship) compared to behavioral evidence (five of seven studies find a relationship).

Fifty-three studies examined the role of pricing. With regard to behavior, higher prices were related to lower legal sales, though the link to UFS rates was unclear, with only five of 11 studies finding that higher prices were associated with more UFS. Six studies found a relationship between higher prices and lower observed sales of music [39–41] and movies [42, 43] and TV [44], no studies identified a relationship between higher pricing and observed UFS behavior. There was also no clear effect from 27 studies investigating the role of individual participant's income upon UFS.

Legal and financial net utility has been heavily researched in comparison to the other identified utility types with 187 observations. However, there was still significant skew in the type of evidence available as well as the media represented. Half of observations focused on music UFS and purchasing. The evidence for other media types was much smaller at 19% of observations for software and 13% for movies. Only four studies explored TV and videogames, and three investigated e-books. Stated preferences and intentions were common outcome measures (31% and 17% respectively). 16% used observed behavior, and 24% had stated behavior as an outcome.

Experiential Utility

Twenty studies explored *interest in the product* as an experiential factor, though only one used observed behavior [45]. Qualitative research from five studies indicated that enjoying the product was a stated motive for UFS in all media, with the possible exception of software. Konstantakis *et al.* [46] found that computer science students considered software to just be a tool they utilized and there was no emotional engagement with products employing this medium when compared to that with books, games, or other media. Five studies examined the role of interest in the product upon unlawful acquisition and only two found a significant positive association [47, 48].

Only four studies investigated *collecting* (the desire to own a collection) as a motive for UFS. Two studies found that it was associated with the gratification felt from unlawfully obtaining content [49, 50]. However, [51] found that 15% of her sample reported the desire to own a collection was a reason for preferring CDs over p2p files. Hennig-Thurau *et al.* [52] estimated the impact of desiring a large collection on actual behavior, and found that this was associated with downloading more movies unlawfully but not with the number of unlawfully acquired movies actually watched. Of course, having a large collection because of other reasons may have led to post hoc justifications such as stating a desire to own a collection.

13 studies examined the extent to which *sampling* (the desire to gain knowledge about product content) was a motive for UFS. These studies found broad support for the hypothesis that products were acquired unlawfully at least sometimes to try out content prior to purchase. Chen *et al.* [53] found that a reason for preferring the use of p2p services over legal content providers was that the p2p services were considered superior for trying new music (see also, [54]). UFS may also be utilized to obtain *niche content*, i.e. content which is not popular enough to be readily available legally. This possibility was explored in 16 studies. Six qualitative studies and three national surveys found support for this hypothesis, with participants stating that the availability of niche content on p2p services allowed access to content that would be otherwise unavailable. Tzantzara and Economides [55] had participants rank services in terms of the extent of their catalogue and found that p2p services were rated most highly while iTunes, the legal service examined, was ranked as the worst. Two studies provided empirical support that the belief that unlawful networks had the best selection of content was associated with using these services [56, 57]. Experiential utility related to niche content may of course interact with technical utility from the technical availability of the content itself, which is discussed below.

Mateus and Peha [23] tracked the files that were downloaded via p2p networks on a university campus. They were able to demonstrate that content did follow a long tail distribution, implying that much downloaded content was not exceptionally popular.

The experiential utility evidence base was the slimmest, with only 88 outcome estimates. This was again heavily skewed towards music (53%) with other evidence limited; movies were the next most investigated media (15%). Most studies measured the impact of experiential factors on the level of stated behavior (40%), only six estimates (7%) utilized observed behavior.

Technical Utility

The question of the *technical availability* of legal (particularly niche) content was explored by nine studies, five of which were qualitative, a survey, and three which estimated observed behavior. The qualitative studies emphasized the impact of release lags, also identified as a motive for UFS in a large survey of UK residents [35]. The impact of release lags received quantitative support from Danaher and Waldfogel [58], who found that longer release lags between countries for movies were associated with lower box office earnings in cinemas. Danaher *et al.* [44] found that the removal of NBC content from iTunes did not affect physical DVD sales but did increase the amount of UFS activity regarding NBC content on p2p networks. This implies that the physical and digital markets may be separate, with legal and unlawful downloads competing more closely than physical sales. Danaher *et al.* [44]Danaher, Dhanasobhon (44) also found that uploads and downloads of non-NBC content on p2p networks increased following the removal of the legal content. This could mean that, once some users had turned to UFS, they used this medium for more than just the removed content, suggesting that there are fixed costs associated with learning to engage in UFS and, once these are taken up, the technical disutility from engaging in UFS will be lower, leading to increased UFS. In Danaher *et al.* (2010), the restoration of NBC content to iTunes did not significantly reduce UFS activity, indicating that the removal of content had led to UFS becoming habitual.

Thirty-five studies have explored directly the hypothesis that, the easier UFS is, the more consumers engage in it. They have predominantly asked participants about internet access, or estimated it by measuring internet and broadband penetration. The evidence does not support an impact of these variables upon attitudes about UFS or intent to engage in UFS. Similarly the effect upon stated behavior in 12 studies was mixed, with six studies finding that technical ease of UFS was associated with UFS rates or a reduction in sales, four studies finding no effect, and two studies finding mixed effects. Mandel and Suessmuth [59] found that having a broadband connection was associated with engaging in UFS more frequently but not to a greater extent than those without a broadband connection. With regard to observed behavior, estimates of the impact of internet or broadband penetration were that it lowers physical music sales in five of six studies, though of course this can be interpreted in terms of online sales, not necessarily in terms of UFS. The one study with no effect, did find that there may be a relationship when IP law strength is weaker in a nation [39]. The direction of effect between broadband or internet penetration and sales was less clear for software, where a positive association between penetration and sales was found [60], and for movies, where two out of three studies found a positive effect upon sales [42,43, 61]. A particular complication of using broadband or internet penetration as a measure of technical ease of UFS is that it is confounded by other variables such as legal online sales, wealth, legal strength, and national infrastructure. Similarly, there are difficulties with establishing a causal relationship between the availability of internet or broadband connections and UFS.

An alternative approach is to estimate the impact of the availability of UFS technology or websites upon sales. Danaher and Waldfogel [58] found that, after the introduction of the BitTorrent protocol, longer release windows were associated with lower box office revenues. This implied that pre-release movie UFS significantly impacted upon sales once UFS became easier to perform. Danaher and Smith [62] explored the impact of the shutdown of a major file sharing website (this paper has since been accepted for publication in the International Journal of Industrial Organization after peer review). They checked for differences in the use of this website between countries and identified a statistically significant increase in digital movie sales. However, it is impossible to determine from this study whether the observed increase would last beyond the 18 week follow up period. Poort and Leenheer [63] found that the blocking of the Pirate Bay website had led to 21% of participants reporting less UFS, but had had no effect on 72%, while 5% said they downloaded more. Of course, the effects may be moderated by the availability of substitute websites.

The evidence from 33 studies overwhelmingly indicates a relationship between perceived*technical skills* to engage in and having more positive attitudes towards UFS, and having a greater intent to file share. However only six studies estimated the impact of such perceptions upon stated behaviors. Although four of these six studies did find a positive relationship, there is a lack of evidence based upon observed behavior. Estimates of the impact of technical skill upon UFS were estimated by 31 studies. The evidence was reasonably consistent that greater technical skill was associated with a greater propensity to UFS behavior, however this was not found for three studies specifically examining software UFS [64–66].

One function of technical skill may be mitigating the *technical risk* posed by viruses and malware, which was explored by 19 studies. Qualitative studies and surveys including participants that did not file share found technical risks to be a disincentive for UFS. However, within samples of file sharers, technical risks were not consistently related to intent to file share or stated behavior. This may reflect that the perception of technical risks are more significant than the actual barriers themselves which once overcome no longer have any effect upon behavior [67]; alternatively, it may be related to the gap between intentions and actual behavior.

Seven studies suggested that one motive for UFS was having an *interest in technology*. Users who file share were found to be early adopters of technology [51, 68, 69] and qualitative evidence suggested that some file sharers do so to "push the envelope" [38]. Relatedly, UFS was perceived as being more convenient in terms of time taken to identify and acquire media and more flexible with regard to how files could be manipulated and used once acquired [51, 57, 70–73]. The use of digital rights management (DRM) and the requirement to continually relicense software products was opposed by users [74].

Technical factors associated with UFS have been relatively extensively researched, with 218 observations. Although music was still the most explored media type (39%), software (21%) and movies (16%) also had a number of relevant observations. However fewer than 10 observations each explored the influence of technical factors upon UFS and purchases of TV, videogames, and books. Stated behaviors, intentions and preferences were all explored to a similar extent (27%, 26% and 21% of outcomes respectively).

Social Utility

A large number of observations (78) investigated *normative beliefs*, that is the extent the beliefs and behaviors of others could influence perceptions of UFS and UFS behaviors. There was widespread evidence that the perceived beliefs and behaviors of others were correlated to individual's beliefs, intentions, and stated behaviors regarding engagement in UFS. One specific channel could be by moderating the effect of perceived legal strength. Of course, it may be that behavior—determined by other utility sources—may be determining responses in these studies. According to these studies, social norms may be more influential when norms are congruent with attitudes [75], when media is intended to be enjoyed socially rather than alone [76] and in collectivist versus individualist cultures [77]. The role of collectivist cultures upon UFS was separately analyzed in nine studies and within them UFS was perceived more acceptable and engaged in more frequently. Denegri-Knott [78] analyzed comments on a website that was set up in opposition to the RIAA and found that a number of them made reference to the fact that the internet itself may have a collectivist culture.

Social norms may in part reflect wider cultural moral beliefs and we focus on moral utility below.

An additional social motive identified for engaging in UFS was maintenance of *social prestige*. Maintaining or enhancing reputation through knowledge of media was identified as a motive for UFS in nine qualitative studies. That said, three studies found a relationship between social-status seeking and UFS and three did not. Kwan [79] found that the relationship between the expectation of social gain from UFS and intent to file share was stronger for hedonistic media, movies and music, than for software. Social prestige may also be more important for providing content than for acquiring it [80, 81], but it is very difficult to know from this literature whether and how actual behavior would change as a result of changes in this potential source of social net utility. Social prestige may interact with experiential utility from the collecting motive, which we have discussed above.

A final social factor that may be related to UFS and legal purchases is *reciprocation*, that is the formation of reciprocal relationships. Qualitative studies identified that within file sharing networks it was felt that downloaders should contribute back into the system, and some networks enforce this by slowing download speeds for those that don't contribute or barring non-contributory users entirely [73, 82]. Cenite *et al.* [70] found via interviews with students that there was also a sense of reciprocity with creators and that content that is enjoyed should be purchased. However, no studies have so far estimated the impact of reciprocity upon downloading behavior.

Most of the 168 sources of social net utility investigated music (40%) or software (26%). Movie UFS was the next most studied media (13%). TV series, books and videogames were investigated in less than five samples each. The most popular outcome measure was at the level of intentions (33%), followed by stated preferences (27%) and stated behaviors (22%). Only eight outcomes measured observed behaviors (5%).

Moral Utility

Six studies directly compared the effects of participants basing their moral beliefs upon what was legal or not. Those participants that used the law to frame their own moral beliefs were more likely to perceive UFS as morally wrong, while, in a Swedish sample that considered UFS morally acceptable, the correctness of the laws was questioned [83].

Twelve studies examined the role different *moral frameworks* may have upon UFS. The contrast between absolutist versus relativist morals may have an impact upon both attitudes about and intention to engage in UFS [84] as well as reported behaviors [85] with absolutist moral frameworks being more likely to view UFS negatively. Research examining whether or not participants consider UFS to be a moral issue at all also found a division between those that utilized more absolute stances and those that instead used contextual information to inform their moral beliefs. Zamoon and Curley [86] performed a content analysis of the five most popular US newspapers, with articles on unlawful software file sharing coded according to their moral arguments for or against UFS. They found that arguments in favor of UFS were less likely than arguments against UFS to be based upon moral justifications. Arguments against UFS were centered upon a small number of key concerns, in particular economic harms to producers. Jambon and Smetana [48] asked participants to complete a survey when considering a scenario in which an artist receives 90% of the profits and a scenario in which industry receives 90% of the profits from sales. They found that it was argued that UFS was a personal and not a moral choice more often when artists were perceived to be the primary beneficiary of sales. It was proposed that, while arguments against UFS tend to focus on absolutes and are relatively constant, the arguments in favor of UFS are more fluid and shift depending upon context. Not considering UFS to be an ethical problem was found to be associated with UFS behaviors in both qualitative and quantitative studies [46, 87, 88].

37 studies tried to estimate the relationships between moral beliefs about UFS, and various*moral justifications* regarding UFS and behavior. Appealing to higher loyalties was a technique utilized more often by those that engaged in UFS more frequently indicating that a belief that UFS enhances social welfare may motivate such behavior [89]. Nine studies directly estimated this possibility and the evidence was consistent that the belief UFS enhanced social welfare was associated with attitudes, intentions, and stated behaviors regarding UFS. A further 15 studies investigated the role of participants awareness of causing harm via UFS and there was a general perception that little or no harm was caused, and while participants had more sympathy when harm was presented as being caused to creators rather than industry, there was still a perception that such harm could be absorbed easily.

Moral net utility was examined by 154 observations. Music was still the most common medium investigated (42%). Software was also fairly well represented in this literature (23%), with movies being researched to a lesser extent (12%). However, it was common to not specify media types when exploring moral factors (17%). As with other utility sources, videogames, TV series and books were only weakly represented. Measured outcomes were most commonly stated preferences, intentions and stated behaviors (34%, 29% and 23% respectively), but there was a paucity of evidence estimating observed behavior, with only two observations (1%).

DISCUSSION

We have outlined the relevant factors that determine the proposed utilities which the extant literature has identified as predictive of UFS behavior. Fig 3 and Table 6 illustrate the identified factors and their proposed links in a conceptual model.

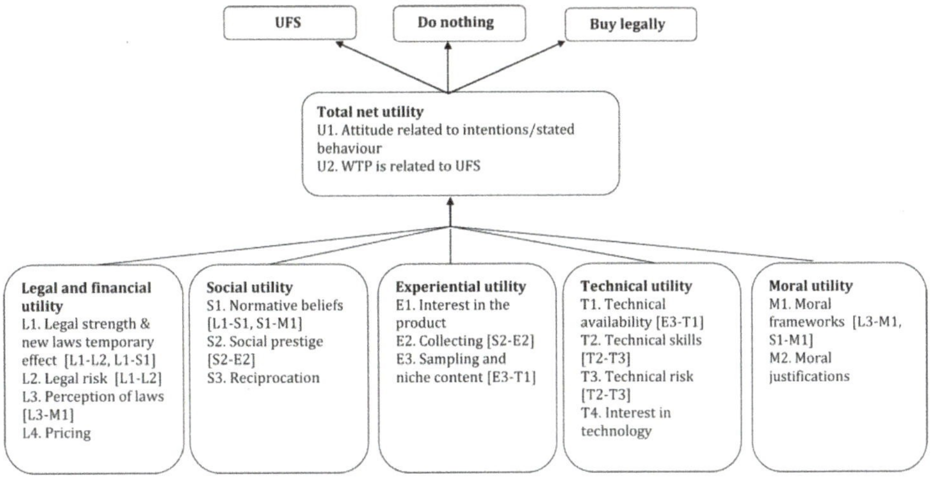

Figure 3. A conceptual framework on the decision to engage in UFS. Note: utility categories are as defined and the links between category elements (in squared brackets) are as described in Table 6.

Table 6. Definition of categories and links in conceptual framework on UFS.

Utility		Definition
Total net utility		Overall assessments regarding how beneficial a behavior is (e.g. attitudes or the results of a cost-benefit analysis), or a reported intent to engage in a behavior in future
Legal and financial net utility		Factors associated with financial outlay for legal purchasing as well as the perceived likelihood and legal and financial consequences of detection whilst engaged in unlawful activity, such as monetary fines
Experiential net utility		Factors associated with perceptions of goods themselves such as individuals' interest in a media type or a desire to experience goods
Technical net utility		Factors associated with individuals' perceived or actual ability to unlawfully file share, for example their technical skill or the availability of broadband connections
Social net utility		Factors associated with the influence others can have upon the behavior of an individual. For example, whether or not peers engage in unlawful file sharing or perceive the behavior to be acceptable or not
Moral net utility		Factors associated with how right or wrong unlawful file sharing is perceived to be by an individual, and how mismatches between individuals moral beliefs and their actual behaviors behavior are managed
Link	Connects	Description
L1-L2	Legal strength—Legal risk	Stronger legal IP regimens are associated with enhanced legal risks.
L1-S1	Legal strength—Normative beliefs	Different cultures have different beliefs about file sharing, which impact upon legal enforcement.
L3-M1	Perception of laws—Moral frameworks	UFS does not always feel like a crime, and in cultures that consider UFS moral the validity of the laws may questioned rather than the appropriateness of UFS.
S2-E2	Collecting—Social prestige	Having content to provide to others can enhance social prestige as well as increase the library for personal consumption.
E3-T1	Sampling and niche content—Technical availability	The technical availability of niche content via UFS networks allows users to indulge an interest in media not (widely) available legally.
T1-T2	Technical skills—Technical risk	Greater technical skill permits a lower risk of contracting malware and damaging equipment.
S1-M1	Normative beliefs—Moral frameworks	Social norms in part reflect wider cultural moral beliefs.

Note: the links are as defined in Fig 3.

doi:10.1371/journal.pone.0127921.t006

Table 6 defines the different utility categories as emerging from the literature. Under the category of *legal and financial utility*, we have considered the legal strength and risks associated to different legal protection regimes as acting as deterrent of UFS; it appears that stricter laws increase purchasing and decrease UFS, with relevant qualifications discussed in the previous section. We have also considered how the perception of laws and pricing matter. The evidence for actual price effects is only unequivocal regarding purchasing; there is mixed evidence for the effect of price on UFS. At a national level stronger laws decrease UFS but this evidence is confounded by culture and national wealth. There is also evidence that the effect of new laws or lawsuits is only temporary—it may be that people are initially concerned by the risk but quickly habituate or adapt their behavior around the new laws.

Under the category of *social utility*, we have considered the role of moral beliefs, social prestige and reciprocation in creating a social environment conducive to UFS. Social norms can potentially increase UFS. Under the category of *experiential utility*, we have noted how interest in the product, a collecting motive, sampling and niche content may increase UFS. For example, UFS is used to learn about a product. Under the category of *technical utility*, we have noted how the technical availability or otherwise of a legal alternative affects UFS, as do the technical skills and risk; UFS is used to obtain hard to access, unreleased or technically flexible media which are not offered by legal means. UFS increases due to legally unavailable content are maintained even when the content becomes legally available, suggesting some form of habit formation. An interest in technology potentially increases UFS. Under the category of *moral utility*, we have identified the role of moral frameworks and justifications in being consistent or not with UFS. UFS not feeling like a crime is consistent with more UFS. People who base their moral beliefs on the law or other absolutist frameworks view UFS negatively whereas relativist moral frameworks or further considerations such as social welfare have a positive view of UFS.

Crucially, different categories can be expected to interact with one another, i.e. it cannot be presumed that their effect on UFS is linearly additive. Fig 3 identifies a number of links between category elements emerging from our review, and Table 6 lists them and describes them. For example, experiential utility and technical utility may interact in two ways: technical availability facilitates a sampling and niche content seeking motive and, while generally being a disincentive to engage in UFS, technical risks of viruses are less of an issue to more experienced file sharers. As a third example, in this case related to an interaction between moral and legal utility, if UFS does not feel like a crime, this may interact with the perception of laws, as their validity may be questioned rather than the appropriateness of UFS.

The five utility categories combine to provide a total utility value of engaging in UFS, buying legally and doing nothing. We can normalize the total utility from this last option to 0. The consumer will then buy the product legally if he or she gains positive total utility from doing so and this is higher than that from engaging in UFS. Vice versa, he or she will engage in UFS if he or she gains positive total utility from doing so and this is higher than buying legally. The connection between willingness to pay (WTP) and increases in purchasing and decreases in UFS is clear from the existing literature, and there does remain considerable if circumstantial evidence that some decrease in UFS (e.g. due to file sharing website closure) creates some increase for sales. Our model therefore permits the complexity of UFS behavior to be represented in a comparatively simple framework that is grounded in the available empirical data (Ritchie & Spencer, 1994).

Another outcome of this review is the apparent difference across media types. Although some studies treat all media as a single entity, and few studies compare media types, we did observe some media specific effects regarding software. There is evidence that, while music is an inferior good whose sales decrease with income, software is a normal good whose legal sales increase with income. Interest in the product and technical skill was predictive of UFS for most media types except software; software is perceived just be a tool they utilized with no emotional engagement. Internet access decreased physical music sales but increased software sales. This suggests that software acquisition is not elective; that the UFS decision is driven by practical considerations such as affordability and availability. Interestingly no differences were observed between primarily visual or primarily acoustic media, nor between media requiring the relatively small or relatively large data transfers.

Limitations

The technological landscape is constantly changing and this review is the product of the time in which the research was conducted. Most of the factors studied will remain influential, as people will remain concerned by legal and financial costs and motivated by experiential, moral and social factors. However, technical factors and available media continue to change. The media focus reflects currently popular media. Historically, small music files were most easily bought or file shared and the focus of much of the research. The increasing ability to download or stream large files makes TV and Movie lawful and unlawful streaming services increasingly important. Legal availability is also changing and adapting to consumer demand.

One limitation, observable from Fig 2, is the comparative scarcity of studies that employ observed behavior as a measured outcome, whether from the experimental laboratory or from the natural world. This scarcity is especially severe for moral net utility but also experiential net utility and social net utility. This makes conclusions such as one that stronger IP laws may be ineffective if set against the moral beliefs or social norms of the society (Svennson and Larsson, 2009), virtually impossible to evaluate at present. The reason for the limited use of observed behavior as the measured outcome may reflect on the one side the lack of familiarity with laboratory experimental methods in most of this literature, and on the other side the ethical and technical complexities of observing unlawful behavior in a manner that has little to no risk for participants whilst providing robust empirical evidence. Nonetheless this quality of evidence is necessary if the objective is to state with confidence which variables can be demonstrated to be causally associated with UFS behavior. The focus upon intent to file share as an outcome is also somewhat concerning given that very few studies seek to establish a relationship between intentions and stated behavior, and given that that some variables, including legal deterrents, may impact upon intentions more strongly than they do upon actual behavior.

The second limitation concerns the fact that the vast majority of the studies employ cross sectional surveys, which makes attributions of causality extremely difficult. There is a clear need for longitudinal studies to better determine causality links, e.g. from stated moral beliefs into future behavior while controlling for past behavior.

A third limitation is that the UFS debate seems to have been played out largely, in relation to evidence, in terms of music files. Movies and software are a distant second, and not well represented for all potential net utility sources. There is very little on videogames, books, or TV content, and the pornography market was ruled out from our cubic representation as we found no studies on it. One study does hint at the consequences of ignoring pornography as a media. Mateus and Peha [23] found that, for participants that use p2p networks to access pornography, 96% of users also download other copyrighted material compared to 65% of users that do not use p2p networks to download pornography. Another example of a notable gap is videogames, traditionally seen as a past-time associated with technically savvy younger adults. The extremely limited evidence identified suggests that despite their technical knowhow, videogame players may choose to not file share, or at least do so to a far lesser extent than consumers of other media [90]. This finding requires replication, and, if robust, the reasons for this could be valuable for those seeking to encourage legal sales in other media.

A fourth limitation is the comparatively widespread use of generic estimates of UFS that are not specific to particular media. We have highlighted that the different elements of the proposed utility model may vary in importance depending upon media. Therefore it would appear to be problematic to assume that the motives of UFS are identical between media; given this, the use of generic dependent variables is a limitation to consider.

CONCLUSIONS

We employed a scoping review methodology to consider and assess the existing evidence on the determinants of UFS in as a systematic and transparent way as possible. Of course, research on UFS is continuing beyond the period considered in this scoping review. For example, a recent paper by Poort *et al.* [91] looks at the effects of legally blocking access to the Pirate Bay in the Netherlands and a survey was carried out by Karaganis and Renkema [92] which compared copying in the US and Germany. Neither the paper nor this survey contradict the findings presented in our review.

We presented a conceptual framework that considers the decision of a consumer to engage in unlawful downloading, purchase a legal copy or do nothing, depending on the utilities obtained from five interacting sources: legal and financial, experiential, technical, social and moral utility. This framework enables us to represent the studies on the determinants of UFS along the three dimensions of a 'cubic' space, where the dimensions are the net utility source, the market medium and the outcome measure. We find a complex relationship between UFS and purchasing, limitations for legal influence, but alternative social, moral, technical and experiential avenues of influence for which more research would be useful, as would be for media other than music files, and particularly videogames, books, or TV content.

ACKNOWLEDGMENTS

Funding for this project was from the RCUK via the Centre for Copyright and New Business Models in the Creative Economy (CREATe), AHRC Grant Number AH/K000179/1, and from the University of East Anglia. The authors wish to acknowledge the assistance of Martin Kretschmer and Lilian Edwards for helping to refine the scope of this review as well as helping to identify sources of grey literature. Joost Poort provided advice which also helped to refine the scope of the review; Elisavet Patouris and Harriet Miller provided research assistance with regard to the design of the data extraction form and the collection of data; Axel Sonntag provided assistance with the figures; Martin Kretschmer helped refine the terminology. Earlier drafts of this report have benefitted from comments from Brett Danaher, Martin Kretschmer, Derek McAuley, Joost Poort and Michael Smith. We thank participants at the "UK Music and Academics" seminar hosted by UK Music on the 6th September 2013, a CREATe BFI meeting on the 8th January 2014, a launch event at Stationers' Hall, London, on the 2nd April 2014 and a CREATe workshop on 15th September 2014 for feedback on presentations of this research.

AUTHOR CONTRIBUTIONS

Analyzed the data: PF SWJ DZ. Wrote the paper: PF SWJ DZ. Responsible for data collection: SWJ. Designed study and interpreted the data: PF SWJ DZ.

REFERENCES

1. Arksey H, O'Malley L. Scoping studies: towards a methodological framework. Int J Soc Res Methodol. 2005;8(1):19–32. doi: 10. 1080/1364557032000119616.
2. Crooks V, Kingsbury P, Snyder J, Johnston R. What is known about the patient's experience of medical tourism? A scoping review. BMC Health Serv Res. 2010;10(1):266. doi: 10. 1186/1472-6963-10-266 pmid:10. 1186/1472-6963-10-266.
3. DCMS. Creative Industries Economic Estimates: Full Statistical Release. Department for Culture, Media and Sport, 2011. Available:http://www. gov. uk/government/publications/creative-industries-economic-estimates-december-2011:
4. Nathan M, Rosso A, Gatten T, Majmudar P, Mitchell A. Measuring the UK's digital economy with big data; 2013. Available:http://niesr. ac. uk/sites/default/files/publications/SI024_GI_NIESR_Google_Report12. pdfNational
5. Ofcom. OCI Tracker Benchmark Study wave 4: Ofcom; 2013. Available:http://stakeholders. ofcom. org. uk/binaries/research/telecoms-research/online-copyright/w4/OCI_MAIN_REPORT_W4_FINAL. pdf.
6. Peha JM, Mateus AM. Policy implications of technology for detecting P2P and copyright violations. Telecomm Policy. 2014;38(1):66–85. doi: 10. 1016/j. telpol. 2013. 04. 007.

7. Bakker P. File-sharing—fight, ignore or compete: Paid download services vs. P2P-networks. Telematics and Informatics. 2005;22(1–2):41–55. http://dx. doi. org/10. 1016/j. tele. 2004. 06. 004.
8. Hemingway P, Brereton N. What is a systematic review? Available:http://www. medicine. ox. ac. uk/bandolier/painres/download/whatis/Syst-review. pdf.
9. Easley RW, Madden CS, Dunn MG. Conducting marketing science: The role of replication in the research process. J Bus Res. 2000;48(1):83–92. doi: 10. 1016/S0148-2963(98)00079-4.
10. Gough D, Oliver S, Thomas J. Introducing systematic reviews. In: Gough D, Oliver S, Thomas J, editors. An Introduction to Systematic Reviews. London: Sage; 2012. p. 1–16.
11. Levac D, Colquhoun H, O'Brien KK. Scoping studies: advancing the methodology. Implement Sci. 2010;5(1):69. doi: 10. 1186/1748-5908-5-69.
12. Brunton J, Stansfield C, Thomas J. Finding relevant studies. In: Gough D, Oliver S, Thomas J, editors. An Introduction to Systematic Reviews. London: Sage; 2012. p. 107–34.
13. Thomas J, Harden A, Newman M. Synthesis: Combining results systematically and appropriately. In: Gough D, Oliver S, Thomas J, editors. An Introduction to Systematic Reviews. London: Sage; 2012. p. 179–226.
14. Hetrick SE, Parker AG, Callahan P, Purcell R. Evidence mapping: illustrating an emerging methodology to improve evidence-based practice in youth mental health. J Eval Clin Pract. 2010;16(6):1025–30. doi: 10. 1111/j. 1365-2753. 2008. 01112. x. pmid:20337833
15. Huygen A, Helberger N, Poort J, Rutten P, Van Eijk N. Ups and downs; economic and cultural effects of file sharing on music, film and games. TNO Information and Communication Technology Series. IViR, 2009.
16. van Eijk N, Poort J, Rutten P. Legal, Economic and Cultural Aspects of File Sharing. Communications and Strategies. 2010;77(1st Quarter):35–54. http://www. idate. org/en/Digiworld/Communications-Strategies/Archives/Archives_50_. html. pmid:1106293 Alternate Accession Number: EP52543981.
17. Hunt R, Williams P, Nicholas D, Rowlands I. Copycats? Digital consumers in the online age: Strategic Advisory Board for Intellectual Property Policy, IPO; 2009. Available: http://www. ipo. gov. uk/ipresearch-copycats-200905. pdf.
18. Ritchie J, Spencer L. Qualitative data analysis for applied policy research. In: Bryman A, Burgess RG, editors. Analysing Qualitative Data. London: Routledge; 1994. p. 173–94.
19. Ritchie J, Spencer L, O'Connor W. Carrying out qualitative analysis. In: Ritchie J, Lewis J, editors. Qualitative Research practice: A Guide for Social Science Students and Researchers. London: Sage; 2003. p. 219–62.
20. Mishra A, Akman I, Yazici A. Organizational software piracy: an empirical assessment. Behav Inf Technol. 2007;26(5):437–44. doi: 10. 1080/01449290500483577 pmid:WOS:000248721500009.
21. Molteni L, Ordanini A. Consumption patterns, digital technology and music downloading. Long Range Plann. 2003;36(4):389–406. doi: 10. 1016/s0024-6301(03)00073-6 pmid:WOS:000184050800006.
22. Peukert C, Claussen J. Piracy and movie revenues: Evidence from Megaupload. 2012. Available: http://papers. ssrn. com/sol3/papers. cfm?abstract_id=2176246.
23. Mateus AM, Peha JM. Dimensions of P2P and digital piracy in a university campus. Proceedings of 2008 Telecommunications Policy Research Conference; Arlington, VA, USA, 2008.
24. Wolfe SE, Higgins GE, Marcum CD. Deterrence and digital piracy: A preliminary examination of the role of viruses. Soc Sci Comput Rev. 2008;26(3):317–33. doi: 10. 1177/0894439307309465 pmid:WOS:000258004700004.
25. Fetscherin M, Lattemann C. Motives and willingness to pay for digital music. In: Delgado J, Ng K, Nesi P, Bellini P, editors. Axmedis 2007: Third International Conference on Automated Production of Cross Media Content for Multi-Channel Distribution; Barcelona, Spain, 2007. p. 189–96.
26. Hsu JL, Shiue CW. Consumers' willingness to pay for non-pirated software. J Bus Ethics. 2008;81(4):715–32. doi: 10. 1007/s10551-007-9543-9 pmid:WOS:000258315800001.
27. Waldfogel J. Music file sharing and sales displacement in the iTunes era. Information Economics and Policy. 2010;22(4):306–14. doi: 10. 1016/j. infoecopol. 2010. 02. 002 pmid:WOS:000286293800004.
28. Walls WD. Cross-country analysis of movie piracy. Appl Econ. 2008;40(5):625–32. doi: 10. 1080/13504850600707337 pmid:WOS:000253730600007.
29. Long X. Intellectual property rights protection and recorded music sales: Focus on 26 OECD countries panel data. Frontiers of Economics in China. 2011;6(2):211–28. doi: 10. 1007/s11459-011-0129-1 pmid:1243663.
30. Adermon A, Liang CY. Piracy, music, and movies: A natural experiment. 2011. Available: http://papers. ssrn. com/sol3/papers. cfm?abstract_id=1752224.
31. Blackburn D. Essays on the economics of copying with an application to the recorded music industry: Harvard University; 2005.
32. Danaher B, Smith M, Telang R, Chen S. The effect of graduated response anti-piracy laws on music sales: evidence from an event study in France. 2012. Available:http://papers. ssrn. com/sol3/papers. cfm?abstract_id=1989240.
33. Bhattacharjee S, Gopal RD, Lertwachara K, Marsden JR. Impact of legal threats on online music sharing activity: An analysis of music industry legal actions. J Law Econ. 2006;49(1):91–114. doi: 10. 1086/501085 pmid:WOS:000238437700004.
34. Grolleau G, Mzoughi N, Sutan A. Please do not pirate it, you will rob the poor! An experimental investigation on the effect of charitable donations on piracy. J Socio

Econ. 2008;37(6):2417–26. doi: 10. 1016/j. socec. 2008. 02. 001 pmid:2008-14865-014.

35. Ofcom. OCI Tracker Benchmark Study Q3 2012: Ofcom; 2012. Available:http://stakeholders. ofcom. org. uk/binaries/research/telecoms-research/online-copyright/Kantar-Media. pdf.

36. Bahanovich D, Collopy D. Music experience and behaviour in young people. University of Hertfordshire, UK, 2009.

37. BMRB Social Research. Future copyright development. Intellectual Property Office, UK, 2009.

38. Ofcom. Qualitative research into online digital piracy: Ofcom; 2011. Available:http://stakeholders. ofcom. org. uk/binaries/research/telecoms-research/filesharing/gfk. pdf.

39. Montoro Pons JdD, Cuadrado Garcia M. Legal origin and intellectual property rights: an empirical study in the prerecorded music sector. European Journal of Law and Economics. 2008;26(2):153–73. doi: 10. 1007/s10657-008-9056-8 pmid:WOS:000259477600003.

40. Montoro-Pons JD, Cuadrado-García M, editors. Digital goods and the effects of copying: an empirical study of the music market. 14th International Conference on Cultural Economics; 2006; Vienna, Austria.

41. Boorstin ES. Music sales in the age of file sharing: Princeton University; 2004.

42. Sung T-W. An economic analysis of new peer-to-peer transfer activities: Claremont Graduate University; 2007.

43. Zentner A. Measuring the impact of file sharing on the movie industry: An empirical analysis using a panel of countries. 2010.

44. Danaher B, Dhanasobhon S, Smith MD, Telang R. Converting pirates without cannibalizing purchasers: The impact of digital distribution on physical sales and internet piracy. Marketing Science. 2010;29(6):1138–51. doi: 10. 1287/mksc. 1100. 0600 pmid:WOS:000285342700014.

45. Aguiar L, Martens B. Digital Music Consumption on the Internet: Evidence from Clickstream Data Institute for Prospective Technological Studies Digital Economy Working Paper 2013/04: European Commission; 2013. Available:http://ipts. jrc. ec. europa. eu/publications/pub. cfm?id=6084.

46. Konstantakis NI, Palaigeorgiou GE, Siozos PD, Tsoukalas IA. What do computer science students think about software piracy? Behav Inf Technol. 2010;29(3):277–85. doi: 10. 1080/01449290902765076 pmid:WOS:000277200000006.

47. Bonner S, O'Higgins E. Music piracy: ethical perspectives. Management Decision. 2010;48(9):1341–54. doi: 10. 1108/00251741011082099 pmid:WOS:000286485900002.

48. Jambon MM, Smetana JG. College students' moral evaluations of illegal music downloading. J Appl Dev Psychol. 2012;33(1):31–9. doi: 10. 1016/j. appdev. 2011. 09. 001 pmid:WOS:000301220200004.

49. Sheehan B, Tsao J, Pokrywczynski J. Stop the music! How advertising can help stop college students from downloading music illegally. J Advert Res. 2012;52(3):309–21. doi: 10. 2501/jar-52-3-309-321 pmid:WOS:000308854700006.

50. Sheehan B, Tsao J, Yang S. Motivations for gratifications of digital music piracy among college students. Atl J Commun. 2010;18(5):241–58. doi: 10. 1080/15456870. 2010. 521471 pmid:55567669.

51. Balducci F. Music or hi-tech lovers? Inferring into the determinants of music consumption. Rivista Italiana Degli Economisti. 2009;14(2):361–90. doi: 10. 1427/30395.

52. Hennig-Thurau T, Henning V, Sattler H. Consumer file sharing of motion pictures. J Mark. 2007;71(4):1–18. doi: 10. 1509/jmkg. 71. 4. 1 pmid:WOS:000250316600001.

53. Chen Y-C, Shang R-A, Lin A-K. The intention to download music files in a P2P environment: Consumption value, fashion, and ethical decision perspectives. Electron Commer Res Appl. 2008;7(4):411–22. doi: 10. 1016/j. elerap. 2008. 02. 001 pmid:WOS:000261183800005.

54. Kinnally W, Lacayo A, McClung S, Sapolsky B. Getting up on the download: College students' motivations for acquiring music via the web. New Media & Society. 2008;10(6):893–913. doi: 10. 1177/1461444808096250 pmid:WOS:000260839500005.

55. Tzantzara K, Economides A A. Gender differences in digital music distribution methods. Peer-to-Peer Networking and Applications. 2010;3(2):161–71. doi: 10. 1007/s12083-009-0056-4 pmid:WOS:000284094000007.

56. Rochelandet F, Le Guel F. P2P music sharing networks: Why the legal fight against copiers may be inefficient. Review of Economic Research on Copyright Issues. 2005;2(2):69–82. http://www. serci. org/default. asp. pmid:0824347.

57. Sandulli FD. CD music purchase behaviour of P2P users. Technovation. 2007;27(6–7):325–34. doi: 10. 1016/j. technovation. 2006. 12. 007 pmid:WOS:000247198600001.

58. Danaher B, Waldfogel J. Reel piracy: The effect of online film piracy on international box office sales. 2012. Available: http://papers. ssrn. com/sol3/papers. cfm?abstract_id=1986299.

59. Mandel P, Suessmuth B. Determinants of digital piracy: A re-examination of results. Jahrb Natl Okon Stat. 2012;232(4):394–413. pmid:WOS:000306152600001.

60. Won SJ, Jang J. Nonlinear income inequality effect on software piracy. The Korean Journal of Economics. 2012;19(2):213–42. doi: 10. 2139/ssrn. 1478907.

61. Smith MD, Telang R. Piracy or promotion? The impact of broadband Internet penetration on DVD sales. Information Economics and Policy. 2010;22(4):289–98. doi: 10. 1016/j. infoecopol. 2010. 02. 001 pmid:WOS:000286293800002.

62. Danaher B, Smith M. Gone in 60 seconds: The impact of the megaupload shutdown on movie sales. 2013. Available: http://papers. ssrn. com/sol3/papers. cfm?abstract_id=2229349.

63. Poort J, Leenheer J. File sharing 2©12: Downloading from illegal sources in the Netherlands. IViR, 2012.

Available:http://www. ivir. nl/publications/poort/Filesharing_2012. pdf.

64. Garbharran A, Thatcher A. The impact of occupational field of expertise on intention to pirate software. Int J Psychol. 2012;47(s1):404–. doi: 10. 1080/00207594. 2012. 709107 pmid:WOS:000307377704285.

65. Higgins GE, Makin DA. Self-control, deviant peers, and software piracy. Psychological Reports. 2004;95(3):921–31. doi: 10. 2466/pr0. 95. 3. 921–931 pmid:WOS:000225896900033.

66. Siponen M, Vartiainen T. Attitudes to and factors affecting unauthorized copying of computer software in Finland. Behav Inf Technol. 2005;24(4):249–57. doi: 10. 1080/01449290512331321857 pmid:2005-07985-002.

67. Liao C, Lin HN, Liu YP. Predicting the use of pirated software: A contingency model integrating perceived risk with the Theory of Planned Behavior. J Bus Ethics. 2010;91(2):237–52. doi: 10. 1007/s10551-009-0081-5 pmid:WOS:000273320800007.

68. Plouffe CR. Examining "peer-to-peer" (P2P) systems as consumer-to-consumer (C2C) exchange. Eur J Mark. 2008;42(11–12):1179–202. doi: 10. 1108/03090560810903637 pmid:WOS:000261633400006.

69. Frank N. Magid Associates. Introducing Hollywood's best customers: Vuze user vs. general internet: Comparative data 2009. Available:http://www. magid. com/sites/default/files/pdf/vuze. pdf.

70. Cenite M, Wang MW, Peiwen C, Chan GS. More than just free content: Motivations of peer-to-peer file sharers. J Commun Inq. 2009;33(3):206–21. doi: 10. 1177/0196859909333697 pmid:42526075.

71. Filiciak M, Hofmokl J, Tarkowski A. The circulations of culture—on social distribution of content. 2012. Available: http://papers. ssrn. com/sol3/papers. cfm?abstract_id=2246508.

72. Steinmetz KF, Tunnell KD. Under the pixelated jolly roger: A study of on-line pirates. Deviant Behavior. 2013;34(1):53–67. doi: 10. 1080/01639625. 2012. 707536 pmid:WOS:000310613500005.

73. Holt TJ, Copes H. Transferring subcultural knowledge on-line: Practices and beliefs of persistent digital pirates. Deviant Behavior. 2010;31(7):625–54. doi: 10. 1080/01639620903231548 pmid:WOS:000281313300003.

74. Karakaya M. Analysis of the key reasons behind the pirated software usage of Turkish Internet users: Application of routine activities theory: University of Baltimore; 2011.

75. Higgins GE, Fell BD, Wilson AL. Low self-control and social learning in understanding students' intentions to pirate movies in the United States. Soc Sci Comput Rev. 2007;25(3):339–57. doi: 10. 1177/0894439307299934 pmid:WOS:000248946800004.

76. Taylor SA, Ishida C, Wallace DW. Intention to engage in digital piracy a conceptual model and empirical test. Journal of Service Research. 2009;11(3):246–62. doi: 10. 1177/1094670508328924 pmid:WOS:000262678400003.

77. Al-Rafee S, Dashti AE. A cross cultural comparison of the extended TPB: The case of digital piracy. Journal of Global Information Technology Management. 2012;15(1):5–24. doi: 10. 1080/1097198X. 2012. 10845610 pmid:WOS:000298733100002.

78. Denegri-Knott J. Sinking the online "music pirates": Foucault, power and deviance on the web. J Comput Mediat Commun. 2004;9(4):No Pagination Specified. doi: 10. 1111/j. 1083-6101. 2004. tb00293. x pmid:2004-17333-002.

79. Kwan SSK. End-user digital piracy: Contingency framework, affective determinants and response distortion: Hong Kong University of Science and Technology; 2008.

80. Xia M, Duan W, Huang Y, Whinston AB. Unravel the drivers of online sharing communities: An empirical investigation. 2006. Available:http://search. ebscohost. com/login. aspx?direct=true&db=eoh&AN=1005526&site=ehost-livehttp://www. business. uiuc. edu/Working_Papers/papers/06-0109. pdf.

81. Xia M, Huang Y, Duan W, Whinston AB. To continue sharing or not to continue sharing? An empirical analysis of user decision in peer-to-peer sharing networks. Information Systems Research. 2012;23(1):247–59. doi: 10. 1287/isre. 1100. 0344 pmid:WOS:000301522800015.

82. Beekhuyzen J, von Hellens L, Nielsen S. Underground online music communities: Exploring rules for membership. Online Information Review. 2011;35(5):699–715. doi: 10. 1108/14684521111176453 pmid:WOS:000296928700002.

83. Svensson M, Larsson S. Social norms and intellectual property. Online norms and the European legal development. Research Report in Sociology of Law, Vol 12009. Available: https://lup. lub. lu. se/search/publication/1510388.

84. Aleassa H, Pearson JM, McClurg S. Investigating software piracy in jordan: An extension of the theory of reasoned action. J Bus Ethics. 2011;98(4):663–76. doi: 10. 1007/s10551-010-0645-4 pmid:WOS:000286608200010.

85. Chan RYK, Lai JWM. Does ethical ideology affect software piracy attitude and behaviour? An empirical investigation of computer users in China. Eur J Inf Syst. 2011;20(6):659–73. doi: 10. 1057/ejis. 2011. 31 pmid:WOS:000296931100004.

86. Zamoon S, Curley S. Ripped from the headlines: What can the popular press teach us about software piracy? J Bus Ethics. 2008;83(3):515–33. doi: 10. 1007/s10551-007-9636-5.

87. Cockrill A, Goode MM. DVD pirating intentions: Angels, devils, chancers and receivers. Journal of Consumer Behaviour. 2012;11(1):1–10. doi: 10. 1002/cb. 357 pmid:2012-02303-001.

88. Coyle JR, Gould SJ, Gupta P, Gupta R. "To buy or to pirate": The matrix of music consumers' acquisition-mode decision-making. J Bus Res. 2009;62(10):1031–7. doi: 10. 1016/j. jbusres. 2008. 05. 002 pmid:WOS:000269428000017.

89. Ingram JR, Hinduja S. Neutralizing music piracy: an empirical examination. Deviant Behavior. 2008;29(4):334–66. doi: 10. 1080/01639620701588131 pmid:WOS:000255248400002.

90. Fukugawa N. How serious is piracy in the videogame industry? Empirical Economics Letters. 2011;10(3):225–33. http://www. eel. my100megs. com/. pmid:1296055.

91. Poort J, Leenheer J, van der Ham J, Dumitru C. Baywatch: Two approaches to measure the effects of blocking access to The Pirate Bay. Telecomm Policy. 2014;38(4):383–92. doi: http://dx. doi. org/10. 1016/j. telpol. 2013. 12. 008. pmid:24976304

92. Karaganis J, Renkema L. Copy Culture in the US and Germany. Available:http://piracy. americanassembly. org/wp-content/uploads/2013/01/Copy-Culture. pdf:New York: Columbia University, The American Assembly, 2013.

CHAPTER 19

THE AFFECTIVE SLIDER: A DIGITAL SELF-ASSESSMENT SCALE FOR THE MEASUREMENT OF HUMAN EMOTIONS

Alberto Betella[1], Paul F. M. J. Verschure[1,2]

[1] SPECS Lab, N-RAS, DTIC, Universitat Pompeu Fabra, Barcelona, Spain

[2] Institució Catalana de Recerca i Estudis Avançats, Barcelona, Spain

ABSTRACT

Self-assessment methods are broadly employed in emotion research for the collection of subjective affective ratings. The Self-Assessment Manikin (SAM), a pictorial scale developed in the eighties for the measurement of pleasure, arousal, and dominance, is still among the most popular self-reporting tools, despite having been conceived upon design principles which are today obsolete. By leveraging on state-of-the-art user interfaces and metacommunicative pictorial representations, we developed the Affective Slider (AS), a digital self-reporting tool composed of two slider controls for the quick assessment of pleasure and arousal. To empirically validate the AS, we conducted a systematic comparison between AS and SAM in a task involving the emotional assessment of a series of images taken from the International Affective Picture System (IAPS), a database composed of pictures representing a wide range of semantic categories often used as a benchmark in psychological studies. Our results show that the AS is equivalent to SAM in the self-assessment of pleasure and arousal, with two added advantages: the AS does not require written instructions and it can be easily reproduced in latest-generation digital devices, including smartphones and tablets. Moreover, we compared new and normative IAPS ratings and found a general drop in reported arousal of pictorial stimuli. Not only do our results demonstrate that legacy scales for the self-report of affect can be replaced with new measurement tools developed in accordance to modern design principles, but also that standardized sets of stimuli which are widely adopted in research on human emotion are not as effective as they were in the past due to a general desensitization towards highly arousing content.

INTRODUCTION

Psychological research on emotions has a long past dating back to the second half of the 19th century with Charles Darwin who explained affective states as means of communication to (ultimately) survive [1] and the, so called, James-Lange theory, which defined the manifestation of emotions as a consequence of physiological changes in arousal [2]. Nonetheless, despite the increasing adoption of psychophysiological measures for the inference of human affect, the field still relies extensively on self-reporting tools. Physiological data, in fact, are prone to artifacts and can present drawbacks, in particular when acquired in ecologically-valid conditions [3–5]. For this

Citation: Betella A, Verschure PFMJ (2016) The Affective Slider: A Digital Self-Assessment Scale for the Measurement of Human Emotions. PLoS ONE 11(2): e0148037. doi:10.1371/journal.pone.0148037.

reason, a common practice is to couple such measures to self-assessment scales or questionnaires.

One of the most popular among the existing self-reporting tools is the Self-Assessment Manikin (SAM) proposed by Bradley and Lang in 1994 [6], which is broadly adopted in psychological studies as well as in a wide range of fields that span from marketing to advertising. SAM is a scale that measures the dimensions of pleasure, arousal and dominance (also called "PAD") using a series of graphic abstract characters horizontally arranged according to a 9-points scale (even though 5-, 7-points and other variants exist). Pleasure ranges from a frowning to a smiling figure, arousal spans from a sleepy to a widely awake figure showing an incremental explosion at the center, while dominance ranges from a very small to a very large character (Fig 1). The original SAM paper [6] has collected in total over 3200 citations since its publication and it was cited in more than 2200 peer-reviewed scientific articles in the last 5 years alone (source: Google Scholar,http://scholar.google.com).

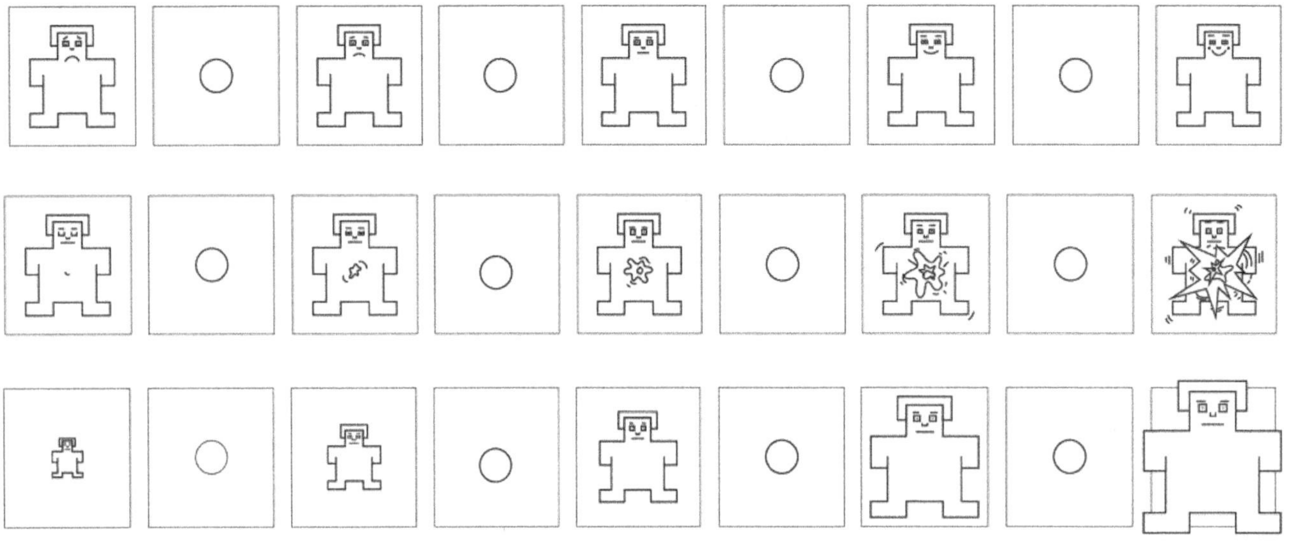

Figure 1. The Self-Assessment Manikin (SAM), adapted with permission from Bradley and Lang 1994 [6]. SAM is a pictorial tool designed in the eighties that measures pleasure (top), arousal (middle) and dominance (bottom) on a discrete scale. It is available in two main versions: paper-and-pencil (5-, 7-, 9-points) and computer program (20-points). Participants can rate their affective state by placing an X over or between any figure.

We have regularly adopted SAM at our laboratory (generally paired with behavioral and phsychophysiological measures) to conduct studies on human emotion because it was the best established tool available for the quick collection of self-reported affective data. Although our participants were administered the official rating instructions, they frequently asked to the experimenter to further clarify the meaning of the pictographic representations, hence raising a pragmatic concern about the intuitiveness of SAM. It should not be surprising indeed that a scale which was designed more than two decades ago might not be understood today as intuitively as it was in the past.

As a matter of fact, the paper-and-pencil design principles upon which SAM was based are distant from the theories that underlie graphical user interfaces at the present-day. We live in an era where advanced interfaces, digital media, social networks and mobile applications changed the way people communicate and, in a broader sense, shaped new paradigms of interaction [7]. By exploiting contemporary design standards for user interfaces along with modern metacommunicative graphical representations of emotions, it is possible to develop novel and more effective tools for psychological research.

For this reason, we designed a new digital scale for the self-assessment of emotion that we called the "Affective Slider" (AS) (Fig 2). The AS is composed of two slider controls that measure basic emotions in terms of pleasure and arousal on a continuous scale that we have systematically calibrated to the SAM in a number of experiments which involved emotional ratings.

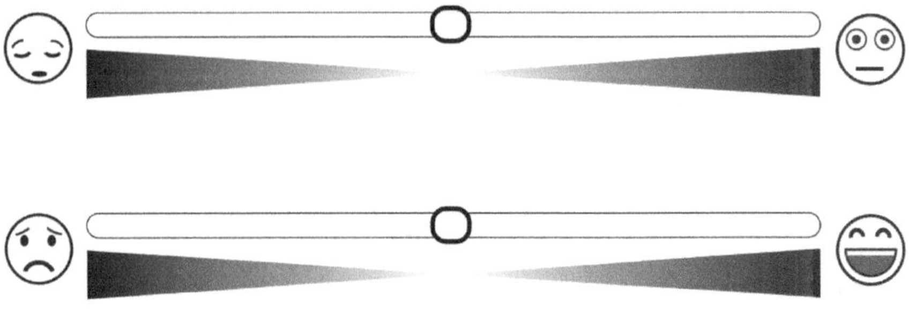

Figure 2. The "Affective Slider" (AS) is a digital self-reporting tool composed of two sliders that measure arousal (top) and pleasure (bottom) on a continuous scale. The AS does not require written instructions and it is intentionally displayed using a neutral chromatic palette to avoid bias in ratings due to the emotional connotation of colors. See text for more details.

Interface elements such as (physical or digital) slider controls have been sparsely adopted in psychological research in tasks related to affective assessment, including video corpora annotation [8] and affective measurements [9, 10]. Yet, the use of sliders in past studies was mainly grounded in intuition. When designing a novel research tool, it is crucial to conduct an empirical validation which allows to compare new methods to their state-of-the-art counterparts. This is precisely what we did with the AS.

Here, we present the results of an experiment which consisted of a systematic comparison between AS and SAM ratings collected through a task that involved the emotional assessment of a series of images taken from the International Affective Picture System (IAPS), a standardized database containing pictures representing a wide range of semantic categories, which had been previously calibrated using the PAD affective dimensions measured through the SAM [11].

The experiment we conducted also allowed us to replicate the original IAPS study through the collection of present-day SAM ratings that we compared to the previous IAPS norms. By doing so, we aimed to validate our hypothesis that the stimuli from this collection (most of which are dated back to the end of the eighties [12]) don't trigger today the same affective responses as they did in the past. Our society, in fact, is increasingly stimulated with highly arousing media content through the massive exposure to media. This plausibly leads to a desensitization towards such content which has been also highlighted in a number of earlier studies [13–15]. Our assumptions are grounded in previous research that observed general trends of lower arousal associated to the IAPS pictures when compared to their normative ratings [16, 17] without, however, drawing definitive conclusions on this specific outcome.

The current study provides a relevant contribution to the field of emotion research by raising new challenges for current methodologies and by introducing a novel tool for the measurement of affect.

MATERIALS AND METHODS

The Affective Slider

The "Affective Slider" (AS) is a digital scale for the self-assessment of emotion composed of two separate slider controls (or "sliders") that measure pleasure and arousal.

In the AS, the two independent controls are located one on top of the other (in random order over subsequent trials).

Underneath each slider two isosceles triangles are placed (symmetrically mirrored from the topmost vertex) that serve as a visual cue for intensity.

Stylized facial expressions (also called "emoticons") visually representing bipolar affective states from Mehrabian and Russell's emotionality scales (i.e. unhappy/happy for pleasure and sleepy/wide-awake for arousal) [18] lie at the two ends of each slider. Previous studies demonstrated the existence of universal trends in the attribution of affect to colors [19, 20]. To avoid potential biases in ratings, in the design of the AS we adopted a monochromatic neutral color scheme (Fig 2).

Contrary to SAM, the AS does not measure dominance. We excluded this dimension for two main reasons: first, Russel's bipolar emotional space constitutes the, so called, "core affect" and is sufficient alone to measure basic emotion [21]. As a result, dominance can be considered redundant and seen as a consequence of core affect. Second, this dimension has not shown consistent effects across studies [16].

The introduction of SAM as a non-verbal pictorial scale for the self-assessment of affect tackled most of the issues typical of pre-SAM verbal scales, which were language-dependent and required complex statistical factorial analyses [6]. However, written instructions are still necessary in order to illustrate how to properly use the SAM tool (SAM instructions normally account for more than 500 English words [11]). In this context, the AS constitutes a further advance since, by leveraging on today's practical knowledge of user interface elements (e.g. sliders) and metacommunicative pictorial representations (i.e. emoticons), it does not require written instructions.

Another advantage of slider controls is the possibility of collecting ratings on continuous scales that allow for more accurate high-resolution measurements, as opposed to the SAM which records data upon a relatively condensed Likert scale.

Due to the obsolescence of the original SAM software version (first developed in 1987), a few researchers more recently implemented their own digital SAM variants which, however, are currently hard to find and not fully-functional. In contrast, the AS can be easily reproduced in any modern digital device, including smartphones and tablets. Its source code and graphic elements, along with examples of implementation, are publicly available under a Creative Commons license (http://AS.specs-lab.com). Moreover, to facilitate researchers in the development of custom-tailored versions of the AS (e.g. integration into existing software packages), we provide detailed design guidelines and recommendations.

Experimental Protocol

We designed an experiment where 400 volunteers were asked to rate a set of 60 pictures randomly selected from the International Affective Picture System (IAPS) [22].

The aim of our study was to empirically validate the AS by correlating the collected affective dimensions to the corresponding SAM ratings and to systematically compare new and normative IAPS ratings. We expected to find a) a strong correlation between the SAM and the AS scales and b) consistently lower ratings of arousal associated to the IAPS pictures when compared to the normative ratings.

We divided our sample into two groups of equal size and assigned each participant to either the SAM or the AS condition, following a between-subjects design (see Section Sample and data pre-processing for more details). The dependent variables measured were "pleasure" and "arousal".

Previous research empirically demonstrated that psychological studies which involve the administration of internet-based surveys deliver equivalent results to laboratory settings [23,24]. For this reason, we developed an on-line questionnaire composed of 4 main sections: a) consent form and demographic data collection, b) instructions, c) pictures rating and d) debriefing.

The protocol of the experiment was approved by the local Ethical Committee "Clinical Research Ethical Committee

(CEIC) Parc de Salut Mar" (Barcelona, Spain). After having electronically signed the consent form and answered the demographic questions (i.e. gender, age, nationality and level of education), participants were presented with the instructions. We administered the original IAPS instructions [11] to both the experimental groups, with minor changes due to the different medium (e.g. we modernized the references to the "booklet" for the affective ratings and to the "projector" that displayed the pictures). In addition, for the AS condition we removed all the mentioning of SAM along with its instructions and simply asked participants to "move the sliders to express how you actually feel while watching the picture".

In the same page, and prior to the confirmation button, we included a notification where the subjects were asked to put their web browser in full-screen mode to maximize the questionnaire resolution and avoid external distractions such as software running in the background. Moreover, we displayed a warning message explaining that repeated dummy ratings (e.g. skipping to the following picture too quickly or without actually interacting with the scales) would be automatically detected by the system, with the consequence of a sudden termination and exclusion from the experiment.

A series of 60 separated pictorial stimuli followed, each of which was sequentially presented in a dedicated page and pseudo-randomly selected (i.e. shuffled) from the entire IAPS collection. Each page was split into two vertical sections that displayed simultaneously the IAPS image on one side, along with the SAM (digital 9-points version we implemented) or the AS on the other (Fig 3).

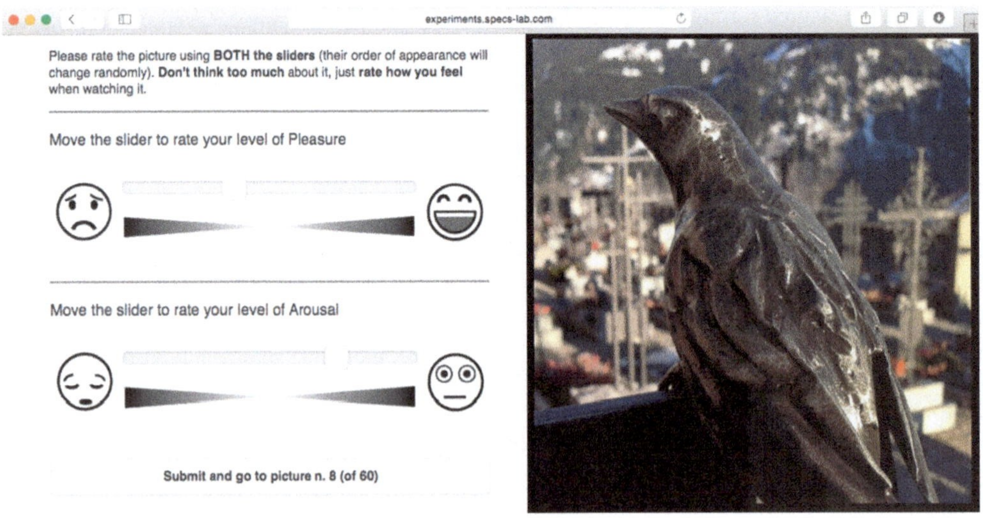

Figure 3. Screenshot of the web-based questionnaire showing a single experimental trial using the AS. The picture (in this example just a placeholder and not part of the IAPS collection) is randomly displayed either on the left or on the right side of the screen. Similarly, the order of the pleasure and arousal dimensions is randomized.

To prevent potential automaticity in the rating process, the content of these two vertical sections was randomly interchanged for each new trial. Similarly, the order of presentation of the two affective dimensions in the administered scale was randomized.

Once the participant completed the rating of one pictorial stimulus, it was possible to proceed to the following trial by pressing the "Submit and Continue" button, until all of the pictures were presented. A 5-seconds black mask covering the entire screen space was displayed between each trial.

Upon completion of all the trials, a debriefing page was presented to the participant, which included the physical and email addresses of the experimenter for further clarifications or questions.

Sample and Data Pre-Processing

400 volunteers were recruited using Amazon's Mechanical Turk (mturk.com), a popular web service that in recent years has been increasingly employed in the conduction of experiments in psychology and social sciences. Previous research demonstrated that the experimental data collected via Mechanical Turk can be considered as reliable as those obtained via traditional methods [25]. Participants were equally assigned to one of the two experimental conditions (AS or SAM) and they all received a monetary compensation.

Although on-line recruitment and internet-based questionnaires present several advantages, web technologies in scientific research have a shortcoming: there is no straightforward way to ensure that participants follow precisely the given instructions. To systematically control for possible errors or misconduct, along with the data explicitly collected through the questionnaire, we logged into our database the time-stamp of each of the 60 trials associated to the participant's unique ID (which was also locally stored using a "cookie"), as well as some anonymous information including (partially masked) IP address and browser inner-window resolution of the client.

Indeed, after conducting a preliminary analysis of the dataset aggregated from the entire sample, we observed that 22% of the volunteers did not successfully complete the questionnaire, submitted more than 60 ratings or participated in the experiment twice (probably due to a manual refresh of the web page or to an incorrect use of the "back" button of the browser). Moreover, from the analysis of the browser window size, we found volunteers that used resolutions below 800x500 pixels (i.e. the minimum size to ensure that the pages of our questionnaire were properly displayed).

For these reasons, and to avoid any inconsistency in our data, we automatically excluded all those participants that did not meet the original criteria, either due to inadvertence or negligence, resulting in a final sample of 309 participants (110 females, mean age 36.26±11.15SD), 87% of which held a university or master degree and whose nationality was mainly American (42.4%) and Indian (53.7%).

Among the 309 valid participants, 153 were exposed to the SAM experimental condition (47 females, mean age 36.3±10.7SD), while 156 to the AS condition (63 females, mean age 36.15±11.6SD).

The mean time for the completion of the entire experiment was 19±9 minutes.

RESULTS

We collected a total of 18540 single ratings, equally divided between SAM and AS on a picture set composed of 1178 different images from the IAPS database, each of which was rated on average 15.2±3.9 times. We averaged the collected scores, thus obtaining mean values of pleasure and arousal for both the AS and the SAM ratings associated with each of the IAPS stimuli. First, we compared the affective ratings between AS and SAM by looking for correlations between the two scales. Second, we compared the new SAM ratings we collected to the normative SAM ratings provided with IAPS. The statistical analysis included the calculation of Spearman's correlation coefficients and Wilcoxon rank-based tests due to the non-Gaussianity of the distributions as assessed through Kolmogorov–Smirnov tests with Lilliefors correction.

AS versus SAM

In order to establish the similarity of the ratings obtained with AS and those rendered through SAM, we calculated the Spearman's correlation coefficient between the measured affective dimensions. We found a strong correlation between AS and SAM for both pleasure ($r_s(1176) = .852$, $p < .001$) and arousal ($r_s(1176) = .860$, $p < .001$) (Fig 4)

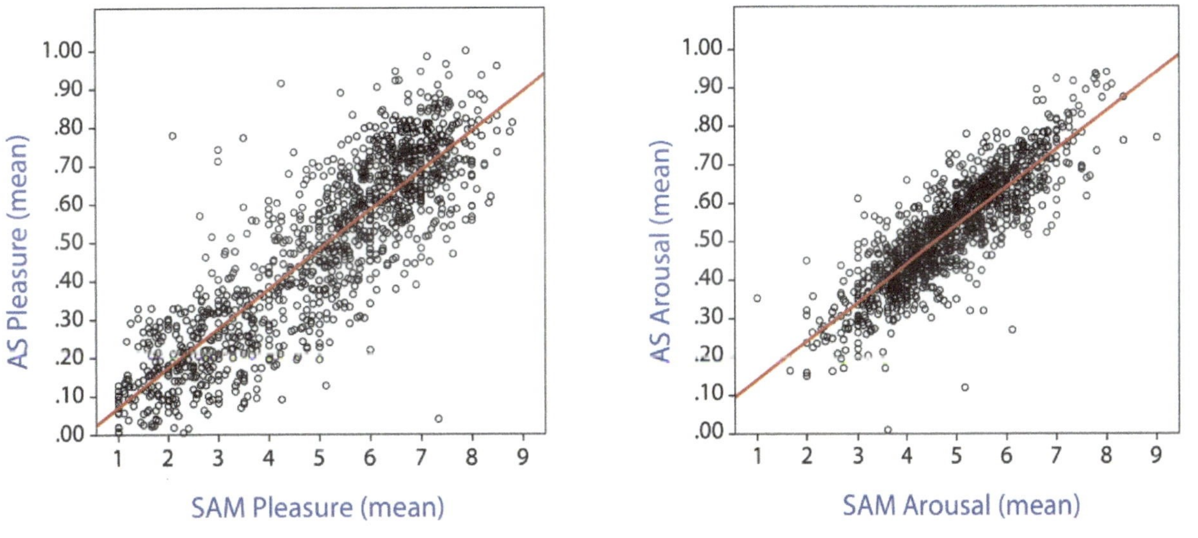

Figure 4. Scatterplots representing the linear correlation between AS and SAM pleasure (r_s **= .852) and arousal (**r_s **= .860).** The red line indicates the best fit.

Comparison between Normative and New IAPS Ratings

By taking into consideration the experimental group assigned to the SAM condition alone (N = 153), we compared our ("new") ratings of pleasure and arousal to the ("old") normative ones provided with the IAPS database. Both old and new ratings were collected using SAM on a 9-points scale and averaged across all subjects. We computed a Spearman's rank correlation coefficient between old and new ratings of pleasure and obtained a very strong correlation ($r_s(1176) = .9$, $p < .001$).

Similarly, we calculated the Spearman's correlation coefficient between the old and the new ratings of arousal. The results of the test only showed a moderate correlation for the arousal dimension ($r_s(1176) = .58$, $p < .001$). To further analyze this outcome, we split the IAPS collection into two equal parts divided by the overall normative median arousal and we called the newly created categories "low arousal" (mean arousal ≤4.8, N = 570) and "high arousal" (mean arousal >4.8, N = 608). For each of these categories, we conducted correlation tests between old and new arousal ratings. We found a moderate correlation for the low arousal category ($r_s(568) = .42$, $p < .001$) and a weak correlation for the high arousal category ($r_s(606) = .3$, $p < .001$), suggesting that IAPS pictures that were originally categorized as highly arousing were not perceived as such in our study. To follow up these findings, we excluded a subset of pictures associated to central arousal values in the original IAPS dataset (normative Mdn arousal = 4.85, mean arousal = 4.81±1.15) and distributed our data into two more extreme categories that we called "very low arousal" (mean arousal ≤4, N = 313) and "very high arousal" (mean arousal ≥6, N = 204). We submitted both categories to a Spearman's test to look for correlations between old and new arousal ratings. We found a weak correlation for the very low arousal category ($r_s(311) = .3$, $p < .001$), while the very high arousal category did not show any significant correlation between the old and the new arousal ratings with a correlation coefficient roughly equal to zero ($r_s(202) = .02$, $p > .1$). We conducted a Wilcoxon Signed-

Ranks test for the pictures belonging to the very high arousal category (N = 204) and compared the old ratings of arousal (Mdn arousal = 6.46, mean arousal = 6.48±0.35) to the new ones (Mdn arousal = 5.81, mean arousal = 5.82±1). The results of the test indicated that the new ratings were significantly lower that the old ones (Z = -7.6, $p < .001$).

CONCLUSION

Emotion research has made considerable progress in recent years, in particular due to the increasing diffusion of methods for the inference of affect grounded in direct and indirect physiological responses modulated by the Autonomic Nervous System. Because such measures are easily contaminated with artifacts [26, 27] and the state of the art about their interpretation is still growing, it is a common practice to couple them with self-assessment tools which provide a complementary source of information. Although psychological research on emotion is flourishing in terms of novel approaches and materials, some aspects of the field remain anchored to legacy methods. The Self-Assessment Manikin (SAM), for instance, is one of the most diffused self-reporting scales, despite having been designed more than two decades ago. In the past years, a number of experiments we conducted at our laboratory highlighted the need for a more intuitive and modern tool for the self-assessment of affect. This is precisely why we designed the Affective Slider (AS), a non-verbal digital scale which, by using two separate slider controls, allows to collect in real-time self-reported ratings of pleasure and arousal.

In this study, we present the results of an empirical validation where we compared the affective ratings we collected through SAM and AS from a fairly large sample using a series of pictures from the IAPS collection, one of the most popular and widely adopted set of pictorial stimuli covering a broad range of affective semantic categories.

The purpose of our experiment was twofold. On the one hand, our goal was to systematically validate the AS as a reliable scale for the quick measurement of the affective dimensions of pleasure and arousal. On the other hand, we aimed to find whether the normative ratings provided with the original IAPS study from Lang et al. 1999 [28], a benchmark in psychological research, could be replicated today.

Our results show a very strong correlation between the SAM and AS ratings, hence empirically demonstrating that the AS can replace SAM in the self-reporting of pleasure and arousal, with the additional advantages of being self-contained and easily reproducible in latest-generation digital devices.

In contrast to SAM, in fact, the AS exploits new universal skills acquired through the large diffusion of modern electronic devices (e.g. interaction with interface elements such as sliders) and it does not require written instructions thus relying exclusively on non-verbal cues. For these reasons, we will henceforth adopt the AS in tasks that involve the self-reporting of pleasure and arousal. We invite other researchers to do the same and, to facilitate this, we provide detailed guidelines along with the source code and graphic elements to easily reproduce the AS in future studies.

In addition, grounded in previous research that highlights a general desensitization towards high arousing visual content [13–15], we compared the new IAPS ratings collected through SAM to the normative data.

When taking into account the entire spectrum of IAPS stimuli, we only found a moderate correlation for the arousal dimension between new and old SAM ratings. This result clearly indicates a drop in the population's sensitivity when exposed to arousing content. Most importantly, by partitioning the set of IAPS stimuli into lower and higher extremes, we found that the new arousal ratings for pictures categorized as highly arousing in IAPS (204 pictures with mean normative arousal ≥6 on a 9-points scale) were significantly lower than and utterly uncorrelated with the normative ones ($r_s = 0.02$).

Previous studies that involved comparisons between more recent and normative IAPS ratings found similar results. Libkuman et al. [16], for instance, obtained lower arousal ratings than the IAPS norms. However, their work mainly aimed to extend a subset of 703 IAPS pictures through the collection of new dimensions and adopted a different protocol that involved the use of 14 different Likert scales rather than SAM. Since these changes might have acted as confounding variables, the authors limit their interpretation of this outcome to a speculation about the factors that might have led to it. Similarly, Grühn and Scheibe [17], while evaluating the impact of age on IAPS ratings using a pictorial set composed of 504 stimuli, found a lower correlation between new and normative arousal ratings.

We have no evidence that the methods we applied in our research might have interfered with the obtained outcome. For the collection of IAPS ratings, we systematically followed a setup that reflected the original experimental settings, including the instructions administered to the participants. Moreover, our results perfectly replicate the normative ratings of pleasure with a very strong correlation ($r_s = 0.9$), thus confirming the coherence of this dimension in the IAPS database across time and consequently implying that the significant effect we found for arousal is genuine.

To the best of our knowledge, our investigation constitutes the most comprehensive and recent study that purposefully replicated the IAPS norms. Our results are in complete agreement with those obtained in previous studies and further extend them to a broader pool of stimuli (i.e. 1178 IAPS pictures). In addition, our findings show that the most arousing IAPS subset consisting of over 200 pictures is perceived today as significantly less arousing, hence suggesting that the use of highly arousing visual content from standardized databases such as IAPS as a benchmark to elicit strong affective responses measured through self-assessment, psychophysiological signals or neuroimaging techniques can lead to inaccurate results, since those stimuli are not calibrated to contemporary sensitivity.

Not only do our results demonstrate that legacy scales for the self-report of affect such as the SAM can be replaced with more intuitive measurement tools developed in accordance to modern design principles, but also that affective responses might combine both invariant and variant components, suggesting a larger plasticity in emotional appraisal and expression than initially expected. This raises the specific question to what extent human emotional experience and expression can be further molded by experience in particular along the dimensions of pleasure and arousal.

Further improvements will consist in the creation of a new set of original pictorial stimuli able to trigger strong responses in arousal. Such database could be implemented using an open web-based collaborative platform (e.g. a Wiki) where researchers can contribute with novel pictures that will be collectively rated using the AS.

AUTHOR CONTRIBUTIONS

Conceived and designed the experiments: AB PV. Performed the experiments: AB. Analyzed the data: AB. Contributed reagents/materials/analysis tools: AB PV. Wrote the paper: AB PV.

REFERENCES

1. Darwin C. The Expression of the Emotions in Man and Animals. Phoenix Books. University of Chicago Press; 1965.
2. James W. What is an Emotion? Mind. 1884;9(34):pp. 188–205. doi: 10. 1093/mind/os-IX. 34. 188.
3. Picard RW, Healey J. Affective wearables. Personal Technologies. 1997;1(4):231–240. doi: 10. 1007/BF01682026.
4. Fahrenberg J, Myrtek M, Pawlik K, Perrez M. Ambulatory Assessment—Monitoring Behavior in Daily Life Settings. European Journal of Psychological Assessment. 2007 Jan;23(4):206–213. doi: 10. 1027/1015-5759. 23. 4. 206.
5. Betella A, Zucca R, Cetnarski R, Greco A, Lanatà A, Mazzei D, et al. Inference of Human Affective States from Psychophysiological Measurements Extracted under Ecologically Valid Conditions. Frontiers in Neuroscience. 2014;8(286). doi: 10. 3389/fnins. 2014. 00286. pmid:25309310
6. Bradley MM, Lang PJ. Measuring emotion: The self-assessment manikin and the semantic differential. Journal of Behavior Therapy and Experimental Psychiatry. 1994 Mar;25(1):49–59. doi: 10. 1016/0005-7916(94)90063-9. pmid:7962581
7. MacKenzie IS. Human-Computer Interaction: An Empirical Research Perspective. Elsevier Science; 2012.
8. Ringeval F, Sonderegger A, Sauer J, Lalanne D. Introducing the RECOLA multimodal corpus of remote collaborative and affective interactions. 2013 10th IEEE International Conference and Workshops on Automatic Face and Gesture Recognition (FG). 2013 Apr;p. 1–8.
9. Lottridge D, Chignell M. Emotional bandwidth: information theory analysis of affective response ratings using a continuous slider. Human-Computer Interaction–INTERACT 2009. 2009;p. 111–114. doi: 10. 1007/978-3-642-03655-2_12.
10. Laurans G, PMa Desmet, Hekkert P. The emotion slider: A self-report device for the continuous measurement of emotion. In: 2009 3rd International Conference on Affective Computing and Intelligent Interaction. Amsterdam: Ieee; 2009.
11. Lang PJ, Bradley MM, Cuthbert BN. International affective picture system (IAPS): Affective ratings of pictures and instruction manual. Gainesville, FL: University of Florida, Center for the Study of Emotion and Attention; 2008. A-8.
12. Lang PJ, Greenwald MK, Bradley MM. The International Affective Picture System (IAPS) standardization procedure and initial group results for affective judgments (Tech. Rep. Nos. 1A–1D). Gainesville, FL: University of Florida, Center for the Study of Emotion and Attention; 1988.
13. Carnagey NL, Anderson CA, Bushman BJ. The effect of video game violence on physiological desensitization to real-life violence. Journal of Experimental Social Psychology. 2007;43(3):489–496. doi: 10. 1016/j. jesp. 2006. 05. 003.
14. Krahé B, Möller I, Huesmann LR, Kirwil L, Felber J, Berger A. Desensitization to media violence: Links with habitual media violence exposure, aggressive cognitions, and aggressive behavior. Journal of personality and social psychology. 2011;100(4):630. doi: 10. 1037/a0021711. pmid:21186935
15. Romer D, Jamieson PE, Bushman BJ, Bleakley A, Wang A, Langleben D, et al. Parental Desensitization to Violence and Sex in Movies. Pediatrics. 2014;.
16. Libkuman TM, Otani H, Kern R, Viger SG, Novak N. Multidimensional normative ratings for the international affective picture system. Behavior research methods. 2007;39(2):326–334. doi: 10. 3758/BF03193164. pmid:17695361
17. Grühn D, Scheibe S. Age-related differences in valence and arousal ratings of pictures from the International Affective Picture System (IAPS): Do ratings become more extreme with age? Behavior Research Methods. 2008;40(2):512–521. doi: 10. 3758/BRM. 40. 2. 512. pmid:18522062
18. Mehrabian A, Russell JA. An approach to environmental psychology. the MIT Press; 1974.
19. Valdez P, Mehrabian A. Effects of color on emotions. Journal of Experimental Psychology: General. 1994;123(4):394–409. doi: 10. 1037/0096-3445. 123. 4. 394.
20. Betella A, Inderbitzin M, Bernardet U, Verschure PFMJ. Non-anthropomorphic Expression of Affective States through Parametrized Abstract Motifs. In: Affective Computing and Intelligent Interaction (ACII), 2013 Humaine Association Conference on; 2013. p. 435–441.
21. Russell JA, Barrett LF. Core affect, prototypical emotional episodes, and other things called emotion: dissecting the elephant. Journal of personality and social psychology. 1999;76(5):805. doi: 10. 1037/0022-3514. 76. 5. 805. pmid:10353204
22. Bradley MM, Lang PJ. The International Affective Picture System (IAPS) in the study of emotion and attention. In: Coan JA, Allen JJB, editors. Handbook of emotion elicitation and assessment. Oxford, New York: Oxford University Press; 2007. p. 29–46.
23. Krantz JH, Dalal R. Chapter 2—Validity of Web-Based Psychological Research. In: Birnbaum MH, editor. Psychological Experiments on the Internet. San Diego: Academic Press; 2000. p. 35–60.

24. Meyerson P, Tryon W. Validating Internet research: A test of the psychometric equivalence of Internet and in-person samples. Behavior Research Methods, Instruments, & Computers. 2003;35(4):614–620. doi: 10. 3758/BF03195541.

25. Buhrmester M, Kwang T, Gosling SD. Amazon's Mechanical Turk: A New Source of Inexpensive, Yet High-Quality, Data? Perspectives on Psychological Science. 2011;6(1):3–5. doi: 10. 1177/1745691610393980. pmid:26162106

26. Cacioppo J, Tassinary L, Berntson G. Handbook of psychophysiology. 3rd ed. Cambridge University Press; 2007.

27. Boucsein W. Electrodermal activity. 2nd ed. Springer; 2012.

28. Lang PJ, Bradley MM, Cuthbert BN. International affective picture system (IAPS): Technical manual and affective ratings. Gainesville, FL: The Center for Research in Psychophysiology, University of Florida; 1999.

CHAPTER 20

DESIGN AND IMPLEMENTATION OF A CLOUD COMPUTING ADOPTION DECISION TOOL: GENERATING A CLOUD ROAD

Iñaki Bildosola[1], Rosa Río-Belver[2] , Ernesto Cilleruelo[1] , Gaizka Garechana[3]

[1] Foresight, Technology and Management (FTM) Group, Industrial Organization and Management Engineering Department, Faculty of Engineering in Bilbao (ETSI Bilbao), University of the Basque Country UPV/EHU, Basque Country, Spain

[2] Foresight, Technology and Management (FTM) Group, Industrial Organization and Management Engineering Department, University College of Engineering of VitoriaGasteiz, University of the Basque Country UPV/EHU, Basque Country, Spain

[3] Foresight, Technology and Management (FTM) Group, Industrial Organization and Management Engineering Department, Escuela Universitaria de Estudios Empresariales de Bilbao, University of the Basque Country UPV/EHU, Basque Country, Spain

ABSTRACT

Migrating to cloud computing is one of the current enterprise challenges. This technology provides a new paradigm based on "on-demand payment" for information and communication technologies. In this sense, the small and medium enterprise is supposed to be the most interested, since initial investments are avoided and the technology allows gradual implementation. However, even if the characteristics and capacities have been widely discussed, entry into the cloud is still lacking in terms of practical, real frameworks. This paper aims at filling this gap, presenting a real tool already implemented and tested, which can be used as a cloud computing adoption decision tool. This tool uses diagnosis based on specific questions to gather the required information and subsequently provide the user with valuable information to deploy the business within the cloud, specifically in the form of Software as a Service (SaaS) solutions. This information allows the decision makers to generate their particular Cloud Road. A pilot study has been carried out with enterprises at a local level with a two-fold objective: to ascertain the degree of knowledge on cloud computing and to identify the most interesting business areas and their related tools for this technology. As expected, the results show high interest and low knowledge on this subject and the tool presented aims to readdress this mismatch, insofar as possible.

INTRODUCTION

Although there is no general definition of cloud computing [1], [2], one of the most used definitions is from the National Institute of Standards and Technology (NIST) which states: "cloud computing is a model for enabling ubiquitous, convenient, on-demand network access to a shared pool of configurable computing resources that can be rapidly provisioned and released with minimal management effort or service provider interaction". Its most important features can be summarized as follows: on-demand self-service, broad network access, resource pooling, rapid elasticity or expansion, and measured service [3]. In cloud computing IT service providers offer their services grouped into three categories, Infrastructure as a Service (IaaS), allowing users to deploy hardware computing resources as a service, Platform as a Service (PaaS), providing all the necessary components for creating a new software application, and Software as a Service (SaaS),

Citation: Bildosola I, Río-Belver R, Cilleruelo E, Garechana G (2015) Design and Implementation of a Cloud Computing Adoption Decision Tool: Generating a Cloud Road. PLoS ONE 10(7): e0134563. doi:10.1371/journal.pone.0134563.

offering the consumer a wide variety of applications provided by service providers and running on the infrastructure of the cloud [4–7]. In addition, there are four deployment models: Private, the cloud infrastructure is operated solely for an organization; Community, the cloud infrastructure is shared by several organizations; Public, the cloud infrastructure is made available to the general public and is owned by an organization selling cloud services; Hybrid, The cloud infrastructure is a composition of two or more clouds (private, community, or public) [3].

A study conducted by the Cisco company [8] revealed the following impressive figures concerning the cloud computing impact sphere. Global cloud traffic:

- Annual global cloud IP traffic will reach 5.3 zettabytes (10^21 bytes) by the end of 2017. By 2017, global cloud IP traffic will reach 443 exabytes (10^18 bytes) per month (up from 98 exabytes per month in 2012)
- Global cloud IP traffic will increase nearly 4.5-fold over the next 5 years. Overall, cloud IP traffic will grow at a Compound annual growth rate of 35 percent from 2012 to 2017
- Global cloud IP traffic will account for more than two-thirds of total data center traffic by 2017

In addition, cloud computing is expected to be the main driving force behind IT sector development and SMEs will be the strategic market. Moreover, it is forecasted that 13.8 million jobs will be created over the 2011–2015 period [9].

North America represents the largest opportunity for SaaS, as well as being the most mature of the regional markets [10]. Furthermore, Gartner says that European cloud adoption will lag behind U.S. by at least two years. The main reasons for this statement are European privacy rules, multi-country business processes, a deep euro crisis and a lingering recession [11]. The introduction to cloud technology occurs in different ways and depends largely on company size, in the case of Spain, for example, 100 percent of large companies are expected to adopt it by 2015. However, only 69% of SMEs will implement it [12]. The largest increase occurs in SMEs, reaching 69% in 2015, up from 13.9% in 2011 [13]. Experts unanimously agree that the trend for large companies will be the hybrid model and all kinds of families (IaaS, PaaS and SaaS). Nevertheless, SMEs will focus on the public model and the demand will be for SaaS applications [14].

It should be pointed out that cloud computing goes hand in hand with three other cutting edge information technologies, namely: big data and analytics, social networking and mobile computing, which are creating the 3rd platform [15] also known as Big Services Era [16]. These technologies are deeply interrelated, as will be made clear when analyzing the test results in the fifth section of this work.

It should be highlighted that there is a lack of knowledge concerning what cloud computing is, as well as its most significant benefits. In particular, 54.9% of microenterprises and SMEs confess that they have no knowledge of cloud technology. This circumstance results in a loss of SME competitiveness, contrasted with the fact that this technology model is particularly beneficial for SMEs [17], [18]. Furthermore, the lack of knowledge regarding the benefits (63.1%) is stressed as the greatest obstacle to entry into the cloud [14].

Migrating to cloud computing is not an easy issue, all the more when there is no widely accepted standard for cloud services and a need to develop guidelines and criteria to help entities understand their requirements. Linked with that, decision support tools that aid decision makers to migrate IT systems to the cloud are also required [19]. In fact, as it is an adoption of an emerging technology, it is regarded as a management innovation challenge related with technological innovations, where managerial interventions in organizational routines will be needed in order to overcome the ineffectiveness of familiar practices within the organization for dealing with a new technology. In addition to which, introducing a new innovation can result in employee resistance, thus, senior decision-makers in organizations need to prepare employees for this new learning curve by providing training and communication in advance of cloud implementation. To this effect, there has to be an awareness of what is being introduced, specially focused on the benefits it will bring [20].

Several frameworks have been presented as guides to make decisions on cloud technology implementation. From theoretical frameworks to specific examples, a few of them have gone beyond the theoretical paper-based approach and have developed an interface for the decision makers, in an attempt to make the process more user friendly. This paper describes the process of making a cloud computing technology adoption decision tool and its assessment performed via a pilot study, conducted with different local companies at Basque Country autonomous community (Spain) level. It should be noted that the Basque Country's industry structure is based on SMEs, in fact 93.4% of the companies have less than 10 employees whereas 5.5% have between 10 and 49. In addition to this, the community ranks number one in Spain in terms of investment in research and development as a percentage of GDP (2.1%). Ultimately, the utilization of the tool, i.e. carrying out the diagnosis, shall permit the users to initiate their own Cloud Road, which will allow implementation of cloud computing technologies in order to enhance the efficiency of their business strategies.

METHODS

Related Work

Generally speaking, a commonly selected criterion when it comes to analyze the adoption of cloud computing is to analyze the corresponding return on investment (ROI). Though current surveys find cloud computing highly suitable for small and medium enterprises, a deeper analysis of the economic aspects of migration to cloud architecture can provide very valuable information. Thus, various types of cloud cost-benefit analysis have been reported [21–23]. An evaluation of IT infrastructures to support the decision of whether to move information systems into the cloud or not was attempted in Khajeh-Hosseini et al. [24], where a Cost Modeling tool is presented and evaluated using a case study of an organization that is considering migration of some of its IT systems to the cloud, analyzing the specific resource usage and the deployment options being used by a system. A more generic model, containing variables which should be applicable to any company, was presented in [25], where a ROI model is implemented, identifying the factors that need to be considered and returning a certain profitability valuation from the change. Here, the concept of "initial information" is considered as a scenario definition, based on the entity's IT utilization level and managed data characteristics. The tool includes some intangible benefits to give a broader picture. No supporting software was developed for the tool.

A multi-criteria approach could also be followed, to give a more generalized point of view, in order to support the decision about implementing cloud computing. In this sense, the decision is based by taking issues such as cost, benefits, opportunities, goals or risks, among other things into account. Several approaches have been presented based on this concept, focused on the outsourcing of IT technologies; such as Wang and Yang [26] and Udo [27], where initial information was not considered and no software tool adaptable to different decision-making goals was developed. A multi-criteria decision tool is presented in Menzel et al. [28], where a customized evaluation method is developed, and where generic multi-criteria frameworks are adapted to IT infrastructure solutions and more specifically to cloud computing, to be used as a decision tool. The evaluation method is selected and configured based on specific criteria and requirements in order to perform the evaluation itself, all this supported by a user interface via web application.

A more practical standpoint is provided by some web based initiatives. For instance, Cloud Harmony [29] is presented as a benchmarking tool, where a set of benchmarks is provided in order to objectively compare different cloud providers, analyzing the corresponding IaaS or PaaS provided. The benchmarks rank cloud providers accordingly with their network throughput, latency, performance (CPU, disk I/O and others) and service availability. With Cloud Sleuth [30], best practices and resources for deploying and managing applications in the cloud are provided, as well as applications to compare the performance and availability of PaaS and IaaS providers. The main approach of this kind of tool is not to provide a framework per se to the decision maker but as much information as possible.

Rather than focusing on the IT technology itself, several studies have focused on a more practical point of view, analyzing SaaS implementation in order to enhance business-specific processes. As a new concept, enterprise resource planning (ERP) software that is deployed into a cloud environment becomes "Cloud ERP Software" [31], with the addition of the fact that different business tasks could be migrated independently, so tailoring needs is perfectly feasible. To this effect, studies like Gerhardter and Ortner [32] try to analyze the success factors for SaaS implementation. These factors are determined by studying those which were successful from a classical ERP implementation and then by reconceiving them with the new cloud scenario.

Several frameworks have been presented when it comes to decide whether to adopt cloud computing or not and how to do it, based on business models or specific business processes. This concept is developed in Chang et al. [33], where an already proven theoretical framework called "Cloud Computing Business Framework" is described. Here the relation between the business model and the IT services is examined, and cloud adoption is presented as a project itself, identifying four key factors, namely "Business Model Classification" where the importance of the business model is stressed; "Organizational Sustainability Modeling" where an ROI is included; "Service Portability" from desktop to Cloud and between Clouds, and "Linkage" where linkage between different cloud services, and between business and services is explained. Some studies have been carried out in order to specify an approach based on one specific business activity, such as the "supply chain" approach in Wu et al. [34], where the circumstances that affect a firm's intention to adopt cloud computing technologies in support of its supply chain operations are investigated, and a conceptual framework model is presented.

Finally it should be stated that few works have made the effort to clarify those variables that work as drivers (or barriers) when it comes to cloud computing adoption. Shimba F in [35], conducted a survey among several workers of both technical and non-technical job-roles and organizations in an attempt to identify these drivers and barriers. In the work he states that the biggest driving force for cloud adoption for most organizations was the need for flexible and scalable IT resources, followed by the need for resource optimization. Accordingly, costs were not the biggest driving force by themselves. However, Iyer EK et al. [36] reached a different conclusion in a later work which also aimed defining such drivers. Here the four gain vectors in the context of potential SME cloud adopters are provided based on a Delphi method process with industry experts, and cost saving gains take 80% of the perceived gain spectrum. Providing different reasons in order to explain this dominance, the paper states that perhaps the cloud computing industry (in terms of its communication to the market) has emphasized the cost gain element more than other non-monetizable ones. In addition to this, it is argued that the SME industry is, to a certain extent, always strapped for cash, and it can be safely surmised that any cost related benefit will tend to override other considerations.

Regarding this fact, it can be concluded that the potential initial drivers for cloud adoption, linked with its technological advantages, have been replaced for those directly related with cost savings, from a clear business approach. Linked to this, Marston et al. in [37] states that while the researchers and practitioners in the computer science community are making rapid strides in realizing cloud computing advantages in technological terms, an equally important discussion needs to start from a business perspective. Thus, our research aims at contributing increased knowledge in that perspective and, accordingly, the proposed model which is described in the next section follows this cost saving issue approach, based on the company perspective through its main strategies of competitive improvement, via general-purpose tools and SaaS recommendations.

Proposed Cloud Adoption Decision Tool

Most of the existing approaches are based on a theoretical framework to aid the decision makers when adopting cloud computing. In fact, few of them have developed real tools. The provided information mainly comes from the analysis of adopting cloud computing or not, and in affirmative cases the migration of the already implemented IT technology is proposed. However, in order to obtain maximum practicality, our work aims to aid the decision makers when it comes to choose the most adequate software related to cloud computing, i.e. SaaS. In this sense, based on the recommendations given by the developed tool, the decision maker should be able to generate their own Cloud Road: the roadmap to implement cloud computing solutions in their company. Our work fills the existing gap from the explained approaches to the last step, the adoption of the cloud. This final step is no more than the SaaS selection, which is especially helpful for SMEs as discussed before. Furthermore, the developed framework is not only theoretical but a real tool which can be used several times in order to clarify the information and options provided.

The design process of a pilot tool was presented in Zabalza-Vivanco et al. [38], presented here is the final complete design, where all the functionalities and results are integrated. The methodology used in the research is summarized in Fig 1. The preparation phase of the decision tool is described in more detail below; this can be divided into two distinct stages: the development of the decision tree (S1 Fig) and its implementation.

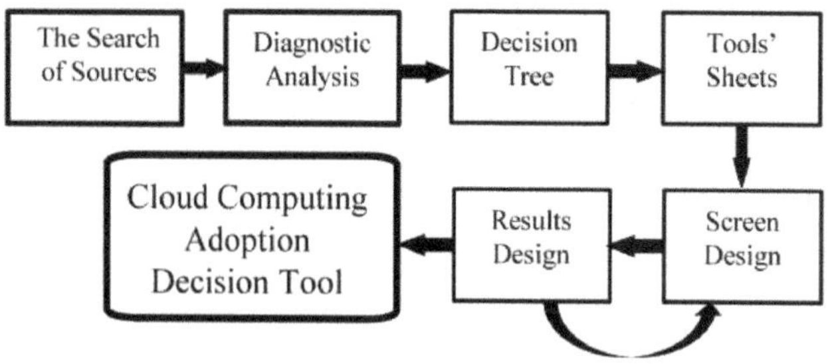

Figure 1. Research Methodology. The methodology used in the research is summarized in the figure, from the initial research to the achievement of the adoption decision tool.

Stage One: The Creation of a Decision Tree

A decision tree is a diagram that shows conditions and actions in a sequential way [39]. Furthermore, this method allows us to show the relationship between each condition and the set of possible actions associated with it. Moreover, it provides a graphical view to aid the decision making process, indicating the variables that are assessed and what actions should be taken as well as the sequence in which decision-making must be executed.

The decision tree and consequently the designed decision tool is based on a diagnosis whose approach is enterprise level for the adoption of the cloud computing tools, mainly focused on SMEs. The goal of the tool is to identify the best actions for each company based on its strategy of competitive improvement. The model used is based on the postulates of Porter et al. [40], who described the competitive strategy as the offensive or defensive strategies of a company that create defendable positions within an industry.

Porter identified three generic strategies which could be used individually or combined in order to create a long-term defendable position: Cost leadership (consequently quality, service and cost reduction); Focus or Niche Strategy (focus on a particular buyer group, product segment, or geographical market); Differentiation (that offered by a firm means creating something that is perceived industry-wide as being unique). Later on in 1990 [41], he recognized the instability of those three generic strategies facing new market circumstances and the need of more dynamic models to design the competitive advantage. Following this approach, the competitive strategy of a given company must be constructed based on its competitive strengths and it should continue improving the most vulnerable areas. Thus, our decision tree and consequently the decision tool itself have been produced from a company perspective. In this sense, the company is questioned according to the main strategies of competitive improvement, consequently questions on offensive actions are particular to each company: the nature of the industry and its competitive position in terms of "company type", "market/client diversification", "product/service diversification"; together with the defensive actions where Porter's generic strategy is followed in terms of cost leadership, hence the identification of which areas, resources and capacities the company wishes to improve is performed. For this purpose, "Clients", "Government and Financial Institutions", "Suppliers" and "HR" where included.

The complete decision tree is provided (separately due to its size), where the method of how to combine the aforementioned variables is shown. In this sense, the variables and their related tools are combined based on the priority levels set out by the company, which are the decision tree conditions: high, medium and low preference. For that purpose, an expert committee was created with members of all the agents involved in the project: staff from the Qmedia and Serikat companies; staff from the Tecnalia research center; and researchers from the Industrial Organization and Management Engineering Department of the University of the Basque Country. The main task of the committee was to evaluate each tool, generate a complete sheet for each and assign a grade to link them with the different variables; the whole process was conducted through several meetings until the final set was obtained. These sheets provide the information to generate the links within the decision tree and ultimately the combination of the variables themselves.

In order to select the proposed tools/SaaS within the decision tool consideration was given to the fact that business strategy was leading the way and accordingly those tools which can be used to increase the competitiveness of the company were prioritized. As a result, the approach taken is mainly based on Marston et al [37], which states that computing applications which are general-purpose in nature are the most appropriate to move to the cloud, since they offer tremendous economies of scale. Thus, based on the recommendations of that work, our decision tool follows this logic sequence when it comes to make recommendations: firstly general-purpose applications such as "office", "email" and "collaboration", applications with no specific requirements for any particular organization;

after that standalone applications such as CRM, which are easy to deploy in a cloud; and lastly applications with intricate interdependence to the cloud. Several cloud applications available on the SaaS market were examined such as [42], taking into account all the aforementioned facts. The result was a set of 51 SaaS applications and tools which are grouped into different sections or functionalities. These functionalities are identified as: On-line Billing, On-line Accounting, Personal Management, Project Management, Backup and Storage, Document Management, Content Management System (CMS), Customer Relationship Management (CRM), e-Commerce, e-Mailing Marketing, Social Networking Management, Feeds Management, e-learning, Event Organization, Collaborative Platforms, Web Development, Video, Communication, Business Intelligence, Production Management, Warehouse Management, Diagrams, Enterprise Resource management (ERP), Quality Management, and Customer Service and Support.

Stage Two: The Development of the Decision Tool

The decision tool was implemented in C#, designed by a local company called Openaula which collaborated in the project with a design aimed at ease of use. It includes branching (conditions), templates and provides basic statistical analysis in order to process the results.

The tool gathers information through eleven steps. Step 1 is used to obtain the size and sector of the entity. The following ten steps use the same procedure: the entity identifies ten different business areas with high, medium or low priority in order to improve the company situation by means of cloud computing adoption. In each step, some recommended functionalities will be shown which will improve those areas; the level of detail depends on the priority level. Finally, SaaS applications which allow the company to implement these actions will be suggested. The following captures (Figs 2–6) show the whole diagnosis process graphically, with different kinds of functionalities and tools provided to illustrate the diagnosis and recommendation process.

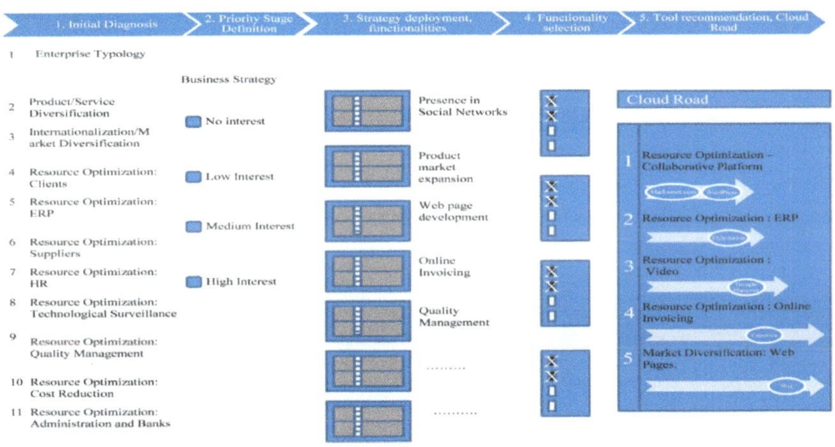

Figure 2. The decision tool operation: whole diagnosis and recommendation process. The whole process graphically represented, showing the different steps to be done by the tool user and the final recommendations to enhance the business areas and deploy the business strategy within the cloud.

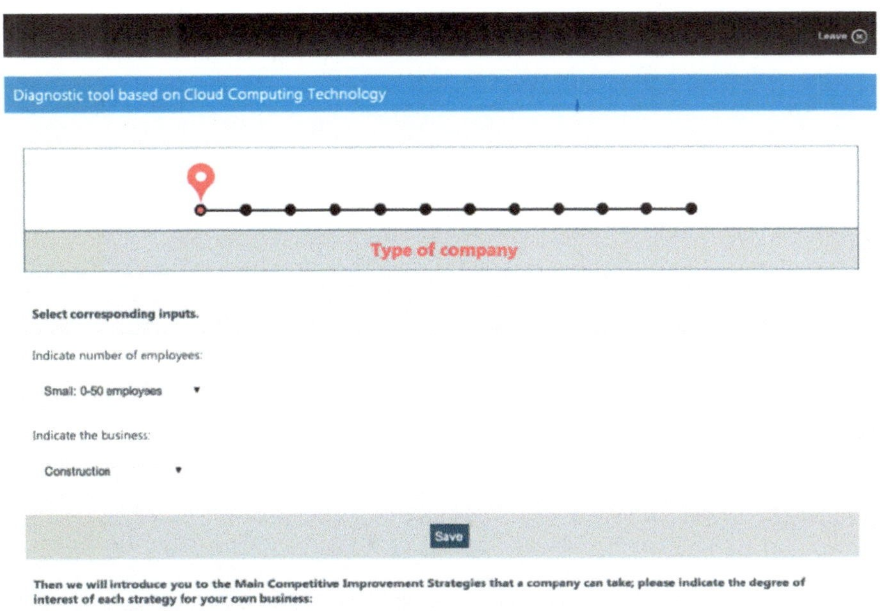

Figure 3. Step 1: Enterprise typology identification. The first step window capture, the tool gathers the user's company size and sector.

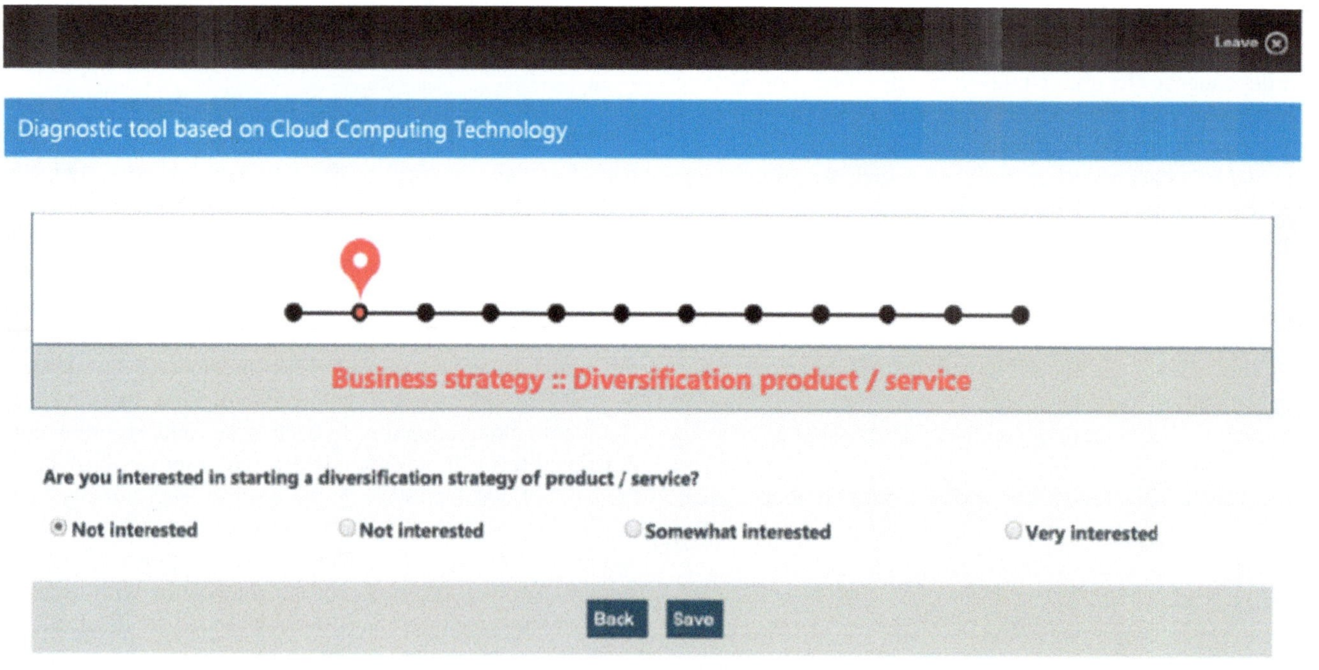

Figure 4. Step 2–11: Identification of the business area priority level. Standard window capture, steps 2–11 of the diagnosis, in which the user must indicate the priority level for each business area. The priority level goes from no interest to high interest.

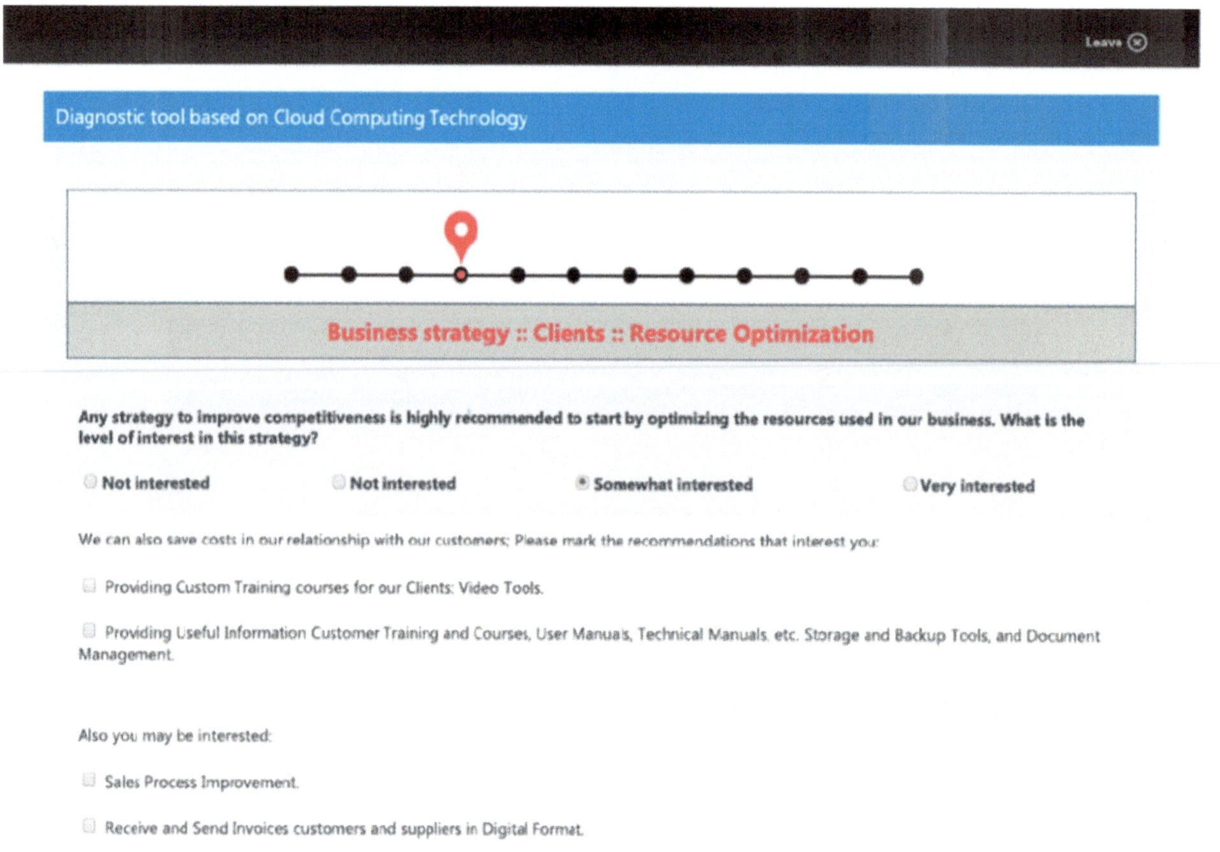

Figure 5. Step 2–11: Recommended functionalities and its selection to enhance business areas. Standard window capture, steps 2–11 of the diagnosis, in which the tool recommends several functionalities to enhance the corresponding business area, and the user selects the preferred ones.

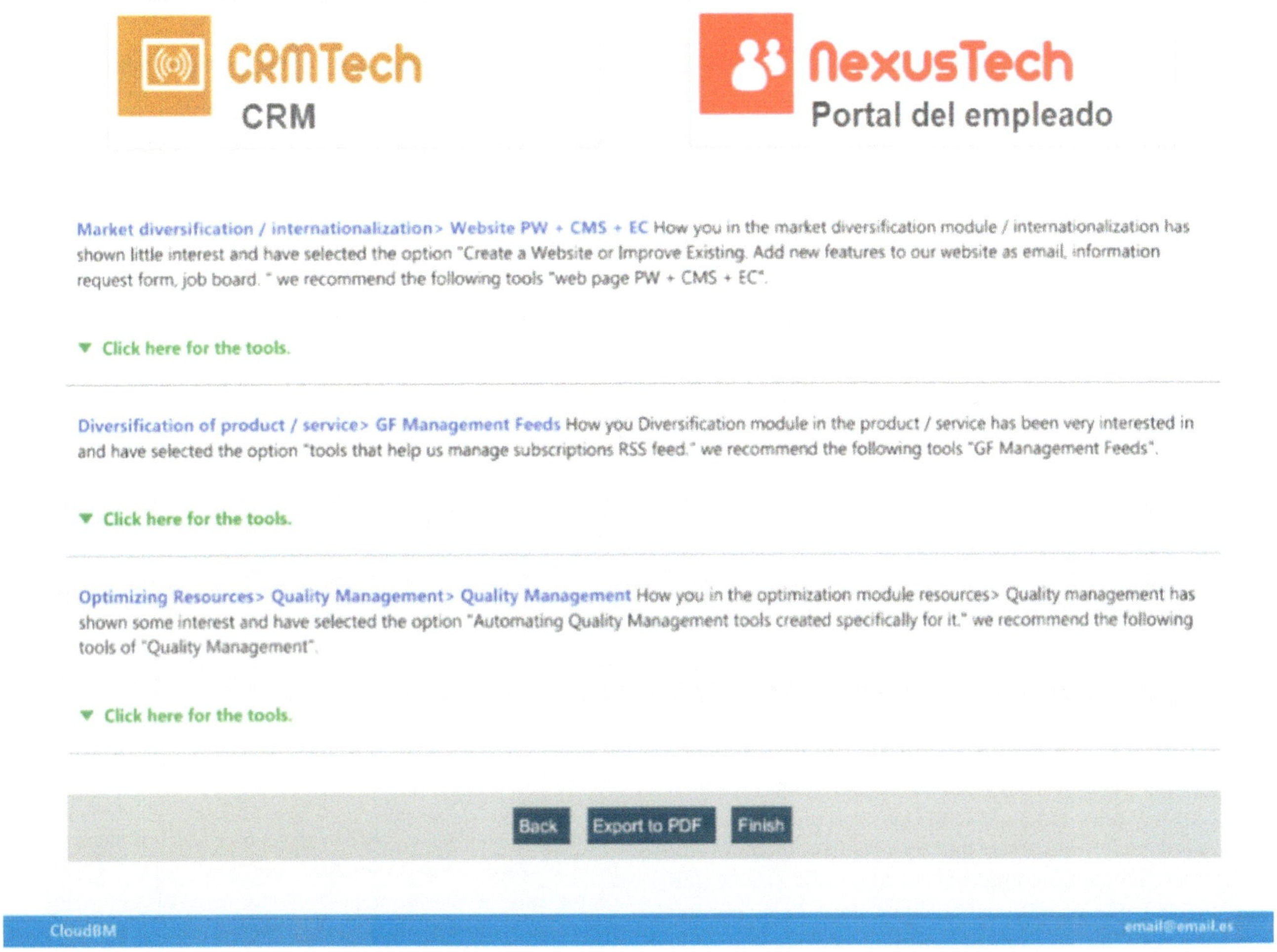

Figure 6. Recommendation of the decision tool to implement the selected functionalities. Final window capture, the decision tool offers and describes different solutions, basically in the form of SaaS, to enhance and deploy the business strategy within the cloud, based on the user's previous selections.

The resulting benefit of using this decision tool lies in the fact that, as a result, companies obtain a number of cloud solutions or tools that will enable them to improve their priority areas, generating a Cloud Road to implement cloud technology via SaaS. This is especially profitable for SMEs as discussed in the previous section, which are indeed the main target of this tool. Bear in mind that SMEs have reduced investment capacity and that the cloud's business model, based on "on-demand service", allows them to implement their priorities more tightly. Consequently, by means of this set of cloud SaaS solutions which fit the needs of each company, entities can reduce costs, improve the management of their customers, suppliers, employees and other agents such as public administration and banks. Furthermore, it is an aid for growth into new markets, as well as enhancing the task of creating new products or services. Note that on the final screen the basic features of each cloud tool are shown. In addition, clicking on any tool name, directs the user to the supplier's webpage. Finally, it is worth pointing out that a tool ranking is generated: the different tools are ranked by the number of clicks received, which indicates how many times they have been visited. All these features are accessible in the tool:http://cloudbm.net/corporativa/default.aspx.

RESULTS AND DISCUSSION

Methodology

In order to pursue a more objective assessment of our tool, a pilot study has been conducted among some SMEs in order to check which areas and features of the tool are more demanded and to check the overall behavior of the diagnosis. Accordingly, the most logical option was to conduct the study at the Basque Innovation Agency, named "Innobasque", a private, nonprofit organization created to coordinate innovation in the Basque Country and to encourage entrepreneurial spirit and creativity. Innobasque membership is made up of all types of organizations, distributed as shown in the Fig 7. It has to be emphasized that 80% of the corporations are SMEs.

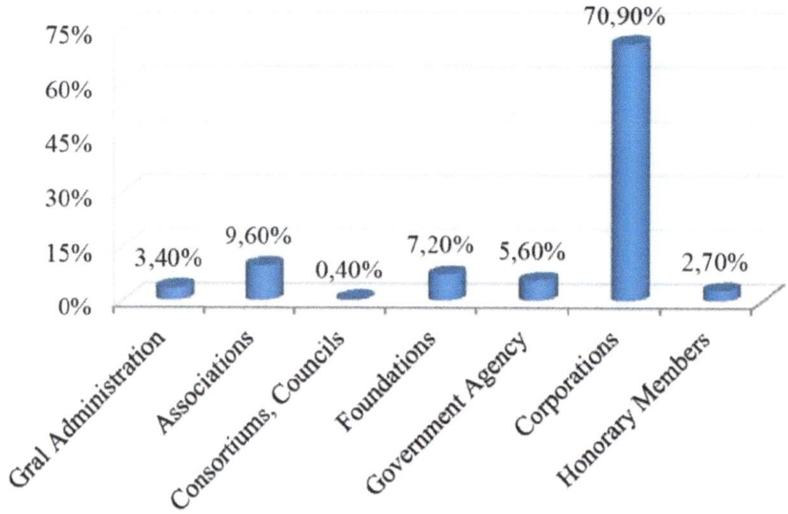

Figure 7. Profile of potential pilot study participants. The chart shows the profile of the potential participants of the pilot study using the tool.

The method used to disseminate information about the tool was to mail all the members an introductory text describing it and providing the access link, supported by a news item published on the Innobasque website. This mailshot was sent on December 2013. In addition to this, once the project had been publicized, a forum was held at Innobasque's premises in April 2014. The forum was used to directly present the tool itself: its functionalities, the diagnosis process and the results. The forum was attended by several enterprise decision makers and the pilot study was carried out. As a result of the pilot study 13 different companies completed the diagnosis satisfactorily, from which some provisional findings have been obtained, as will be seen in the following section. It should be noted that the participants validated the need of a tool to generate a cloud road and most of them reported having implemented the proposed tools. However, the tool is considered to be a live element and even though this first evaluation was centered on its design and usability, due to the continuous variability of the SaaS market, further results shall have to be gathered in order to evaluate the proposed tools and consider adding new solutions or removing some of the included.

Pilot Study Results

First of all, the tool gathers information regarding the enterprise's sector and size, in order to generate a simple profile of each case. Different sectors are represented in the results since innovation does not clash with any specific sector and, as mentioned, sooner or later all enterprises will face cloud computing adoption. When it comes to size, most of the enterprises fall within the 0–50 employees category, whereas larger ones are less represented. It should be noted for future work that the 0–50 scale should be further subdivided, considering that most of the participants will be SMEs. The exact values are shown in Fig 8.

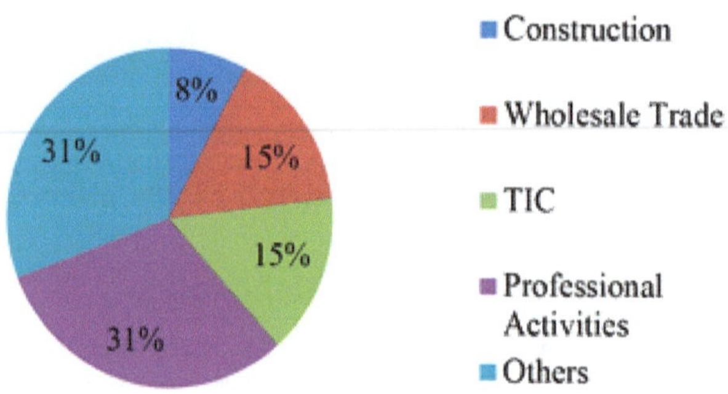

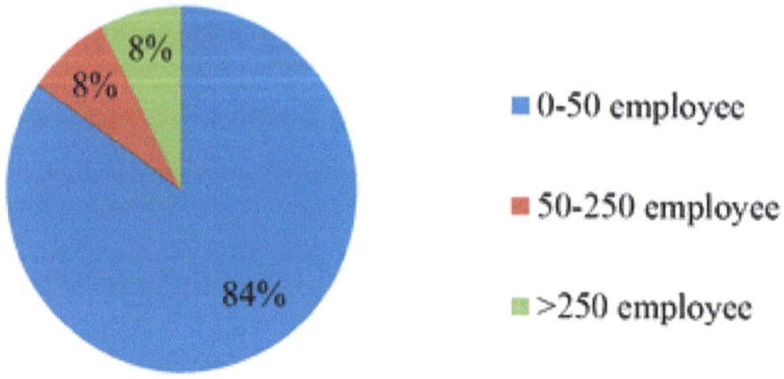

Figure 8. Typology of pilot study participants. The chart shows the typology of the final group of pilot study participants using the tool.

The analysis based on the participants' answers is two-fold:

- On the one hand it is a discussion about business areas and priority levels.
- On the other hand the functionalities for each business area and the different solutions (i.e. SaaS) for those functionalities can be discussed.

Thus, when it comes to business areas, it is important to distinguish the participants' preferences in terms of which business areas have attracted most interest. As a result, the tool asks the user to evaluate their interest in each of them by selecting from high, medium, low and no priority levels. There are 10 business areas reflected in the diagnosis and, as seen in Fig 9, not all of them obtain the same interest from the users.

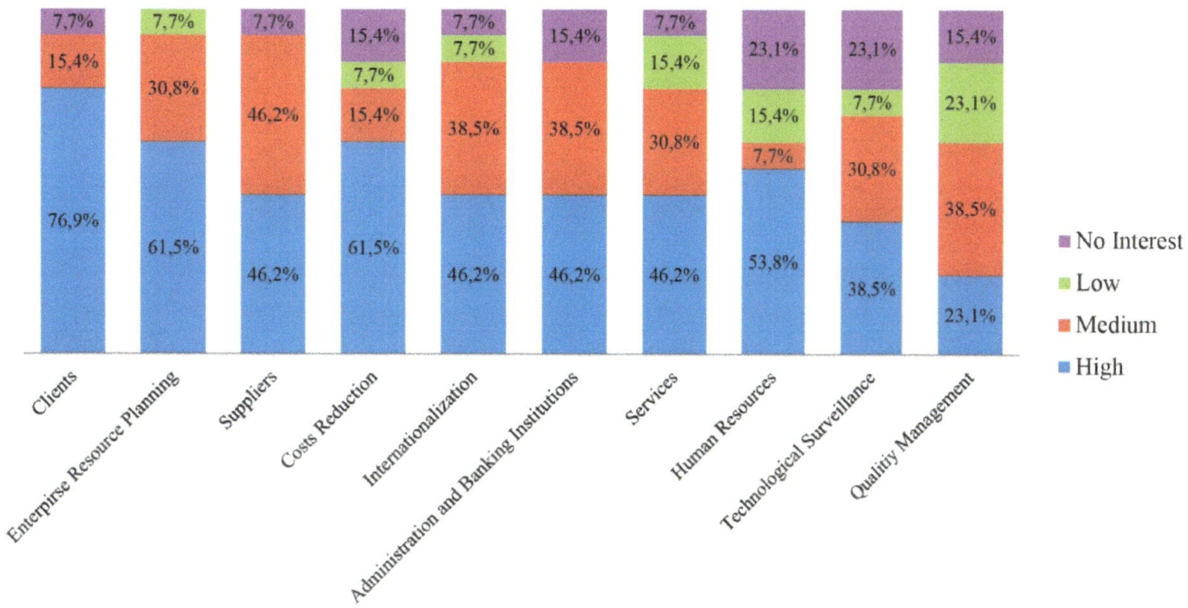

Figure 9. Participants' interest level by business area. The chart shows the initial interest generated by each business area, among the pilot study participants.

The arrangement on the graph is performed by weighting the priority with 5, 3, 1 and 0 respectively from high to no interest. It is worth noting that the Clients business area has obtained more than 70% of high interest, along with ERP and Suppliers areas on the positive side of the balance, which obtain more than 80% of high and medium interest. At the other end lie the Human Resources and Quality Management areas which obtain 60% of that kind of interest. This may be due to the fact that cloud computing offers clear advantages when dealing with clients and ERP management in terms of ubiquity and flexibility, whereas Quality Management and probably Human Resources are not particularly benefited by the irruption of cloud computing. This has been well perceived by the participants. More surprising still is the poor ranking of Technology Surveillance, a clear cutting-edge business area apparently not yet well-known by firms within the study, but a must in the short-term.

In order to distinguish those interests but differentiating the enterprise sector, a deeper subdivision has been performed. Thus, the same information is offered, divided by business sector, in Figs 10–13.

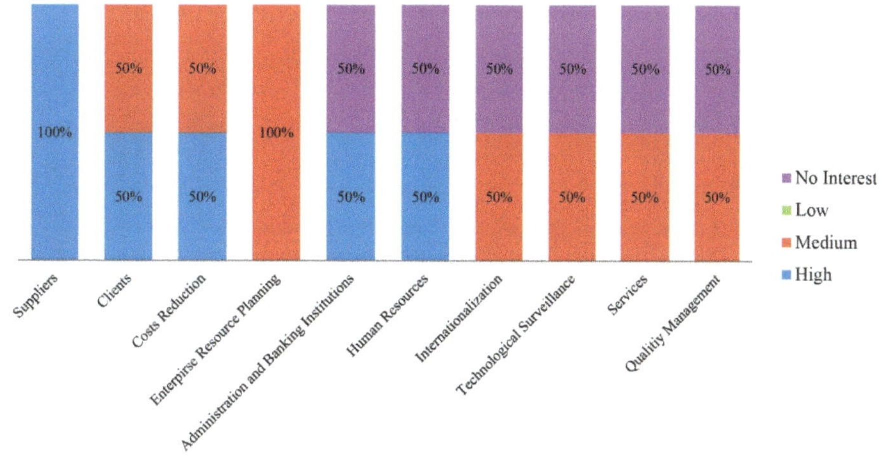

Figure 10. Participants' interest level by business area. Wholesale sector companies. The chart shows the initial interest generated by each business area, among the pilot study participants pertaining to the wholesale sector.

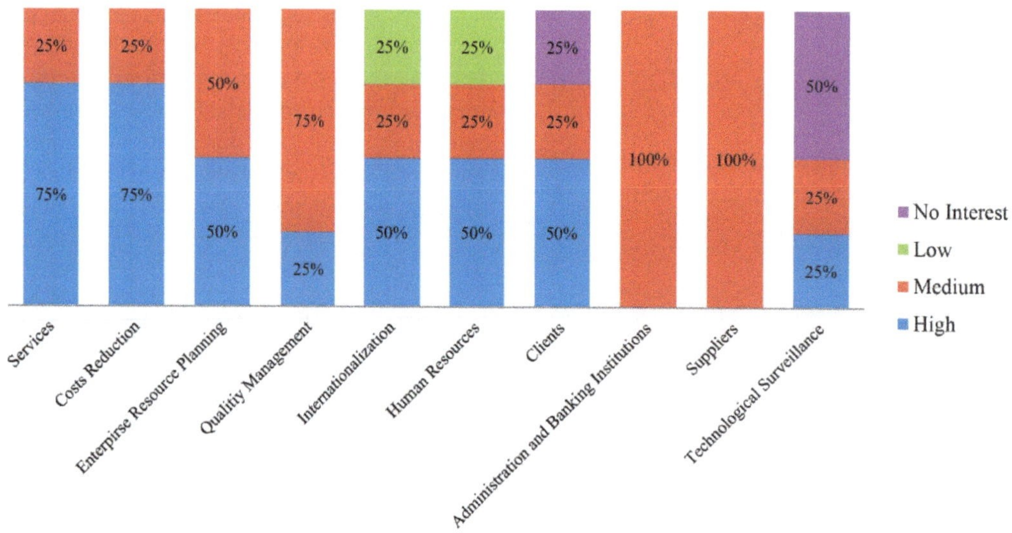

Figure 11. Participants' interest level by business area. Professional activities sector companies. The chart shows the initial interest generated by each business area, among the pilot study participants pertaining to the professional activities sector.

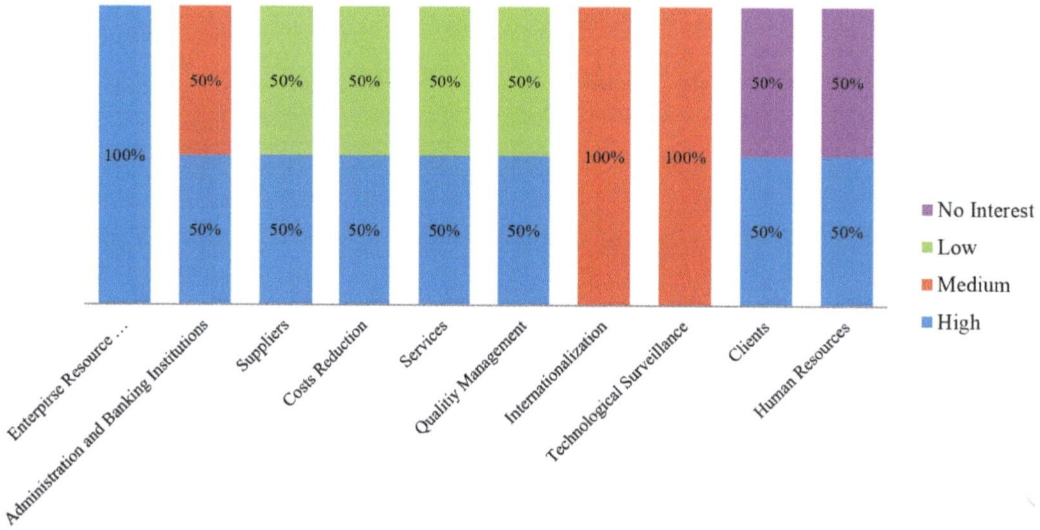

Figure 12. Participants' interest level by business area. Information and communication technologies sector companies. The chart shows the initial interest generated by each business area, among the pilot study participants pertaining to the information and communication technologies sector.

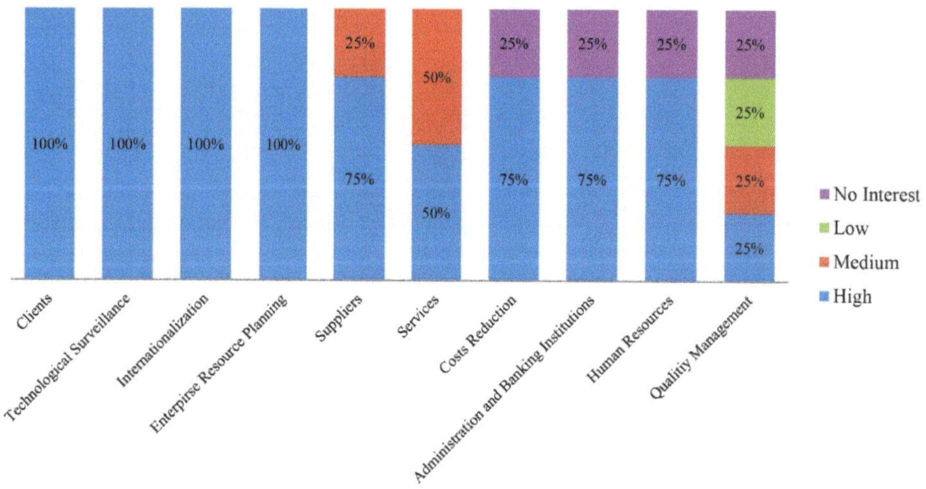

Figure 13. Participants' interest level by business area. Other sector companies. The chart shows the initial interest generated by each business area, among the pilot study participants pertaining to other sectors.

The sample size does not permit any reliable conclusions to be drawn for each sector, however, the tool's potential for the task is clear. Even if the ability to identify preferred business areas is valuable information when it comes to adopt cloud computing technology, a breakdown by enterprise sector offers a far more in-depth view of specific strategies. Thus, the results make it possible to conclude that even if the breakdown is performed, uniformity of preferences is not assured, as can be seen in the "Professional Activities" sector, where different kinds of priority levels are selected in most of the business areas. This inconsistency would be overcome when using larger sample sizes. Analyzing different sectors in order to discover similarities shall allow them to be grouped by their interest patterns revealing, at least in part, which areas of business should be exploited by cloud computing technology in each sector.

When it comes to analyze the functionalities of each business area and the solutions to those functionalities it should be noted that those solutions can be either a specific existing SaaS or a different kind of solution (i.e. a social network such as Facebook), so for the sake of clarity, both will be identified generically as tools. With regard to the functionalities and the tools analyzed in the diagnosis, the first interesting point is to show which specific tools have been recommended more frequently. Accordingly, Fig 14 shows the top ten tools based on how many times they have been proposed. It should be noted that some specific functionalities and the corresponding tools are included in different business areas, as it is the case, for instance, with the "Subscription to Social Networks" functionality and its specific proposed solutions LinkedIn, Facebook and Twitter, which appear in four different business areas, namely Services, Suppliers, Technological Surveillance and Cost Reduction. This of course influences the number of recommendations received by these functionalities, however, it is not less significant that they are placed logically within different business areas so they deserve to be recommended more often than others. Thus, when a group of tools is involved in more than one business area, it is identified with a number in brackets corresponding to that number of areas. The specific total figures do not provide meaningful information, even less for this pilot study, nonetheless the appearance or absence of some specific tools in this top ten provides valuable information. To such effects, those tools which provide a solution to videoconference functionality can be found at the very top, these are tools designed to facilitate collaboration between employees and clients and to reduce communication costs, such as Google Hangout and Skype, among others. This kind of functionality is applicable to different business areas such as Internationalization, Suppliers, Human Resources, Costs Reduction and Administration and Bank Institutions and has generated high interest among participants. Together with these tools, the tools which provide the solution to subscribe to different social networks are ranked in second place. These go hand in hand with those used to manage subscriptions, such as Hootsuite and TweetDeck, ranked fourth. There is no doubt that despite these tools not being pure cloud computing technologies, they are the primary drivers of the incorporation of current enterprises into the cloud. This further demonstrates an increase of business interest in being aware of online reputation.

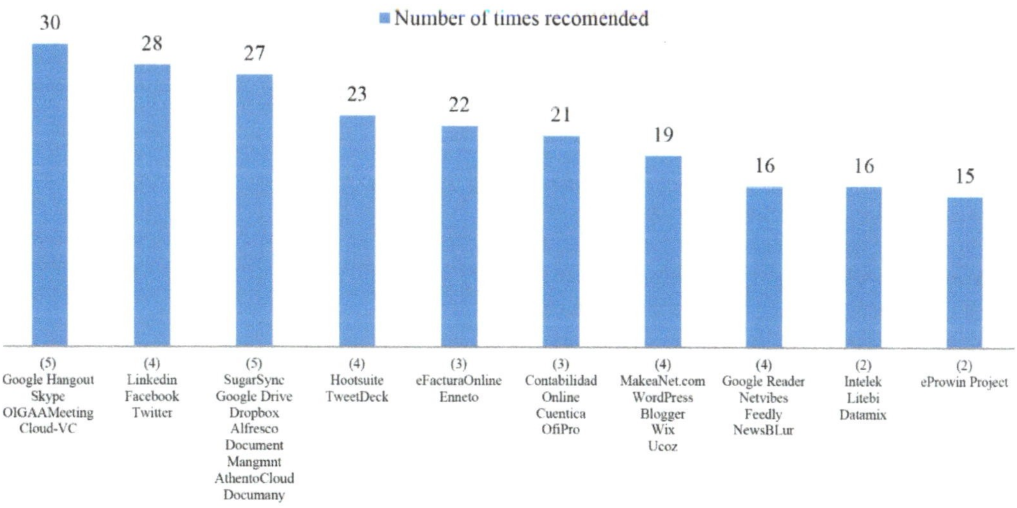

Figure 14. Top ten tools by number of times recommended. The chart shows the top ten tools, arranged by the total number of times recommended to the participants in the pilot study. In brackets the number of business areas in which each tool appears.

It is worth mentioning that the fifth and the sixth positions are occupied by tools aimed at solving accounting tasks, such as eFactura Online and Enneto for Online Billing functionality and Contabilidad Online and Cuentica for Online Accounting and invoicing. These solutions are proposed within Clients, Suppliers and Cost Reduction areas, and take advantage of one of cloud computing's main characteristics, accessibility of different agents from different places. The collaboration between employees, suppliers and clients is based on the functionalities Collaborative Platforms which provide real-time collaboration through web conferencing and Content Management Systems which allow content to be published, edited and modified from a central interface. This is a pure example of cloud computing technology and it is well placed in the seventh position with specific tools such asMakeaNet.com and WordPress. The Feed Readers functionality solutions allow the companies to be aware of competitors' actions, even to perform self-assessments. This activity has become an unavoidable task for current enterprises and it is well covered by cloud computing. These tools have generated enough interest to be placed in the eighth position, with solutions such as Google Reader (which stopped working in July 2013) and Netvibes. The technology surveillance tools such as Intelek and Litebi are included within the Services and Technology Surveillance areas in the diagnosis, providing decision making functionality; even if the importance of technology surveillance is not yet well-known by the majority of the enterprises, most of the participants have expressed interest in this functionality, as a result of which it appears in the top ten, so an increase in demand for such tools can expected. Finally the tenth most demanded functionality has been Online Project Management, with the eProwin Project tool. Even if it is only offered within the Human Resources and Cost Reduction business areas it has been one of the most demanded functionalities. In fact, the project management task requires a continuous updating and this probably needs to be done by various agents; cloud computing provides a satisfactory solution to that.

Functionalities and tool analysis gives us some deeper insights. Each business area has its own functionalities, for instance the Services area is described through seven functionalities whereas Internationalization does it through eight. In this regard, it is interesting to show which areas have gained greater interest in terms of the average percentage of functionalities selected by the participants in each area, which can be seen in Fig 15.

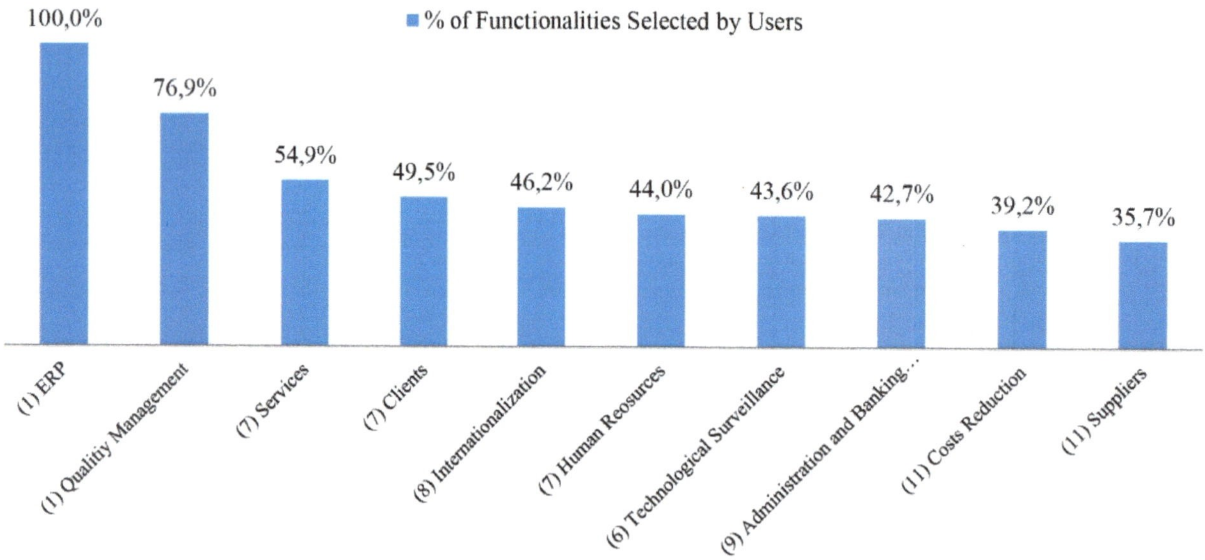

Figure 15. Business areas ranked by percentage of selection of its functionalities. The chart shows the business areas analyzed by the tool, arranged in terms of percentage of selection of the functionalities pertaining to each business area. In brackets the number of functionalities belonging to each business area.

The percentage gives us a good measure about how the participants have reacted to the different areas; in fact, a high percentage means that most of its functionalities have attracted the interest of the participants, whereas a low percentage means the opposite. It is worth checking the differences between the preliminary priority levels (shown in Fig 9), which are gathered before describing the functionalities themselves, against the percentage of selection described in this figure. The most surprising case is that of Quality Management, which was placed in last position in terms of interest but ranked second in percentage of selection. This is partially explained by the fact that it only has one functionality: Online Automation of Quality Management, nonetheless it is remarkable that even though the participants were not initially interested in it, once the functionalities are described they feel at least curious, behavior which can be extrapolated to cloud computing as a whole. In addition to this, as seen in Fig 15, the ERP's functionality is selected by all the participants, it was well placed within the preliminary priority levels and none of the participants miss the opportunity to find out about the tool related to it. Most of the others are placed approximately in the same position in both figures, with the exception of Cost Reduction and Suppliers, which were placed third and fourth in Fig 9, yet in contrast they occupy the last positions in Fig 15. Both of them are described with 11 functionalities, a number apparently too large for the participants, as a result of which the percentage of selection was fewer than 40%. In conclusion, even if a business area arouses interest, enterprises are not ready to handle so many different tools, at most they select three or four. When analyzing these percentages, bear in mind that these only deals with advice about the tools, so when it comes to discuss adopting the tools, the percentages will be smaller.

Finally, the pilot study provides an opportunity to perform a further breakdown in order to identify the preferred functionalities and the corresponding tools for each business area. The following figures show two examples (Figs 16 and 17) for two different business areas. In the case of Suppliers, the participants have mostly selected the Online Accounting & Invoicing tools such as Cuentica, a traditionally cumbersome task which can be integrated and simplified through cloud computing. On the other hand the Marketplace functionality has attracted little interest, perhaps too ambitious a tool. In the case of the Cost Reduction area, Online Accounting & Invoicing is once again at the top, a clear interesting solution for the participants wherever it appears. In this case the Incident Management System closes the list, a tool most related to those businesses with strong after-sales services.

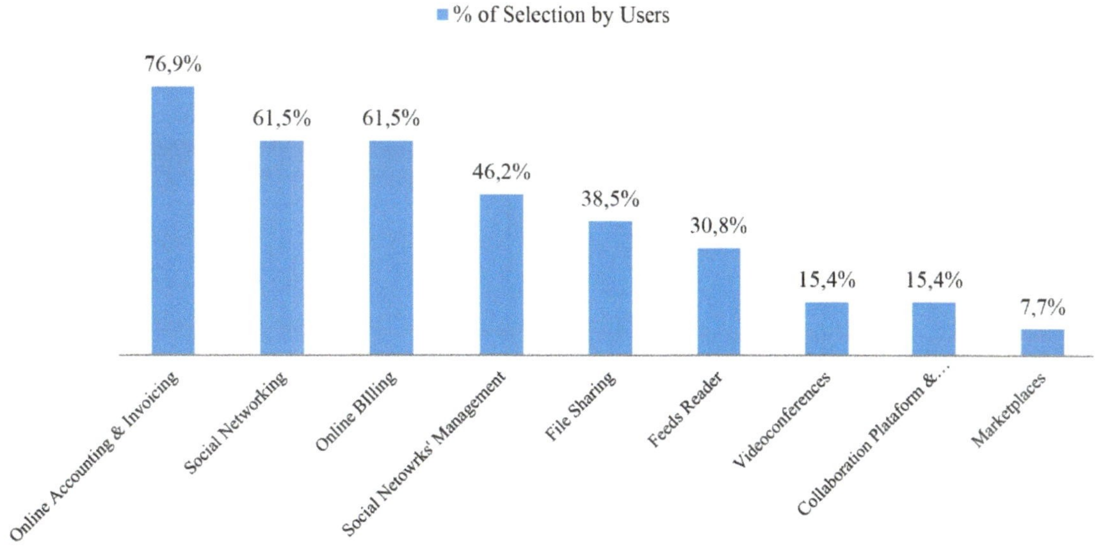

Figure 16. Ranking of functionalities and tools, Suppliers business area. The chart shows the functionalities and its tools belonging to the Suppliers business area, arranged by the percentage of selection by the pilot study participants.

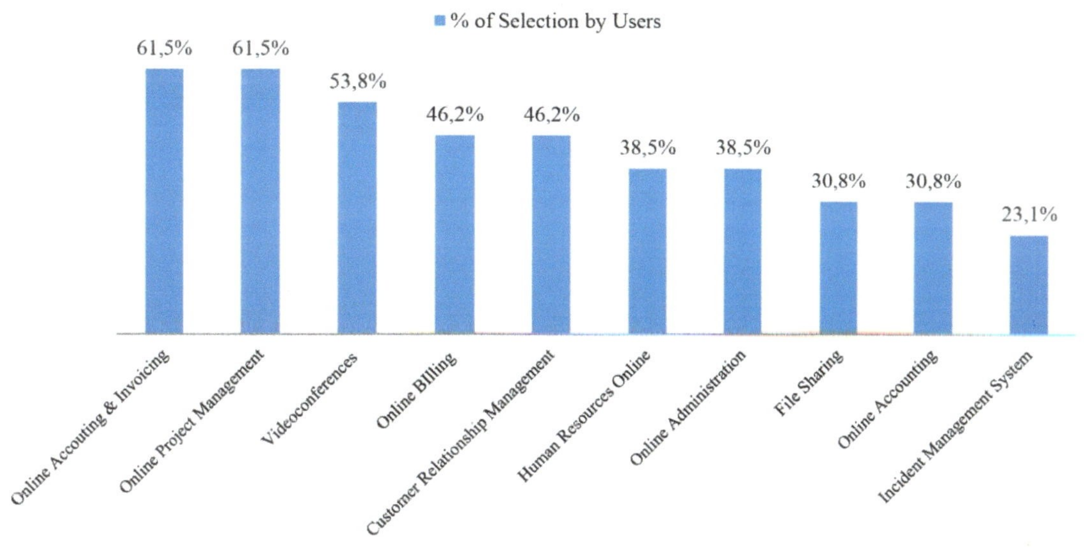

Figure 17. Ranking of functionalities and tools, Cost Reduction business area. The chart shows the functionalities and its tools belonging to the Cost Reduction business area, arranged by the percentage of selection by the pilot study participants.

CONCLUSIONS

Although, it could be argued that this is now a reality, it is also a fact that a large number of companies, especially SMEs, are not yet aware of either the existence of cloud technology or its benefits for the business sector. Therefore, it is necessary to implement mechanisms to overcome these problems which can be considered as barriers for cloud adoption. Consequently, a cloud computing adoption decision tool has been created, the main aim of which is to show the different SaaS applications available on the market and how these applications can enhance and manage business priority areas. Via the pilot study performed with different kinds of SMEs at local level, some interesting results have been established. Participants' initial preferences were upgraded once the functionalities were explained; the fear of the unknown is a clear barrier which has to be overcome. There are certain areas more likely to boom in cloud computing, at least initially, whereas other areas need longer to get the market, as discussed in the results section. In this sense, an aid to all stakeholders involved could be an endeavor as with Bildosola et al. [43], where a methodology is presented to depict the cloud computing technology evolution path. In addition to this, each enterprise should recognize where its own path to the cloud is, its own Cloud Road.

The newcomers to the cloud should take into account several factors. From one side it is clear that SaaS applications are deployed in a cross-cutting manner in the whole company rather than in particular areas. Moreover, Commercial and Sales areas along with others such as Productive aspects, Finance Management, Quality, Human Resources and Innovation can be emphasized. On the other hand, the SaaS market is still in its infancy in many countries, so there are many bogus solutions within the cloud concept which create confusion in the market. It is important to remember that SaaS service offerings do not usually mention the migration process, which should be taken into account given its difficulty. Thus it must be analyzed carefully.

It can be concluded by saying that cloud computing is especially beneficial for startup companies, SMEs, entrepreneurs and companies that need to make new investments or do not have a stable infrastructure. For these companies this technology leads to a significant saving, in addition to increasing flexibility and competitiveness. This work is a try to help these actors to get into the cloud.

Supporting Information

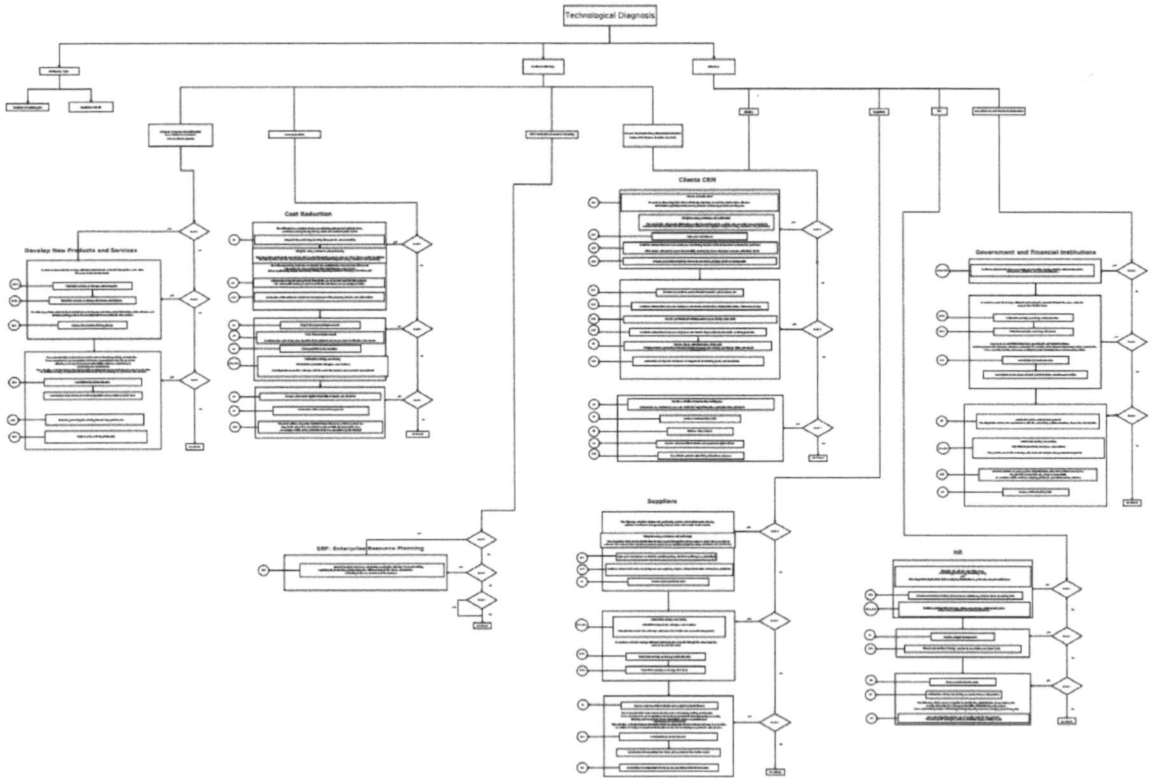

S1 Figure. Decision Tree. The figure shows all the variables and conditions used to construct the decision tree. The decision tool is based on this decision tree and as a result of the combination of these variables and conditions different tools are proposed to the user.

doi:10.1371/journal.pone.0134563.s001

ACKNOWLEDGMENTS

The authors are grateful to the enterprise Open Aula, especially to Jose Antonio Crespo for his leadership and Aitor Ferandez for programming the tool. The authors would like to thank the company Tecnalia, namely Francisco Javier Acera for his open collaboration. Finally, thanks to the Basque Innovation Agency (Innobasque), in particular to Mariana Ruiz for the support in the dissemination of the work.

AUTHOR CONTRIBUTIONS

Conceived and designed the experiments: RR. Performed the experiments: IB RR. Analyzed the data: IB. Wrote the paper: IB. Revising the work critically for important intellectual content: GG. Final approval of the version to be published: EC.

REFERENCES

1. Grossman RL (2009) The case for cloud computing. IT professional 11(2): 23–27. doi: 10. 1109/mitp. 2009. 40
2. Voas J, Zhang J (2009) Cloud computing: new wine or just a new bottle?. IT professional 11(2): 15–17. doi: 10. 1109/mitp. 2009. 23
3. Mell P, Grance T (2011) The NIST definition of cloud computing. Available:http://csrc. nist. gov/publications/nistpubs/800-145/SP800-145. pdf. Accessed 2 Feb 2013.
4. Zabalza-Vivanco, J, Rio-Belver R, Cilleruelo E, Garechana G, Gavilanes J (2012) Benefits Related to cloud computing in the SMEs. In XVI Congreso de Ingeniería de Organización: Vigo, 18 a 20 de julio de 2012: 637–644.
5. Miller H, Veiga GJ (2009) Cloud computing: Will commodity services benefit user long term?. IT Professional 11(6): 57–59. doi: 10. 1109/mitp. 2009. 117
6. Sultan N, (2010) Cloud computing for education: A new dawn?. International Journal of Information Management 30(2): 109–116. doi: 10. 1016/j. ijinfomgt. 2009. 09. 004
7. Talukder AK, Zimmerman L, Prahalad HA (2010) Cloud economics: Principles, costs, and benefits. In Antonopoulos N, Gillam L, editors. Cloud computing. pp. 343–360.
8. Cisco (2013) White Paper: Cisco Global Cloud Index: Forecast and Methodology, 2012–2017. Available: http://www. cisco. com/c/en/us/solutions/collateral/service-provider/global-cloud-index-gci/Cloud_Index_White_Paper. html. Accessed 17 September 2014.

9. Gantz JF, Minton S, Toncheva A (5 April 2012) cloud computing's Role in Job Creation. IDC. Available:http:// news. microsoft. com/download/features/2012/IDC_Cloud_jobs_White_Paper. pdf. Accessed 17 September 2014.
10. Merz S, Eschinger C, Eid T, Pang C, Wurster L (2012) Forecast: Software as a Service, worldwide, 2010–2015, 1H11 Update. Market Analysis and Statistics. 17 p.
11. Gartner (27 Mar 2012) Gartner Says Worldwide Software-as-a-Service Revenue to Reach $14. 5 Billion in 2012. Gartner press release. Available:http://www. gartner. com/newsroom/id/1963815. Accessed 6 October 2014.
12. CB Consulting (3 Nov 2012) cloud computing y Virtualización en España 2012–2015. Available: http:// carlosborrasdelahoz. com/?p=272. Accessed 6 October 2014.
13. CB Consulting (6 Sep 2012) El cloud computing y su situación en España. Available: http:// carlosborrasdelahoz. com/?p=180. Accessed 6 October 2014.
14. Urueña A, Ferrari A, Blanco D, Valdecasa E (2012) cloud computing. Retos y Oportunidades. ONTSI. 341p.
15. Gens F, (2012) IDC Predictions 2013: Competing on the 3rd Platform. Int. Data Corporation.
16. Zhang LJL (2012) Editorial: Big services era: Global trends of cloud computing and big data. IEEE Transactions on Services Computing (4): 067–468. doi: 10. 1109/tsc. 2012. 36
17. Nabil AS (2011) Reaching for the "cloud": How SMEs can manage. International Journal of Information Management 31(3): 272–278. doi: 10. 1016/j. ijinfomgt. 2010. 08. 001
18. Kloch C, Petersen E, Madsen O (2011) Cloud based infrastructure, the new business possibilities and barriers. Wireless Personal Communications 58(1): 17–30. doi: 10. 1007/s11277-011-0286-7
19. Wang H, He W, Wang FK (2012) Enterprise cloud service architectures. Information Technology and Management 13(4): 445–454. doi: 10. 1007/s10799-012-0139-4
20. Morgan L, Conboy K (2013) Factors Affecting The Adoption Of cloud computing: An Exploratory Study. In Proceedings of the 21st European Conference on Information Systems: 1–13.
21. Hinchcliffe D (22 Aug 2009) What does cloud computing actually cost? An analysis of the top vendors, ebiz: the Insider's Guide to Business and IT Agility. Available:http://www. ebizq. net/blogs/ enterprise/2009/08/what_does_cloud_computing_actu. php. Accessed 11 October 2014.
22. Ghag SS (24 Dec 2008) Financial implications of the cloud, Infosys Microsoft Alliance and Solutions Blog. Available:http://www. infosysblogs. com/ microsoft/2008/12/financial_implications_of_the_1. html. Accessed 11 October 2014. Accessed 11 October 2014.
23. Rosenberg D (12 Jan 2012) The cost of cloud adoption. Available:http://news. cnet. com/8301-13846_3-10140303-62. html. Accessed 11 October 2014.
24. Khajeh-Hosseini A, Greenwood D, Smith JW, Sommerville I (2012) The Cloud Adoption Toolkit: supporting cloud adoption decisions in the enterprise. Softw: Pract. Exper (42): 447–465. doi: 10. 1002/spe. 1072
25. Misra SC, Mondal A (2011) Identification of a company's suitability for the adoption of cloud computing and modelling its corresponding Return on Investment. Mathematical and Computer Modelling 53(3): 504–521. doi: 10. 1016/j. mcm. 2010. 03. 037
26. Wang J, Yang D (2007) Using a hybrid multi-criteria decision aid method for information systems outsourcing. Computers & Operations Research 34(12): 3691–3700. doi: 10. 1016/j. cor. 2006. 01. 017
27. Udo G (2000) Using analytic hierarchy process to analyze the information technology outsourcing decision. Industrial Management and Data Systems 100(8): 421–429. doi: 10. 1108/02635570010358348
28. Menzel M, Schönherr M, Tai S (2013) (MC2)2: criteria, requirements and a software prototype for Cloud infrastructure decisions. Software: Practice and experience 43(11): 1283–1297. doi: 10. 1002/spe. 1110
29. Cloud Harmony. Available: http://cloudharmony. com/ benchmarks. Accessed 13 October 2014.
30. Cloud Sleuth. Available: https://cloudsleuth. net/about. Accessed 13 October 2014.
31. Raihana GFH (2012) Cloud ERP–A Solution Model. International Journal of Computer Science and Information Technology & Security 2(1): 76–79.
32. Gerhardter A, Ortner W (2013) Flexibility and Improved Resource Utilization Through Cloud Based ERP Systems: Critical Success Factors of SaaS Solutions in SME. In: Piazolo F, Felderer M, editors. Springer Berlin Heidelberg:171–182.
33. Chang V, Walters RJ, Wills G (2013) The development that leads to the cloud computing Business Framework. International Journal of Information Management: 33(3): 524–538. doi: 10. 1016/j. ijinfomgt. 2013. 01. 005
34. Wu Y, Cegielski CG, Hazen BT, Hall DJ (2013) Cloud computing in support of supply chain information system infrastructure: understanding when to go to the cloud. Journal of Supply Chain Management 49(3): 25–41. doi: 10. 1111/j. 1745-493x. 2012. 03287. x
35. Shimba F (2010) Cloud Computing:Strategies for Cloud Computing Adoption. Masters Dissertation. Dublin Institute of Technology.
36. Iyer EK, Pandey N, Lamba PS, Panda T (2013) Decision variables influencing Cloud adoption by SME Sector: A Conjoint Analysis Mapping. In National Conference on Business Analytics & Business Intelligence.
37. Marston S, Li Z, Bandyopadhyay S, Zhang J, Ghalsasi A (2011) Cloud computing-The business perspective. Decision Support Systems 51(1):176–189 doi: 10. 1016/j. dss. 2010. 12. 006

38. Zabalza-Vivanco J, Rio-Belver R, Cilleruelo E, Acera-Osa, FJ; GarechanaG (2013) Decision Tool Based on cloud computing Technology. In: Proceedings ofthe 7th International Conference on Industrial Engineering and Industrial Management: 137–145.

39. Quinlan JR (1986) Induction of decision trees. Machine Learning 1(1): 81–106. doi: 10. 1007/bf00116251

40. Porter ME (1980) Competitive Strategy: Techniques for Analyzing Industries and Competitors. New York: Free Press.

41. Porter ME (1990) The Competitive Advantage of Nations. Harvard Business Review 68(2): 73–93.

42. SaaS Directory. Online Software and Applications. Available:http://www. saasdirectory. com/. Accessed 13 October 2014.

43. Bildosola I, Rio-Bélver R, Cilleruelo E (2015) Forecasting the Big Services Era: Novel Approach Combining Statistical Methods, Expertise and Technology Roadmapping. In Enhancing Synergies in a Collaborative Environment. Springer International Publishing: 371–379.

CHAPTER 21 DYNAMICROOTS: A SOFTWARE PLATFORM FOR THE RECONSTRUCTION AND ANALYSIS OF GROWING PLANT ROOTS

Olga Symonova[1], Christopher N. Topp[2], Herbert Edelsbrunner[1]

[1] IST Austria, Klosterneuburg, Austria

[2] Donald Danforth Plant Science Center, St. Louis, Missouri, USA

ABSTRACT

We present a software platform for reconstructing and analyzing the growth of a plant root system from a time-series of 3D voxelized shapes. It aligns the shapes with each other, constructs a geometric graph representation together with the function that records the time of growth, and organizes the branches into a hierarchy that reflects the order of creation. The software includes the automatic computation of structural and dynamic traits for each root in the system enabling the quantification of growth on fine-scale. These are important advances in plant phenotyping with applications to the study of genetic and environmental influences on growth.

INTRODUCTION

Root system architecture plays a key role in plant fitness and crop productivity. Climate change, a growing global population, and unsustainable use of fertilizers are responsible for the pressing need to understand how root systems grow and interact with their environment, with the goal to develop robust and efficient crops [1–3]. Studying plant roots systems has been hindered by their complex three-dimensional branching topology, environmental growth plasticity, as well as the opacity of the soil. In recent years, however, various imaging technologies have been applied to monitor the formation and development of roots non-disruptively and throughout a time period: X-ray [4–8], MRI [9], PET-MRI [10], laser [11], and optical imaging [12, 13]. These technologies reconstruct the 3D shape of a root system and enable the assessment of traits that were impossible to quantify by hand measurements before [5, 12–15]. Most of the existing tools compute traits for static shapes, and if more than one shape representing the same root system is available, the global traits are computed without separating the contributions of individual branches [16]. Software that analyzes a time-series of 2D root images but requires significant user input to track growth has been introduced in [17, 18]. Several high-throughput platforms were developed for the analysis of video clips of growing dicot roots [19–21]. Advances in the fields of computer graphics and computer vision make it possible to quickly align large shapes that are at least partially similar [22, 23]. These methods can be used to improve the analysis of time-series but have not yet been exploited for plant phenotyping.

Citation: Symonova O, Topp CN, Edelsbrunner H (2015) DynamicRoots: A Software Platform for the Reconstruction and Analysis of Growing Plant Roots. PLoS ONE 10(6): e0127657. doi:10.1371/journal.pone.0127657.

In this paper, we present the DynamicRoots software designed to automatically process a time-series of 3D reconstructions of a growing root system. It registers the 3D shapes in a common coordinate system and creates a data structure that records the growth. Using this data structure, we estimate dynamic traits of individual branches, which we aggregate to global traits. Our contributions to the state-of-the-art are:

- a geometric graph representation of a root system that reflects its hierarchical structure;
- an algorithm that guarantees temporal coherence of the hierarchical decomposition and computes the time function recording the growth process;
- a suite of structural and dynamic root traits including elongation rates and branching frequency.

The computed traits facilitate the analysis of root systems in unprecedented resolution of time and space. We illustrate the software by analyzing several time-series of reconstructed rice and maize roots.

Outline. The Methods section gives a detailed description of the algorithm that constructs the growth record for a time-series of 3D root shapes, and lists the structural and dynamic traits computed from this record. The Results section explains how we validate the software and presents experimental results for rice and maize root systems. We conclude the paper with a discussion of current limitations and future research directions.

METHODS

The goal of this work is to acquire the shape of a growing root system, to compactly represent it in a unified data structure, and to compute traits that reflect the structural and dynamic properties of the root system. We divide the process into five steps:

- Take 2D images of root systems and construct a time-series of 3D shapes.
- Align the shapes to define depth as the geodesic distance from consistently detected seed areas.
- Use the depth function to decompose each shape into a hierarchy of branches.
- Construct the time function and reorganize the hierarchy by repairing inconsistencies between depth and time of growth.
- Use the time function on the branch hierarchy to compute structural and dynamic traits of the root system.

Correspondingly, we have five subsections explaining the steps in appropriate detail. Step 1 relies on prior work presented elsewhere, while the other four steps are novel contributions reported for the first time in this paper. Steps 2 to 4 construct the growth record, and Step 5 makes use of this unifying data structure.

Background and Assumptions

We review the prior work to the extent necessary to provide the context for our work. To overcome the obstacle of opaque soil, we grow rice and maize plants in gel with nutrients inside transparent cylindrical containers [13], monitoring the development of the root system for several weeks. To construct the 3D shape of a root system, we place the container on a rotating table connected to a camera and a computer, and we take 40 images at 9° increments. Currently, 20 of these images are used to reconstruct the shape of the root system represented as a collection of voxels in 3D space [24]. Letting t be the time of the acquisition, we write $\mathbb{V}_t$ for the reconstructed shape. Depending on the purpose, we will think of $\mathbb{V}_t$ as a subset of $\mathbb{R}^3$, a collection of voxels, or a graph whose nodes are the voxels and whose arcs connect neighboring voxels. Drawn as straight line segments ending at voxel centers, the arcs have length 1, $\sqrt{2}$, or $\sqrt{3}$ times the length of a voxel edge.

In order to analyze the growth of a root system, the same plant is reconstructed at different moments in time. We thus get a time-series of shapes $\mathbb{V}_t$, for $t = 0,1, \ldots, T$, which provides a much richer source of information about the root system than a single such shape. However, harvesting this information is more difficult since we need to compare, quantify similarities and differences, and resolve occasional contradictions. To do this automatically within our software platform, we make use of the following three assumptions:

- A_1: A root system grows in only two ways: by generating a new branch at a fork, and by elongating an existing branch at the tip.
- A_2: A root system is connected and contractible. In other words, the branches do not form loops, and they do not surround voids in space.
- A_3: The time-series is dense enough to observe the correct root hierarchy: when a side branch first appears at a fork, it is shorter than the parent branch.

While we have biological reasons to believe that A_1 and A_2 are true, both assumptions are sometimes violated by the reconstructed shapes. Our software can tolerate mild violations of all of the three assumptions but will fail when the reconstructed shapes contain gross contradictions to our expectations.

Depth, Seed, and Alignment

In this and the next two subsections, we explain how to construct the *growth record* of a root system, which provides a decomposition into a hierarchy of branches together with the time of growth. As a first step, we equip each reconstructed shape with a function φ_t: $_t \to \mathbb{R}$ that maps each voxel to its geodesic distance from a *seed area*, a concept we will explain shortly. We call this distance the *depth* of the voxel, and we call φ_t the *depth function* of $\mathbb{V}_t$. After fixing a set of voxels $S_t \subseteq \mathbb{V}_t$ as the seed area, we compute φ_t using Dijkstra's shortest path algorithm [25]. Running this algorithm on the graph of voxels is straightforward, but the result crucially depends on the choice of S_t, which is inspired by the biological idea that the root grows from a particular first location. It will be more important that the location of this area is consistent among all shapes in the time-series than to correctly identify the biological beginnings of the root system. We therefore compute S_T, and propagate its location to the other shapes after computing an initial alignment of all shapes in the time-series. We will explain the alignment first and return to computing the seed area thereafter.

Note that Assumption A_1 implies $\mathbb{V}_s \subseteq \mathbb{V}_t$ for all $0 \leq s \leq t \leq T$. To align the two shapes, we can therefore use an algorithm that requires that the first shape be contained in the second. Our algorithm of choice is the *4-point congruent sets (4PCS) algorithm* described in [22]. To apply it, we think of $\mathbb{V}_s$ as a collection of points in R^3, namely the centers of its voxels. The algorithm selects four approximately coplanar points from $\mathbb{V}_s$ and searches for a congruent configuration of four points in $\mathbb{V}_t$. Let M be the matrix of the rigid motion that moves the 4-point configuration in $\mathbb{V}_t$ to that in $\mathbb{V}_s$. While the 4PCS algorithm is fast, the alignment it produces can often be improved, and we use the *iterative closest point (ICP) algorithm*originally described in [26] for this purpose. It computes a second matrix M', and we set $M_{st} = M' \cdot M$ so that $M_{st}(\mathbb{V}_t)$ is aligned with $\mathbb{V}_s$. To align all $T + 1$ shapes in the time-series, it suffices to compute T rigid motions, and we choose to compute M_{0t} for $t = 1, 2, \ldots, T$. To align V_t with V_s, we then use $M_{st} = M_{0s}^{-1} \cdot M_{0t}$. Suppose now that we have computed the seed area in the last shape, $S_T \subseteq \mathbb{V}_T$. Using the rigid motions, we get $S_t \subseteq \mathbb{V}_t$ as the set of voxels closest to $M_{tT}(S_T)$, for $0 \leq t \leq T$.

To detect the seed area in $\mathbb{V}_T$, we perform *principal component analysis* (PCA) on a small neighborhood of a radius R around every voxel. Covariance matrices with three similar eigenvalues indicate a similar spread of points along the principal axes, which in 3D space corresponds to a spherical neighborhood. We find the biggest connected component of voxels with roughly spherical neighborhoods and form the seed area by adding voxels with offset at most R from this component. For the results reported in this paper, we used $R = 3$ and we suggest that this parameter is set to a value from the interval $[r, 2r]$, in which r is the average radius of the branches. If the seed was not detected—for example when the set of voxels with roughly spherical neighborhoods is empty or larger than an allowed fraction of the total volume—we choose a voxel in the center of the topmost horizontal slice of the root system as the seed area.

Branch Hierarchy

As a second step in the construction of the growth record, we decompose each shape in the time-series into branches, which we organize hierarchically. This decomposition is inspired by the path decompositions of trees used in the design of efficient data structures; see e.g. [27]. Each branch starts at its tip at the bottom and extends upward, ending right before its fork, which lies somewhere between the two ends of the parent branch; we therefore represent each branch by the triplet of these entities: $\mathbb{B}^i = (\text{Tip}^i, \text{Fork}^i, \text{Parent}^i)$. An exception is the topmost branch, which does not have a parent. Among all possible branch decompositions, we are interested in the one defined by the depth function.

To construct the decomposition, we traverse the voxels in the order of decreasing depth, adding an arc right after its second endpoint. With each visited voxel, we create a new component, and with each visited arc, we either form an additional connection within the component, or we merge two components into one. After visiting all voxels and arcs, they are part of a single component representing the entire root system, and we recover the branches and the relations between them by analyzing the history of events. To make this concrete, we equip each voxel, v, with a pointer to another voxel, $\rho(v)$. In the beginning, each voxel points to itself. After completion of the algorithm, each voxel points to the tip of its branch, except for the tip itself, which points to the tip of the parent branch. A *tip* is therefore identified by having other voxels point to it, a *branch* is represented by its tip and consists in addition of all voxels pointing to this tip, and the *parent branch* is given by the pointer stored at the tip.

The only interesting event during the course of the algorithm is when it encounters an arc that connects two components. Let its endpoints be the voxels u and v, and write $p = \rho(u)$ and $q = \rho(v)$ for the corresponding tips, noting that $p \neq q$ by assumption. Assume without loss of generality that q is deeper than p: $\varphi(p) < \varphi(q)$. If the difference in depth between $u$and p is smaller than some fixed threshold, then we declare the entire branch to be a part of the branch of q by updating the pointer: $\rho(p) = q$. Otherwise, we consolidate the branch of $p$by declaring v as its fork and the branch of q as its parent.

As mentioned earlier, each branch is represented by its tip, p, and consists of all voxels $u$with $\rho(u) = p$, together with p. To avoid possible confusions arising from the two different uses of the ρ-pointer, we save the pointer to the parent branch by setting $\text{Parent}(p) = \rho(p)$, and thereafter set $\rho(p) = p$ to indicate that it belongs to the branch it represents. In addition, we store a pointer $\text{Fork}(p)$ to the fork in the parent branch. The thus linked branches form what we call a *branch hierarchy*. At this moment, the hierarchy is determined by depth: a branch has a tip that is necessarily less deep than the tip of the parent branch. Ultimately, we would like the hierarchy be determined by age. In the next section, we will explain how the hierarchy can be modified to achieve this goal.

Time Function

We are now ready to compute the time function of the last shape in the time-series, $\tau; \to R$ with $\mathbb{V} = \mathbb{V}_T$. Compressing the information of the time-series into a single shape, it maps every voxel of $\mathbb{V}$ to the moment in time the voxel was created. The time function is piecewise constant, with possibly large steps in particular but not exclusively at forks. We note that the time function is the central piece of the growth record that enables the dynamic analysis of the root system.

To prepare the computation, we initialize the time function to $\tau(v) = T$ for every voxel $v \in \mathbb{V}$. Traversing the other shapes in the time-series from back to front, we use the Euclidean distance between voxels to match the branches of $\mathbb{V}_t$ with those of $\mathbb{V}$. It is therefore important that the shapes in the time-series are aligned and registered into a common coordinate system, which we henceforth assume. Specifically, for each tip in $\mathbb{V}_t$, we find the closest voxel $v \in \mathbb{V}$, and we match the branch of the tip with the branch $\mathbb{J}$ in $\mathbb{V}$ that contains v. Finally, we set $\tau(u) = t$ for all voxels u of $\mathbb{J}$ whose depth satisfies $\varphi_T(u) \leq \varphi_T(v)$.

After running the algorithm, the set of voxels $u \in \mathbb{V}$ with $\tau(u) \leq t$ would ideally be the set of voxels in $\mathbb{V}_t$, for every $0 \leq t \leq T$. Of course, this will never be the case in practice, but there is a reason other than the inevitable noise in the system that may lead to discrepancies between the computed and the ideal time function, namely possible inconsistencies between the decompositions into branches between $\mathbb{V}_t$ and $\mathbb{V}$. Instead of detecting inconsistencies between the branch decompositions, we repair the time function. Suppose $v \in \mathbb{V}$ is a fork at which the classification into main branch and side branch is incorrect.

By Assumption A_3, we get a conflict between the depth and the time. Specifically, we observe neighbors u of v for which

$$\varphi(u) < \varphi(v) \text{ and } \tau(u) > \tau(v). \quad (1)$$

If we detect such a fork, we repair the inconsistency by an operation we call a *switch*. Letting p and q be the tips of the two branches at v, with v = Fork(p) but $v \neq w$ = Fork(q), we note that q = Parent(p). To perform the switch, we reassign the part of the branch of q between v and w to the branch of p; see Fig 1. In addition, the time at any voxel u within this part is set to the minimum of the current value and the value at v.

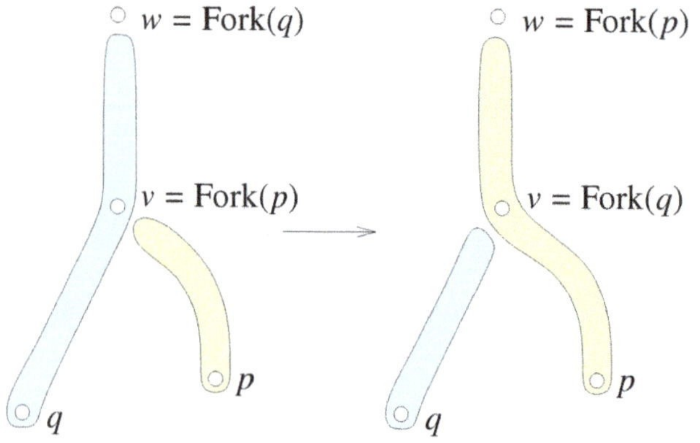

Figure 1. A switch at the fork v.

Root Traits

Using the growth record explained above, we compute a suite of traits that describe a root system captured in a time-series. Denoting the growth record by $\mathbb{V} = \mathbb{V}_T$, we make essential use of the decomposition into branches, which we denote as $\mathbb{B}^i$. Recall that $\mathbb{B}^i_t \subseteq \mathbb{B}^i$ is the sublevel set of the time function on the branch. We call the voxel $u \in \mathbb{B}^i_t$ with maximum depth the *tip* of the branch at time t. We compute the following traits for every branch $\mathbb{B}^i$ and at every moment of time $0 \leq t \leq T$:

- **volume**: the number of voxels in $\mathbb{B}^i_t$;
- **depth of tip**: the geodesic depth of the tip of $\mathbb{B}^i_t$;
- **location of tip**: the three Cartesian coordinates of the tip;
- **length**: the difference between the geodesic depth values of the tip and the fork;
- **switch event**: a logical variable that indicates whether or not $\mathbb{B}^i_t$ is longer than its parent branch;
- **tortuosity**: the ratio between the length of a branch and the Euclidean distance between tip and fork;
- **average radius**: the square root of the volume divided by π times the length;
- **angle to gravity**: the angle between the major PCA axis of $\mathbb{B}^i_t$ and the vertical direction;
- **angle to parent branch**: the angle between the major PCA axes of $\mathbb{B}^i_t$ and of its parent branch;
- **number of children**: the number of branches that have $\mathbb{B}^i_t$ as parent branch.

There is an ambiguity about which part of a branch should be taken into account when computing the root emergence angle or direction of growth. In order to avoid this uncertainty, we use the major PCA axis of the branch which shows the main direction of the spread of all the voxels forming this branch.

Only two of the measurements relate the root system to the surrounding, namely the location of the tip and the angle to gravity. Both are useful to study the reaction of the root system to nutrients and other local environmental conditions. The measurements we output for each branch can of course be accumulated to obtain overall traits of the root system, such as the **total volume**, the **total length**, the **total average radius**, and so on. Similarly, we can take differences to compute dynamic traits, as for example the **amount of growth** from time t to time $t + 1$. Beyond the traits listed above, we compute the following characteristics of the seed area:

- **seed volume**: the number of voxels in the seed area of the root system;
- **seed orientation**: the angle between the major PCA axis of the seed area and the vertical direction.

Comparing the seed volume with the total volume, we get the **volume fraction** of the seed area. The concrete representation of the seed area is useful in turning the geometric hierarchy of the branches into a biologically more meaningful one. The former is defined by assigning the index 0 to the topmost branch and increasing the index by 1 whenever we pass from a branch to a child branch. A biologically more meaningful classification is into

- *crown roots*, which emerge above the seed area;
- *seminal roots* with forks located within the seed area;
- the *primary root* corresponding to the topmost branch;
- *lateral roots*, which are the children of other branches.

Unfortunately, crown roots often emerge from the stem above the reconstructed space, which results in disconnected branches. The reconstruction software used in this study [24] enforces connectivity and tries to find the shortest path between the biggest component of the root system and a disconnected branch. This shortest path does not always join the branch in a biologically correct manner, making the classification into biological classes more challenging. At the moment, we explore other ways to differentiate between crown, seminal, and lateral roots. In particular, elongation rates might provide a good clue for detecting crown roots as their initiation is developmentally delayed but typically proceeds faster than of the other root types, see Fig 2.

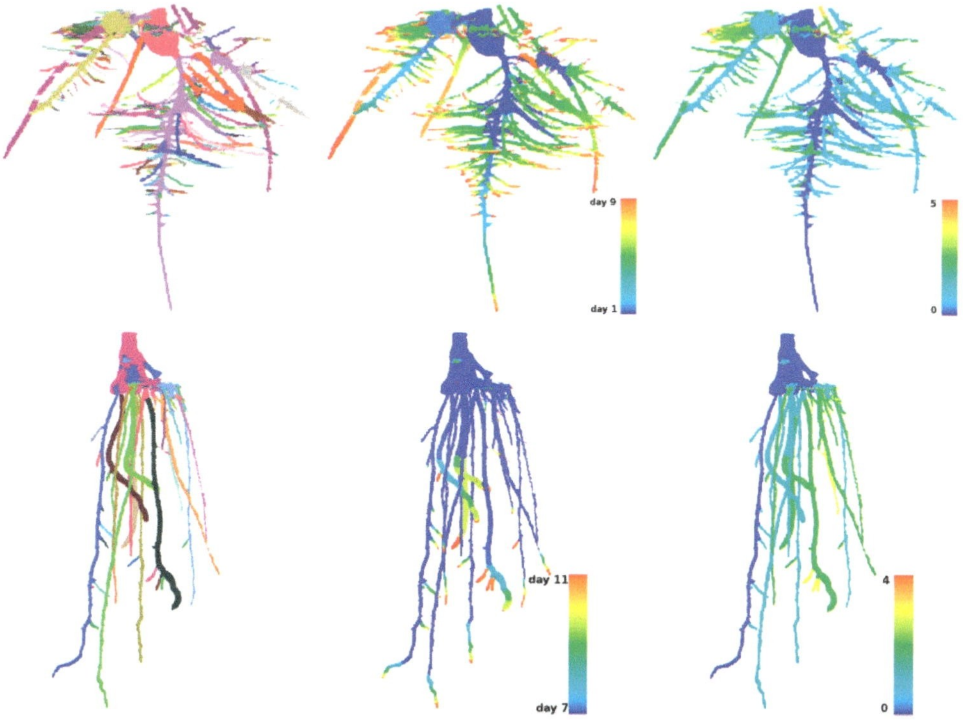

Figure 2. Structural and dynamical analysis of a root system. *Top row*: images of a maize plant imaged between the first and ninth days after planting. *Bottom row*: images of a rice plant imaged between the seventh and eleventh days after planting. *Left*: decomposition into a seed area and branches distinguished by color. *Center*: the color-coded time function. *Right*: the color-coded branch hierarchy.

RESULTS

Applying our methods, we obtain insights into the growth behavior of rice and maize plants. We note, however, that this is primarily a Methods paper, so we have limited the experiments to a few examples selected to illustrate useful features of the DynamicRoots software. The source code and the pre-compiled executable file for 64-bit Windows can be downloaded from http://dynamicroots.sourceforge.net/. The software has a command-line interface. In addition, we provide a python script, which organizes the input files and passes them as arguments to scripts that perform format conversion, data alignment, and time-series processing. The DynamicRoots software was developed in C++ using the Approximate Nearest Neighbor (http://www.cs.umd.edu/mount/ANN/) and ALGLIB (http://www.alglib.net/) libraries. DynamicRoots is an open source software distributed under the terms of the BSD license.

Datasets and Validation

We use the software to analyze four different time-series of 3D shapes, three obtained by imaging growing rice and maize plants, and one artificially created to validate the software. The latter consists of three models forming a caricature of a growing root system; see Fig 3. Created from a collection of discretized algebraic curves, the models are obtained by sweeping balls of varying radii along the curves to get branches with prescribed thickness. Observe that the time-series satisfies Assumptions A_1 to A_3 stated in Section 1. After designing the models, we 3D-printed them from resin, imaged the three shapes, reconstructed the 3D shapes from the 2D images, and finally processed the result with our software. Table 1 compares the hand measurements of *branch length*, *depth of tip*, *volume*,*average radius*, and *tortuosity* with the values computed by our software. The agreement in branch length and depth of tip is remarkably high, with a somewhat larger relative error only for very short branches. The tortuosity of a branch depends on the estimation of its length and agrees fairly well with our hand measurements, with only 6% average relative error. The volume and therefore the average radius are slightly underestimated by the software because the reconstruction of the 3D shapes tends to lose some of the thickness due to small misalignments of the 2D images. Nonetheless, the total volume estimated by our software differs on average only by 5.2% from the volume computed as a product of the mass of the printed model and the resin density. In order to validate the values of the angle to parent branch, we represent the each branch as a line segment passing through the tip and the fork and compute the angle between them. We note that the software computes the angle between the branches using PCA and it is impossible to measure this value by hand. Nevertheless, we observe a similar behavior in the values measured by hand and computed with the software: the angles decrease as branches elongate. Unfortunately, there is no a common way to measure branch angles, and DynamicRoots offers a new approach to estimate this trait.

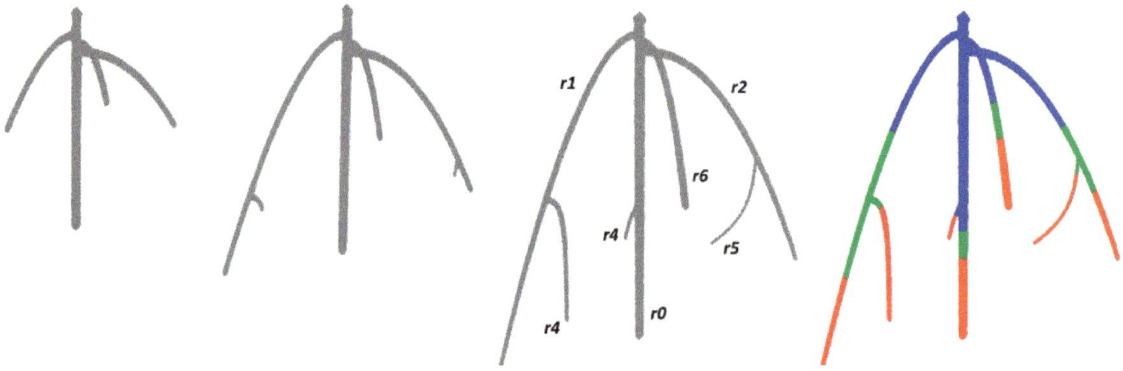

Figure 3. A series of three 3D models mimicking a growing root system designed to facilitate the validation of our software. The branches are labeled as in Table 1. The color-coded model at the far *right*illustrates the time function.

Table 1. Comparison of traits measured by hand and computed with DynamicRoots. Length, vertical depth, and radius are given in millimeters (mm), volume in cubic millimeters (mm^3), angle in degrees, and tortuosity is dimensionless. The last column gives the average error of the DynamicRoots results compared to hand measurements.

Trait		Hand measurements			DynamicRoots results			Error
		t = 0	*t* = 1	*t* = 2	*t* = 0	*t* = 1	*t* = 2	
branch r0	Length	63.800	71.100	95.220	64.068	72.275	98.383	0.018
	Depth	63.800	71.100	95.220	62.083	69.683	95.348	0.016
	Volume	450.976	502.576	673.071	444.766	491.641	621.281	0.037
	Radius	1.500	1.500	1.500	1.488	1.473	1.418	0.027
	Tortuosity	1.000	1.000	1.000	1.030	1.040	1.030	0.033
	Angle to parent	0.000	0.000	0.000	0.000	0.000	0.000	0.000
branch r1	Length	35.770	76.110	102.680	36.198	84.020	112.870	0.072
	Depth	36.860	76.620	99.610	34.443	75.388	100.940	0.032
	Volume	112.375	239.107	322.579	96.219	203.297	248.516	0.174
	Radius	1.000	1.000	1.000	0.920	0.878	0.838	0.122
	Tortuosity	1.140	1.050	1.058	1.120	1.120	1.120	0.048
	Angle to parent	41.957	27.139	25.140	27.600	20.360	18.700	0.283
branch r2	Length	42.980	66.770	99.060	46.173	72.208	98.910	0.052
	Depth	36.530	55.890	78.230	32.820	53.085	74.885	0.065
	Volume	135.026	209.764	311.206	131.938	187.922	229.125	0.130
	Radius	1.000	1.000	1.000	0.953	0.910	0.858	0.093
	Tortuosity	1.075	1.136	1.237	1.120	1.160	1.180	0.036
	Angle to parent	57.645	49.580	40.981	55.200	43.570	36.840	0.088
branch r3	Length		7.000	37.550		4.335	39.833	0.221
	Depth		57.960	83.350		55.803	81.983	0.027
	Volume		17.224	92.395		8.516	54.703	0.457
	Radius		0.885	0.885		0.790	0.660	0.181
	Tortuosity		1.127	1.097		1.000	1.110	0.062
	Angle to parent		90.000	40.030		45.360	15.980	0.548
branch r4	Length			9.270			7.940	0.143
	Depth			66.480			65.203	0.019
	Volume			13.665			6.875	0.497
	Radius			0.685			0.525	0.234
	Tortuosity			1.150			1.070	0.070
	Angle to parent			38.432			15.49	0.597
branch r5	Length		4.300	27.830		3.538	32.415	0.171
	Depth		51.190	71.190		47.538	69.125	0.050
	Volume		6.339	41.025		2.484	19.609	0.565
	Radius		0.685	0.685		0.473	0.440	0.334
	Tortuosity		0.883	0.984		1.000	1.110	0.130
	Angle to parent		62.507	60.122		24.510	8.940	0.730
branch r6	Length	27.490	35.010	53.730	25.753	36.245	56.103	0.048
	Depth	30.260	36.970	54.370	24.633	33.623	50.628	0.115
	Volume	86.362	109.987	168.798	76.719	103.422	155.781	0.083
	Radius	1.000	1.000	1.000	0.975	0.953	0.940	0.044
	Tortuosity	1.180	1.113	1.130	1.070	1.100	1.110	0.041
	Angle to parent	49.957	46.420	35.918	43.190	36.200	27.890	0.193
total	Length	170.040	260.290	425.340	172.190	272.620	446.453	0.037
	Volume	784.738	1084.997	1622.737	749.641	997.281	1335.891	0.101
	Mass x Density	694.000	967.000	1397.00	749.641	997.281	1335.891	0.052

doi:10.1371/journal.pone.0127657.t001

The first of the three natural datasets consists of 478 time-series of 3 shapes each, reconstructing root systems of growing rice plants on Days 12, 14, 16 after planting. Using static traits, this data has been used in [16] to study the genetic control of shape and development of the root architecture. We intend to extend this study with the dynamic traits and the information about the branch hierarchy available from our software. The second natural dataset consists of 4 time-series of 25 shapes each, reconstructing root systems of growing rice plants imaged every two hours from 8am to 4pm for five days starting from Day 7 after planting. The third natural dataset consists of 3 time-series of 23 shapes each, reconstructing root systems of growing maize plants images from Day 1 to Day 9 after planting.

The relatively high temporal resolution in the last two datasets leads to detailed characteristics of the root development not available in the first dataset.

Traits

The traits described in Section 1 are output in a file for each time-series; see the supplementary material, which includes the file for the maize plant shown in the top row of Fig 2. For complete disclosure, our software also outputs files containing the color-coded geometry of the root system, representing the time function and the branch hierarchy, among other information; see Fig 2.

We use the remainder of this subsection to demonstrate how DynamicRoots can be used to analyze growth dynamics. As a first example, we look at the dynamic addition of volume to the shapes for the two displayed time-series. Each vertical bar in Fig 4 represents the root system at a moment in time, with the colored segments representing branches in the decomposition. The displayed behavior reveals a remarkable dynamics in the growth process: the volume of the maize root almost doubles in the course of just a few hours, with the bulk of the additional volume contributed by newly formed branches (see Fig 4 top, between 72 and 96 hours).

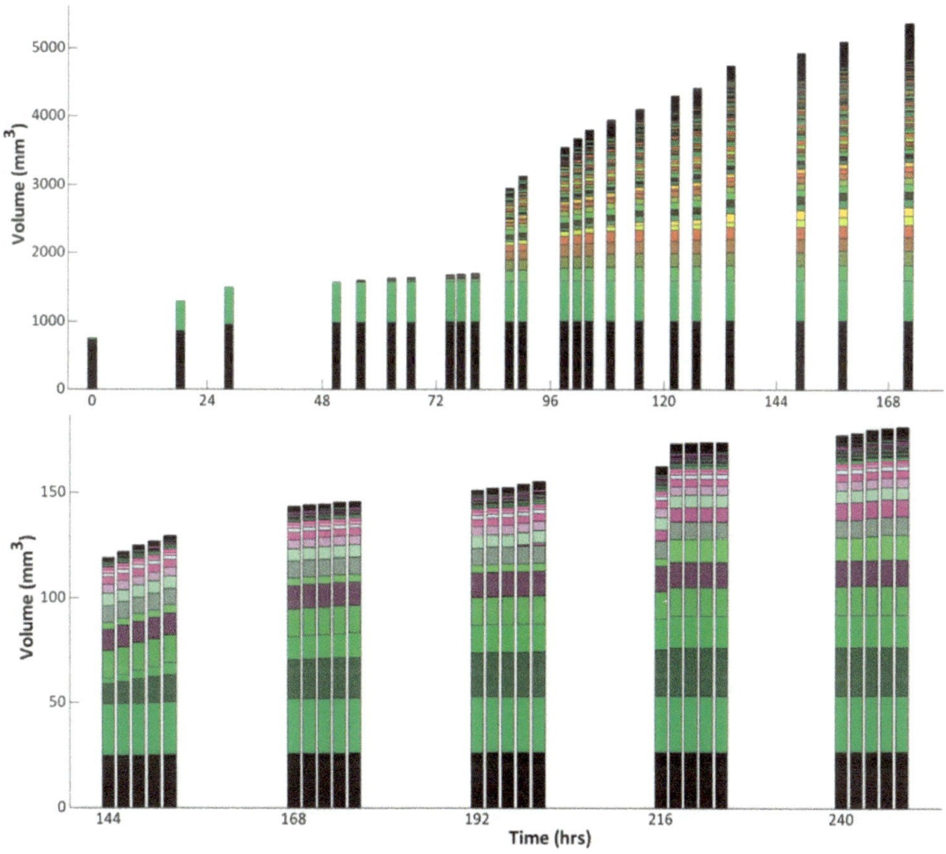

Figure 4. Volume dynamics of the root systems in Fig 2; maize at the *top* **and rice at the** *bottom*. The colored segments within each vertical bar show the volume contributed by individual branches.

As a second example, we look at the branching dynamics, and in particular at the difference between the number of branches formed during day- and night-time. Fig 5 shows the number of branches as graphs over time for four rice plants. Observing the root systems during five consecutive days, we note that there are more branches formed during day-time than during night-time. The rice plants grew in the 12-hour cycle with the temperature of 28°C and 25°C at day and night. In [28] the authors studied diurnal elongation rates in*Arabidopsis thaliana* and observed higher elongation rates at night time than during the day. In [29] the authors demonstrated that growth conditions have a great impact on the diurnal growth patterns in sorghum and rice plants, they did not find differences in day-night elongation rates when the temperature was constant. In our data, we did not see differences in elongation rates at day and night time for plants in Fig 5. While more experiments are needed to understand the branching dynamics of root systems, it is clear that DynamicRoots can be of valuable assistance in collecting and analyzing the data.

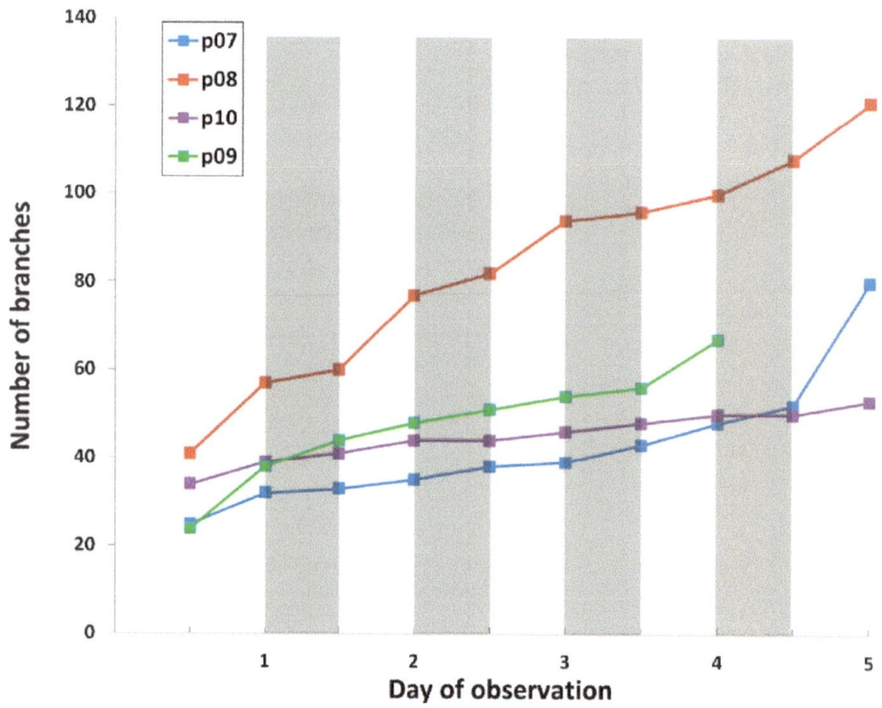

Figure 5. The branching dynamics of rice plants during five consecutive days. The shading distinguishes day- from night-time, highlighting that more branches are formed during day-time.

Performance

We distinguish between performance characteristics that pertain to the speed and the correctness of the software. In addition to the traits discussed above, the software outputs performance statistics, including the **running time**, the **average distance** between aligned 3D shapes, and the **number of switch events**. For example, the average running time for one time-series from our first dataset, including file format conversion, graphical file output, shape alignment and processing, is 51 seconds on an Intel Core 3.4GHz desktop computer.

We use the remainder of this subsection to illustrate how we make use of the performance measurements. A delicate step in our algorithm is the alignment of the 3D shapes in a time-series. We underline the fact that the alignment performs quite accurately due to the property of the 4PCS algorithm which can robustly align shapes even with small overlap, noise, and outliers [22]. To shed light on the quality of the alignment, we compute the average distance between the aligned shapes and provide the result as an indicator of the quality of the achieved alignment. More precisely, we sample 10% of the voxels in the first shape, $\mathbb{V}_0$, and we compute the Euclidean distance to the closest voxels in $\mathbb{V}_1$ to $\mathbb{V}_T$. For a high quality alignment, the average distance will be small, namely less than the edge length of a voxel. In the first dataset, there are several time-series for which the accuracy is compromised by technical difficulties with the imaging platform. For these series, the average distance we observe is significantly larger than for series that do not suffer from these imaging artefacts: e.g. 5.03 versus 0.84 times the length of an edge. In our analysis of the first dataset, we have used a threshold of 10.00 edge lengths for the average distance of the alignment beyond which a shape was excluded from the computations.

Another measurement that varies significantly with the quality of the alignment is the number of switch events. On average, we observe 9.04 switches between shapes in the first dataset. However, in the time-series affected by the mentioned image artefacts, this number increases to 58.96. The number of switches by itself can be an interesting biological trait as it measures how often a branch out-grows its parent branch. However, if the number is significantly higher than the average, then this may be reason for concern since it might be caused by technical difficulties in the acquisition pipeline rather than biological reality.

DISCUSSION

The DynamicRoots software provides novel capabilities for the analysis of growing root systems of plants. The analyzed shapes come from plants grown in a gel substrate, but can be derived from any growth and imaging system. A logical next step is the genome-wide analysis of dynamic traits for root systems of agricultural plants. Given the availability of the decomposition into branches and the detailed per-branch information, it is time to study the local and global response of plants to localized nutrients in the environment.

While we hope that our software finds many users and contributes to our understanding of root systems, it is important to point out that there are pitfalls in using it. Most root systems we considered have 3D reconstructions with touching branches that lead to violations of our Assumption A_2. As a consequence, there are loops in the reconstructed shape which leads to faulty decompositions into branches. Fortunately, such mistakes are local and do not affect branches away from the loops. Ideally, the software would have the built-in capability to remove loops by separating touching branches, but this is a challenging problem that awaits a satisfactory solution.

Nonetheless, the framework described here represents a major advance in root phenotyping methodology. For the first time, the growth dynamics of each branch in a complex three-dimensional root system can be automatically tracked and quantified over time. Thus, DynamicRoots will enable high-throughput analysis of local growth response to a wide-range of biotic and abiotic plant-environment interactions, as well as provide a powerful tool to answer fundamental questions such as: "How is root growth regulated over the circadian clock?", and "How do local growth decisions of each root tip contribute to global root architecture?".

ACKNOWLEDGMENTS

OS thanks Niloy Mitra for sharing the 4CPS alignment code and Szymon Rusinkiewicz for publishing the trimesh2 library containing the implementation of the ICP algorithm. CNT thanks Ni Jiang for providing the 3D reconstructions of the validation models shown in Fig 3.

AUTHOR CONTRIBUTIONS

Conceived and designed the experiments: OS CNT HE. Performed the experiments: OS CNT. Analyzed the data: OS. Contributed reagents/materials/analysis tools: OS CNT. Wrote the paper: OS CNT HE. Designed and developed the software: OS.

REFERENCES

1. de Dorlodot S, Forster B, Pages L, Price A, Tuberosa R, Draye X. Root system architecture: opportunities and constraints for genetic improvement of crops. Trends in Plant Science 2007; 12:474–481. doi: 10. 1016/j. tplants. 2007. 08. 012. pmid:17822944
2. Lynch J. Root architecture and plant productivity. Plant Physiol. 1995; 109:7–13. pmid:12228579
3. Tester M, Langridge P. Breeding technologies to increase crop production in a changing world. Science 2010; 327:818–822. doi: 10. 1126/science. 1183700. pmid:20150489
4. Gregory PJ, Hutchison DJ, Read DB, Jenneson PM, Gilboy WB, Morton EJ. Non-invasive imaging of roots with high resolution X-ray micro-tomography. Plant and Soil 2003; 255:351–359. doi: 10. 1023/A:1026179919689.
5. Hargreaves CE, Gregory PJ, Bengough AG. Measuring root traits in barley (Hordeum vulgare ssp vulgare and ssp spontaneum) seedlings using gel chambers, soil sacs, and X-ray microtomography. Plant and Soil 2009; 316:285–297. doi: 10. 1007/s11104-008-9780-4.
6. Heeraman DA, Hopmans JW, Clausnitzer V. Three dimensional imaging of plant roots in situ with x-ray computed tomography. Plant and Soil 1997; 189:167–179. doi: 10. 1023/B:PLSO. 0000009694. 64377. 6f.
7. Perret JS, Al-Belushi ME, Deadman M. Non-destructive visualization and quantification of roots using computed tomography. Soil Biology & Biochemistry 2007; 39:391–399. doi: 10. 1016/j. soilbio. 2006. 07. 018.
8. Tracy SR, Roberts JA, Black CR, McNeill A, Davidson R, Mooney SJ. The X-factor: visualizing undisturbed root architecture in soils using X-ray computed tomography. Journal of Experimental Botany 2010; 61:311–313. doi: 10. 1093/jxb/erp386. pmid:20051353
9. Van AH, Scheenen T, Vergeldt FJ. MRI of intact plants. Photosynthesis Research 2009; 102:213–222. doi: 10. 1007/s11120-009-9486-3.
10. Jahnke S, Menzel MI, van Dusschoten C, Roeb GW, Böhler G, Minwuyelet S, et al. Combined MRI-PET dissects dynamic changes in plant structures and functions. Plant Journal 2009; 59:634–644. doi: 10. 1111/j. 1365-313X. 2009. 03888. x. pmid:19392708
11. Fang S, Yan X, Liao H. 3D reconstruction and dynamic modeling of root architecture in situ and its application to crop phosphorus research. Plant Journal 2009; 60:1096–1108. doi: 10. 1111/j. 1365-313X. 2009. 04009. x. pmid:19709387
12. Clark RT, MacCurdy RB, Jung JK, Shaff JE, McCouch SR, Aneshansley DJ, et al. Three-dimensional root phenotyping with a novel imaging and software platform. Plant Physiology 2011; 156:455–465. doi: 10. 1104/pp. 110. 169102. pmid:21454799
13. Iyer-Pascuzzi AS, Symonova O, Mileyko Y, Hao Y, Belcher H, Harer J, et al. Imaging and analysis platforms for automatic phenotyping and classification of plant root systems. Plant Physiol. 2010; 152:1148–1157. doi: 10. 1104/pp. 109. 150748. pmid:20107024
14. Galkovskyi T, Mileyko Y, Bucksch A, Moore B, Symonova O, Price CA, et al. GiA Roots: software for the high throughput analysis of plant root system architecture. BMC Plant Biology 2012; 12:116–127. doi: 10. 1186/1471-2229-12-116. pmid:22834569
15. Pound MP, French AP, Atkinson J, Wells DM, Bennett MJ, Pridmore T. RootNav: Navigating images of complex root architectures. Plant Physiol. 2013; 164:1802–14. doi: 10. 1104/pp. 113. 221531.
16. Topp CN, Iyer-Pascuzzi AS, Anderson JT, Lee CR, Zurek PR, Symonova O, et al. 3D phenotyping and quantitative trait locus mapping identify core regions of the rice genome controlling root architecture. PNAS 2013; 110(18):E1695–E1704. doi: 10. 1073/pnas. 1304354110. pmid:23580618
17. Le Bot J, Serra V, Fabre J, Draye X, Adamowicz S, Pages L. DART: a software to analyse root system architecture and development from captured images. Plant and Soil 2010; 326:261–273. doi: 10. 1007/s11104-009-0005-2.
18. Lobet G, Pages L, Draye X. A novel image-analysis toolbox enabling quantitative analysis of root system architecture. Plant Physiology 2011; 157:29–39. doi: 10. 1104/pp. 111. 179895. pmid:21771915
19. French A, Ubeda-Tomas S, Holman TJ, Bennett MJ and Pridmore T. High-throughput quantification of root growth using a novel image-analysis tool. Plant Physiology 2009; 150:1784–1795. doi: 10. 1104/pp. 109. 140558. pmid:19515787
20. Miller ND, Durham Brooks TL, Assadi AH, Spalding EP. Detection of a gravitropism phenotype in glutamate receptor-like 3. 3 mutants of Arabidopsis thaliana using machine vision and computation. Genetics 2010; 186:585–593. doi: 10. 1534/genetics. 110. 118711. pmid:20647506
21. Yazdanbakhsh N, Fisahn J. High throughput phenotyping of root growth dynamics, lateral root formation, root

architecture and root hair development enabled by PlaRoM. Functional Plant Biology 2009; 36:938–946. doi: 10. 1071/FP09167.

22. Aiger D, Mitra NJ, Cohen-Or D. 4-points congruent sets for robust pairwise surface registration. ACM Trans. Graph. 2008; 27(3): 85:1–85:10. doi: 10. 1145/1360612. 1360684.

23. Rusinkiewicz S, Levoy M. Efficient variants of the ICP algorithm. In Proc. of 3DIM 2001; 145–152.

24. Zheng Y, Gu S, Edelsbrunner H, Tomasi C, Benfey P. Detailed reconstruction of 3D plant root shape. In Proc. 13th Internat. Conf. Comput. Vision 2011; 2026–2033.

25. Dijkstra EW. A note on two problems in connexion with graphs. Numerische Mathematik 1959; 1:269–271. doi: 10. 1007/BF01386390.

26. Besl PJ, McKay ND. A method for registration of 3-D shapes. IEEE Trans. Patt. Anal. Mach. Intel. 1992; 14:239–256. doi: 10. 1109/34. 121791.

27. Tarjan RE. Data Structures and Network Algorithms. SIAM, Philadelphia, Pennsylvania, 1983.

28. Yazdanbakhsh N, Fisahn J. Stable diurnal growth rhythms modulate root elongation of Arabidopsis thaliana. Plant Root 2011; 5:17–23. doi: 10. 3117/plantroot. 5. 17.

29. Iijima M, Oribe Y, Horibe Y, Kono Y. Time lapse analysis of root elongation rates of rice and sorghum during the day and night. Annals of Botany 1998; 81:603–607. doi: 10. 1006/anbo. 1998. 0611.

INDEX

N

O

P

Q

R

S

T

U

V

W